Basics

Wiley Automotive Series

John Remling   **Brakes**
John Remling   **Steering and Suspension**
John Remling   **Basics**

Forthcoming titles
Mark Kovach   **Electrical**

Basics

John Remling

Board of Cooperative Educational Services
Valhalla, New York

John Wiley & Sons
New York   Chichester
Brisbane   Toronto

This book was printed and bound by Halliday Press.
It was set in Helvetica Light by Waldman Graphics, Inc.
Linda Sadovnick supervised production.
Deborah Herbert supervised the editing.

Cover and text design by Edward A. Butler.
Drawings on chapter opening pages by Mario Stasolla.
Cover painting by Edward A. Butler.

Library of Congress Cataloging in Publication Data:

Remling, John, 1928-
   Basics.
   (Wiley automotive series)
   Includes bibliographical references and index.
   1. Automobiles—Maintenance and repair.
I. Title.
TL152.R415   629.28'7'22   79-19868
ISBN 0-471-04762-7

Printed in the United States of America

10 9 8 7 6 5 4 3 2

To the Reader

You may think that all it takes to be a good mechanic is the ability to remove and install a few parts—that all the skills needed are in your hands. It is true that a mechanic must have some highly developed hand skills. But hand skills are useless unless you know when and where to apply them. How will you know which part to replace or to adjust? How will you know what to do to keep that part from failing again? As a mechanic you must check automotive systems to find the causes of many kinds of problems. But that is not enough. You must check related systems and parts to be sure that the problems will not occur again. This kind of checking requires a skill called *diagnosis*. Diagnosis is the basis of all repair, and it requires knowledge.

As a mechanic you must have a working knowledge of all of the systems that make up an automobile. You must know the ways in which those systems work and relate to one another. Without this knowledge you cannot make an accurate diagnosis. Without an accurate diagnosis you may do unnecessary work, and you may replace parts that do not need replacing. As an auto mechanic you will use your knowledge to diagnose problems and to determine needed repairs. You will then use your hand skills to make the repairs.

As an auto mechanic you will need—knowledge, diagnostic skills, and repair skills. Specifically, you will need—

Knowledge of:

1. The function and operation of automotive systems and their parts
2. The names of parts
3. Automotive theory
4. Measurement and related mathematics and science
5. Hand tools and other equipment
6. Shop practices and safety

Diagnostic skills such as:

1. Recognizing malfunctions
2. Isolating sources of trouble

3. Using test equipment
4. Interpreting test results
5. Analyzing failure
6. Evaluating completed repairs

Repair skills such as:

1. Lubricating and adjusting parts
2. Repairing, overhauling, or replacing parts

This book can help you acquire some of this knowledge and some of these skills.

John Remling

Contents

*For the remaining chapters we list in a developmental sequence, jobs whose learning objective is either knowledge (K), diagnostic skills (D), or repair skills (R).

Introduction

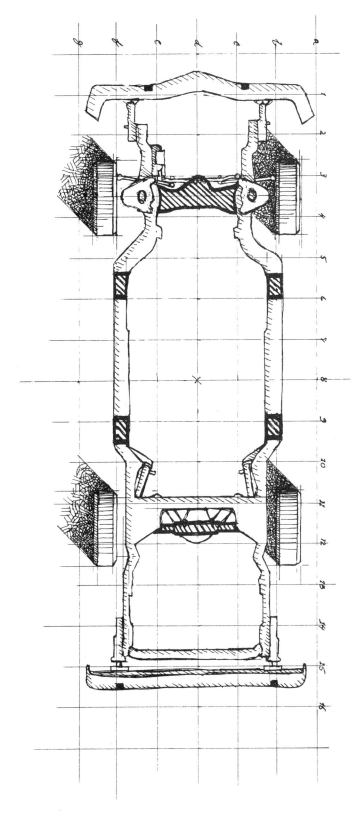

This textbook, one of several in a series dealing with a broad range of automotive service areas, covers the area of basic automotive maintenance. It has been developed to help you gain the basic knowledge, diagnostic skills, and repair skills required of an automobile mechanic.

In studying the various automotive systems, you will find many words with which you are familiar. But some of these words will have meanings that are different from those you already know. For example, a brake spoon in no way resembles an item of tableware. You will also find some words with which you are not familiar. Although many of those words are descriptive, what they describe is not always clear. Some steering systems use drag links, but the links had better not drag.

Like any other technical field, automotive service has a language all its own. A mechanic may use the language of a layperson, especially when explaining to a car owner the need for a certain repair. But that same mechanic must understand and use the language of the trade when talking to a parts dealer or to another mechanic and when reading a service manual.

In this book you will find the language of the trade easy to learn. When a new technical term is first used, it is printed in *italic* type. Also, a definition or explanation of the term is provided. To help yourself add the new term to your vocabulary, you should study the pictures related to the text. Studying the pictures will help you in three ways.

1 It will help you better understand the definition or explanation.
2 It will help you recognize various automobile parts when you see them on a car.
3 It will help you understand the function or operation of the parts and their relationship to one another.

Throughout this book you will be advised to consult the service manual for the car on which you are working. Not all car makers use the same types of systems. Many variations are used, even among cars built by the same manufacturer. Different systems require different service procedures. Service manuals provide you with drawings and photos that show where and how to perform certain service procedures on the particular make and model of car on which you are working. At times a special tool is required, and its use is shown and explained. Sometimes a special sequence of steps is given that will save you time. Precautions are given so that you may perform the procedures without damaging parts or injuring yourself.

Even if you know the correct procedure for any given job, you still need the car maker's service manual. It provides specifications. Specifications are measurements that must be taken before, during, and after assembling the components of automotive systems. Only by working according to specifications can you be sure that the complete job is well done.

In most chapters of this book you will find pages that present jobs for you to perform. Some of the jobs will require you to identify parts or the function of parts. Such jobs are really tests to help you determine if you have learned the information presented in the text material that precedes them. They require you to furnish information within a certain time. Do not attempt to perform a job until you are sure you understand the text material that precedes it.

Some jobs will require that you adjust, replace, or overhaul certain parts in a particular system. Those jobs are tests also. They test your skills in performing service procedures to the

specifications of the car manufacturer. They require you to complete the procedure within a specified time. Such jobs should be started only after you have practiced them and have gained the necessary skills.

Each job is a checkpoint that you must pass to achieve your goals. It is placed at a point where you can measure the knowledge, diagnostic skills, or repair skills you have gained. Since the material that follows each job is built on the preceding material, you should use the job to determine whether or not you are ready to advance. If you do not achieve a satisfactory performance on a particular job, you know that you have not gained sufficient knowledge or skills to move on. You should review the material preceding the job and, when necessary, practice the procedures that revealed your weakness.

At the end of each chapter, you will find a self-test. The test is provided so that you can see how well you have learned the material presented in the chapter. All of the self-test questions and incomplete statements are of the multiple-choice type. They are all similar in form and content to the questions used in the Auto Mechanics Certification Examination given by NIASE. When taking the self-test, read each incomplete statement or question very carefully. Read each of the answers or completion choices and choose the one that best answers the question or best completes the statement. After responding to all of the test items, check your responses against the answer key located at the back of the book. If you have chosen an incorrect response, review the appropriate material. The answer key also indicates where that material can be found.

Chapter 1 Basic Automotive Maintenance

The proper maintenance of an automobile is important for many reasons. These reasons are most obvious in the following areas:

1
Safety. If the various systems of an automobile are kept in good working order, accidents caused by system failures are minimized.

2
Economy. The advantages of properly maintaining an automobile are apparent not only in low operating costs but in high resale value.

3
Fuel Conservation. A well-maintained automobile uses less fuel. The importance of fuel conservation cannot be minimized.

4
Air Pollution. A properly maintained automobile emits fewer pollutants into the atmosphere.

This chapter provides an overview of the basic jobs performed in routine maintenance. It also explains the need for service manuals and other reference materials. And it explains why mechanics supply their own hand tools. Three jobs are provided. The completion of these jobs is your objective in this chapter. These jobs are as follows:

1 Locate specifications in manufacturer's manuals
2 Locate specifications in a comprehensive service manual
3 Identify basic hand tools

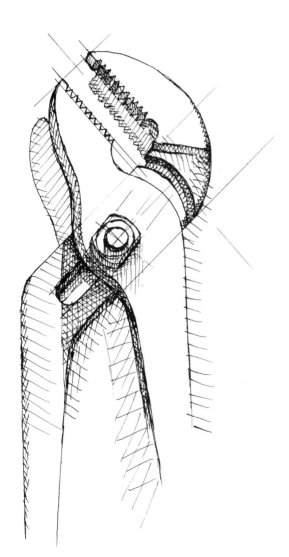

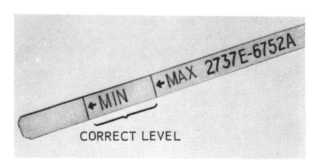

Figure 1.1 Typical markings on an engine oil dipstick. Checking the oil level in an engine is simple job, yet it is a very important part of basic maintenance (Ford Motor Company).

AUTOMOTIVE MAINTENANCE

The automobile is a very complicated piece of machinery. It contains thousands of parts connected and fitted so that they all work together. In many instances, the failure of one part will cause the failure of one or more other parts. Extensive repairs are then required. Most part failures cannot be blamed on defects in the parts. Lack of proper adjustment, insufficient lubrication, and corrosion cause many failures. Proper maintenance will eliminate many of these causes, and thus minimize part failure.

The most efficient type of maintenance is preventive maintenance. Preventive maintenance emphasizes the simple jobs. Checking and adjusting the level of oil in an engine is a simple job. Yet if the oil level drops too low, extensive engine damage will result. Checking and adjusting the pressure in tires is another simple job. Yet underinflation is the most common cause of excessive tire wear. As you learn about the automobile, you will find that the simple jobs are the most important.

Basic Under-Hood Services You are probably familiar with many of the checks and adjustments in this area. They are often performed by a service station attendant while a car is being refueled. Many car owners perform these checks themselves. They have found that a properly maintained car requires fewer repairs and is more economical to operate. The services are simple, but certain knowledge is required to perform them correctly.

The basic under-hood services cover checking and adjusting fluid levels. Those fluids include oil, coolant, brake fluid, transmission fluid, power steering fluid, and water.

Engine Oil You have probably had occasion to check the level of oil in an engine. (See Figure 1.1.) And you may have added oil if it was needed. But did you add oil of the proper viscosity? Did the oil have the correct service classification for that particular car? In performing the jobs in this text, you will check and adjust oil levels. And you will learn how to select oil by its viscosity and its service classification.

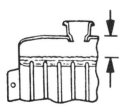

Figure 1.2 A radiator should not be overfilled. The coolant level in the radiator of a cold system should be approximately 1½ inches (37 mm) below the base of the filler neck. This allows room for coolant expansion (Ford Motor Company).

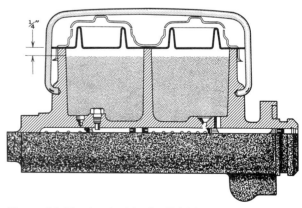

Figure 1.3 The level of brake fluid in a master cylinder should be about ¼ inch (6 mm) below the top of the reservoir (Chevrolet Service Manual, Chevrolet Motor Division, GM).

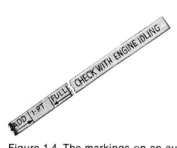

Figure 1.4 The markings on an automatic transmission dipstick. The measurement is accurate only when the fluid is hot and while the engine is running (Buick Motor Division, GM).

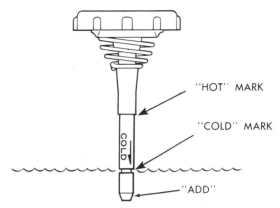

Figure 1.5 A typical power steering fluid dipstick. Note that markings are provided for hot and cold fluid (Chevrolet Service Manual, Chevrolet Motor Division, GM).

Coolant You may have also checked the coolant level in a radiator. And you may have added water if you thought that the level was too low. But did you know that a radiator can be overfilled? (See Figure 1.2.) And that if you added water, you may have diluted the coolant and thus decreased the efficiency of the cooling system? This text will help you to learn about coolant and will show you how to check and adjust its level.

Brake Fluid Most cars have hydraulically operated brake systems. Hydraulic systems transmit pressure by means of fluids. This means that the only link between the driver and the brakes at each wheel is the fluid in the system. Not only must the correct fluid level be maintained, but the correct fluid must be used. The use of an incorrect fluid in the system can result in brake failure. This text will show you how to check and adjust the level of fluid in brake systems. (See Figure 1.3.) And it will tell you how to identify the correct fluid.

Transmission Fluid Many cars have automatic transmissions. These transmissions are hydraulically operated, and the maintenance of the fluid level is very important. Different types of fluid are required for different types of transmissions. The use of the wrong fluid can effect the operation of a transmission and can result in damage to certain components.

By performing the jobs in this text you will learn how to check the fluid level in an automatic transmission. (See Figure 1.4.) You will also learn how to select the correct fluid.

Power Steering Fluid Power steering systems are also hydraulically operated. On some cars, they use automatic transmission fluid. On others, a special fluid must be used. This text will show you how to determine which fluid to use and how to check and adjust the fluid level. (See Figure 1.5.)

Water The fluid in a battery is called electrolyte. It consists of sulfuric acid and water. As a battery is alternately discharged and charged, the water in the electrolyte evaporates. While the water vapor is trapped in some batteries, it is lost to the atmosphere with others. The electrolyte level in batteries with removable vent caps must be checked at frequent intervals. (See Figure 1.6.) If the electrolyte level is low, water must be added. This procedure and the related safety precautions are covered in the text.

Basic Under-Car Services The performance of some maintenance services requires that you work under the car. In many shops, a jack is used to raise a car. (See Figure 1.7.) Car stands are then placed under the car to

ELECTROLYTE
LEVEL
TOO LOW

ELECTROLYTE
AT CORRECT
LEVEL

Figure 1.6 Typical views of the surface of the electrolyte in a battery cell. Note that the surface appears distorted when the electrolyte is at the correct level (Buick Motor Division, GM).

Figure 1.8 A pair of adjustable car stands. Car stands should always be used to support a car after you raise it with a jack (courtesy of Hein-Werner Corporation).

support its weight. (See Figure 1.8.) Some shops have lifts that both raise and support a car. An improperly placed jack or lift can cause considerable damage. Improperly placed car stands can allow a car to fall while you are working under it. (See Figure 1.9.) This text covers several methods of raising and supporting cars without damaging them and without risking injury.

Under-car services include checking and adjusting the level of the lubricant in transmissions and differentials. Also included is the lubrication of the parts in the various chassis

systems. Changing engine oil and replacing oil filters are other jobs that are usually performed from under a car. Procedures for performing these operations together with information regarding lubricants are provided in this text.

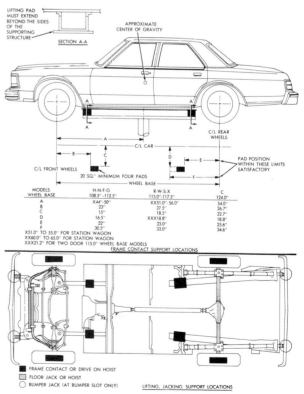

Figure 1.9 Typical lifting and support locations on a car of unit body design. Because a separate frame is not used, the jacks and car stands must be placed under reinforced areas of the floor pan (courtesy Chrysler Corporation).

Figure 1.7 A hydraulic floor jack similar to those used in most auto shops (courtesy of Hein-Werner Corporation).

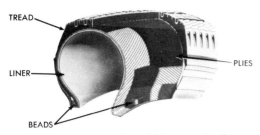

Figure 1.10 Construction differences in the most widely used types of tires (courtesy Chrysler Corporation).

Tire and Wheel Service Four small areas of rubber are the only connections between a car and the road. The frictional contact provided by the tires enables the driving wheels to push against the road. That contact also allows the front wheels to steer the car. And it enables the brakes to bring the car to a stop.

Because of their importance, tires, and the wheels on which they are mounted, are given considerable coverage in this text. Through job performance, you will learn to identify the various types of tires and to recognize their differences. (See Figure 1.10.) The causes of abnormal tire wear are covered so that you can diagnose those causes. Other jobs enable you to develop various repair skills. These skills include tire rotation, tire repair, tire replacement, and balancing. (See Figure 1.11.)

Battery Service The lead-acid storage battery used in most automobiles is a device for storing energy. It does not store electricity, but stores chemical energy that can be converted to electrical energy. A knowledge of how a battery operates is an essential foundation on which you can build many diagnostic and repair skills. This text provides you with the means to gain that knowledge.

Battery failure is a major cause of automotive problems requiring road service. Preventive maintenance can minimize these failures and the related inconvenience and expense. Certain services can extend the service life of a battery. And certain tests can enable you to determine if a battery can be recharged or if

Figure 1.11 A typical bubble balancer. Many service stations use an instrument such as this to static balance wheel and tire assemblies (courtesy AMMCO Tools, Inc.)

it should be replaced. (See Figure 1.12.) Those services and tests are covered in this text. Jobs are provided so that you can develop the required skills.

Jumper cables are often used to start a car that has a discharged battery. The improper use of jumper cables can damage certain electrical components on a car. And failure to observe certain precautions can result in a battery explosion. This text provides a procedure you should follow to jump start a car with-

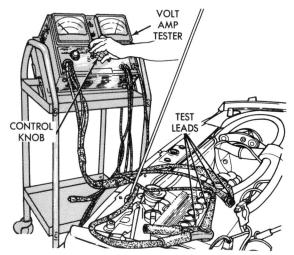

Figure 1.12 Load testing a battery (courtesy Chrysler Corporation).

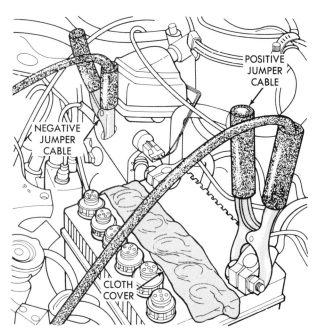

Figure 1.13 When attempting to jump start a car, the vent caps of both the discharged battery and the booster battery should be removed. The openings to the cells should be covered with cloth. The negative jumper cable should be connected to a good ground on the engine (courtesy Chrysler Corporation).

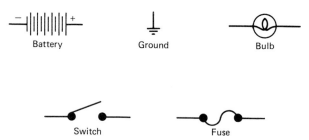

Figure 1.14 Symbols used to represent automotive electrical parts. These symbols are often used in wiring diagrams.

out causing damage or injury. (See Figure 1.13.)

Many replacement batteries are manufactured and sold without electrolyte. These dry-charged batteries require the addition of electrolyte and other services before they can be used. This text provides the required activation procedures.

Basic Electrical Services There are many electrical circuits in an automobile. Maintenance service in these circuits is based on diagnosis, and that diagnosis is based on knowledge. To enable you to gain that knowledge, this text provides an introduction to basic circuitry. The types and functions of conductors, loads, controls, and protection devices are covered. The differences between series circuits and parallel circuits are explained and shown in symbolized drawings. (See Figure 1.14.)

The operation of the bulbs, switches, flashers, and fuses most commonly used in lighting circuits is also covered. Jobs are provided so that you may become skilled in the replacement of these parts. The various types of sealed beam headlight bulbs are listed, and their differences are explained. Other jobs provide for skill development in replacing and aiming these bulbs. (See Figure 1.15.)

Fuel System Service Maintenance of the fuel system includes replacing and cleaning filters and making minor checks and adjust-

Figure 1.15 A typical headlight aiming kit. Note the various adaptors that allow the aimers to be used on all types and sizes of headlights (courtesy American Motors Corporation).

FAST IDLE CAM

FAST IDLE
SPEED—
ADJUSTING
SCREW

FAST IDLE
LEVER

CURB IDLE SPEED
ADJUSTING SCREW

Figure 1.16 The locations of the curb idle adjusting screw and the fast idle adjusting screw on a typical carburetor (Ford Motor Company).

ments. Although the jobs may be termed simple, they cannot be correctly performed without some knowledge of engine operation, fuel systems, and fuel.

This text explains how an engine releases the heat energy in gasoline and converts that energy to mechanical energy. Gasoline octane ratings and their meaning are also explained. Jobs are provided to reinforce the knowledge you gain in these areas.

The function of the various parts in the fuel system are covered, and the required service procedures are outlined. Jobs are provided so that you may develop skills in servicing air cleaners, replacing fuel filters, and adjusting carburetors. (See Figure 1.16.)

Many different emission control devices are found on late model cars. Some of these devices are built into the fuel system. Other emission control devices are used in separate systems, but these systems interact with the fuel system. The operation of evaporation emission control systems and positive crankcase ventilation systems is explained. Procedures for testing these systems and replacing

certain parts are given. And jobs are provided to help you to develop skills in performing these procedures. (See Figure 1.17.)

Cooling System Service Much of the heat energy released from gasoline in an engine is not converted to mechanical energy. That sur-

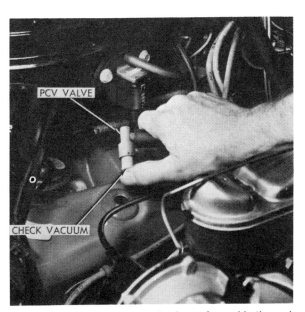

PCV VALVE

CHECK VACUUM

Figure 1.17 One of the quick checks performed in the maintenance of a PCV system. A strong vacuum should be felt at the PCV valve when the engine is running (courtesy Chrysler Corporation).

plus heat must be taken away from the engine and passed off to the atmosphere. High engine temperatures cause a loss of proper lubrication and excessive wear, resulting in extensive engine damage.

Low engine temperatures also cause problems. Automobile engines operate most efficiently in a temperature range that extends from 195°F (90°C) to 240°F (115°C). At lower temperatures, less usable energy is obtained from the fuel. In addition, more pollutants are emitted in the exhaust gases, and the engine oil becomes contaminated with fuel and water.

The cooling system must allow an engine to reach its most efficient operating temperature as quickly as possible. It then must maintain that temperature regardless of the loads placed on the engine or the temperature of the outside air. The cooling system requires very little maintenance, but that maintenance is vital to its trouble-free operation.

This text explains how the system operates and how its various parts function. The reasons for the use of coolant instead of water are fully covered, and charts are provided so that coolant ratios can be determined. Coolant testing and pressure testing procedures are

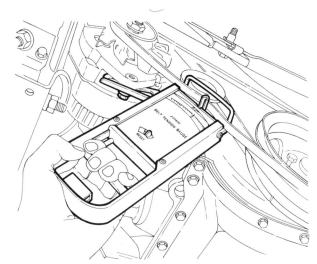

Figure 1.19 Fan belts should be adjusted to the tension specification of the car manufacturer (courtesy American Motors Corporation).

outlined, and jobs are provided to help you develop these diagnostic skills. (See Figure 1.18.) Repair procedures are outlined for flushing a system, replacing hoses and thermostats, and adjusting belts. You can develop skills in these procedures by performing the jobs provided. (See Figure 1.19.)

Wheel Bearing Service On most cars, the front wheels rotate on small axles called spindles. To minimize friction, bearings are used between the spindles and the hubs of the wheels. These bearings must allow free rotation of the wheels, and yet support the weight of the front of the car. Most automobile manufacturers use tapered roller bearings in the front wheels of their cars. Properly maintained, these bearings almost never require replacement.

Wheel bearing service consists of removal, cleaning, inspection, lubrication, installation, and adjustment. Where maintenance has been neglected or improperly performed, bearing replacement is required. This text provides outlines for all the procedures required to service and replace wheel bearings. It also provides the information needed to diagnose the cause of bearing failures. Jobs are pro-

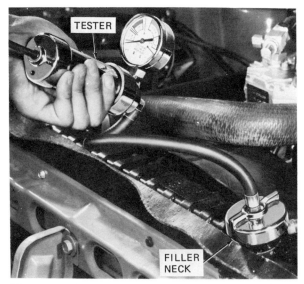

Figure 1.18 Pressure testing a cooling system (courtesy American Motors Corporation).

Figure 1.20 Front wheel bearings should be adjusted with the aid of a torque wrench (Ford Motor Company).

vided so that you can develop the necessary diagnostic and repair skills. (See Figure 1.20.)

Brake System Service The brake system is considered by many to be the most important system on a car. A car in motion has a considerable amount of kinetic energy. Kinetic energy can be thought of as the energy of weight in motion. That energy must be converted to another form of energy if the car is to be brought to a stop. The brake system converts kinetic energy to heat energy. It does that through the friction created by forcing brake shoes against rotors or drums attached to the wheels. The heat created is then passed off to the atmosphere.

This text explains the operation of brake systems and the function of their parts. Because a knowledge of brake systems is important in performing the various maintenance inspections, jobs are provided to reinforce these explanations.

Because brakes are friction devices, they are subject to a considerable amount of wear. The brake shoes are covered with an asbestos lining. If that lining wears excessively, braking will be impaired and the rotors and drums will be damaged. On most cars, maintenance of the brake system consists of various inspections. On some cars, certain adjustments must be made. The replacement of worn and damaged parts involves procedures that are beyond the scope of basic maintenance.

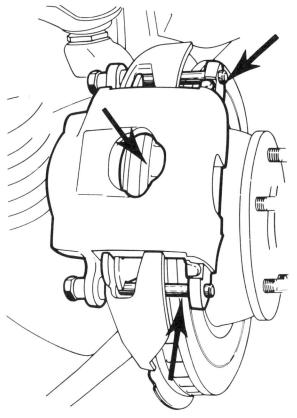

Figure 1.21 Lining inspection areas on a typical disc brake assembly (Pontiac Motor Division, GM).

Because both disc brakes and drum brakes are in common use, this text provides inspection procedures for each type. Adjustment procedures are provided for those cars that require that service. Each of the procedures is accompanied by a job so that you can perform the procedures and develop the required skills. (See Figure 1.21.)

Suspension and Steering System Services The suspension and steering systems are so closely related that it is difficult to separate them. In most instances, a failure in one system will have an effect on the other system. In terms of safety, the suspension and steering systems are considered to be just as important as the brake system.

There are several different types of suspension and steering systems in common use. A knowledge of these systems and their parts is necessary in the performance of maintenance inspections and repairs. This text contains an overview of the various systems and their parts. And it explains how the systems are dependent on each other. (See Figure 1.22.)

In addition to lubrication, maintenance of the systems consists primarily of inspections for wear and damage, and the replacement of minor parts. (See Figure 1.23.) Alignment and the replacement of major components exceeds the scope of basic maintenance. This text includes the procedures for inspecting ball joints and shock absorbers. Procedures are also provided for the replacement of shock absorbers and for power steering belt adjustment. Each procedure is followed by a job to provide the opportunity for skill development.

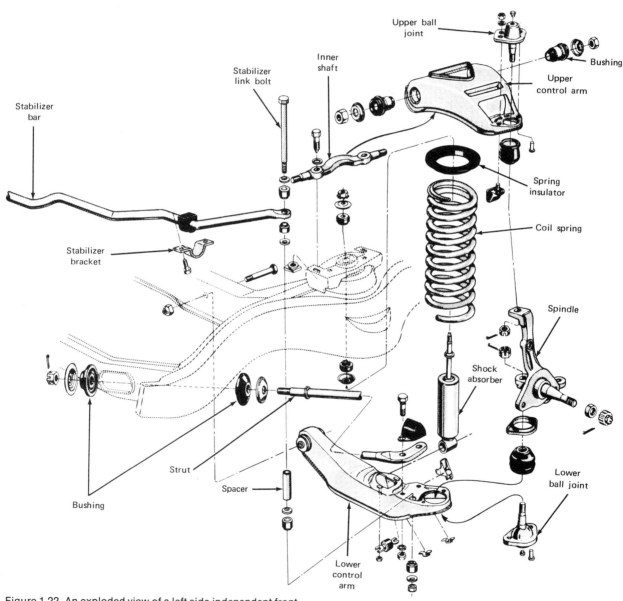

Figure 1.22 An exploded view of a left side independent front suspension system (Ford Motor Company).

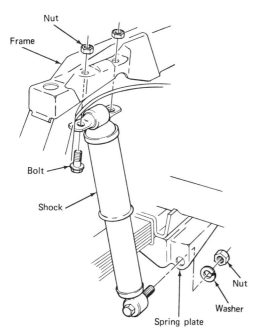

Figure 1.23 A typical rear shock absorber mounting (Buick Motor Division, GM).

Ignition System Secondary Circuit Service A complete diagnostic tune-up includes many operations beyond those considered a part of routine maintenance. But routine main-

tenance does include certain inspections, adjustments, and part replacements in the ignition system. Proper maintenance of ignition systems requires an understanding of their operating principles. This text will help you gain that understanding.

An introduction to both breaker type and breakerless ignition systems is given. The parts used in these systems and the functions of these parts are listed and explained. (See Figures 1.24 and 1.25.) Learning is reinforced through the inclusion of jobs.

Although there are many different types of ignition systems in use, their secondary circuits are similar. Information on various types of secondary circuit components is given to facilitate diagnosis. To aid in the development of diagnostic skills, jobs are provided where you will identify spark plug operating conditions, and inspect and test spark plug wires. (See Figure 1.26.)

Procedures for several secondary circuits repairs are included, and jobs are provided for skill development. These jobs include spark plug replacement, spark plug reconditioning, and distributor cap replacement.

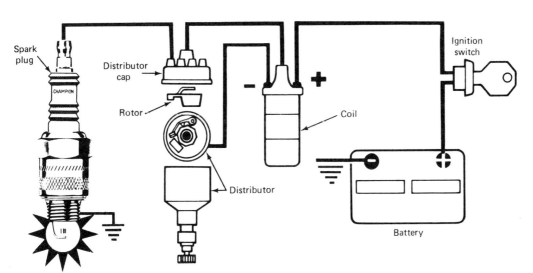

Figure 1.24 A basic breaker point type ignition system (Courtesy of Champion Spark Plug Company).

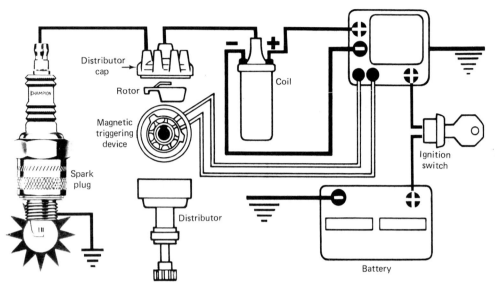

Figure 1.25 A basic electronic ignition system (courtesy of Champion Spark Plug Company).

Ignition System Primary Circuit Service Routine maintenance of the ignition system also includes some services in the primary circuit. This text provides the information and procedures necessary to perform these services. The means to obtain diagnostic skills are provided by jobs. These jobs include the inspection of the primary circuit, and dwell and timing checks. The development of repair skills is aided by the inclusion of jobs requiring you to adjust dwell and adjust timing. (See Figure 1.27.)

Starting System Service Routine maintenance of the starting system includes circuit

testing, cleaning and tightening connections, and the replacement of components found to be faulty. Because a basic knowledge of sys-

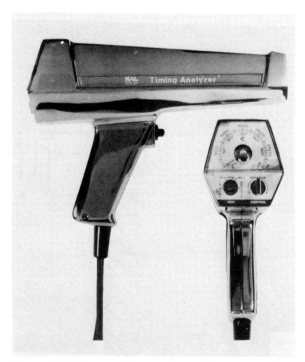

Figure 1.27 A timing light combined with a spark advance meter. This instrument will check initial spark timing and measure both centrifugal and vacuum spark advance (Kal-Equip Company).

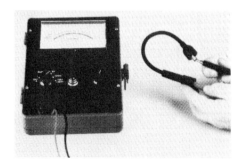

Figure 1.26 Using an Ohmmeter to check the resistance of a spark plug wire (courtesy American Motors Corporation).

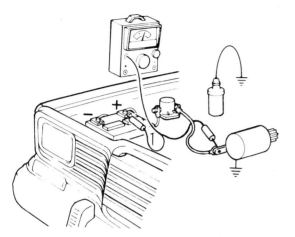

Figure 1.28 Meter connections for performing a voltage drop test of the "hot" side of the starting system motor circuit (courtesy American Motors Corporation).

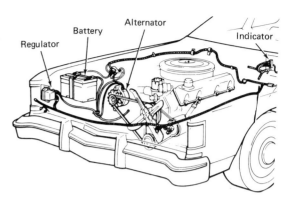

Figure 1.29 A typical charging system circuit (Ford Motor Company).

tem operation is necessary, the various system parts and their functions are explained. The three types of starter motors in common use are discussed. And the differences in solenoids and relays are explained.

The diagnostic procedures in the text include testing for starter current draw and testing for excessive voltage drop in the motor circuit. Jobs are provided for skill development in these procedures. Procedures for the replacement of relays and starter motors are also included and are followed by jobs for skill development. (See Figure 1.28.)

Charging System Service The charging system requires maintenance if it is to function correctly. The adjustments and replacements required should be determined by diagnosis. And that diagnosis must be based on an understanding of the operation of the system. This text explains the operation of the three systems most commonly used. The parts of these systems are described, and their differences are explained. Jobs are provided to help you gain knowledge of these parts and their functions. (See Figure 1.29.)

Diagnostic procedures include a basic test of the entire system. That procedure is followed by procedures for determining causes of un-

dercharging and overcharging. Jobs are provided so that you can develop skills in the performance of these tests. (See Figure 1.30.)

TOOLS OF THE TRADE The performance of maintenance services requires more than knowledge, diagnostic skills, and repair skills. You also need tools. As an auto mechanic, you will require two different types of tools. The first type includes hand tools, power tools, instruments, and equipment. These tools enable your hands to perform diagnostic and repair procedures. The second type consists of service manuals and other reference materials. These are tools that tell you how those procedures should be performed. And they provide the specifications that must be used.

Service Manuals Throughout this text you will be advised to consult an appropriate manual to determine specific procedures and specifications. The various systems used in all cars usually follow the same basic operating principles. But those systems are not always the same. Many variations are used, even among cars built by the same manufacturer. Different systems require different service procedures. Service manuals provide you with drawings and photos that show where and how to perform certain procedures on the

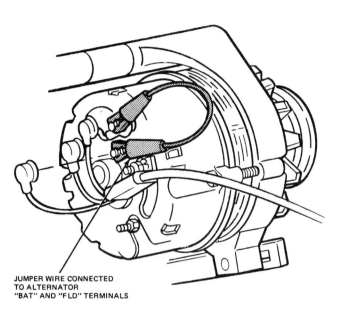

JUMPER WIRE CONNECTED
TO ALTERNATOR
"BAT" AND "FLD" TERMINALS

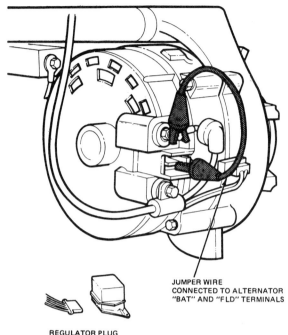

REGULATOR PLUG
REMOVED
FROM REGULATOR

JUMPER WIRE
CONNECTED TO ALTERNATOR
"BAT" AND "FLD" TERMINALS

Figure 1.30 During some alternator tests, jumper wires are used to bypass the regulator (Ford Motor Company).

particular car on which you are working. At times a special tool is required, and its use is shown and explained. Sometimes a special sequence of steps is given that will save you time. Precautions are given so that you may perform the procedures without damaging parts or injuring yourself.

Even if you know the correct procedure for a particular job, you still need a service manual. A service manual provides specifications. Specifications are measurements that must be taken before, during, and after assembling components of automotive systems. Only by working to specifications can you be sure that the completed job has been performed correctly.

Two types of service manuals are in common use. One type includes the manuals published by the various car manufacturers. The other type includes the comprehensive manuals published privately.

Manufacturer's Service Manuals Most car makers publish a complete manual or set of manuals for each model year of the cars they build. (See Figure 1.31.) These manuals provide the best source of information for the cars they cover. The information in these manuals is arranged in groups, or sections. As shown in Figure 1.32, each group, or section, covers a different system or area of repair. Each group, or section, has its own index to enable you to locate specific information. The pages within each group, or section, are numbered in a separate sequence, as are the pages in each chapter of this text.

Although all manufacturer's manuals are similar, each manufacturer uses different groupings and different methods of presentation. You should look through some of the manuals published by different manufacturers so that you will become familiar with these differences.

Sources of manufacturer's service manuals are listed in the Appendix of this text.

CHRYSLER
CORPORATION

Service Manual

1978
Plymouth
Horizon

Dodge Omni

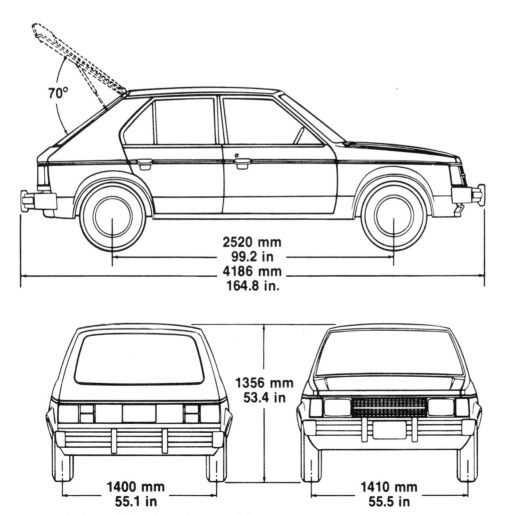

Figure 1.31 A typical manufacturer's service manual (courtesy Chrysler Corporation).

Foreword

This Chrysler Corporation Omni, Horizon Service Manual has been prepared with the latest service information available for use on 1978 models. Diagnosis, disassembly, repair, assembly and installation procedures coupled with complete specifications and tightening references can be found in each group. It will prove an invaluable aid in properly performing any phase of service necessary to maintain or restore the fine performance and reliability characteristics designed, engineered and manufactured into these outstanding automobiles.

Index

Symbols are shown in the index tab which identify the group subject. The symbol is also located at the end of the page title, located at the left or right top of each page.

Page Numbers

All page numbers consist of two sets of digits separated by a dash. The digits preceding the dash identify the group. The digits following the dash represent the consecutive page number within the particular group. The page numbers are found on the page title at the top of each page.

Group Index

The first page in each main group has a contents of the subjects included in that group. The first page also contains an index listing particular components within a certain subject.

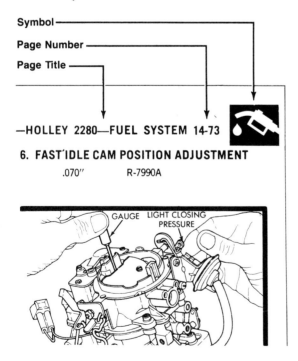

Symbol
Page Number
Page Title

—HOLLEY 2280—FUEL SYSTEM 14-73

6. FAST IDLE CAM POSITION ADJUSTMENT

.070″   R-7990A

GAUGE LIGHT CLOSING PRESSURE

Chrysler Corporation reserves the right to make changes in design or to make additions to or improvements in its products without imposing any obligations upon itself to install them on its products previously manufactured.

Figure 1.32 The table of contents in a typical manufacturer's service manual (courtesy Chrysler Corporation).

Job 1a

LOCATE SPECIFICATIONS IN MANUFACTURER'S MANUALS

SATISFACTORY PERFORMANCE

A satisfactory performance on this job requires that you do the following:

1 Locate the specifications requested below for the two cars assigned.

2 Using appropriate manufacturer's manuals, complete the job within 30 minutes.

3 Fill in the blanks under "Information."

PERFORMANCE SITUATION

Description of cars assigned

Car no. 1 Year, make, model _____

Engine identification _____

Transmission type _____

Car no. 2 Year, make, model _____

Engine identification _____

Transmission type _____

INFORMATION

Car no. 1

Reference used_____

Specification for	Specification	Page Number
Spark plug gap	_____	_____
Cooling system capacity	_____	_____
Cooling system pressure cap rating	_____	_____
Engine oil capacity	_____	_____
Alternator belt tension	_____	_____

Car no. 2

Reference used_____

Specification for	Specification	Page Number
Spark plug gap	_____	_____
Cooling system capacity	_____	_____
Cooling system pressure cap rating	_____	_____
Engine oil capacity	_____	_____
Alternator belt tension	_____	_____

Comprehensive Service Manuals The most commonly used specifications and procedures for the most frequently performed service operations for recent model cars are compiled in these manuals. Published yearly, the manuals provide the best single source of reference material you will need in your daily work.

Comprehensive service manuals are usually divided into two sections. The first section contains procedures and specifications that apply to specific makes and models of cars. That section is indexed alphabetically by car name. The second section contains general service information and procedures.

The material in manuals from different publishers is arranged and presented differently. All the manuals are easy to use when you are familiar with their differences. You should look through the manuals you have available to become acquainted with them.

The titles and publishers of the most commonly used comprehensive service manuals are listed in the Appendix of this text. It is advisable that you obtain a manual of this type for your reference library.

Job 1b

LOCATE SPECIFICATIONS IN A COMPREHENSIVE SERVICE MANUAL

SATISFACTORY PERFORMANCE

A satisfactory performance on this job requires that you do the following:

1 Locate the specifications requested below for the two cars assigned.

2 Using a comprehensive service manual, complete the job within 15 minutes.

3 Fill in the blanks under "Information."

PERFORMANCE SITUATION

Description of cars assigned

Car no. 1 Year, make, model _____

Engine identification _____

Transmission type _____

Car no. 2 Year, make, model _____

Engine identification _____

Transmission type _____

INFORMATION

Car no. 1

Reference used _____

Specification for	Specification	Page Number
Spark plug gap	_____	_____
Cooling system capacity	_____	_____
Cooling system pressure cap rating	_____	_____
Engine oil capacity	_____	_____
Alternator belt tension	_____	_____

Car no. 2

Reference used _____

Specification for	Specification	Page Number
Spark plug gap	_____	_____
Cooling system capacity	_____	_____
Cooling system pressure cap rating	_____	_____
Engine oil capacity	_____	_____
Alternator belt tension	_____	_____

Manuals, Catalogs, and Other Reference Material Published by Manufacturers of Parts, Tools, and Equipment The makers of the parts, tools, and equipment that you will use in servicing automobiles publish a variety of reference material. Much of that material contains information not only about the items that they produce, but about the automotive systems in which they are used. In most instances, these materials supplement the information found in manufacturer's service manuals and in comprehensive service manuals.

Many manufacturers offer material free of charge upon request. You can assemble a very useful automotive reference library by taking advantage of these offerings. A partial listing of these manufacturers is provided in the Appendix of this text.

Tools It is almost universally accepted that an auto mechanic must supply personally owned hand tools. There are many reasons for this requirement. Hand tools enable you to perform tasks that exceed your physical limitations. You cannot tighten nuts, bolts, and screws with your fingers. But you can easily perform these operations by using wrenches and screwdrivers.

The need for hand tools is obvious. What may not be obvious is the relationship between the tool and the hand that holds it. That relationship is one of the main reasons why mechanics supply their own tools. When you use a tool for any length of time, you become accustomed to that particular tool. Each tool has its own "feel." This "feel" is developed between your hands and that particular tool. It is because of that "feel" that baseball players select particular bats and musicians select particular instruments.

As you repeatedly perform a certain operation, you become skilled in that performance. But some of the skill you develop is in the use of the particular tools you handle. If you own the tools you use, you will develop skills more rapidly and more easily. And you will have control over one of the variables that effects the application of those skills.

There are other reasons why mechanics supply their own tools. A mechanic must not only complete jobs to specifications, but must complete them within a reasonable amount of time. In some shops, mechanics' wages are based not only on the quality of the work performed, but on the amount of work completed. With personally owned tools, a mechanic saves the time that would be lost in borrowing tools from another mechanic or from a tool room.

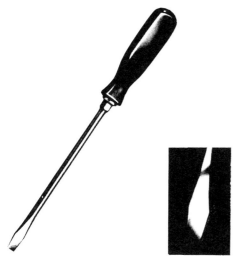

Figure 1.33 A screwdriver with a standard tip (courtesy of Snap-on Tools Corporation).

Responsibility is another reason for tool ownership. Carelessness in performing a job in the starting system may result in inconvenience to the car owner. But carelessness in performing a job in the brake system may result in a serious accident. When you perform a job, you must accept the responsibility for that job. If you are not willing to accept the responsibility for supplying your own tools, you may not be ready to accept the responsibility for the jobs you perform.

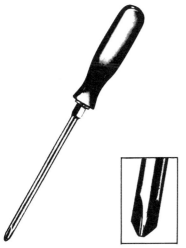

Figure 1.34 A screwdriver with a Phillips tip (courtesy of Snap-on Tools Corporation).

Pride is probably the best reason for tool ownership. You should be proud of your abilities and of the skills that you develop. If you feel that you are a good mechanic, you will want to work with good tools. Many employers check a mechanic's tool box before hiring the mechanic. Quality tools, kept clean and properly maintained, are considered a sign of a good mechanic.

The Basic Tool Kit There is no one set of tools that will meet the needs of every situation. Rather than purchase a set of tools, it is usually better to purchase individual tools as you need them. It is recommended that you purchase tools of high quality. Cheap tools have a short service life and often distort, slip, or break while in use. A tool that fails can damage the parts you are servicing and cause you injury. The following tools are suggested for your consideration:

Screwdrivers Screwdrivers are always needed, but two screwdrivers will be sufficient for your immediate needs. One should have a standard tip. The other should have a #2 Phillips tip. Both should have blades from 4 to 6 inches in length. Figures 1.33 and 1.34 show screwdrivers of these types.

Pliers There are hundreds of different types of pliers available, but you will find that two are used most often. A pair of interlocking jaw pliers about 8 or 9 inches long is especially handy. Pliers of that description are shown in Figure 1.35. Most of your cutting needs can be handled by a pair of diagonal cutters about 7 inches long. These pliers are shown in Figure 1.36.

Wrenches You will eventually find that you need both box wrenches and open end wrenches. A box wrench, shown in Figure 1.37, completely encircles a nut or the head of a bolt. A wrench of this type is not apt to slip and cause damage or injury. An open end

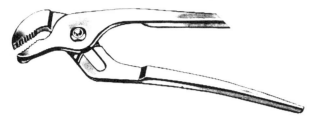

Figure 1.35 A pair of interlocking jaw pliers. Pliers of this type are also referred to as water pump pliers (courtesy of Snap-on Tools Corporation).

Figure 1.36 A pair of diagonal cutting pliers (courtesy of Snap-on Tools Corporation).

wrench, as its name implies, has an open end as shown in Figure 1.38. An open end wrench can often be used where a box wrench cannot be used, but an open end wrench is more liable to slip. It is suggested that you purchase combination wrenches. As shown in Figure 1.39, a combination wrench has a box wrench on one end and an open end wrench on the other end. The three most useful sizes are $7/16$ inch, $1/2$ inch, and $9/16$ inch. Smaller and larger wrenches may be added as necessary.

Sockets   A set of sockets, a ratchet handle, and a few extensions will enable you to perform many jobs that cannot be performed with combination wrenches. Although all the individual tools can be purchased separately, it is usually more economical to purchase a small set similar to the one shown in Figure 1.40. The socket set should be of $3/8$ inch drive. $1/4$ inch drive sets are too small for general use, and $1/2$ inch drive sets are too large. The purchase of those sets can be postponed until they are needed. Spark plug sockets for $5/8$ inch and $13/16$ inch spark plugs should be added to the set if they are not included. A typical spark plug socket is shown in Figure 1.41.

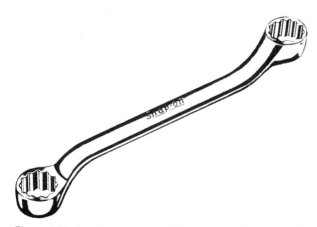

Figure 1.37 A typical box wrench (courtesy of Snap-on Tools Corporation).

Figure 1.38 A typical open end wrench (courtesy of Snap-on Tools Corporation).

Additional tools can be added to your basic kit as you find you need them. Where special tools are used in the procedures in this text, those tools are described and shown. It is suggested that you add tool catalogs to your automotive reference library. A study of those catalogs will help you to select the tools you need. Several manufacturers of automotive tools are listed in the Appendix of this text.

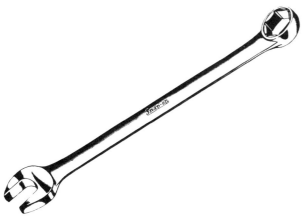

Figure 1.39 A typical combination wrench (courtesy of Snap-on Tools Corporation).

Figure 1.40 A basic ⅜-inch drive socket set complete with a ratchet, two extensions, and a universal joint (courtesy of Snap-on Tools Corporation).

Figure 1.41 A typical spark plug socket. Note that the socket has a hex-shaped head so that it can be turned with a box wrench or an open end wrench (courtesy of Snap-on Tools Corporation).

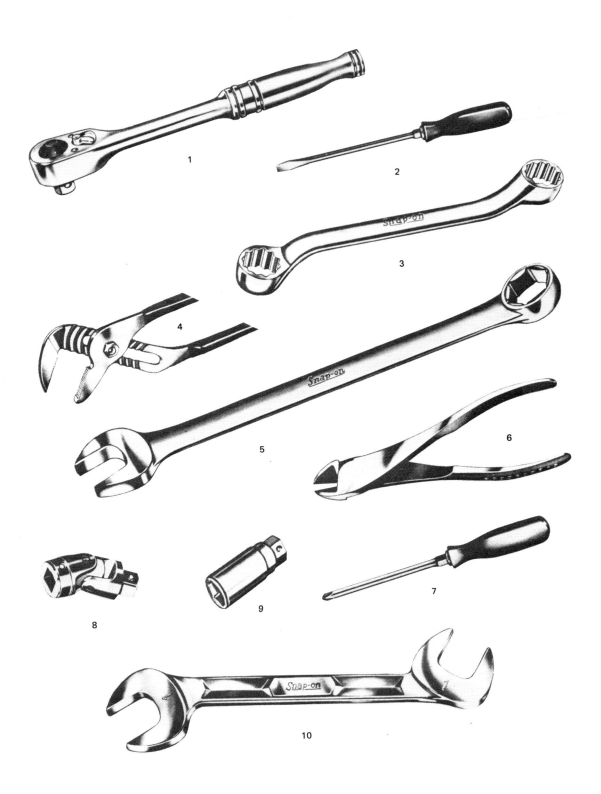

Illustration for Job 1c.

Job 1c

IDENTIFY BASIC HAND TOOLS

SATISFACTORY PERFORMANCE
A satisfactory performance on this job requires that you do the following:

1 Identify the hand tools shown by placing the number of each tool in front of the correct tool name.

2 Complete the job within 10 minutes.

PERFORMANCE SITUATION

_____Spark plug socket   _____Ratchet

_____Slip joint pliers   _____Phillips bit screwdriver

_____Diagonal cutters   _____Open end wrench

_____Universal joint   _____Interlocking jaw pliers

_____Combination wrench   _____Standard tip
                                           screwdriver

_____Box wrench

                                   _____Flare nut wrench

SUMMARY

By completing this chapter you learned of some of the basic jobs that are performed as a part of automotive maintenance. Those jobs consist of simple checks and adjustments, and the replacement of certain parts. You also learned that service manuals and other reference materials are required to provide the correct procedures for those jobs. And even when the correct procedures are known, manuals must be used to obtain the specifications needed.

You learned that to perform these jobs correctly, knowledge, diagnostic skills, and repair skills are required. That knowledge must be gained by study, and those skills must be developed by performance. If you wish to become a good mechanic, you must accept the responsibility for gaining that knowledge and developing those skills. If you accept that responsibility, you are well on your way toward your goal.

SELF-TEST

Each incomplete statement or question in this test is followed by four suggested completions or answers. In each case select the *one* that best completes the sentence or answers the question.

1 Two mechanics are discussing battery service.
Mechanic A says that the electrolyte level should be adjusted by adding water.
Mechanic B says that the electrolyte level should be adjusted by adding acid.
Who is right?
A. A only
B. B only
C. Both A and B
D. Neither A nor B

2 A battery converts
A. heat energy to electrical energy
B. chemical energy to electrical energy
C. mechanical energy to electrical energy
D. electrical energy to mechanical energy

3 Two mechanics are discussing the cable connections for jump starting a car that has a discharged battery.
Mechanic A says that the positive jumper cable should be connected to the positive battery terminal.
Mechanic B says that the negative jumper cable should be connected to the engine away from the battery.
Who is right?
A. A only
B. B only
C. Both A and B
D. Neither A nor B

4 A positive crankcase ventilation system is an emission control system that interacts with the
A. fuel system
B. cooling system
C. electrical system
D. lubrication system

5 Automobile engines operate most efficiently in a temperature range that extends from
A. 105°F (40°C) to 150°F (65°C)
B. 150°F (65°C) to 195°F (90°C)
C. 195°F (90°C) to 240°F (115°C)
D. 240°F (115°C) to 285°F (140°C)

6 Two mechanics are discussing front wheel bearings.
Mechanic A says that the bearings are located between the spindles and the wheel hubs.
Mechanic B says that most manufacturers use ball bearings.
Who is right?
A. A only
B. B only
C. Both A and B
D. Neither A nor B

7 Two mechanics are discussing service manuals.
Mechanic A says that manufacturer's manuals are usually published for each model year.
Mechanic B says that comprehensive manuals contain service procedures and specifications for many model years and for many different cars.
Who is right?
A. A only
B. B only
C. Both A and B
D. Neither A nor B

8 This text provides a list of sources of manuals and other reference material. Where is that list located?
A. The Appendix
B. The Glossary
C. The Bibliography
D. The Introduction

9. In performing automotive maintenance services, the most commonly used Phillips screwdriver has a
A. #1 tip
B. #2 tip
C. #3 tip
D. #4 tip

10 The two most commonly used spark plug socket sizes are
A. 3/8 inch and 9/16 inch
B. 9/16 inch and 5/8 inch
C. 5/8 inch and 13/16 inch
D. 13/16 inch and 7/8 inch

Chapter 2 Basic Under-Hood Services

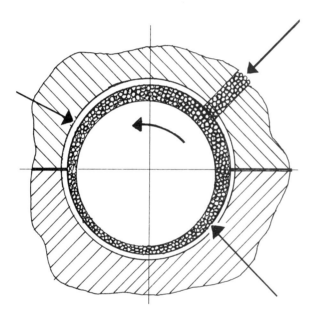

Some of the most important maintenance services include those simple checks and adjustments that are usually made when a vehicle is refueled or at other frequent intervals. You have probably performed some of these checks and adjustments without realizing their importance.

In this chapter you will learn how to perform some of the basic maintenance services. In performing these services, you will gain certain skills. You will learn about lubricants, coolant, and other fluids. You will also gain knowledge of the parts and the systems on which those services are performed.

Your specific objectives are to perform the following jobs:

1
Identify terms relating to engine oil.
2
Check and adjust engine oil level.
3
Check and adjust coolant level.
4
Check and adjust brake fluid level.
5
Check and adjust automatic transmission fluid level.
6
Check and adjust power steering fluid level.
7
Check and adjust battery electrolyte level.

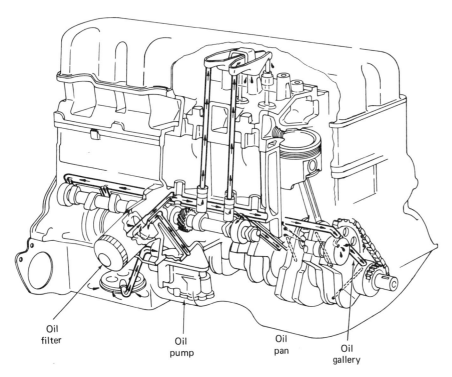

Oil
filter

Oil
pump

Oil
pan

Oil
gallery

Figure 2.1 A typical six-cylinder engine lubrication system
(courtesy American Motors Corporation).

**ENGINE LUBRICATION SYSTEM SERV-
ICES** The most commonly performed under-
hood services are the checking of engine oil
level and the addition of engine oil. Although
those jobs can be considered simple, a good
mechanic realizes the importance of the simple jobs. The use of the incorrect type of oil,
allowing the oil level to drop too low, and even
the addition of too much oil, all can cause serious engine damage. Those so-called simple
jobs require some knowledge of engine lubrication before they can be properly performed.

The Engine Lubrication System Every engine must have a lubrication system to provide
a quantity of oil sufficient to lubricate the engine's moving parts. Typical lubrication systems are shown in Figures 2.1 and 2.2. A study
of these illustrations will help you understand
how a lubrication system works. The *oil pan*
at the bottom of the engine acts as a reservoir

and holds the supply of oil. When the engine
is running, the *oil pump* pulls oil from the oil
pan and forces it through an *oil filter*. The filter
removes any particles of dirt and grit so that
they will not be pumped through the system.
After passing through the filter, the oil is
forced through a series of passages called *oil
galleries*. These passages direct the oil to the
various moving parts of the engine. Some
parts receive oil directly from the oil galleries.
Other parts are lubricated by oil that is allowed to run over them. Still others are lubricated by oil that is splashed on them by other
moving parts. After the oil has done its job, it
drains back into the oil pan and is recirculated
by the pump.

Oil The oil that flows through the lubrication
system performs many functions. The most important function is that of a *lubricant*. Any motion between parts in contact creates friction,

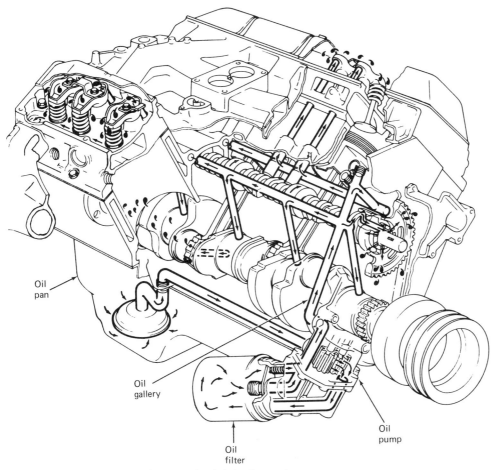

Figure 2.2 A typical eight-cylinder engine lubrication system (courtesy American Motors Corporation).

and friction causes wear. To minimize wear, friction must be minimized. A lubricant reduces friction by flowing between parts in contact and providing a thin film that acts to separate the parts. The effect of a lubricating film is shown in Figure 2.3. As this lubricating film can be wiped off or squeezed out by the motion of the parts, a constant supply of oil must be provided to maintain continuous lubrication.

Oil also helps to cool an engine. Because the oil comes in contact with hot parts, the oil absorbs some of the heat and carries it back to the oil pan. Much of this heat is passed off, or *dissipated*, through the sides and bottom of the oil pan. The oil also tends to equalize the

temperature of the engine parts by transmitting some of its heat to cooler parts.

Among the other functions oil performs is that of a *sealant*. The film of oil that forms between

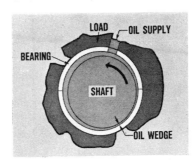

Figure 2.3 A cross-sectional view of an oil film. Note that the oil film separates the bearing and the shaft, and thus minimizes friction and wear (courtesy American Motors Corporation).

the cylinder walls and the piston rings helps in obtaining a seal between those parts.

The remaining functions of oil are for the most part handled by the *additives* in the oil. Additives are chemical compounds that are blended into the oil when it is refined and processed. Those additives include *detergents* which are similar to the soaps and detergents used to wash clothes. Detergents in the oil act to dissolve dirt, sludge, and varnish deposits in the engine. If used continuously in new engines, oil containing detergents will keep the insides of engines from becoming dirty. Usually included with detergents are *dispersants* which act to keep any dirt in suspension in the oil. If the dirt is kept in suspension, it cannot build in the engine. Large dirt particles are trapped by the filter. The remaining dirt drains out with the old oil when it is changed.

Other additives include *viscosity index improvers* and *pour point depressants* which help to control the change of oil thickness with temperature change, and various *inhibitors* which decrease or prevent oxidation, rust, and corrosion. Additional agents reduce foaming and improve lubricating qualities.

Any oil that you pour into an engine must perform these functions under all possible driving conditions. As an aid in selecting the correct oil, engine manufacturers provide oil specifications. To understand these specifications, you must have a knowledge of *viscosity* and *service classification*.

Viscosity Oil is available in different thicknesses. Oil can be as thin as water and flow very easily, or it can be as thick as honey and flow very slowly. Viscosity is a measurement of how easily a liquid will flow. Oil for use in automobile engines is graded in a viscosity index system developed by the Society of Automotive Engineers (SAE). In this system, oils are assigned numbers in relation to their thickness. Thin oils are given low numbers, and higher numbers are assigned to thicker oils.

To help assure good cold and hot starting, as well as maximum engine life, fuel economy, and oil economy, select the proper viscosity from the temperature range anticipated from the following chart:

RECOMMENDED SAE VISCOSITY GRADES

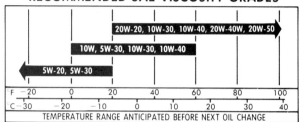

NOTE: SAE 5W-30 oils are recommended for all seasons in vehicles normally operated in Canada. SAE 5W-20 oils are not recommended for sustained high-speed driving. SAE 30 oils may be used at temperatures above 40°F (4°C).

Figure 2.4 Typical oil viscosity recommendations based on temperature (Chevrolet Service Manual, Chevrolet Motor Division, GM).

The most commonly specified oil viscosities for automobile engines range from SAE 5 or SAE 5W (Winter) for cold climate use to SAE 50 for use under high temperature conditions. Figure 2.4 shows the oil viscosities recommended by one manufacturer for use within normal temperature ranges on the North American continent.

When oil is heated, it tends to thin out. An oil with a low viscosity will flow easily between parts. This may provide excellent lubrication when a cold engine is first started. But when the engine reaches normal operating temperatures, the oil may be too thin and allow excessive wear. An oil with a higher viscosity may be ideal for high temperature operation. However, it may not flow between the parts when the engine is cold, and thus allow wear when the engine is first started. To provide proper lubrication over a broad temperature range, *multi-grade* or *multi-viscosity* oils were developed.

In use, a multi-viscosity oil performs as a low viscosity oil when it is cold. When it is heated, it performs as a high viscosity oil. As an example, an SAE 10W-30 oil flows as an SAE 10W oil when cold, but flows as an SAE 30 oil when hot. Multi-viscosity oils are produced by the addition of viscosity index improvers mentioned previously. These additives keep the oil from becoming too thin when heated.

Service Classification   This system was developed by the American Petroleum Institute (API). It provides a means of selecting an engine oil based on the service conditions under which a particular engine is operated. At present there are five classifications in the "S" (Service Station, Garages, New Car Dealers, etc.) category. The API lists these categories as follows:

SA   (Utility Gasoline and Diesel Engine Service)

Oils with this classification can be used in engines which are operated under such mild conditions that the protection afforded by oils containing additives is not required. This classification has no performance requirements.

SB   (Minimum Duty Gasoline Engine Service)

Oils with this classification can be used in gasoline engines operated under such mild conditions that only minimum protection afforded by oils containing additives is desired. Oils designed for this service have been used since the 1930s and provide only antiscuff capability, and resistance to oil oxidation and bearing corrosion.

SC   (1964 through 1967 Gasoline Engine Warranty Maintenance Service)

Oils with this classification can be used in gasoline engines in 1964 through 1967 models of passenger cars, and in light trucks operating under the manufacturer's warranties in effect during these model years. Oils designed for this service provide control of high and low temperature deposits, wear, rust, and corrosion in gasoline engines.

SD   (1968 through 1970 Gasoline Engine Warranty Maintenance Service)

Oils with this classification can be used in gasoline engines in 1968 through 1970 (and certain 1971) models of passenger cars, and in light trucks operating under the manufacturer's warranties in effect during those model years. Oils designed for this service provide more protection against high and low temperature engine deposits, wear, rust, and corrosion than oils classified SC.

SE   (1972 through Present Gasoline Engine Warranty Maintenance)

Oils with this classification can be used in gasoline engines in 1972 (and certain 1971) through present models of passenger cars, and in light trucks operating under the manufacturer's warranties. Oils designed for this service provide more protection against oil oxidation, high temperature engine deposits, rust, and corrosion than do oils classified SD.

The API Service Classification System is "open-ended" in that it allows the addition of new classifications as they become necessary. When engine design, operating conditions, or lubricant performance require a new classification, SF will be added. With 21 letters of the alphabet remaining, this system should remain in use indefinitely.

All engine oil distributed by reputable refiners and manufacturers is labeled to identify its SAE Viscosity and its API Service Classification. Typical container markings are shown in Figure 2.5.

Job 2a

IDENTIFY TERMS RELATING TO ENGINE OIL

SATISFACTORY PERFORMANCE

A satisfactory performance on this job requires that you do the following:

1 Identify terms and abbreviations relating to engine oil by placing the number of each term or abbreviation in front of the phrase that best describes it.

2 Correctly identify all the terms within 15 minutes.

PERFORMANCE SITUATION

1 SA   6 Detergent
2 Dispersant   7 Viscosity Index Improver
3 SE   8 Additives
4 SAE   9 Inhibitors
5 Viscosity   10 API

_____ dissolves dirt and sludge in engines

_____ an oil classification that has no performance requirements

_____ American Petroleum Institute

_____ Super Activated

_____ additives that decrease or prevent oxidation and rust

_____ chemical compounds added to engine oil

_____ an oil classification meeting current warranty requirements

_____ a measurement of the ability of a liquid to flow

_____ Severe Aeration Eliminator

_____ an additive that controls viscosity change

_____ Society of Automotive Engineers

_____ an additive that holds dirt in suspension in the oil

Figure 2.5 Typical oil container markings that identify the SAE viscosity and API Service Classification (courtesy of Pennzoil Co.).

CHECKING ENGINE OIL LEVEL If there is insufficient oil in an engine, the engine parts may not receive proper lubrication and the oil may be overheated. If there is too much oil in an engine, excessive oil consumption may result. An oil level that is too high may also result in the oil being *aerated*. That condition can occur when the rotating crankshaft and the ends of the connecting rods strike the surface of the oil in the oil pan. This action whips the oil so that air bubbles are mixed with it. Air bubbles and foam in the system provide poor lubrication. An engine lubricating system will function properly only when the correct oil level is maintained.

The level of the oil is easily checked by means of a dipstick located on the engine. A typical dipstick location is shown in Figure 2.6. Most dipsticks have markings that indicate a safe oil level range, as shown in Figures 2.7 and 2.8. Oil level must be checked only when the engine is not running and when the car is parked in a level position. Oil level should not be checked immediately after stopping an engine. Time must be allowed for all the oil to drain back into the oil pan. An accurate check can be made only when the engine has been off for at least 3 minutes.

The following steps outline a procedure for accurately checking engine oil level:

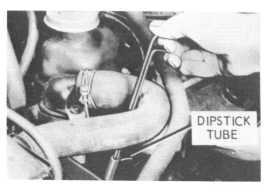

Figure 2.6 A typical engine oil dipstick location (Ford Motor Company).

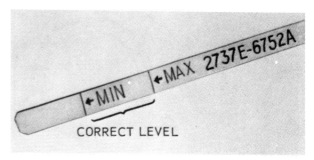

Figure 2.7 Typical dipstick markings. On this dipstick, minimum and maximum levels are indicated, with the safe range between these two markings (Ford Motor Company).

1 Locate and remove the engine oil dipstick.

2 Using a clean rag or a paper towel as shown in Figure 2.9, wipe all traces of oil from the dipstick.

3 Study the markings on the dipstick so that you can determine the location of the safe oil level range.

4 Insert the dipstick into its tube, pushing it down as far as it will go.

5 Remove the dipstick and hold it with the handle up as shown in Figure 2.10.

Note: If you hold the dipstick so that the end is pointed upward, the oil will run down the dipstick and give you a false reading.

6 Read the oil level shown on the dipstick.

7 Insert the dipstick into its tube.

CORRECT LEVEL

Figure 2.8 Variant dipstick markings. On this dipstick, the safe range is indicated (Ford Motor Company).

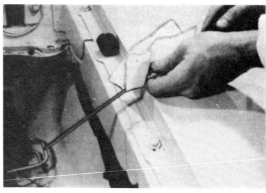

Figure 2.9 The dipstick should be wiped clean before inserting it to check oil level (Ford Motor Company).

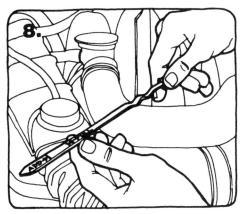

Figure 2.10 The dipstick should be held with the tip downward while checking the oil level (Ford Motor Company).

Figure 2.11 A typical engine oil filler cap. On this engine, it is located on the left side valve cover (reproduced by permission of Ashland Oil, Inc. "VALVOLINE" is a registered trademark of Ashland Oil, Inc., Ashland, Kentucky, U.S.A.).

Adjusting the Oil Level If the oil level is within the safe range, no adjustment is necessary.

If the oil level is below the safe range, add 1 quart of oil to the engine. The oil filler cap is usually located in a valve cover at the top of the engine. Figure 2.11 shows the location of a typical filler cap. The use of a *canspout*, shown in Figure 2.12, minimizes the possibility of spilling oil on the engine. After adding oil, wait a few minutes for it to drain down into the pan. Recheck the oil level. If the oil level is still below the safe range, add another quart and repeat the oil level check. Never add oil so that the oil level goes above the safe range.

If the oil is above the safe range, the excess oil should be drained. That procedure is explained in Chapter 3.

In most instances you will use a multi-viscosity oil of SAE 10W-30 or SAE 10W-40 with an API Service Classification of SE. However, that selection will not be correct in all instances. You should always consult the manufacturer's manual for specifications for the oil to be used in a particular engine.

Job 2b

CHECK AND ADJUST ENGINE OIL LEVEL

SATISFACTORY PERFORMANCE
A satisfactory performance on this job requires that you do the following:

1 Check the oil level in the engine assigned and adjust the oil level if required.
2 Following the steps in the "Performance Outline," complete the job within 10 minutes.
3 Fill in the blanks under "Information."

PERFORMANCE OUTLINE

1 Remove, clean, and insert the dipstick.
2 Remove the dipstick and determine the oil level.
3 Adjust the oil level if necessary.

INFORMATION

Vehicle identification _____

Reference used_____ Page(s)_____

Oil specified   SAE viscosity_____ API classification_____

Oil level was   Correct_____   Too low_____   Too high_____

Was oil added?   Yes_____   No_____

Oil added —   SAE viscosity_____   API classification_____

COOLING SYSTEM SERVICE Most of the automobile engines you will work on have liquid cooling systems similar to the one shown in Figure 2.13. Cooling system maintenance includes a few simple jobs, but there is some information you should know before you attempt these jobs.

Coolant Although many people refer to liquid cooled engines as "water cooled" engines, no manufacturer recommends the use of water alone in the cooling system. The liquid specified, called *coolant*, is a mixture of water and *ethylene glycol*. (See Figure 2.14.) Ethylene glycol is commonly known as "permanent" antifreeze. Although the need for antifreeze when the temperature drops below 32°F (0°C) is obvious, its use in hot weather may seem strange.

Permanent antifreeze does more than lower the freezing point of water. It also raises the boiling point of water. Therefore, a mixture of water and permanent antifreeze provides a solution that has a low freezing point and a high boiling point. A half-and-half (50 percent water and 50 percent ethylene glycol) mixture provides a coolant that will remain liquid down to a temperature of about −34°F (−37°C). That same mixture will not boil until heated to a temperature of about 227°F (108.3°C).

The use of permanent antifreeze provides other benefits. Permanent antifreeze contains

Figure 2.12 Adding oil to an engine. The use of a funnel or a canspout helps to avoid spillage (reproduced by permission of Ashland Oil, Inc. "VALVOLINE" is a registered trademark of Ashland Oil, Inc., Ashland, Kentucky, U.S.A.).

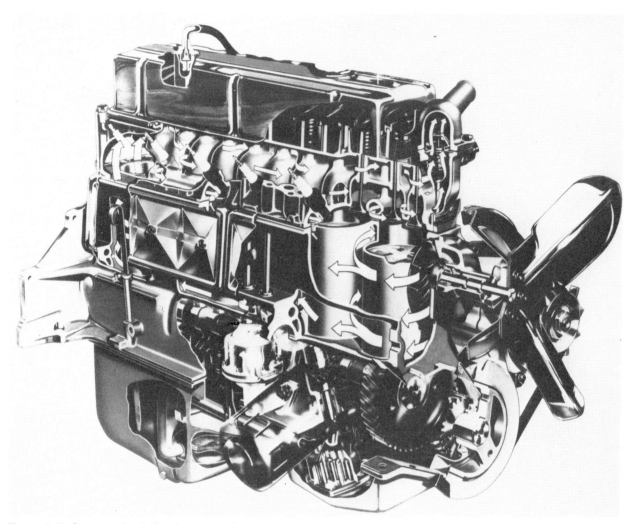

Figure 2.13 Coolant circulation in a six-cylinder engine (Chevrolet Service Manual, Chevrolet Motor Division, GM).

additives. Some of those additives reduce the formation of rust. Others lubricate the water pump and other moving parts in the system. Still others reduce the tendency of the coolant to foam. To obtain all the benefits of coolant, the cooling systems of all cars are filled with coolant when they leave the factory.

When checking cooling systems, you will find cars that require additional coolant to bring the level up the correct point. Never attempt to adjust the coolant level by adding water alone. To do so may affect the operation of the cooling system. If additional coolant is required, a 50-50 mixture of water and permanent antifreeze should be used.

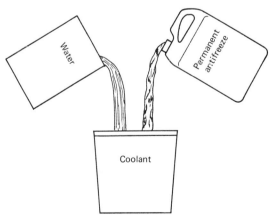

Figure 2.14 Coolant is a mixture of water and permanent antifreeze.

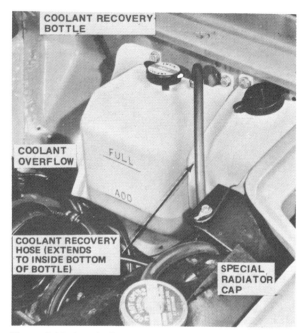

Figure 2.15 A typical coolant recovery system. Note that the coolant recovery hose connects to the radiator filler neck below the radiator cap (courtesy American Motors Corporation).

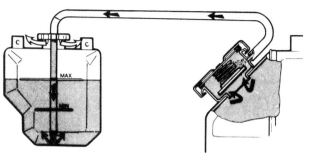

Figure 2.16 When coolant is heated and expands in the radiator, the excess coolant flows to the recovery bottle (Ford Motor Company).

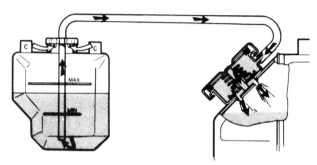

Figure 2.17 When the engine cools, the coolant contracts. Coolant then returns to the radiator from the recovery bottle (Ford Motor Company).

CHECKING COOLANT LEVEL Although this too is a simple job, there are several things you should know before you attempt it. This information concerns (1) coolant expansion and (2) pressurized cooling systems.

Coolant Expansion Most liquids expand when they are heated. When pure water is heated to a temperature of about 200°F (93°C), it expands at a rate of approximately ¼ pint per gallon (.12 l per 3.8 l). The addition of ethylene glycol increases that rate of expansion. A 50-50 mixture of water and ethylene glycol will expand at a rate of approximately ⅓ pint per gallon (.16 l per 3.8 l) when heated to the same temperature. This means that a cooling system which contained 18 quarts (17.1 l) of coolant would have an excess of about 1½ pints (.7 l) when it reached normal operating temperature.

To allow for this excess coolant, most cars have a *coolant recovery system* similar to the one shown in Figure 2.15. A coolant recovery system consists of a reservoir or *recovery bottle* mounted near the radiator and connected to it by a hose. When the coolant expands, excess coolant flows into the reservoir as shown in Figure 2.16. While the engine is cooling after operation, the coolant contracts. As the coolant contracts, it returns to the radiator. This action is shown in Figure 2.17.

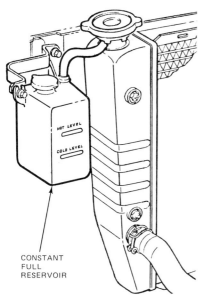

Figure 2.18 A coolant recovery bottle marked to indicate levels for hot and cold coolant (Ford Motor Company).

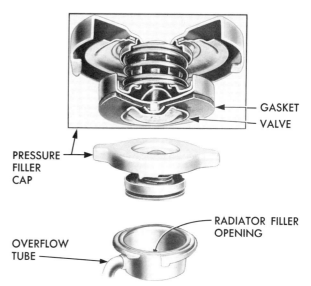

Figure 2.19 A typical pressure cap (courtesy Chrysler Corporation).

On most cars the coolant recovery bottle is marked to indicate the correct coolant level. Usually, two levels are marked as shown in Figure 2.18. The "Hot Level" indicates the normal level of expanded coolant. The "Cold Level" indicates the correct level of coolant in a cold engine. In place of those markings, some manufacturers use the words "Full" and "Add," or "Max" and "Min." (Refer to Figures 2.15 and 2.18.) The use of these markings eliminates the need for you to remove the radiator cap. The coolant level can be checked simply by looking at the coolant bottle. If the coolant level is below the "Cold Level" or "Add," additional coolant is required.

Pressurized Cooling Systems All cars of recent production have pressurized cooling systems. The pressure in the system is provided by the expansion of the coolant. This pressure is obtained by the use of a *pressure cap* on the filler neck of the radiator. A typical pressure cap is shown in Figure 2.19. The pressure cap seals the system and allows no coolant to escape to the recovery bottle until the pressure in the system reaches about 15 psi (pounds per square inch) 1.05 kg per sq cm). Pressurized cooling systems are used because they allow the coolant to be heated above its normal boiling point without boiling. This in turn increases the efficiency of the radiator in dissipating heat. The cooling system dissipates heat by transfering it to the air that passes through the radiator.

Because the coolant in a pressurized system may be at a temperature well above its normal boiling point, any release of pressure could allow the coolant to instantly boil. If you remove the radiator cap from a system that is at its normal operating temperature, the

Figure 2.20 The coolant level in the radiator of a hot cooling system may be base of the filler neck (Ford Motor Company).

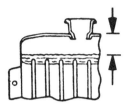

Figure 2.21 The coolant level in the radiator of a cold system should be approximately 1½ inches (37 mm) below the base of the filler neck. This allows room for coolant expansion (Ford Motor Company).

steam released by the boiling coolant could force the coolant out of the radiator filler neck and cause severe burns. For this reason, you should never remove the radiator cap when the system is hot. In most instances, a slight adjustment of the coolant level can be made by adding coolant to the recovery bottle.

The following steps outline procedures for checking and adjusting coolant level:

Cooling Systems with Recovery Bottles

1 Check the coolant level by observing the level of the coolant in the recovery bottle.

2 If additional coolant is required, add a mixture of 50 percent water and 50 percent ethylene glycol to the recovery bottle so that the level is at the correct marking.

Cooling Systems Without Recovery Bottles

WARNING: NEVER REMOVE THE RADIATOR CAP WHILE THE ENGINE IS RUNNING. FAILURE TO FOLLOW THIS ADVICE COULD CAUSE SERIOUS BURNS AND POSSIBLE DAMAGE TO THE COOLING SYSTEM. AS SCALDING HOT COOLANT OR STEAM MAY ERUPT FROM THE RADIATOR FILLER NECK, USE EXTREME CARE WHEN REMOVING A RADIATOR FILLER CAP. IT IS BEST TO WAIT UNTIL THE ENGINE HAS COOLED.

1 When the engine has cooled, wrap a heavy rag or wiper around the radiator filler cap.

2 Turn the radiator filler cap counterclockwise (to the left) until you feel it stop at its first "stop" or *detent*. This position releases the pressure in the system.

Note: If pressure is released, stand away from the radiator until you are sure that all pressure is released. Do not attempt to remove the cap in one motion. The pressure in the system could force hot coolant or steam to erupt from the filler neck.

3 Wiggle the cap to be sure that it is loose and has released all the pressure in the system.

4 Push down on the cap and slowly turn it counterclockwise to its second "stop" and lift the cap from the filler neck.

5 Observe the level of coolant in the radiator. If the system is hot,

the coolant level should be near the bottom of the filler neck. (See Figure 2.20.) If the system is cold, the coolant level may be from 1 to 2 inches (25 to 50 mm) below the bottom of the filler neck, as shown in Figure 2.21.

Note: **You should never completely fill the radiator when the system is cold. When the coolant is heated, it will expand and be lost through the overflow.**

6 Adjust the coolant level if necessary. Use a 50-50 mixture of water and ethylene glycol.

7 Install the radiator cap, turning it clockwise past the first "stop" until it is tight.

Job 2c

CHECK AND ADJUST COOLANT LEVEL

SATISFACTORY PERFORMANCE

A satisfactory performance on this job requires that you do the following:

1 Check the coolant level in the cooling system of the car assigned. Add coolant if necessary.
2 Following the steps in the "Performance Outline," complete the job within 10 minutes.
3 Fill in the blanks under "Information."

PERFORMANCE OUTLINE

1 Check the coolant level, removing the radiator cap only if necessary.
2 Add coolant if it is required.

INFORMATION

Vehicle identification _____

Reference used_____Page(s)_____

Coolant level was checked at the

     Coolant recovery bottle_____ Radiator_____

Coolant level was   Too low_____   OK_____   Too high_____

Was coolant added? Yes_____   No_____

Ratio of coolant (water/antifreeze) added   Water_____

                                 Antifreeze_____

Cooling system capacity _____quarts

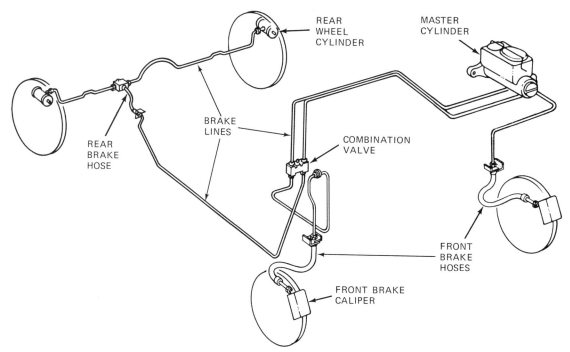

Figure 2.22 A typical hydraulic brake system showing the major components and the connecting lines and hoses (courtesy American Motors Corporation).

BRAKE SYSTEM SERVICE When you step on the brake pedal of a car, your effort is transmitted to the braking mechanism at each wheel by fluid. This fluid passes through a system of lines and hoses similar to the one shown in Figure 2.22. If the fluid level in the brake system is not maintained, the system will not function. If the wrong type of fluid is added, the system can be seriously damaged. Because brake fluid is so important, there are certain things that you must know about it before you attempt to check and adjust its level.

Brake Fluid Because the brake system is vital to the safe operation of an automobile, the fluid which is used in that system must meet certain standards. Those standards have been set by the Society of Automotive Engineers (SAE) and the Department of Transportation (DOT). Before using a brake fluid, you should check the container to be sure that the fluid has SAE and DOT approval. (See Figure 2.23.)

Figure 2.23 Brake fluid containers marked to indicate that the fluid meets or exceeds SAE and DOT specifications (courtesy EIS Division, Parker Hannifin Corporation).

All brake fluid sold by reputable manufacturers meets or exceeds SAE and DOT specifications. You should never use a brake fluid of questionable origin, and you should always check the container to see that it is marked DOT 3 or DOT 4.

Fluid meeting DOT 3 specifications is suitable for use in drum and disc brake systems. Fluid meeting DOT 4 specifications is also suitable for drum and disc systems. However, it is recommended for extra-heavy duty. It will withstand higher temperatures than fluid meeting DOT 3 specifications.

A brake fluid must not rust or corrode metals such as iron, brass, and aluminum. Many parts of the brake system are made of those metals. Furthermore, brake fluid must not cause rubber to swell or dissolve. Brake hoses and certain other parts of the brake system are made of rubber. For this reason, you should never use oil or any petroleum-based fluid in a hydraulic brake system. If the fluid in a brake system is contaminated with a petroleum product, the system will have to be taken apart and thoroughly flushed out. Moreover, all the rubber parts will have to be replaced with new ones.

Brake fluid must also have a low freezing point and a high boiling point. A low freezing point is necessary because a vehicle may be operated in very cold temperatures. A high boiling point is necessary because much of the heat of braking is transmitted to the fluid. Brake fluid must be chemically stable within the ranges of temperature and pressure to which it is subjected. The fluid must not break down, and it must not form sludge deposits that may gum up the system. Also, the fluid must provide lubrication for the pistons and other moving parts in the system.

Finally, brake fluid must be *miscible*. That is, it must mix well with other brake fluids. As the brake lining wears, the pistons in the calipers and wheel cylinders move outward. This creates more space in the system. To fill that space, you must add more fluid, but you have

no way of knowing the brand of fluid which is already in the system. Any fluid you add must mix well with the fluid already there, and it must mix without causing any chemical action that may damage the system.

Brake Fluid and Water Brake fluid is *hydroscopic*. In other words, it tends to absorb water, and it can even absorb moisture from the air. For this reason, brake fluid should always be stored in a closed, air-tight container. Even small amounts of water in a brake system will lower the boiling point of the fluid. In severe usage, such as during panic stops or repeated braking, the temperature of the fluid is raised to well above the boiling point of water. When the water in the system boils, a steam pocket forms in the system.

Unlike a fluid, steam can be compressed. Therefore, when there is steam in the brake system, the pressure in the system is wasted in compressing the steam. This results in a lack of pressure, and the brake shoes may not be pushed against the rotors and drums with enough force. To stop the car, the driver must push the brake pedal down farther than usual. In extreme cases, the pedal goes all the way down to the floor without developing enough pressure to stop the car.

Water in a brake system can cause problems other than a loss of pressure. Because water is heavier than brake fluid, it settles in the lowest parts of the system. This leads to rust and corrosion inside the calipers and wheel cylinders, and to the eventual failure of those parts.

Most brake systems have a reservoir for reserve fluid built as part of the *master cylinder*. The master cylinder is usually located under the hood on the left side of the car. Figure 2.24 shows a master cylinder and its reservoir cover. This cover must be removed to check the level of the brake fluid. Most master cylinder reservoir covers have a *diaphragm*, or *bellows seal*, as shown in Figure 2.25. The diaphragm is folded so that it will move up

Figure 2.24 A typical master cylinder. Note how the reservoir cover is secured by the bail (courtesy Chrysler Corporation).

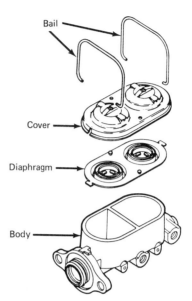

Figure 2.25 A typical dual master cylinder with the cover removed to show the position of the diaphragm (Chevrolet Service Manual, Chevrolet Motor Division, GM).

and down with changes in the fluid level and yet will seal out air. The diaphragm cuts down on the amount of moisture that the fluid can absorb from the air.

CHECKING BRAKE FLUID LEVEL The master cylinder reservoir should be checked regularly to maintain the reserve level of fluid. The steps in the procedure for checking and adjusting the fluid level are outlined below. You should refer to an appropriate manual for the specific procedures that may be necessary on particular cars.

1 Open the hood and place a fender cover on the left (driver's side) front fender.

2 Clean the reservoir cover thoroughly so that no dirt can fall into the reservoir when the cover is removed.

3 Use a screwdriver to pry the *bail,* or clasp, to one side as shown in Figure 2.26. Hold the cover with your free hand to avoid dropping it.

Note: Some master cylinders have plastic reservoirs with threaded caps as shown in Figure 2.27. As the reservoir contains two separate compartments, both caps must be removed when checking the fluid level.

4 Lift the cover, turn it over, and check the diaphragm. If the seal is unfolded or distorted, refold it so that it lies flat.

Note: Brake fluid attacks and removes paint. Do not hold the cover over, or place it on, any painted surface.

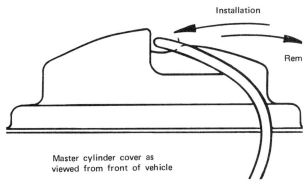

Figure 2.26 Removal and installation of the bail or clasp used to secure the cover on a master cylinder reservoir (Chevrolet Service Manual, Chevrolet Motor Division, GM).

Figure 2.27 A plastic master cylinder reservoir with threaded caps. The fluid level in both compartments should be maintained at ¼ inch (about 6 mm) below the reservoir top (courtesy Chrysler Corporation).

5 Check the fluid level. Add fluid, if necessary, to raise the level to within ¼ inch (about 6 mm) of the top of the casting as shown in Figures 2.27 and 2.28.

Note: **Be careful not to spill any fluid. Remember that it dissolves paint.**

6 Carefully set the cover back in place so that the seal is not distorted.

7 Using a screwdriver, carefully pry the bail up and into place in its retaining groove in the cover.

8 Remove the fender cover.

Job 2d

CHECK AND ADJUST BRAKE FLUID LEVEL

SATISFACTORY PERFORMANCE

A satisfactory performance on this job requires that you do the following:

1 Check the level of fluid in the master cylinder reservoir of the car assigned and adjust the fluid level if necessary.
2 Following the steps in the "Performance Outline," complete the job within 10 minutes.
3 Fill in the blanks under "Information."

PERFORMANCE OUTLINE

1 Protect the fender of the car with a fender cover.
2 Remove the reservoir cover.
3 Check the diaphragm seal and refold it if necessary.
4 Adjust the fluid level if necessary.
5 Install the cover.
6 Remove the fender cover.

INFORMATION

Vehicle identification _____

Reference used_____ Page(s) _____

Was fluid needed? Yes_____ No_____

Was fluid added? Yes_____ No_____

Fluid added was DOT_____

AUTOMATIC TRANSMISSION SERVICE The majority of the cars you will service have automatic transmissions. The most commonly performed maintenance services on automatic transmissions are the checking and adjusting of the fluid level. To make it easy to perform those services, most automobile manufacturers provide a filler tube containing a dipstick. The filler tube extends from the transmission up to the engine compartment so that it is accessible from under the hood. As shown in Figure 2.29, the tube and dipstick are usually located near the rear of the engine at the right (passenger's) side of the car. As with checking and adjusting engine oil and coolant levels, there are a few things you must know before you can check and adjust transmission levels accurately.

Automatic Transmission Fluid Different types of transmissions require different types of fluid. The use of the wrong fluid in a transmission can lead to harsh shifting, slipping, and eventual transmission failure. To avoid the possibility of causing those problems, you should always consult the owner's manual or the manufacturer's service manual to determine the type of fluid specified for a particular transmission.

The most commonly used types of automatic transmission fluids (ATF) are *Dexron, Type F,* and *Type CJ*. Dexron is usually recommended for use in the automatic transmissions in cars built by General Motors, Chrysler Corporation, and American Motors. Dexron is also recommended for use in older model transmissions that originally required a fluid known as *Type A*. Some of the automatic transmissions used in cars built by Ford Motor Company require Type F. Others require Type CJ.

Different types of fluid are necessary because of the design differences in the transmissions. The designs used by General Motors, Chrysler Corporation, and American Motors require a fluid with "high lubricity" to provide smooth shifting. The transmission designs of Ford Motor Company require that a "frictional additive" be blended with the fluid to provide proper shifting. In most instances, the different fluids are not *compatible*. That is, they will not perform properly if mixed together. The addition of only one quart of the wrong fluid to a transmission will affect the operation of the unit.

CHECKING AUTOMATIC TRANSMISSION FLUID LEVEL Most manufacturers specify that the level of fluid in their transmissions be checked when the fluid is at normal operating temperature, the engine idling, the selector lever in PARK or NEUTRAL position, and the car parked on a level surface. The following steps outline a typical procedure, but you should check an appropriate manual for the procedure that may be necessary for the car on which you are working:

1 Check that the transmission fluid is at normal operating temperature. In most instances the temperature of the fluid should be about 190°F (88°C).

Note: **The transmission fluid will be at its normal operating temperature if the car has been driven so that its coolant is at normal operating temperature.**

2 Be sure that the car is parked in a level position.

3 Apply the parking brake.

4 Place the transmission selector lever in the PARK position and start the engine.

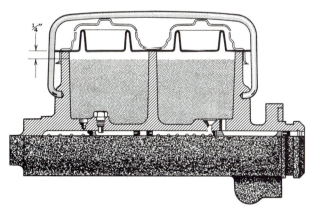

Figure 2.28 A sectioned view of a dual master cylinder showing the correct level of fluid (Chevrolet Service Manual, Chevrolet Motor Division, GM).

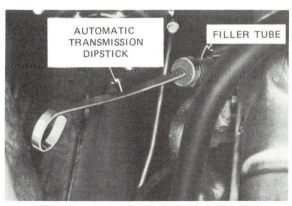

Figure 2.29 A typical automatic transmission dipstick as it appears under the hood. The dipstick is usually located at the rear of the engine on the right side (Buick Motor Division, GM).

Figure 2.30 Typical automatic transmission dipstick markings (Buick Motor Division, GM).

5 Remove the transmission dipstick and wipe it dry with a clean wiper or paper towel.

6 Insert the dipstick into the filler tube and push it down as far as it will go.

7 Remove the dipstick and note the fluid level indicated.

Note: Most dipsticks indicate a ''safe'' range between FULL and ADD as shown in Figure 2.30.

8 Insert the dipstick into the filler tube and push it down as far as it will go.

At times it will be necessary to check the transmission fluid level in a vehicle that cannot be driven sufficiently to bring the fluid to its normal operating temperature. The level of fluid at room temperature of about 70°F (22°C) can be checked in the following manner:

1 Apply the parking brake.

2 Place the selector lever in the PARK position and start the engine.

3 Allow the engine to run at idle speed.

4 Holding your foot on the brake pedal, move the selector lever slowly through all its positions.

5 Place the selector lever in the PARK position and immediately check the fluid level as outlined in steps 4, 5, and 6 of the preceding procedure.

Note: The level of fluid at room temperature will be approximately ¼ inch (6 mm) lower on the dipstick than the level of fluid at its normal operating temperature. When heated, the fluid will expand and the level will rise approximately ¼ inch (6 mm).

Adjusting Automatic Transmission Fluid Level If the level of fluid in an automatic transmission is too low, slipping, loss of drive, and eventual transmission failure may result. If the level is too high, aeration or foaming may occur, and fluid may be forced out of the filler tube as the fluid expands. The fluid must be maintained at the correct level if those problems are to be avoided. Be sure to check the owner's manual or an appropriate shop manual to determine the correct type of fluid to add.

With the dipstick removed, fluid can be added to a transmission by means of a funnel similar to the one shown in Figure 2.31. Because the difference between the ADD and FULL markings on most dipsticks is equal to about 1 pint (.47 l), you should add fluid in small amounts. (Refer to Figure 2.30.) One way to avoid overfilling is to add fluid one cupful (about .25 l) at a time, checking the fluid level after each addition.

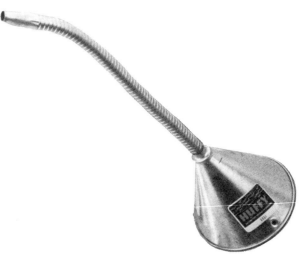

Figure 2.31 An automobile transmission funnel with a flexible metal spout (courtesy of Huffy Automotive Products).

Job 2e

CHECK AND ADJUST AUTOMATIC TRANSMISSION FLUID LEVEL

SATISFACTORY PERFORMANCE

A satisfactory performance on this job requires that you do the following:

1 Check the level of fluid in the automatic transmission of the car assigned and adjust the fluid level if necessary.
2 Following the steps in the "Performance Outline" and the procedures and specifications of the manufacturer, complete the job within 10 minutes.
3 Fill in the blanks under "Information."

PERFORMANCE OUTLINE

1 Determine the temperature of the fluid.
2 Check the fluid level by the method appropriate to the fluid temperature.
3 Adjust the fluid level if necessary.

INFORMATION

Vehicle identification _____

Reference used_____ Page(s)_____

Fluid temperature — Normal operating temperature_____

Room temperature_____

ATF specified for this transmission_____

Was fluid added? Yes_____ No_____

Fluid level indicated on dipstick

Below ADD_____ At ADD_____ Between ADD and FULL_____

At FULL_____ Above FULL_____

POWER STEERING SERVICE Cars that have power steering are equipped with a booster unit in the steering system. When the effort required to turn the steering wheel exceeds a certain limit, hydraulic pressure boosts the effort of the driver. That hydraulic pressure is provided by a pump mounted near the front of the engine. The pressure is transmitted to the steering gear by fluid flowing through connecting hoses. A typical power steering system is shown in Figure 2.32.

The reservoir on the pump must contain the correct amount of fluid for the system to function properly. Excessive noise, poor steering assist, and erratic operation may result from a low fluid level. Routine maintenance re-

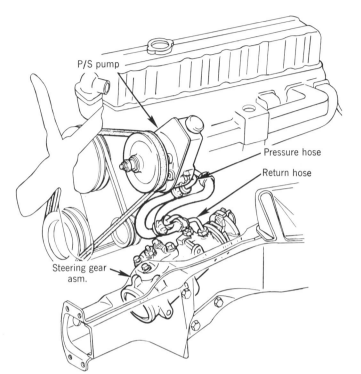

Figure 2.33 A typical power steering pump reservoir and dipstick (courtesy Chrysler Corporation).

Figure 2.32 A typical power steering system (Chevrolet Service Manual, Chevrolet Motor Division, GM).

quires that the level of fluid in the reservoir be checked regularly and adjusted when necessary. Some car makers recommend the use of ATF in their power steering systems. Others specify a special power steering fluid. The use of the wrong fluid could affect the operation of the system. You should always check an appropriate manual to determine the correct fluid for the system on which you are working.

CHECKING THE POWER STEERING FLUID LEVEL Most power steering pump reservoirs have a dipstick under the filler cap, as shown in Figure 2.33. Some manufacturers recommend that the fluid level be checked when the fluid is "cold" (at a room temperature of about 70°F (21°C). Others specify that it be checked only when the fluid is "hot," usually in the 150° to 175°F (65° to 79°C) range. Because fluid expands when it is hot, on some cars an accurate check can be made only when the fluid is at normal operating temperature. For those cars, a check made when the fluid is cold results in a false (low) reading. If fluid is added as a result of that reading, the reservoir becomes overfilled. When the fluid is heated during operation, it expands and leaks from the overfilled reservoir. If necessary, cold fluid can be heated to normal operating temperature in a short time by the following method:

1 Start the engine.

2 Turn the steering wheel repeatedly as far as it will go in both directions.

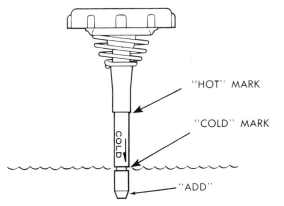

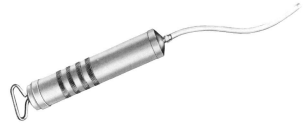

Figure 2.35 A suction gun. A gun of this type is useful in removing excess fluid from a power steering reservoir (courtesy of Lincoln St. Louis, Div. McNeil Corp., St. Louis, Missouri).

Figure 2.34 A power steering fluid dipstick with markings for checking fluid when hot and when cold (Chevrolet Service Manual, Chevrolet Motor Division, GM).

Note: Do not hold the steering wheel in the extreme left or right positions for more than 5 seconds.

3 Check the fluid temperature.

Note: The sides of the reservoir should be very hot to the touch. A more accurate check can be obtained by inserting a thermometer in the filler neck of the reservoir.

4 When the fluid reaches its normal operating temperature, turn off the engine.

Many dipsticks are marked so that you can check the fluid level both when hot and when cold. A dipstick with dual markings is shown in Figure 2.34. The steps listed below outline the procedure that should be followed to check the level of fluid in the reservoir:

1 Clean the filler cap and the area around it so that no dirt will fall into the reservoir when the cap is removed.

2 Turn the cap counterclockwise to unlock it, and lift it straight up.

3 Read the level of fluid on the dipstick.

Note: If the fluid level is difficult to see, wipe the dipstick clean and dry, insert it in the reservoir, and remove it again.

4 If the fluid level is below the correct marking, add small amounts of the fluid specified by the manufacturer, rechecking until the correct level is obtained.

Note: If too much fluid is added, the excess fluid must be removed with a suction gun. A gun similar to the one shown in Figure 2.35 is ideal for that use. Overfilling will cause the reservoir to leak.

5 Install the filler cap, turning it clockwise to lock it in place.

Job 2f

CHECK AND ADJUST POWER STEERING FLUID LEVEL

SATISFACTORY PERFORMANCE

A satisfactory performance on this job requires that you do the following:

1 Check the level of the power steering fluid on the car assigned and adjust the level if necessary.
2 Following the steps in the "Performance Outline" and the specifications of the manufacturer, complete the job within 5 minutes.
3 Fill in the blanks under "Information."

PERFORMANCE OUTLINE

1 Determine if the fluid must be checked while hot or while cold.
2 Protect the fender with a fender cover.
3 Check the fluid level.
4 Add the specified fluid if necessary.
5 Install the filler cap.
6 Remove the fender cover.

INFORMATION

Vehicle identification _____

Reference used_____Page(s)_____

Type of fluid specified _____

Temperature of fluid when checked _____Hot _____Cold

Was fluid added? _____ Yes _____ No

BATTERY SERVICE The battery in an automobile serves four important functions:

1 It furnishes the electrical energy that cranks the engine for starting.
2 It supplies the current needed to operate the ignition system while starting.
3 It provides current to the electrical system when the demands of the system exceed the output of the charging circuit.
4 It acts as a stabilizer or "cushion" in the electrical system to minimize variations in system voltage.

Unless the battery performs each of these functions, the electrical system and its related systems will not operate properly.

Battery Construction and Operation Most automobile batteries are of the lead-acid type. The lead is in the form of plates that are arranged together in *cells* or compartments as shown in Figure 2.36. The acid is a mixture of sulfuric acid and water called *electrolyte*.

Because electrolyte is an acid, you should be extremely careful when working on or near a battery. Electrolyte can damage painted finishes. It can corrode metals. It can eat holes

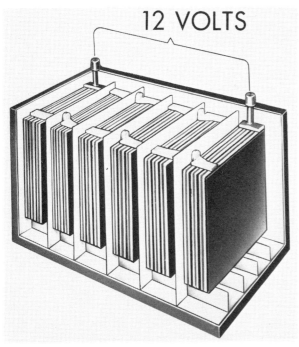

12 VOLTS

Figure 2.36 Internal battery construction. Note that groups of plates are arranged in separate compartments or cells (Chevrolet Service Manual, Chevrolet Motor Division, GM).

ARRESTOR CAP

SEALED TERMINALS

Figure 2.38 A battery with removable cell caps. These batteries require regular inspection and the addition of water (Chevrolet Service Manual, Chevrolet Motor Division, GM).

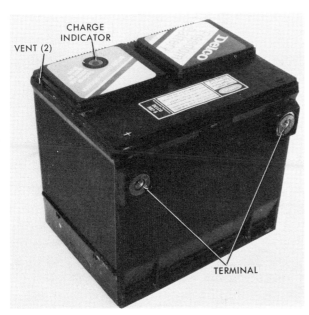

CHARGE INDICATOR

VENT (2)

TERMINAL

Figure 2.37 A sealed battery. These batteries do not require the addition of water (Chevrolet Service Manual, Chevrolet Motor Division, GM).

in your clothing. It can cause painful burns if spilled on your skin, and can cause blindness if splashed in your eyes.

There are two different battery designs in common use. One design, shown in Figure 2.37, has a sealed top. Because of its design and its internal chemistry, a sealed battery does not require the addition of water. The remaining design, shown in Figure 2.38, is not sealed. Each cell is provided with a vented cap. These caps allow you to check the level of the electrolyte in each cell and to add water if the level is low.

When a battery is operating an electrical device or when it is being charged by the alternator or by a charger, the battery is said to be "working." A battery that is working gives off gases. Those gases include hydrogen, which is an explosive. Sparks or flame may ignite the hydrogen and cause an explosion which may burst the battery. (See Figure 2.39.) To avoid the possibility of an explosion, you should take the following precautions when you work near a battery:

1 Wear safety glasses or goggles.
2 Remove jewelry such as rings and watches.

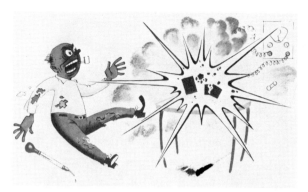

Figure 2.39 The explosive gases given off by a battery can be ignited by a spark or a flame (Chevrolet Service Manual, Chevrolet Motor Division, GM).

3 Never smoke near a battery.
4 Never short across the battery terminals or place tools on the top of a battery.
5 Never disconnect a cable from a battery when the battery is working. A spark usually occurs when a circuit is broken.

CHECKING AND ADJUSTING ELECTROLYTE LEVEL

A battery with removable cell caps will normally use water at the rate of 1 to 2 ounces (30 to 60 ml) per cell per month. If a car is driven extensively, especially in hot weather, the water loss may be higher. Only the water in the electrolyte is lost, not the acid. Therefore, only water should be added to adjust a low electrolyte level. In most batteries, the correct electrolyte level is indicated by a distortion of the surface of the electrolyte. That distortion usually appears as shown in Figure 2.40. If the surface of the electrolyte is not distorted, water should be added slowly until the distortion appears. Only water that is pure, colorless, odorless, and safe for drinking should be used. Because electrolyte expands when heated, you should be careful not to overfill the cells. Overfilling will cause electrolyte to leak through the vented caps when the battery temperature rises during operation.

The following steps outline a procedure for checking and adjusting the level of electrolyte in a battery:

1 Place a fender cover on the fender near the battery.
2 Clean the battery top if it is dirty.

ELECTROLYTE
LEVEL
TOO LOW

ELECTROLYTE
AT CORRECT
LEVEL

Figure 2.40 Typical views of the surface of the electrolyte in a battery cell. Note that the surface appears distorted when the electrolyte is at the correct level (Buick Motor Division, GM).

Figure 2.41 Because each cell is a separate compartment, the electrolyte level in all cells must be checked. The caps should be placed on top of the battery while checking the electrolyte level (Ford Motor Company).

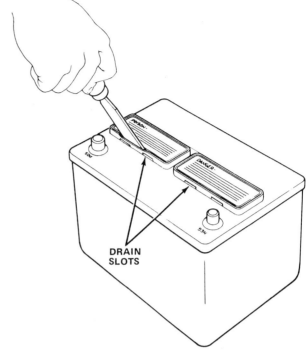

DRAIN SLOTS

Figure 2.42 On some batteries, the cell caps must be removed by prying them up with a putty knife (courtesy American Motors Corporation).

Note: Use wet paper towels to clean the battery top and discard the towels in a waste receptacle when finished. Use care during this step because there may be acid on the battery top.

3 Remove the cell caps and place them carefully on the battery top as shown in Figure 2.41.

Note: Some batteries have special caps that must be removed with the aid of a putty knife or a similar flat-bladed tool as shown in Figure 2.42.

4 Check the electrolyte level in each cell. (Refer to Figure 2.40.)

Note: Use a flashlight if the surface of the electrolyte cannot be easily seen.

5 If the electrolyte level is too low in any of the cells, use a clean syringe or a battery filler of the type shown in Figure 2.43 to slowly add water.

Note: Do not overfill the battery. Add water only until the surface of the electrolyte appears distorted.

6 Install the cell caps.

7 If any water has spilled on the battery top, clean and dry the top of the battery with paper towels. Discard the paper towels when finished.

8 Remove the fender cover.

Figure 2.43 A typical battery water filler. Note the valve on the spout that helps to prevent overfilling (courtesy of Snap-on Tools Corporation).

Job 2g

CHECK AND ADJUST BATTERY ELECTROLYTE LEVEL

SATISFACTORY PERFORMANCE

A satisfactory performance on this job requires that you do the following:

1 Check the level of the electrolyte in the battery of the car assigned and adjust the level if necessary.

2 Following the steps in the "Performance Outline," complete the job within 10 minutes.

3 Fill in the blanks under "Information."

PERFORMANCE OUTLINE

1 Protect the fender of the car with a fender cover.
2 Clean the battery top
3 Remove the cell caps
4 Check the electrolyte level in each cell.
5 Add water if necessary.
6 Install the cell caps.
7 Clean the battery top
8 Remove the fender cover.

INFORMATION

Vehicle identification _____

Was water needed? Yes_____   No_____

Was water added? Yes_____   No_____

SUMMARY

By completing this chapter you have developed skills in performing many of the routine maintenance services required to keep an automobile running properly. You also learned some of the reasons that these services are so important.

You used manufacturer's service manuals and other reference sources to locate specifications. You used these specifications to perform checks and adjustments. You are aware of the SAE viscosity numbering system and the API Service Classifications. You can use that knowledge to check correctly and adjust engine oil level. You are now knowledgeable of the composition of coolant and can check and adjust coolant level. You can check and adjust the level of brake fluid in master cylinder reservoirs and you realize the importance of the use of the correct brake fluid.

You now know about the different types of ATF and can check and adjust automatic transmission fluid levels. You can correctly check and adjust the level of electrolyte in batteries, and you are aware of the precautions you should take while working with electrolyte. You are now aware of the importance of the so-called simple jobs.

SELF-TEST

Each incomplete statement or question in this test is followed by four suggested completions or answers. In each case select the *one* that best completes the sentence or answers the question.

1 Engine oil for use in a 1979 model automobile should meet API Service Classification
   A. SB
   B. SC
   C. SD
   D. SE

2 Which of the following additives is used in engine oil to keep dissolved dirt in suspension?
   A. Dissolvers
   B. Inhibitors
   C. Detergents
   D. Dispersants

3 Coolant is a mixture of
   A. 10 percent water and 90 percent ethylene glycol
   B. 30 percent water and 70 percent ethylene glycol
   C. 50 percent water and 50 percent ethylene glycol

D. 70 percent water and 30 percent ethylene glycol

4 Most automobile cooling systems are pressurized to
   A. raise the boiling point of the coolant
   B. lower the boiling point of the coolant
   C. raise the freezing point of the coolant
   D. lower the freezing point of the coolant

5 Two mechanics are discussing brake fluid.
   Mechanic A says that brake fluid meeting DOT 3 specifications should *not* be used in cars with disc brakes.
   Mechanic B says that brake fluid meeting DOT 4 specifications can be used in cars with drum brakes.
   Who is right?
   A. A only
   B. B only
   C. Both A and B
   D. Neither A nor B

6 Most master cylinder reservoirs are fitted with a diaphragm seal under the cover to
   A. prevent fluid evaporation
   B. prevent the passage of fluid between the reservoirs
   C. maintain a slight residual pressure on the brake fluid
   D. minimize the amount of moisture absorbed by the brake fluid.

7 Two mechanics are discussing ATF.
   Mechanic A says that automatic transmissions in cars built by American Motors require Dexron ATF.
   Mechanic B says that automatic transmissions in cars built by General Motors require Type F ATF.
   Who is right?
   A. A only
   B. B only
   C. Both A and B
   D. Neither A nor B

8 Two mechanics are discussing batteries.
   Mechanic A says that most automobile batteries are of the lead-acid type.

Mechanic B says that electrolyte is a mixture of sulfuric acid and water.
Who is right?

A. A only
B. B only
C. Both A and B
D. Neither A nor B

9 Two mechanics are discussing battery service.

Mechanic A says that sealed batteries require no routine maintenance.

Mechanic B says that batteries with removable cell caps require the addition of water to adjust the electrolyte level.
Who is right?

A. A only
B. B only
C. Both A and B
D. Neither A nor B

10 A battery cell is considered full when the electrolyte surface

A. appears distorted
B. is at the top of the filler neck
C. is about ¼ inch (6 mm) below the filler neck
D. is about 1 inch (25 mm) below the filler neck

Chapter 3 Basic Under-Car Services

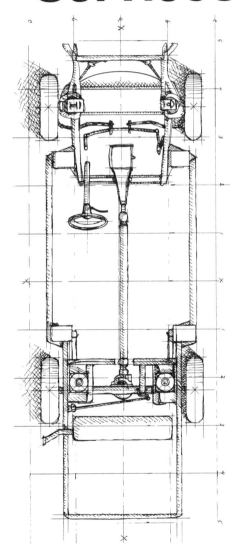

Many routine maintenance jobs must be performed under a car. The most common of those jobs include checking and adjusting the lubricant levels in manual transmissions and differentials, lubricating chassis components, and changing engine oil and filters. To perform those jobs you must raise the car from the floor and support it so that you can work under it safely.

This chapter contains the information you need to know to perform routine under-car services. It provides the procedures you should follow so that the jobs will be performed correctly.

Your specific objectives in this chapter are to perform satisfactorily the following jobs:

1
Raise a car and support it by the frame.
2
Raise a car and support it by the suspension system.
3
Raise and support a car on a frame contact lift.
4
Raise and support a car on a suspension contact lift.
5
Check and adjust transmission and differential lubricant levels.
6
Lubricate chassis components.
7
Change engine oil.
8
Replace an engine oil filter.

page 3-1

Figure 3.1 A hydraulic floor jack similar to those used in most auto shops (courtesy of Hein-Werner Corporation).

Figure 3.2 A pair of adjustable car stands. Car stands should always be used to support a car after you raise it with a jack (courtesy of Hein-Werner Corporation).

RAISING AND SUPPORTING A CAR

Many of the jobs you will perform require that you work under a car. Therefore, to do these jobs, you must raise the car off the floor. Most of the time a car is raised by means of a floor jack similar to the one shown in Figure 3.1. Whenever you raise a car with a floor jack, you must be careful where you place the jack. An improperly placed jack may let the car fall or may damage parts under the car. The proper placement of a jack depends on the type of frame and suspension system on the car. Many different types of frames and suspension systems are in use. Therefore, before raising a car with a floor jack you should check the car manufacturer's service manual. The manual will help you find the areas under the car that will provide a safe, solid place for you to position the jack.

When using a jack you should always remember that it is made to raise cars, not to support them. Working on a car that is held off the floor by a jack is very dangerous, because the car can easily slide off the jack. Anytime you raise a car, even for a few minutes, you should place *car stands* under the car to support its weight. Typical car stands are shown

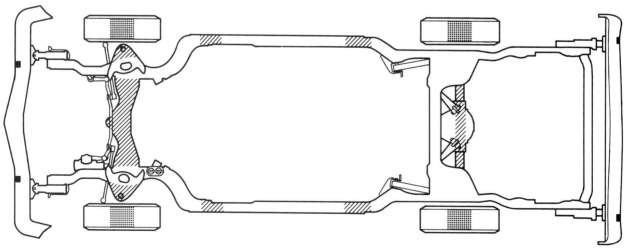

Figure 3.3 A drawing of a typical frame, showing where it is safe to place a jack and car stands (Chevrolet Service Manual, Chevrolet Motor Division, GM).

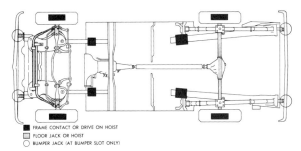

Figure 3.4 Typical lifting and support locations on a car of unit body design. Because a separate frame is not used, the jacks and car stands must be placed under reinforced areas of the floor pan (courtesy Chrysler Corporation).

in Figure 3.2. The manufacturer's service manual will show you where it is safe to place those stands. Figures 3.3 and 3.4 are typical of the drawings found in service manuals. They show areas where it is safe to place a jack and car stands.

Although there are many different areas under a car where car stands can be positioned, there are only two ways a car can be supported. One is by the frame; the other is by the suspension systems. When a car is supported by the frame, the wheels are free to drop down to the limits of their suspension systems. When a car is supported by the suspension systems, the wheels are held up in the approximate position they are in when the car is on the floor. Both methods are used for the jobs you will perform. The method chosen depends on the particular job to be done. The proper methods of raising and supporting a car are very important to your safety.

On many cars, the fuel tank is attached to the frame ahead of the rear bumper. In that position, it may be damaged while using a jack to raise or lower a car. When both the front and the rear wheels of a car must be raised from the floor, the rear of the car should be raised and supported first. The front of the car can then be raised. When the car is lowered to the floor, the front of the car should be lowered before the rear of the car is lowered. Those procedures will minimize the possibility of fuel tank damage and the dangers of fuel leakage.

RAISING A CAR AND SUPPORTING IT BY THE FRAME The steps that follow outline a typical procedure for raising a car with a jack and supporting it with car stands placed under the frame. You should check the manual for the car on which you are working for the correct lifting and support points:

Rear 1 Roll a jack under the rear of the car. Raise the jack slightly, and adjust its position so that it is centered under the rear axle housing. (See position C in Figure 3.5.)

2 Operate the jack to raise the car until the wheels are clear of the floor by at least 10 inches (25 cm).

3 Place car stands under the frame side rails just ahead of the bend in the frame. (See positions D in Figure 3.5.) Raise the car stands as close as possible to the frame.

4 Lower the jack so that the car is supported by the stands.

5 Remove the jack.

Front 1 Roll a jack under the front of the car. Raise the jack slightly, and adjust its position so that it is centered under the front crossmember of the frame. (See position A in Figure 3.5.)

2 Operate the jack to raise the car until the wheels are clear of the floor by about 6 inches (15 cm).

3 Place the car stands under the frame side rails just behind the

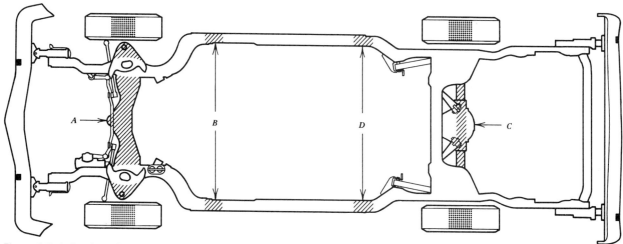

Figure 3.5 A drawing of a typical chassis, showing locations for raising a car with a jack (*A* and *C*) and positions where car stands should be placed (*B* and *D*) for supporting the car by the frame (Chevrolet Service Manual, Chevrolet Motor Division, GM).

bend in the frame. (See positions *B* in Figure 3.5.) Raise the car stands as close as possible to the frame.

4 Lower the jack so that the car is supported by the stands.

5 Remove the jack.

Job 3a

RAISE A CAR AND SUPPORT IT BY THE FRAME

SATISFACTORY PERFORMANCE

A satisfactory performance on this job requires that you do the following:

1 Using a hydraulic floor jack, raise a car from the floor and support it with car stands placed under the frame.

2 Following the steps in the "Performance Outline" and the recommendations of the car manufacturer regarding jack and car stand positioning, complete the job within 15 minutes.

3 Fill in the blanks under "Information."

PERFORMANCE OUTLINE

1 Raise the rear of the car.
2 Support the rear of the car with car stands.
3 Raise the front of the car.
4 Support the front of the car with car stands.
5 Lower the car to the floor.

INFORMATION

Vehicle identification _____

Reference used_____ Page(s)_____

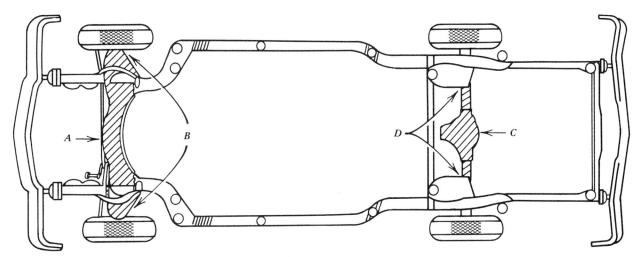

Figure 3.6 A drawing of a typical chassis, showing locations for raising a car with a jack (*A* and *C*) and positions where car stands should be placed (*B* and *D*) for supporting the car by the suspension systems (Chevrolet Service Manual, Chevrolet Motor Division, GM).

RAISING A CAR AND SUPPORTING IT BY THE SUSPENSION SYSTEMS The following steps outline a typical procedure for raising a car with a jack and supporting it with car stands placed under the suspension systems. Be sure the check the manual for the car on which you are working for the correct lift and support points.

Rear 1 Roll a jack under the rear of the car. Raise the jack slightly, and adjust its position so that it is centered under the rear axle housing. (See position *C* in Figure 3.6)

2 Operate the jack to raise the car until the wheels are clear of the floor by at least 6 inches (15 cm).

3 Place car stands under the rear axle housing as close as possible to the wheels. (See positions *D* in Figure 3.6.) Raise the car stands as close as possible to the housing.

4 Lower the car so that the car is supported by the stands.

5 Remove the jack.

Front 1 Roll a jack under the front of the car. Raise the jack slightly, and adjust its position so that it is centered under the front crossmember of the frame. (See position *A* on Figure 3.6.)

2 Operate the jack to raise the car until the wheels are clear of the floor by about 6 inches (15 cm).

3 Place car stands under the lower control arms as close as possible to the wheels. (See positions *B* in Figure 3.6.) Raise the car stands as close as possible to the lower control arms.

4 Lower the jack so that the car is supported by the stands.

5 Remove the jack.

Job 3b

RAISE A CAR AND SUPPORT IT BY THE SUSPENSION SYSTEM

SATISFACTORY PERFORMANCE

A satisfactory performance on this job requires that you do the following:

1 Using a hydraulic floor jack, raise a car from the floor and support it with car stands placed under the suspension systems.

2 Following the steps in the "Performance Outline" and the recommendations of the car manufacturer regarding jack and car stand positioning, complete the job within 15 minutes.

3 Fill in the blanks under "Information."

PERFORMANCE OUTLINE

1 Raise the rear of the car.

2 Support the rear of the car with car stands.

3 Raise the front of the car.

4 Support the front of the car with car stands.

5 Lower the car to the floor.

INFORMATION

Vehicle identification _____

Reference used_____Page(s)_____

Raising a Car with a Lift Many shops are equipped with hydraulic or electric lifts that raise and support cars. Most of those lifts are capable of raising a car high enough so that a mechanic can stand while working under the car. All of those lifts incorporate some type of safety system in their construction so that a car cannot drop suddenly in case of equipment failure. Some of these safety systems are automatic. Others must be manually set. Before you attempt to use a lift, you should be sure that you understand the operation of its safety device.

Although there are many different types of lifts in use, they all support a car in one of two ways. One is by the frame. The other is by the suspension systems.

Because there is such a variety of lifts in use, it is beyond the scope of this book to provide specific operating instructions for all of them. Lift manufacturers provide instruction manuals for the operation of each of the designs they make. You should read the manual provided with the lift you have available. Lacking the manual, you should receive instructions from someone who is familiar with the operation of the lift you intend to use. Although the following steps do not apply to the operation of some lifts, they outline procedures that are common to most lifts.

Frame Contact Lifts A typical frame contact lift is shown in Figure 3.7. They are usually made with adjustable arms and contact pads. This allows the pads to be positioned to contact the correct lifting points on any car. As you learned when raising a car with a jack, the correct lifting points for any car can be found in the service manual for that car. Figure 3.8 shows the location of the lifting points specified by one manufacturer. The following steps outline a typical procedure for the operation of a frame contact lift:

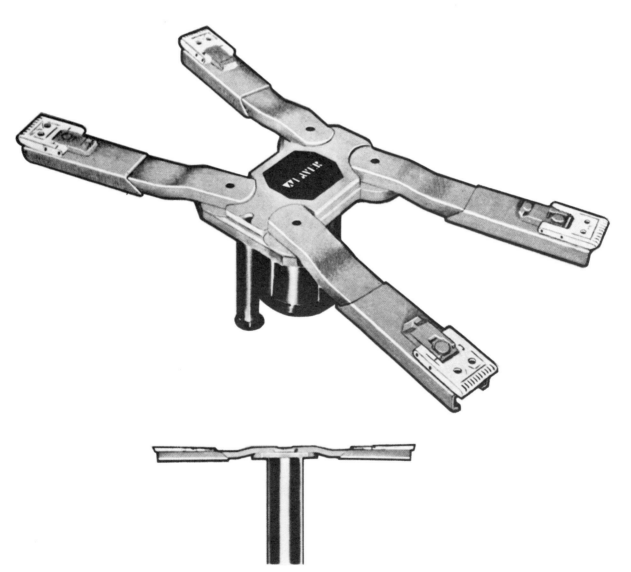

Figure 3.7 A frame engaging lift. The arms are adjustable in both length and angle, and the adapters at the ends of the arms are adjustable for different heights (courtesy of Weaver-Paris Div. Dura Corp.).

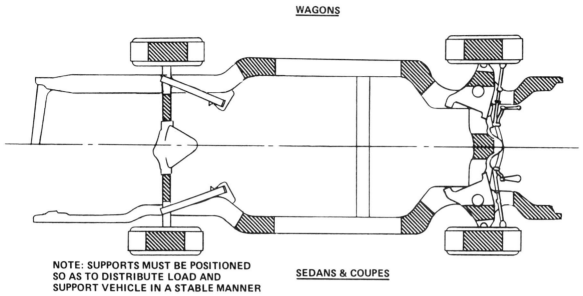

Figure 3.8 Typical lift points specified by one manufacturer.
(Pontiac Motor Division, GM).

Preparation 1 Check that the lift is all the way down and that the arms and pads will not come in contact with the underbody of a car driven over the lift. Lower the lift and move these parts if necessary.

2 Slowly drive the car over the lift so that the car is centered. Position the car so that the wheels are in place in the trough or against the stops on the floor. Turn off the engine, leave the parking brake off, and place the shift lever in the NEUTRAL position.

3 Check to see that the car is centered over (or between) the lift posts. Reposition the car if necessary.

4 Consult an appropriate manual to determine the correct lifting points.

5 Adjust the position of the arms and pads so that they are directly under the lifting points.

Note: When positioning the pads and arms, try to keep the approximate center of gravity of the car over the post(s) as shown in Figure 3.9.

Lifting 1 Carefully operate the lift controls so that the lift rises from the floor. Stop the lift when the pads contact the car.

2 Check the position of each pad so you are sure that they are in firm contact with the correct lifting areas.

Note: The pads should extend beyond the sides of the frame or underbody supporting structure as shown in Figure 3.10.

3 Raise the car until the tires are clear of the floor by about 1 inch

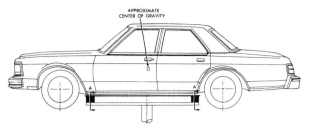

Figure 3.9 A car positioned on a frame contact lift. Note that the approximate center of gravity is directly over the center post(s) of the lift (courtesy Chrysler Corporation).

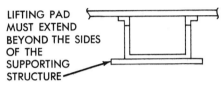

LIFTING PAD MUST EXTEND BEYOND THE SIDES OF THE SUPPORTING STRUCTURE

Figure 3.10 A sectioned view showing how the lifting pads should be positioned under the frame or supporting structure (courtesy Chrysler Corporation).

(25 mm). By pushing on the bumpers and fenders, try to push the car off the lift.

Note: It is better to have the car slip off the lift now, when there is little danger of damage or injury, than to have it slip off when raised several feet.

4 If the car is secure on the lift, continue to raise the car to the desired height.

5 Set and lock any manually operated safety devices that may be present.

Lowering 1 Clear the area under the car of any tools, equipment, wires, and hoses.

2 Release the safety device.

3 Carefully operate the controls to lower the car to the floor.

4 Adjust the position of the arms and pads under the car so that the car may be driven off the lift.

Job 3c

RAISE AND SUPPORT A CAR WITH A FRAME CONTACT LIFT

SATISFACTORY PERFORMANCE

A satisfactory performance on this job requires that you do the following:

1 Using a frame contact lift, raise and support the car assigned.

2 Following the steps in the "Performance Outline," the lift manufacturer's operating instructions, and the car manufacturer's specifications regarding lifting points, complete the job within 15 minutes.

3 Fill in the blanks under "Information."

PERFORMANCE OUTLINE

1 Align the car on the lift and adjust the lift so that the pads will contact the lifting points and so that the car's approximate center of gravity is over the post(s).

2 Raise the car slightly and test the security of the points of contact.

3 Raise the car and engage the safety device.

4 Lower the car to the floor and clear the lift so that the car can be removed.

INFORMATION

Vehicle identification _____

Lift identification and type _____

Reference used_____ Page(s)_____

SUSPENSION CONTACT LIFTS Figure 3.11 shows a typical suspension contact lift. The posts or heads can be adjusted so that a car is lifted by the front lower control arms and the rear axle housing. Figure 3.12 shows how these lifting points are specified by one manufacturer. The following steps outline a typical procedure for the operation of a frame contact lift:

Preparation 1 Check that the lift is all the way down and that the heads will not come into contact with the suspension system or underbody of a car driven over the lift. Lower the lift and move those parts if necessary.

2 Slowly drive the car over the lift so that the car is centered. Position the car so that the wheels are in the troughs or against the stops on the floor. Turn off the engine, leave the parking brake off, and place the shift lever in the NEUTRAL position.

3 Check to see that the car is centered over the heads. Reposition the car if necessary.

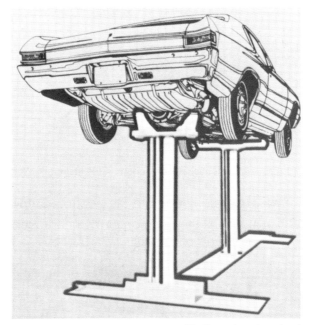

Figure 3.11 A suspension contact lift. Note that the wheels are held in the approximate position they are in when the car is on the floor (courtesy of Weaver-Paris Div. Dura Corp.).

4 Consult an appropriate manual to determine the correct lifting points.

5 Adjust the position of the heads so that they are directly under the lifting points.

Lifting 1 Carefully operate the lift controls so that the lift rises from the floor. Stop the lift when the heads contact the lower control arms and the rear axle housing.

2 Check the position of the heads to be sure that they are in firm contact and in the proper position. (See Figure 3.13.)

3 Raise the car until the tires are clear of the floor by about 1 inch (25 mm). By pushing on the bumpers and fenders, try to push the car off the lift.

Note: It is better to have the car slip off the lift now, when there is little danger of damage or injury, than to have it slip off when raised several feet.

4 If the car is secured on the lift, continue to raise the car to the desired height.

5 Set and lock any manually operated safety devices that may be present.

Lowering 1 Clear the area under the car of any tools, equipment, wires, and hoses.

2 Release the safety device.

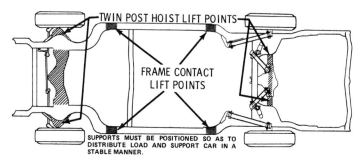

Figure 3.12 Typical locations of lifting points when using a twin post suspension contact lift (Oldsmobile Division, GM).

3 Carefully operate the controls to lower the car to the floor.

4 Adjust the position of the heads under the car so that the car may be driven off the lift.

Job 3d

RAISE AND SUPPORT A CAR WITH A SUSPENSION CONTACT LIFT

SATISFACTORY PERFORMANCE

A satisfactory performance on this job requires that you do the following:

1 Using a suspension contact lift, raise and support the car assigned.
2 Following the steps in the "Performance Outline," the lift manufacturer's operating instructions, and the car manufacturer's specifications regarding lifting points, complete the job within 15 minutes.
3 Fill in the blanks under "Information."

PERFORMANCE OUTLINE

1 Align the car on the lift and adjust the heads so that they will contact the lifting points.
2 Raise the car slightly and test the security of the points of contact.
3 Raise the car and engage the safety device.
4 Lower the car to the floor and clear the lift so that the car can be removed.

INFORMATION

Vehicle identification _____

Lift identification and type _____

Reference used_____ Page(s)_____

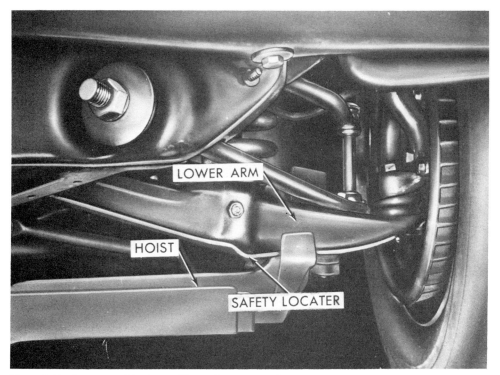

Figure 3.13 Correct positioning of lift on a lower control arm. As shown, some lower control arms incorporate a safety locator to guide the placement of the lift head (Cadillac Motor Car Division, GM).

MANUAL TRANSMISSION AND DIFFERENTIAL LUBRICATION

As with automatic transmissions, manual transmissions in different cars require different lubricants. Most car makers specify a multi-purpose gear lubricant, API classification GL-5, with a viscosity of SAE 80 or SAE 90. Some manufacturers specify that ATF be used.

The specifications for differential lubricants also vary. Most manufacturers specify that gear lubricant with API classification of GL-5 and a viscosity of SAE 80 or SAE 90 should be used in standard differentials. Limited-slip differentials, sometimes referred to as "Positraction" or "Sure-Grip" units, require special lubricants. These lubricants contain additives essential to the proper operation of the units. The use of regular lubricants in those units can lead to their failure.

The correct lubricant for any transmission and differential is best determined by consulting the manual for the car on which you are working.

CHECKING TRANSMISSION LUBRICANT LEVEL Although the level of the fluid in an automatic transmission can be checked from under the hood, you must go under a car to check the lubricant level in a manual transmission. Most manual transmissions have a filler hole in the right side of the transmission case as shown in Figure 3.14. This hole is threaded for a plug, and is placed so that it is just above the proper lubricant level. When the plug is

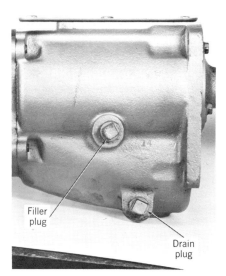

Filler
plug

Drain
plug

Figure 3.14 The filler and drain plugs on a manual transmission (courtesy American Motors Corporation).

removed, the surface of the lubricant should be near the bottom edge of the hole. If you can touch the lubricant with the first joint of your finger placed in the filler hole, the level can be considered to be correct. If lubricant drains out when the plug is removed, the level is too high. You should allow the excess lubricant to drain out into a waste oil container.

The steps that follow outline a typical procedure for checking the level of lubricant in a manual transmission. You should consult an appropriate manual or lubrication chart for the specific lubricants and procedures that may be necessary for the particular car on which you are working.

1 Raise and support the car so that it is level.

2 Remove the filler plug on the side of the transmission.

Note: Most transmissions have two plugs. (Refer to Figure 3.14.) Be sure you remove the upper plug. The lower plug is used to drain the lubricant from the transmission.

3 Check the level of the lubricant.

Note: Sufficient lubricant is present if you can touch it with the first joint of your finger inserted in the filler hole.

4 Add the specified lubricant if the level is low. A hand-operated suction gun similar to the one shown in Figure 3.15 can be used for this purpose.

Note: If too much lubricant is added, the excess should be allowed to drain out until the lubricant seeks its own level at the bottom edge of the filler hole. Don't forget to use a drain pan to catch the excess lubricant.

Figure 3.15 A hand-operated suction gun. Such a gun can be used to add lubricant to manual transmissions and differentials (courtesy of Lincoln St. Louis, Div. McNeil Corp., St. Louis, Missouri).

5 Install the filler plug.

Note: The filler plug should be tightened with a short wrench about 6 inches (15 cm) long. The use of a short wrench will minimize the chance of your overtightening the plug.

6 Lower the car to the floor.

CHECKING DIFFERENTIAL LUBRICANT LEVEL Checking the level of lubricant in a differential also requires that you go under the car. Differentials have filler holes too, but they can be in different locations. Figure 3.16 shows a filler plug located in the rear cover of the differential. Some differentials have the filler plug in the side of the housing in front of the axle. Such a location is shown in Figure 3.17. As with manual transmissions, the plug is positioned so that the correct level of lubricant is present when the surface of the lubricant is near the bottom edge of the hole. The location and size of the filler hole in some differentials make it difficult, if not impossible, to use your finger as a gauge. In those units,

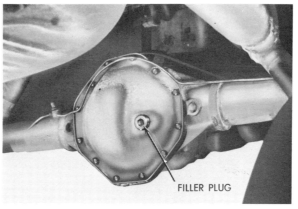

FILLER PLUG

Figure 3.16 A rear axle filler plug located in the housing cover (courtesy Chrysler Corporation).

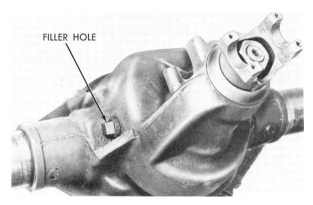

Figure 3.17 A rear axle filler plug located in the side of the housing (courtesy Chrysler Corporation).

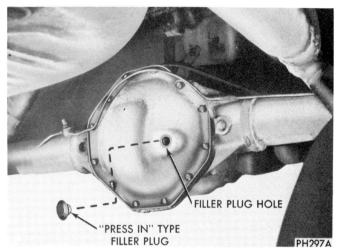

Figure 3.18 A "press in" plug made of synthetic rubber is used in some differentials (courtesy Chrysler Corporation).

you can bend a piece of welding rod or coat hanger wire to form a dipstick. If excess lubricant is found, it should be allowed to drain out.

The following steps outline a typical procedure for checking the level of lubricant in a differential. You should consult an appropriate manual or lubrication chart for the specific lubricants and procedures that may be necessary for the car on which you are working:

1 Raise and support the car so that it is level.

2 Remove the filler plug on the differential. (Refer to Figures 3.16 and 3.17.)

Note: Some differentials are fitted with "press in" type filler plugs made of synthetic rubber. A plug of this type is shown in Figure 3.18. Plugs of this type must be pried out carefully to avoid damage to the plug.

3 Check the level of the lubricant.

Note: If you cannot insert your finger into the filler hole, fashion a small dipstick from a short length of wire.

4 Add the specified lubricant if the level is low. A suction gun can

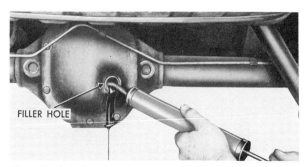

Figure 3.19 Using a suction gun to add lubricant to a differential (courtesy Chrysler Corporation).

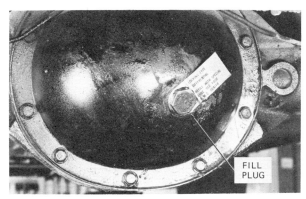

Figure 3.20 Some limited-slip or locking-type differentials are identified by a tag or plate (courtesy American Motors Corporation).

be used to add lubricant, as shown in Figure 3.19. Excess lubricant should be allowed to drain out.

Note: Check to see if the differential is of the limited-slip type. Most limited-slip differentials require a special lubricant. Some limited-slip differentials are identified by a tag as shown in Figure 3.20. Others are identified by a code number or letter on the vehicle identification plate. Be sure that you add the correct lubricant.

5 Install the filler plug.

Note: Tighten the filler plug with a short wrench to avoid over-tightening. If the plug is of the "press in" type, be sure that it is fully seated in the axle cover.

6 Lower the car to the floor.

Job 3e

CHECK AND ADJUST TRANSMISSION AND DIFFERENTIAL LUBRICANT LEVELS

SATISFACTORY PERFORMANCE

A satisfactory performance on this job requires that you do the following:

1 Check, and if necessary, adjust the transmission and differential lubricant levels on the car assigned.
2 Following the steps in the "Performance Outline" and the procedures and specifications of the car manufacturer, complete the job within 30 minutes.
3 Fill in the blanks under "Information."

PERFORMANCE OUTLINE

1 Raise and support the car so that it is level.
2 Check the transmission lubricant level and adjust it if necessary.
3 Check the differential lubricant level and adjust it if necessary.

4 Lower the car to the floor.

INFORMATION

Vehicle identification _____

Reference used_____ Page(s)_____
Transmission lubricant specified _____

Transmission lubricant level was (check one)
Correct_____ Too low_____ Too high_____
If too low, was lubricant added? Yes_____ No_____
If yes, indicate API classification and SAE viscosity_____

_____

Differential type Standard_____ Limited-slip_____
Differential lubricant specified _____

Differential lubricant level was (check one)
Correct_____ Too low_____ Too high_____
If too low, was lubricant added? Yes_____ No_____
If yes, indicate API classification and SAE viscosity_____

_____

CHASSIS LUBRICATION The suspension system, the steering system, and the drive train have many moving parts. Movement between parts in contact produces friction, which causes wear. Whenever there is motion between metal parts in contact, a lubricant must be used. The lubricant coats the parts, minimizing friction and wear.

The lubricant specified by most car makers is a semisolid, lithium-based, multi-purpose grease. However, not all lubricants are compatible. If you use the wrong grease to lubricate a car, the new grease may react with the old grease to break down the lubricating properties of both. This may result in excessive wear. For this reason, you should always check the car manufacturer's manual to determine the correct lubricant before attempting to lubricate chassis components.

Depending on the particular car, chassis components require lubrication at regular intervals of from 6,000 to 35,000 miles (9,600 to 56,000 km). Here again you should consult the car manufacturer's manual for recommendations. The number of parts requiring lubrication also differs from one make of car to another. Figures 3.21 and 3.22 show the manner in which the various lubrication points are shown in some manuals.

In most cases, a grease gun is used to force lubricant into parts through *grease fittings*. Figure 3.23 illustrates some of the many fittings used. Those fittings, sometimes called *Zerk fittings*, contain a check valve that allows grease to enter but closes to keep it from leaking out. The grease fittings are usually threaded into the parts as shown in Figure 3.24. Although many shops have high-pressure grease guns operated by compressed air, the use of such guns is not recommended

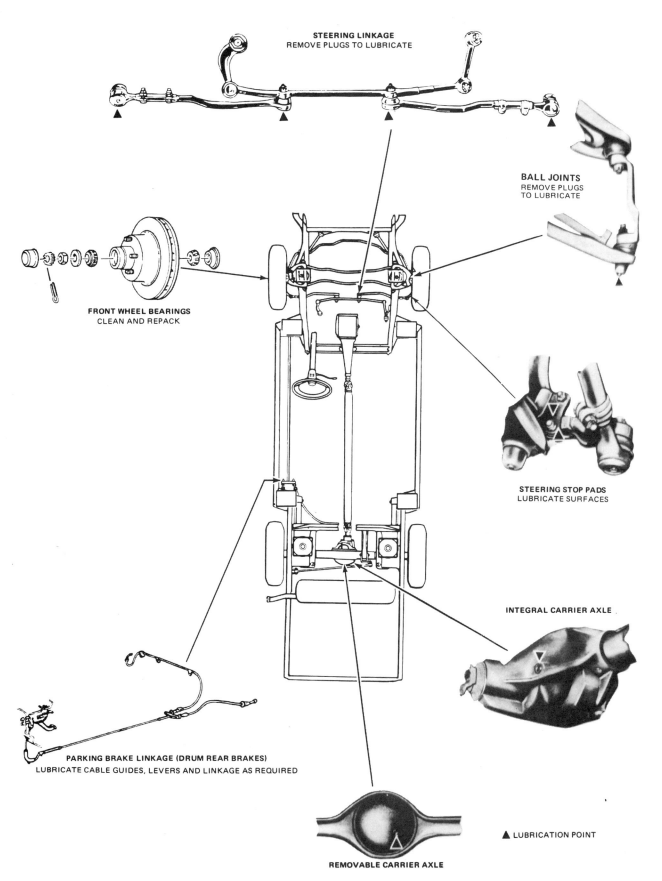

STEERING LINKAGE
REMOVE PLUGS TO LUBRICATE

BALL JOINTS
REMOVE PLUGS
TO LUBRICATE

FRONT WHEEL BEARINGS
CLEAN AND REPACK

STEERING STOP PADS
LUBRICATE SURFACES

INTEGRAL CARRIER AXLE

PARKING BRAKE LINKAGE (DRUM REAR BRAKES)
LUBRICATE CABLE GUIDES, LEVERS AND LINKAGE AS REQUIRED

▲ LUBRICATION POINT

REMOVABLE CARRIER AXLE

Figure 3.21 Typical chassis lubrication points (Ford Motor Company).

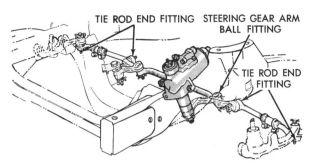

Figure 3.22 Location of grease fittings on a steering linkage (courtesy Chrysler Corporation).

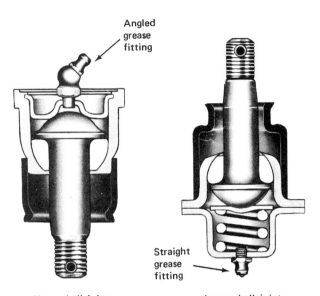

Upper ball joint   Lower ball joint

Figure 3.24 A pair of ball joints fitted with straight and angled grease fittings (Buick Motor Division, GM).

by most car manufacturers. Hand-operated grease guns, similar to the one shown in Figure 3.25, develop sufficient pressure. They are also less likely to damage the seals and boots on the parts being lubricated. Various types of seals and boots of the type shown in Figure 3.26 are used by most manufacturers to keep the lubricant inside the part and to keep out dirt and water.

Some chassis parts are not fitted with grease fittings. Plugs are threaded into the holes where the grease fittings would normally be. The plugs are installed by the car manufacturer after the parts have been lubricated during assembly. Those plugs discourage lubrication by persons who may not know the proper lubricant, the proper service interval, or about the damage that can be caused by the use of high-pressure equipment. When these parts require lubrication, you should remove the plugs and install fittings. After the

proper lubricant has been pumped in, the fittings should be removed and the plugs reinstalled. Some shops use adapters on their grease guns so that fittings do not have to be installed. These adapters fit into the threaded hole and allow you to pump grease directly into the part. An adapter of that type is shown in Figure 3.27.

Some chassis parts have no provision for lubrication. They are filled with grease during manufacture. Special seals are used to keep the grease in and to keep dirt and water out.

Rubber Bushings Where motion between metal parts is slight, rubber bushings are often

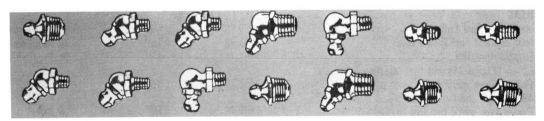

Figure 3.23 An assortment of grease fittings showing the various threads and angles available (courtesy of Dorman Products, Inc.)

Figure 3.25 A typical hand-operated grease gun suitable for lubricating chassis components (courtesy of Lincoln St. Louis, Div. of McNeil Corp., St. Louis, Missouri).

used to eliminate metal-to-metal contact. Rubber bushings of this type are shown in Figure 3.28. In most instances, rubber bushings are held tightly by the metal parts they separate. Thus, the bushing *flexes*, or stretches, without moving. This means that there is no actual motion between parts in contact and thus no friction. Rubber bushings require no lubrication. In fact, a petroleum-based lubricant applied to a rubber bushing could attack the rubber and destroy the part. If a rubber bushing is noisy, it is moving in relation to one of the parts it separates. Noisy bushings should be replaced.

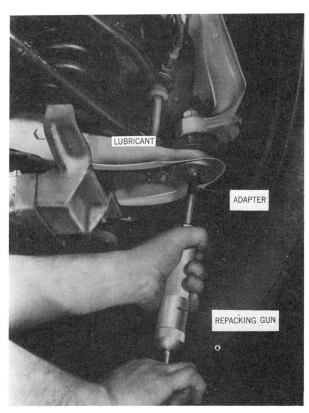

Figure 3.27 A hand-operated grease gun fitted with an adapter to allow lubrication through the plug hole (Cadillac Motor Car Division, GM).

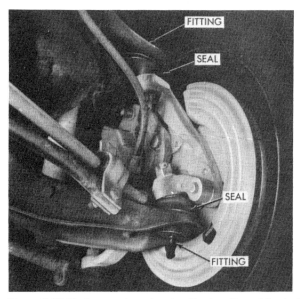

Figure 3.26 Under-car view showing the location of the ball joint fittings and seals (courtesy Chrysler Corporation).

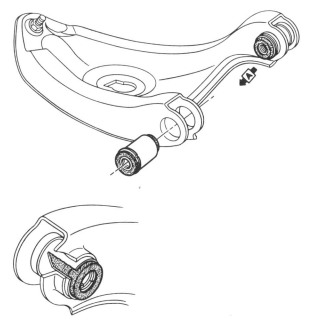

Figure 3.28 A lower control arm using rubber bushings. Note that the bushing is held between two metal sleeves (Pontiac Motor Division, GM).

LUBRICATING CHASSIS COMPONENTS The steps that follow outline a typical procedure for lubricating chassis components. Lubricant specifications and procedures that may be necessary for the particular car on which you are working should be obtained from an appropriate manual or lubrication chart:

1 Raise and support the car.

2 Using a manual or a chart, locate the lubrication points.

3 Clean the grease fittings or plugs and the areas around them so that dirt will not be forced into the part along with the grease.

4 Using a hand-operated grease gun, force grease through the fittings until the rubber boots on the parts start to expand or until grease leaks from a "bleed" hole provided in the boot.

Note: If the parts are fitted with plugs, you must remove them. Install grease fittings or use an adapter on the grease gun so that grease can be forced into the part. Reinstall the plugs after lubricating the parts.

5 Apply a dab of grease to each of the steering stops as shown in Figure 3.29.

Note: Most cars have protrusions on the lower control arms and on the steering arms. Those protrusions, called *steering* stops, limit the amount the front wheels can be turned in steering.

6 If the car is equipped with a manual transmission, check the lubricant level. Add lubricant if needed.

7 Check the level of the lubricant in the differential. Add the specified lubricant if needed.

8 Lower the car to the floor.

Figure 3.29 Most manufacturers recommend that grease be applied to the steering stops during a chassis lubrication (courtesy American Motors Corporation).

Job 3f

LUBRICATE CHASSIS COMPONENTS

SATISFACTORY PERFORMANCE

A satisfactory performance on this job requires that you do the following:

1 Lubricate the chassis components on the car assigned.

2 Following the steps in the "Performance Outline" and the recommendations and specifications of the car manufacturer, complete the job within 30 minutes.

3 Fill in the blanks under "Information."

PERFORMANCE OUTLINE

1 Raise and support the car.

2 Locate and clean the lubrication points.

3 Lubricate the parts as specified by the manufacturer.

4 Check the transmission lubricant level. Adjust the level if necessary.

5 Check the differential lubricant level. Adjust the level if necessary.

6 Lubricate the other points specified by the manufacturer.

7 Lower the car to the floor.

INFORMATION

Vehicle identification _____

Reference used_____ Page(s)_____

Number of grease fittings _____

Transmission lube level OK_____ Lube added_____

Differential lube level OK_____ Lube added_____

CHANGING ENGINE OIL As with chassis lubrication, the automobile manufacturers specify the intervals at which the engine oil in their cars should be changed. Oil change intervals are found in the appropriate service manuals and in the owner's manuals furnished with each car. Although changing engine oil is an easy task, it could result in extensive engine damage if it is improperly performed.

Oil Change Precautions Changing the engine oil requires that you remove the drain plug at the bottom of the oil pan. The location of a drain plug is shown in Figure 3.30. That drain plug is removed and installed many times during the life of an engine. Thus, the plug, its gasket, and the threaded hole in the oil pan may be worn or damaged by improper service procedures. If the damage of those

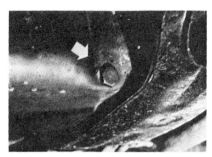

Figure 3.30 The oil drain plug. On this car it is located on the side of the oil pan (reproduced by permission of Ashland Oil, Inc. "VALVOLINE" is a registered trademark of Ashland Oil, Inc., Ashland, Kentucky, U.S.A.).

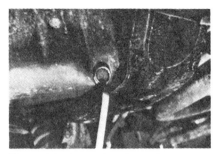

Figure 3.31 Removing the drain plug with a box wrench (reproduced by permission of Ashland Oil, Inc. "VALVOLINE" is a registered trademark of Ashland Oil, Inc., Ashland, Kentucky, U.S.A.).

parts allows oil to leak from the oil pan, the engine can be ruined by lack of lubrication.

To avoid the possibility of causing damage and to avoid installing parts that may have been damaged in the past, you should take the following precautions:

1 Remove the drain plug with a socket wrench or a box wrench as shown in Figure 3.31. The use of these tools will minimize the possibility of "rounding-off" the corners of the hex-shaped top of the plug.
2 After the plug is removed, clean and examine the threads on the plug. If they appear worn, rounded, or contain metal slivers, replace the plug with a new one.
3 Clean and examine the gasket. If the gasket is crushed, cracked, or broken, replace it with a new one.
4 Examine the threads in the oil pan drain hole by carefully threading the plug approximately halfway into the hole. The plug should not feel loose in the

hole and should resist any effort to pull it straight out. If the plug "wobbles" in the threads, or can be pulled out, repeat the test with a new plug. If the fit is improved with a new plug, discard the old plug. If the fit is not improved when tested with a new plug, an oversize replacement plug should be installed. An oversize replacement plug, shown in Figure 3.32, is made of hardened steel and will re-cut the worn threads in the drain hole as it is installed.
5 When installing the drain plug, start the plug by hand and thread it in place with your fingers to avoid cross-threading.
6 Tighten the drain plug carefully. A box wrench or a socket wrench should again be used. The plug should not be tightened with a great amount of force, but should be "snugged up" just tight enough to compress the gasket slightly. One method you can use to avoid overtightening is to hold the wrench about 6 inches (15 cm) away from the plug. This will reduce the amount of leverage you can apply.

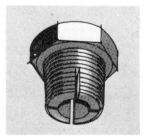

Figure 3.32 An oversize drain plug. A plug of this type should be used when the threads in the oil pan drain hole are worn or stripped (courtesy of Dorman Products, Inc.)

OIL CHANGE PROCEDURE Ideally, engine oil should be changed when it is hot. If the oil is cold, it is advisable to run the engine for about 5 minutes before draining the oil. You should consult an appropriate manual for the specifications and amount of the new oil to be added. The following steps outline a typical procedure:

1 Raise and support the car.

2 Place a drain pan under the engine.

3 Locate the drain plug on the engine oil pan. The plug is usually positioned on the bottom or low on the side of the oil pan. (Refer to Figure 3.30.)

4 Using a socket wrench or a box wrench, loosen the drain plug by turning it counterclockwise. (Refer to Figure 3.31.)

5 Position the drain pan under the plug and remove the plug.

Note: Hot engine oil can cause severe burns. When draining hot oil it is advisable to remove the plug with a socket on an extension, or to protect your hand with a folded wiper or rag.

6 Clean and examine the plug and the gasket. Replace any worn or damaged parts.

7 Examine the drain hole in the oil pan. Fit a new or oversize plug if required.

8 Carefully install the drain plug, make sure the gasket is in place.

Note: Thread the plug in by hand to avoid cross-threading.

9 Using a socket wrench or a box wrench, carefully tighten the drain plug.

10 Remove the drain pan from under the engine and pour the old oil into a waste oil receptacle or other suitable container for disposal. Clean the drain pan.

11 Lower the car to the floor.

12 Fill the crankcase with the correct amount and type of oil specified by the car manufacturer.

13 Start the engine and allow it to run at idle speed. Check to see that the oil pressure warning light goes out or that the oil pressure gauge indicates that the engine has sufficient oil pressure.

14 Check the drain plug and the floor under the car for any evidence of leakage. Correct any leaks found.

15 Turn off the engine. After allowing a few minutes for the oil to drain back into the oil pan, check the oil level. Correct the oil level if necessary.

Job 3g

CHANGE ENGINE OIL

SATISFACTORY PERFORMANCE

A satisfactory performance on this job requires that you do the following:

1 Change the engine oil of the car assigned.
2 Following the steps in the "Performance Outline" and the specifications of the manufacturer, complete the job within 30 minutes.
3 Fill in the blanks under "Information."

PERFORMANCE OUTLINE

1 Raise and support the car.
2 Drain the oil into a suitable container.
3 Examine the plug, the gasket, and the drain hole. Replace parts as required.
4 Install the plug.
5 Discard the waste oil and clean the drain pan.
6 Lower the car to the floor.
7 Fill the crankcase with the amount and type of oil specified by the manufacturer.
8 Check for leaks and correct oil level.

INFORMATION

Vehicle identification _____

Reference used_____ Page(s)_____

Oil used

Amount _____quarts   SAE viscosity_____

API Classification_____

CHANGING THE OIL FILTER All automobile engines in current production use a "full-flow" oil filtration system. As shown in Figure 3.33, all the oil that is pumped from the oil pan must flow through a filter before lubricating the internal parts of the engine. Because it is the job of the filter to trap dirt and other particles that contaminate the engine oil, the filter must be changed at regular intervals.

As with chassis lubrication and engine oil changes, the manufacturer of the vehicle specifies those intervals. In many instances it is recommended that the filter be replaced during every other oil change. About 1 pint (.47 l) of old oil remains in the filter when the oil is changed. That old oil mixes with the new oil if the filter is not changed at the same time. Because of this mixing, some manufacturers recommend that the filter be changed with each oil change.

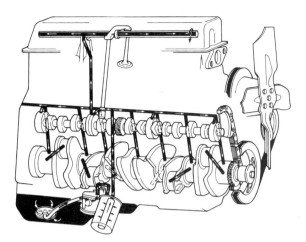

Figure 3.33 A typical lubrication system in a six-cylinder engine. Note that all the oil flows through the oil filter before it lubricates the engine parts (courtesy of American Motors Corporation).

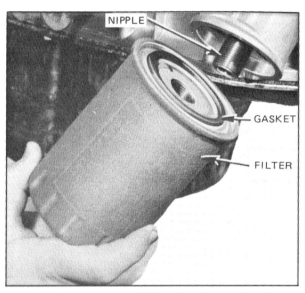

Figure 3.34 A disposable oil filter. Note that the filter fits on a threaded nipple on the engine block and that the gasket is cemented to the filter (Buick Motor Division, GM).

OIL FILTER REPLACEMENT Most manufacturers use a disposable screw-on filter of the type shown in Figure 3.34. The filter mounts on the engine block as shown in Figures 3.35 and 3.36. You will need a special *oil filter wrench* similar to those shown in Figures 3.37 and 3.38 to loosen the filter. You should consult an appropriate manual for the specific instructions that may be necessary for the car on which you are working. The following steps outline a typical procedure:

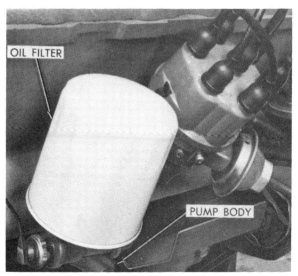

Figure 3.35 An oil filter mounted on the side of a six-cylinder engine (courtesy Chrysler Corporation).

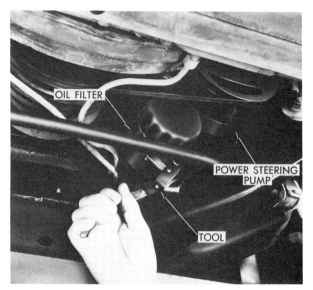

Figure 3.36 An oil filter mounted under an eight-cylinder engine (courtesy Chrysler Corporation).

1 Raise and support the car.

2 Position a drain pan beneath the filter.

3 Using an oil filter wrench as shown in Figure 3.39, turn the filter counterclockwise to loosen it.

4 Remove the wrench and unscrew the filter by hand.

Note: **If the filter is hot, protect your hand with a folded wiper or rag.**

5 Clean the part of the engine block where the filter gasket seats.

6 Lubricate the gasket on the new filter by using your fingertip to coat the gasket with clean engine oil as shown in Figure 3.40.

Note: **Lubricating the gasket aids in installation and minimizes the possibility of gasket distortion when you tighten the filter.**

7 Screw the new filter in place by hand and continue turning it until it makes contact with the engine block.

8 Tighten the filter by turning it ⅔ to ¾ of a turn from the point where the filter gasket made initial contact with the block.

Note: **The tightening specification is usually indicated on the filter or on the filter box. Although it is recommended that the filter be tightened by hand, it is sometimes necessary to use a filter wrench.**

9 Remove the drain pan from under the engine. Dispose of the old filter. Clean the pan.

10 Lower the car to the floor.

Figure 3.37 A universal oil filter wrench. The handle not only provides leverage, but tightens the band around the filter (courtesy of K-D Tools).

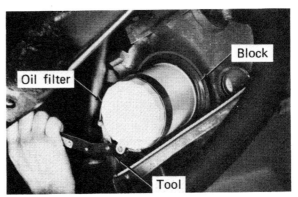

Figure 3.39 Using an oil filter wrench to loosen an oil filter (courtesy Chrysler Corporation).

Figure 3.38 A square drive filter wrench designed for hard-to-reach filters. This wrench can be turned with a ⅜-inch extension and ratchet (courtesy of K-D Tools).

Figure 3.40 Lubricating the oil filter gasket (reproduced by permission of Ashland Oil, Inc. "VALVOLINE" is a registered trademark of Ashland Oil, Inc., Ashland, Kentucky, U.S.A.).

11 Check the engine oil level. Adjust the oil level if necessary.

12 Start the engine and allow it to run at idle speed. Check to see that the oil pressure warning light goes out or that the oil pressure gauge indicates that the engine has sufficient oil pressure.

Note: If oil pressure is not indicated within 10 seconds turn off the engine and check for leaks.

13 If oil pressure is indicated, allow the engine to run for a few minutes.

14 Check the oil filter for leaks.

15 Turn off the engine. After allowing a few minutes for the oil to drain back to the oil pan, check the oil level. Adjust the oil level if necessary.

Job 3h

REPLACE AN ENGINE OIL FILTER

SATISFACTORY PERFORMANCE
A satisfactory performance on this job requires that you do the following:

1 Replace the engine oil filter on the car assigned.
2 Following the steps in the "Performance Outline" and the specifications of the manufacturer, complete the job within 20 minutes.
3 Fill in the blanks under "Information."

PERFORMANCE OUTLINE

1 Raise and support the car.
2 Remove the oil filter.
3 Clean the filter mounting area.
4 Lubricate the filter gasket.
5 Install the replacement filter.
6 Lower the car to the floor.
7 Check for leaks.
8 Adjust the oil level if necessary.

INFORMATION
Vehicle identification _____

Reference used_____Page(s)_____

Filter make_____ Part number_____

Tightening specification_____ turns after contact

SUMMARY

In this chapter you have learned some of the basic under-car services that are performed as a part of routine automotive maintenance. You have learned about the different methods of raising and supporting an automobile and have developed skills in performing these operations. You now know how to lubricate various chassis components, check and adjust lubricant levels, change engine oil, and replace oil filters.

SELF-TEST

Each incomplete statement or question in this test is followed by four suggested completions or answers. In each case select the *one* that best completes the sentence or answers the question.

1 Two mechanics are discussing the methods of raising and supporting a car.
Mechanic A says that when a car is to be supported by the frame, the jack should be placed under a control arm.
Mechanic B says that when a car is raised by placing a jack under the front crossmember, car stands are not needed for support.
Who is right?
A. A only
B. B only
C. Both A and B
D. Neither A nor B

2 Two mechanics are discussing the position of car stands so that a car is supported by the suspension systems.
Mechanic A says that the stands should be placed under the torsion bars.
Mechanic B says that the stands should be placed under the spring shackles.
Who is right?
A. A only
B. B only
C. Both A and B
D. Neither A nor B

3 When supporting the front of a car so that the wheels will be in approximately the

same position they are in when the car is on the floor, the car stands should be placed under the
A. torsion bars
B. frame side rails
C. frame crossmember
D. lower control arms

4 Two mechanics are discussing the use of a frame contact lift.
Mechanic A says that the lift pads should be placed under the frame crossmembers.
Mechanic B says that the center of gravity of the car should be placed over the center of the lift.
Who is right?
A. A only
B. B only
C. Both A and B
D. Neither A nor B

5 Two mechanics are discussing the rubber bushings used in suspension systems.
Mechanic A says that the rubber bushings eliminate friction between metal parts.
Mechanic B says that the rubber bushings should be lubricated with a lithium-based lubricant.
Who is right?
A. A only
B. B only
C. Both A and B
D. Neither A nor B

6 When lubricating a part in the front suspension system, the grease should be pumped into the part through the fitting until
A. the part will accept no more lubricant
B. the seal or boot starts to balloon or expand
C. the lubricant is forced out around the threads of the Zerk fitting
D. you can touch the lubricant with the first joint of your finger inserted into the filler hole

7 Two mechanics are discussing the boots used to seal parts in the steering and suspension systems.
Mechanic A says that the boots keep the grease in contact with the parts.
Mechanic B says that the boots keep dirt and water from entering the parts.
Who is right?
A. A only
B. B only
C. Both A and B
D. Neither A nor B

8 Two mechanics are discussing the changing of engine oil.
Mechanic A says that the oil pan drain plug should be removed with an open end wrench.
Mechanic B says that the drain plug should be replaced if the threads are rounded.
Who is right?
A. A only
B. B only
C. Both A and B
D. Neither A nor B

9 A mechanic has threaded an oil filter in place so that its gasket is just touching the gasket seat on the engine block. To complete the installation, the filter should be tightened an additional
A. ⅓ to ½ turn
B. ⅔ to ¾ turn
C. ¾ to 1 turn
D. 1 to 1½ turns

10 Two mechanics are discussing oil filters.
Mechanic A says that oil filters should be replaced when the oil appears dirty.
Mechanic B says that oil filters should be replaced when the filter contains less than 1 pint of oil.
Who is right?
A. A only
B. B only
C. Both A and B
D. Neither A nor B

Chapter 4
Tire and Wheel Service

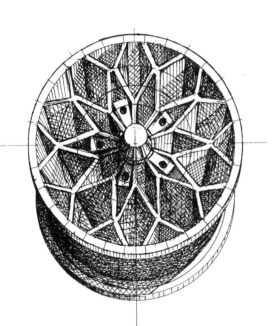

Four small areas of tire tread are the only contact between a car and the road. That frictional contact is very important. It allows the power developed by the engine to start a car in motion and keep it in motion. It allows the steering system to control a car's direction. And it allows the brakes to bring the car to a stop. Those four small areas of contact actually determine the roadability and handling qualities of a car.

In this chapter you will study the construction of various types of tires. You will become aware of the different systems used in tire measurement and identification. And you will learn how to interpret tire wear patterns. You will also dismount, mount, and repair tires. And you will perform other jobs related to tire maintenance.

Your specific objectives are to perform the following jobs:

1
Identify tire types and parts.
2
Check and adjust tire pressures.
3
Rotate tires.
4
Identify the causes of abnormal tire wear.
5
Dismount and mount a tire.
6
Repair a punctured tubeless tire.
7
Static balance a wheel and tire assembly on a bubble balancer.

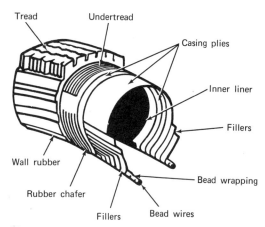

Figure 4.1 Cutaway views of a tubeless tire (Chevrolet Service Manual, Chevrolet Motor Division, GM).

TIRES Tires serve two basic functions. First, they act as primary shock absorbers, cushioning the car from the jarring effects of rough roads. Second, they provide the car's frictional contact with the road. This contact allows the rear wheels to start the car in motion and to keep it moving. It allows the front wheels to steer the car. And it allows the brakes to slow the car or bring it to a stop.

As shown in Figure 4.1, tires are made of layers of cords. Those layers are called *plies*. The cords are usually made of nylon, rayon, or polyester fiber. The layers of cords are impregnated with rubber. They are then placed over a donut-shaped form. Coils of steel wire are placed at the *beads*, or open edges of the tire. The rubber for the tread and sidewalls is laid on over the plies. The entire assembly is then placed in a special mold, where heat and pressure cause the rubber to flow. This process, called *vulcanizing*, bonds all the parts of the tire together. The mold also determines the sidewall and tread designs.

Tire Types There are three types of tires in common use. They are (1) the bias ply, (2) the bias belted, and (3) the radial ply. Each type has a different construction.

Bias Ply Tires Bias ply tires, sometimes called cross-biased ply tires, usually have 2 or 4 plies. As shown in Figure 4.2, those plies crisscross the centerline of the tire at an angle of about 35°. The alternate plies cross at opposite angles and extend from bead to bead.

Bias Belted Tires Bias belted tires are bias ply tires that have two or more "belts" under the tire tread. As shown in Figure 4.3, the belts extend across the full width of the tread surface. They help make the tread more rigid than it would be without them. The greater rigidity reduces the amount of tread motion when the tread contacts the road. The reduced motion prolongs tread life.

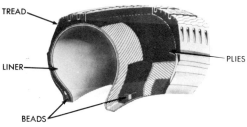

Figure 4.2 A sectioned view of a bias ply tire (courtesy Chrysler Corporation).

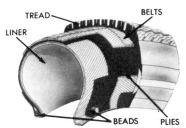

Figure 4.3 A sectioned view of a bias belted tire (courtesy Chrysler Corporation).

Radial Ply Tires   Radial ply tires have cords that run from bead to bead, crossing the tire centerline at a 90° angle as shown in Figure 4.4. In effect, the cords radiate from the centerpoint of the tire. Two or more belts are placed under the tread area. This construction increases tread rigidity, but it also increases the flexibility of the sidewalls.

Tire Sizes and Size Markings   As you know, tires come in many sizes. There are several methods of indicating tire sizes. However, all methods are based on two measurements. One is the rim diameter. The other is the cross-section width.

Rim Diameter   Most cars use wheels that have a rim diameter of 13 inches, 14 inches, or 15 inches. Rim diameter is measured as shown in Figure 4.5. This measurement, in inches, is the last two-digit number in any given indication of tire size. For example, a tire marked 7.75-14 fits a wheel that has a rim diameter of 14 inches.

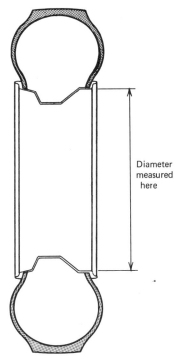

Figure 4.5 Wheel rim diameter.

Cross-Section Width   The cross-section width of a tire can be given in three different ways. These are (1) numerical designation in inches, (2) numerical designation in metrics, and (3) alphabetic designation.

Numerical Designation in Inches   In this method of designating tire size the first number refers to the approximate cross-section

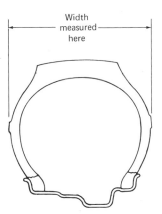

Figure 4.6 Tire cross-section width (Chevrolet Service Manual, Chevrolet Motor Division, GM).

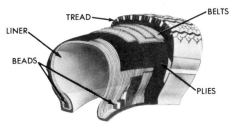

Figure 4.4 A sectioned view of a radial ply tire (courtesy Chrysler Corporation).

Bias	Low-Profile Bias and Bias Belted				Radial	
	Series 78	Series 70	Series 60	Metric	Series 78	Series 70
6.00-13				165 R 13		
	A78-13	A70-13			AR78-13	AR70-13
6.50-13	B78-13	B70-13		175 R 13	BR78-13	BR70-13
	C78-13	C70-13			CR78-13	CR70-13
7.00-13				185 R 13		
		D70-13			DR78-13	DR70-13
				195 R 13		
		E70-13			ER78-13	ER70-13
				155 R 14		
		A70-14				AR70-14
6.45-14				165 R 14		
6.00-14						
	B78-14	B70-14			BR78-14	BR70-14
6.95-14				175 R 14		
	C78-14	C70-14			CR78-14	CR70-14
6.50-14						
	D78-14	D70-14			DR78-14	DR70-14
7.35-14				185 R 14		
7.00-14						
	E78-14	E70-14			ER78-14	ER70-14
7.75-14				195 R 14		
7.50-14						
	F78-14	F70-14	F60-14		FR78-14	FR70-14
8.25-14				205 R 14		
8.00-14						
	G78-14	G70-14	G60-14		GR78-14	GR70-14
8.55-14				215 R 14		
8.50-14						
	H78-14	H70-14	H60-14		HR78-14	HR70-14
9.00-14 8.85-14				225 R 14		
	J78-14	J70-14	J60-14		JR78-14	JR70-14
		K70-14				KR70-14
9.50-14						
		L70-14	L60-14			LR70-14

Figure 4.7 Comparative size listing of popular 13-inch and 14-inch tires.

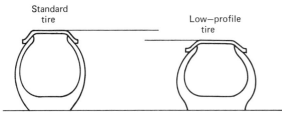

Figure 4.8 Comparison of a conventional tire with a low-profile tire.

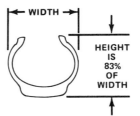

Figure 4.9 Conventional tires have a profile ratio of 83 (courtesy American Motors Corporation).

width, in inches, of a fully inflated tire. This dimension is shown in Figure 4.6. The measurement is given in decimals. A tire that measures 7¾ inches wide is designated 7.75. If the same tire is made to fit a 14-inch rim, the complete size designation is 7.75-14. For other common sizes designated in inches see the columns headed "Bias" in Figure 4.7.

Numerical Designation in Metrics Many radial tires use a combination of metric and inch measurements. The first number in the size refers to the cross-section width in millimeters. (Refer to Figure 4.6.) The second number refers to the rim diameter in inches. A tire almost the same size as a 7.75-14 might bear the designation 195-14.

Alphabetic Designation The tires used on cars of recent production are of an improved low-profile design. As shown in Figure 4.8, these tires have a wider cross-section and a reduced height compared with tires of conventional design. Low-profile tires are classified in "series" sizes. The cross-section width of the tire is not directly stated. It is expressed as a ratio between the section height and the width. This ratio is referred to as the *profile ratio*, or the *aspect ratio*.

Conventional tires have a profile ratio of 83. This means that the height of the tire is 83 percent of its width. This ratio is shown in Figure 4.9. Low-profile tires are commonly found in three "series" sizes—series 78, 70, and 60. Series 78 means that the tire is 78 percent as

high as it is wide. A series 70 tire is 70 percent as high as it is wide. A series 60 tire is the widest, having a height that is only 60 percent of its width. These tires are shown in Figure 4.10.

The actual width of a series tire is given in an alphabetic range. The smallest width is A, and the sizes run progressively wider through the alphabet.

Tire sizes are not duplicated in all the different measuring systems. The columns headed "Low-Profile" in the chart in Figure 4.7 list the comparative sizes of tires that fit 13-inch and 14-inch rims.

Radial Tire Markings Federal law requires that radial tires be marked as such on the sidewalls. For this reason, the letter *R* is usually included in the size designation of radial tires. Thus, a 195-14 radial tire would be marked *195 R 14*. Similarly, the radial equivalent of an F78-14 tire would be marked FR78-14. The closest metric equivalent is marked *205 R 14*. (See the columns headed "Radial" in Figure 4.7.)

Many domestic cars are now fitted with metric-sized radial tires as standard equipment. Those tires are marked to identify the (1) tire type, (2) section width, (3) aspect (profile) ratio, (4) construction type, and (5) rim diameter. The marking system used is explained in Figure 4.11.

Other Tire Markings The markings on the sidewall of a tire can tell you more than the size of a tire and whether it has radial con-

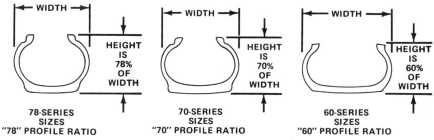

Figure 4.10 A comparison of the most popular low-profile tires (courtesy American Motors Corporation).

struction. Here is a list of typical tire markings and their meanings:

DOT These letters are the abbreviation for the Department of Transportation. They indicate that the tire meets certain government standards for safety. When the tire maker's name is not on the tire, the letters *DOT* are followed by a code number. That number identifies the manufacturer.

METRIC TIRE SIZES

P 195 / 75 R 14

TIRE TYPE
P - PASSENGER
T - TEMPORARY
C - COMMERCIAL

ASPECT RATIO
(SECTION HEIGHT)
(SECTION WIDTH)
70
75
80

RIM DIAMETER
(INCHES)
13
14
15

SECTION WIDTH
(MILLIMETERS)
185
195
205
ETC.

CONSTRUCTION TYPE
R - RADIAL
B - BIAS - BELTED
D - DIAGONAL (BIAS)

SECTION WIDTH

SECTION HEIGHT

Figure 4.11 Metric tire size markings (Pontiac Motor Division, GM).

PLY RATING The ply rating usually marked on passenger car tires is *4 Ply Rating / 2 Ply*. This means that the tire is of 2-ply construction but has the same load-carrying capacity as the most recently built 4-ply tire of the same size at the same inflation pressure. Because there is no industry-wide definition of ply rating, it is being replaced by *load range*.

LOAD RANGE This term refers to the service limitations of a tire. It is identified by an alphabetic system. A particular load limit and inflation pressure is specified. Load Range *B* is the approximate equivalent of a 4-ply rating. It is most commonly found on passenger car tires.

MAX. LOAD _____ LBS. @ _____ PSI MAX. PRESSURE This type of marking prescribes the load limit of the tire and the maximal pressure to which it should be inflated when cold. The correct inflation pressure for any tire is determined by the manufacturer of the car on which the tire is installed.

TUBELESS This word must appear on a tire if the tire is designed for use without a tube.

TUBE-TYPE This marking indicates that the tire must be used with an inner tube.

Job 4a

IDENTIFY TIRE TYPES AND PARTS

SATISFACTORY PERFORMANCE

A satisfactory performance on this job requires that you do the following:

1 Identify each tire shown below by placing its identifying letter before the word or phrase that best describes the tire's construction.
2 Identify the parts of the tires shown by placing each part number in front of the correct part name.
3 Correctly identify all the tires and tire parts within 15 minutes.

PERFORMANCE SITUATION

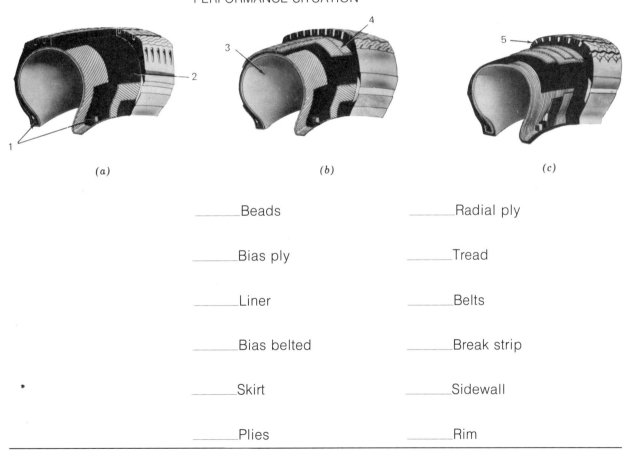

(a)   (b)   (c)

_____Beads   _____Radial ply

_____Bias ply   _____Tread

_____Liner   _____Belts

_____Bias belted   _____Break strip

_____Skirt   _____Sidewall

_____Plies   _____Rim

TIRE INFLATION Many car owners forget to maintain proper tire pressures. Their forgetfulness often leads to the need for repairs to the steering and suspension systems and for the replacement of ruined tires. Routine maintenance should always include checking and adjusting the air pressure in all four tires. An accurate tire gauge, similar to the one

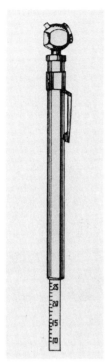

Figure 4.12 A pocket type tire pressure gauge. The one shown is calibrated to 50 pounds in one pound units (courtesy of H. B. Egan Manufacturing Company, Muskogee, Oklahoma 74401).

shown in Figure 4.12, is one of the most important instruments to have in your tool box.

Many problems are caused by improper tire inflation. A properly inflated tire provides full contact with the road, as shown in Figure 4.13. The proper tire pressures for any car vary with the type and size of the tires on the car. They

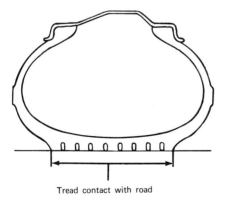

Tread contact with road

Figure 4.13 A properly inflated tire. Note that the tread is in full contact with the road (Chevrolet Service Manual, Chevrolet Motor Division, GM).

also vary with the loads the car is to carry. Proper tire pressures are listed in shop manuals, owner's manuals, and usually on a plate or decal affixed to the car. Figure 4.14 shows how tire inflation pressures are specified in the manual of one manufacturer. Inflation pressures are usually given in psi (pounds per square inch). However, you will also find inflation pressures specified in *kilopascals* (kPa). A conversion chart for commonly used pressures is provided in Figure 4.15.

Underinflation Normal air loss combined with owner neglect often results in tires that are underinflated. Underinflated tires not only bulge out at the sidewalls, but provide poor contact between the tread and the road surface. An underinflated tire is shown in Figure 4.16. Underinflated tires cause the following problems:

1 Increased steering effort and poor steering response.
2 A tendency toward skidding and poor control on turns as the tire tread deflects and distorts with side thrust loads.
3 Poor directional stability because of wander or pull in the steering.
4 Early tire failure brought on by the heat generated by excessive flexing of the tire sidewalls.
5 Abnormal wear on the outer edges of the tread.
6 Increased possibilities of tire and rim damage on impact with broken pavement.
7 Erratic braking action.
8 Increased fuel consumption because of increased friction and reduced rolling diameter.

Overinflation Overinflated tires are found less frequently than underinflated tires. An overinflated tire, shown in Figure 4.17, does not allow full tread contact with the road. Overinflated tires cause the following problems:

1 Decreased tread contact with the road surface.
2 The transmission of excessive road shock to the steering and suspension systems.
3 A less comfortable ride.
4 Abnormal wear in the center of the tread.

TIRE SIZE

MATADOR — COUPE	E78		ER 78		FR78		F 78		G78		GR78		GR70		H78		HR78		HR70	
	F	R	F	R	F	R	F	R	F	R	F	R	F	R	F	R	F	R	F	R
Six-Cylinder less air cond.	24	24*	24	24	24	24	24	24	24	24										
Six-Cylinder with air cond.	26	24*	24	24	24	24	24	24	24	24										
304 V-8 less air cond.	26*	26*	24*	24*	24*	24*	24*	24*	24	24	24	24								
304 V-8 with air cond.			26	24*	26	24*	26	24*	24	24	24	24								
360 V-8 or 401 V-8 less air cond.			24*	24*	24*	24*	24*	24*	24	24	24	24								
360 V-8 or 401 V-8 with air cond.			26*	24**	26*	24**	26	24**	24	24	24	24								
SEDAN																				
Six-Cylinder All Models	24*	24**	24	24*	24	24*			24	24										
304 V-8 — All models			24*	24*	24*	24*			24	24	24	24	24	24	24	24	24	24	24	24
360 V-8 or 401 V-8 less air cond.			24*	24**	24*	24*			24	24	24	24	24	24	24	24	24	24	24	24
360 V-8 or 401 V-8 with air cond.			26	26*	26	26*			24	24	24	24	24	24	24	24	24	24	24	24
WAGONS																				
Six-Cylinder and all V-8 models									20	28	20	28			20	28	20	28	20	28

* Add 2 psi for Full Load.
** Add 4 psi for Full Load.

Figure 4.14 A typical list of tire pressure specifications (courtesy American Motors Corporation).

Checking and Adjusting Tire Pressures

Tire pressures should be checked when the tires are cool. The most accurate readings are obtained when the car has been parked for at least 3 hours or before it has been driven more than 3 miles. Tire temperatures increase as a car is being driven, and increased temperatures cause an increase in tire pressure. Heavy loads, high road-surface temperatures, and high-speed driving can raise tire pressures as much as 10 psi (70 kPa). This pressure build-up is normal. Therefore, no air should be released from a hot tire in order to lower the pressure.

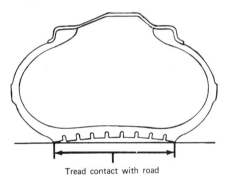

Tread contact with road

Figure 4.16 An underinflated tire. Note that the center of the tread is not held in firm contact with the road surface (Chevrolet Service Manual, Chevrolet Motor Division, GM).

INFLATION PRESSURE CONVERSION CHART (KILOPASCALS TO PSI)			
kPa	psi	kPa	psi
140	20	215	31
145	21	220	32
155	22	230	33
160	23	235	34
165	24	240	35
170	25	250	36
180	26	275	40
185	27	310	45
190	28	345	50
200	29	380	55
205	30	415	60
Conversion: 6.9 kPa = 1 psi			

Figure 4.15 kPa to psi conversion chart (Pontiac Motor Division, GM).

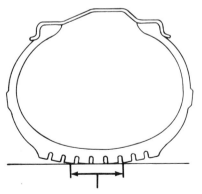

Tread contact with road

Figure 4.17 An overinflated tire. Note that the edges of the tread do not contact the road surface (Chevrolet Service Manual, Chevrolet Motor Division, GM).

Figure 4.18 Typical tire valves (courtesy of H. B. Egan Manufacturing Company, Muskogee, Oklahoma 74401).

Figure 4.19 Typical tire valve caps (courtesy of H. B. Egan Manufacturing Company, Muskogee, Oklahoma 74401).

Before you check tire pressures, you should always determine the pressures recommended by the car manufacturer. If the tire pressure specifications are not on a plate or decal on the car, you should check the owner's manual or an appropriate shop manual. Be sure to check the tire size. As mentioned earlier, proper tire pressure depends partly on tire size.

All tire valve stems contain valves similar to those shown in Figure 4.18. Those valves are designed to hold pressure during inflating and pressure checking operations. They are not designed to hold pressure indefinitely. All valve stems are threaded for valve caps similar to those shown in Figure 4.19. Valve caps provide a positive seal and keep dirt and water from entering the valve. After checking and adjusting tire pressures, you should be sure that all the valve stems are fitted with caps. If any caps are missing or damaged, new caps should be installed.

Job 4b

CHECK AND ADJUST TIRE PRESSURES

SATISFACTORY PERFORMANCE

A satisfactory performance on this job requires that you do the following:

1 Check and adjust the pressure in the tires of the car assigned.
2 Following the steps in the "Performance Outline" and the specifications of the manufacturer, complete the job within 10 minutes.
3 Fill in the blanks under "Information."

PERFORMANCE OUTLINE

1 Determine the correct tire pressures for the front and rear tires.
2 Check the pressure in each tire, and add or release air to obtain the correct pressure.

INFORMATION
Vehicle identification _____

Reference used _____ Page(s) _____

Size of tires on vehicle _____

Tire pressures specified   Front _____ psi   Rear _____ psi

Pressures at completion of job

Front _____ psi   Rear_____ psi

Tires were Cool _____   Hot _____

Are valve caps in place on all valve stems? Yes _____

No _____

TIRE USAGE Different types of tires impart different handling characteristics to a car. Certain combinations of different tire types on the same car can dangerously impair roadability. For that reason tire usage should be governed by the following rules:

1 Except in an emergency, radial tires should not be used with bias ply or bias belted tires on the same car. If radial tires are to be used, they should be used on all four wheels.

2 If radial tires must be used with bias ply or bias belted tires, they should be used in pairs on common axles. The radial tires should be installed on the rear wheels. Radial tires should never be used on the front wheels when bias ply or bias belted tires are used on the rear wheels.

3 Bias ply and bias belted tires, also, may be used on the same car only in pairs on common axles. The bias belted tires should be used on the rear wheels.

4 Tires in different series sizes may be used on the same car only in pairs on common axles. Also, the tires on the front and those on the rear should be no more than one series apart. The widest tires should be placed on the rear wheels. For example, 78 series tires may be used on the front wheels with 70 series on the rear wheels.

TIRE MAINTENANCE As mentioned earlier, the most important procedure in tire care is to maintain proper tire pressure. Other important procedures include (1) tire rotation and (2) tire inspection.

Tire Rotation Most car makers recommend rotating tires at regular intervals of from 5,000 to 10,000 miles (8,000 to 16,000 km). Tires should be rotated so that they will not remain in the same position throughout their lifetime. Tire rotation equalizes wear and minimizes tire noise. Tires should be rotated in a definite pattern, and the same pattern should be followed each time they are rotated. All five tires should be rotated when possible. However, when the spare is in poor condition or when a "stowaway" or "compact" spare tire is used, only the four tires already on the axles can be rotated.

Bias ply and bias belted tires should be rotated in a pattern similar to that shown in Figure 4.20.

Radial ply tires should be rotated so that they remain on one side of a car. The longest possible tread life for radial tires is obtained when the tires always revolve in the same direction.

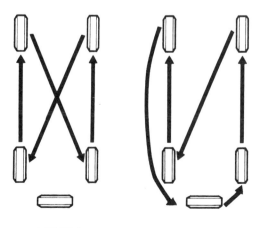

4 WHEELS   5 WHEELS

Figure 4.20 Typical tire rotation patterns for bias ply and bias belted tires (Chevrolet Service Manual, Chevrolet Motor Division, GM).

RADIAL TIRES

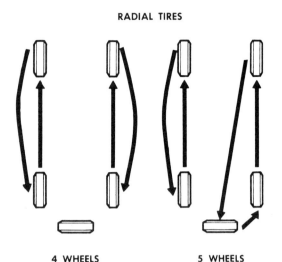

4 WHEELS   5 WHEELS

Figure 4.21 Typical tire rotation patterns for radial tires (Chevrolet Service Manual, Chevrolet Motor Division, GM).

Figure 4.21 shows the preferred rotation patterns for radial tires.

Removing Wheels To rotate tires, you must remove the wheels from the car. Most shops use *impact wrenches* similar to the one shown in Figure 4.22 to remove the lug nuts that hold the wheels in place. Impact wrenches are like drill motors, but instead of spinning a drill bit they spin a socket wrench with a hammering

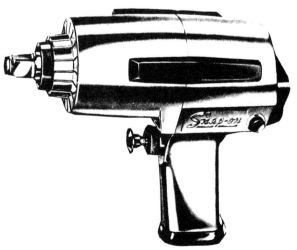

Figure 4.22 A typical impact wrench (courtesy of Snap-on Tools Corporation).

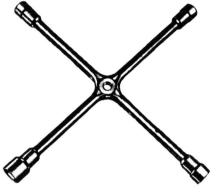

Figure 4.23 A typical lug wrench (courtesy of Snap-on Tools Corporation).

action. Impact wrenches are great timesavers, but they are not always available. In many instances you will have to use a muscle-powered lug wrench. A lug wrench is shown in Figure 4.23.

Have you ever tried to loosen a lug nut when the wheel is off the ground? You turn the wrench and the wheel turns. You can apply the parking brakes, but they hold only the rear wheels. Maybe you can get a friend to sit in the car and press down on the brake pedal until you can loosen the nuts. But what if you are working alone?

If you are going to remove the wheels from a car, remove the wheel covers and loosen the lug nuts before you raise the car off the floor. This procedure is easy, and it requires far less energy than trying to loosen the lug nuts after the car is off the floor. Once the car is up in the air, you can spin the loosened nuts off with little effort.

Installing Wheels As a mechanic, you will find that many problems are caused by improper wheel installation. For example, if the lug nuts are left too loose, the wheel may come off. If the lug nuts are tightened too much, the wheel and the hub may be distorted. This distortion leads to vibrations in the steering system. In the brake system it can cause problems which become evident through pulsation of the brake pedal. Lug nuts, then, should be tightened just enough to keep them from loosening, but not so much that they will distort the wheel or hub. For that reason, lug nuts should be tightened to a torque specification. *Torque* can be defined as a turning or twisting effort. When you turn a wrench, you are applying torque to a nut or a bolt. By measuring that torque, you can tell how much you are tightening it.

To measure torque, you must use a *torque wrench*. A torque wrench is a wrench whose handle indicates how much torque, or twisting effort, is being applied to a nut or a bolt. There are many types of torque wrenches. Some have a wand, or pointer, that moves across a scale as you pull on the wrench. Some torque wrenches of that type are shown in Figure 4.24. Other torque wrenches indicate torque

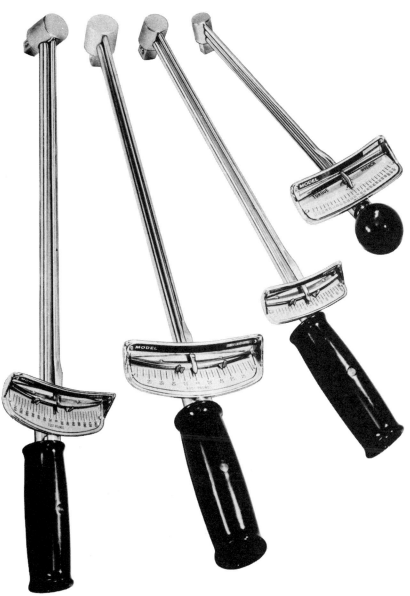

Figure 4.24 Four different beam-type torque wrenches (courtesy AMMCO Tools, Inc.).

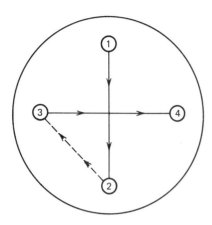

Figure 4.25 "Cross" pattern, recommended as the sequence for tightening lug nuts on a four-hole wheel.

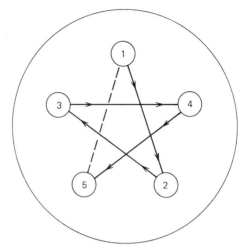

Figure 4.26 "Star" pattern, recommended as the sequence for tightening lug nuts on a five-hole wheel.

by means of a pointer on a dial. Some give off a loud click when a preset torque is reached. There are even some which have a lamp that lights when the nut is tight enough.

Torque is measured in foot-pounds (ft lbs) or in Newton meters (N m). Suppose you had a wrench that was 12 inches (30 cm) long and you applied a force of 20 pounds (9 kg) to the handle. Then, the nut or bolt you were tightening would be tightened to 20 ft lbs (270 cm kg) (27 N m) or torque. There are hundreds of nuts and bolts on a car that must be tightened to a specified torque. This is one reason that the manufacturer's service manuals are so important to you. They contain the torque specifications you need to turn out a quality job.

Tightening the lug nuts to the right amount of torque is only half the job. The nuts must also be tightened in a sequence. The proper sequence for four-hole and five-hole wheels is shown by numerals and arrows in Figures 4.25 and 4.26. The proper sequence for four-hole wheels is represented by a "cross" pattern. For five-hole wheels it is represented by a "star" pattern.

If you used an impact wrench to remove the lug nuts, you can use it for installing them. Just remember that it should be used only to run the nuts up snug. After you lower the car to the floor, you should use a torque wrench to tighten the nuts to specifications.

ROTATING TIRES The steps that follow outline a typical procedure for rotating tires:

1 Check all five tires and determine the rotation pattern to be used.

2 Remove the spare if it is to be used.

3 Remove the wheel covers and loosen the lug nuts.

4 Raise and support the car.

5 Remove the wheels and install them in their new locations.

6 Install the lug nuts.

Note: Be sure that you install the nuts with the tapered, or cone-shaped, end toward the wheel as shown in Figure 4.27.

7 Lower the car to the floor.

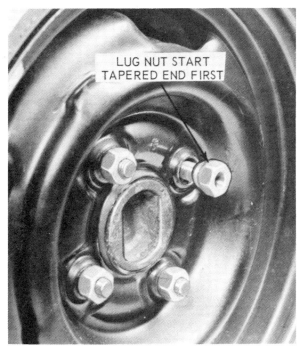

Figure 4.27 Lug nuts should be installed so that the tapered, or cone-shaped, end of the nut is toward the wheel (Ford Motor Company).

8 Tighten the lug nuts to the torque specification in the correct sequence.

9 Install the wheel covers.

10 Install the spare.

11 Check and adjust the tire pressures.

Job 4c

ROTATE TIRES

SATISFACTORY PERFORMANCE

A satisfactory performance on this job requires that you do the following:

1 Rotate the tires on the car assigned.
2 Following the steps in the "Performance Outline" and the recommendations and specifications of the manufacturer, complete the job within 60 minutes.
3 Fill in the blanks under "Information."

PERFORMANCE OUTLINE

1 Determine the rotation pattern to be used.
2 Rotate the tires to the new positions.
3 Tighten the lug nuts to the torque specification.

4 Check and adjust the tire pressures.

INFORMATION

Vehicle identification _____

Specified tire pressures Front _____ Rear_____

Lug nut torque specification _____

Reference used _____ Page(s) _____

Indicate the rotation pattern used

<--- Front

Tire Inspection Tires should be inspected during each rotation and at regular intervals between rotations. Any tire that has a tread depth of less than $1/16$th of 1 inch (1.6 mm) should be replaced. To aid you in determining when a tire requires replacement, tread wear indicators are molded into the tire when it is built. When the tread wears to a depth of less than $1/16$th of an inch (1.6 mm), bands approximately ½ inch (1.3 cm) wide will appear, as shown in Figure 4.28. When those indicators are visible in two or more adjacent tread grooves, the tire should be replaced.

Tread wear should be evenly distributed across the entire tread. Any uneven wear should be considered abnormal, and its cause should be determined and corrected. A listing of the most commonly found abnormal wear patterns, their causes, and corrections is provided in Figure 4.29. You should study those wear patterns so that you will recognize them when you find them during a tire inspection.

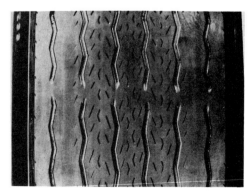

Figure 4.28 A tread wear indicator strip (courtesy Chrysler Corporation).

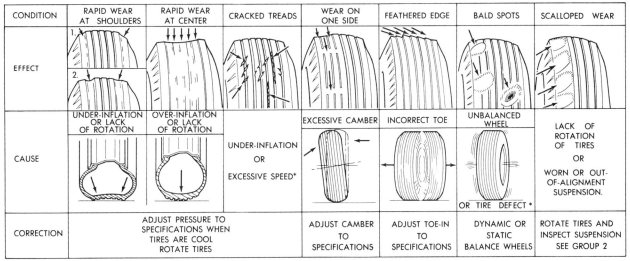

CONDITION	RAPID WEAR AT SHOULDERS	RAPID WEAR AT CENTER	CRACKED TREADS	WEAR ON ONE SIDE	FEATHERED EDGE	BALD SPOTS	SCALLOPED WEAR
EFFECT	1. / 2.						
CAUSE	UNDER-INFLATION OR LACK OF ROTATION	OVER-INFLATION OR LACK OF ROTATION	UNDER-INFLATION OR EXCESSIVE SPEED*	EXCESSIVE CAMBER	INCORRECT TOE	UNBALANCED WHEEL OR TIRE DEFECT*	LACK OF ROTATION OF TIRES OR WORN OR OUT-OF-ALIGNMENT SUSPENSION.
CORRECTION		ADJUST PRESSURE TO SPECIFICATIONS WHEN TIRES ARE COOL ROTATE TIRES		ADJUST CAMBER TO SPECIFICATIONS	ADJUST TOE-IN TO SPECIFICATIONS	DYNAMIC OR STATIC BALANCE WHEELS	ROTATE TIRES AND INSPECT SUSPENSION SEE GROUP 2

*HAVE TIRE INSPECTED FOR FURTHER USE.

Figure 4.29 Typical tire wear patterns (courtesy Chrysler Corporation).

Job 4d

IDENTIFY THE CAUSES OF ABNORMAL TIRE WEAR

SATISFACTORY PERFORMANCE

A satisfactory performance on this job requires that you do the following:

1 Determine the cause of the abnormal wear patterns shown in the illustration below.
2 Place the number of each wear pattern in front of its most probable cause in the list of causes provided.
3 Complete the job within 15 minutes.

PERFORMANCE SITUATION

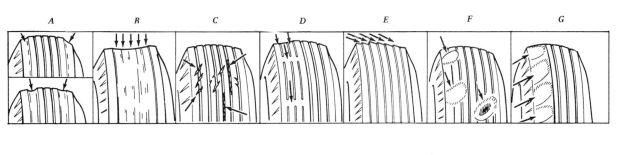

_____Unbalanced wheel and tire   _____Incorrect toe-in

_____Incorrect camber

4-18 **Tire and Wheel Service**

_____Underinflation

_____Incorrect caster

_____Worn suspension parts

_____Overinflation

_____Excessive speed

TIRE SERVICE Tire service involves repairing punctures and replacing tires. Removing and installing tires will be easier for you if you understand certain facts about the design of wheels.

Wheel Design Most cars are fitted with steel wheels as standard equipment. A typical steel wheel is shown in Figure 4.30. Of two-piece construction, the *spider*, or center section, of the wheel is electrically welded to the *rim*. The rim, shown in Figure 4.31, is made with a

dropped center. This lowered area, or well, is necessary for tire installation and removal. One part of the bead can be held in the dropped center so the other part can be slipped over the rim flange. Most wheels incorporate small raised sections, or *safety ridges*, on the inner portion of the rim. When the tire is inflated, the beads of the tire are forced over these ridges. The safety ridges serve two purposes: (1) They aid in preventing the beads from slipping inward during hard cornering. (2) They help hold the tire in position on the wheel in case of a tire failure.

Most manufacturers advise against any attempt to repair a damaged wheel. They suggest that wheels be replaced when any of the following conditions are found:

1 The wheel is bent or dented.
2 The wheel has excessive *runout* or "wobble."
3 Air is leaking through the welds.
4 The bolt holes are enlarged or elongated.
5 The wheel is heavily rusted.

Some cars are fitted with wheels made of cast aluminum alloy as shown in Figure 4.32. As protection against corrosion, many of those

SPIDER
(CENTER SECTION)

RIM

Figure 4.30 Typical construction of a standard steel wheel (courtesy American Motors Corporation).

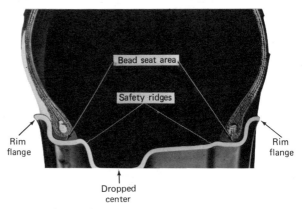

Figure 4.31 Wheel rim nomenclature (courtesy Chrysler Corporation).

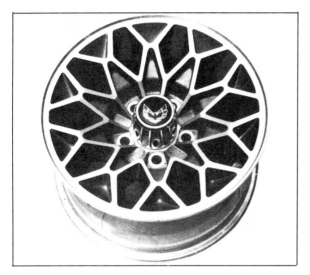

Figure 4.32 A wheel made of cast aluminum alloy (Pontiac Motor Division, GM).

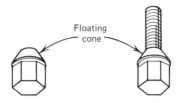

Figure 4.33 Special lug nuts and bolts are used with aluminum wheels.

alloy wheels are coated with a clear lacquer. When working with alloy wheels, you should be careful not to scratch or chip that protective coating. Because aluminum is relatively soft, special lug nuts and lug bolts are usually used with aluminum wheels. Some of those nuts and bolts have a steel sleeve or tube that fits into the hole in the wheel and protects it. Others, similar to the ones shown in Figure 4.33, have a cone-shaped end that is free to turn. Those special nuts and bolts prevent gouging and tearing the holes in the wheels as the nuts and bolts are tightened.

DISMOUNTING AND MOUNTING TIRES

In most shops, a tire machine is used to dismount and mount tires. One such tire machine is shown in Figure 4.34. Regardless of the type of machine you use, the job will be much easier and you will minimize your chances of injury if you follow these basic precautions:

1 Remove the valve core from the valve stem. (This will insure that all the pressure is released from the tire.)

2 Mount the wheel and tire assembly on the machine so that the dropped center of the rim is facing up as shown in Figure 4.35. (This will allow the beads of the tire to slip easily over the rim flange.)

3 After breaking both beads loose from the rim, thoroughly lubricate the upper bead with rubber lubricant. (This decreases the friction between the bead and the rim flange. It also minimizes the possibility of bead damage.)

4 After removing the tire from the wheel, inspect the bead seat area of the rim. Use a wire brush, sandpaper, or coarse steel wool to clean the bead seat of all old lubricant, rubber deposits, and rust.

5 Before mounting the replacement tire, apply a liberal amount of rubber lubricant to both beads.

6 Do not stand over the tire when inflating it. (There have been instances where bead wires have broken when the bead was forced over the safety ridge. This can cause you serious injury.)

Figure 4.34 A popular type of tire machine (The Coats Co., Inc., La Vergne, Tenn.).

7 Never exceed 40 psi (275 kPa) pressure when inflating a tire. (If a bead will not seat, deflate the tire, relubricate the bead, and reinflate the tire.)

The procedure you will follow in dismounting and mounting tires is largely determined by the machine you have available. You should study the instruction manual furnished with the tire machine before you attempt to dismount and mount tires. The procedure that follows can be considered typical. Refer to Figure 4.36 for the machine parts and controls mentioned in the procedural steps:

Dismounting 1 Examine the wheel rim to determine the location of the dropped center. (Refer to Figure 4.35.)

2 Place the wheel and tire assembly over the center post so that the dropped center is near the top.

3 Rotate the wheel and tire assembly so that the valve is facing the front of the machine and the positioning pin is protruding from one of the wheel lug holes.

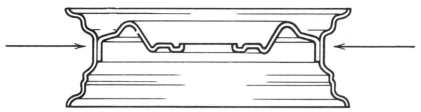

Figure 4.35 When mounting a wheel and tire assembly on a tire machine, the dropped center of the rim should be toward the top (courtesy American Motors Corporation).

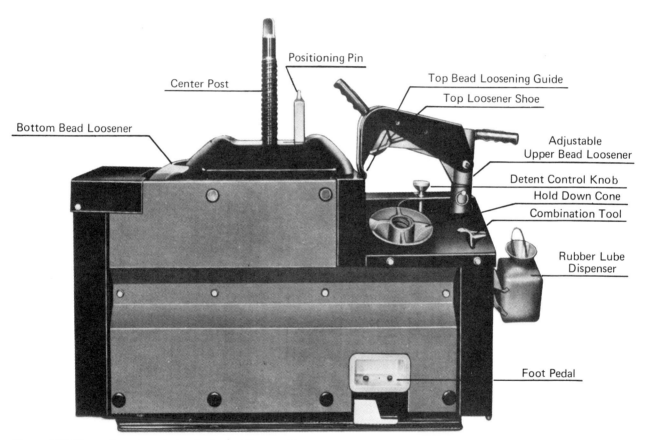

Figure 4.36 The parts and controls of a typical tire machine (The Coats Co., Inc., La Vergne, Tenn.).

Figure 4.37 Tightening the hold down cone to secure the wheel and tire assembly to the tire machine (The Coats Co., Inc., La Vergne, Tenn.).

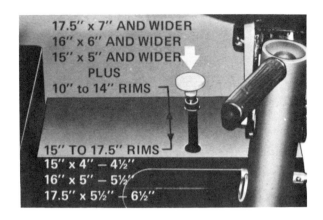

Figure 4.38 The tire machine is adjustable for different size wheels by the detent control shown above (The Coats Co., Inc., La Vergne, Tenn.).

4 Place the hold down cone over the center post and turn it down so that the small end of the cone enters the center hole in the wheel. Tighten the cone hand tight. (See Figure 4.37.)

5 Remove the valve core from the valve stem.

6 Adjust the detent control to the proper wheel size as shown in Figure 4.38.

7 Lift the top bead loosener and place the shoe on the tire next to the rim. The bead loosening guide should contact the rim as shown in Figure 4.39.

8 Remove your hands from the machine and step down on the foot pedal. This will activate both the top bead loosener and the bottom bead loosener. Release the foot pedal after the top bead loosener has completed its downward stroke.

Note: A single stroke of the machine will usually loosen both the upper and lower beads. Repeat step 8 if the beads do not break loose.

Figure 4.39 Positioning the top bead loosener. Note that the bead loosener shoe contacts the tire and the guide contacts the inside of the rim (The Coats Co., Inc., La Vergne, Tenn.).

Figure 4.40 Lubricating the top bead with rubber lubricant (The Coats Co., Inc., La Vergne, Tenn.).

Figure 4.41 Prying the bead over the rim (The Coats Co., Inc., La Vergne, Tenn.).

Figure 4.42 Positioning the combination tool over the center post key (The Coats Co., Inc., La Vergne, Tenn.).

9 Apply a liberal amount of rubber lubricant all around the bead surfaces as shown in Figure 4.40.

10 Align the combination tool with the center post key and insert the tool between the tire and the rim. Hold the tool as shown in Figure 4.41 and pry the bead of the tire over the rim.

11 Continue pushing on the combination tool until it slides over the center post key as shown in Figure 4.42.

12 Holding the combination tool in place, step down on the foot pedal. This will cause the center post key to rotate counterclockwise, turning the combination tool and lifting the bead off the rim.

Note: If you lift upward on the tire in the location of the arrow in Figure 4.43, the bead will lift off more easily.

13 Repeat steps 10, 11, and 12 to remove the bottom bead.

Figure 4.43 Starting to demount the upper bead. If you use your other hand to lift up on the tire at the position indicated by the arrow, the bead will dismount more easily (The Coats Co., Inc., La Vergne, Tenn.).

Figure 4.45 Positioning the tire on the rim (The Coats Co., Inc., La Vergne, Tenn.).

Figure 4.44 Applying rubber lube to both beads of a tire before mounting (The Coats Co., Inc., La Vergne, Tenn.).

Mounting 1 Apply a liberal amount of rubber lubricant to both beads as shown in Figure 4.44.

2 Position the tire over the wheel so that it is tipped to the right as shown in Figure 4.45. Do not attempt to push the lower bead into the dropped center.

3 Hook the large end of the combination tool over the rim and place it over the center post key as shown in Figure 4.46. Hold the tool in this position with your right hand.

4 With your left hand, slide the tire clockwise as shown in Figure 4.47 until the lower bead contacts the hollow area at the end of the combination tool. This will hold the tool in place.

Figure 4.46 The combination tool in position for mounting the tire. Note that the hooked part of the tool is in contact with the rim and the lipped part is facing upward (The Coats Co., Inc., La Vergne, Tenn.).

Figure 4.47 Sliding the tire so that the bead comes in contact with the groove between the hook and the lip on the end of the combination tool (The Coats Co., Inc., La Vergne, Tenn.).

Figure 4.48 Mounting the lower bead. Note the correct positions of your hands while the combination tool is moving (The Coats Co., Inc., La Vergne, Tenn.).

5 Using both hands, continue to slide the tire clockwise until the lower bead is positioned in the dropped center of the rim.

6 Position your hands as shown in Figure 4.48 and step down on the foot pedal. This will turn the combination tool. Follow the tool with your right hand, pushing down on the tire to keep the lower bead in the dropped center. The lower bead will drop in place.

Note: Always position your hands so that your fingers are over the tire tread and away from the bead. (Refer to Figure 4.48.) This will keep you from getting your fingers caught between the bead and the rim.

7 Repeat steps 2 through 6 to mount the upper bead.

INFLATING During shipping and storage, new tires are compressed so that the sidewalls are pushed together. When the tires are mounted, especially on wide rims, it may be very difficult to get the beads to contact the bead seats so that the tire can be inflated. To help push the beads out so that they contact the bead seats, some shops use a bead expander band similar to the one shown in Figure 4.49. This tool is placed around the tread of the tire and tightened so that the sidewalls bulge out. This expands the beads so that the tire can be inflated in the normal manner. If you use a band-type bead expander, never exceed 5 psi (35 kPa) pressure in the tire while the tool is in place.

Most shops use an air ring to inflate a collapsed tire. The air ring is positioned around the tire, and seats the bead by forcing a surge of air between the bead and the bead seat. As shown in Figure 4.50, many tire machines are fitted with an air ring. The ring is mounted

57x24

Figure 4.49 Expanding tire beads so that they contact the bead seats on the rim (courtesy Chrysler Corporation).

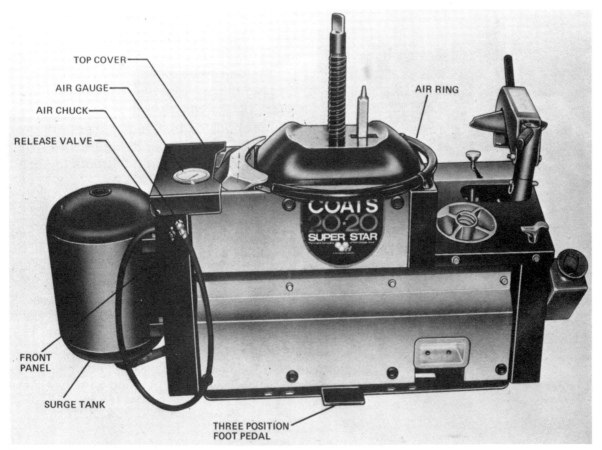

Figure 4.50 A tire machine fitted with an air ring to aid tire inflation. Note the surge tank that stores air for inflation and the three-position foot pedal control (The Coats Co., Inc., La Vergne, Tenn.).

Figure 4.51 Connecting the air chuck (The Coats Co., Inc., La Vergne, Tenn.).

Figure 4.52 Lifting the tire so that the upper bead contacts the rim (The Coats Co., Inc., La Vergne, Tenn.).

so that air is blown in between the bottom bead and the bead seat. The following procedure for inflating tires is typical when using a machine of that type. Refer to Figure 4.50 for the machine parts and controls mentioned in the procedural steps:

1 Connect the air chuck to the tire valve stem as shown in Figure 4.51.

2 Grasp the tire with both hands as shown in Figure 4.52 and lift the tire so that the top bead contacts the edge of the bead seat.

3 Step down hard on the foot pedal to push it into position 3 (Seal). See Figure 4.53. Hold the pedal down for about 2 seconds. This action releases a surge of air that enters the gap between the lower bead and the bead seat, expanding the tire and sealing the bead.

4 Check the position of the beads after releasing the foot pedal.

Note: If the beads are not seated, repeat steps 2 and 3.

5 When the beads are seated, loosen the hold down cone one full turn.

6 Step down on the foot pedal, holding it in position 2. (Refer to Figure 4.53.) Release the foot pedal after a few seconds and check the air gauge for the tire pressure.

7 Continue to inflate the tire by depressing the foot pedal for short intervals, checking the air gauge until the beads snap into place in the bead seats.

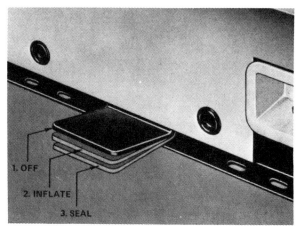

Figure 4.53 Valve operation of the three-position foot pedal (The Coats Co., Inc., La Vergne, Tenn.).

Note: Never exceed 40 psi (275 kPa) pressure while attempting to seat the beads. If the beads will not seat, remove the air, and check and deflate the tire. Relubricate the beads and repeat steps 6 and 7.

8 When the beads are seated, remove the air chuck and install the tire valve core.

9 Inflate the tire to the pressure recommended by the car manufacturer.

10 Remove the wheel and tire assembly from the tire machine.

Job 4e

DISMOUNT AND MOUNT A TIRE

SATISFACTORY PERFORMANCE

A satisfactory performance on this job requires that you do the following:

1 Dismount and mount the tire from the wheel and tire assembly assigned.
2 Following the steps in the "Performance Outline" and the instructions for using the tire machine you have available, complete the job within 15 minutes.
3 Fill in the blanks under "Information."

PERFORMANCE OUTLINE

1 Mount the assembly on the machine.
2 Break the beads loose from the rim.
3 Lubricate the upper bead.
4 Remove the tire from the wheel.
5 Inspect the wheel and clean the bead areas.

6 Lubricate the tire beads.

7 Install the tire on the wheel.

8 Inflate the tire to the recommended pressure.

9 Remove the wheel and tire assembly from the machine.

INFORMATION

Tire size_____ Recommended inflation pressure _____

PUNCTURE REPAIRS Tires punctured in the tread area shown in Figure 4.54 can be repaired if the puncture does not exceed ¼ of 1 inch (6.4 mm) in diameter. Never attempt to repair a tire that has any of the following defects:

1 A sidewall puncture.

2 Cuts or cracks extending into the tire fabric.

3 Tread wear indicators showing.

4 Loose cords.

5 Evidence of ply separation.

6 Tread separation.

7 Broken or otherwise damaged bead wires.

A permanent repair requires that you (1) patch the puncture from the inside and (2) plug the hole. For this reason most manufacturers recommend a plug-type patch applied from the inside of the tire. A typical patch of this type is shown in Figure 4.55. Several tools are available that will enable you to permanently seal a puncture without removing the tire from the wheel. One such tool is shown in Figure 4.56. This tool will insert rivet-like rubber plugs into a puncture from the outside of the tire. The following procedure outlines the steps to

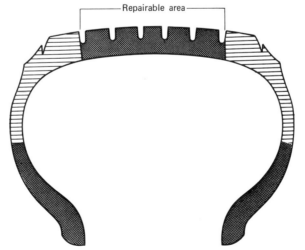

Figure 4.54 The repairable area of a tire (courtesy American Motors Corporation).

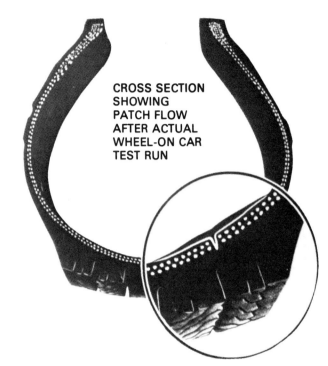

CROSS SECTION
SHOWING
PATCH FLOW
AFTER ACTUAL
WHEEL-ON CAR
TEST RUN

Figure 4.55 A cross section of a punctured tire that has been repaired internally. Note that the patch has flowed into the hole (courtesy of H. B. Egan Manufacturing Company, Muskogee, Oklahoma 74401).

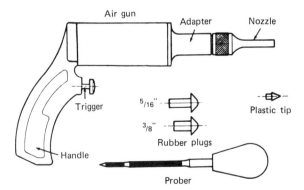

Air gun   Adapter   Nozzle

Trigger $^5/_{16}''$ Plastic tip

Handle $^3/_8''$ Rubber plugs

Prober

Figure 4.56 A tubeless tire repair kit containing an air gun that installs rivet-like rubber plugs in punctures. Note the plugs, plastic tips, and the prober used with the gun (Tyler Manufacturing Co., Inc., Hawthorne, Calif.).

Figure 4.57 Using the prober to locate the direction of the hole and to coat the hole with vulcanizing cement (Tyler Manufacturing Co., Inc., Hawthorne, Calif.).

Figure 4.58 Removing the nozzle of the air gun (Tyler Manufacturing Co., Inc., Hawthorne, Calif.).

Figure 4.59 Inserting the plug into the air gun (Tyler Manufacturing Co., Inc., Hawthorne, Calif.).

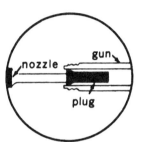

Figure 4.60 Using the reversed nozzle as a plunger to push the plug back into the gun (Tyler Manufacturing Co., Inc., Hawthorne, Calif.).

follow when using a tool of this type:

1 Locate the puncture in the tire.

2 Dip the probing tool in vulcanizing cement.

3 Carefully push the prober into the puncture, feeling for the direction of the hole. See Figure 4.57.

Note: Do not force the prober as you may cause another puncture.

4 Remove the prober. Repeat steps 2 and 3 several times so that the hole will be well coated with cement. Leave the prober in the hole.

5 Remove the nozzle from the gun as shown in Figure 4.58.

6 Insert the stem of a lubricated plug into the gun as shown in Figure 4.59.

Note: The plugs are prelubricated, but if the lubricant has dried or has been removed, wet the plugs with the lubricant supplied with the repair kit.

7 Reverse the nozzle and, using it as a plunger as shown in Figure 4.60, push the head of the plug back into the gun.

Note: The flexible head of the plug will fold back, allowing the plug to enter the gun easily.

Figure 4.61 Installing a plastic tip on the nozzle of the air gun (Tyler Manufacturing Co., Inc., Hawthorne, Calif.).

Figure 4.62 Inserting the nozzle of the gun into the puncture (Tyler Manufacturing Co., Inc., Hawthorne, Calif.).

8 Install the nozzle on the gun.

9 Install a plastic tip on the nozzle of the gun. See Figure 4.61.

10 Remove the prober from the tire and insert the nozzle of the gun, following the direction of the puncture as determined with the prober. See Figure 4.62.

11 Press the trigger of the gun to fire the plug. Release the trigger.

Note: The trigger must be released before attempting to withdraw the gun. Failure to do so may stretch the stem of the plug and allow the repair to leak.

12 Withdraw the gun from the tire.

13 Cut off the protruding end of the plug to within ⅛ of 1 inch (3 mm) of the tread surface.

14 Inflate the tire to the pressure recommended by the manufacturer.

15 Test the repair for leakage.

Job 4f

REPAIR A PUNCTURED TUBELESS TIRE

SATISFACTORY PERFORMANCE

A satisfactory performance on this job requires that you do the following:

1 Repair a punctured tubeless tire by using a puncture repair gun to install a rubber plug.
2 Following the steps in the "Performance Outline" and the instructions furnished by the manufacturer of the tool, complete the job within 15 minutes.
3 Fill in the blanks under "Information."

PERFORMANCE OUTLINE

1 Use a probing tool to locate the direction of the hole and coat the hole with cement.
2 Load the gun.

3 Fire the plug into the hole.
4 Cut off the excess plug.
5 Inflate the tire and test the repair.

INFORMATION

Tire size and type_____

Make of repair gun used _____

Size of rubber plug used _____

Tire inflation pressure _____

Method used to test repair_____

Was the repair successful?   Yes_____   No_____

WHEEL AND TIRE IMBALANCE When a car is in motion, its tires are subjected to many forces. Those forces vary with the weight the tire is carrying and with the speed at which the tire is rotating. These forces may cause a wheel and tire assembly to bounce up and down or to wobble from side to side. In most cases, these problems are caused by *imbalance*. Imbalance is the condition caused when the weight of the wheel and tire assembly is unevenly distributed. Most tires have some imbalance because of the variety of materials and the many operations used in their manufacture.

Static Balance Static balance means "balance at rest." In a wheel and tire assembly it is the equal distribution of weight around the axis of rotation. A wheel and tire assembly that is in static balance has no tendency to rotate on its spindle, or axle, by itself. You will rarely find a wheel and tire assembly that is perfectly balanced. In most cases, the fault is in the tire. In the manufacture of a tire, the fabric and the rubber are sometimes unevenly distributed. This results in heavy spots and light spots in the tire. To bring the wheel and tire assembly into balance, you must attach weights to the

wheel rim opposite any heavy spot in the tire. Typical wheel weights, shown in Figure 4.63, are made of lead alloy. They are attached to the rim by a steel clip.

A wheel and tire assembly that is not in static balance causes *wheel tramp*. Wheel tramp is a vertical movement of the spindle as shown in Figure 4.64. Wheel tramp occurs when the heavy part of a tire moves up and down while the tire is rotating. This motion causes a vibration as shown in Figure 4.65. This vibration annoys the driver and causes premature wear of steering and suspension parts.

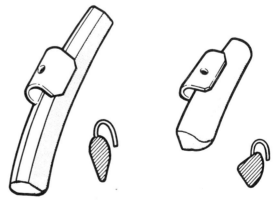

Figure 4.63 Typical wheel weights. The steel clip holds the weight to the rim (Ford Motor Company).

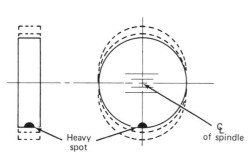

Figure 4.64 Wheel tramp. The heavy spot in the tire causes the spindle to move up and down as the wheel spins (Pontiac Motor Division, GM).

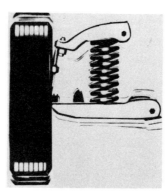

Figure 4.65 Vibration caused by wheel tramp (Ford Motor Company).

Figure 4.66 A typical bubble balancer (courtesy AMMCO Tools, Inc.).

Static balance is easily obtained through the use of a *bubble balancer*. A bubble balancer is shown in Figure 4.66. The wheel and tire assembly is placed horizontally on the balancer. Weights are placed on the wheel rim until the bubble level is centered. Figure 4.67 shows a typical bubble level.

Although the bubble balancer can show you the location of the heavy portion of the tire, you have no way of knowing the exact location of the heavy spot. So, you must assume that it is directly under the tread. For this reason, the total amount of weight needed must be "split." Half the weight must be attached to the outside of the wheel, and half attached to the inside, as shown in Figure 4.68.

A *B*

Figure 4.67 A bubble level typical of those used in static wheel balancers. *A* shows the bubble off-center, indicating an imbalance condition. *B* shows the bubble centered, indicating perfect static balance.

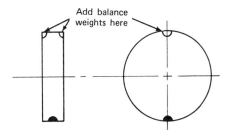

Figure 4.68 Correction for static imbalance. Note that the amount of weight required to correct the imbalance is "split" and placed on both sides of the wheel (Pontiac Motor Division, GM).

STATIC BALANCING The procedure that follows is typical for static balancing a wheel and tire assembly with a bubble balancer. You should follow the procedure specified by the maker of the balancer you have available for zeroing the instrument and for positioning the weights:

1 Remove all stones and dirt from between the tread ribs.

2 Remove all mud and dirt deposits from both sides of the wheel.

3 Zero the balancer as specified by the manufacturer.

4 Carefully place the wheel and tire assembly on the balancer so that the centering cone enters the center hole in the wheel.

5 If the balancer has a locking lever, release the lock so that the bubble is free to move.

6 Allow the bubble to come to rest. If the bubble is centered, the wheel and tire assembly is in static balance. If the bubble is not centered, remove the wheel and tire from the balancer and continue with step 7.

7 Remove any existing weights from the wheel.

8 Carefully place the wheel and tire assembly on the balancer so that the centering cone enters the center hole in the wheel.

9 Release the lock (if necessary) and allow the bubble to come to rest.

10 Carefully place a weight on the rim in line with the bubble.

11 Continue to add weights until the bubble is centered.

Note: You may have to shift the weights to either side to perfectly center the bubble.

12 With chalk, mark the position of the weights (the light spot) on the tire.

13 Determine the total amount of weight added to achieve balance.

14 Remove the wheel and tire assembly from the balancer.

15 Divide in half the amount of weight needed.

Note: This determines the amount of weight you must install on each side of the wheel. For example, if 4 ounces of weight are required to balance the assembly, you will need two 2-ounce weights.

16 Install one weight on the outside wheel rim in line with the chalk mark on the tire.

17 Install the remaining weight on the inside rim in line with the outside weight. (Refer to Figure 4.68.)

Note: Some balancer manufacturers recommend the use of four weights spread out equally from the light spot. For the proper method, check the instruction manual for the balancer you are using.

18 Place the wheel and tire assembly back on the balancer and check that static balance has been obtained.

Job 4g

STATIC BALANCE A WHEEL AND TIRE ASSEMBLY ON A BUBBLE BALANCER

SATISFACTORY PERFORMANCE

A satisfactory performance on this job requires that you do the following:

1 Static balance the wheel and tire assembly provided so that the bubble is centered within the inner ring of the indicator.

2 Following the steps in the "Performance Outline" and the instructions of the balancer manufacturer, complete the job within 15 minutes.

3 Fill in the blanks under "Information."

PERFORMANCE OUTLINE

1 Clean the wheel and tire.
2 Zero the balancer.
3 Position the wheel and tire assembly.
4 Install the weights required.
5 Check that proper balance was obtained.

INFORMATION

Total weight required _____

Amount attached to the inside of the wheel_____

Amount attached to the outside of the wheel_____

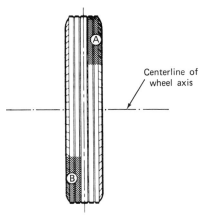

Figure 4.69 A tire in static balance. The weight on both sides of the axis centerline (positions A and B) is equal (Ford Motor Company).

Dynamic Balance Dynamic balance means "balance in motion." It requires that the wheel and tire assembly be in static balance. It also requires that the weight of the wheel and tire assembly be evenly distributed on both sides of the tire centerline. Figure 4.69 illustrates the condition that exists when a wheel and tire assembly is in static balance. The weight of the assembly is distributed even around the axis of rotation. Figure 4.70 illustrates the con-

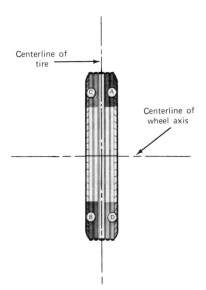

Figure 4.70 A tire in dynamic balance. The total weight of positions A and C equals the total weight of positions B and D. Also, the weight at position A equals the weight at position C and the weight at position B equals the weight at position D (Ford Motor Company).

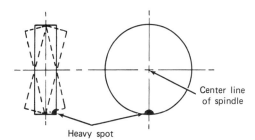

Figure 4.71 Shimmy. The heavy spot in the tire causes the wheel to shake or "wobble" as the wheel spins (Pontiac Motor Division, GM).

dition that exists when a wheel and tire assembly is in dynamic balance. The weight on both sides of the tire centerline must also be considered.

When you static balance a wheel and tire assembly on a bubble balancer, you must assume that the heavy spot of the tire is under the center of the tread. But in many cases it is under one of the sidewalls. A wheel and tire assembly may be in static balance but out of dynamic balance.

A wheel and tire assembly that is not in dynamic balance will cause *shimmy*. Shimmy is a wobbling movement of the spindle as shown in Figure 4.71. This movement is caused by *centrifugal force*. Centrifugal force is a tendency of a rotating body to move away from its axis of rotation. When a wheel and tire assembly is rotating, the heavy parts of the tire tend to move outward and toward the centerline of the tire. This movement is shown in Figure 4.72. Above certain car speeds, usually about 45 mph (72 km/h), this movement can cause a vibration, or shimmy, as shown in Figure 4.73. This vibration can cause violent shaking of the steering wheel and rapid wearing of steering and suspension parts.

As in the correction of static imbalance, dynamic imbalance is also corrected with weights. However, the amount of weight used and the position of the weights must be determined while the wheel and tire assembly is spinning. There are many types of dynamic wheel balancers in use. Some require that you remove the wheel and tire assembly from the

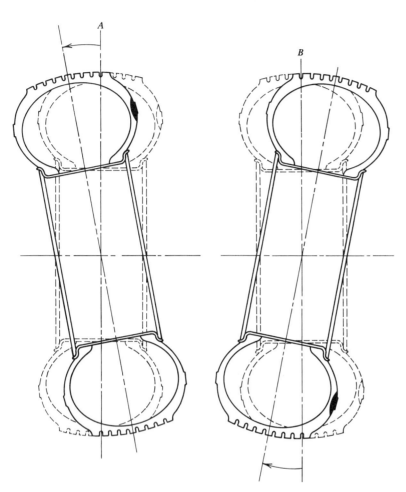

Figure 4.72 The effect of dynamic imbalance. In view *A* centrifugal force causes the heavy spot to move outward from the axis of rotation and toward the tire centerline. In this case the heavy spot tips to the left. View *B* shows the same tire after it has rotated 180°. Centrifugal force now causes the heavy spot to tip to the right. Centrifugal force increases with the speed of rotation. At high speeds dynamic imbalance causes severe vibration.

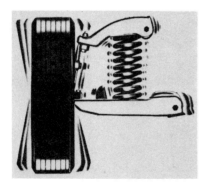

Figure 4.73 A vibration caused by shimmy (Ford Motor Company).

car. Others allow you to balance the assembly while it is on the car.

SUMMARY

In this chapter you learned how the most popular types of tires are constructed. You can now read and interpret the various markings on these tires. You learned the proper methods of removing and installing wheel and tire assemblies, and how to rotate tires to equalize wear. You can now inspect tires, interpret wear patterns, and identify the causes of abnormal wear. You can now perform many tire services including replacing a tire on a tire machine, repairing a puncture in a tubeless tire, and statically balancing a wheel and tire assembly. You have met your objectives and are closer to your goal.

SELF-TEST

Each incomplete statement or question in this test is followed by four suggested completions or answers. In each case select the *one* that best completes the sentence or answers the questions.

1. Two mechanics are discussing tires.
   Mechanic A says that a 78-14 tire is 78 percent as high as it is wide.
   Mechanic B says that an F70-14 tire is wider than an F78-14 tire.
   Who is right?
   A. A only
   B. B only
   C. Both A and B
   D. Neither A nor B

2. A tire marked "4 ply Rating / 2 Ply" will be classified by which of the following load ranges?
   A. A
   B. B
   C. C
   D. D

3. Which of the following would *not* be caused by underinflated tires?
   A. Erratic braking action
   B. Abnormal wear in the center of the tire treads
   C. Increased steering effort and poor steering response
   D. Poor directional stability because of wander or pull in the steering

4. An inspection of the tires on a car reveals that the front tires have excessive wear at the outer edges of the treads. Which of the following would *not* cause this type of wear?
   A. Underinflation
   B. Incorrect toe-in
   C. Lack of rotation
   D. High-speed cornering

5. Two mechanics are discussing the installation of wheels. Mechanic A says that lug nuts should be tightened to a torque specification.

Mechanic B says that lug nuts should be tightened in a torque sequence.
   Who is right?
   A. A only
   B. B only
   C. Both A and B
   D. Neither A nor B

6. To allow for mounting and dismounting tires, one-piece steel wheels have a
   A. rim flange
   B. safety ridge
   C. center section
   D. dropped center

7. When tread wear indicator strips appear across the tread of a tire, the tread has worn to a depth of less than
   A. $1/32$ in. (0.8 mm)
   B. $2/32$ in. (1.6 mm)
   C. $3/32$ in. (2.4 mm)
   D. $4/32$ in. (3.2 mm)

8. Two mechanics are discussing the removal of a tire from a wheel.
   Mechanic A says that the wheel and tire assembly should be placed on a tire machine so that the dropped center of the rim faces upward.
   Mechanic B says that the upper bead should be dismounted before the lower bead is broken loose from the rim.
   Who is right?
   A. A only
   B. B only
   C. Both A and B
   D. Neither A nor B

9. Two mechanics are discussing the repair of tubeless tires.
   Mechanic A says that a punctured sidewall can be plugged if the hole does not exceed ¼ of 1 inch (6.4 mm) in diameter.
   Mechanic B says that sidewall punctures can be repaired without removing the tire from the wheel if a special rivetlike plug is used.
   Who is right?
   A. A only
   B. B only

C. Both A and B
D. Neither A nor B

10 Two mechanics are discussing wheel balance.
Mechanic A says that static imbalance will cause wheel tramp.
Mechanic B says that a bubble balancer can be used to dynamically balance a wheel and tire assembly.
Who is right?
A. A only
B. B only
C. Both A and B
D. Neither A nor B

Chapter 5 Battery Service

All too often, the battery in a car is ignored until it fails to crank the engine. Annual surveys repeatedly list battery failure as one of the most common reasons for requiring road service. Failure to maintain the battery in a car can cause more than inconvenience. Lack of proper maintenance will considerably shorten the useful life of a battery.

The most commonly performed battery services include cleaning, testing, charging, and replacement. These services require certain knowledge, diagnostic skills, and repair skills. In this chapter you will be given the opportunity to gain that knowledge and those skills. Your specific objectives are to perform the following jobs:

1
Identify terms relating to battery operation and construction
2
Clean battery posts and cable clamps
3
Remove and install a battery
4
Test the specific gravity of battery electrolyte
5
Load test a battery
6
Charge a battery
7
Use a booster battery to start a car
8
Activate a dry charged battery

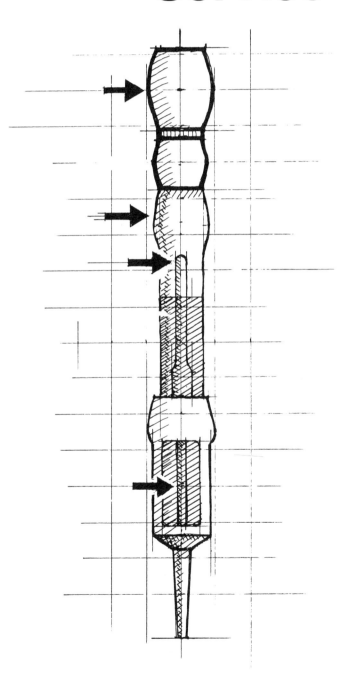

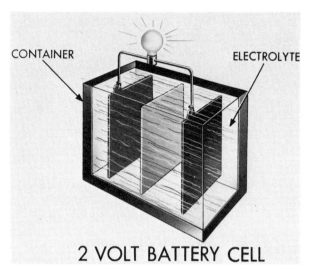

Figure 5.1 The difference in pressure between the plates of a simple cell causes the flow of current. In this example, the current flows through the filament of a bulb (Chevrolet Service Manual, Chevrolet Motor Division, GM).

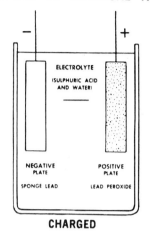

Figure 5.2 The composition of a simple lead acid cell (ESB, Inc.).

THE BATTERY While a battery may sometimes be referred to as a "storage battery," a battery does not store electricity. A battery stores chemicals that react to produce electrical energy. Battery service includes certain chemical and electrical tests. But it is not enough to be able to perform the tests. You must also be able to interpret the results of those tests. To do that, you must be knowledgeable about certain facts regarding battery operation and construction.

Battery Operation A battery operates through the application of a simple scientific principle. When two different metals are immersed in an acid solution, a difference in electrical pressure exists between them. Figure 5.1 shows how that pressure causes the flow of electricity.

As you learned in Chapter 2, most batteries used in automobiles are of the lead-acid type. In a lead-acid battery, the different metals are *lead peroxide* and *sponge lead*. The lead peroxide forms the *positive* (+) plate. The sponge lead forms the *negative* (−) plate. The acid is electrolyte, a mixture of sulfuric acid and water. A simple lead-acid cell is shown in Figure 5.2.

Electrochemical Action A lead-acid cell can be repeatedly discharged and charged. This is possible because the chemical action in the cell can be reversed. The energy used to start an engine can be restored by the charging system when the engine is running. If such were not the case, a battery would have to be discarded after a short period of use. Throughout its life, a battery is *cycled*, or partially discharged and recharged, thousands of times. At any time in its life, a battery will be in one of the following states:

Charged Figure 5.3 shows the chemical condition of a fully charged battery. The positive plate consists of lead peroxide, the negative plate is sponge lead, and the electrolyte is at its full strength.

Discharging When a load is placed across the plates, the battery discharges. The difference in electrical pressure between the plates causes current to flow. While that current is flowing, a chemical change takes place in the plates and in the electrolyte. As shown in Figure 5.4, the electrolyte becomes diluted and the plates become *sulfated*. Actually, the electrolyte (H_2SO_4) divides into hydrogen (H_2) and a sulfate radical (SO_4). The hydrogen (H_2)

DIAGRAM OF CHEMICAL ACTION

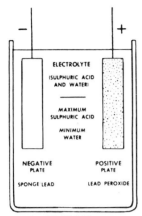

CHARGED

Figure 5.3 The chemical condition of a fully charged battery (ESB, Inc.).

combines with some of the oxygen (O) formed at the positive plate and produces additional water (H_2O). The sulfate (SO_4) combines with the lead (Pb) in both plates and forms lead sulfate ($PbSO_4$).

Discharged If a continuous load is placed on a battery, the chemical action continues until the battery is discharged. As shown in Figure 5.5, the electrolyte has been depleted and diluted until it is mostly water. The plates have both become lead sulfate, and they are no longer dissimilar.

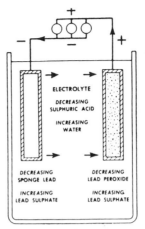

DISCHARGING

Figure 5.4 The chemical condition of a battery that is discharging (ESB, Inc.).

Charging When a battery is being charged, the chemical action is reversed as shown in Figure 5.6. The lead sulfate ($PbSO_4$) is broken down, restoring the plates to their original composition (PbO_2 and Pb). The sulfate (SO_4) combines with the hydrogen (H_2) in the water (H_2O) to form sulfuric acid (H_2SO_4). The sulfuric acid increases the strength of the electrolyte.

Cell Voltage Electrical pressure is measured in units called *volts*. A fully charged lead-acid cell produces a maximum pressure of about 2.2 volts. Internal resistance reduces that pressure slightly, and a lead-acid cell is

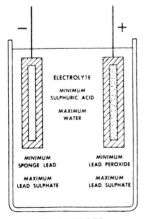

DISCHARGED

Figure 5.5 The chemical condition of a discharged battery (ESB, Inc.).

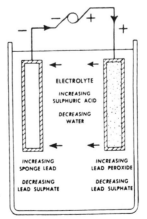

CHARGING

Figure 5.6 The chemical condition of a battery that is being charged (ESB, Inc.).

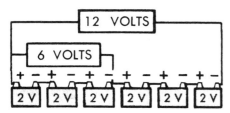

Figure 5.7 Cells are connected in series to form batteries. A 6-volt battery has three cells. A 12-volt battery has six cells.

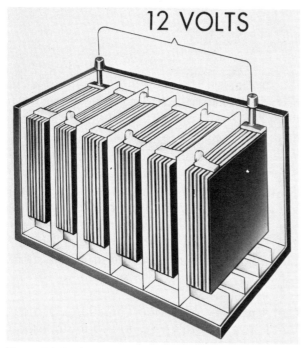

Figure 5.8 Typical arrangement of the cells of a 12-volt battery (Chevrolet Service Manual, Chevrolet Motor Division, GM).

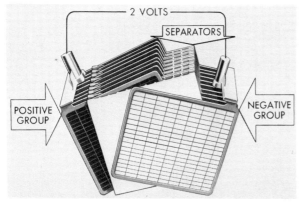

Figure 5.9 A group of positive plates and a group of negative plates are combined to form a compound element. Insulating separators are used to keep the plates from touching each other (Chevrolet Service Manual, Chevrolet Motor Division, GM).

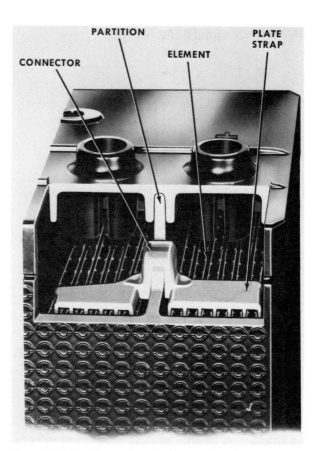

Figure 5.10 A cutaway view of a battery showing the internal connections between the cells (Chevrolet Service Manual, Chevrolet Motor Division, GM).

usually referred to as a 2-volt cell. Increasing the size of the plates, or increasing the number of plates in a cell will not increase the voltage. In order to obtain higher voltage, cells must be connected in *series*, positive to negative, as shown in Figure 5.7.

Battery Construction Most cars use what is commonly called a 12-volt battery. A 12-volt battery consists of six cells connected in series as shown in Figure 5.8. Each cell contains a *compound element*. As shown in Figure 5.9, a compound element consists of a group of positive plates and a group of negative plates. The plates are *porous*, or spongy, so that electrolyte can flow through them. Because the plates must not touch each other, insulating *separators* are placed between them. The separators too are porous, allowing the flow of electrolyte.

The element in each cell is connected to the element in the adjoining cell by a *connector*, as shown in Figure 5.10. The connectors pass through the partition walls of the battery case. The positive group of the element in the first cell is connected to the positive (+) terminal of the battery. The negative group of the element in the last cell is connected to the negative (−) terminal.

Job 5a

IDENTIFY TERMS RELATING TO BATTERY OPERATION AND CONSTRUCTION

SATISFACTORY PERFORMANCE

A satisfactory performance on this job requires that you do the following:

1 Identify terms relating to battery operation and construction by placing the number of each term in front of the phrase that best describes it.
2 Correctly identify all the terms within 15 minutes.

PERFORMANCE SITUATION

1 Sponge lead	5 Lead peroxide
2 Voltage	6 Compound element
3 Electrolyte	7 Lead sulfate
4 Separator	

_____ The composition of the positive plate in a fully charged lead-acid cell.

_____ A measurement of electrical pressure.

_____ The composition of the plates in a discharged cell.

_____ The material used to make separators.

_____ The composition of the negative plate in a fully charged lead-acid cell.

_____ A mixture of sulfuric acid and water.

_____ An assembly of a positive group and a negative group.

_____ An insulator used between plates.

BATTERY SERVICE Although some batteries do not require the addition of water, all batteries require routine maintenance services. Those services include visual inspection, cleaning, testing, and charging.

Visual Inspection Battery service should begin with a thorough visual inspection. A visual inspection may reveal the need for other services. Figure 5.11 illustrates some of the more common faults that may be found.

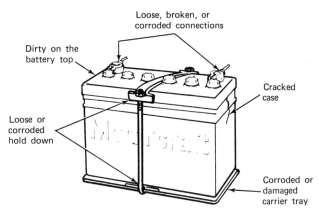

Figure 5.11 Battery service should begin with a thorough visual inspection of the battery, its connections, and its mounting (Ford Motor Company).

A loose or broken hold down will allow a battery to move. If a battery is not securely mounted, movement and vibration will damage the battery. A hold down should be tightened snugly so that the battery cannot move, but not so tight that the battery case is distorted. If a hold down is damaged so that it cannot be tightened, it should be replaced.

A cracked case will allow electrolyte to leak from the battery. Even if that leakage is slight, the electrolyte will corrode the battery carrier tray and its surrounding parts. A battery with a cracked case should be replaced.

Corrosion caused by spilled electrolyte should be removed and neutralized. This can be done by cleaning the parts with a solution made by dissolving a teaspoonful of baking soda in a cup of water. After the parts have dried, they should be protected from further corrosion by a coating of oil or light grease.

Dirt on the top of a post-type battery may hold spilled electrolyte. Because electrolyte conducts electricity, that coating may cause a battery to self-discharge. The top of a battery should always be kept clean and dry.

Loose, broken, or corroded connections may restrict current flow. In an electrical circuit, a restriction to current flow is called *resistance*. The resistance in such connections often causes problems that may be incorrectly blamed on the battery or on the starter motor. Broken and damaged cables should be replaced. Connections should be kept clean, tight, and in good condition.

CLEANING BATTERY CONNECTIONS A visual inspection of battery connections may reveal some of the faults shown in Figure 5.12. Although these faults require correction, a more serious fault may escape detection. Oxidation and corrosion between the battery post and the cable clamp, as shown in Figure 5.13, are a common cause of high resistance. To eliminate this resistance, the cables must be removed from the posts and all parts thoroughly cleaned. The following steps outline a suggested procedure:

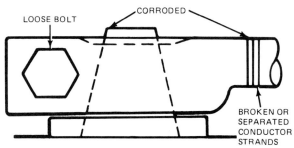

Figure 5.12 A cable clamp should be clean, tight, and exhibit no broken or separated conductor strands (Ford Motor Company).

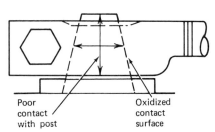

Figure 5.13 Although a cable clamp may appear clean and tight, internal oxidation can create a bad connection (Ford Motor Company).

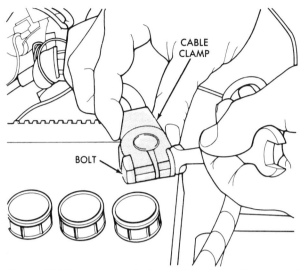

Figure 5.14 Loosening a battery cable clamp. The ground cable should be removed first to minimize the danger of arcing and a possible battery explosion (courtesy Chrysler Corporation).

Figure 5.15 Typical battery pliers. This tool is designed for the removal of cable clamp nuts which are so corroded that a wrench cannot be used (courtesy of K-D Tools).

1 Make sure that all switches and controls are in the OFF position.

2 Loosen the clamp connecting the ground cable to the battery as shown in Figure 5.14. On most cars, the ground cable is connected to the negative (−) battery post.

Note: If the nut on the clamp bolt is corroded or worn so that a wrench cannot be used, a pair of battery pliers similar to those shown in Figure 5.15 will prove helpful.

3 Remove the cable clamp from the battery post.

Note: Never attempt to pry or twist a cable clamp from a battery post. To do so could damage the battery. If a clamp will not slide off easily, a cable puller similar to the one shown in Figure 5.16 should be used. Positioned over the clamp as shown in Figure 5.17, a puller will enable you to remove a clamp without damage to the battery.

4 Remove the remaining cable clamp.

Figure 5.16 A typical battery cable clamp puller (courtesy of K-D Tools).

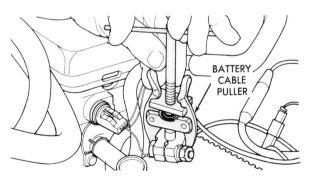

Figure 5.17 Using a puller to remove a battery cable clamp from a battery post (courtesy Chrysler Corporation).

Figure 5.18 A typical battery post and clamp cleaning brush (courtesy of K-D Tools).

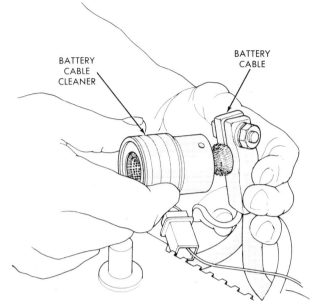

BATTERY
CABLE
CLEANER

BATTERY
CABLE

Figure 5.19 Cleaning the inside surfaces of a battery cable clamp (courtesy Chrysler Corporation).

5 Using a battery post and clamp cleaning brush similar to the one shown in Figure 5.18, clean the inside of the battery clamps. This operation is shown in Figure 5.19.

6 Clean the battery posts as shown in Figure 5.20.

7 Clean the top of the battery. A solution of baking soda and water applied with a brush is ideal for cleaning as it will neutralize any spilled acid. See Figure 5.21.

Note: Use care so that the solution does not enter the cells. The baking soda and water solution will weaken the electrolyte.

8 Install the cable that connects the battery to the starter motor or starter switch. On most cars, this cable connects to the positive (+) post on the battery.

Note: This cable should be installed first to minimize the dangers of arcing and possible battery explosion.

9 Install the ground cable. On most cars, the ground cable is connected to the negative (−) post.

Note: The ground cable should always be installed last to minimize the dangers of arcing and possible battery explosion.

10 Coat the cable clamps with a thin coating of a petroleum-based grease.

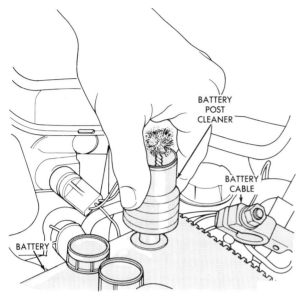

Figure 5.20 Cleaning a battery post (courtesy Chrysler Corporation).

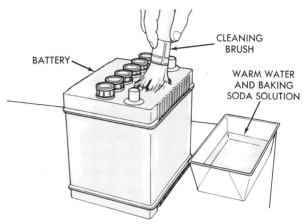

Figure 5.21 Cleaning the top of a battery with a solution of baking soda and water (courtesy Chrysler Corporation).

Job 5b

CLEAN BATTERY POSTS AND CABLE CLAMPS

SATISFACTORY PERFORMANCE

A satisfactory performance on this job requires that you do the following:

1 Clean the battery posts and cable clamps in the car assigned.
2 Following the steps in the "Performance Outline" and the recommendations and specifications of the manufacturer, complete the job within 30 minutes.
3 Fill in the blanks under "Information."

PERFORMANCE OUTLINE

1 Disconnect the cables from the battery.
2 Clean the cable clamps and the posts.
3 Clean the battery top.
4 Install the battery cables.

INFORMATION

Vehicle identification _____

Battery type _____Post terminal _____Side terminal

Which cable was disconnected first?   _____ Positive

                                                      _____ Negative

Which cable was connected last?   _____ Positive

                                                      _____ Negative

---

REMOVING AND INSTALLING BATTERIES Many times you will be required to remove the battery from a vehicle. Battery removal may be necessary for a thorough battery inspection and cleaning, recharging, gaining access to other parts, or installing a replacement battery. The steps that follow outline a procedure which will enable you to safely remove and install a battery. You should follow the vehicle manufacturer's torque specifications when tightening clamps and hold down bolts:

Removal 1 Make sure that all switches and controls are in the OFF position.

2 Disconnect the ground cable from the battery.

Note: **On most cars, the ground cable is connected to the negative (−) battery post or terminal.**

3 Disconnect the remaining cable from the battery.

4 Remove the battery hold down. Penetrating oil applied to the threads of the hold down will make this operation easier.

Note: **On some cars, the battery hold down is located at the bottom of the battery as shown in Figure 5.22. On other cars the hold down is positioned across the top of the battery as shown in Figure 5.23.**

5 Lift the battery from the battery tray and remove it from the car.

Note: **Take care in performing this operation. Batteries are very heavy and contain acid. To avoid the possibility of dropping the battery, you should use a battery carrier. Figure 5.24 shows a battery carrier strap commonly used with post-type batteries. Side terminal batteries can be safely lifted with a carrier similar to the one shown in Figure 5.25. That type of carrier is attached to the battery by screws that thread into the battery terminals. Some shops use a clamp-type carrier similar to the one shown in Figure 5.26. That type of carrier can be used on both post-type and side terminal batteries as shown in Figure 5.27.**

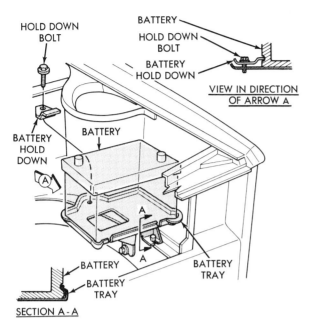

SECTION A-A

Figure 5.22 A typical battery hold down. This type of hold down secures the battery to the battery tray by means of grooves formed in the bottom edges of the battery case (courtesy Chrysler Corporation).

Figure 5.24 A typical battery carrier strap. This type is for use with post-type batteries (courtesy of K-D Tools).

Figure 5.25 A battery carrier strap designed for use with side terminal batteries. Knurled headed screws provide a means of attaching the strap to the terminals (courtesy of K-D Tools).

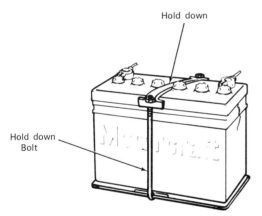

Figure 5.23 A hold down that passes over the top of the battery (Ford Motor Company).

Figure 5.26 A clamp-type battery carrier (courtesy of Snap-on Tools Corporation).

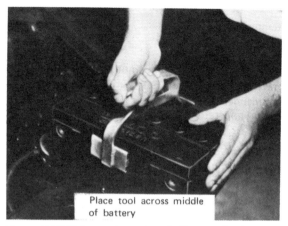

Place tool across middle of battery

Figure 5.27 Using a clamp-type battery carrier to remove a battery. The tool should be positioned across the center of the battery (Buick Motor Division, GM).

Figure 5.28 Battery terminal spreading pliers. A tool of this type is useful for opening the clamp so that the cable can be installed on a new battery (courtesy of K-D Tools).

Installation 1 Inspect the battery tray. If any corrosion is present, clean the tray with a solution of baking soda and water. After drying the tray, it should be coated with light oil to retard future corrosion.

2 Using a battery carrier, carefully place the battery in the tray. Be sure the posts are in the correct position.

Note: **If the original battery is to be installed, clean the posts and the battery top before placing the battery in the tray.**

3 Install the hold down and tighten the attaching bolt(s) to the manufacturer's torque specification.

4 Clean the cable clamps.

5 Install the battery cables, connecting the ground cable last.

Note: **If the clamps will not fit over the battery posts, they may be spread with the use of a tool similar to the one shown in Figure 5.28.**

6 Tighten the clamp nuts or terminal bolts to the torque specification of the manufacturer.

7 Coat the cable clamps with a thin coating of a petroleum-based grease.

Job 5c

REMOVE AND INSTALL A BATTERY

SATISFACTORY PERFORMANCE

A satisfactory performance on ttis job requires that you do the following:

1 Remove and install the battery in the car assigned.

2 Following the steps in the "Performance Outline" and the specifications of the car manufacturer, complete the job within 30 minutes.
3 Fill in the blanks under "Information."

PERFORMANCE OUTLINE
1 Disconnect the battery cables.
2 Remove the hold down.
3 Remove the battery.
4 Inspect and clean the carrier tray.
5 Clean the battery posts and the cable clamps.
6 Install the battery and secure it with the hold down.
7 Connect the battery cables.

INFORMATION

Vehicle identification _____

Reference used_____ Page(s)_____

Type of hold down used   _____Top mounted

                              _____Bottom mounted

Type of battery   _____Post-type terminals

                              _____Side terminals

BATTERY TESTING Routine maintenance requires that a battery be tested at regular intervals. Two different tests should be made to determine the condition of a battery. The first test, called a specific gravity test, determines the state of charge of a battery. The second test, called a high-rate discharge test or load test, determines the battery's capacity to deliver energy.

SPECIFIC GRAVITY TESTING Specific gravity may be defined as "exact weight." The specific gravity of pure water is 1.000. The specific gravity of sulfuric acid is about 1.835. Thus, any mixture of water and sulfuric acid has a specific gravity of more than 1.000 and less than 1.835. One commonly used electrolyte consists of a mixture of 64 percent water and 36 percent acid. As shown in Figure 5.29, that electrolyte has a specific gravity of 1.270.

Most manufacturers consider a battery to be fully charged if the electrolyte in the battery has a specific gravity of from 1.250 to 1.265. The specific gravity of the electrolyte in a battery is easily measured with a *hydrometer*. A hydrometer, shown in Figure 5.30, is a syringe-

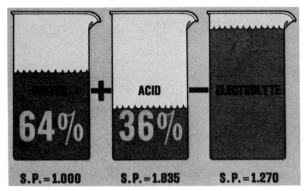

Figure 5.29 The composition of a typical battery electrolyte (courtesy American Motors Corporation).

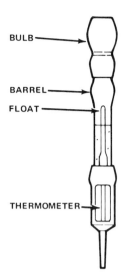

Figure 5.30 A typical battery hydrometer (courtesy American Motors Corporation).

type device which enables you to withdraw a sample of electrolyte from a battery. As the electrolyte rises in the glass barrel of the hydrometer, it causes a calibrated float to rise. The float is marked for various specific gravities. If the electrolyte is heavy, as it is in a fully charged battery, the float will be high and will indicate a high specific gravity. If the electrolyte is light, as in a discharged battery, the float will be low and indicate a low specific gravity.

As you learned earlier in this chapter, the electrolyte in a battery changes to water as the battery discharges. Thus, the electrolyte becomes lighter as the battery discharges. This change of weight, shown in Figures 5.31 through 5.34, provides a reliable indication of the battery's state of charge. The percentage of charge for various ranges of specific gravity is given in Figure 5.35.

The specific gravity of a liquid changes with its temperature. As a liquid is heated, it expands and becomes less dense. Thus, its specific gravity becomes lower. As a liquid is cooled, it contracts and becomes more dense. Thus, its specific gravity becomes higher. Because of this, a partially discharged battery may appear to be fully charged if it is tested when it is cold. For the same reason, a fully charged battery may appear to be partially discharged if it is tested when it is hot.

The specific gravity readings and specifications for electrolyte are accurate only when the electrolyte is at 80°F (27°C). If the electrolyte is at any other temperature, the hydrometer readings must be corrected. Most hydrometers contain a thermometer which enables you to determine the temperature of the electrolyte. Electrolyte temper-

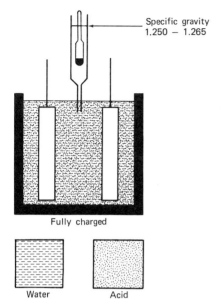

Figure 5.31 The electrolyte in a fully charged battery has a high concentration of acid and thus a high specific gravity.

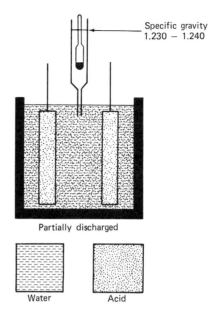

Figure 5.32 As the battery discharges, the acid combines chemically with the plates, and the specific gravity drops.

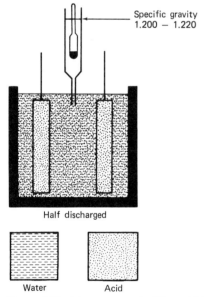

Figure 5.33 A large amount of the acid in the electrolyte has combined with the plates. A battery in this condition may not have sufficient energy to start an engine.

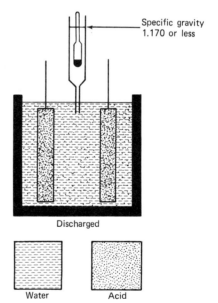

Figure 5.34 Most of the acid in the electrolyte has combined with the plates. Since the electrolyte now consists mainly of water, it has a very low specific gravity.

PERCENT OF CHARGE	SPECIFIC GRAVITY RANGES
100	1.260–1.265
95	1.250–1.260
75	1.230–1.240
50	1.200–1.220
25	1.170–1.190

Batteries containing electrolyte with a lower specific gravity should be considered discharged.

Figure 5.35 Approximate percentages of the state of charge for various ranges of battery electrolyte specific gravity.

ature must always be considered when using a hydrometer to determine the state of charge of a battery.

The temperature correction chart in Figure 5.36 provides an easy method by which you can correct specific gravity readings within a wide range of temperature. That chart reflects a .004 change in specific gravity for each 10°F (5.5°C) change in temperature. For every 10°F (5.5°C) over 80°F (27°C), .004 must be added to the hydrometer reading. For every 10°F (5.5°C) under 80°F (27°C), .004 must be subtracted from the hydrometer reading.

The following steps outline a procedure for measuring the specific gravity of the electrolyte in a battery:

1 Place a fender cover over the fender nearest the battery.

Note: Electrolyte is an acid and is highly corrosive. Use care not to spill or splash any electrolyte during this procedure.

2 Remove the vent caps or covers from the cells and place them on the battery as shown in Figure 5.37.

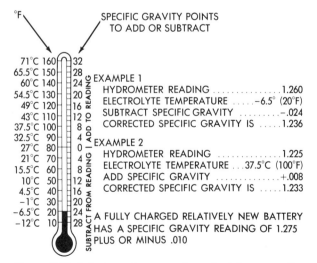

Figure 5.36 A hydrometer correction chart for correcting specific gravity readings for various electrolyte temperatures (courtesy Chrysler Corporation).

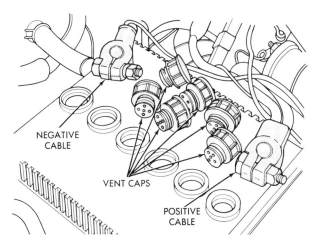

NEGATIVE
CABLE

VENT CAPS

POSITIVE
CABLE

Figure 5.37 All vent caps and covers should be removed prior to testing specific gravity. Placing the caps on the battery minimizes the possibility of electrolyte damage to other surfaces (courtesy Chrysler Corporation).

3 Squeeze the suction bulb of the hydrometer and insert the pick up tube into the cell closest to the positive (+) post.

Note: Do not force the tube into the cell; you might damage the plates and separators.

4 Slowly release the bulb and draw in sufficient electrolyte to half fill the barrel.

Note: If there is insufficient electrolyte in the cell, an accurate test cannot be made. Water must be added to the cell and the battery must be charged so that the water will mix with the electrolyte.

5 Slowly squeeze the bulb to return the electrolyte to the cell.

Note: This step adjusts the temperature of the hydrometer to that of the electrolyte and provides for a more accurate first reading.

6 Slowly release the bulb again and draw in sufficient electrolyte to cause the float to rise.

Note: The hydrometer should be held in a vertical position so that the float will not drag against the inside of the barrel.

7 Read the specific gravity indicated on the float. Be sure that the float is drifting free in the electrolyte and that it is not in contact with the spacer at the top of the barrel.

Note: An accurate reading requires that you bend down so that the reading is taken at eye level, as shown in Figure 5.38. Do not remove the hydrometer from the battery, as that will allow electrolyte leakage.

8 Note the temperature indicated by the thermometer.

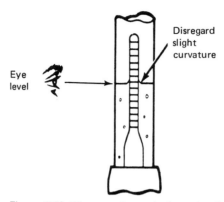

Figure 5.38 When reading a hydrometer, it should be held vertical so that the float does not touch the sides of the barrel. To obtain an accurate reading, the liquid should be at eye level (courtesy American Motors Corporation).

9 Slowly squeeze the bulb and return all the electrolyte to the cell.

10 Record the specific gravity and the electrolyte temperature.

11 Repeat steps 3 through 10 for the remaining cells.

12 Install the vent caps or covers.

13 Clean and dry the top of the battery.

Interpreting Test Results If the electrolyte temperature was approximately 80°F (27°C), the specific gravity readings may be considered accurate as recorded. Specific gravity readings of electrolyte at any other temperature must be corrected. Refer to Figure 5.36 to correct the specific gravity. Refer to Figure 5.35 to determine the state of charge.

Batteries with electrolyte whose specific gravity is less than 1.240 may be charged to increase the specific gravity. Batteries with electrolyte whose specific gravity is less than 1.200 should be charged before any further testing is attempted.

Job 5d

TEST THE SPECIFIC GRAVITY OF BATTERY ELECTROLYTE

SATISFACTORY PERFORMANCE

A satisfactory performance on this job requires that you do the following:

1 Test the specific gravity of the electrolyte in the battery assigned.

2 Following the steps in the "Performance Outline" and the specifications of the car manufacturer, complete the job within 15 minutes.

3 Fill in the blanks under "Information."

PERFORMANCE OUTLINE

1 Remove the vent caps.

2 Measure and record the specific gravity and the temperature of the electrolyte in each cell.
3 Install the vent caps.
4 Clean and dry the battery top.
5 Correct the specific gravity readings if necessary and determine the state of charge of the battery.

INFORMATION

Vehicle identification _____

Battery identification _____

Reference used_____ Page(s)_____

Measurements obtained

Cell No.	Specific Gravity	Temperature
1	_____	_____
2	_____	_____
3	_____	_____
4	_____	_____
5	_____	_____
6	_____	_____

Corrections and interpretations

Cell No.	Corrected Specific Gravity	Percent of Charge
1	_____	_____
2	_____	_____
3	_____	_____
4	_____	_____
5	_____	_____
6	_____	_____

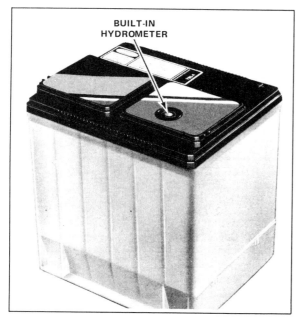

Figure 5.39 A sealed battery with a built-in temperature-compensated hydrometer (Pontiac Motor Division, GM).

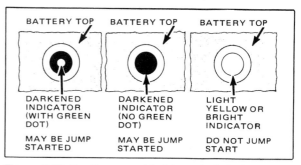

Figure 5.40 Readings provided by a built-in hydrometer (Pontiac Motor Division, GM).

Specific Gravity Testing of Sealed Batteries Some batteries are completely sealed except for a small vent hole. Those batteries have no removable vent caps or covers. Therefore, a conventional hydrometer cannot be used to determine the state of charge. Most sealed batteries incorporate a built-in temperature-compensated hydrometer as shown in Figure 5.39. Although the built-in hydrometer does not provide a measurement of the spe-

cific gravity of the electrolyte, it does provide sufficient information for diagnosis.

As shown in Figure 5.40, the most commonly used type of built-in hydrometer provides three indications:

1 *Green Dot Visible.* Any green appearance should be considered a "green dot." This indicates that the state of charge is satisfactory and that the battery is ready for further testing.

2 *Dark—Green Dot Not Visible.* A dark appearance without a green dot indicates that the battery is partially discharged. Further testing is required to determine if the battery can be charged or if it should be replaced.

3 *Clear or Light Yellow.* A clear or light yellow appearance usually indicates that the battery is defective. If a clear or light yellow appearance is accompanied by a failure to crank the engine, the battery should be replaced. DO NOT ATTEMPT TO CHARGE, TEST, OR JUMP START.

LOAD TESTING Although a hydrometer test can be used to determine the state of charge of a battery, it cannot measure the battery's ability to deliver energy. A load test provides a method of determining the serviceability of a battery. As its name implies, load testing consists of testing a battery while it is working under a load.

Many different instruments and procedures may be used to load test a battery. However, all of those instruments and procedures require that battery voltage be measured while the battery is being discharged at a high rate. For this reason, a load test is often referred to as a high rate discharge test.

A tester similar to the one shown in Figure 5.41 is most commonly used to load test a battery. In addition to various selector switches, the tester contains an adjustable resistance unit, an ammeter, and

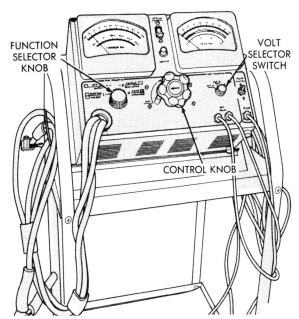

FUNCTION
SELECTOR
KNOB

VOLT
SELECTOR
SWITCH

CONTROL KNOB

Figure 5.41 A typical tester used to load test batteries (courtesy Chrysler Corporation).

a voltmeter. The adjustable resistance unit is usually a *carbon pile*. A carbon pile is a stack of carbon discs that can be squeezed together to form a low resistance unit capable of handling large amounts of current. The ammeter measures the amount of current flowing through the carbon pile. The voltmeter measures the battery voltage.

In use, the tester is connected across the terminals of a battery as shown in Figure 5.42. The carbon pile is adjusted by means of the control knob until a specified current is shown on the ammeter. The voltage indicated by the voltmeter is read after the load has been maintained for 15 seconds.

The following steps outline a typical procedure for load testing a battery. You should consult an appropriate manual for the correct load to place on the battery you are testing:

1 Test the specific gravity of the battery. If the specific gravity is less than 1.200, the battery should be charged before a load test is attempted.

2 Disconnect the cables from the battery.

Note: **Disconnect the ground cable first. This will minimize the possibility of arcing and a resultant battery explosion.**

3 Turn the control knob on the battery tester to the OFF position.

4 If the tester is fitted with a function control switch, turn the switch to the BATTERY TEST position.

5 If the tester is fitted with a volt selector switch, turn the switch so that a voltage exceeding battery voltage is selected.

6 Connect the heavy ammeter leads to the battery terminals. The positive (+) lead must be connected to the positive (+) terminal. The negative (−) lead to the negative (−) terminal.

Note: When testing batteries with side terminals, adapters similar to those shown in Figure 5.43 should be used so good connections can be obtained.

7 Connect the voltmeter leads to the battery terminals. The positive (+) lead must be connected to the positive (+) terminal, the negative (−) lead to the negative (−) terminal.

Note: The voltmeter leads should contact the battery terminals or adapters. If the voltmeter leads are connected to the clamps on the ammeter leads, an inaccurate voltmeter reading may be obtained.

8 Refer to an appropriate manual for the correct load to place on the battery being tested.

Note: Some manufacturers provide specific discharge rates for their batteries. An example of those specific loads is shown in Figure 5.44. Other manufacturers recommend that the battery be discharged at a rate equal to three times the ampere hour rating of the battery.

9 Turn the control knob clockwise as shown in Figure 5.45 until the desired discharge rate is indicated by the ammeter.

10 Maintain the desired discharge rate for 15 seconds and note the voltage indicated by the voltmeter.

11 Immediately turn the control knob counterclockwise to the OFF position.

Note: It is not advisable to maintain the load for more than 15 seconds.

12 Disconnect the tester from the battery.

13 Connect the battery cables.

Note: Connect the cable to the starter motor or starter switch first. Connect the ground cable last.

Interpreting Test Results A battery in good condition will maintain a voltage of at least 9.6 volts while the specified load is applied. Because the battery temperature will affect the indicated voltage, the chart in Figure 5.46 lists the minimum voltage allowable for temperatures lower than 70°F (21°C).

If the indicated voltage during a load test drops below those listed in Figure 5.46, the battery is defective and should be replaced.

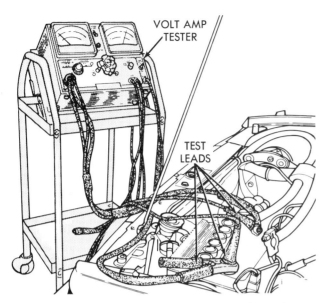

Figure 5.42 A volt-amp tester connected to perform a battery load test (courtesy Chrysler Corporation).

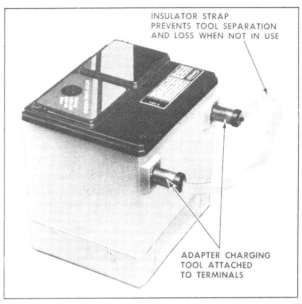

Figure 5.43 Adapters can be attached to side terminal batteries to facilitate testing (Pontiac Motor Division, GM).

Conventional Batteries	
Battery Capacity	Discharge Rate
(Ampere Hours)	(Amperes)
36	155
41	145
45	190
53	175
54	225
68	220
77	228

Maintenance-Free Batteries	
Battery Capacity	Discharge Rate
(Ampere Hours)	(Amperes)
53	200
63	215
68	235

Figure 5.44 Discharge rates specified by one manufacturer for batteries of different ampere hour capacities.

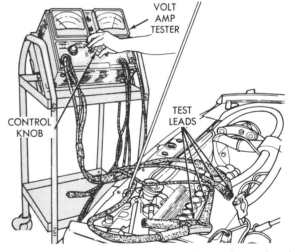

Figure 5.45 A load is applied to the battery by turning the control knob clockwise (courtesy Chrysler Corporation).

MINIMUM VOLTAGE	BATTERY TEMPERATURE	
UNDER SPECIFIED LOAD	°F	°C
9.6	70	21
9.5	60	16
9.4	50	10
9.3	40	4
9.1	30	−1
8.9	20	−7
8.7	10	−12
8.5	0	−18

Figure 5.46 Minimum voltages during load testing.

Job 5e

LOAD TEST A BATTERY

SATISFACTORY PERFORMANCE

A satisfactory performance on this job requires that you do the following:

1 Perform a load test or high rate discharge test on the battery assigned.
2 Following the steps in the "Performance Outline" and the specifications of the manufacturer, complete the job within 15 minutes.
3 Fill in the blanks under "Information."

PERFORMANCE OUTLINE

1 Test the specific gravity of the battery.
2 Disconnect the battery cables.
3 Connect the tester.
4 Apply the specified load.
5 Read the voltage while the battery is under load.
6 Remove the load.
7 Disconnect the tester.
8 Connect the battery cables.

INFORMATION

Vehicle identification _____

Battery identification _____

Reference used_____ Page(s)_____

Battery ampere hour capacity _____

Discharge rate (test load) _____

Tester identification _____

Amount of time load was maintained _____

Voltage indicated while under load _____

Approximate battery temperature _____

Recommendations (check one)

    Battery should be returned to service   _____

    Battery should be charged and returned to service _____

    Battery should be replaced   _____

BATTERY CHARGING A battery in good condition may occasionally fail. This is usually noticed by the car owner when the battery is unable to crank the engine fast enough to make it start. The most common causes of a failure of this type are as follows:

1 The lights or other accessories were accidentally left on overnight.
2 Poor battery maintenance, including failure to maintain electrolyte level, loose connections, dirty connections, or an improperly secured battery.
3 Problems in the charging system, including loose drive belts, a faulty generator, a faulty regulator, or high resistance in connections and components.
4 Trips of short duration that do not allow sufficient time for the charging system to restore the energy used for starting.
5 Defects in the electrical system such as short circuits.
6 The application of electrical loads exceeding the capacity of the generator. This is usually caused by the use of after-market equipment such as radio systems, air conditioners, and special lighting systems.
7 Battery self-discharge during a long period of inactivity.

A discharged battery in good condition can be charged and returned to service. To prevent a reoccurrence, the cause of the discharged condition should be determined and corrected, if possible.

Many types of battery chargers are in use, but all chargers operate on the same principle. They apply an electrical current to the battery to reverse the chemical action in the cells.

WHEN A BATTERY IS BEING CHARGED, AN EXPLOSIVE GAS MIXTURE IS RELEASED FROM THE ELECTROLYTE. THAT GAS IS PRESENT IN THE CELLS AND IN THE AREA SURROUNDING THE BATTERY. TO AVOID THE POSSIBILITY OF IGNITING THAT GAS YOU SHOULD OBSERVE THE FOLLOWING PRECAUTIONS:

1. Never connect or disconnect live charger leads to a battery or otherwise break a live circuit at a battery. To do so may cause arcing and possibly ignite the gas. The charger should be turned OFF before the leads are connected, disconnected, or otherwise disturbed.
2. Keep all open flames away from a battery.
3. Do not smoke near a battery on charge or near a battery that has recently been charged.

Slow Charging If time permits, slow charging should be used to recharge a discharged battery. Slow charging consists of charging a battery at a rate of about 5 amperes for a time sufficient to bring the specific gravity to its highest reading. Depending on the existing state of charge of the battery, slow charging may require from 12 to 24 hours or more. During the charging period, the electrolyte temperature should not exceed 110°F (43°C). If the electrolyte temperature rises above 110°F (43°C), the charging rate should be decreased.

A battery on slow charge is considered fully charged when the electrolyte is *gassing*, or steaming freely, and when no further rise in specific gravity is noted during three successive hydrometer readings taken at intervals of 1 hour. A sealed battery should be slow charged until the green dot appears. In some instances a sealed battery must be tipped or shook to allow the green dot to appear.

Fast Charging If time is not available to slow charge a battery, fast charging at a high rate is permissible. Although fast charging will not fully recharge a battery, it will restore the charge sufficiently to allow the battery to be used. If the charging system in the car is operating correctly, the battery will continue charging in service.

Fast charging consists of charging a battery at a rate of from 10 to 50 amperes. The exact charging rate depends on the construction of the battery and the time available. The temperature of the electrolyte provides an indication of the correct charging rate. If the electrolyte temperature rises to above 125°F (65.5°C), the charging rate is too high and should be reduced. Because a high charging rate and the resultant high temperatures can

Watt Rating	5 Amperes	10 Amperes	20 Amperes	30 Amperes	40 Amperes	50 Amperes
Below 2450	10 Hours	5 Hours	2½ Hours	2 Hours		
2450-2950	12 Hours	6 Hours	3 Hours	2 Hours	1½ Hours	
Above 2950	15 Hours	7½ Hours	3¼ Hours	2 Hours	1¾ Hours	1½ Hours

*Initial rate for constant voltage taper rate charger.
To avoid damage, charging rate must be reduced or temporarily halted if:
    1. Electrolyte temperature exceeds 125° F.
    2. Violent gassing or spewing of electrolyte occurs.
Battery is fully charged when over a two hour period at a low charging rate in amperes
all cells are gassing freely and no change in specific gravity occurs. **For the most satisfactory
charging, the lower charging rates in amperes are recommended.**
Full charge specific gravity is 1.260 - 1.280 corrected for temperature with electrolyte level
at split ring.

Figure 5.47 Typical charging rates and times for fully discharged batteries as recommended by one car manufacturer (Buick Motor Division, GM).

damage a battery, a battery should be charged at the lowest possible rate. Most car manufacturers specify the charging rates and charging times for their batteries. Figure 5.47 shows the specifications provided in the manual of one car manufacturer.

CHARGING A BATTERY The following steps outline a procedure for charging a battery. You should consult the instructions provided with the charger you have available. The charging specifications should be obtained from an appropriate manual.

1 Place a fender cover over the fender nearest the battery.

2 If the battery is not a sealed battery, check the electrolyte level in all the cells and adjust the level if necessary.

3 If the battery is a sealed battery, check the built-in hydrometer. Do not attempt to charge the battery if the indicator appears clear or light yellow. Refer to Figure 5.40.

4 Disconnect the battery cables. This will prevent possible damage to electrical components in the car during charging.

Note: **Disconnect the ground cable first to minimize the possibility of arcing.**

5 Clean the battery terminals and the battery top.

6 Consult an appropriate manual and determine the charging rate and time.

7 Turn the charger switch to the OFF position.

8 Connect the charger leads to the battery. The positive (+) lead must be connected to the positive (+) terminal. The negative (−) lead to the negative (−) terminal.

9 Turn the charger switch to the ON position.

Note: **On some chargers, the timer must be set to turn the charger ON.**

10 Adjust the charging rate.

11 Adjust the timer.

12 Check the charging rate and the battery temperature after the battery has been charging for about 15 minutes. Adjust the charging rate if required.

13 Continue charging until the allotted time has elapsed or until the battery is fully charged.

14 Turn the charger switch to the OFF position.

15 Disconnect the charger from the battery.

16 Connect the battery cables.

Note: **Connect the cable to the starter motor or starter switch first. Connect the ground cable last.**

Job 5f

CHARGE A BATTERY

SATISFACTORY PERFORMANCE

A satisfactory performance on this job requires that you do the following:

1 Recharge the battery assigned.
2 Following the steps in the "Performance Outline" and the charging recommendations of the manufacturer, complete the job within 30 minutes plus the charging time.
3 Fill in the blanks under "Information."

PERFORMANCE OUTLINE

1 Check the electrolyte level and adjust the level if required.
2 Disconnect the battery cables.
3 Clean the battery terminals and the battery top.
4 Determine the charging rate and time.
5 Connect the charger and adjust the charging rate and time.
6 Check the charging rate and the battery temperature.
7 Turn the charger OFF when completed.
8 Disconnect the charger.
9 Connect the battery cables.

INFORMATION

Vehicle identification _____

Battery identification _____

Reference used_____ Page(s)_____

Recommended charging rate_____amperes for_____hours.

Battery was charged at the rate of _____amperes.

Battery temperature during period of charge. _____

Length of time battery was charged. _____

Specific gravity of electrolyte at completion._____

JUMP STARTING A *booster battery* is often used to "jump start" the engine of a vehicle that has a discharged battery. The booster battery may be a separate battery brought to the disabled vehicle. Or, it may be the battery in another vehicle. Jumper cables similar to those shown in Figure 5.48 are commonly used to connect the booster battery to the car with the discharged battery. Properly connected, a booster battery enables you to provide an important emergency service. Improperly connected, a booster battery can cause damage to automotive electrical systems and may even cause a battery explosion.

The following precautions should be observed when using a booster battery:

1 Wear safety glasses or other appropriate eye protection.
2 Do not allow electrolyte to come in contact with your eyes, skin, clothing, or the finish of the vehicle(s).
3 Do not lean over a battery when connecting or disconnecting cables.
4 Do not allow the jumper cable clamps to touch each other.
5 Keep open flame and sparks away from batteries.
6 Do not connect a booster battery directly to a discharged battery.

Figure 5.48 A pair of jumper cables (courtesy of Applied Power, Inc.).

USING A BOOSTER BATTERY TO JUMP START A CAR The following steps outline a typical procedure for using a booster battery to jump start a car. Some car manufacturers have established alternate procedures to protect certain electrical components used in their products. You should consult an appropriate manual for the jump starting procedures recommended by the manufacturer of the car you wish to start.

1 Check to see that all switches and other electrical controls in the car are in the OFF position.

2 If the discharged battery is a sealed battery, check the charge indicator. If the charge indicator is light, as shown in Figure 5.40, DO NOT attempt to jump start the car. Replace the battery.

3 If the discharged battery has removable vent caps, remove the caps and check the electrolyte level.

Note: During cold weather, the electrolyte in a discharged battery may freeze. If the electrolyte is not visible, or if it appears that the electrolyte is frozen, DO NOT attempt to jump start the car. A frozen battery may rupture or explode if a booster battery is connected to it. A frozen battery should be thawed by placing it in a warm area. After the battery has been warmed, the electrolyte level should be adjusted as necessary. The battery should then be tested and charged in the normal manner.

4 If the electrolyte is not frozen, and if the level is above the tops of the plates, cover the openings with a cloth as shown in Figure 5.49.

Note: This will minimize the possibility of electrolyte spewing from the openings.

5 If the booster battery has vent caps, remove them and cover the openings with a cloth as you did with the discharged battery.

6 Connect one jumper cable between the positive (+) terminal of the booster battery and the positive (+) terminal of the discharged battery as shown in Figure 5.50.

Note: Be sure that the clamps on the jumper cable are firmly connected to the battery terminals.

7 Connect one end of the remaining cable to the negative (−) terminal of the booster battery. (Refer to Figure 5.50.)

8 Attach the remaining end of the jumper cable to a good ground on the engine. (Refer to Figure 5.50.)

Note: Some manufacturers recommend that the negative (−) jumper cable be connected to the alternator bracket or to the air conditioning compressor bracket as shown in Figure 5.51. Do not attach the cable to any part of the fuel system.

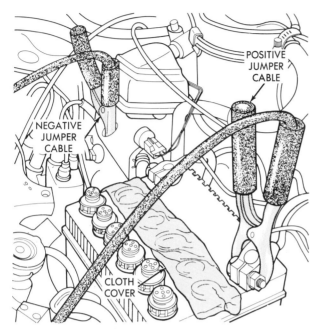

Figure 5.49 When attempting to jump start a car, the vent caps of both the discharged battery and the booster battery should be removed. The openings to the cells should be covered with cloth (courtesy Chrysler Corporation).

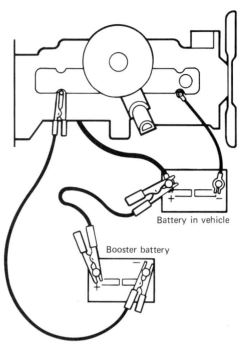

Figure 5.50 The correct placement of jumper cables when a booster battery is used to start a car. Note that the negative (−) jumper cable is connected to the engine (courtesy American Motors Corporation).

9 Attempt to start the engine in the normal manner.

10 After the engine has started (or if the engine fails to start), the jumper cables should be disconnected in the reverse order by which they were connected.

Note: The negative jumper cable should be disconnected from the ground on the engine FIRST.

11 Remove and discard the cloths that were used to cover the battery openings.

12 Install the vent caps on the batteries.

Job 5g

USE A BOOSTER BATTERY TO START A CAR

SATISFACTORY PERFORMANCE

A satisfactory performance on this job requires that you do the following:

1 Use a booster battery to start the engine of the car assigned.

2 Following the steps in the "Performance Outline" and the procedure and specifications of the manufacturer, complete the job within 15 minutes.

3 Fill in the blanks under "Information."

ATTACH NEGATIVE
JUMPER CABLE HERE

Figure 5.51 Some manufacturers recommend that the negative (−) jumper cable be connected to the alternator bracket
or to the air conditioner compressor bracket as shown (Pontiac Motor Division, GM).

PERFORMANCE OUTLINE

1 Determine that the battery in the vehicle is in a
condition which will allow safe starting.

2 Connect the booster battery to the car.

3 Start the engine.

4 Disconnect the booster battery.

INFORMATION

Vehicle identification _____

Vehicle battery condition

Electrolyte level _____ Above tops of plates

_____ Below tops of plates

Electrolyte temperature   _____ Above 40°F (4°C)

   _____ Below 40°F (4°C)

The positive (+) booster cable was connected to

   _____ the positive (+) post on the car's battery

   _____ a good ground on the engine

The negative (−) booster cable was connected to

   _____ the negative (−) post on the car's battery

   _____ a good ground on the engine

Which cable was connected first?   _____Positive

   _____Negative

Which cable was disconnected first?   _____Positive

   _____Negative

DRY CHARGED BATTERIES Dry charged batteries are manufactured with dry, charged plates. They are shipped, stocked, and sold without electrolyte in the cells. Dry charged batteries offer certain advantages over "wet" batteries. Shipping costs are lower, especially where electrolyte is available from local sources. Their lower weight allows easier handling and storage. But their greatest advantage is their long shelf life.

As you learned, a "wet" battery will self-discharge if it is not used. A battery starts to self-discharge as soon as acid is added to the cells. If a "wet" battery is not placed in service within a short period of time, it will require recharging before it can be used. If a "wet" battery remains in storage too long, the plates may become sulfated. Recharging may not restore the battery to its original condition and the service life of the battery will be shortened.

Dry charged batteries are not only manufactured without electrolyte; the cells are sealed so that moisture, even moisture in the air, cannot enter the battery. Because of this, no chemical action takes place in the battery, and thus the battery cannot self-discharge and deteriorate.

When you replace a defective battery with a dry charged battery, you must first activate the dry charged battery.

ACTIVATING DRY CHARGED BATTERIES The following steps outline a procedure for activating a dry charged battery. The specifications given for electrolyte specific gravity, battery temperature, and charging rates may differ with batteries from various manufacturers. You should read the instructions furnished with the battery you are activating and follow the specifications provided:

1 Carefully unpack the battery and place it on a level surface.

Note: Do not install the battery and attempt to activate it in the car. It is recommended that a dry charged battery be activated on the floor near a floor drain. This will enable you to flush away any electrolyte that may be spilled.

2 Check the electrolyte supplied with the battery. It should be battery grade sulfuric acid with a specific gravity of 1.265.

3 Remove the vent seals.

Note: Some batteries are sealed with disposable caps. Others have a thin plastic disc under the vent caps. Those discs must be pushed down into the cells with the special extended vent cap provided.

4 Carefully open the electrolyte container.

Note: Use extreme care during this step and the steps that follow. Remember that electrolyte is an acid and can cause you painful burns.

5 Using a plastic or glass funnel, slowly add electrolyte to the cells.

Note: Add the electrolyte slowly and stop often to check the electrolyte level. It is easy to overfill the cells. Excess electrolyte must be removed with a syringe or with a hydrometer. Spilled electrolyte must be washed away.

6 After all the cells are full, carefully tip the battery from side to side to release any air bubbles that may be trapped in the cells.

7 Check the electrolyte level in each cell and adjust the levels as required.

8 Check the specific gravity and the temperature of the electrolyte. The specific gravity should be at least 1.250. The temperature should be at least 80°F (27°C).

9 If the specific gravity or the temperature does not meet the above specifications, the battery should be placed on charge at a rate of approximately 30 amperes for about 15 minutes.

10 If the specific gravity and the temperature meet the above specifications, the battery may be installed without charging.

Note: A battery that meets the above specifications is not fully charged, but is charged sufficiently for use.

11 Drain and rinse the empty acid container in running water. Crush or mutilate the container so that it cannot be reused and dispose of it where it is not likely to be handled.

12 Flush away any spilled electrolyte. Discard any rags that are wet with electrolyte.

Job 5h

ACTIVATE A DRY CHARGED BATTERY

SATISFACTORY PERFORMANCE

A satisfactory performance on this job requires that you do the following:

1 Activate the dry charge battery assigned.
2 Following the steps in the "Performance Outline" and the instructions and specifications furnished with the battery, complete the job within 30 minutes.
3 Fill in the blanks under "Information."

PERFORMANCE OUTLINE

1 Place the battery where spills can be easily washed away.
2 Remove the vent seals.
3 Fill the cells with electrolyte.
4 Test the battery.
5 Charge the battery if necessary.
6 Clean up any spilled electrolyte and dispose of the empty container.

INFORMATION

Vehicle identification _____

Battery identification _____

Reference used_____ Page(s)_____

Specific gravity of electrolyte used _____

Specific gravity of electrolyte in battery _____

Temperature of electrolyte in battery _____

Was boost charge necessary? _____ Yes _____ No

Charging rate of boost charge _____

SUMMARY

By completing this chapter you have gained knowledge of the lead-acid battery and its operation. By performing the jobs you have developed some of the skills required to correctly service batteries. You can identify terms relating to battery operation and construction. You can clean battery terminals and clamps and you can remove and install batteries. You can perform certain chemical and electrical tests and interpret the results. You can charge a battery, use jumper cables to start an engine, and activate a dry charged battery. By accomplishing your objectives you have moved closer to your goal.

SELF-TEST

Each incomplete statement or question in this test is followed by four suggested completions or answers. In each case select the *one* that best completes the sentence or answers the question.

1 Two mechanics are discussing the construction of a lead-acid storage battery.
Mechanic A says that the positive plates are made of lead peroxide.
Mechanic B says that the negative plates are made of sponge lead.
Who is right?
A. A only
B. B only
C. Both A and B
D. Neither A nor B

2 A 12-volt battery consists of
A. 3 cells connected in series
B. 3 cells connected in parallel
C. 6 cells connected in series
D. 6 cells connected in parallel

3 Which of the following may cause a battery to self-discharge?
A. Loose connections
B. Dirty connections
C. A loose hold down
D. Dirt and electrolyte on the battery top

4 The electrolyte in a fully charged battery has a specific gravity of approximately
A. 1.205 to 1.220
B. 1.220 to 1.235
C. 1.235 to 1.250
D. 1.250 to 1.265

5 A test of a cold battery reveals that the electrolyte has a specific gravity of 1.240 at 30°F (−1°C). The temperature corrected specific gravity is
A. 1.205
B. 1.220
C. 1.235
D. 1.250

6 Two mechanics are discussing the effect of temperature on electrolyte.
Mechanic A says that as electrolyte is heated, it expands and becomes less dense.
Mechanic B says that as electrolyte is heated, its specific gravity becomes lower.
Who is right?
A. A only
B. B only
C. Both A and B
D. Neither A nor B

7 Two mechanics are discussing a sealed battery whose built-in hydrometer appears light yellow in color.
Mechanic A says that the battery should be charged at the rate of 30 amperes for 60 minutes.
Mechanic B says that the battery should be load tested at a rate of 60 amperes for 15 seconds.
Who is right?
A. A only
B. B only
C. Both A and B
D. Neither A nor B

8 If a specific discharge rate for load testing a battery cannot be found, the battery may be discharged at a rate equal to

A. 3 times the ampere hour rating of the battery

B. 6 times the ampere hour rating of the battery

C. 9 times the ampere hour rating of the battery

D. 12 times the ampere hour rating of the battery

9 Two mechanics are discussing the procedure for charging a discharged battery.
Mechanic A says that the battery should be charged until the specific gravity of the electrolyte is 1.290.
Mechanic B says that the battery should be charged until the temperature of the electrolyte reaches 150°F (65.5°C).
Who is right?

A. A only

B. B only

C. Both A and B

D. Neither A nor B

10 Two mechanics are discussing jump starting a car by using a booster battery.
Mechanic A says that the positive (+) jumper cable should be connected first.
Mechanic B says that the negative (−) jumper cable should be connected to a good ground at the engine.
Who is right?

A. A only

B. B only

C. Both A and B

D. Neither A nor B

Chapter 6
Basic Electrical System Service

The electrical energy available from the battery is used in many systems. The starting system uses electrical energy to crank the engine. The ignition system uses electrical energy to ignite the fuel-air mixture in the engine. And the lighting system uses electrical energy to illuminate the road, to signal the driver's intent to stop and turn, and to light the car so that it can be seen by other drivers. Although all of these systems are important, for safety reasons the lighting system is the most important.

Routine maintenance of the lighting system requires that you perform certain services in many different circuits. In this chapter you will learn about basic circuitry, circuit control, and circuit protection. With this knowledge, you will gain an understanding of how these circuits operate. You will then learn about various circuit components and develop skills in testing and replacing those components.

Your specific objectives are to perform the following jobs:

1
Identify circuit parts and their definitions
2
Replace a fuse
3
Replace a flasher
4
Replace a small bulb
5
Replace a sealed beam bulb
6
Adjust headlight aim
7
Replace a switch

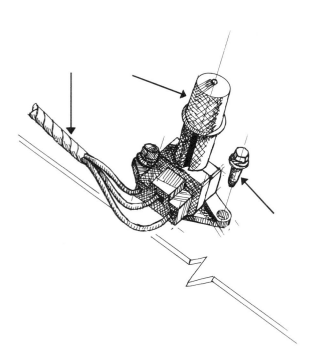

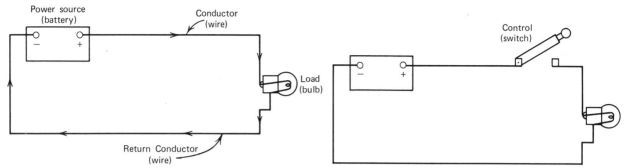

Figure 6.1 A simple circuit. Current flows from the battery through a wire to the bulb. After flowing through the filament of the bulb, the current flows back to the battery through the return wire.

Figure 6.2 A simple circuit with a switch as a control. Opening the switch opens the circuit and stops the flow of current.

BASIC ELECTRICAL CIRCUITRY From your work with batteries, you know that a battery converts chemical energy to electrical energy. Electrical energy can be converted to other forms of energy such as light, heat, and motion. Before the electrical energy of a battery can be put to work, the battery must be connected in a circuit.

Circuits A circuit is nothing more than a path for electricity. Before electricity will flow in a circuit, the circuit must be *closed*, or complete. This means that the path must be continuous. It must provide a route for the current to flow from the battery. And it must also provide a route for the current to return to the battery.

A circuit must have a minimum of three components.

1 *A Power Source*. This can be the battery or, when the engine is running, the generator.
2 *Conductors*. These can be wires and the metal parts of the automobile.
3 *A Load*. This can be a light, motor, or other device that converts electrical energy to another form of energy.

Figure 6.1 shows how those components can be connected to form a simple lighting circuit. In this circuit, a wire conducts current to a bulb. The current flows through the *filament* of the bulb. The filament is a fine wire that gets white hot, or *incandescent*, when current flows

through it. After passing through the filament, the current flows back to the battery through the return wire. The electrical energy of the battery is converted to light energy because the circuit is closed.

Circuit Control The circuit shown in Figure 6.1 has several disadvantages. One is that the circuit cannot be controlled. The light will continue to burn until all the electrical energy is converted to light energy. By adding a control that will *open*, or break, the circuit, the light can be turned on and off. A control that opens and closes a circuit is called a *switch*. Figure 6.2 shows how a switch can be installed in a circuit.

Ground Return Another disadvantage of the circuit shown in Figure 6.1 is that it requires too much wire. Figure 6.3 shows how most of the return wire can be eliminated. Because the frame and body of the car are made of metal, these parts can form the return conductor. When the metal parts of a car form the return conductor, that part of the circuit is referred to as the *ground*. Most automotive circuits use the ground as a return conductor. If an automobile had only a few circuits, a few extra lengths of wire would be of no concern. However, an automobile has hundreds of separate circuits. If the ground was not used as the return conductor, the amount of wire used in a car would be doubled.

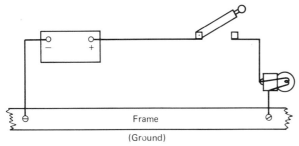

Figure 6.3 A simple circuit using the automobile frame and body as the return conductor.

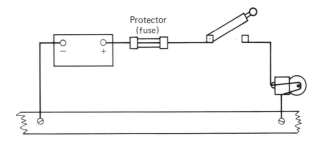

Figure 6.4 A simple circuit protected by a fuse. Note that the fuse is placed "first" in the circuit directly after the power source.

Circuit Protection Another disadvantage of the circuit shown in Figure 6.1 is that it has no protection against overload. If the load in the circuit is increased, or if an additional load is added, the wires and switch may be unable to carry the extra current required. The wires and the switch will overheat and will be damaged. The heat may also cause an electrical fire.

One method of providing circuit protection is to install a *fuse* in the circuit. A fuse is a "sacrifice" conductor which will *blow*, or burn out, when the current that flows through it exceeds a certain limit. Because a fuse protects only those parts of the circuit "downstream" from its location, a fuse is usually located as close as possible to the power source. Figure 6.4 shows how a fuse is placed in a circuit.

Symbols The circuits shown in Figures 6.1 through 6.4 are in pictorial form. The parts of the circuit are drawn to resemble the actual parts. This method is often used for simple circuits with few parts. But it has limited usage in showing automotive circuits.

Most automotive circuits are shown by *wiring diagrams*. The parts in those drawings are often represented by *symbols*. Symbols are codes or signs that have been adopted by the automotive industry to indicate certain parts and conditions. Symbols are a part of the written language of the automotive trades. Figure 6.5 shows some of the most commonly used symbols. These symbols are used in Figure

6.6 to diagram the same circuit shown in Figure 6.4. Compare those two illustrations. You will see that a diagram with symbols is not difficult to understand.

Types of Circuits There are only two major types of circuits—*series circuits* and *parallel circuits*. Both types are used in automotive electrical systems. At times, both are combined. A circuit of this type is called a *series-parallel circuit*.

Series Circuits The simple circuit that was developed in Figures 6.1 through 6.6 is a series circuit. When a circuit contains only one

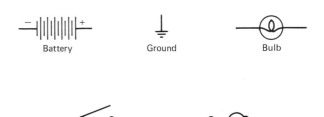

Figure 6.5 Symbols commonly used in wiring diagrams.

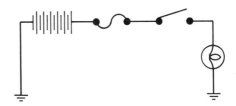

Figure 6.6 A wiring diagram for a simple circuit.

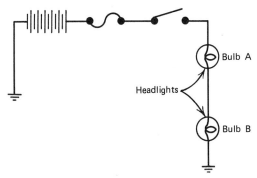

Figure 6.7 A pair of headlights connected in a series circuit. If either bulb "A" or bulb "B" burns out, it will break the circuit. The remaining bulb then cannot operate.

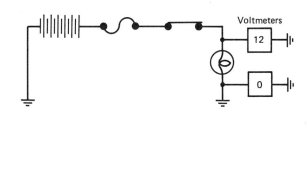

Figure 6.8 Voltage in a series circuit. Two voltmeters connected as shown will indicate that full voltage is present before the load, and that there is no voltage after the load.

load and one power source, it can only be a series circuit. A series circuit has one continuous path for the flow of current. Therefore, current flows through all the parts in a sequence. If any of the parts fail, or if the circuit is broken at any point, current stops flowing in the entire circuit. Some examples of series circuits used in automobiles include the starter circuit and the primary circuit of breaker point ignition systems.

A series circuit provides only one path for the flow of current. Therefore, it is seldom used for a lighting circuit containing two or more loads. Figure 6.7 shows a pair of headlights connected in a series circuit. As shown, the failure of one headlight would result in an open circuit. Current flow would stop and the other headlight would go out.

Series circuits have other disadvantages that relate to voltage and current flow. You know that most automobiles have a 12-volt battery. You also know that voltage is a unit of electrical pressure. A 12-volt battery provides a 12-volt pressure to push current through a circuit. The load in the circuit is designed to operate at that pressure. The load is built so that its resistance allows a pressure of 12 volts to push sufficient current through the load so that it functions properly. In effect, the load "uses up" the voltage in the circuit as it converts electrical energy to energy of another form. Assuming no losses through bad connections,

the voltage in a circuit just before the load is the full circuit voltage. The voltage just after the load is zero. This can be proven by using a voltmeter as shown in Figure 6.8.

If a second similar load were placed in the circuit, the resistance of the circuit would be doubled. The 12-volts pressure from the battery would be insufficient to make both loads operate correctly. This voltage would push only half as much current through the loads. A voltmeter test in a circuit of this type would reveal the results shown in Figure 6.9.

Adding a third similar load to the circuit as shown in Figure 6.10 further increases the resistance. This causes a greater drop in voltage and in current flow. As you can see, series circuits containing two or more loads do not allow efficient use of electrical energy.

Parallel Circuits A parallel circuit is one where two or more loads are connected so that each is provided with its own return path to the power source. Figure 6.11 shows a pair of headlights connected in a parallel circuit. Compare that illustration with Figure 6.7. When wired in parallel, the failure of either bulb will not affect the operation of the remaining bulb. This is one reason that automotive lighting systems use parallel circuits.

A parallel circuit offers another advantage. Each load receives full system voltage as shown in Figure 6.12. Also, when loads are

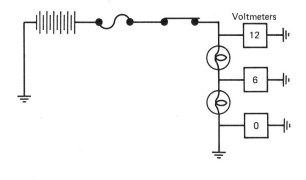

Figure 6.9 Voltage in a circuit with two loads in series. The voltmeters show the effect of the increased resistance.

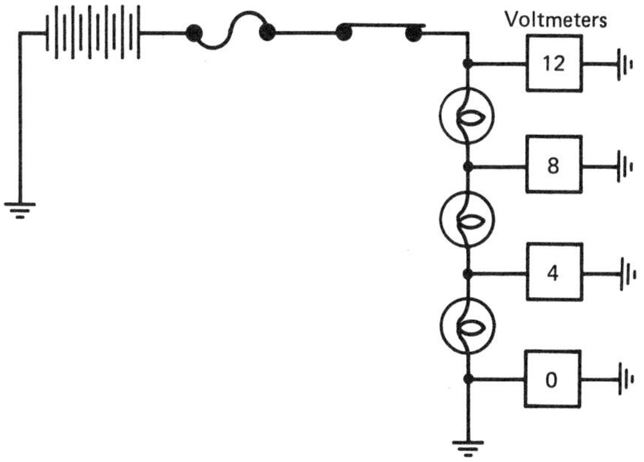

Figure 6.10 Voltage in a circuit with three loads in series. The voltmeters show the further effects of the increased resistance.

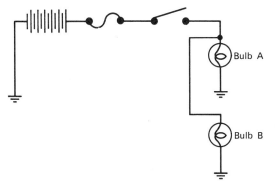

Figure 6.11 A pair of headlights connected in a parallel circuit. If either bulb "A" or bulb "B" burns out, the remaining bulb will not be affected.

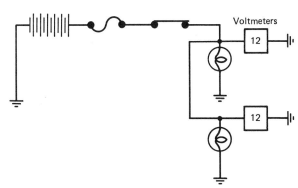

Figure 6.12 Voltage in a parallel circuit. Two voltmeters connected as shown will indicate that full voltage is present before each load.

connected in parallel, the total circuit resistance drops because of the additional return paths provided. Therefore, more current can flow in the circuit and the loads can operate at full efficiency. This is another reason that parallel circuits are used in automotive lighting systems.

Job 6a

IDENTIFY CIRCUIT PARTS AND THEIR DEFINITIONS

SATISFACTORY PERFORMANCE

A satisfactory performance on this job requires that you do the following:

1 Identify the symbolized circuit parts in the diagram below by placing the number of each part in front of the correct part name.

2 Identify the definition of each part by placing the number of each part in front of its correct definition.

3 Correctly identify all the parts and their definitions within 15 minutes.

PERFORMANCE SITUATION

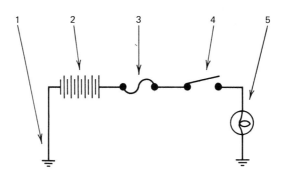

_____ Fuse　　　　　　_____ Switch

_____ Ground　　　　　_____ In-line fuse

_____ Bulb　　　　　　_____ Battery

_____ a connection to the metal parts of a car

_____ a power source

_____ a device that boosts voltage in a circuit

_____ a control device that opens and closes a circuit

_____ a device that converts electrical energy to light energy

_____ a "sacrifice" part that protects a circuit

LIGHTING SYSTEM SERVICE Basic maintenance of the lighting system includes the replacement of various components. Before you attempt to replace any component, you should check to determine that the suspected component is defective. Replacing a part which does not require replacement is not only time consuming but embarrassing. Simple diagnosis of electrical problems requires (1) a knowledge of basic circuitry and (2) a _test light_.

The Test Light In most instances, a simple test light of the type shown in Figure 6.13 can be used to determine the cause of a problem in a lighting circuit. A test light consists of a bulb wired to a sharp steel probe and to a length of wire fitted with an alligator clip. For convenience, the bulb is usually enclosed in a plastic handle to which the probe is attached.

When the alligator clip is attached to ground, the bulb will light when the probe is touched

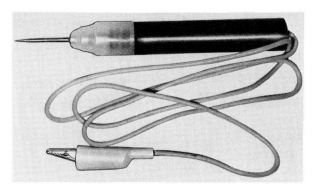

Figure 6.13 A simple test light (courtesy American Motors Corporation).

to any current-carrying conductor which is not on the ground side of the load in a circuit. Figure 6.14 shows some test points in a simple circuit.

Fuses   A blown fuse is one of the most common causes of circuit failure. As you know, a fuse is a "sacrifice" part that blows, or burns out, when too much current flows through it. When a fuse blows, it opens its circuit and thus protects all the other circuit parts from damage.

Glass Cartridge Fuses   The most commonly used fuse consists of a strip of metal that has a low melting point. The strip is enclosed in a glass tube and is connected to a metal cap at each end. The metal strip is designed to handle a limited amount of current. When the current flowing through the fuse exceeds that limit, the strip melts. Figure 6.15 shows a good fuse and one that has blown.

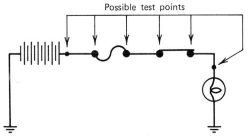

Figure 6.14 A test light will glow when connected between ground and any of the test points shown.

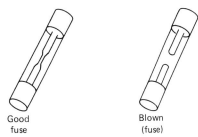

Figure 6.15 Typical glass cartridge fuses of the type used in automotive electrical systems.

Glass cartridge fuses are available in many ratings and sizes. Figure 6.16 shows some of the more commonly used ratings and sizes. A replacement fuse should always be of the same rating and size as the one removed. If you install a fuse with a lower rating, it may not be able to handle the normal current flow in the circuit. If you install a fuse with a higher rating, it will allow too much current to flow in the circuit. The excess current could damage other components.

Most cars have a *fuse block* located under the instrument panel. A fuse block provides a convenient, single location for most, if not all, of the fuses in a car. Figure 6.17 shows such a fuse block. At times, a particular circuit will not have its fuse located in the fuse block. These circuits use an *in-line fuse holder* of the

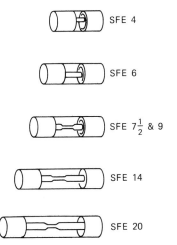

Figure 6.16 A few of the more popular fuse sizes and ratings.

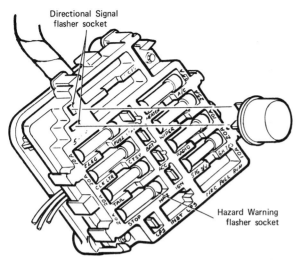

Figure 6.17 Most automobiles have a fuse block of this type mounted beneath the instrument panel. Note that the fuses, when installed, are recessed below the surface of the fuse block (Chevrolet Service Manual, Chevrolet Motor Division, GM).

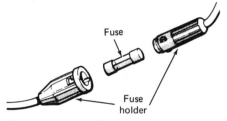

Figure 6.18 An in-line fuse holder. Fuse holders of this type are often used in accessory circuits (Ford Motor Company).

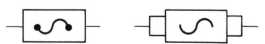

Figure 6.19 Two symbols commonly used to represent an in-line fuse.

type shown in Figure 6.18. In wiring diagrams, an in-line fuse holder is usually symbolized as shown in Figure 6.19. In-line fuse holders are often used in the wiring of accessories that have been added to a car. Those accessories include radios, tape decks, and special auxiliary lights.

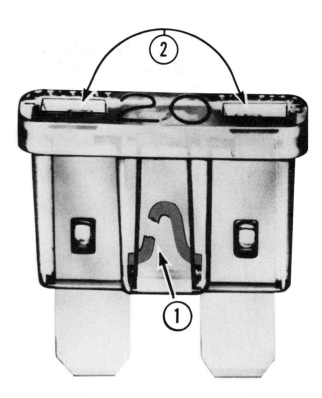

TO TEST FOR BLOWN MINI-FUSE:

(1) **PULL FUSE OUT AND CHECK VISUALLY.**

(2) **WITH THE CIRCUIT ACTIVATED, USE A TEST LIGHT ACROSS THE POINTS SHOWN.**

MINI-FUSE COLOR CODES

RATING	COLOR
5 AMP	TAN
10 AMP	RED
20 AMP	YELLOW
25 AMP	WHITE

Figure 6.20 An enlarged view of a miniaturized fuse. Note that the fuse is blown (Pontiac Motor Division, GM).

Miniaturized Fuses Many late model cars use a miniaturized fuse, or *mini-fuse*, as shown in Figure 6.20. These fuses also use a strip of metal which melts. Mini-fuses plug into special fuse blocks and cannot be interchanged with glass cartridge fuses. A miniaturized fuse block is shown in Figure 6.21.

As with glass cartridge fuses, mini-fuses should be replaced only with fuses of the same rating. The rating of a mini-fuse is indicated by number and by color code. (Refer to Figure 6.20.)

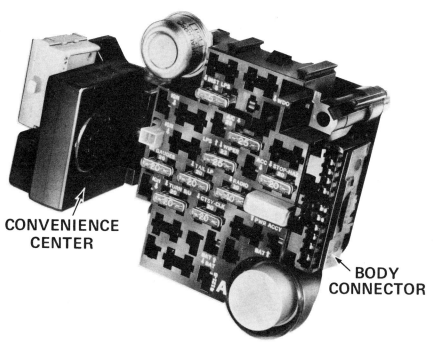

CONVENIENCE CENTER

BODY CONNECTOR

Figure 6.21 A miniaturized fuse block (Pontiac Motor Division, GM).

TESTING FUSES When it is suspected that a fuse is blown, it is easier to test the fuse in the circuit than to remove it for testing. You can make the job even easier by using an appropriate manual. The manual will tell you where the fuse block is located. It will also show you the location of each fuse and the correct fuse rating. Figure 6.22 shows how that information is given in one manual.

Glass Cartridge Fuses Glass cartridge fuses can often be checked visually. With the aid of a flashlight you can usually see if the fuse is blown. (Refer to Figure 6.15.) A positive test can be made by using a test light in the following manner:

1 Check the operation of the test light by connecting it across the terminals of a battery.

2 Turn ON the circuit that you wish to test.

3 Connect the test light alligator clip to a good ground.

4 Touch the probe of the test light to each end of the suspected fuse. Three results are possible:

A. The test light glows when touched to either end of the fuse. This means that the fuse is good.

B. The test light glows only when touched to one end of the fuse. This means that the fuse is blown or defective.

C. The test light does not glow when touched to either end of the fuse. This means that the circuit is not turned ON, or that the

FUSES

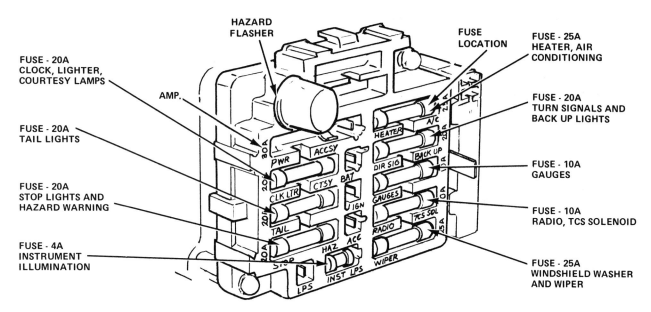

FUSE - 20A
CLOCK, LIGHTER,
COURTESY LAMPS

AMP.

HAZARD
FLASHER

FUSE
LOCATION

FUSE - 25A
HEATER, AIR
CONDITIONING

FUSE - 20A
TAIL LIGHTS

FUSE - 20A
TURN SIGNALS AND
BACK UP LIGHTS

FUSE - 20A
STOP LIGHTS AND
HAZARD WARNING

FUSE - 10A
GAUGES

FUSE - 4A
INSTRUMENT
ILLUMINATION

FUSE - 10A
RADIO, TCS SOLENOID

FUSE - 25A
WINDSHIELD WASHER
AND WIPER

DO NOT USE FUSES OF HIGHER AMPERAGE RATING THAN THOSE SPECIFIED

Figure 6.22 Fuse locations and specifications as found in a
typical manufacturer's service manual (Buick Motor Division,
GM).

circuit is broken between the fuse and the power source. It can also mean that you have a bad ground connection at the alligator clip.

Mini-Fuses It is almost impossible to see if a mini-fuse is blown without removing it from the fuse block. These fuses can easily be checked by using a test light in the following manner:

1 Check the operation of the test light by connecting it across the terminals of a battery.

2 Turn ON the circuit that you wish to test.

3 Connect the test light alligator clip to a good ground.

4 Touch the probe of the test light to each of the test points exposed on the top of the fuse. (Refer to Figure 6.20.) Three results are possible:

A. The test light glows when touched to either of the test points. This means that the fuse is good.

B. The test light glows only when touched to one of the test points. That means that the fuse is blown or defective.

C. The test light does not glow when touched to either of the test points. This means that the circuit is not turned ON, or that the circuit is broken between the fuse and the power source. It can also mean that you have a bad ground connection at the alligator clip.

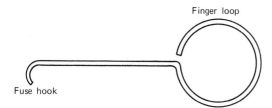

Figure 6.23 A fuse hook. A piece of stiff wire bent to the shape above will enable you to remove fuses from a fuse block.

Replacing Fuses When a glass cartridge fuse is mounted in a fuse block, it is almost impossible to remove it with your fingers. A hook made of stiff wire such as welding rod or coat hanger wire should be used. You can make that tool by following the sketch in Figure 6.23. The replacement fuse is easily pushed in place with your fingertips. (Refer to Figure 6.17.)

Fuses contained inside in-line fuse holders are removed by grasping the ends of the fuse holder, pushing them together, and twisting the ends counterclockwise. The locking lugs will release and the ends can be pulled apart. After the replacement fuse is inserted, the ends are pushed together and twisted clockwise.

Mini-fuses are easily removed. Just grasp the top and pull straight out. The replacement fuse is merely plugged in.

Job 6b

REPLACE A FUSE

SATISFACTORY PERFORMANCE

A satisfactory performance on this job requires that you do the following:

1 Check the fuses in the vehicle assigned and replace the defective fuse.
2 Following the steps in the "Performance Outline" and the procedure and specifications of the manufacturer, complete the job within 15 minutes.
3 Fill in the blanks under "Information."

PERFORMANCE OUTLINE

1 Locate the fuse block or fuse holder.
2 Locate the defective fuse.
3 Install a replacement fuse.
4 Test the fused circuit.

INFORMATION

Vehicle identification _____

Reference used_____Page(s)_____

Circuit in which defective fuse was found _____

Location of fuse _____Fuse block _____In-line fuse holder

Type of fuse _____Glass cartridge fuse _____Mini-fuse

Fuse identification and rating _____

Did the circuit operate properly after the fuse was replaced?

_____Yes _____No

Flashers   Most automotive lighting systems contain two flashers. The directional signal circuit includes one flasher. The hazard warning circuit contains the other. Flashers are controls, or switches, that automatically open and close a circuit. Because they are switches, flashers are placed in series in a circuit. This means that all the current which flows in the circuit passes through the flasher. Any failure of the flasher will affect the entire circuit.

As shown in Figure 6.24, a flasher is operated by heat. The current that passes through a flasher flows through and heats a special *bimetallic* conductor. That conductor is termed bimetallic because it is made of two strips of different metals bonded together. When heated, the different metals expand at different rates, causing the conductor to bend. This motion opens a set of switch contacts and breaks the circuit. Because the flow of current stops, the bimetallic conductor cools and returns to its original shape. This motion closes the switch contacts and the cycle is repeated.

Testing a Flasher   The easiest way to test a flasher is by *substitution*. A replacement flasher which is known to be good is substituted for the one that is suspected of being bad.

Replacing a Flasher   Replacing a flasher is easy. In fact, at times it is more difficult to locate a flasher than it is to replace it. Because of this, the easiest method of replacing a flasher is to use an appropriate manual to find where the flasher is located.

Flashers are usually mounted under the instrument panel, but the exact locations vary, even among cars built by the same manufacturer. On some cars, both flashers are located on the fuse block. (Refer to Figure 6.17.) On other cars, only one flasher will be found on the fuse block. (Refer to Figure 6.22.) The remaining flasher is mounted in some other location. Figure 6.25 shows the location chosen by one manufacturer to mount both flashers in one model car. On some cars, one of the flashers is taped to part of the wiring harness.

Most flashers have two prongs as shown in Figure 6.26. Unplugging the old flasher and plugging in the replacement is usually all that is required.

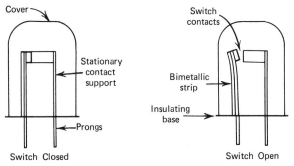

Figure 6.24 The operation of a flasher. Current flowing through the bimetallic strip causes the strip to bend, opening the contacts. When the strip cools, it returns and the contacts close.

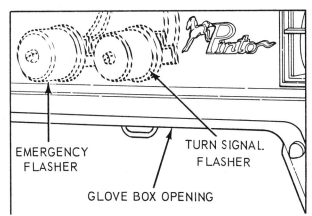

Figure 6.25 Flasher locations vary with each model car. On this model they are mounted above the glove box (Ford Motor Company).

Job 6c

REPLACE A FLASHER

SATISFACTORY PERFORMANCE

A satisfactory performance on this job requires that you do the following:

1 Replace the designated flasher on the car assigned.
2 Following the steps in the "Performance Outline" and the manufacturer's procedure and specifications, complete the job within 15 minutes.
3 Fill in the blanks under "Information."

PERFORMANCE OUTLINE

1 Determine the location of the designated flasher.
2 Remove the old flasher.
3 Install the correct replacement flasher.
4 If necessary, secure the flasher.
5 Test the operation of the circuit.

INFORMATION

Vehicle identification _____

Flasher replaced Directional signal _____

Hazard warning _____

Reference used_____ Pages(s)_____

Flasher location _____

Part number of old flasher _____

Part number of replacement flasher _____

Was the circuit working correctly after the flasher was replaced?

_____Yes _____ No

Small Bulbs A small bulb consists of a filament enclosed in a ball-shaped glass envelope. To prevent the filament from burning out, the air is evacuated from the bulb and it is sealed. Most automotive bulbs have a metal base that fits into a socket. That base is referred to as a *bayonet base* as it has lugs, or pins, on its side that engage with locking slots in the socket. Bulbs with threaded bases are not used in automobiles because they tend to become loose with vibration. The construction of a typical small bulb is shown in Figure 6.27.

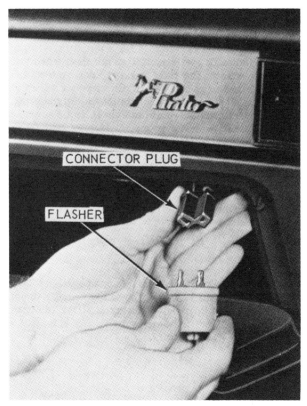

Figure 6.26 Replacing a flasher. Note that the flasher has two prongs which plug into a socket or quick disconnect (Ford Motor Company).

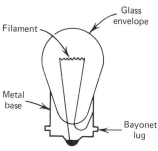

Figure 6.27 A sectioned view of a typical small bulb. The air is evacuated from the glass envelope so the filament can glow white hot without burning.

Figure 6.28 A sectioned view of a bulb with two filaments. Note that the center wire is attached to the metal base and forms a common ground for both filaments.

Some bulbs contain two filaments. These bulbs are used where one light must serve two functions. An example of where a bulb of this type is used is in a parking light which is also used as a directional signal. On many cars, the function of tail lights and stop lights is served by bulbs of this construction. A small bulb with two filaments is shown in Figure 6.28.

There are dozens of small bulbs used in every car. These bulbs are of many different designs. They range from the wedge type used to illuminate the instruments to the double filament designs used in parking lights and tail lights. Bulbs are identified by a universal numbering system which is used by all American car manufacturers. Figure 6.29 shows some of the more commonly used bulb types.

Testing Small Bulbs In most instances, a bulb can be checked visually. If the filament is broken or missing, the bulb is defective. A bulb can be tested by using a jumper wire as shown in Figure 6.30 to connect it across the terminals of a battery. But, because the bulb must be removed for testing, it is usually easier to test it by substitution. Just install a replacement bulb known to be good and turn the circuit ON. If the replacement bulb lights, you can assume that the old bulb was defective.

Replacing Small Bulbs in Exterior Lights Before you can replace a bulb, you must gain access to it. On most cars, the designs of parking lights, tail lights, and marker lights change annually with the styling of the car. These changes often require a change in service procedure. The correct procedure for any particular car should be found in the manufacturer's service manual.

In general, you can gain access to a bulb in one or two ways. You can remove the lens, or you can remove the socket. As shown in Figure 6.31, the lens on some parking lights and back-up lights is secured by screws. Remov-

Figure 6.29 Small bulbs most commonly used in automotive lighting circuits.

ing those screws will allow you to remove the lens. On some cars, the space between the bulb and the sides of the reflector is very limited and it is hard to get a grip on the bulb. In such instances, and where the bulb may be tight in its socket, you may find it helpful to use a pair of bulb-gripping pliers of the type shown in Figure 6.32. Another similar pair of pliers, shown in Figure 6.33, can be used to remove the base of a broken bulb. Those tools can help you to avoid cuts from broken bulbs.

On other cars, you must remove the socket from the rear of the reflector. Figure 6.34

shows two different types of removable sockets. Both types must be pushed in and turned counterclockwise for removal. Sockets of these types usually have locating keys or tabs that allow installation in only one position. When installing these sockets, you must align the tabs, push the socket in, and turn clockwise to lock it. Access to those sockets may be from inside the trunk, or luggage compartment, behind the grille, behind the bumper, or inside the fender. Figures 6.35 and 6.36 show two of those locations.

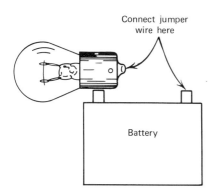

Figure 6.30 A small bulb can be tested by using a jumper wire to connect the bulb across the terminals of a battery.

Figure 6.31 On some cars, the bulbs in the parking lights and back-up lights can be reached by removing the lens (Ford Motor Company).

Figure 6.32 A pair of pliers designed for removing bulbs. The soft, plastic-coated jaws grip the bulb securely and minimize breakage (courtesy of K-D Tools).

Figure 6.33 A pair of pliers designed for removing the bases of broken bulbs (courtesy of K-D Tools).

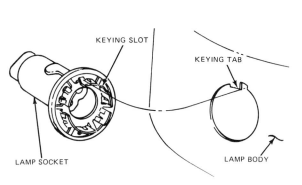

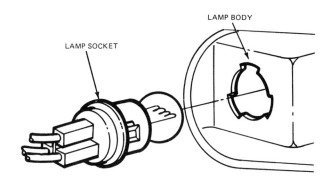

Figure 6.34 Different sockets have different types of alignment and locking keys (Ford Motor Company).

Replacing Small Bulbs in Interior Lights Quite often, the bulbs used inside a car outnumber those used for exterior lighting. Figure 6.37 shows the location of all the bulbs used in a typical instrument panel. Bulbs used to illuminate instruments are usually of the wedge type. The bulb is pushed into a plastic adapter cap which has bayonet lugs. The cap in turn is installed in the back of the instrument panel with the same push-and-twist motion used to install bayonet base bulbs. Some of the bulbs are accessible by reaching under the instrument panel. In many instances, the instrument cluster must be removed in order to change a bulb. Figure 6.38 shows the bulb locations in an instrument cluster that has been removed. The procedure for removing the instrument cluster from any particular car must be obtained from an appropriate manual.

Bulbs used to illuminate the passenger compartment will be found with all types of bases. (Refer to Figure 6.29.) In most instances, the lens of the light must be removed to replace the bulb. Lenses on some cars are retained by screws. On other cars, the lens snaps in place and is removed by squeezing the lens or by prying it loose as shown in Figure 6.39. Because of the many different designs used, you should consult the manufacturer's manual for the correct removal procedure.

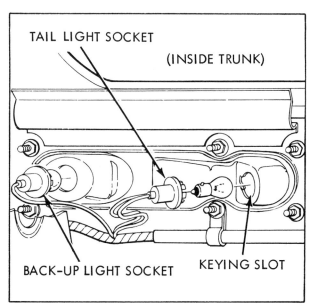

Figure 6.35 On many cars, the bulbs in the rear lights are accessible from inside the trunk, or luggage compartment (Ford Motor Company).

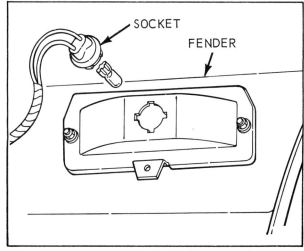

Figure 6.36 Access to the bulbs in side marker lights is obtained from inside the fenders (Ford Motor Company).

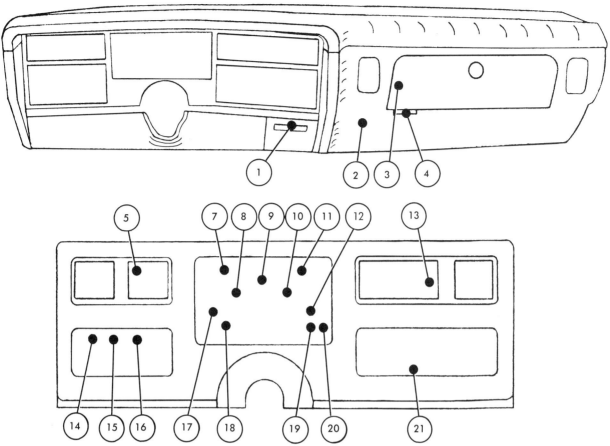

Figure 6.37 Bulb locations in the instrument panel of a typical automobile (courtesy Chrysler Corporation).

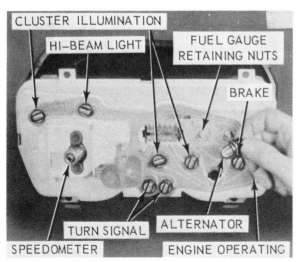

Figure 6.38 The rear of an instrument cluster that has been removed from an instrument panel. Note the caps that hold the wedge base bulbs (Ford Motor Company).

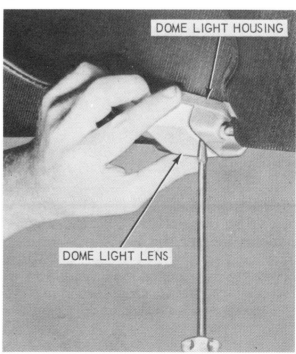

Figure 6.39 Some interior light lenses are removed by carefully prying the lens loose from its housing (Ford Motor Company).

Job 6d

REPLACE A SMALL BULB

SATISFACTORY PERFORMANCE

A satisfactory performance on this job requires that you do the following:

1 Replace the designated bulb on the car assigned.
2 Following the steps in the "Performance Outline" and the procedure and specifications of the manufacturer, complete the job within 200 percent of the manufacturer's suggested time.
3 Fill in the blanks under "Information."

PERFORMANCE OUTLINE

1 Remove any parts necessary to gain access to bulb.
2 Remove the defective bulb.
3 Install the replacement bulb.
4 Install any parts removed to gain access.
5 Test the operation of the bulb.

INFORMATION

Vehicle identification _____

Location of bulb replaced _____

Number of the bulb replaced _____

Reference used_____Page(s)_____

Bulb was replaced by Removing lens _____Removing socket _____

Was the light working correctly after the bulb was replaced?

_____Yes _____No

Sealed Beam Bulbs A sealed beam bulb is actually an assembly of a bulb, a lens, and a reflector. The lens and the reflector are fused together into one unit. The filament is mounted in the reflector and positioned so that the light is most efficiently reflected. Because the unit is sealed and all air evacuated from it, the thin glass envelope used on small bulbs is not needed. The lens has small prisms molded on its inner surface. Those prisms bend the light rays so that the desired beam shape is projected. A typical sealed beam bulb is shown in Figure 6.40.

Some sealed beam bulbs have two filaments. One filament provides a *high beam* that projects a concentrated, high intensity beam of light straight ahead. The high beam is intended for use only when it cannot interfere with the vision of the drivers of oncoming cars. The remaining filament provides a *low beam*.

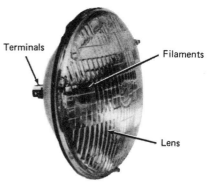

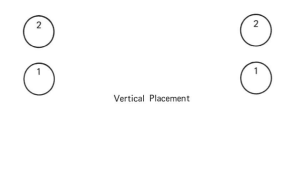

Vertical Placement

Figure 6.40 A typical sealed beam headlight bulb (Guide Lamp Division, GM).

Horizontal Placement

Figure 6.42 The sealed beam bulbs in dual headlight systems are arranged so that the bulbs with two filaments are the upper bulbs or the outer bulbs. Small bulbs are used, and they may be round or rectangular.

Figure 6.41 Large sealed beams with two filaments are used in systems using two headlights. The bulbs may be round or rectangular.

The low beam provides a less concentrated distribution of light that is aimed slightly downward and toward the right. The low beam is intended for use in traffic and at other times when the high beam could disturb other drivers.

Sealed beam bulbs with two filaments are usually marked "2" or "2B" on the lens. They are easy to identify even without that marking. Sealed beam bulbs with two filaments have three prongs, or terminals, projecting from the rear of the reflector.

Some sealed beam bulbs have only one fila-

ment. This filament is used as a high beam. Bulbs of this type are used as the inner or lower bulbs in systems using four sealed beam bulbs. Sealed beam bulbs with only one filament are often marked "1" or "1B." Because they have only one filament, they require only two prongs, or terminals.

Sealed beam bulbs used as automobile headlights are built in two shapes, round and rectangular. Two sizes are available in each shape. The larger bulbs are for use in systems that have two headlights. The smaller bulbs are for use in dual systems. These systems are shown in Figures 6.41 and 6.42.

REPLACING SEALED BEAM BULBS The following steps outline a typical procedure for replacing a sealed beam headlight bulb. It is suggested that you consult an appropriate manual for alternate procedures that may be necessary on some cars:

1 Remove the screws holding the headlight *door*, or trim ring. (See Figure 6.43.)

2 Remove the headlight door.

3 Remove the small screws holding the headlight retainer ring. Do not loosen or remove the adjusting screws. (See Figure 6.44.)

Note: Some cars have a spring that holds one side of the retainer ring. This spring can easily be disconnected by using the tool

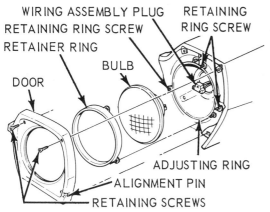

WIRING ASSEMBLY PLUG
RETAINING RING SCREW
RETAINER RING
DOOR
BULB
RETAINING RING SCREW
ADJUSTING RING
ALIGNMENT PIN
RETAINING SCREWS

Figure 6.43 A typical headlight assembly (Ford Company).

VERTICAL ADJUSTING SCREWS
BULB RETAINING SCREWS
HORIZONTAL ADJUSTING SCREWS

Figure 6.44 When replacing a headlight bulb, only the retaining screws should be removed. The adjusting screws should not be disturbed (Ford Motor Company).

you made to remove fuses. (Refer to Figure 6.23.)

4 Remove the retainer ring.

5 Carefully pull the sealed beam bulb forward and disconnect the wiring assembly plug.

6 Align the prongs of the replacement sealed beam bulb with the wiring assembly plug and push the parts together so that the prongs are fully seated.

7 Position the bulb in the adjusting ring so that the alignment tabs on the rear edge of the bulb fit into the slots in the ring.

Note: The alignment tabs are located so that the bulb will fit properly in only one position.

8 Install the retainer ring.

Note: The screw holes in the edge of the ring are located so that the ring will fit properly in only one position.

9 Check the operation of the bulb.

10 Install the headlight door.

Job 6e

REPLACE A SEALED BEAM BULB

SATISFACTORY PERFORMANCE

A satisfactory performance on this job requires that you do the following:

1 Replace the designated headlight bulb on the car assigned.

2 Following the steps in the "Performance Outline" and the procedure and specifications of the manufacturer, complete the job within 200 percent of the manufacturer's suggested time.

3 Fill in the blanks under "Information."

PERFORMANCE OUTLINE
1 Remove the headlight door.
2 Remove the bulb retaining ring.
3 Replace the bulb.
4 Install the retaining ring.
5 Check the operation of the bulb.
6 Install the headlight door.

INFORMATION

Vehicle identification _____

Location of bulb replaced _____Right side _____Left side

_____Upper _____Upper

_____Lower _____Lower

_____Inner _____Inner

_____Outer _____Outer

Number marked on bulb replaced _____1(B) _____2(B)

Part number of replacement bulb _____

Was the light working correctly after the bulb was replaced?

_____Yes _____No

Aiming Headlights To provide effective lighting, headlights must be aimed. Routine maintenance of any vehicle requires that the aim of the headlights be periodically checked and adjusted. The aim of the headlights can be changed by road shock, minor accidents, and changes in the suspension system. Most manufacturers suggest that headlight aim be checked at least once each year and after the replacement of a sealed beam bulb.

Most shops use headlight aiming devices to obtain the proper adjustment. Lacking those devices, headlights can be aimed by observing the spots of light projected on a wall chart or on a marked wall.

AIMING HEADLIGHTS BY USING MECHANICAL AIMERS The following steps outline a procedure for aiming headlights using mechanical aimers of the type shown in Figure 6.45. It is suggested that you consult the manual furnished with the aimers you have available:

Figure 6.45 A typical mechanical headlight aiming kit. Note the various adapters furnished so the aimers can be used on all types and sizes of bulbs (courtesy American Motors Corporation).

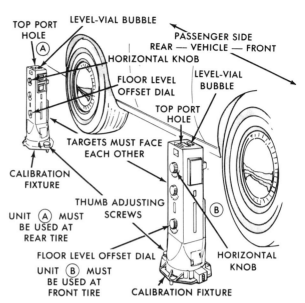

Figure 6.47 The slope of the floor can be compensated for by measurements taken with the aimers positioned at the front and rear wheels of the car (courtesy Chrysler Corporation).

Figure 6.46 A calibration fixture attached to a headlight aimer (courtesy Chrysler Corporation).

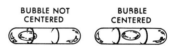

Figure 6.48 Bubble levels are used to adjust the level of the aimers (courtesy Chrysler Corporation).

Adjusting the Aimers The aimers are furnished with calibration fixtures that enable you to adjust the aimers to compensate for any slope in the floor.

1 Attach the calibration fixtures to the aimers as shown in Figure 6.46.

Note: **The calibration fixtures snap in place when properly aligned.**

2 Stand the aimers on the floor next to the car as shown in Figure 6.47. Aimer "A" must be aligned with the center of the rear wheel. Aimer "B" must be aligned with the center of the front wheel. The adjusting knobs must face outward and the targets must face each other.

3 Adjust the level of each aimer by turning the thumb adjusting screw on each calibration fixture. (Refer to Figure 6.46.) The adjustment is correct when the bubble in the top level vial is centered as shown in Figure 6.48.

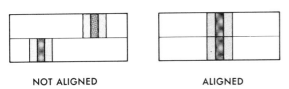

NOT ALIGNED   ALIGNED

Figure 6.49 The "split image" is aligned by turning the horizontal knob (courtesy Chrysler Corporation).

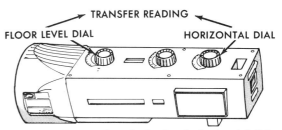

Figure 6.50 The reading obtained at the horizontal dial must be transfered to the floor level dial. This adjusts the aimer to compensate for the slope of the floor (courtesy Chrysler Corporation).

4 Look down into the top port hole in aimer "A." (Refer to Figure 6.47.) You should see an image similar to those shown in Figure 6.49.

Note: Moving your head from side to side will enable you to locate the image. At times you may have to rotate one or both of the aimers slightly to correct their alignment.

5 While watching the image, turn the horizontal knob back and forth slowly until the split image is aligned. (Refer to Figure 6.49.)

6 Lift aimer "A" and observe the plus (+) or minus (−) reading indicated on the horizontal dial.

7 Adjust the floor level dials on both aimers to that reading. (See Figure 6.50.)

Note: The floor level dials are self-locking. They must be pushed in slightly before they can be turned.

8 Remove the calibration fixtures from the aimers.

Mounting the Aimers The aimers must be fitted with adapters before they can be mounted on the headlights.

1 Clean the headlight lenses with a wet paper towel.

Note: The suction cups in the aimers will not hold on dirty lenses.

2 Select the adapters required to fit the sealed beam bulbs used and install them on the aimers. Figure 6.51 shows the various adapters and their application.

3 Check the accessibility of the adjusting screws. Remove the headlight doors if necessary.

Note: On some cars, the headlight doors are notched as shown in Figure 6.52. Those notches enable you to reach the adjusting screws without removing the doors.

4 Position aimer "A" on the left (driver's side) headlight. Check to see that the steel inserts in the adapter are in contact with the guide points that project from the edge of the lens. (See Figure 6.53.)

USE FOR FIVE INCH CIRCULAR HEADLAMP

USE FOR SEVEN INCH CIRCULAR HEADLAMP

USE FOR 4 x 6.5 INCH (100 x 165 MM) RECTANGULAR HEADLAMP

USE FOR 142 x 200 MM (5.6 x 7.9 INCH) RECTANGULAR HEADLAMP

Figure 6.51 Headlight aimer adapters and their application (courtesy Chrysler Corporation).

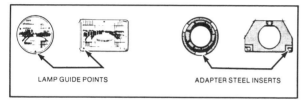

LAMP GUIDE POINTS   ADAPTER STEEL INSERTS

Figure 6.53 All sealed beam headlight bulbs have guide points molded into the edge of the lens. The steel inserts in the adapters must contact those points when the aimers are installed (Pontiac Motor Division, GM).

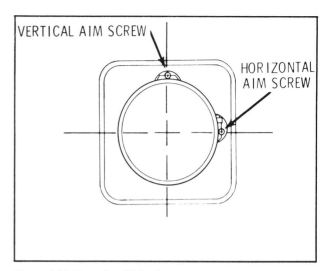

Figure 6.52 Some headlight doors are notched for access to the adjusting screws (Chevrolet Service Manual, Chevrolet Motor Division, GM).

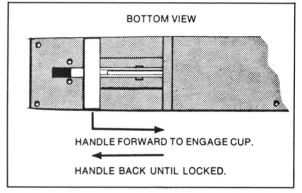

Figure 6.54 The operation of the piston handle on the headlight aimer (Pontiac Motor Division, GM).

5 Holding the aimer in position, push the piston handle forward to force the suction cup against the lens. Immediately pull the handle back until it locks in place. (See Figure 6.54.)

6 Repeat steps 4 and 5 to mount aimer "B" on the right side headlight.

Horizontal Adjustment 1 Adjust the horizontal dial on aimer "A" to zero. (See Figure 6.55.)

2 Look down into the viewing port on aimer "A." You should see the split image lines. (Refer to Figure 6.49.)

Note: If the lines are not visible, you may have to rotate one or both of the aimers slightly to shift the position of the sight openings.

3 Using a screwdriver, slowly turn the horizontal adjusting screw located at the side of the headlight. (Refer to Figure 6.52.) Turn the

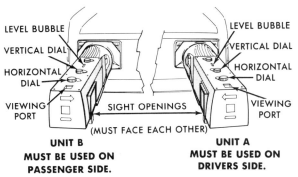

Figure 6.57 The vertical adjusting screw is turned to center the bubble (courtesy Chrysler Corporation).

Figure 6.55 The location of the parts of the aimers when they are mounted on headlights (courtesy Chrysler Corporation).

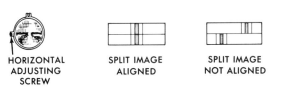

Figure 6.56 The horizontal adjusting screw is turned to align the split image (courtesy Chrysler Corporation).

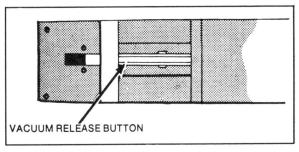

Figure 6.58 The vacuum release button is used to release the suction cup from the headlight lens (Pontiac Motor Division, GM).

screw in or out as required until the split image is aligned. (See Figure 6.56.)

4 Repeat steps 1 through 3 at the opposite headlight.

Vertical Adjustment 1 Set the vertical dial knob on aimer "A" to zero.

Note: **The motor vehicle laws of your state may require a different setting.**

2 Using a screwdriver, slowly turn the vertical adjusting screw located at the top of the headlight. (Refer to Figure 6.52.) Turn the screw in or out as required until the bubble in the level is centered. (See Figure 6.57.)

3 Repeat steps 1 and 2 at the opposite headlight.

4 Check the alignment of the split image at both aimers.

Note: **A slight readjustment at one or both lights may be necessary.**

5 Remove the aimers by holding them securely and pressing the vacuum release button on the piston handle. (See Figure 6.58.)

If the car is equipped with dual headlights, the steps listed under Mounting the Aimers, Horizontal Adjustment, and Vertical Adjustment must be performed on the second pair of headlights.

AIMING HEADLIGHTS BY OBSERVING THE PROJECTED LIGHT Headlights can be aimed by observing the location of the high intensity areas of projected light. This method is often used when aiming devices are not available. The special chart may be used,

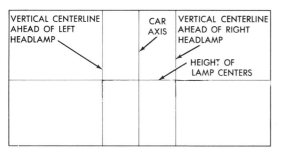

Figure 6.59 The lines that must be marked on a chart or wall to aim headlights. The locations of the lines must be determined by measurements made on the particular car (courtesy Chrysler Corporation).

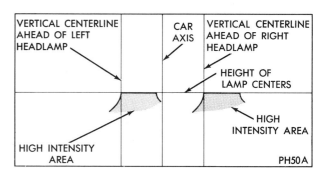

Figure 6.60 The correct low beam pattern for sealed beam bulbs marked "2" and "2B" (courtesy Chrysler Corporation).

or lines can be taped on a light-colored wall. A typical procedure follows:

Preparation Because the horizontal and vertical centerlines of the headlights on various cars differ, certain measurements must be made for each car. These measurements are used to locate lines on a chart or on a wall as shown in Figure 6.59.

1 Position the car on a level floor so that it squarely faces a vertical chart or wall.

2 Adjust the position of the car so that the headlights are 25 feet (750 cm) from the chart or wall.

3 Tape a vertical line in alignment with the centerline of the car. (Refer to Figure 6.59.)

Note: **The centerline of the car can be determined by standing behind the car and carefully sighting through the rear window at the chart or wall.**

4 Measure the distance between the centers of the headlights.

5 Transfer that measurement to the chart or wall and tape vertical lines representing the vertical centerlines of the headlights. (Refer to Figure 6.59.)

Note: **If the car is equipped with dual headlights, two sets of vertical centerlines must be marked.**

6 Measure the distance from the floor to the center of the headlights.

7 Transfer that measurement to the chart or wall, and tape a horizontal line to represent the horizontal centerline of the headlights. (Refer to Figure 6.59.)

Adjustment of Type 2 and Type 2B Bulbs Bulbs with two filaments marked "2" and "2B" should be adjusted with the low beams on.

1 Turn the vertical adjusting screws so that the high intensity areas are located just below the horizontal centerline as shown in Figure 6.60.

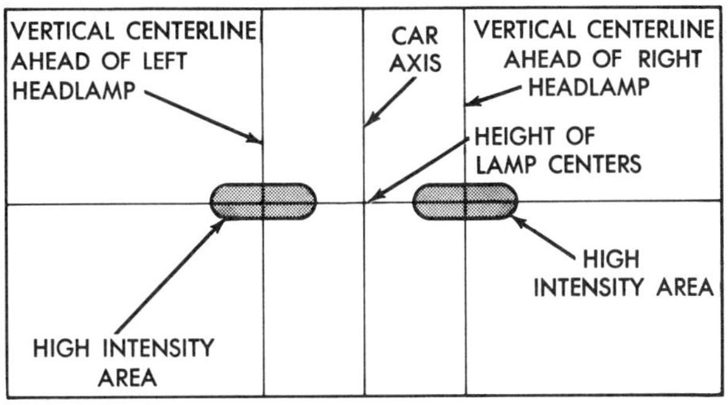

Figure 6.61 The correct high beam pattern for sealed beam bulbs marked "1" and "1B" (courtesy Chrysler Corporation).

2 Turn the horizontal adjusting screws so that the high intensity areas are positioned just to the right of the vertical centerlines. (Refer to Figure 6.60.)

Adjustment of Type 1 and Type 1B Bulbs Bulbs with one filament marked "1" or "1B" should be adjusted with the high beams on. The type 2 or type 2B bulbs used in the system should be covered while adjusting the type 1 or type 1B bulbs.

1 Turn the vertical adjusting screws so that the high intensity areas are centered on the horizontal centerline as shown in Figure 6.61.

2 Turn the horizontal adjusting screws so that the high intensity areas are centered on the vertical centerlines. (Refer to Figure 6.61.)

Job 6f

ADJUST HEADLIGHT AIM

SATISFACTORY PERFORMANCE

A satisfactory performance on this job requires that you do the following:

1 Adjust the aim of the headlights on the car assigned.
2 Following the steps in the "Performance Outline" and the procedure and specifications of the manufacturer, complete the job within 45 minutes.
3 Fill in the blanks under "Information."

PERFORMANCE OUTLINE
1 Prepare for adjustment.
2 Adjust the horizontal and vertical headlight aim.

INFORMATION

Vehicle identification _____

Headlight system _____Single _____Dual

Reference used_____ Page(s)_____

Method used to adjust aim ⎯⎯⎯⎯⎯Mechanical aimers

⎯⎯⎯⎯⎯Projected light

Identification of instrument used ⎯⎯⎯⎯⎯⎯⎯⎯⎯⎯⎯⎯⎯

Was car positioned on a level floor? ⎯⎯⎯⎯Yes ⎯⎯⎯⎯No

Was instrument adjusted for the floor slope?

⎯⎯⎯⎯⎯Yes ⎯⎯⎯⎯⎯No

The bulbs marked "2" or "2B" were adjusted on ⎯⎯High beam

⎯⎯Low beam

The bulbs marked "1" or "1B" were adjusted on ⎯⎯High beam

⎯⎯Low beam

Switches Every car has a variety of switches that open and close the different lighting circuits. Some of these switches, including the headlight switch and the turn signal switch, are operated manually. Other switches, such as those that control the stop lights and the back-up lights, are operated remotely.

Replacing Switches The following replacement procedures are typical for the switches listed. Many variations of switch design and mounting are used. Because of this, the replacement procedure for a specific switch on a particular car should be obtained from the manufacturer's manual:

Dimmer Switches On most cars, the headlight dimmer switch is located on the floor where it can be controlled by the driver's left foot. In most instances, access to the switch is obtained by lifting the mat or carpet. The switch is usually attached to the floor by two self-tapping screws, as shown in Figure 6.62. The switch has prongs or terminals that plug

into a socket at the end of the wire harness. The switch is removed by removing the two screws and unplugging the connection. Installation of the replacement switch is performed by reversing those steps.

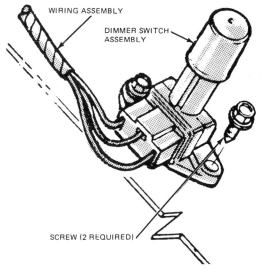

Figure 6.62 A typical dimmer switch installation. The switch plugs into a socket on the wiring harness and is secured to the floor by two screws (Ford Motor Company).

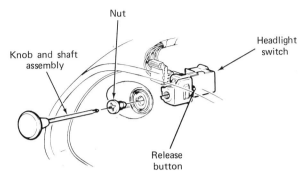

Figure 6.63 A typical headlight switch installation. Note the release button that is used to remove the knob and shaft assembly (Chevrolet Service Manual, Chevrolet Motor Division, GM).

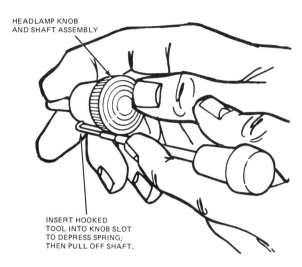

Figure 6.64 Removing the knob from the shaft of a headlight switch (Ford Motor Company).

Headlight Switches In most instances, headlight switches are removed from behind the instrument panel. Before you attempt to remove a headlight switch, disconnect the ground cable from the battery. The headlight switch on most cars is held to the instrument panel by a nut, as shown in Figure 6.63. Before that nut can be removed, the knob or the knob and shaft assembly must be removed. On most cars, the shaft is released by pushing a knob release button located on the switch. (Refer to Figure 6.63.) The switch must be in the ON position while the release button is pushed. On some cars, the knob is held to the shaft by a spring clip. This clip can be released by using a stiff wire hook, as shown in Figure 6.64.

After the knob or the knob and shaft assembly have been removed, the retaining nut can be removed. The switch is then lowered and unplugged from its socket. The replacement switch is installed by reversing the procedure.

Stop Light Switches The stoplight switch on most cars is located under the instrument panel and above the brake pedal. Some of those switches are similar to the one shown in Figure 6.65. The switch fits into a hole in a mounting bracket and is secured with a lock nut. Prongs on the back of the switch plug into a socket on the wires. The switch is removed by disconnecting the wires and removing the

lock nut. The replacement switch is installed by reversing those steps. The switch should be adjusted so that it closes the stoplight circuit when the brake pedal is depressed about ¼ inch (6 mm) to ⅝ inch (15 mm) from its fully released position. On some cars, the bracket is adjustable. (Refer to Figure 6.65.) On other cars, the hole in the mounting bracket is threaded. Turning the switch in or out provides the adjustment.

Figure 6.66 shows another type of stoplight switch in common use. A switch of this type fits on the pin that connects the brake pedal to the master cylinder push rod. Switches of

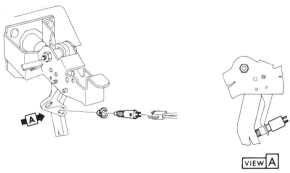

Figure 6.65 A typical stoplight switch installation. When the brake pedal is depressed, the spring-loaded plunger moves outward, turning the switch on (Chevrolet Service Manual, Chevrolet Motor Division, GM).

this type are nonadjustable. The switch closes the stoplight circuit when the pedal is moved the small distance allowed by the oversize hole in the eye of the push rod. The operation of the switch is shown in Figure 6.67.

To remove a switch of this type, you must unplug the wire connector. Then pull out the hairpin-shaped retainer and slide the switch and the push rod off the pedal pin. The replacement switch is aligned with the push rod, the bushing, and the washer, and slipped over the pin. Installing the retainer and connecting the wires completes the installation. (Refer to Figure 6.66.)

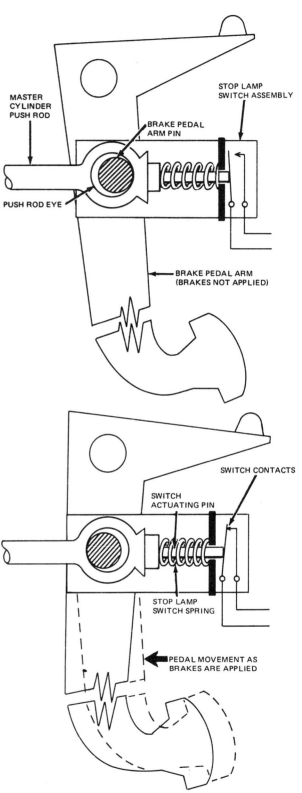

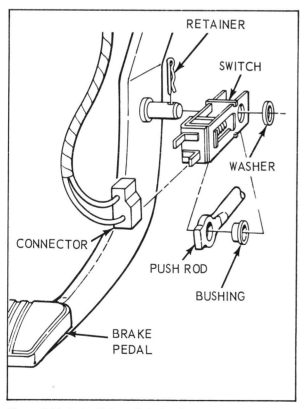

Figure 6.66 A stoplight switch that is mounted on the brake pedal linkage (Ford Motor Company).

Figure 6.67 The operation of a linkage mounted stoplight switch. The switch is operated by the movement allowed by the oversize hole in the push rod eye (Ford Motor Company).

Job 6g

REPLACE A SWITCH

SATISFACTORY PERFORMANCE

A satisfactory performance on this job requires that you do the following:

1 Replace the designated switch on the car assigned.

2 Following the steps in the "Performance Outline" and the procedure and specifications of the manufacturer, complete the job within 200 percent of the manufacturer's suggested time.

3 Fill in the blanks under "Information."

PERFORMANCE OUTLINE

1 Remove the designated switch.

2 Install the replacement switch.

3 Check the operation of the circuit.

INFORMATION

Vehicle identification _____

Switch replaced _____

Reference used_____ Page(s)_____

SUMMARY

By completing the jobs in this chapter you gained knowledge and developed diagnostic skills. You learned about electrical circuits and can identify some of the symbols used in wiring diagrams. You learned about various types of fuses and developed skill in testing and replacing them. You learned about the different types of small bulbs, their construction, and their locations. You have learned how to replace these bulbs in various lights.

You learned about sealed beam bulbs and can identify the various types, shapes, and sizes. You can replace sealed beam bulbs and can adjust them to correct their aim. You learned about some of the many switches used in a car, and you developed skills in replacing these switches.

SELF-TEST

Each incomplete statement or question in this test is followed by four suggested completions or answers. In each case select the *one* that best completes the sentence or answers the question.

1 A circuit device that converts electrical energy to another form of energy is called a
  A. load
  B. control
  C. conductor
  D. power source

2 When a circuit is protected with a fuse, the fuse is usually located between the
  A. load and the ground
  B. control and the load
  C. ground and the power source
  D. power source and the control

3 Two mechanics are discussing electrical circuits.
Mechanic A says that a parallel circuit provides only one path for the flow of current.
Mechanic B says that a series circuit provides more than one path for the flow of current.
Who is right?
A. A only
B. B only
C. Both A and B
D. Neither A nor B

4 Two mechanics are discussing fuses.
Mechanic A says that glass cartridge fuses are used in fuse blocks.
Mechanic B says that mini-fuses are used in in-line fuse holders.
Who is right?
A. A only
B. B only
C. Both A and B
D. Neither A nor B

5 Two mechanics are discussing mini-fuses.
Mechanic A says that the rating of a mini-fuse is marked on the fuse.
Mechanic B says that the rating of a mini-fuse is indicated by a color code.
Who is right?
A. A only
B. B only
C. Both A and B
D. Neither A nor B

6 Two mechanics are discussing flashers.
Mechanic A says that a flasher is a temperature operated switch.
Mechanic B says that a flasher is connected in series in a circuit.
Who is right?
A. A only
B. B only
C. Both A and B

D. Neither A nor B

7 A small bulb without a metal base is called
A. a wedge base bulb
B. an index base bulb
C. a bayonet base bulb
D. a filament base bulb

8 Two mechanics are discussing sealed beam headlight bulbs.
Mechanic A says that bulbs marked "2" are used in dual headlight systems.
Mechanic B says that bulbs marked "2" have 2 terminals or prongs at the rear of the reflector.
Who is right?
A. A only
B. B only
C. Both A and B
D. Neither A nor B

9 The three guide points molded into the edge of the lens of a sealed beam headlight bulb are provided for
A. proper alignment of the headlight door
B. accurate mounting of mechanical aimers
C. proper positioning of the bulb in its housing
D. accurate placement of the bulb retaining ring

10 Two mechanics are discussing the replacement of a headlight switch.
Mechanic A says that the battery should be disconnected before attempting to remove the switch.
Mechanic B says that the knob or the knob and shaft assembly must be removed before attempting to remove the switch.
Who is right?
A. A only
B. B only
C. Both A and B
D. Neither A nor B

Chapter 7
Fuel System Service

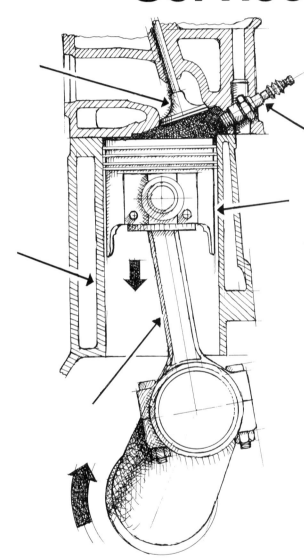

An engine will develop sufficient power only when it receives the correct fuel mixture. The four-stroke cycle engine used in most automobiles burns a fuel mixture of gasoline and air. This chapter will cover the basic operating principles of this engine and its fuel system.

The fuel system stores and delivers gasoline and mixes it with air in the correct proportions. In addition, the fuel system must limit the emissions of both burned and unburned gases that pollute the atmosphere.

In this chapter you will learn about fuel system parts, their function, and their location in the system. You will learn about fuel and fuel air mixtures. And you will perform a series of jobs that will reinforce your knowledge and aid you in developing diagnostic and repair skills.

Your specific objectives are to perform the following jobs:

1
Identify the four strokes of the four-stroke cycle engine
2
Identify the definition of terms relating to gasoline
3
Identify the function of fuel system parts
4
Service an air filter
5
Service a PCV system
6
Replace a fuel filter
7
Service an evaporation emission control system
8
Measure engine idle speed
9
Adjust engine idle speed

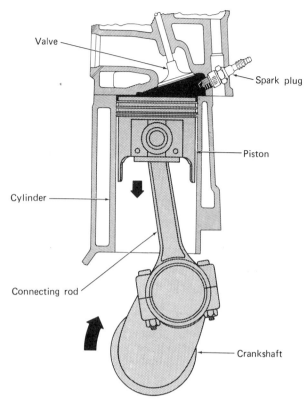

Figure 7.1 The major parts of a four-stroke cycle engine (Ford Motor Company).

ENGINE OPERATION Most automobiles are powered by an *internal combustion* engine fueled by gasoline. An internal combustion engine is one that burns fuel internally, converting heat energy to the energy of motion. The most popular type of engine operates on the *four-stroke cycle* principle. Before you attempt to work on a fuel system or any other engine system, you should have an understanding of the four-stroke cycle.

The Four-Stroke Cycle A four-stroke cycle engine utilizes a piston that moves up and down in a cylinder. By means of a connecting rod, the piston is connected to a crankshaft. Through this arrangement, the *reciprocating*, or up and down, motion of the piston is converted to rotary motion. Figure 7.1 shows a four-stroke cycle engine and identifies the major parts. You should study this illustration so that you will be familiar with these parts.

During each stroke of the piston, the crankshaft rotates one-half turn (180°). Therefore, a complete four-stroke cycle requires that the crankshaft rotate two full turns (720°). Fuel is burned and power is delivered to the crankshaft only during one stroke. The remaining three strokes are required to fill the cylinder with a fuel-air mixture, to compress the mixture, and to exhaust the burned gases.

The Intake Stroke The intake stroke starts with the piston at the extreme top of the cylinder. This position is called *Top Dead Center* or *TDC*. As the crankshaft turns, the piston is pulled down in the cylinder as shown in Figure 7.2. The intake valve opens, allowing atmospheric pressure to push a mixture of gasoline vapor and air into the cylinder. The intake

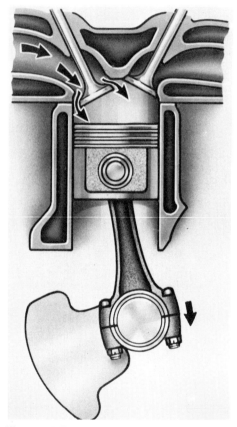

Figure 7.2 The intake stroke. The intake valve opens and the piston is pulled down in the cylinder, creating a partial vacuum. Atmospheric pressure forces the fuel-air mixture into the cylinder through the intake port (Chevrolet Service Manual, Chevrolet Motor Division, GM).

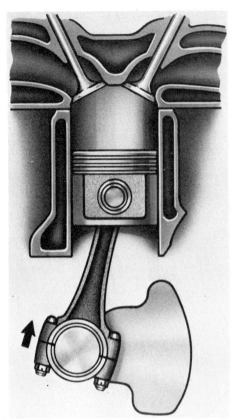

Figure 7.3 The compression stroke. The piston is pushed up in the cylinder while both valves remain closed. The fuel-air mixture is compressed into the combustion chamber (Chevrolet Service Manual, Chevrolet Motor Division, GM).

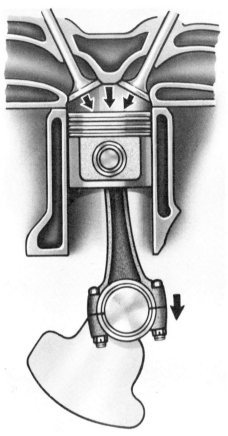

Figure 7.4 The power stroke. The fuel-air mixture is ignited and the pressure of the burning mixture pushes the piston down in the cylinder (Chevrolet Service Manual, Chevrolet Motor Division, GM).

stroke is completed when the piston reaches the limit of its travel at the bottom of the cylinder. This position is called *Bottom Dead Center* or *BDC*.

The Compression Stroke The fuel-air mixture in the cylinder must be squeezed, or *compressed*, for efficient burning. The intake valve closes and the rotating crankshaft forces the piston back up into the cylinder as shown in Figure 7.3. Because the fuel-air mixture cannot escape, it is compressed into a small space between the cylinder head and the top of the piston. This space is called the *combustion chamber*. (Refer to Figure 7.1.) The compression stroke is completed when the piston reaches TDC.

The Power Stroke A spark produced at the spark plug located in the combustion chamber ignites the compressed mixture. Both valves remain closed and the expansion of the burning mixture forces the piston down as shown in Figure 7.4. The fuel mixture is completely burned and the power stroke is completed when the piston reaches BDC.

The Exhaust Stroke The cylinder is now filled with burned gases which must be expelled. As shown in Figure 7.5, the exhaust valve opens. The rotating crankshaft pushes the piston back up into the cylinder, forcing the burned gases out through the exhaust port. When the piston reaches TDC, the exhaust stroke is completed and the cycle is repeated.

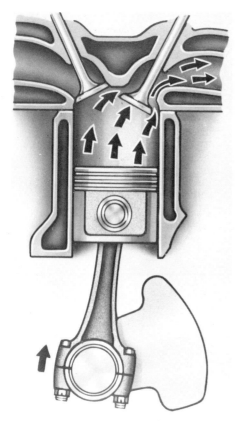

Figure 7.5 The exhaust stroke. The exhaust valve opens and the piston is pushed up in the cylinder. The burned gases are forced out of the cylinder through the exhaust port (Chevrolet Service Manual, Chevrolet Motor Division, GM).

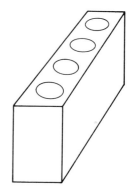

Figure 7.6 Cylinder arrangements of in-line engines.

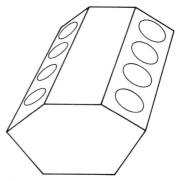

Figure 7.7 Cylinder arrangements of V-type engines.

Multi-Cylinder Engines A single cylinder engine delivers power to the crankshaft only once during two revolutions. Therefore, these engines run roughly, especially at low speed. The use of multiple cylinders provides a smoother running engine. Most automobile engines have four, six, or eight cylinders. The power strokes of all the cylinders are timed so that they occur within the same two revolutions of the crankshaft. In a four-cylinder engine, a power stroke occurs during each 180° of crankshaft rotation. In most six-cylinder engines, a power stroke occurs every 120°. In eight-cylinder engines, power is delivered to the crankshaft during each 90° of crankshaft rotation.

Cylinder Arrangement Although many different cylinder arrangements have been used, the most popular are the *in-line* and the *V*. These cylinder arrangements are shown in Figures 7.6 and 7.7. Most four-cylinder engines are in-line. To avoid excessive length, most eight-cylinder engines are of the V-type. Six-cylinder engines are built in both in-line and V designs. Sectioned views of in-line and V-type engines are shown in Figures 7.8 and 7.9.

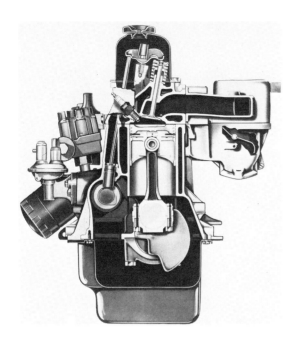

Figure 7.8 A sectional view of a typical in-line engine as seen from the front (courtesy American Motors Corporation).

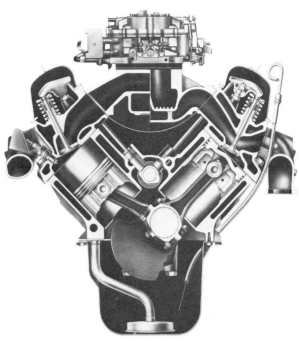

Figure 7.9 A sectional view of a typical V-type engine as seen from the front (courtesy American Motors Corporation).

Job 7a

IDENTIFY THE FOUR STROKES OF THE FOUR-STROKE CYCLE AND RELATED ENGINE PARTS

SATISFACTORY PERFORMANCE

A satisfactory performance on this job requires that you do the following:

1 Identify the four strokes of the four-stroke cycle shown by placing the letter of each stroke in front of the correct stroke name.

2 Identify the numbered engine parts shown by placing the number of each part in front of the correct part name.

3 Correctly identify all the strokes and parts with 10 minutes.

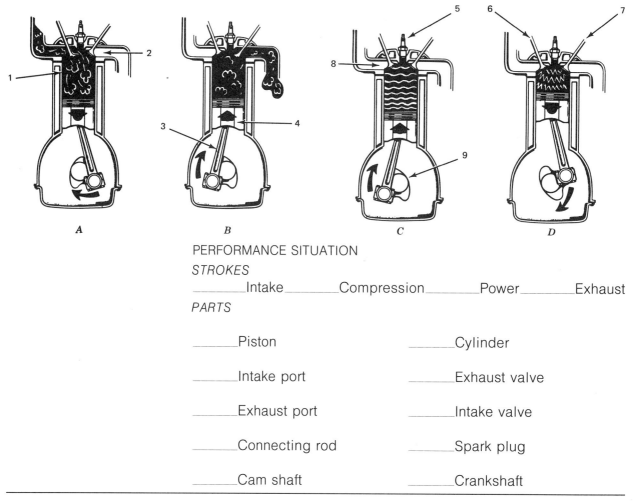

A   B   C   D

PERFORMANCE SITUATION

STROKES

_____Intake_____Compression_____Power_____Exhaust

PARTS

_____Piston	_____Cylinder
_____Intake port	_____Exhaust valve
_____Exhaust port	_____Intake valve
_____Connecting rod	_____Spark plug
_____Cam shaft	_____Crankshaft

GASOLINE Gasoline is a mixture of *hydro-carbons*. Hydrocarbons are chemical compounds made up of hydrogen and carbon. Although gasoline is purchased in liquid form, liquid gasoline will not burn in an engine. Before the energy in gasoline can be harnessed, the gasoline must be *vaporized*, or changed from a liquid to a vapor. When gasoline is vaporized and mixed with air, it is referred to as a fuel-air mixture. If the proportions of fuel and air are within a certain range, the mixture will burn rapidly and release a great amount of heat energy.

Fuel-Air Ratios Fuel-air ratios are determined by weight. As shown in Figure 7.10, about 9000 gallons of air are required to burn 1 gallon of gasoline. By converting these amounts from volume to weight, the numbers are easier to work with. A mixture of 15 pounds of air and 1 pound of gasoline has a ratio of 15 to 1 and can be considered an average mixture. A mixture that contains less air (or more gasoline) is called a *rich mixture*. A mixture that contains more air (or less gasoline) is called a *lean mixture*. As shown in Figure 7.11, a mixture richer than 8 to 1 usually will not burn in an engine. At the other extreme, a mixture leaner than 18.5 to 1 will also fail to burn.

Rich Mixtures A rich mixture may be needed at times when maximum power is required. However, the gasoline in a rich mixture is not completely burned during combustion. In addition to providing poor fuel economy, mixtures that are too rich will cause (1) the spark plugs to become carbon fouled, (2) carbon

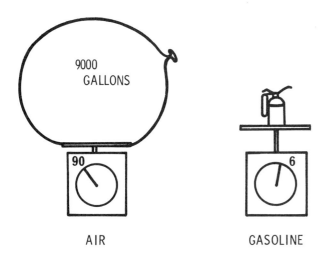

9000 GALS. ARE NEEDED TO BURN 1 GAL.
90 LBS. ARE NEEDED TO BURN 6 LBS.
15 LBS. ARE NEEDED TO BURN 1 LB.

Figure 7.10 Approximately 9000 gallons of air are required to burn 1 gallon of gasoline in an engine (Chevrolet Service Manual, Chevrolet Motor Division, GM).

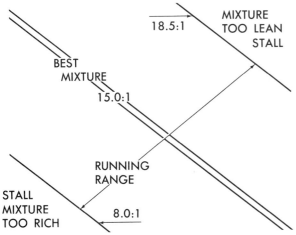

Figure 7.11 Fuel-air ratio running range (Chevrolet Service Manual, Chevrolet Motor Division, GM).

deposits to build up in the engine, and (3) the engine to emit polluting unburned hydrocarbons.

Lean Mixtures A lean mixture is desirable for reasons of economy and because it burns more completely. By burning more completely, a lean mixture emits fewer unburned hydrocarbons, resulting in less pollution. The use of a mixture that is too lean for a particular engine can result in engine damage. A lean

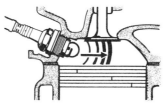

When the spark plug ignites the fuel-air mixture, a flame front moves across the combustion chamber. The burning is controlled and the energy released exerts a push against the piston.

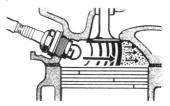

The flame front continues across the combustion chamber and the pressure and temperature of the unburned mixture ahead of the flame front increases.

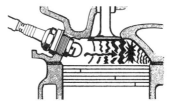

The temperature of the unburned mixture rises so high that the mixture starts to burn at another location. When the opposing flame fronts collide, an explosion occurs.

Figure 7.12 Detonation of a fuel-air mixture (Ford Motor Company).

mixture usually creates combustion chamber temperatures that are higher than normal. This excess heat can (1) damage spark plugs, (2) cause valves to burn, and (3) cause piston damage.

Detonation Ideally, the fuel-air mixture should burn at a controlled rate. In this manner, the released energy acts to push the piston down in the cylinder rather than to drive it down. Detonation occurs when the smooth, progressive burning of the fuel-air mixture is interrupted by an explosion. Figure 7.12 shows how detonation occurs. When the mixture *detonates*, or explodes, its energy is released too rapidly. This sudden release of energy imparts a hammer-like blow to the piston and can cause extensive engine damage. Figure 7.13 shows a piston damaged by detonation.

Figure 7.13 Piston damage caused by the explosive force of detonation (courtesy of Champion Spark Plug Company).

Because detonation is an explosion, it can often be heard. Detonation is usually heard when an engine is under load, such as when a car is accelerating or when it is climbing a hill. Audible detonation is often referred to as *pinging* or *spark knock*.

Detonation results when a fuel-air mixture is exposed to a combination of temperature and pressure too great for it to withstand. Engine design, operating conditions, and even weather conditions are factors that affect detonation. In many instances, detonation can be minimized by using a fuel that burns slower. Slower burning fuels are usually identified by a high octane rating.

Octane Ratings The octane rating of a fuel provides an indication of the fuel's ability to resist detonation. The octane rating of a fuel can be adjusted during the refining process by blending different hydrocarbons, and by using additives.

The octane number assigned to a fuel is based on the results of comparative testing. A sample of fuel is burned in a special laboratory engine. The antiknock quality of the fuel is then matched to that of a control fuel composed of *isooctane* and *heptane*. These two hydrocarbons have widely differing antiknock qualities. Isooctane is rated at 100, whereas heptane is rated at 0. If the fuel tested has the same antiknock quality as a mixture of 80 percent isooctane and 20 percent heptane, the fuel is rated at 80 octane.

Gasoline Safety When gasoline is burned in an engine, the heat energy released is harnessed and put to work. If gasoline is ignited outside an engine, the energy released can rarely be controlled. Gasoline fires have caused staggering property losses, extremely painful and disfiguring injuries, and much loss of life. When working on an automobile or in an auto shop, you should always remember that gasoline and gasoline vapors are usually present. The observance of the following safety rules will help you to avoid a serious accident:

1 Never use gasoline to wash parts or equipment.
2 Never smoke while in the vicinity of gasoline or where gasoline vapors may be present.
3 Use care when working on parts of a fuel system. Fuel is usually spilled when lines are disconnected and parts removed.
4 Never attempt to start an engine if gasoline has been spilled on the engine. Dry up all spills with rags and dispose of the rags outdoors where the fuel can evaporate.
5 Do not attempt to weld or braze on or near fuel system parts.
6 When gasoline must be stored in other than underground tanks, it should be stored only in small quantities in special gasoline safety cans.
7 Never refuel a vehicle indoors. A buildup of gasoline vapors will occur. Outdoor refueling allows fuel vapors to dissipate.

Job 7b

IDENTIFY THE DEFINITIONS OF TERMS RELATING TO GASOLINE

SATISFACTORY PERFORMANCE

A satisfactory performance on this job requires that you do the following:

1 Identify terms relating to gasoline by placing the number of each term in front of the phrase that best defines it.
2 Correctly identify all the terms within 15 minutes.

PERFORMANCE SITUATION

1	Hydrocarbon	6	Detonation
2	Octane rating	7	Rich mixture
3	Lean mixture	8	Vaporization
4	Isooctane	9	Heptane
5	Spark knock	10	Gasoline

_____ An explosion that occurs when a fuel is subjected to excessive pressure and temperature.

_____ A hydrocarbon that has a very high resistance to detonation.

_____ A fuel composed of a mixture of hydrocarbons.

_____ A chemical compound made up of hydrogen and carbon.

_____ A fuel additive that increases the amount of energy released during combustion.

_____ An indication of a fuel's ability to resist detonation.

_____ A hydrocarbon that has very little resistance to detonation.

_____ An audible indication of detonation.

_____ A fuel-air mixture that has an excess of fuel.

_____ The changing of a vapor to a liquid.

_____ A fuel-air mixture that has an excess of air.

_____ The changing of a liquid to a vapor.

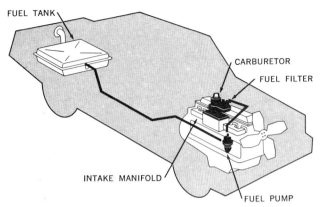

FUEL TANK

CARBURETOR

FUEL FILTER

INTAKE MANIFOLD

FUEL PUMP

Figure 7.14 A basic automotive fuel system (Ford Motor Company).

THE FUEL SYSTEM An automotive fuel system must (1) store fuel, (2) deliver the fuel to the engine, and (3) vaporize the fuel and mix it with the correct amount of air. In addition, the system should contain devices that filter the fuel, filter the air, and prevent the escape of polluting fuel vapors. Figure 7.14 shows the major parts of a typical fuel system. You should study this illustration so that you become familiar with the location of these parts.

The Fuel Tank Although some plastic fuel tanks will be found, most fuel tanks are made of sheet steel. The tank is usually attached to the frame or underbody of the car as shown in Figure 7.15. Most fuel tanks have a filler pipe, an outlet tube, and one or more vent tubes. Some fuel tanks incorporate a fuel return tube. An electrical device using a movable float operates the fuel gauge on the instrument panel, as shown in Figure 7.16.

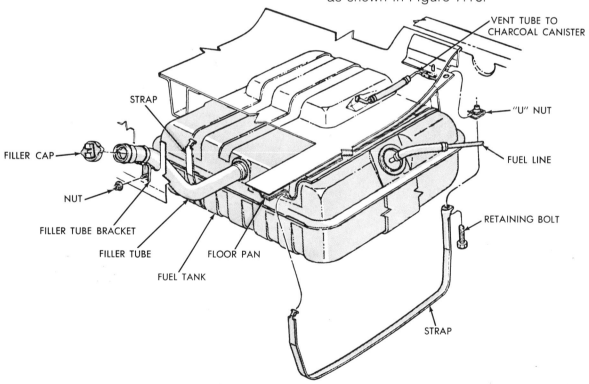

VENT TUBE TO CHARCOAL CANISTER

STRAP

"U" NUT

FILLER CAP

FUEL LINE

NUT

RETAINING BOLT

FILLER TUBE BRACKET

FILLER TUBE

FLOOR PAN

FUEL TANK

STRAP

Figure 7.15 A typical fuel tank assembly. Note that the tank is secured to the car's floor pan by straps (courtesy Chrysler Corporation).

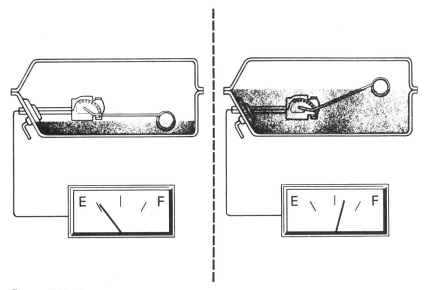

Figure 7.16 The operation of an electric fuel gauge. The movable float operates a variable resistance which in turn operates the gauge (Ford Motor Company).

Fuel tanks on cars that require unleaded gasoline have a restricted filler pipe. The small opening prevents refueling from pumps that dispense leaded gasoline. As shown in Figure 7.17, some filler pipes incorporate a spring-loaded valve. This valve cannot be opened by the nozzle of a leaded gasoline pump.

The outlet tube is connected to the fuel line that runs to the fuel pump. The vent tube(s) allow air to enter the tank as the fuel is used. The vent tube(s) also prevent pressure

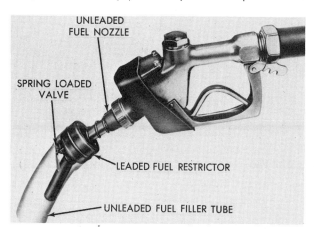

Figure 7.17 A filler pipe used on cars that require unleaded gasoline. Note that the restrictor has a spring loaded valve that must be pushed open by the fuel nozzle (courtesy Chrysler Corporation).

changes in the tank when the fuel expands or contracts with temperature changes.

The Fuel Pump The fuel pump must perform two jobs. It must pull gasoline from the fuel tank, and it must push gasoline to the carburetor. Most cars use a mechanically operated diaphragm pump mounted on the engine. As shown in Figure 7.18, a pump of this type is operated by an eccentric on the camshaft. Some cars will be found to have electric fuel pumps. Electric fuel pumps are often mounted in the fuel line between the tank and the carburetor. Electric fuel pumps are mounted inside the fuel tanks of some cars. An installation of this type is shown in Figure 7.19.

The Carburetor A carburetor is a device which mixes gasoline and air in the correct amounts so that the mixture can be burned in the engine. As shown in Figure 7.20, the carburetor must perform three functions. It must (1) *meter*, or measure out, the correct amount of fuel, (2) *atomize*, or break up, the liquid gasoline into a fine mist, and (3) mix the atomized fuel with the air flowing into the engine.

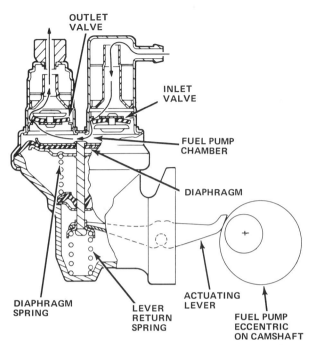

Figure 7.18 A typical mechanical fuel pump. An eccentric on the camshaft moves an actuating lever. As the diaphragm moves downward, fuel is pulled from the tank. When the diaphragm is returned by the spring, fuel is pushed to the carburetor (courtesy American Motors Corporation).

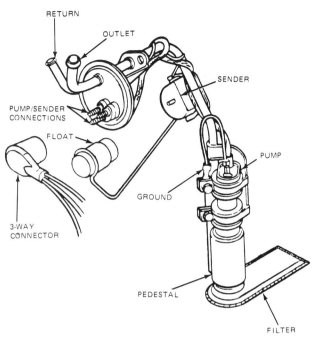

Figure 7.19 A typical in-tank electric fuel pump. Note that the pump is combined with the fuel gauge sender unit (Ford Motor Company).

Filters All automobile fuel systems include filters. These filters remove dirt and other foreign matter from both the fuel and the air that is mixed with the fuel. Dirt in the fuel can plug the small passages in the carburetor. Dirt in the air can cause abrasive wear in the engine and shorten its life.

Fuel Filters Most automobiles have at least two filters in the fuel system. A primary filter is usually used in the fuel tank. As shown in Figure 7.21, this filter is attached to the end of the outlet pipe. The primary filter prevents much of the dirt that accumulates in the tank from entering the fuel line. A secondary filter is usually installed between the fuel pump and the carburetor. This filter removes any dirt that passes through the primary filter.

The most commonly used secondary filters are the *in-line filter* and the *fuel inlet filter*. An in-line filter, as its name implies, is installed in the fuel line between the fuel pump and the

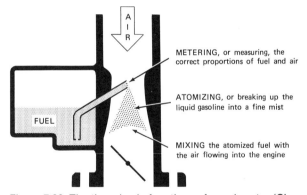

Figure 7.20 The three basic functions of a carburetor (Chevrolet Service Manual, Chevrolet Motor Division, GM).

carburetor. Figure 7.22 shows such an installation. A fuel inlet filter, shown in Figure 7.23, is housed in the carburetor where the fuel line is connected.

Air Filters Most car makers use an air filter made of porous paper. The paper is pleated, or accordian folded, so that a large filtering area is provided. As shown in Figure 7.24, the filter is contained in a sheet metal housing that is mounted on the top of the carburetor.

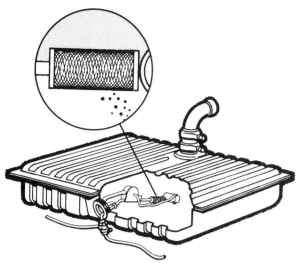

Figure 7.21 Most manufacturers install a mesh filter on the pickup end of the outlet tube in the fuel tank (Ford Motor Company).

Figure 7.22 An in-line filter installed in the fuel line between the fuel pump and the carburetor (courtesy Chrysler Corporation).

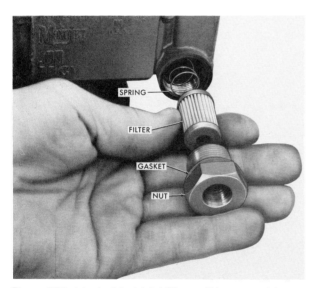

Figure 7.23 A typical fuel inlet filter as it is removed from a carburetor (Chevrolet Service Manual, Chevrolet Motor Division, GM).

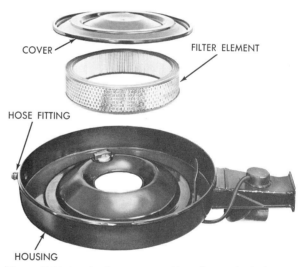

Figure 7.24 An air cleaner assembly using a pleated paper filter (courtesy Chrysler Corporation).

Additional filtering is provided on some cars by a porous band of polyurethane wrapped around the paper filter. A two-stage filter of this type is shown in Figure 7.25.

Pollution Control Devices It is estimated that about 50 percent of the pollutants which poison our atmosphere is emitted by automobiles. Most of these pollutants are emitted from the engine and from the fuel system. Automobile emissions can be traced to three sources: (1) engine exhaust, (2) fuel evaporation, and (3) crankcase vapors.

Engine Exhaust Emissions Engine exhaust is responsible for about 60 percent of automotive pollution. The exhaust from a gasoline engine contains three products that are polluting:

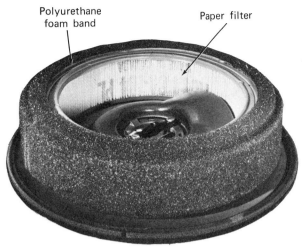

Figure 7.25 To provide additional filtering, some cars are fitted with a polyurethane band that encloses the paper filter (courtesy American Motors Corporation).

1 *Unburned Hydrocarbons (HC).* Because it is almost impossible to burn all the fuel in a fuel-air mixture, some unburned fuel is present in the exhaust. Under certain conditions, unburned hydrocarbons combine with sunlight to form a compound called *photochemical smog*. Photochemical smog is an eye and lung irritant.

2 *Nitrogen Oxides (NOx).* Nitrogen oxides are various compounds of nitric oxide and nitrogen dioxide. They are formed when the nitrogen and oxygen in the air are exposed to high temperatures. Oxides of nitrogen aid the formation of smog under certain conditions.

3 *Carbon Monoxide (CO).* Carbon monoxide is a normal by-product of combustion, but it is produced in quantities larger than normal when the fuel-air mixture is rich. Carbon monoxide is an invisible, odorless, poisonous gas.

Exhaust emissions are controlled by many means. The devices and methods used vary with each engine design. The maintenance of exhaust emission control devices is a specialized area and is not within the scope of this text.

Fuel Evaporation Emissions Gasoline vapors from the fuel tank and from the carburetor amount to about 20 percent of automotive emissions. On modern cars, the fuel tank and the carburetor bowl are vented into a cannister containing activated charcoal. The charcoal absorbs the gasoline vapors which are then

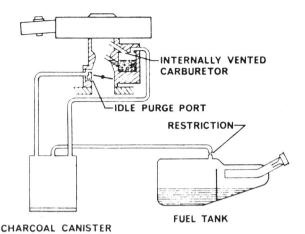

Figure 7.26 An evaporation emission control system prevents the escape of fuel vapors to the atmosphere (Pontiac Motor Division, GM).

drawn into the engine and burned. A typical evaporation emission control system is shown in Figure 7.26.

Crankcase Vapor Emissions During the power stroke, a small amount of unburned fuel and some burned gases leak past the piston and enter the crankcase. This leakage is called *blow-by* and amounts to about 20 percent of automotive emissions. On most cars, the unburned fuel and the burned gases are removed by a *Positive Crankcase Ventilation (PCV)* system. This system, shown in Figure 7.27, draws fresh air through the crankcase and directs the harmful gases to the engine, where they are burned.

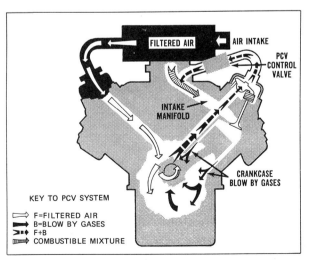

Figure 7.27 The operation of a typical PCV system (Chevrolet Service Manual, Chevrolet Motor Division, GM).

Job 7c

IDENTIFY THE FUNCTION OF FUEL SYSTEM PARTS

SATISFACTORY PERFORMANCE

A satisfactory performance on this job requires that you do the following:

1 Identify the function of the listed parts by placing the part number in front of the phrase that best describes its function.
2 Correctly identify nine parts within 15 minutes.

PERFORMANCE SITUATION

1 Carburetor	6 Restricted filler pipe
2 Fuel tank vent	7 Fuel tank
3 PCV system	8 Fuel inlet filter
4 In-line fuel filter	9 Fuel evaporation cannister
5 Fuel pump	10 Air filter

_____ Stores fuel vapors so they can be burned in the engine

_____ Pulls fuel from the fuel tank and pushes it to the carburetor

_____ Measures and atomizes fuel and mixes it with air

_____ Vaporizes fuel before it reaches the fuel pump

_____ Cleans the air that enters the carburetor

_____ Stores fuel in liquid form

_____ Removes dirt from the fuel as it passes through the line between the fuel pump and the carburetor

_____ Draws clean air into the crankcase and removes the harmful vapors so they can be burned

_____ Prevents refueling from the nozzle of a leaded gasoline pump

_____ Mixes air with the gasoline as it flows through the fuel line

_____ Minimizes pressure differences in the fuel tank as the fuel expands and contracts with temperature changes

_____ Removes dirt and other foreign matter from the fuel as it enters the carburetor

FUEL SYSTEM SERVICE The services necessary to maintain a fuel system are specified by the vehicle manufacturer. Mileage intervals are given for the inspection, cleaning, and replacement of parts. Routine maintenance of the fuel system requires certain knowledge and skills. You now know the major parts of the system and are aware of their functions. The skills required are easily developed.

Air Filter Service Air filters require periodic service if they are to function properly. An air filter that is plugged with dirt will restrict the flow of air to the carburetor. The reduced air flow will cause the fuel-air mixture to be too rich. This will result in poor fuel economy and increased pollution. The filter may be damaged or installed so that all the dirt is not removed from the air. If dirt and dust are allowed to enter the engine, they can cause rapid wear of the moving parts.

Air filters should be serviced at intervals of from 5,000 to 30,000 miles. The correct interval will be specified in the owner's manual or in the manufacturer's manual for the vehicle on which you are working. If the vehicle is operated under dusty conditions, the air filter should be checked at intervals more frequent than specified.

CLEANING AN AIR FILTER Within mileage limitations, a pleated paper filter can be cleaned and reused. The following steps outline a typical procedure. You should consult an appropriate manual for the correct service interval:

1 Remove the wing nut holding the cover to the air cleaner. (See Figure 7.28.)

2 Lift the cover and remove the air filter, as shown in Figure 7.29.

3 If the filter is fitted with a polyurethane band, carefully remove the band.

4 Wash the band in cleaning solvent and, as shown in Figure 7.30, squeeze the band as dry as possible. Set the band aside.

Note: Never attempt to wring the band dry as this could tear the band. A torn or damaged band must be replaced.

5 Using a compressed air blowgun, blow through the filter from the inside as shown in Figure 7.31. By blowing in the reverse direction of normal air flow, most of the dust and dirt will be dislodged from the filter.

Note: Always wear safety goggles during this operation. Avoid placing the blowgun too close to the filter as the concentrated air blast can puncture the paper.

6 If the filter was fitted with a polyurethane band, dip the band in light engine oil. Squeeze the band to remove the excess oil.

7 Carefully install the band around the air filter. The edges of the band should overlap the edges of the paper filter. (Refer to Figure 7.28.)

8 Using a rag or wiper dampened with cleaning solvent, wipe out the inside of the air filter housing.

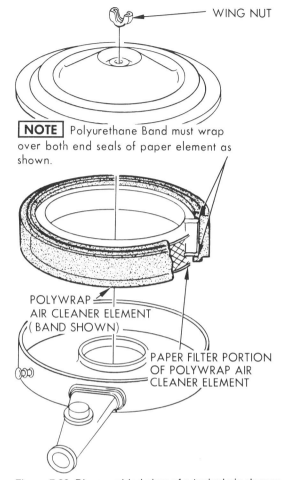

WING NUT

NOTE Polyurethane Band must wrap over both end seals of paper element as shown.

POLYWRAP
AIR CLEANER ELEMENT
(BAND SHOWN)

PAPER FILTER PORTION
OF POLYWRAP AIR
CLEANER ELEMENT

Figure 7.28 Disassembled view of a typical air cleaner. Note that the filter uses a polyurethane band (Chevrolet Service Manual, Chevrolet Motor Division, GM).

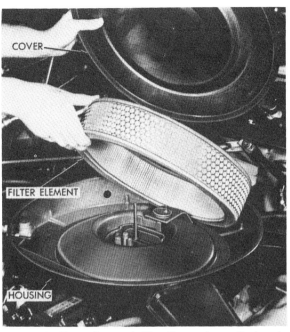

COVER

FILTER ELEMENT

HOUSING

Figure 7.29 Removing an air filter. On most cars, the housing need not be removed from the carburetor to gain access to the filter (courtesy Chrysler Corporation).

Figure 7.30 A polyurethane filter band should be carefully washed and squeezed dry. The band is easily torn or damaged by rough handling (Chevrolet Service Manual, Chevrolet Motor Division, GM).

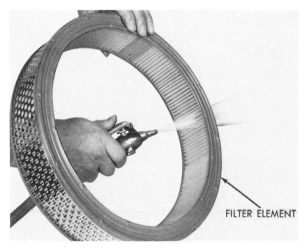

FILTER ELEMENT

Figure 7.31 Cleaning an air filter. The air blast should be directed in the reverse direction of normal air flow (courtesy Chrysler Corporation).

9 Install the filter in the housing.

10 Install the cover and the wing nut.

Job 7d

SERVICE AN AIR FILTER

SATISFACTORY PERFORMANCE

A satisfactory performance on this job requires that you do the following:

1 Service the air filter on the car assigned.
2 Following the steps in the "Performance Outline" and the specifications of the manufacturer, complete the job within 15 minutes.
3 Fill in the blanks under "Information."

PERFORMANCE OUTLINE

1 Remove the filter from its housing.
2 Clean the filter.
3 Install the filter.

INFORMATION

Vehicle identification _____

Reference used_____

Type of air filter used

_____Paper filter _____Polyurethane band _____Other

PCV System Service A positive crankcase ventilation system pulls fumes from the crankcase by intake manifold vacuum. The flow of air and fumes through the system must be controlled so that the fuel-air mixture is not affected. A *PCV valve*, shown in Figure 7.32, provides this control. The PCV valve is located between the intake manifold and the crankcase. Figure 7.33 shows a typical location.

A PCV valve functions in three positions. These positions are determined by intake manifold vacuum which must move the valve against spring pressure.

Partially Open When the engine is idling or when the car is decelerating, intake manifold vacuum is very high. As shown in Figure 7.34, this high vacuum pulls the valve plunger, or shuttle, off its rear seat. As the valve is pulled to the limit of its travel, the nose of the plunger partially restricts the flow of air. This results in a minimum flow.

Fully Open When the engine is running at higher speeds, manifold vacuum decreases. As shown in Figure 7.35, the spring pushes the plunger back slightly. This changes the position of the tapered nose on the plunger and allows the maximum flow of air.

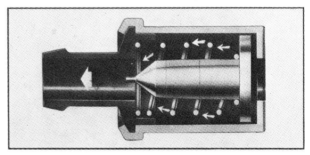

Figure 7.32 A sectioned view of a typical PCV valve (Chevrolet Service Manual, Chevrolet Motor Division, GM).

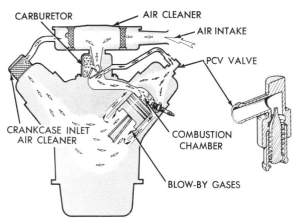

Figure 7.33 The location of the parts in a typical PCV system (courtesy Chrysler Corporation).

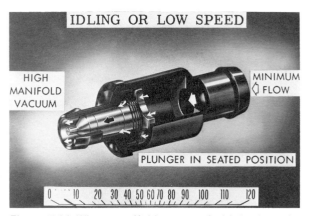

Figure 7.34 When manifold vacuum is high, the valve plunger is pulled off its seat. The nose of the plunger restricts the air flow to a minimum (Chevrolet Service Manual, Chevrolet Motor Division, GM).

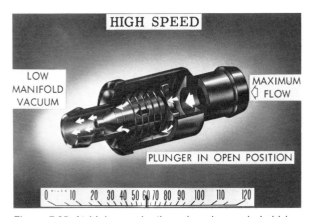

Figure 7.35 At high speeds, the valve plunger is held in a middle position, allowing the maximum flow of air (Chevrolet Service Manual, Chevrolet Motor Division, GM).

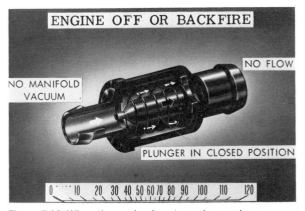

Figure 7.36 When the engine is not running, spring pressure closes the valve. The valve also closes when the engine backfires (Chevrolet Service Manual, Chevrolet Motor Division, GM).

Closed When the engine is turned off, manifold vacuum drops to zero. The spring then closes the valve, as shown in Figure 7.36. The valve also closes during periods of heavy acceleration and high road speeds. If the engine backfires, the PCV valve acts as a check valve and closes. If flame from a backfire enters the crankcase, the vapors could ignite and explode.

As fumes are removed from the crankcase, fresh, filtered air must be allowed to enter. Some systems use a small air cleaner that mounts on a valve cover. An air cleaner of this type is shown in Figure 7.37. Other systems use a small filter fitted inside the air filter hous-

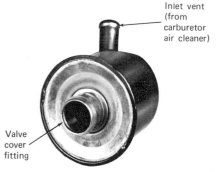

Figure 7.37 An air cleaner used to filter the air that enters the crankcase (courtesy Chrysler Corporation).

Figure 7.38 On some cars, the filter for the PCV system is located in the air filter housing (Chevrolet Service Manual, Chevrolet Motor Division, GM).

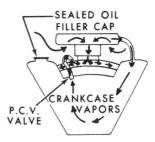

NORMAL IDLE OR
ROAD SPEEDS

Figure 7.39 The normal flow of crankcase vapors when the PCV valve is open (Pontiac Motor Division, GM).

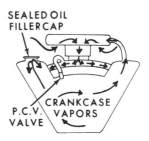

HEAVY ACCELERATION OR
HIGH ROAD SPEED

Figure 7.40 The flow of crankcase vapors when the PCV valve is closed (Pontiac Motors Division, GM).

ing, as shown in Figure 7.38. In all instances the air enters through a hose connected to the air filter housing.

All PCV systems now in use are *closed systems*. This means that both the inlet and outlet hoses are connected so that all crankcase fumes will be burned by the engine. Figure 7.39 shows the normal air flow when the PCV valve is open. During the short periods of time

when the PCV valve is closed, crankcase pressures rise and force fumes out through the inlet hose. Figure 7.40 shows the air flow during these periods.

CHECKING THE OPERATION OF A PCV SYSTEM Three simple tests should be made to determine if a PCV system is functioning properly. The procedures for making these checks follow:

1 Locate the PCV valve and disconnect it from the engine.

Note: The PCV valve is usually located at the end of a hose that leads to the intake manifold. On most engines, the PCV valve plugs into a rubber *grommet*, or ring, on a valve cover.

2 Holding the hose, shake the PCV valve as shown in Figure 7.41. You should hear a clicking or rattling noise, which indicates that the valve plunger, or shuttle, is free to move.

3 Apply the parking brake.

4 If the car has an automatic transmission, place the transmission

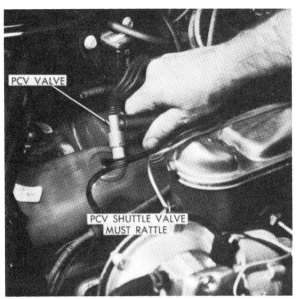

Figure 7.41 When shaken, a PCV valve should rattle. This indicates that the valve is not sticking (courtesy Chrysler Corporation).

Figure 7.42 A strong vacuum should be felt at the PCV valve when the engine is running (courtesy Chrysler Corporation).

selector lever in the PARK position. If the car has a standard transmission, place the shift lever in the NEUTRAL position.

5 Start the engine and allow it to operate at idle speed.

6 Listen to the PCV valve. A hissing noise should be heard as air passes through the valve.

7 Place one of your fingers over the valve opening as shown in Figure 7.42. You should feel a strong vacuum.

8 Push the PCV valve back into its grommet.

9 Locate and remove the inlet air cleaner or hose.

Note: The cap or hose is usually located in a valve cover.

10 Position a piece of stiff paper, such as a parts tag, over the inlet opening, as shown in Figure 7.43. As the pressure drops in the crankcase, the paper should be pulled against the opening with a noticeable force.

11 Install the inlet cap or hose.

12 Turn the engine OFF.

If the PCV system fails to pass any of the tests previously described, the PCV valve should be replaced. The tests should then be repeated. If a new PCV valve does not improve the operation of the system, additional diagnosis is required.

Figure 7.43 Suction in the crankcase can be checked by the use of a stiff piece of paper (courtesy Chrysler Corporation).

Job 7e

SERVICE A PCV SYSTEM

SATISFACTORY PERFORMANCE

A satisfactory performance on this job requires that you do the following:

1 Service the PCV system on the vehicle assigned.
2 Following the steps in the "Performance Outline" and the procedure established by the vehicle manufacturer, complete the job within 15 minutes.
3 Fill in the blanks under "Information."

PERFORMANCE OUTLINE

1 Test the PCV valve for freedom of movement.
2 Test the PCV valve for the passage of air.
3 Test for the presence of a vacuum in the crankcase.
4 Check the condition of the PCV system air filter.
5 Clean or replace parts as necessary.

INFORMATION

Vehicle identification _____

Reference used_____

Location of PCV valve _____

Did the valve rattle or click when shaken? _____Yes _____No

Did air flow through the valve?   _____Yes _____No

Did you detect a vacuum in the
crankcase? _____Yes _____No

Did the PCV valve require replacement? _____Yes _____No

Was the PCV system air filter dirty? _____Yes _____No

Was the PCV system air filter serviced? _____Yes _____No

Fuel Filter Service Fuel filters are designed to trap and hold dirt and other foreign matter which may be present in the fuel. Therefore, if a fuel filter is working properly, it will eventually become clogged or restricted. Most fuel filters cannot be cleaned, but must be replaced. Auto manufacturers suggest that fuel filters be replaced at regular service intervals. These intervals are specified in the service manuals, and vary from 12,000 miles (19,200 km) to 30,000 miles (48,000 km).

Replacing a Fuel Filter In most instances, the fuel filter is located between the fuel pump and the carburetor. In this location, the fuel is under slight pressure, even when the engine is not running. This pressure will cause a certain amount of fuel to leak when the filter is disconnected. Because of the possibility of fire, you should never attempt to change a fuel filter while the engine is hot. Place a rag or cloth wiper under the filter to catch leaking fuel before you loosen any connections. When the fuel has stopped leaking, the rag should be disposed of outdoors where the fuel vapors can dissipate.

In-line Filters The typical in-line filter is connected in the fuel line by two short hoses. (Refer to Figure 7.22.) The filter is easily removed by loosening or removing the hose clamps. Many replacement filters are furnished with new hoses and clamps. The replacement of all these parts is recommended for a leak-proof installation.

Most fuel filters are *directional*. This means that the fuel should flow through the filter in a certain direction. To aid in proper installation, in-line filters are usually marked with an arrow to indicate the correct direction of fuel flow. The filter should be installed so that the arrow points toward the carburetor. Some in-line filters incorporate a vapor return fitting, as shown in Figure 7.44. Filters of this type should be installed so that the vapor return fitting is positioned at the top.

In-line Filters at the Carburetor As shown in Figure 7.45, some in-line filters have a threaded outlet that screws into the carburetor.

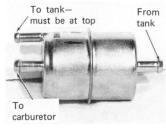

Figure 7.44 An in-line filter that contains a vapor vent (courtesy American Motors Corporation).

Figure 7.45 An in-line filter that is threaded into the carburetor inlet (Ford Motor Company).

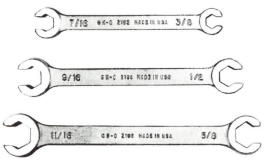

Figure 7.46 A set of flare nut wrenches. Flare nut wrenches should always be used when loosening and tightening fuel line fittings (courtesy of K-D Tools).

Figure 7.47 A fuel inlet filter and its related parts must be installed in this order (Pontiac Motor Division, GM).

When removing these filters, the hose should be disconnected before attempting to turn the filter. Carburetor castings are made of very soft metal. Therefore, the replacement filter should be threaded into place by hand to avoid stripping the threads in the carburetor. A wrench should be used only for the final tightening. Here, too, it is suggested that a new hose and new clamps be used to complete the installation.

Fuel Inlet Filters Fuel inlet filters are housed inside the carburetor body. (Refer to Figure 7.23.) The fuel inlet fitting, or nut, must be removed to gain access to the filter. Before the nut can be removed, the fuel line must be disconnected. When loosening or tightening a fuel line fitting, you should always use a *flare nut wrench*. Flare nut wrenches, shown in Figure 7.46, are designed so that they will not damage fuel line fittings. When disconnecting the fuel line, the nut should be held with a large open end wrench while the fitting is turned with a flare nut wrench.

Fuel inlet filters are directional. They must be installed so that the open end of the filter faces outward. To function properly, the filter must be held against the nut by a spring. Figure 7.47 shows the order in which the filter and its related parts must be installed.

The threads on the nut and in the carburetor body are very fine. Thus, the threads in the soft carburetor body are easily stripped. When installing a fuel inlet filter, be sure the gasket is in place on the nut. Then, carefully screw the nut all the way in with finger pressure only. A wrench should be used for the final tightening.

Job 7f

REPLACE A FUEL FILTER

SATISFACTORY PERFORMANCE
A satisfactory performance on this job requires that you do the following:

1 Replace the designated fuel filter on the vehicle assigned.

2 Following the steps in the "Performance Outline" and the procedure and specifications of the manufacturer, complete the job within 200 percent of the manufacturer's suggested time.
3 Fill in the blanks under "Information."

PERFORMANCE OUTLINE
1 Position a rag to catch any spilled gasoline.
2 Remove the filter and its related parts.
3 Install the replacement filter.
4 Start the engine and check for leakage.

INFORMATION

Vehicle identification _____

Reference used _____ Page(s)_____

Type of filter replaced

_____In-line _____In-line at carburetor _____Fuel inlet

Part number of replacement filter _____

Evaporation Emission Control Service

Evaporation emission control systems are relatively simple. Their sole function is to prevent the escape of fuel vapors to the atmosphere. Vapors from the fuel tank and from the carburetor bowl are conducted to a vapor storage canister by hoses. While the engine is running, the vapors are pulled into the engine and burned. Vapors that form while the engine is not running are absorbed by and stored in a bed of activated charcoal. When the engine is started, the canister is *purged*, or cleaned, as shown in Figure 7.48. The amount of fuel vapors that are burned at any time is very small. The burning of these vapors has no effect on engine performance or on fuel economy.

Evaporation emission control systems require little service. An inspection of the hoses and their connections and, on some cars, a replacement of a filter is all that is needed. Disconnected or damaged hoses could allow fuel vapors to escape. A quick check of the hoses will disclose these faults. A hose with a split end can often be cut back and reinstalled. If

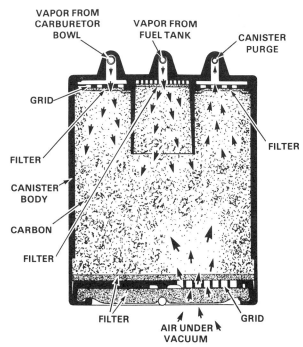

Figure 7.48 The flow of air and fuel vapors in a vapor storage canister (Pontiac Motor Division, GM).

a hose is damaged so that it must be replaced, only hoses suitable for fuel systems should be used.

Most canisters are fitted with a filter. (Refer to Figure 7.48.) This filter should be replaced at the mileage interval specified by the manufacturer. Because the filter is usually located at the bottom of the canister, you may have to remove the canister to replace the filter. Before you disconnect the canister hoses, mark them so that they will be connected to the proper location. As shown in Figure 7.49, the filter is easily replaced with your fingers.

Figure 7.49 In most instances, an evaporation emission control canister must be removed and inverted to replace the filter (courtesy Chrysler Corporation).

Job 7g

SERVICE AN EVAPORATION EMISSION CONTROL SYSTEM

SATISFACTORY PERFORMANCE

A satisfactory performance on this job requires that you do the following:

1 Service the evaporation emission control system on the car assigned.
2 Following the steps in the "Performance Outline" and the procedure and specifications of the manufacturer, complete the job within 200 percent of the manufacturer's suggested time.
3 Fill in the blanks under "Information."

PERFORMANCE OUTLINE

1 Check the condition of the hoses and their connections.
2 Repair or replace hoses as required.
3 Check the condition of the canister filter.
4 Replace the filter if required.

INFORMATION

Vehicle identification _____

Reference used _____ Page(s)_____

Condition of hoses and connections _____OK _____NG

Were hoses repaired or replaced? _____Yes _____No

Condition of filter _____OK _____NG

Was filter replaced? _____Yes _____No

The manufacturer's recommended service interval for filter replacement is _____ miles.

Carburetor Service The carburetor is responsible for providing the fuel-air mixture that is burned in an engine. The mixture must be rich enough to provide sufficient power. It must be lean enough to provide good fuel economy. And it must burn in such a manner that it does not cause excessive exhaust emissions.

If an engine were operated at a constant speed and under a constant load in a controlled environment, the ideal fuel-air ratio could be determined. A relatively simple carburetor could then be used.

When an engine is used to power an automobile, it must operate under all possible combinations of speed and load. And it must operate within wide ranges of temperature, humidity, and barometric pressure. These varying conditions require different fuel-air ratios. Therefore, the carburetor used on an automobile engine must automatically adjust itself to meet these requirements.

All carburetors follow the same principles of operation, yet many different designs are in use. In many instances you will find different carburetors on similar cars built by the same manufacturer. The factors that determine the choice of a particular carburetor design are numerous. So numerous in fact, that the choice is usually based on the results of a computerized study.

Each different carburetor design requires many different adjustments. Each adjustment must be performed in a special procedure and to a particular specification. The specifications are established to keep emission levels below the limits set by federal and state laws. In most instances, the adjustments require the use of special tools and instruments. Adjustments made without the use of such equipment may cause emissions to exceed legal limits.

Idle Speed If the idle speed of an engine is too low, the engine may stall frequently if pressure is not maintained on the accelerator pedal. If the idle speed is too high, fuel is wasted. Also, cars with automatic transmissions will *creep*, or move, excessively with no pressure on the accelerator pedal.

The correct idle speed for any engine is listed on the *Emission Control Information Label* or *"Decal."* This label is located on the engine or in a conspicuous place in the engine compartment. Examples of the various labels used are shown in Figures 7.50 through 7.53. If the vehicle on which you are working does not have such a label, you must obtain the idle speed specification from an appropriate manual.

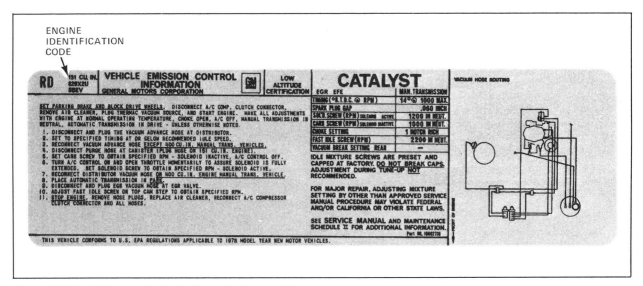

Figure 7.50 An Emission Control Information Label of the type found on vehicles built by General Motors Corporation (Pontiac Motor Division, GM).

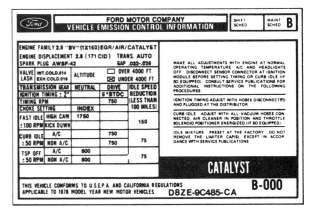

Figure 7.51 An Emission Control Information Label of the type found on vehicles built by Ford Motor Company (Ford Motor Company).

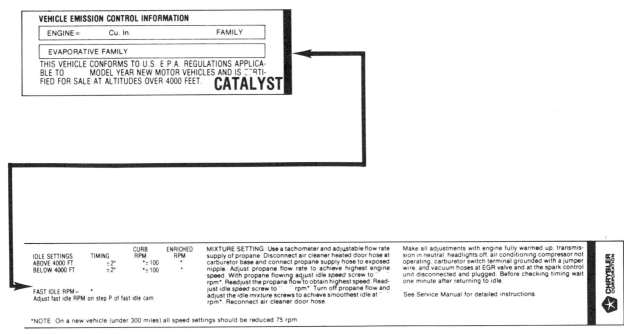

Figure 7.52 An Emission Control Information Label of the type found on vehicles built by Chrysler Corporation (courtesy Chrysler Corporation).

AMC VEHICLE EMISSION CONTROL INFORMATION	ENGINE FAMILY ENGINE C.I.D. EVAPORATIVE FAMILY EMISSION CONTROL SYSTEM		
THIS VEHICLE CONFORMS TO U.S. E.P.A. REGULATIONS APPLICABLE TO 1978 MODEL YEAR NEW MOTOR VEHICLE INTENDED FOR SALE AT ALTITUDE 4000 FEET.	SPECIFICATIONS	TRANSMISSION	
		AUTO.	MANUAL
	IGNITION TIMING ± 2° BTDC @ R.P.M.		
PROPER MAINTENANCE AND ADJUSTMENT ARE NECESSARY FOR CONTINUED EFFECTIVENESS. MAKE ADJUSTMENTS WITH ENGINE AT NORMAL OPERATING TEMPERATURE, AIR CLEANER ON, AIR CONDITIONING OFF. SET IGNITION TIMING WITH DISTRIBUTOR VACUUM OFF AND PLUGGED, SOLENOID DISCONNECTED.	CARB. IDLE SPEED ± 100 R.P.M.		
	HIGH IDLE SPEED ± 100 RPM(N)SEC. STEP		
	IDLE MIXTURE LEAN IDLE DROP		
	SPARK PLUG GAP		
	HOT VALVE INTAKE LASH EXHAUST		
	CAM DWELL		
SEE OWNER OR SERVICE MANUAL FOR INSTRUCTIONS. "POUR PLUS DE RESEIGNEMENTS, VEUILLEZ VOUS REPORTER AU MANUEL DU PROPRIÉTAIRE OU DENTRETIEN."			

Figure 7.53 An Emission Control Information Label of the type found on vehicles built by American Motors Corporation (courtesy American Motors Corporation).

MEASURING IDLE SPEED Engine speed specifications are given in revolutions per minute, usually abbreviated as *rpm*. To adjust idle speed you must use a *tachometer*. A tachometer is an instrument that measures engine speed. Most shops use a *Tach-Dwell meter* similar to the one shown in Figure 7.54. A Tach-Dwell meter combines a tachometer with a *Dwell meter*. The Dwell meter is used in various ignition system tests.

Figure 7.54 A typical Tach-Dwell Meter (courtesy of Snap-on Tools Corporation).

Most Tach-Dwell meters have a function switch, as shown in Figure 7.55. This switch allows you to match the meter to the test you wish to perform. For greater accuracy at low speeds, most Tach-Dwell meters have two rpm scales. A scale indicating speeds to 1000 rpm is provided for idle speed measurement. A scale indicating speeds to 5000 rpm is provided for those tests where speeds greater than 1000 rpm must be measured. The appropriate scale is selected by a switch. (Refer to Figure 7.55.)

Another switch matches the Tach-Dwell meter to the number of cylinders in the engine on which you are working. Some Tach-Dwell meters do not provide a switch position for four-cylinder engines. When using meters of this type, the eight-cylinder mode is selected. The meter reading must then be doubled to obtain the true rpm. (Refer to Figure 7.55.)

The steps below outline a procedure for measuring engine idle speed. You should consult the instruction manual furnished with the meter you have available for the correct meter adjustments and connections. To obtain an accurate measurement of idle speed, vehicle manufacturers establish special procedures for various models. If these procedures are not listed on the decal, you must locate them in an appropriate manual. (Refer to Figure 7.50.)

The function switch allows you to match the meter to the test you wish to perform

The cylinder selector switch enables you to match the meter to the number of cylinders in the engine

Figure 7.55 Typical Tach-Dwell Meter controls (courtesy of Snap-on Tools Corporation).

1 Place the function switch of the Tach-Dwell meter in the TACH position.

2 Position the cylinder selector switch to match the number of cylinders in the engine.

Note: Remember that on some meters you must place the switch in the eight-cylinder position, and double the indicated speed when working on four-cylinder engines.

3 Place the scale selector switch in the 0-5000 rpm position.

Note: Placing the scale selector switch in the high speed position minimizes the possibility of meter damage which may occur when starting the engine.

4 Connect the Tach-Dwell meter to the DIST (−) terminal on the coil and to a good ground as shown in the diagram in Figure 7.56.

Note: Figures 7.57 and 7.58 show the coil connections that must be made on some cars with electronic ignition systems.

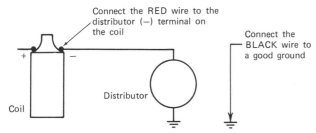

Figure 7.56 A Tach-Dwell Meter is connected to the coil primary wire leading to the distributor and to a good ground.

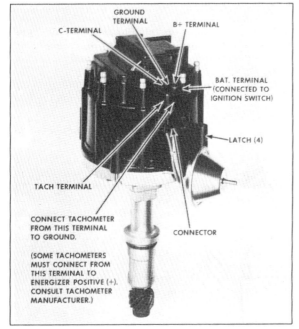

Figure 7.58 A special TACH terminal is provided on the H.E.I. distributor used in cars made by General Motors (Pontiac Motor Division, GM).

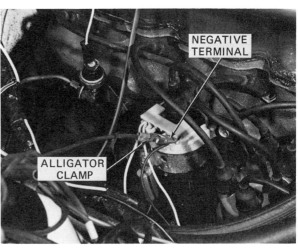

Figure 7.57 On cars using a coil connector of the type shown, an alligator clamp can be used to contact the negative terminal (courtesy American Motors Corporation).

5 Check the decal or an appropriate manual for the idle measurement procedure and specifications.

Note: On some cars, the idle speed must be checked while the transmission is in DRIVE. In some instances certain hoses must be disconnected and plugged. Other requirements include turning on the air conditioner and headlights, and removing the air cleaner.

6 Apply the parking brake.

Note: If the transmission must be placed in DRIVE for the idle speed measurement, block the wheels of the car so that it cannot move.

7 If the car has an automatic transmission, place the transmission selector lever in PARK. If the car has a standard transmission, place the shift lever in NEUTRAL.

8 Start the engine and allow it to operate at idle speed.

Note: If the engine is cold, the engine will idle fast. Idle speed can be accurately measured only when the engine has reached its normal operating temperature.

9 When the engine has reached its normal operating temperature, "tap" the accelerator pedal once or twice and allow the engine to idle.

10 If required, place the transmission selector lever in DRIVE.

Note: Do not attempt to accelerate the engine while the transmission is in DRIVE.

11 Place the scale selector switch on the Tach-Dwell meter in the 0-1000 rpm position and read the speed indicated by the meter.

Note: Do not forget to double the reading if you are working on a four-cylinder engine and the meter is in the eight-cylinder position.

12 Record the idle speed and compare it with the specifications.

13 Turn the ignition switch to the OFF position.

14 Disconnect and remove the Tach-Dwell meter.

15 Connect all hoses that were disconnected. Install all components that were removed.

Job 7h

MEASURE ENGINE IDLE SPEED

SATISFACTORY PERFORMANCE
A satisfactory performance on this job requires that you do the following:

1 Measure the engine idle speed of the vehicle assigned.
2 Following the steps in the "Performance Outline" and the procedure of the manufacture, complete the job within 20 minutes.
3 Fill in the blanks under "Information."

PERFORMANCE OUTLINE
1 Adjust the meter.
2 Connect the meter.
3 Check the manufacturer's procedure and specifications.
4 Start the engine.
5 Read the indicated rpm.
6 Turn the engine OFF.

INFORMATION

Vehicle identification _____

Reference used _____ Page(s)_____

Identification of instrument used_____

Number of cylinders in engine _____4 _____6 _____8

Was engine at normal operating
temperature?   _____Yes _____No

Was transmission placed in DRIVE?   _____Yes _____No

Were the wheels blocked?   _____Yes _____No

Were the headlights on?   _____Yes _____No

Was the air conditioner on?   _____Yes _____No

Indicated idle speed was _____ rpm.

Manufacturer's specified idle speed is _____ rpm.

ADJUSTING IDLE SPEED If the engine idle speed does not meet specifications, it should be adjusted. Most carburetors have an adjustment screw for this purpose. This screw is often referred to as the *curb idle speed adjusting screw*. This designation is used to distinguish it from the *fast idle adjusting screw*. The fast idle adjusting screw controls the idle speed only while the engine is cold and while the choke is closed or partially closed. This adjustment should not be disturbed.

Most carburetors also have *idle mixture adjusting screws*. These screws adjust the fuel-air ratio of the idle mixture. The idle mixture adjusting screws are usually covered by *limiter caps*. These plastic caps are installed to discourage adjustment. Any adjustment of the idle mixture without the use of specialized equipment could raise emission levels above legal limits. Figures 7.59 through 7.61 show the location of the curb idle speed adjusting screw on some typical carburetors.

Some carburetors have no curb idle speed adjusting screw. On these carburetors, the curb idle is adjusted at a *solenoid*. The solenoid is an electromagnetic device that acts as a movable throttle stop. While the ignition switch is in the ON position, a plunger extends from the solenoid and holds the throttle in the idle position. When the ignition switch is turned to the OFF position, the plunger moves back into the solenoid and the throttle closes. This action stops the air supply to the engine, eliminating the tendency of the engine to *diesel* (or continue to run), after the switch has been turned off.

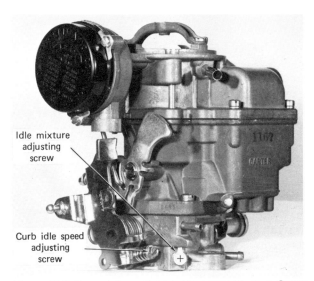

Figure 7.59 Two of the adjustments provided on a Carter Model YF single-barrel carburetor. Note the plastic limiter cap on the idle mixture adjusting screw (courtesy American Motors Corporation).

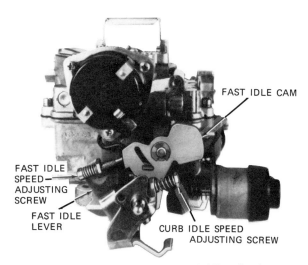

Figure 7.60 The locations of the curb idle adjusting screw and the fast idle adjusting screw on a Holley Model 1946 carburetor (Ford Motor Company).

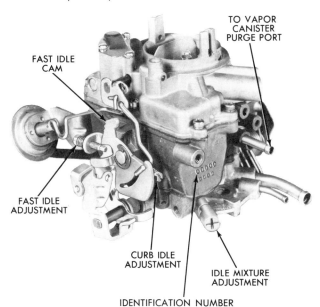

Figure 7.61 The location of the adjustment screws on a Holley Model 1945 carburetor (courtesy Chrysler Corporation).

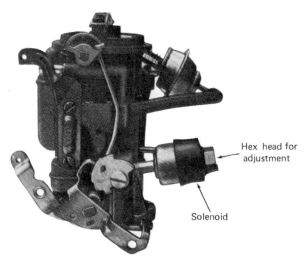

Figure 7.62 A typical single-barrel Rochester carburetor equipped with an idle stop solenoid. Idle speed adjustment is obtained by threading the solenoid in or out (Chevrolet Service Manual, Chevrolet Motor Division, GM).

There are several different methods of adjusting the curb idle on a carburetor equipped with a solenoid. Figure 7.62 shows one type of solenoid installation. On this type, the solenoid is turned by means of a wrench fitted to a hexagon head on the solenoid. Turning the solenoid clockwise increases the idle speed.

Figure 7.63 illustrates a solenoid commonly used on two-barrel and four-barrel carburetors. This type of solenoid is adjusted by turning the threaded plunger with a wrench. On these installations, the plunger is turned counterclockwise to increase the idle speed.

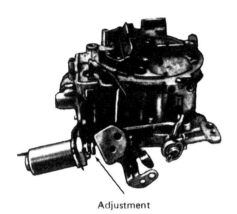

Adjustment

Figure 7.63 A solenoid installation of this type is used on certain Rochester two-barrel and four-barrel carburetors. Adjustment is provided by a threaded plunger (Chevrolet Service Manual, Chevrolet Motor Division, GM).

IDLE MIXTURE SCREW AND LIMITER CAP

SOLENOID ADJUSTING SCREW

Figure 7.64 Some carburetors have an adjustment screw that contacts the solenoid plunger, as on this Holley-Weber Model 5210 (courtesy American Motors Corporation).

The solenoid shown on the carburetor in Figure 7.64 is not adjustable. An adjustment screw contacts the plunger. When turned clockwise, this screw increases the idle speed. On the carburetor shown in Figure 7.65, the solenoid is mounted on a movable base. Turning an adjustment screw clockwise moves the solenoid toward the throttle lever and increases the idle.

The following steps outline a procedure for adjusting curb idle speed. Because of the many different carburetor designs in use, you should consult an appropriate manual for the location of the adjustment:

1 Adjust a Tach-Dwell meter and connect it to the engine.

Note: You may wish to refer to the previously outlined procedure in this chapter.

2 Check the decal or an appropriate manual for the idle adjustment procedure and specifications.

Note: On some cars, the idle speed must be adjusted while the transmission is in DRIVE. In some instances certain hoses must be disconnected and plugged. Other requirements include turning on the air conditioner and headlights, and removing the air cleaner.

3 Apply the parking brake.

Note: If the transmission must be placed in DRIVE for the idle speed adjustment, block the wheels of the car so that it cannot move.

4 If the car has automatic transmission, place the transmission selector lever in PARK. If the car has a standard transmission, place the shift lever in NEUTRAL.

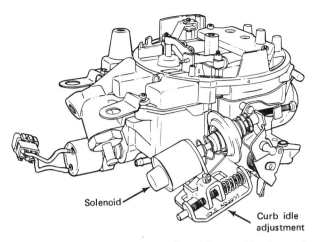

Figure 7.65 A solenoid on an adjustable mounting is used on the Motorcraft Model 2700 VV two-barrel carburetor (Ford Motor Company).

5 Start the engine and allow it to operate at idle speed.

Note: **If the engine is cold, the engine will idle fast. Idle speed can be accurately adjusted only when the engine has reached its normal operating temperature.**

6 When the engine has reached its normal operating temperature, "tap" the accelerator pedal once or twice and allow the engine to idle.

7 If required, place the transmission selector lever in DRIVE.

Note: **Do not attempt to accelerate the engine while the transmission is in DRIVE.**

8 Observe the speed indicated by the Tach-Dwell meter.

9 Following the manufacturer's procedure, adjust the idle speed to the specifications.

10 Turn the ignition switch to the OFF position.

11 Disconnect and remove the Tach-Dwell meter.

12 Connect all hoses that were disconnected. Install all components that were removed.

Job 7i

ADJUST ENGINE IDLE SPEED

SATISFACTORY PERFORMANCE
A satisfactory performance on this job requires that you do the following:

1 Adjust the engine idle speed of the vehicle assigned.
2 Following the steps in the "Performance Outline" and the procedure and specifications of the manufacturer, complete the job within 20 minutes.
3 Fill in the blanks under "Information."

PERFORMANCE OUTLINE
1 Adjust the meter.
2 Connect the meter.
3 Check the manufacturer's procedure and specifications.
4 Start the engine.
5 Read the indicated rpm.
6 Adjust the idle speed to the specifications.
7 Turn the engine OFF.

INFORMATION

Vehicle identification _____

Reference used_____Page(s)_____

Identification of instrument used _____

Number of cylinders in engine _____4_____6_____8

Was engine at normal operating
temperature?   _____Yes   _____No

Was transmission placed in DRIVE?   _____Yes   _____No

Were the wheels blocked?   _____Yes   _____No

Were the headlights on?   _____Yes   _____No

Was the air conditioner on?   _____Yes   _____No

Type of adjustment provided _____Adjustment screw

_____Adjustable solenoid

_____Adjustable solenoid plunger

_____Adjustable solenoid mounting

Manufacturer's specified idle speed _____rpm

Idle speed before adjustment _____rpm

Idle speed after adjustment _____rpm

SUMMARY

In this chapter, you learned how a four-stroke cycle engine burns fuel to produce power. You learned how the fuel system stores, delivers, and mixes this fuel efficiently while producing a minimum of pollution. You are aware of the many parts in the fuel system, how they function, and where they are located. By performing the jobs, you used your knowledge to develop diagnostic and repair skills. These skills include servicing air filters, PCV systems, and evaporation emission control systems. You also learned how to replace fuel filters and to adjust engine curb idle speed.

SELF-TEST

Each incomplete statement or question in this test is followed by four suggested completions or answers. In each case select the _one_ that best completes the sentence or answers the question.

1 During the four strokes of the four-stroke cycle, the crankshaft makes
A. one revolution (360°)
B. two revolutions (720°)
C. three revolutions (1080°)
D. four revolutions (1440°)

2 The sequence of the four strokes in the four-stroke cycle is
A. intake, compression, power, and exhaust
B. power, compression, intake, and exhaust
C. intake, power, compression, and exhaust
D. power, intake, compression, and exhaust

3 Two mechanics are discussing fuel-air ratios.
Mechanic A says that fuel-air ratios are determined by weight.
Mechanic B says that a ratio of 15 to 1 is too rich and will not burn in an engine.
Who is right?
A. A only
B. B only
C. Both A and B
D. Neither A nor B

4 Two mechanics are discussing detonation.
Mechanic A says that detonation can be minimized by using a fuel that burns faster.
Mechanic B says that faster burning fuels have higher octane numbers.
Who is right?
A. A only
B. B only
C. Both A and B
D. Neither A nor B

5 Two mechanics are discussing fuel-air mixtures.
Mechanic A says that a lean mixture causes carbon deposits to build up in the engine.
Mechanic B says that a rich mixture causes detonation.
Who is right?
A. A only
B. B only

C. Both A and B
D. Neither A nor B

6 Many cars use a canister of activated charcoal to collect and store
A. blow by
B. fuel vapors
C. carbon monoxide
D. oxides of nitrogen

7 A positive crankcase ventilation (PCV) system removes the vapors from the crankcase and
A. burns them in the engine
B. vents them to the atmosphere
C. stores them in a carbon canister
D. conducts them to the exhaust manifold

8 When adjusting engine idle speed, a tachometer should be connected to a good ground and to the

A. coil terminal marked IGN
B. positive battery terminal
C. coil terminal marked DIST
D. idle stop solenoid terminal

9 The function of the fast idle cam is to increase the engine idle speed
A. during deceleration
B. during rapid acceleration
C. after the idle stop solenoid is energized
D. while the choke is closed or partially closed

10 Limiter caps are used on idle mixture screws to help prevent
A. rich idle mixture adjustments
B. lean idle mixture adjustments
C. the throttle from opening too far
D. the throttle from closing too far

Chapter 8 Cooling System Service

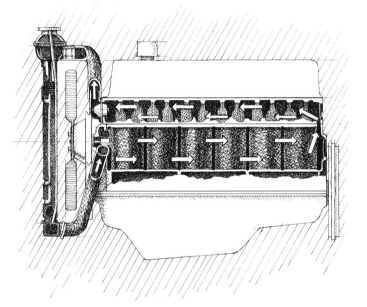

The cooling system must remove about 35 percent of the heat of combustion and dissipate it into the air. Without a cooling system, a car could be driven only a few miles before its engine would be ruined. But the cooling system must not remove too much heat. For efficient operation, an engine must run within a certain temperature range. The cooling system must remove only enough heat to maintain the temperature range.

In this chapter you will learn how the cooling system operates. You will learn about its parts and how they function. You will gain skills in diagnosing problems, making adjustments, and replacing parts. Your specific objectives are to perform the following jobs:

1
Identify cooling system parts and their function.
2
Test coolant mixture and condition.
3
Drain, flush, and refill a cooling system.
4
Pressure test a cooling system and a radiator cap.
5
Replace cooling system hoses.
6
Replace a thermostat.
7
Adjust a fan belt.

THE COOLING SYSTEM The combustion of the fuel-air mixture in an engine can raise internal temperatures to near 5000°F (2760°C). If this heat is not quickly dissipated, considerable engine damage will result. To carry off most of the heat, a typical liquid-cooled engine requires the circulation of up to the equivalent of 7000 gallons (26,600) of coolant per hour. Obviously, this large amount of coolant is not required because the coolant in the system is continuously cooled and recirculated at that rate.

If a cooling system is to operate efficiently, it must receive regular routine maintenance. Most of the tests, adjustments, and repairs you will perform are relatively simple. But you will find that a knowledge of how a cooling system operates is essential for diagnosing problems.

Cooling System Operation Figure 8.1 shows coolant circulation in a cooling system. A *water pump*, driven by a belt from the crankshaft, circulates the coolant. The pump pulls coolant from the lower tank of the radiator through the lower hose. It then pushes the coolant through *water jackets* in the cylinder block. Water jackets consist of passages that surround the cylinders and combustion cham-

FIN AND TUBE

Figure 8.2 A section of a typical "tube and fin" radiator core. Coolant flowing through the tubes passes off heat to the tubes and fins. This heat, in turn, is passed off to the air that flows between the fins and tubes (Ford Motor Company).

bers. As the coolant passes through the block water jackets, it absorbs heat from the cylinder walls.

From the block, the coolant is directed upward into the cylinder head water jackets through holes in the head gasket. As the coolant passes through the head, it absorbs more heat from the combustion chambers and the valve seats. The hot coolant leaves the cylinder head through the upper hose and enters the upper tank of the radiator. The coolant then flows down through the radiator core, a section of which is shown in Figure 8.2. As the coolant flows through the tubes of the core, it passes off heat to the air flowing through the fins. To insure a constant flow of air through the radiator, a fan is attached to the water pump and rotates with it. When the coolant reaches the lower tank, it has cooled sufficiently to be recirculated.

Temperature Control The average liquid-cooled engine operates most efficiently when its temperature is in the 195°F to 240°F (90°C to 115°C) range. In the simple cooling system just described, the engine temperature will change with the outside air temperature and with the loads placed on the engine. To maintain engine temperature within the most efficient range, a *thermostat* is used. A thermo-

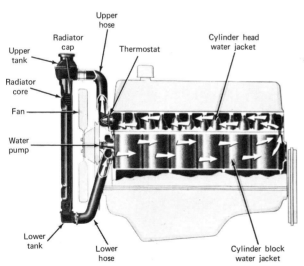

Figure 8.1 Sectioned view of a typical cooling system showing coolant circulation (Ford Motor Company).

Figure 8.3 Various types of thermostats (courtesy Chrysler Corporation).

stat, shown in Figure 8.3, is a heat-operated valve which regulates the amount of coolant that flows through the cooling system. A thermostat is placed in the system at the base of the upper radiator hose. (Refer to Figure 8.1).

When an engine is cold, the thermostat is closed. When the engine is started, the coolant cannot flow from the engine to the radiator. A small amount of coolant is circulated through the block and head by means of a bypass port. While the engine is warming up, this is the only coolant circulation in the system. A typical bypass port is shown in Figure 8.4.

When the coolant in the engine reaches a temperature of about 195°F (90°C), the thermostat starts to open. This allows some coolant to

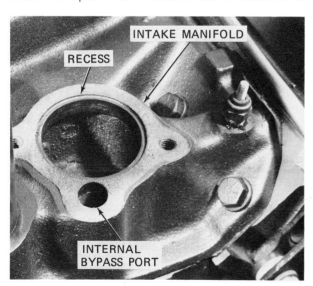

Figure 8.4 The water outlet port of a V-8 engine. The bypass port allows coolant to circulate through the engine when the thermostat is closed (courtesy American Motors Corporation).

flow through the radiator. As the engine temperature increases, the thermostat continues to open and the coolant flow increases. When the coolant reaches a temperature of from 215°F to 220°F (101°C to 104°C), the thermostat is completely open and full circulation is allowed.

If the outside air temperature is very low, the thermostat will open slowly, and may never open completely. This restricts coolant circulation and allows the engine temperature to remain as close as possible to the ideal range. If the outside air temperature is very high, the thermostat opens quickly and completely. This allows full circulation while maintaining the engine temperature within its most efficient range.

During average driving in moderate temperatures, the thermostat will automatically regulate the flow of coolant through the system. It will close slightly to restrict the flow when engine temperature drops. And it will open to increase the flow when engine temperature rises.

Pressure Control As you learned in a previous chapter, most cooling systems are pressurized. A pressurized cooling system is more efficient because it allows the coolant to absorb more heat without boiling. It also allows the coolant to dissipate more heat through the radiator.

The average pressure cap maintains a pressure of about 15 psi (103 kPa) in the system. Because a pressure of 1 psi (6.9 kPa) raises the boiling point of a liquid about 3°F (1.6°C), coolant in the system can be heated to over 250°F (121°C) without boiling.

If the pressure in a system exceeds the rating of the cap, a pressure valve in the cap opens, as shown in Figure 8.5. This allows pressurized coolant to escape through the overflow tube to the coolant recovery bottle. If the car does not have a coolant recovery system, the coolant is lost on the road.

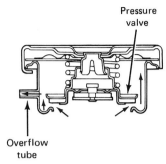

Figure 8.5 Pressure valve operation in a radiator pressure cap. The pressure valve is pushed off its seat and coolant escapes through the overflow tube (courtesy American Motors Corporation).

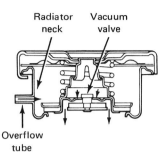

Figure 8.6 Vacuum valve operation in a radiator pressure cap. The vacuum valve is lifted off its seat and coolant returns through the overflow tube (courtesy American Motors Corporation).

As engine temperature drops, the coolant pressure drops. As the coolant contracts, it can form a partial vacuum in the system. As shown in Figure 8.6, the vacuum valve in the cap opens and allows coolant in the recovery system to return to the radiator. If the car does not have a coolant recovery system, air enters the system through the overflow tube until the system pressure is equalized.

Job 8a

IDENTIFY COOLING SYSTEM PARTS AND THEIR FUNCTION

SATISFACTORY PERFORMANCE

A satisfactory performance on this job requires that you do the following:

1 Identify the numbered parts on the drawing by placing the number of each part in front of the correct part name.
2 Identify the function of the numbered parts by placing the number of each part in front of the phrase that best describes its function.
3 Correctly identify all the parts and their functions within 15 minutes.

PERFORMANCE SITUATION

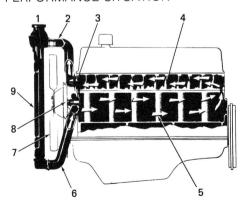

_____Radiator cap   _____Fan

_____Water pump   _____Thermostat

_____Upper hose   _____Recovery tank

_____Radiator   _____Lower hose

_____Cylinder head water   _____Cylinder block water
          jacket   jacket

_____Controls the circulation of coolant

_____Circulates coolant through the system

_____Transfers heat from the coolant to the air

_____Allows coolant to contact the outer surfaces of the cylinder
          walls

_____Carries the coolant from the engine to the radiator

_____Forces the coolant from the head to the block

_____Allows coolant to contact the outer surfaces of the combus-
          tion chambers and valve ports

_____Pulls air through the radiator core

_____Carries the coolant from the radiator to the engine

_____Maintains pressure in the system

COOLANT TESTING   As you learned in a previous chapter, coolant is a mixture of 50 percent water and 50 percent ethylene glycol. Very often you will find that the coolant in a cooling system has been diluted with water. There are two common causes of this dilution:

1 Coolant lost through a leak in the system was replaced by the addition of water.
2 The level of coolant in a system without a recovery bottle was repeatedly raised by the addition of water when the system was cold. When the coolant was heated, it expanded, and the excess coolant was forced out the overflow tube and was lost.

Figure 8.7 A coolant hydrometer, or antifreeze tester. With this type, the number on the float is aligned with the top of the thermometer column to provide temperature corrected freezing and boiling points (courtesy of E. Edelmann & Co., Skokie, Illinois 60076).

Figure 8.8 A dial indicating antifreeze tester. This type provides a temperature compensated direct reading (courtesy of E. Edelmann & Co., Skokie, Illinois 60076).

Diluted coolant may freeze in cold weather and may cause overheating in warm weather. To protect the cooling system and maintain its efficiency, the 50-50 ratio of the coolant mixture should be maintained. As with battery electrolyte, the specific gravity of coolant can be measured. This measurement can be used to determine if sufficient ethylene glycol is present in the coolant.

The specific gravity of coolant is measured with a special hydrometer. Various types of coolant hydrometers, usually called *antifreeze testers*, are available. Some of these testers are shown in Figures 8.7 and 8.8. As you learned when you measured the specific gravity of electolyte, some hydrometers require that you consider the temperature of the liquid. Other hydrometers automatically compensate for different temperatures.

An antifreeze tester is easy to use. A sample of the coolant is drawn into the tester from the upper radiator tank. The tester then indicates the freezing point of the coolant. Because you know that the freezing point of a 50-50 coolant mixture is about −34°F (−37°C), you can determine if the coolant contains sufficient ethylene glycol.

In addition to testing the "strength" of the coolant, an antifreeze tester provides you with a simple way to check the condition of the coolant. Because the body of the tester is usually made of clear glass or plastic, you can examine the coolant for contamination by dirt or rust. Some antifreeze testers contain a series of plastic balls of different weight. The number of balls that float in the coolant indicates its relative "strength." An antifreeze tester of this type is shown in Figure 8.9.

Most ethylene glycol sold as permanent anti-freeze contains a dye that gives it a yellow-green color. This color should be quite obvious in the coolant. If the coolant contains dirt or rust particles, or if it appears dark or dirty, it should be drained and discarded. The cooling system should be flushed to remove loose dirt and rust, and new coolant installed.

Figure 8.9 A pocket type coolant tester that is in common use. The degree of protection is measured by the number of floating balls (courtesy of Thexton Mfg. Co. Inc.).

TESTING COOLANT MIXTURE AND CONDITION The following steps outline a procedure for testing coolant. You should consult the instructions furnished with the anitfreeze tester you have available for the correct use of that instrument:

WARNING: NEVER REMOVE THE RADIATOR CAP WHILE THE ENGINE IS RUNNING. FAILURE TO FOLLOW THIS ADVICE COULD CAUSE SERIOUS BURNS AND POSSIBLE DAMAGE TO THE COOLING SYSTEM. BECAUSE SCALDING HOT COOLANT OR STEAM MAY ERUPT FROM THE RADIATOR FILLER NECK, USE EXTREME CARE WHEN REMOVING A RADIATOR FILLER CAP. IT IS BEST TO WAIT UNTIL THE ENGINE HAS COOLED.

1 Wrap a heavy rag or wiper around the radiator cap.

2 Turn the radiator cap counterclockwise until you feel it stop at its first "stop" or detent. This position releases the pressure in the system.

Note: If pressure is released, stand away from the radiator until you are sure that all pressure is released. Do not attempt to remove the cap in one motion. The pressure in the system could force hot coolant or steam to erupt from the filler neck.

3 Wiggle the cap to be sure that it is loose and has released all the pressure in the system.

4 Push down on the cap and slowly turn it counterclockwise to its second "stop" and lift the cap from the filler neck.

5 Insert the tester into the radiator and draw up a sufficient quantity of coolant to operate the tester.

Note: Some testers are accurate only when the coolant is at or near its normal operating temperature. Be sure to check the instructions furnished with the tester.

6 Read the tester to determine the freezing point of the coolant.

7 Hold the tester up to a light source and check the condition of the coolant.

8 Return the coolant sample to the radiator tank.

9 Repeat steps 5 through 8 to verify your findings.

10 Install the radiator cap.

Determining the Amount of Ethylene Glycol Required The chart shown in Figure 8.10 can be used to determine the amount of ethylene glycol in a cooling system. The capacity of the system and the approximate freezing point of the coolant are all you need to know. The cooling system capacity can be found in the owner's manual or a shop manual. The antifreeze tester provides the approximate freezing point.

COOLING SYSTEM CAPACITY (QUARTS)	QUARTS OF ETHYLENE GLYCOL							
	3	4	5	6	7	8	9	10
6	−34							
7	−17							
8	−7	−34						
9	0	−21						
10	4	−12	−34					
11	8	−6	−23					
12	10	0	−15	−34				
13		3	−9	−25				
14		6	−5	−17	−34			
15		8	0	−12	−26			
16		10	2	−7	−19	−34		
17			5	−4	−14	−27		
18			7	0	−10	−21	−34	
19			9	2	−7	−16	−26	
20			10	4	−3	−12	−22	−34
21				6	0	−9	−17	−28

Figure 8.10 A coolant mixture chart showing the freezing points of various mixtures. All temperatures are in degrees Fahrenheit.

COOLING SYSTEM CAPACITY (QUARTS)	QUARTS OF ETHYLENE GLYCOL							
	3	4	5	6	7	8	9	10
6	−34							
7	−17							
8	−7	−34						
9	0	−21						
10	4	−12	−34					
11	8	−6	−23					
12	10	0	−15	−34				
13		3	−9	−25				
14		6	−5	−17	−34			
15		8	0	−12	−26			
16		10	2	−7	−19	−34		
17			5	−4	−14	−27		
18			7	0	−10	−21	−34	
19			9	2	−7	−16	−26	
20			10	4	−3	−12	−22	−34
21				6	0	−9	−17	−28

Figure 8.11 An example of how the chart can be used to determine the amount of ethylene glycol in a cooling system.

To use the chart, simply read across the line provided for the capacity until you find the approximate freezing point. The number of quarts of ethylene glycol in the coolant is noted above that column.

Once you know how much ethylene glycol is in the coolant, you can easily determine how much, if any, additional ethylene glycol should be added to obtain a 50-50 mixture. The following is an example of how this chart can be used:

A test made of the coolant in a system containing 16 quarts indicates that it will provide protection against freezing down to a temperature of about −20°F (−29°C). As shown in Figure 8.11, in reading across the line for a system with a 16-quart capacity, you will find a box for −19°F. This column indicates that the system contains approximately 7 quarts of ethylene glycol. One additional quart of ethylene glycol should be added to restore the coolant to its correct 50-50 proportions.

Job 8b

TEST COOLANT MIXTURE AND CONDITION

SATISFACTORY PERFORMANCE

A satisfactory performance on this job requires that you do the following:

1 Test the mixture and condition of the coolant in the car assigned.
2 Following the steps in the "Performance Outline" and the instructions supplied with the tester used, complete the job within 15 minutes.
3 Fill in the blanks under "Information."

PERFORMANCE OUTLINE
1 Remove the radiator cap.
2 Determine the freezing point of the coolant.
3 Check the condition of the coolant.
4 Install the radiator cap.

INFORMATION

Vehicle identification _____

Reference used_____Page(s)_____

Cooling system capacity _____

Tester used _____

Indicated freezing point of coolant _____

Temperature of coolant tested _____Hot _____Cold

Is additional antifreeze required? _____Yes _____No

How much antifreeze should be added to bring the freezing point of the coolant to approximately −34°F (−37°C)?

_____

Is the coolant dirty? _____Yes _____No

Should the coolant be changed? _____Yes _____No

COOLING SYSTEM CLEANING Most automobile manufacturers recommend that cooling systems be drained, flushed, and re-filled with fresh coolant at intervals of about two years or 30,000 miles (48,000 km). The antifreeze and antiboil properties of the coolant may still be effective after that period of usage. But the rust and corrosion inhibitors in the mixture are usually depleted. In addition, a considerable amount of rust and dirt particles may be in the coolant. As those particles are circulated through the system, they may build up in certain passages and restrict coolant flow.

A properly maintained cooling system can usually be cleaned by use of a chemical cleaner. Chemical cleaners loosen and dissolve deposits of dirt, rust, and corrosion and hold them in suspension. When the cleaner is drained, the dissolved deposits are removed. Most chemical cleaners contain acids, and they should be handled with respect for the injury and damage that acids can inflict. Depending on the acid content, some cleaners require that the system be treated with a *neutralizer* following the cleaning process. The neutralizer stops the action of any acid that may remain in the system.

CLEANING A COOLING SYSTEM The following steps outline a procedure for cleaning a cooling system by using a chemical cleaner. Because the procedures for use vary with different chemical cleaners, you should carefully read and follow the instructions furnished with the particular cleaner you have available:

1 Drain the coolant from the system.

Note: Most cooling systems can be drained through a *petcock*, or valve, located in the lower radiator tank. Such a valve is shown in Figure 8.12. Although the petcock is located in the lowest part of the system, a considerable amount of coolant will remain in the block water jackets. On some engines, this coolant can be drained by removing threaded plugs from the water jackets. This type of plug and its location are shown in Figure 8.13. Because the plugs may be difficult to remove, many mechanics leave them in place and raise the rear of the car with a jack. This procedure allows more coolant to drain from the radiator petcock.

2 After the coolant has drained, close the petcock and fill the system with clean water to a level of about 2 inches (5 cm) below the base of the filler neck.

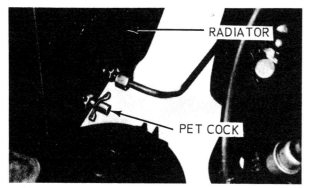

Figure 8.12 Most cooling systems can be drained by means of a petcock located in the lower radiator tank (Ford Motor Company).

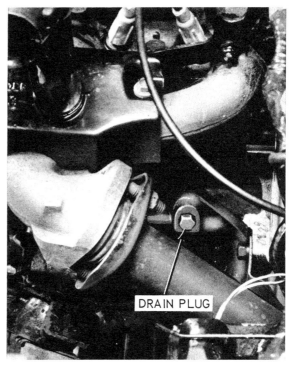

Figure 8.13 Some engines are fitted with plugs in the water jackets so that the coolant may be drained from the block (Ford Motor Company).

3 Apply the parking brake.

4 Place the transmission selector lever in the PARK position and start the engine.

5 Adjust the heater temperature control to its highest position. This allows circulation of coolant through the heating system.

6 Allow the engine to run until it reaches its normal operating temperature.

Note: Check the water level frequently during this period of operation. When the thermostat opens, the water level may drop. Adjust the water level as necessary.

7 Add the chemical cleaner.

8 Allow the engine to run at its normal operating temperature for the period of time specified by the instructions furnished within the cleaner.

9 Turn the engine off and drain the cleaning mixture.

10 After the cleaning mixture has drained, close the petcock and fill the system with clean water.

Note: Some cleaners require that a neutralizer be added to the water at this step.

11 Run the engine for the specified amount of time to dilute and neutralize the cleaner remaining in the system.

Note: **Be sure to check the water level frequently.**

12 Drain the water from the system.

Note: **It is advisable to raise the rear of the car so that sufficient water will drain from the system to allow for the addition of the ethylene glycol.**

13 Check an appropriate manual to determine the capacity of the cooling system.

14 Determine the amount of ethylene glycol required. (Most manufacturers recommend 50 percent of the system capacity.)

15 After the water has drained, close the petcock and add the required amount of ethylene glycol to the system.

16 Add water to the system to a level of about 2 inches (5 cm) below the base of the filler neck.

17 Start the engine and allow it to run until it reaches its normal operating temperature.

Note: **Check the coolant level frequently during this period of operation. When the thermostat opens, the water level may drop. Adjust the coolant level with water as necessary.**

18 Allow the engine to run and check the operation of the heater to be sure that hot coolant is circulating through the heater core.

19 Install the radiator cap.

20 Turn the engine off.

Job 8c

DRAIN, FLUSH, AND REFILL A COOLING SYSTEM

SATISFACTORY PERFORMANCE

A satisfactory performance on this job requires that you do the following:

1 Drain, flush, and refill the cooling system of the car assigned.
2 Following the steps in the "Performance Outline" and the instructions furnished with the chemical cleaner available, complete the job within 60 minutes plus the time required for the circulation of the cleaner.
3 Fill in the blanks under "Information."

PERFORMANCE OUTLINE
1 Drain the coolant.
2 Fill the system with fresh water and flush the system in accordance with the instructions furnished with the cleaner.

4 Add the required amount of ethylene glycol.

5 Adjust the coolant level with water.

6 Check the circulation of the coolant and readjust the coolant level if necessary.

INFORMATION

Vehicle identification _____

Reference used_____Page(s)_____

Chemical cleaner used _____

Was a neutralizer required? _____Yes _____No

Cooling system capacity _____

Amount of ethylene glycol added _____

COOLING SYSTEM LEAKAGE Any leakage in a cooling system can cause a loss of coolant, a loss of pressure, and overheating. A cooling system should be tested for leaks as part of routine maintenance. Many times, a system will not leak until it is hot and is operating near its maximum pressure. Those conditions can be duplicated in the shop by using a *pressure tester* similar to the one shown in Figure 8.14.

A pressure tester consists of a hand pump that can be attached to the radiator filler neck. A gauge on the tester enables you to pressurize the system to the maximum pressure the system will be subjected to in use. Figure 8.15 shows a pressure tester connected to a radiator. The tester can be used to test radiator pressure caps by means of an adapter. This test is shown in Figure 8.16.

Figure 8.14 A typical cooling system pressure tester and adapter (courtesy American Motors Corporation).

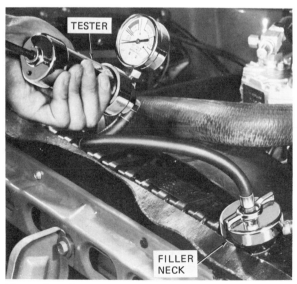

Figure 8.15 Pressure testing a cooling system (courtesy American Motors Corporation).

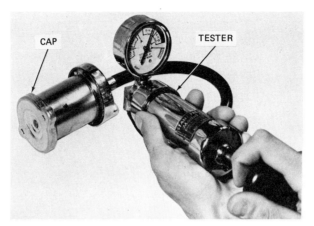

Figure 8.16 Testing a radiator pressure cap (courtesy American Motors Corporation).

PRESSURE TESTING A COOLING SYSTEM The following steps outline a typical procedure for pressure testing a cooling system. You should consult the instruction manual furnished with the tester you have available for any specific procedure that may be necessary for that instrument:

1 Apply the parking brake, place the transmission selector lever in PARK, and start the engine.

2 Allow the engine to run until it reaches its normal operating temperature.

3 Turn off the engine.

4 Wrap a heavy rag or wiper around the radiator cap.

5 Carefully remove the radiator cap.

Note: Do not attempt to remove the cap in one motion. Remember that the pressure in the system could force hot coolant to erupt from the radiator and cause you painful burns.

6 Carefully wipe out the inside of the filler neck and examine the *seat*, or sealing surface, in the neck for dirt or damage that could cause a faulty seal between the seat and the pressure cap. (See Figure 8.17.)

7 Locate the manufacturer's specified cooling system pressure in an appropriate manual.

Note: The pressure cap is usually marked to indicate its opening pressure. Because the cap may be a replacement with an incorrect pressure rating, you should not rely on the cap markings to indicate the system operating pressure.

8 Attach a pressure tester to the filler neck as you would install a radiator cap.

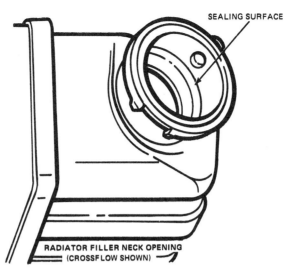

Figure 8.17 The seat inside the radiator filler neck provides the sealing surface for the pressure cap (Ford Motor Company).

9 Operate the tester pump until the gauge indicates that the system is pressurized to the specification. (Refer to Figure 8.15)

10 Observe the gauge:
   A. If the gauge needle holds steady and the pressure is maintained for at least two minutes, the system has no serious leaks.
   B. If the gauge needle drops slowly, seepage or small leaks are indicated. Use a drop light or a flashlight and examine all hoses, connections, and gaskets for leaks.
   C. If the gauge needle drops quickly, serious leaks are indicated.

11 Slowly release the pressure in the system.

Note: **This can be safely done on some testers by tipping the metal "stem" that connects the hose to the tester cap.**

PRESSURE TESTING A RADIATOR PRESSURE CAP The following steps outline a procedure for testing a radiator pressure cap. You should consult the instruction manual furnished with the tester you have available for any specific procedure which may be necessary for that instrument:

1 Clean the rubber seal inside the cap and check it for any dirt or damage that could cause it to leak. (See Figure 8.18.)

2 Wet the rubber seal with water and install the cap on the adapter as you would to install the cap on the radiator.

3 Attach the adapter to the pressure tester.

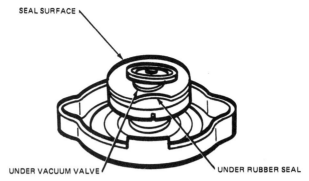

Figure 8.18 Parts of a pressure cap that require cleaning and inspecting (Ford Motor Company).

Note: Some testers require an adjustment before the tester can be fitted to the adapter. Other testers require the use of a spacer washer. The correct method for fitting the adapter is described in the instruction manual furnished with the tester.

4 Operate the tester pump until the gauge indicates its highest reading. (Refer to Figure 8.16.) This reading indicates the cap release pressure and should agree with the manufacturer's specification.

5 Observe the gauge:
    A. If the gauge needle holds steady and pressure is maintained for at least 30 seconds, the cap is in good condition.
    B. If the gauge needle drops rapidly, the cap is defective.

6 Remove the cap from the tester.

Job 8d

PRESSURE TEST A COOLING SYSTEM AND RADIATOR CAP

SATISFACTORY PERFORMANCE

A satisfactory performance on this job requires that you do the following:

1 Pressure test the cooling system and the radiator cap of the car assigned.
2 Following the steps in the "Performance Outline" and the instructions furnished with the tester used, complete the job within 15 minutes.
3 Fill in the blanks under "Information."

PERFORMANCE OUTLINE
1 Bring the engine up to its normal operating temperature.
2 Install the pressure tester.

3 Pressurize the system to the manufacturer's specified pressure.
4 Observe the pressure gauge and locate any leaks indicated.
5 Remove the pressure tester.
6 Using the adapter, pressure test the cap.
7 Remove the cap from the tester and install the cap on the radiator.

INFORMATION

Vehicle identification _____

Reference used_____Page(s)_____

Cooling system operating pressure specification _____

Hoses As you know, the radiator and the engine are connected by hoses. These hoses allow the engine to vibrate and to move slightly in its mounts without damaging the radiator. The radiator hoses installed by car manufacturers as original equipment are usually *molded*, or curved. A pair of molded hoses installed on a radiator is shown in Figure 8.19. Molded hoses are formed to a definite shape so that they will clear the fan and other parts at the front of the engine. Although molded hoses are available as replacement parts, many mechanics use flexible hoses of the type shown in Figure 8.20. These hoses are reinforced with steel wire and can be bent

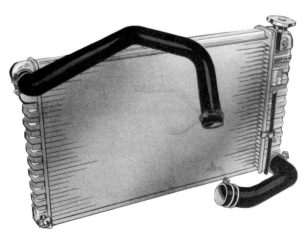

Figure 8.19 A pair of molded radiator hoses correctly positioned on a radiator (Oldsmobile Division, GM).

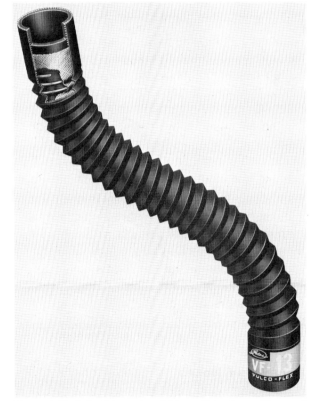

Figure 8.20 A flexible or bendable radiator hose. Hoses of this type can be used to replace many of the molded types (The Gates Rubber Company, Denver, Colorado 80217).

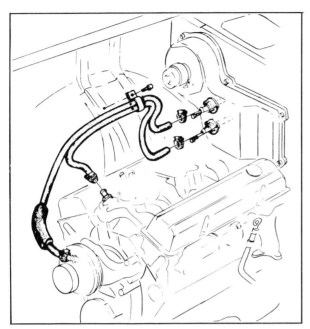

Figure 8.21 Typical heater hose locations. Note that the hose from the upper fitting on the engine is connected to the lower fitting on the heater core (Chevrolet Service Manual, Chevrolet Motor Division, GM).

to duplicate the curves of many molded hoses.

As shown in Figure 8.21, hoses also connect the engine to the heater. These hoses, usually called *heater hoses*, allow hot coolant to circulate through a small radiator called a *heater core*. Air passing through the heater core is heated and used to warm the passenger compartment. Although some heater hoses may be of molded construction, in most instances they are cut from straight lengths of flexible hose.

The hoses in the cooling system are repeatedly subjected to movement, vibration, and extremes in temperature and pressure. Thus, they have a limited service life. Routine maintenance requires that the hoses in a cooling system be inspected at regular intervals. Most manufacturers suggest that all hoses and their connections be checked at least once each year or every 15,000 miles (24,000 km).

Inspecting Hoses A careful check of the hoses in a cooling system may reveal leaks or damage and deterioration which could cause a hose to fail in service. Any hose that fails to pass the following inspections should be replaced:

Visual Inspection Using a drop light or a flashlight, check the outer surface of the hoses. Look for coolant stains and other signs of leakage. Check for cracks, exposed cords, and damage by abrasion. The hoses should appear smooth with no signs of swelling, blisters, or bubbles. Connect a pressure tester to the system and check for leakage, swelling, and blisters while the system is pressurized.

Manual Inspection Remove the pressure tester and squeeze the hoses. They should be firm but not hard. A hose that feels hard is usually brittle and may crack if it is bent. A hose that is rotted internally usually feels soft or spongy. A hose that feels slippery or oily may have been softened by oil or fuel spills.

Hose Clamps A hose that is in good condition will often leak at its connection to the engine or radiator. The clamp holding the hose to its fitting may be loose or defective. Tightening or replacing the clamp may eliminate the leak. Several types of clamps are in common use.

Radial-Type Hose Clamps Clamps of this type, shown in Figure 8.22, are used by many manufacturers as original equipment. A clamp of this type can usually be tightened with a screwdriver. If the clamp is rusted or corroded so that an adjustment cannot be made, it should be replaced. The use of a tool similar to the one shown in Figure 8.23 will enable you to cut off the defective clamp without damage to the hose.

"Perma-Quik" Hose Clamps At times you will find heater hoses and water pump bypass hoses that are secured with clamps of this

Figure 8.22 A radial-type hose clamp (courtesy of K-D Tools).

type. Shown in Figure 8.24, these clamps are designed for one-time use. They are *crimped*, or squeezed, on the hose and are not adjustable. Clamps of this type can be easily removed by cutting them off with a tool similar to the one shown in Figure 8.25.

Screw-Drive Hose Clamps   Clamps of this type, shown in Figure 8.26, are commonly used to replace clamps used as original equipment. Sometimes called *Whittek clamps*, they provide a positive grip over a wide range

of adjustment. In addition, clamps of this type can be opened, allowing you to install them without removing the hose.

Corbin Hose Clamps   Made of heavy spring-steel wire as shown in Figure 8.27, a Corbin clamp is another type of clamp in common use. A Corbin clamp is self-tightening and self-adjusting. A special pair of *hose clamp pliers*, similar to those shown in Figure 8.28, should be used to remove and install a clamp of this type.

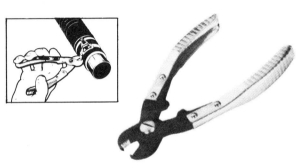

Figure 8.23 A special cutter for removing radial-type hose clamps without damaging the hose. The insert shows how the tool is used (courtesy of K-D Tools).

Figure 8.26 A screw-drive or "Wittek" hose clamp (The Gates Rubber Company, Denver, Colorado 80217).

Figure 8.24 A "Perma-Quik" hose clamp. This type clamp is crimped in place and is not reusable (courtesy of K-D Tools).

Figure 8.27 A Corbin clamp. Clamps of this type are self-tightening (courtesy of K-D Tools).

Figure 8.25 A special cutter for removing "Perma-Quik" hose clamps (courtesy of K-D Tools).

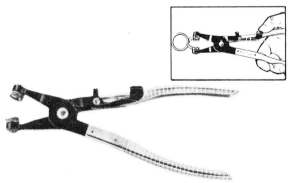

Figure 8.28 Hose clamp pliers used to remove and install Corbin clamps. The insert shows how the pliers are used to grip and expand a clamp (courtesy of K-D Tools).

REPLACING RADIATOR HOSES The following steps outline a procedure for replacing radiator hoses in a typical cooling system:

Removal 1 Drain the coolant into a suitable clean container.

2 Loosen or remove the clamps at the ends of the hose to be replaced.

3 Twist the hose to break its bond with its connections and slide it off the fittings.

Note: Do not force a hose off the fittings, because you may cause damage. If a hose is tight on its fittings, use a sharp knife to carefully split the hose.

Installation 1 Compare the replacement hose with the hose you removed and determine its position.

2 Clean all traces of dirt and old sealer from the hose fittings.

3 Place the clamps on the hose.

Note: Most mechanics prefer to use new clamps when replacing a hose. The old clamps may not provide for a leakproof connection.

4 Install the hose on its fittings, aligning it so that it clears the fan, the belts, and the other parts at the front of the engine.

Note: Some manufacturers advise coating the fittings with a water-resistant sealer before installing a hose.

5 Slide the clamps so that they are positioned approximately ¼ of 1 inch (about 6 mm) from the ends of the hose as shown in Figure 8.29.

6 Tighten the clamps.

Note: Be sure that the *bead*, or ridge, on the fitting is not under the clamp. The clamp should be between the bead and the end of the hose as shown in Figure 8.30.

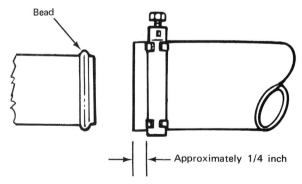

Bead

Approximately 1/4 inch

Figure 8.29 A hose clamp should be positioned so that it is about ¼ inch (6 mm) from the end of the hose (Ford Motor Company).

BEAD UNDER HOSE

Figure 8.30 The clamp should be tightened so that it is between the bead on the fitting and the end of the hose (Ford Motor Company).

7 Fill the system with the drained coolant.

8 Apply the parking brake, place the shift selector lever in PARK or NEUTRAL, and start the engine.

9 Allow the engine to run until the normal operating temperature is reached.

Note: Be sure to check the coolant level repeatedly during the warm-up. The level may drop when the thermostat opens.

10 Turn the engine off.

11 Pressure test the system for leaks.

REPLACING HEATER HOSES The following steps outline a procedure for replacing heater hoses:

Removal 1 Drain the coolant into a suitable clean container.

2 Loosen or remove the clamps at the ends of the hose to be replaced.

3 Twist the hose to break its bond with the fittings, and remove the hose.

Note: Do not attempt to remove a heater hose by force. The fittings at the heater core are easily damaged. If a hose is tight on its fittings, use a sharp knife to carefully split the hose.

4 Free the hose from any brackets or straps that position the hose. (Refer to Figure 8.21.)

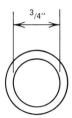

Figure 8.31 Hose size is determined by the inside diameter. The two most commonly used heater hose sizes are ⅝ inch and ¾ inch.

Installation   1 Determine the diameter of the replacement hose required.

Note: Hose size is determined by its inside diameter, as shown in Figure 8.31. The most commonly used sizes are ⅝ inch and ¾ inch.

2 Cut a length of replacement hose to match the length of the hose you removed.

Note: Some mechanics prefer to cut the new hose a few inches longer than the old hose. If the hose proves to be too long, it can be trimmed on installation.

3 Clean all traces of dirt and old sealer from the hose fittings.

4 Place the clamps on the hose.

Note: Most mechanics prefer to use new clamps when replacing a hose. The old clamps may not provide for the leakproof connection.

5 Position the hose in its retaining brackets or straps. (Refer to Figure 8.21.)

6 Install the hose on its connections, aligning it so that it is clear of the exhaust manifold and any other parts which may cause wear or damage.

Note: Some manufacturers advise coating the connections with a water-resistant sealer before installing a hose.

7 Slide the clamps so that they are positioned approximately ¼ of 1 inch (about 6 mm) from the ends of the hose. (Refer to Figure 8.29.)

8 Tighten the clamps.

Note: Be sure that the bead, or ridge, on the fitting is not under the clamp. The clamp should be between the bead and the end of the hose. (Refer to Figure 8.30.)

9 Fill the system with the drained coolant.

10 Apply the parking brake, place the shift selector lever in the PARK or NEUTRAL position, and start the engine.

11 Allow the engine to run until it reaches its normal operating temperature.

Note: Be sure to check the coolant level repeatedly during warm-up. The level may drop when the thermostat opens.

12 Position the heater controls in the HEAT position and check the operation of the heater.

13 Turn the engine off.

14 Pressure test the system for leaks.

Job 8e

REPLACE COOLING SYSTEM HOSES

SATISFACTORY PERFORMANCE

A satisfactory performance on this job requires that you do the following:

1 Replace the designated hose(s) on the car assigned.

2 Following the steps in the "Performance Outline" and the procedure and specifications of the manufacturer, complete the job within 200 percent of the time suggested by the manufacturer.

3 Fill in the blanks under "Information."

PERFORMANCE OUTLINE

1 Drain the coolant.

2 Remove the designated hose(s).

3 Install the replacement hose(s).

4 Check the operation of the system.

5 Pressure test the system.

INFORMATION

Vehicle identification _____

Reference used_____ Page(s)_____

Hose(s) replaced _____Upper radiator _____Lower radiator

_____Heater supply _____Heater return

_____Water pump bypass

Heater hose size _____ ⅝ in. _____ ¾ in.

Cooling system pressure specification_____

Cooling system was tested to _____

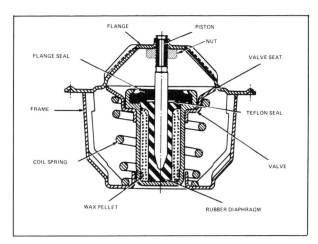

Figure 8.32 Sectional view of a thermostat (Pontiac Motor Division, GM).

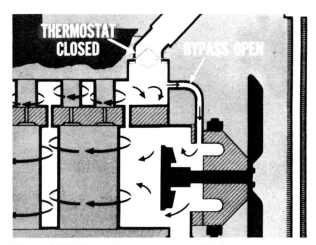

Figure 8.33 When the coolant is cold, the thermostat is closed. The coolant does not flow through the radiator, but is pumped through the water jackets (courtesy Chrysler Corporation).

THERMOSTATS A thermostat is an automatic valve that controls the flow of coolant in the cooling system. The parts of a typical thermostat are shown in Figure 8.32. The valve is actuated by the expansion of a temperature-sensitive material sealed within a cup and piston assembly. When the assembly is heated, the valve opens. When the assembly cools, the temperature-sensitive material contracts and allows a spring to close the valve.

When the engine, and thus the coolant, is cold, the valve remains closed. This prevents the coolant from circulating through the radiator. By means of a bypass, coolant circulates only through the water jackets, as shown in Figure 8.33. This allows the engine to warm up quickly and evenly. As the coolant temperature rises, the valve opens slightly and allows coolant to flow through the radiator. Depending on the temperature of the coolant, the valve opens and closes, permitting the flow of sufficient coolant to keep the engine operating temperature within the specified limits.

Diagnosing Thermostat Problems If the valve in a thermostat remains open or partially open, the following problems may occur:

1 Extended engine warm-up time
2 Engine operating temperature below specifications
3 Insufficient heat from the heater
4 Unacceptable levels of exhaust emissions

If the valve of a thermostat remains closed or does not open sufficiently, the following problems may occur:

1 Overheating
2 Coolant loss
3 Internal engine damage

You may occasionally find that the thermostat is missing from the cooling system of some cars. The thermostat may have been removed by someone in an attempt to "cure" a problem of overheating. A thermostat, even when wide open, provides a restriction in the cooling system. That restriction is designed to slow down the flow of coolant and insure complete circulation through the water jackets.

If the thermostat is removed, coolant flow to the rear of the water jackets is usually decreased. This results in uneven engine temperatures. The front cylinders may be overcooled, whereas the cylinders at the rear of the engine may not be cooled enough. Uneven engine temperatures result in engine wear and damage caused by improper lubrication and improper combustion.

An engine should not be operated without a thermostat in the cooling system. If an engine overheats continuously when the proper thermostat is installed, the thermostat is usually not the cause of the problem. Overheating can be caused by many things including plugged radiator core tubes, improper fan operation, and clogged water jackets. These and many other causes are listed in appropriate service manuals together with the required repairs.

A coolant thermometer similar to the one shown in Figure 8.34 will help you to deter-

Figure 8.34 A typical coolant thermometer (courtesy of K-D Tools).

mine if a thermostat is operating correctly. When inserted in the filler neck of the radiator, it provides you with a fairly accurate measurement of coolant temperature.

REPLACING THERMOSTATS The following steps outline a typical procedure for replacing a thermostat. Because of the many variations in thermostat mounting and placement, you should consult an appropriate manual for the specific procedures and specifications required for the car on which you are working:

Removal 1 Drain the coolant into a suitable clean container.

2 Disconnect the upper radiator hose from the coolant outlet connection. (See Figure 8.35.)

3 Using a socket wrench, remove the bolts that hold the outlet connection to the engine. (See Figure 8.36.)

4 Remove the coolant outlet and the thermostat.

Installation 1 Clean all traces of sealer and old gasket material from the outlet connection and its mating surface on the engine.

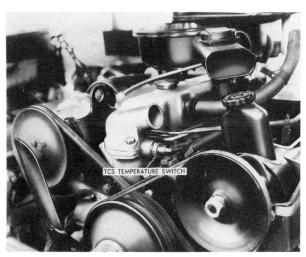

Figure 8.35 The hose should be disconnected from the water outlet before attempting to remove the thermostat (Chevrolet Service Manual, Chevrolet Motor Division, GM).

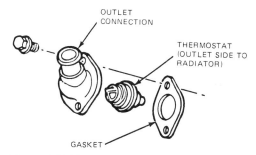

Figure 8.36 Disassembled view of the coolant outlet, thermostat, and gasket (Ford Motor Company).

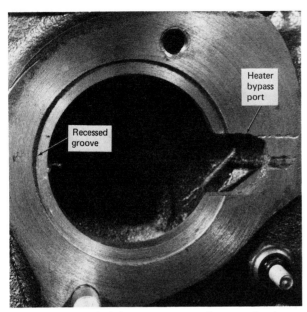

Figure 8.37 A typical thermostat recess in an engine (courtesy American Motors Corporation).

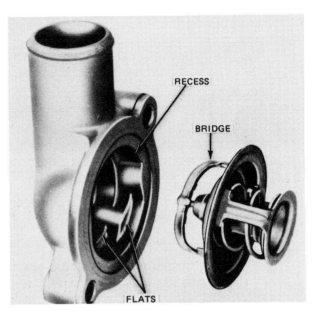

Figure 8.38 A thermostat recess formed in the coolant outlet connection. This outlet also has flats into which the thermostat can be locked to insure proper installation (Ford Motor Company).

2 Check the replacement thermostat to be sure that it is the correct type and that it has the correct opening temperature.

Note: Most thermostats are marked with their opening temperature.

3 Install the thermostat so that the actuating pellet is toward the engine. Most thermostats are marked to indicate the correct position.

Note: The outer edge of a thermostat fits into a recess. On some cars the recess is in the engine, as shown in Figure 8.37. On other cars the recess is in the outlet connection, as shown in Figure 8.38. If the thermostat is not seated in this recess, the outlet connection may crack when the bolts are tightened. Some mechanics place a few small dabs of assembly cement on the rim of the thermostat to insure that it will stay in place in the recess during assembly. Some manufacturers provide a means of locking the thermostat in the recess. The thermostat is inserted in the outlet connection and turned clockwise to lock it in place. (Refer to Figure 8.38.)

4 Coat a new gasket with water-resistant sealer and position the gasket over the thermostat.

5 Position the outlet connection over the engine and install the attaching bolts.

Note: Be careful not to dislodge the thermostat from its position in the recess.

6 Tighten the bolts to the torque specification of the manufacturer.

7 Connect the upper hose.

8 Fill the system with the drained coolant.

9 Pressure test the system for leaks.

10 Apply the parking brake and place the shift selector lever in PARK or NEUTRAL. Start the engine and allow it to run until its normal operating temperature is reached.

Note: **Be sure to check the coolant level repeatedly during the warm-up. The level may drop when the thermostat opens.**

11 Check the temperature of the coolant.

Job 8f

REPLACE A THERMOSTAT

SATISFACTORY PERFORMANCE

A satisfactory performance on this job requires that you do the following:

1 Replace the thermostat in the cooling system of the car assigned.

2 Following the steps in the "Performance Outline" and the procedure and specifications of the manufacturer, complete the job within 200 percent of the manufacturer's suggested time.

3 Fill in the blanks under "Information."

PERFORMANCE OUTLINE

1 Drain the coolant.

2 Disconnect the upper hose.

3 Remove the thermostat.

4 Install the replacement thermostat.

5 Connect the upper hose.

6 Install the coolant.

7 Pressure test the system.

8 Check the operation of the system.

INFORMATION

Vehicle identification _____

Reference used_____Page(s)_____

Manufacturer's specifications for

    Thermostat opening temperature _____

    Coolant outlet connection bolt torque _____

System operating pressure_____

Opening temperature of thermostat installed_____

Location of thermostat recess _____coolant outlet

_____engine

System pressure tested to _____

Coolant temperature at completion of test _____

FAN BELTS Many engine accessories, including the fan and the water pump, are driven by V-belts. These belts are turned by a pulley on the front of the engine crankshaft. On most cars, the fan is attached to the water pump shaft. Thus, the fan and the water pump are driven by the same belt. In addition to driving the fan and the water pump, most *fan belts* also drive the *alternator*, or generator. Figure 8.39 shows some typical belt arrangements. A failure of the fan belt results in the failure of both the cooling and the charging systems. An inspection and adjustment of the fan belt should be considered a part of routine maintenance.

Inspecting Fan Belts Before any attempt to adjust a belt is made, the belt should be inspected. The underside of the belt should have no cracks. If cracks are found, the belt should be replaced. The tapered sides of the belt should be smooth. A loose belt slips, and some slipping belts develop *glazing*. A belt is glazed when its sides have a shiny, glass-like surface. A glazed belt will continue to slip, even after it has been properly adjusted. For this reason, a glazed belt should be replaced. In most cases an oil-soaked belt indicates that the seal at the end of the crankshaft is leaking. An oil-soaked belt must also be replaced, and the location of the leak must be found and the required repair performed.

A loose belt cannot drive the fan, water pump, and alternator at the proper speed. Therefore, a belt that is not cracked, glazed, or oil soaked should be adjusted to increase its tension. Most fan belts are adjusted by moving the alternator in or out on its mountings. This oper-

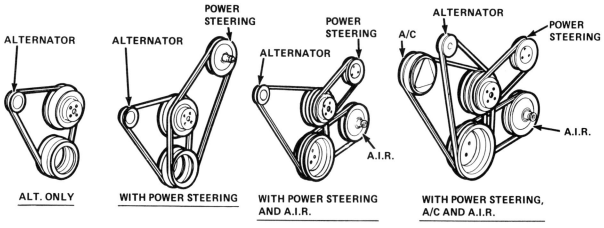

Figure 8.39 Typical belt arrangements (Pontiac Motor Division, GM).

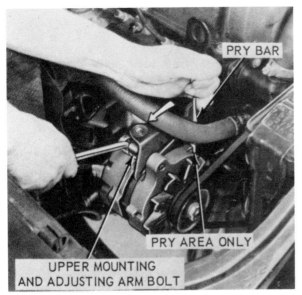

Figure 8.40 On most cars, the fan belt tension is adjusted by prying the alternator outward in its mountings (Ford Motor Company).

Figure 8.41 A typical belt tension gauge (courtesy American Motors Corporation).

ation is shown in Figure 8.40.

Most manufacturers specify the tension to which the belts on their cars should be adjusted. After a belt is inspected, its tension should be measured. Such measurement is possible through the use of a *belt tension gauge*. A typical belt tension gauge is shown in Figure 8.41. The gauge is positioned on the belt as shown in Figure 8.42. The tension indicated on the gauge should be compared with the specifications. If the tension is within the specified range, no adjustment is necessary. If the tension is too low or too high, an adjustment is required.

Figure 8.42 Installing a belt tension gauge on the fan belt. The gauge is placed between the alternator and the water pump (Chevrolet Service Manual, Chevrolet Motor Division, GM).

ADJUSTING A FAN BELT The following steps outline a typical procedure for adjusting a fan belt. You should consult an appropriate manual for the particular procedure and specifications that may be necessary for the car on which you are working:

1 Position a belt tension gauge on the fan belt as shown in Figure 8.43.

2 Loosen the adjustment nuts or bolts on the alternator slightly so that the alternator can be moved on its mountings.

3 Carefully pry the alternator outward until the correct tension is indicated on the gauge.

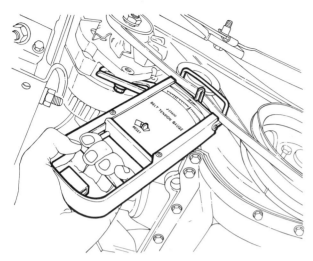

Figure 8.43 Checking fan belt tension with a belt tension gauge. As shown, in some instances it is easier to check the belt tension from under the car (courtesy American Motors Corporation).

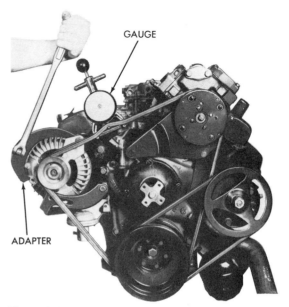

Figure 8.44 Adjusting the tension of a belt using a special tool to grasp the alternator (courtesy Chrysler Corporation).

Note: Some manufacturers provide a special tool that is used with a ½-inch drive ratchet or breaker bar. Such a tool and its use is shown in Figure 8.44.

4 Tighten the adjustment bolts or nuts to the manufacturer's torque specification while maintaining the correct belt tension.

5 Remove the belt tension gauge.

Job 8g

ADJUST A FAN BELT

SATISFACTORY PERFORMANCE

A satisfactory performance on this job requires that you do the following:

1 Adjust the fan belt tension on the car assigned.
2 Following the steps in the "Performance Outline" and the manufacturer's procedure and specifications, complete the job within 200 percent of the manufacturer's suggested time.
3 Fill in the blanks under "Information."

PERFORMANCE OUTLINE

1 Measure the belt tension.
2 Compare the tension with the specifications.
3 Loosen the adjustment bolts or nuts.
4 Adjust the belt tension to the specification.
5 Tighten the nuts or bolts to the torque specification.

6 Remove the gauge.

INFORMATION

Vehicle identification _____

Reference used_____ Page(s)_____

Belt tension specification _____

Belt tension at the start of the job_____

Belt tension at the completion of the job _____

SUMMARY

By completing this chapter you have gained knowledge of the operation of the cooling system. By performing the jobs you have developed skills needed to maintain the system. You can identify cooling system parts and their function. You can test coolant and pressure test a radiator cap and a cooling system. And you can drain and flush a system and refill it with the proper coolant mixture. You can also locate and replace leaking hoses, replace thermostats, and adjust fan belts. Your achievements have brought you closer to your goals.

SELF-TEST

Each incomplete statement or question in this test is followed by four suggested completions or answers. In each case select the *one* that best completes the sentence or answers the question.

1 Two mechanics are discussing the operation of a cooling system.
   Mechanic A says that coolant flows down from the upper radiator tank through the upper hose and into the water jackets in the cylinder head.
   Mechanic B says that the speed of the water pump is controlled by the thermostat.
   Who is right?
   A. A only

B. B only
C. Both A and B
D. Neither A nor B

2 To maintain engine temperature within a certain range, most cooling systems use
   A. a radiator
   B. a thermostat
   C. a water pump
   D. water jackets

3 When the thermostat is closed, water is circulated through the engine water jackets by means of
   A. a bypass
   B. the upper hose
   C. the lower hose
   D. a restrictor valve

4 The coolant mixture specified by most manufacturers consists of
   A. 30 percent water and 70 percent ethylene glycol
   B. 40 percent water and 60 percent ethylene glycol
   C. 50 percent water and 50 percent ethylene glycol
   D. 60 percent water and 40 percent ethylene glycol

5 On most cars, the petcock for draining the cooling system is located in the
   A. block water jacket
   B. thermostat housing
   C. lower radiator tank
   D. water outlet connection

6 When pressure testing a cooling system, the
   A. coolant should be drained
   B. thermostat should be removed
   C. fan belt should be adjusted to the correct tension
   D. engine should be at its normal operating temperature

7 Two mechanics are discussing hoses used in cooling systems.
   Mechanic A says that most radiator hoses are of molded construction.
   Mechanic B says that most heater hoses are cut from straight lengths of hose.
   Who is right?
   A. A only
   B. B only
   C. Both A and B
   D. Neither A nor B

8 The most commonly used sizes of heater hose are
   A. ⅜ inch and ½ inch
   B. ½ inch and ⅝ inch
   C. ⅝ inch and ¾ inch
   D. ¾ inch and ⅞ inch

9 A self-tightening hose clamp made of heavy steel wire is usually referred to as a
   A. Corbin hose clamp
   B. Screw-drive hose clamp
   C. Radial-type hose clamp
   D. Perma-Quik hose clamp

10 Two mechanics are discussing the installation of a thermostat.
   Mechanic A says that the thermostat should be fitted into a recess either in the coolant outlet connection or in the engine.
   Mechanic B says that the thermostat should be installed so that the temperature-sensitive pellet or cup faces the radiator.
   Who is right?
   A. A only
   B. B only
   C. Both A and B
   D. Neither A nor B

Chapter 9
Wheel Bearing Service

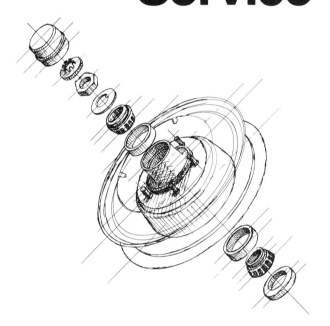

Wheel bearings should be serviced at intervals of from 20,000 to 40,000 miles (32,000 to 64,000 km) and as a part of every brake job. The specified service interval for any car is found in the manufacturer's manual for that car.

Worn or improperly adjusted wheel bearings can cause problems which may appear to be in the steering, suspension, or braking systems. The diagnosis of any problems in these systems should include a check of the wheel bearings. Wheel bearing service includes some simple but important jobs. This chapter will cover those jobs and the importance of performing them correctly. Your specific objectives are to perform the following jobs:

1
Identify wheel bearings and related parts.
2
Identify the function of front hub parts.
3
Adjust wheel bearings.
4
Repack wheel bearings on vehicles with drum brakes.
5
Repack wheel bearings on vehicles with disc brakes.
6
Replace a bearing cup.

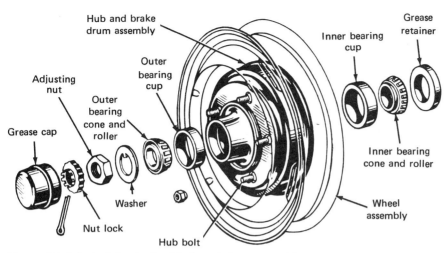

Figure 9.1 A typical front wheel hub and drum assembly showing all component parts in the order of their assembly (Ford Motor Company).

FRONT WHEEL BEARINGS The front wheels of a car are mounted on *hubs*. A hub provides the means for mounting a wheel so that it will rotate on the spindle. The hub is made of cast iron and contains two bearings. These bearings allow the hub to rotate freely, even with the weight of the car pressing down on the wheels.

On cars that have drum brakes, the front drums are mounted on the hubs. A typical hub and drum assembly is shown in Figure 9.1. Study the drawing carefully. To correctly perform the jobs in this chapter, you must be familiar with all the parts and their names.

Bearings The bearings used in front wheels are sometimes referred to as *anti-friction bearings*. These bearings use balls or rollers to provide rolling friction. Rolling friction allows the wheel to rotate very easily on the spindle. The bearings in Figure 9.1 are *tapered roller bearings*. The rollers themselves are tapered, and they roll on a tapered *race*, or ring, which is also called a *cone*. The rollers are held in place on the cone by a *cage*, which is a metal band with a slot for each roller. The cage also keeps the rollers from contacting each other.

The cone, rollers, and cage are assembled as a unit, as shown in Figure 9.2. This allows you to remove the bearing as an assembly without having to work with separate pieces.

There are two cone-and-roller assemblies in each hub. The inner assembly is installed from the rear of the hub. It is the larger of the two. The outer cone-and-roller assembly is the smaller. It is accessible without removing the hub from the spindle. The cone-and-roller assemblies are easily removed.

Bearing Cups The bearing *cups* provide a hard, smooth surface on which the bearing rollers can roll. A bearing cup forms the outer race for the bearing and is tapered to match the taper of the rollers. You can see one of those cups in Figure 9.3. Even though the cups are separate from the cone-and-roller assemblies, they are actually a part of the bearing. They should be replaced any time the cone-and-roller assemblies are replaced.

Grease Retainers The grease retainer, or grease seal, shown in Figure 9.4, is a seal that serves to keep the wheel bearing grease from leaking out. Such leakage would contaminate the brake lining and cause braking problems. The grease retainer fits into the rear of the hub, behind the inner bearing assembly. Grease retainers should be replaced each time the wheel bearings are repacked with grease.

The Spindle Washer The washer, which is flat, fits near the end of the spindle and is very important. In Figure 9.5 you will notice that the washer has a little *key*, or tab, on the inside. This key fits into a *keyway*, or groove, on the spindle and keeps the washer from turning. The washer separates the outer bearing assembly from the adjusting nut. If the bearing assembly were in contact with the nut, it could act to turn the nut.

The Adjusting Nut The adjusting nut, pictured in Figure 9.6, holds the parts of the hub assembly on the spindle and in the proper position. Turning the nut to the right or to the left tightens or loosens the bearings in their cups.

The Nut Lock The nut lock is a pressed steel cover that fits over the adjusting nut. As

shown in Figure 9.7, the nut lock has *castellations*, or notches. Those castellations allow the nut to be locked in any desired position. You will find that some cars do not use nut locks. Some adjusting nuts are castellated and thus do not require additional locks. The nut lock is used by most manufacturers however, and you will find that it allows you to obtain a more accurate wheel bearing adjustment than you can obtain with a castellated adjusting nut.

The Cotter Pin The cotter pin, shown in Figure 9.8, is used to secure the nut lock. It passes through a hole drilled through the end of the spindle, and holds the nut lock by its castellations.

The Grease Cap The grease cap, or hub cap, seals the open end of the hub. Although it does serve to keep the grease in the hub, its primary job is to keep dirt and water out. A car should never be placed in service without grease caps. Figure 9.9 shows a typical grease cap.

Figure 9.2 A typical cone-and-roller assembly (Ford Motor Company).

Figure 9.5 A spindle washer. Note the tab, or key, that fits into the keyway on the spindle (Ford Motor Company).

Figure 9.3 A typical bearing cup (Ford Motor Company).

Figure 9.6 An adjusting nut (Ford Motor Company).

Figure 9.4 A grease retainer, or grease seal (Ford Motor Company).

Castellations

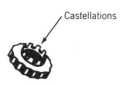

Figure 9.7 A nut lock (Ford Motor Company).

Figure 9.8 A cotter pin (Ford Motor Company).

Figure 9.9 A typical grease cap, or hub cap (Ford Motor Company).

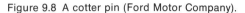

Job 9a

IDENTIFY WHEEL BEARINGS AND RELATED PARTS

SATISFACTORY PERFORMANCE
A satisfactory performance on this job requires that you do the following:

1 Identify the numbered parts on the drawing by placing the number of each part in front of the correct part name.
2 Correctly identify all the parts within 15 minutes.

PERFORMANCE SITUATION

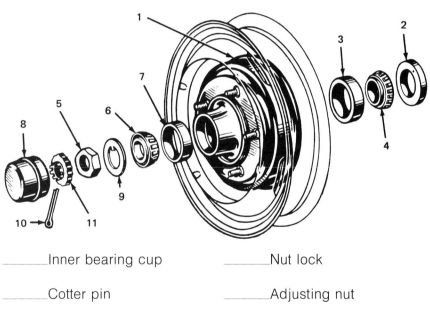

_____ Inner bearing cup	_____ Nut lock
_____ Cotter pin	_____ Adjusting nut
_____ Spindle shim	_____ Hub assembly
_____ Washer	_____ Grease retainer
_____ Outer bearing assembly	_____ Grease cap
_____ Outer bearing cup	_____ Inner bearing assembly

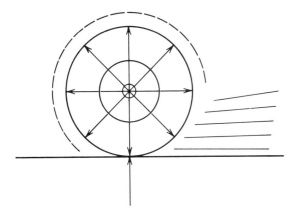

Figure 9.10 A radial load on a wheel.

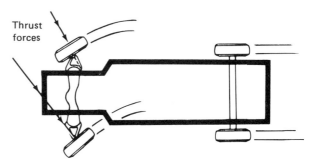

Figure 9.11 Side thrust forces on front wheels during cornering (courtesy American Motors Corporation).

Bearing Loads Wheel bearings are subjected to two major forces. These are radial loads and thrust loads. A *radial* load is a load that acts perpendicular, or at a right angle, to the axis of the wheel. The weight of the car pushes down on the road in a straight line from the spindle to the road. When the wheel rotates, this load still pushes straight down, but the force is carried by another part of the wheel. If you could see these lines of force, they would look like spokes in a wheel. They would radiate from the spindle to the tread of the tire as shown in Figure 9.10.

A *thrust* load is one that acts parallel to the axis of the wheel. It tends to push the wheel off or further onto the spindle. The wheels of a car are subjected to considerable thrust loads, especially when cornering as shown in Figure 9.11. Because of these thrust loads, wheel bearings must do much more than spin freely and support the weight of the car. They must keep the wheels from sliding in or out on their spindles.

Wheel bearings are designed to handle both radial and thrust loads. You may occasionally find ball bearings in the front hubs of some cars, but tapered roller bearings are used in most. Tapered roller bearings have a long life and are capable of handling extreme loads. Figure 9.12 shows a view of a cone-and-roller assembly and a sectioned bearing cup. The

arrows indicate where the thrust loads are applied. You can see that the tapered shape of the bearing assembly and its cup handle these loads.

When installed in a hub, the inner bearing handles the thrust loads that attempt to push the hub further onto the spindle. The outer bearing handles the thrust loads that attempt to push the wheel off the spindle. The position of each bearing is shown in Figure 9.13.

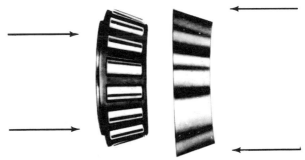

Figure 9.12 A view of a cone-and-roller assembly and a sectioned cup, showing where thrust loads are applied (Pontiac Motor Division, GM).

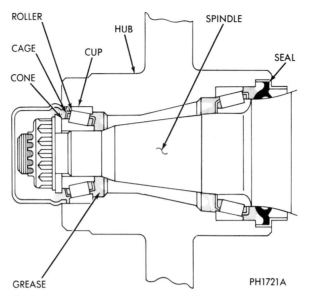

Figure 9.13 The wheel bearings and related parts assembled in a front hub (courtesy Chrysler Corporation).

Job 9b

IDENTIFY THE FUNCTION OF FRONT HUB PARTS

SATISFACTORY PERFORMANCE

A satisfactory performance on this job requires that you do the following:

1 Identify the function of the front hub parts listed below by placing the part number in the space provided in front of the correct part function.
2 Complete the job by identifying the function of all the parts within 15 minutes.

PERFORMANCE SITUATION

1 Grease retainer
2 Spindle nut
3 Nut lock
4 Bearing cone
5 Spindle washer

6 Tapered roller bearing
7 Bearing cup
8 Bearing cage
9 Cotter pin
10 Grease cap

_____Handles both radial and thrust loads

_____Secures the nut lock to the spindle

_____Provides an inner race for the bearing

_____Helps keep dirt and water from entering the hub

_____Keeps the outer wheel bearing from turning the spindle nut

_____Provides an outer race for the bearing

_____Keeps the grease from contaminating the brake lining

_____Secures the wheel to the hub

_____Holds the rollers in place on the cone

_____Provides a means of adjusting the bearings

_____Provides a means of securing the adjustment

WHEEL BEARING SERVICE Wheel bearings should be serviced at regular intervals of from 20,000 to 40,000 miles (32,000 to 64,000 km) as a part of routine maintenance. The adjustment of the bearings should be checked as one of the first steps in diagnosing any problems in the steering, suspension, and brake systems. The condition of the wheel bearings is very important. Worn or loose bearings often cause a car to pull to one side or cause vibrations.

WHEEL BEARING ADJUSTMENT Adjusting wheel bearings properly is a very simple, yet very important job. Tightening the adjusting nut forces the outer bearing in against its cup. The cup, in turn, pushes against the hub, which pushes the inner cup against its bearing. If the nut is overtightened, both bearings will be jammed against their cups. Jamming will increase the friction in the bearings and cause them to wear out very quickly. If the nut is left too loose, the bearings will not be in proper contact with their cups. Bearings that are too loose will also wear out fast. Moreover, they will allow the hub, and thus the wheel, to wobble.

The following adjustment procedure and specifications can be considered typical. However, such procedures and specifications vary with different manufacturers. Therefore, you should always consult the car manufacturer's service manual for the procedure and specifications for the car on which you are working:

1 Raise the front of the car and support it with car stands.

2 Remove the wheel cover from one of the front wheels.

3 Remove the grease cap. A special pair of grease cap pliers similar to those shown in Figure 9.14 can be used for this task.

Note: **Lacking a pair of grease cap pliers, you can use a pair of Channellock pliers, shown in Figure 9.15.**

4 Using a pair of diagonal cutters similar to those shown in Figure 9.16, remove the cotter pin. First, straighten the legs of the pin. Then grasp the head of the pin deep in the jaws of the pliers. By prying upward against the nut lock, you will pull the pin through the hole in the spindle.

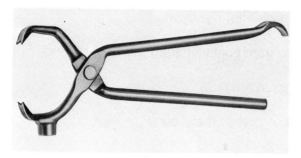

Figure 9.14 A pair of grease cap, or hub cap, pliers (courtesy AMMCO Tools, Inc.).

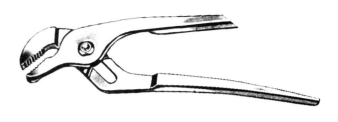

Figure 9.15 Typical Channellock pliers (courtesy of Snap-on Tools Corporation).

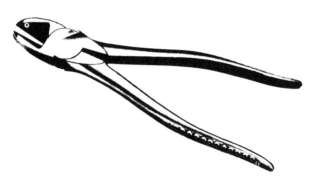

Figure 9.16 A pair of diagonal cutting pliers (courtesy of Snap-on Tools Corporation).

Figure 9.17 Applying the initial torque to seat front wheel bearings. Note that the wheel is turning while this adjustment is made (Ford Motor Company).

5 Remove the nut lock.

6 Using a torque wrench, tighten the adjusting nut to between 17 and 25 foot-pounds (23 to 33 N m) to seat the bearings. As shown in Figure 9.17, rotate the wheel while tightening the nut.

7 Place the nut lock over the adjusting nut so that the castellations on the lock are aligned with the cotter pin hole in the spindle. (See Figure 9.18.)

8 Using a pair of Channellock pliers, back off on the nut and the nut lock together so that the next castellation is aligned with the cotter pin hole.

9 Install a new cotter pin to lock the nut lock in this position.

Note: The cotter pin must fit the hole snugly and be tightly crimped over the nut lock. Figure 9.19 illustrates a correctly secured cotter pin.

10 Install the hub cap.

11 Install the wheel cover.

12 Repeat steps 2 through 11 at the remaining wheel.

13 Lower the car to the floor.

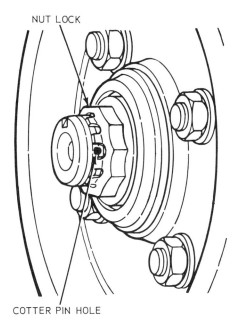

NUT LOCK

COTTER PIN HOLE

Figure 9.18 The nut lock should be installed so that the castellations are aligned with the slot for the cotter pin (Ford Motor Company).

Figure 9.19 A correctly installed cotter pin (Ford Motor Company).

Job 9c

ADJUST WHEEL BEARINGS

SATISFACTORY PERFORMANCE

A satisfactory performance on this job requires that you do the following:

1 Adjust the front wheel bearings on the car assigned.
2 Following the steps in the "Performance Outline" and the manufacturer's procedure and specifications, complete the job within 30 minutes.
3 Fill in the blanks under "Information."

PERFORMANCE OUTLINE

1 Raise and support the front of the car.
2 Remove the cotter pins.
3 Adjust the bearings according to the manufacturer's procedure and specifications.
4 Install new cotter pins.
5 Install all parts removed to gain access to the cotter pin.
6 Lower the car to the floor.

INFORMATION

Vehicle identification _____

Reference used_____ Page(s)_____

Initial tightening torque _____

Amount backed off _____

Size of cotter pin used _____

REPACKING WHEEL BEARINGS—CARS WITH DRUM BRAKES Wheel bearings that are properly adjusted, properly lubricated, and kept free of dirt will usually outlast the car on which they are installed. A good mechanic understands and appreciates the importance of the so-called simple jobs. Adjusting wheel bearings is a simple job, but as you can see, it must be performed carefully.

You are now going to repack wheel bearings. This, too, is a simple job. But you must follow a step-by-step procedure to perform it properly. Be sure to check the adjustment procedure and specifications in the proper manual. A typical procedure follows:

1 Remove the wheel covers.

2 Loosen the lug nuts holding the front wheels to the hubs.

3 Raise the front of the car and support it with car stands.

4 Remove the lug nuts from one of the front wheels.

5 Remove the wheel.

6 Remove the grease cap.

7 Remove the cotter pin.

8 Remove the nut lock, the adjusting nut, the washer, and the outer bearing.

Note: The outer bearing can be easily removed by hitting the edge of the drum with the heel of your hand. This action usually causes the bearing to slide out on the spindle where it can be easily grasped.

9 Grasp the brake drum with both hands, and with a twisting motion, slide it off the spindle.

Note: Never force a drum off if it will not slide off easily. Loosen the brake adjustment to provide more clearance between the drum and the brake shoes. This procedure can be found in the following chapter.

Note: The brake assembly and the inside of the brake drum may contain asbestos dust. Breathing asbestos dust may cause asbestosis and cancer. You should wear an air purifying respirator during all procedures where you may be exposed to asbestos dust.

Figure 9.20 Removing a grease retainer with a puller (Ford Motor Company).

Figure 9.21 Using a blunt punch to remove the inner bearing and the grease retainer (Ford Motor Company).

10 Remove the grease retainer. Figure 9.20 shows how a puller may be used for this operation. Lacking such a puller, the inner bearing and the grease retainer may be removed together by means of a blunt punch, as shown in Figure 9.21.

11 Thoroughly wash all the parts (except the drum) in a suitable solvent such as Kleer-Flo or Agitene.

12 Dry all the parts.

Note: If compressed air is used to dry the parts, be careful not to spin the bearings. Hold the bearings firmly and direct the air between the rollers at the small end of the bearing. This will dry the bearing and will blow out all traces of old grease. Spinning the bearings with an air gun will cause damage to the bearings and may cause personal injury if a roller flies out of the cage.

13 Inspect the bearings. (See Figures 9.22 and 9.23 for diagnosing bearing faults.) Turn the cone and rollers so that all the roller surfaces can be seen. Replace any bearing that shows signs of pitting, discoloration, or scoring. Also check for the presence of any metallic powder or flakes. They usually indicate a defective cone.

FRONT WHEEL BEARING DIAGNOSIS

CONSIDER THE FOLLOWING FACTORS WHEN DIAGNOSING BEARING CONDITION:

1. GENERAL CONDITION OF ALL PARTS DURING DISASSEMBLY AND INSPECTION.
2. CLASSIFY THE FAILURE WITH THE AID OF THE ILLUSTRATIONS.
3. DETERMINE THE CAUSE.
4. MAKE ALL REPAIRS FOLLOWING RECOMMENDED PROCEDURES.

ABRASIVE ROLLER WEAR

PATTERN ON RACES AND ROLLERS CAUSED BY FINE ABRASIVES.

CLEAN ALL PARTS AND HOUSINGS. CHECK SEALS AND BEARINGS AND REPLACE IF LEAKING, ROUGH OR NOISY.

GALLING

METAL SMEARS ON ROLLER ENDS DUE TO OVERHEAT, LUBRICANT FAILURE OR OVERLOAD (WAGON'S)

REPLACE BEARING -- CHECK SEALS AND CHECK FOR PROPER LUBRICATION.

BENT CAGE

CAGE DAMAGE DUE TO IMPROPER HANDLING OR TOOL USAGE.

REPLACE BEARING.

ABRASIVE STEP WEAR

PATTERN ON ROLLER ENDS CAUSED BY FINE ABRASIVES.

CLEAN ALL PARTS AND HOUSINGS. CHECK SEALS AND BEARINGS AND REPLACE IF LEAKING, ROUGH OR NOISY.

ETCHING

BEARING SURFACES APPEAR GRAY OR GRAYISH BLACK IN COLOR WITH RELATED ETCHING AWAY OF MATERIAL USUALLY AT ROLLER SPACING.

REPLACE BEARINGS -- CHECK SEALS AND CHECK FOR PROPER LUBRICATION.

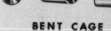

BENT CAGE

CAGE DAMAGE DUE TO IMPROPER HANDLING OR TOOL USAGE.

REPLACE BEARING.

INDENTATIONS

SURFACE DEPRESSIONS ON RACE AND ROLLERS CAUSED BY HARD PARTICLES OF FOREIGN MATERIAL.

CLEAN ALL PARTS AND HOUSINGS. CHECK SEALS AND REPLACE BEARINGS IF ROUGH OR NOISY.

CAGE WEAR

WEAR AROUND OUTSIDE DIAMETER OF CAGE AND ROLLER POCKETS CAUSED BY ABRASIVE MATERIAL AND INEFFICIENT LUBRICATION.

CLEAN RELATED PARTS AND HOUSINGS. CHECK SEALS AND REPLACE BEARINGS.

MISALIGNMENT

OUTER RACE MISALIGNMENT

CLEAN RELATED PARTS AND REPLACE BEARING. MAKE SURE RACES ARE PROPERLY SEATED.

Figure 9.22 Front wheel bearing diagnosis guide (Pontiac Motor Division, GM).

FRONT WHEEL BEARING DIAGNOSIS (CONT'D)

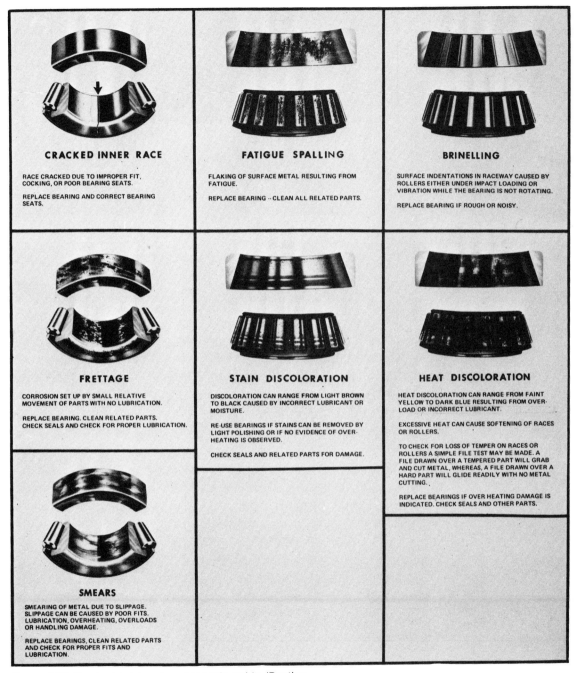

CRACKED INNER RACE

RACE CRACKED DUE TO IMPROPER FIT, COCKING, OR POOR BEARING SEATS.

REPLACE BEARING AND CORRECT BEARING SEATS.

FATIGUE SPALLING

FLAKING OF SURFACE METAL RESULTING FROM FATIGUE.

REPLACE BEARING -- CLEAN ALL RELATED PARTS.

BRINELLING

SURFACE INDENTATIONS IN RACEWAY CAUSED BY ROLLERS EITHER UNDER IMPACT LOADING OR VIBRATION WHILE THE BEARING IS NOT ROTATING.

REPLACE BEARING IF ROUGH OR NOISY.

FRETTAGE

CORROSION SET UP BY SMALL RELATIVE MOVEMENT OF PARTS WITH NO LUBRICATION.

REPLACE BEARING. CLEAN RELATED PARTS. CHECK SEALS AND CHECK FOR PROPER LUBRICATION.

STAIN DISCOLORATION

DISCOLORATION CAN RANGE FROM LIGHT BROWN TO BLACK CAUSED BY INCORRECT LUBRICANT OR MOISTURE.

RE-USE BEARINGS IF STAINS CAN BE REMOVED BY LIGHT POLISHING OR IF NO EVIDENCE OF OVER-HEATING IS OBSERVED.

CHECK SEALS AND RELATED PARTS FOR DAMAGE.

HEAT DISCOLORATION

HEAT DISCOLORATION CAN RANGE FROM FAINT YELLOW TO DARK BLUE RESULTING FROM OVER-LOAD OR INCORRECT LUBRICANT.

EXCESSIVE HEAT CAN CAUSE SOFTENING OF RACES OR ROLLERS.

TO CHECK FOR LOSS OF TEMPER ON RACES OR ROLLERS A SIMPLE FILE TEST MAY BE MADE. A FILE DRAWN OVER A TEMPERED PART WILL GRAB AND CUT METAL, WHEREAS, A FILE DRAWN OVER A HARD PART WILL GLIDE READILY WITH NO METAL CUTTING.

REPLACE BEARINGS IF OVER HEATING DAMAGE IS INDICATED. CHECK SEALS AND OTHER PARTS.

SMEARS

SMEARING OF METAL DUE TO SLIPPAGE. SLIPPAGE CAN BE CAUSED BY POOR FITS, LUBRICATION, OVERHEATING, OVERLOADS OR HANDLING DAMAGE.

REPLACE BEARINGS, CLEAN RELATED PARTS AND CHECK FOR PROPER FITS AND LUBRICATION.

Figure 9.23 Front wheel bearing diagnosis guide (Pontiac Motor Division, GM).

Figure 9.24 A bearing packer (courtesy AMMCO Tools, Inc.).

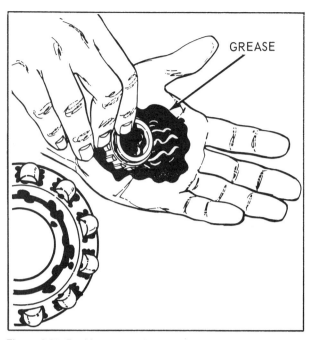

Figure 9.25 Packing grease between the rollers and the cage of a wheel bearing (Ford Motor Company).

Note: Whenever a bearing is replaced, the cup into which the bearing fits must also be replaced, even if it exhibits no apparent damage. Refer to "Replacing Bearing Cups" for the procedure to follow.

14 Inspect the bearing cups. (Refer to Figures 9.22 and 9.23 for diagnosing bearing faults.) Also check for the presence of any metallic powder or flakes. Replace any cups that exhibit those faults.

Note: Whenever a bearing cup is replaced, its mating bearing must also be replaced, even if it exhibits no apparent damage. Refer to "Replacing Bearing Cups" for the procedure to follow.

15 Repack the bearings. Many shops use a bearing packer similar to the one shown in Figure 9.24. Follow the instructions of the manufacturer if you use one of those devices. If a packing device is not available, the grease should be worked up between the rollers by drawing the bearing, large end down, across grease held in the palm of your hand. Figure 9.25 illustrates this method. Continue to push grease into the bearing in this manner until it oozes out at the small end.

Note: Be sure to use only grease which meets the specifications stated in the manufacturer's service manual.

16 Place the inner (large) bearing in its cup.

17 Install a new grease retainer. The new grease retainer should be installed so that the sharp edge of the seal is facing in, as shown in Figure 9.26.

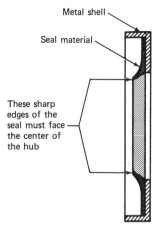

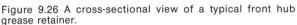

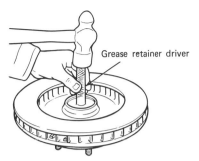

Figure 9.27 Installing a grease retainer (Ford Motor Company).

Figure 9.26 A cross-sectional view of a typical front hub grease retainer.

Note: An installing tool such as the type shown in Figure 9.27 enables you to drive the retainer in place without danger of damaging it. Lacking an installing tool, you can carefully drive the retainer in place with a hammer and a block of wood, as shown in Figure 9.28. Most retainers should be driven in until their outer surface is flush with the surface of the hub.

18 Check to see that there is no dirt, grease, or foreign matter on the inner surfaces of the drum. Carefully slide the hub in place over the spindle.

Note: Use care to center the hub on the spindle. Otherwise, the threads on the spindle could damage the new retainer you just installed.

19 Install the outer bearing on the spindle, sliding it into its cup.

20 Install the washer and adjusting nut.

21 Adjust the bearings and install the nut lock and cotter pin in accordance with the procedure and specifications of the manufacturer.

22 Install the grease cap.

23 Install the wheel and run the lug nuts up snug.

24 Repeat steps 4 through 24 on the remaining wheel.

25 Raise the car with a jack, remove the car stands, and lower the car to the floor.

26 Tighten the lug nuts to the torque specification in the sequence given by the manufacturer.

27 Install the wheel covers.

Figure 9.28 Lacking a special tool, a block of wood can be used to install a grease retainer (Ford Motor Company).

Job 9d

REPACK WHEEL BEARINGS—DRUM BRAKES

SATISFACTORY PERFORMANCE

A satisfactory performance on this job requires that you do the following:

1 Repack the front wheel bearings of the car assigned.

2 Following the steps in the "Performance Outline" and the specifications of the manufacturer, complete the job within 90 minutes.

3 Fill in the blanks under "Information."

PERFORMANCE OUTLINE

1 Raise and support the car.

2 Remove the front wheels.

3 Remove a hub assembly.

4 Clean and inspect all parts.

5 Repack the bearings.

6 Assemble the parts and install the hub on the spindle.

7 Adjust the bearings to the manufacturer's specifications.

8 Install the cotter pin and the grease cap.

9 Repeat steps 3 to 8 on the remaining wheel.

10 Install the wheels and lower the car to the floor.

11 Torque the lug nuts and install the wheel covers.

INFORMATION

Vehicle identification _____

Reference used_____ Page(s)_____

Size of cotter pin used _____

Wheel bearing initial torque specification _____

REPACKING WHEEL BEARINGS—CARS WITH DISC BRAKES The bearings in the front hubs of cars with disc brakes are the same as those used with drum brakes. The procedure for repacking them, however, is more involved. This is because the disc brake caliper must be removed before the rotor, or disc, can be removed from the spindle. There are many different types of calipers in use. Because of this, you should refer to the manufacturer's manual for the specific removal and installation procedures required for the car on which you are working.

Cars Fitted with Delco-Moraine Type Single Piston Calipers The following procedure can be used on cars equipped with Delco-Moraine type single piston calipers. A caliper of this type is shown in Figure 9.29.

1 Remove the wheel covers.

2 Loosen the lug nuts holding the front wheels.

3 Raise the front of the car and support it with car stands.

4 Remove the lug nuts from one of the front wheels.

5 Remove the wheel.

Note: The caliper assembly and the disc brake rotor may be coated with asbestos dust. Breathing asbestos dust may cause asbestosis and cancer. You should wear an air purifying respir-

Figure 9.29 A Delco-Moraine single piston caliper assembly (Oldsmobile Division, GM).

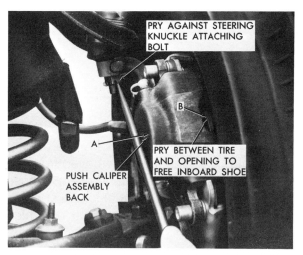

Figure 9.30 Moving disc brake shoes away from the rotor by prying outward on the caliper (Chevrolet Service Manual, Chevrolet Motor Division, GM).

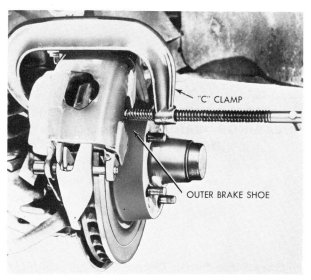

Figure 9.31 Using a "C" clamp to push a caliper piston back in its bore (Chevrolet Service Manual, Chevrolet Motor Division, GM).

ator during all procedures where you may be exposed to asbestos dust.

6 Push the caliper piston back into the caliper a slight distance to separate the brake shoes from the rotor. This will make the caliper easier to remove. The piston can be pushed back by (1) slowly prying the brake caliper outward with a pry bar positioned as shown in Figure 9.30, or (2) by using a "C" clamp positioned over the caliper with the pad of the clamp against the back of the outboard shoe as shown in Figure 9.31.

Note: When using either method, move the caliper only enough to allow the rotor to spin freely.

7 Using a suitable wrench or socket, remove the mounting bolts as shown in Figure 9.32.

8 Lift the caliper up and off the rotor. Support the caliper by placing it securely on a part of the suspension system, as shown in Figure 9.33, or tie it in place with a piece of wire.

Note: Never allow a caliper to hang by the brake hose. To do so would weaken the hose.

9 Remove the grease cap from the hub.

10 Remove the cotter pin.

11 Remove the nut lock, the adjusting nut, the washer, and the outer bearing.

Note: The outer bearing can be easily removed by hitting the edge of the rotor with the heel of your hand. This action usually causes the bearing to slide out on the spindle where it can be easily grasped.

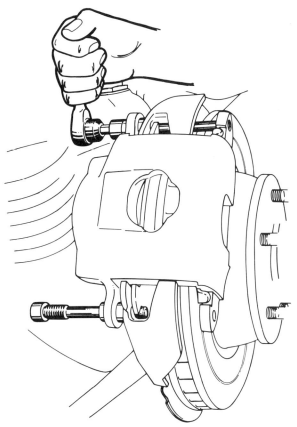

Figure 9.32 Removing the caliper mounting bolts (Pontiac Motor Division, GM).

Figure 9.33 A caliper securely positioned on the front suspension system. A caliper should never be allowed to hang from the brake hose (Pontiac Motor Division, GM).

12 Grasp the rotor with both hands, and carefully slide it off the spindle.

13 Lay the rotor on a bench covered with clean paper. This will protect the inner surface of the rotor from damage and contamination.

14 Remove the grease retainer and the inner bearing. (Refer to Figures 9.20 and 9.21.)

15 Thoroughly wash all the parts (except the rotor) in a suitable solvent such as Kleer-Flo or Agitene.

16 Dry all the parts.

Note: If compressed air is used to dry the parts, be careful not to spin the bearings. Hold the bearings firmly and direct the air between the rollers at the small end of the bearing. This will dry the bearing and will blow out all traces of old grease. Spinning the bearings with an air gun will cause damage to the bearings and may cause personal injury if a roller flies out of the cage.

17 Inspect the bearings. (Refer to Figures 9.22 and 9.23 for diagnosing bearing faults.) Turn the cone and rollers so that all the roller surfaces can be seen. Replace any bearing that shows signs of pitting, discoloration, or scoring. Also check for the presence of any metallic powder or flakes. They usually indicate a defective cone.

Note: Whenever a bearing is replaced, the cup into which the bearing fits must also be replaced, even if it exhibits no apparent damage. Refer to "Replacing Bearing Cups" for the procedure to follow.

18 Carefully clean all traces of grease from the inside of the hub. Inspect the bearing cups. (Refer to Figures 9.22 and 9.23 for diagnosing bearing faults.) Also check for the presence of any metallic powder or flakes. Replace any cups that exhibit these faults.

Note: Whenever a bearing cup is replaced, its mating bearing must also be replaced, even if it exhibits no apparent damage. Refer to "Replacing Bearing Cups" for the procedure to follow.

19 Repack the bearings. Many shops use a bearing packer for this operation. (Refer to Figure 9.24.) Follow the instructions of the manufacturer if you use one of these devices. If a packing device is not available, the grease should be worked up between the rollers by drawing the bearing, large end down, across grease held in the palm of your hand. (Refer to Figure 9.25.) Continue to push grease into the bearing in this manner until it oozes out at the small end.

Note: Be sure to use only grease that meets the specifications stated in the manufacturer's service manual.

20 Place the inner (large) bearing in its cup.

21 Install a new grease retainer. The new grease retainer should be installed so that the sharp edge of the seal is facing in. (Refer to Figure 9.26.)

Note: An installing tool should be used if available. An installing tool enables you to drive the retainer in place without danger of damaging it. (Refer to Figure 9.27.) Lacking an installing tool, you can carefully drive the retainer in place with a hammer and a block of wood. (Refer to Figure 9.28.) Most retainers should be driven in until their outer surface is flush with the surface of the hub.

22 Check to see that there is no dirt, grease, or foreign matter on the surfaces of the rotor. Carefully slide the hub in place over the spindle.

Note: Use care to center the hub on the spindle. Otherwise, the threads on the spindle could damage the new retainer you just installed.

23 Install the outer bearing on the spindle, sliding it into its cup.

24 Install the washer and the adjusting nut.

25 Adjust the bearings and install the nut lock and cotter pin in accordance with the procedure and specifications of the manufacturer.

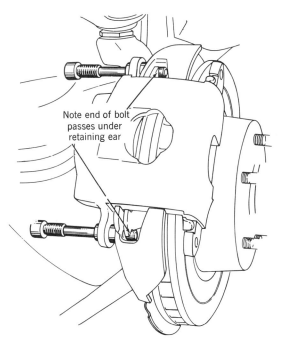

Note end of bolt passes under retaining ear

Figure 9.34 Installing the caliper mounting bolts (Chevrolet Service Manual, Chevrolet Motor Division, GM).

26 Install the grease cap.

27 Push the caliper down over the rotor, and align the holes in the caliper with the holes in the mounting.

28 Push the mounting bolts through the caliper and through the mount as shown in Figure 9.34. Make sure that the bolts pass under the ears on the inboard shoe.

29 Push the bolts through the holes in the outboard shoe and through the holes in the outer caliper ears. Thread the bolts into the mounting bracket, starting the threads by hand to avoid cross-threading.

30 Tighten the bolts to the torque specification of the manufacturer.

31 Pump the brake pedal several times to position the piston and the caliper.

Note: Do not remove the caliper at the remaining wheel until the caliper you just replaced has been positioned.

32 Repeat steps 4 through 31 at the remaining wheel.

33 Install the wheels and run the lug nuts up snug.

34 Raise the car with a jack, remove the car stands, and lower the car to the floor.

35 Tighten the lug nuts to the torque specification and in the sequence given by the manufacturer.

36 Install the wheel covers.

Figure 9.35 A Ford-type, single piston caliper disc brake assembly (Ford Motor Company).

CARS FITTED WITH FORD TYPE SINGLE PISTON CALIPERS The following procedure can be used on cars equipped with Ford type single piston calipers. A caliper of this type is shown in Figure 9.35.

1 Remove the wheel covers.

2 Loosen the lug nuts holding the front wheels.

3 Raise the front of the car and support it with car stands.

4 Remove the lug nuts from one of the front wheels.

5 Remove the wheel.

Note: The caliper assembly and the disc brake rotor may be coated with asbestos dust. Breathing asbestos dust may cause asbestosis and cancer. You should wear an air purifying respirator during all procedures where you may be exposed to asbestos dust.

6 Push the caliper piston back into the caliper a slight distance to separate the brake shoes from the rotor. This will make the caliper easier to remove. The piston can be pushed back by (1) prying the piston back with a screwdriver as shown in Figure 9.36, or (2) using a "C" clamp positioned over the caliper with the pad of the clamp against the outboard shoe. (Refer to Figure 9.31.)

Note: When using either method, move the caliper only enough to allow the rotor to spin freely.

7 Remove the screw holding the caliper retaining key as shown in Figure 9.37.

8 Carefully drive the retaining key and its support spring from the key slot as shown in Figure 9.38.

9 Lift the caliper off the rotor and out of its mounting. To do this, push the caliper downward, then tip the caliper outward as shown in Figure 9.39.

Note: On disc brakes of this type, the inboard shoe will remain

Figure 9.36 Prying a caliper piston back into its bore by means of a screwdriver inserted between the piston and the inboard shoe (courtesy American Motors Corporation).

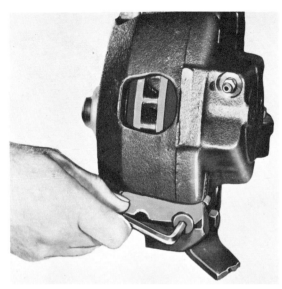

Figure 9.37 Removing the screw that holds the caliper retaining key (Ford Motor Company).

in its mounting behind the rotor. The outboard shoe will remain in place in the caliper as shown in Figure 9.40.

10 Support the caliper by placing it securely on a part of the suspension system, or tie it up in place with a piece of wire. (Refer to Figure 9.33.)

Note: Never allow a caliper to hang by the brake hose. To do so would weaken the hose.

Figure 9.38 Driving out the caliper retaining key (Ford Motor Company).

Figure 9.39 Lifting the caliper out of its mounting (Ford Motor Company).

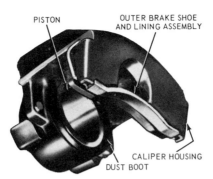

Figure 9.40 Removed caliper with the outboard shoe in place (Ford Motor Company).

11 Remove the grease cap from the hub.

12 Remove the cotter pin.

13 Remove the nut lock, the adjusting nut, the washer, and the outer bearing.

Note: The outer bearing can be easily removed by hitting the edge of the rotor with the heel of your hand. This action usually causes the bearing to slide out on the spindle where it can be easily grasped.

14 Grasp the rotor with both hands, and carefully slide it off the spindle.

15 Lay the rotor on a bench covered with clean paper. This will protect the inner surface of the rotor from damage and contamination.

16 Remove the grease retainer and the inner bearing. (Refer to Figures 9.20 and 9.21.)

17 Thoroughly wash all the parts (except the rotor) in a suitable solvent such as Kleer-Flo or Agitene.

18 Dry all the parts.

Note: If compressed air is used to dry the parts, be careful not to spin the bearings. Hold the bearings firmly and direct the air between the rollers at the small end of the bearing. This will dry the bearing and will blow out all traces of old grease. Spinning the bearings with an air gun will cause damage to the bearings and may cause personal injury if a roller flies out of the cage.

19 Inspect the bearings. (Refer to Figures 9.22 and 9.23 for diagnosing bearing faults.) Turn the cone and rollers so that all the roller surfaces can be seen. Replace any bearing that shows signs of pitting, discoloration, or scoring. Also check for the presence of any metallic powder or flakes. They usually indicate a defective cone.

Note: Whenever a bearing is replaced, the cup into which the bearing fits must also be replaced, even if it exhibits no apparent damage. Refer to "Replacing Bearing Cups" for the procedure to follow.

20 Carefully clean all traces of grease from the inside of the hub. Inspect the bearing cups. (Refer to Figures 9.22 and 9.23 for diagnosing bearing faults.) Also check for the presence of any metallic powder or flakes. Replace any cups that exhibit these faults.

Note: Whenever a bearing cup is replaced, its mating bearing must also be replaced, even if it exhibits no apparent damage. Refer to "Replacing Bearing Cups" for the procedure to follow.

21 Repack the bearings. Many shops use a bearing packer for this operation. (Refer to Figure 9.24.) Follow the instructions of the manufacturer if you use one of these devices. If a packing device is not available, the grease should be worked up between the rollers by drawing the bearing, large end down, across grease held in the palm of your hand. (Refer to Figure 9.25.) Continue to push grease into the bearing in this manner until it oozes out at the small end.

Note: Be sure to use only grease that meets the specifications stated in the manufacturer's service manual.

22 Place the inner (large) bearing in its cup.

23 Install a new grease retainer. The new grease retainer should be installed so that the sharp edge of the seal is facing in. (Refer to Figure 9.26.)

Note: An installing tool should be used if available. An installing tool enables you to drive the retainer in place without danger of damaging it. (Refer to Figure 9.27.) Lacking an installing tool, you can carefully drive the retainer in place with a hammer and a block of wood. (Refer to Figure 9.28.) Most retainers should be driven in until their outer surface is flush with the surface of the hub.

24 Check to see that there is no dirt, grease, or foreign matter on the surfaces of the rotor. Carefully slide the hub in place over the spindle.

Note: Use care to center the hub on the spindle. Otherwise the threads on the spindle could damage the new retainer you just installed.

25 Install the outer bearing on the spindle, sliding it into its cup.

26 Install the washer and the adjusting nut.

27 Adjust the bearings and install the nut lock and cotter pin in accordance with the procedure and specifications of the manufacturer.

28 Install the grease cup.

29 Position the caliper over the rotor so that the lower mounting

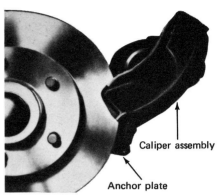

Figure 9.41 First step in caliper installation. Note that the lower mounting groove on the caliper is resting on the anchor plate (Ford Motor Company).

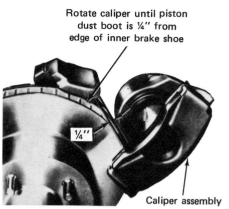

Figure 9.42 Second step in caliper installation (Ford Motor Company).

groove on the caliper rests on the mounting, or anchor plate. (See Figure 9.41.)

30 Pivot the caliper upward and inward toward the rotor until the edge of the dust boot is about ¼ inch (6 mm) away from the edge of the inboard shoe. (See Figure 9.42.)

31 Place a piece of lightweight cardboard between the lower half of the dust boot and the shoe as shown in Figure 9.43. (This prevents the dust boot from getting caught between the piston and the shoe.)

32 Pivot the caliper toward the rotor. When you feel a slight resistance, pull the cardboard down toward the center of the rotor while pushing the caliper over the rotor. This step is shown in Figure 9.44.

33 Remove the cardboard, and push the caliper all the way down over the rotor as shown in Figure 9.45.

34 Slide the caliper up against the machined surface of the upper part of the mounting, or anchor, as shown in Figure 9.46.

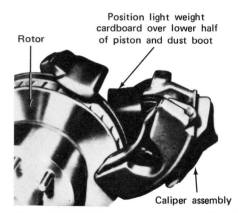

Figure 9.43 Third step in caliper installation. A piece of light cardboard is used to protect the dust boot (Ford Motor Company).

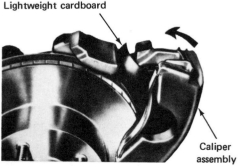

Figure 9.44 Fourth step in caliper installation (Ford Motor Company).

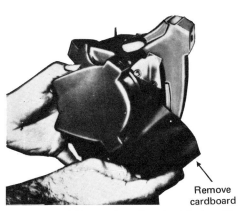

Figure 9.45 Fifth step in caliper installation. The caliper is in place over the rotor and the cardboard is removed (Ford Motor Company).

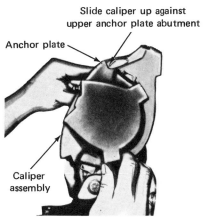

Figure 9.46 Caliper being slid into place against the upper part of its mounting (Ford Motor Company).

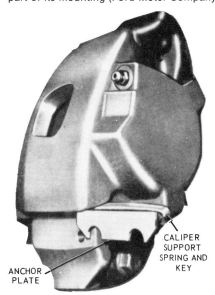

Figure 9.47 Installing the caliper retaining key (Ford Motor Company).

35 Position the lower part of the caliper so that the retaining key and its support spring can be inserted into the opening between the caliper and the anchor plate, as shown in Figure 9.47.

36 Carefully drive the retaining key and its support spring into the slot until the notch on the key aligns with the threaded hole in the anchor plate.

37 Install the retaining screw and tighten it to the manufacturer's torque specification.

38 Pump the brake pedal several times to position the piston and the caliper.

Note: Do not remove the caliper at the remaining wheel until the caliper you just installed has been positioned.

39 Repeat steps 4 through 38 at the remaining wheel.

40 Install the wheels and run the lug nuts up snug.

41 Raise the car with a jack, remove the car stands, and lower the car to the floor.

42 Tighten the lug nuts to the torque specification and in the sequence given by the manufacturer.

43 Install the wheel covers.

Job 9e

REPACK WHEEL BEARINGS—DISC BRAKES

SATISFACTORY PERFORMANCE

A satisfactory performance on this job requires that you do the following:

1 Repack the front wheel bearings of the car assigned.
2 Following the steps in the "Performance Outline" and the specifications of the manufacturer, complete the job within 120 minutes.
3 Fill in the blanks under "Information."

PERFORMANCE OUTLINE

 1 Raise and support the car.
 2 Remove the front wheels.
 3 Remove the disc brake caliper.
 4 Remove the hub and rotor assembly.
 5 Clean and inspect all parts.
 6 Repack the bearings.
 7 Assemble the parts and install the hub and rotor assembly on the spindle.
 8 Adjust the bearings to the manufacturer's specifications.
 9 Install the cotter pin and the grease cap.
10 Install the disc brake caliper.
11 Repeat steps 3 through 10 on the remaining wheel.
12 Install the wheels and lower the car to the floor.
13 Torque the lug nuts and install the wheel covers.

INFORMATION

Vehicle identification _____

Reference used_____ Page(s)_____

Type of caliper _____

Size of cotter pin used _____

Wheel bearing initial torque specification _____

Wheel lug nut torque specification _____

Replacing Bearing Cups Because the rollers of a wheel bearing roll inside their cup, any wear on one part will affect the other. If a worn bearing is replaced without replacing its cup, the new bearing will have a short life. Bearing cups, or races, are fitted very tightly in the hub. This prevents them from turning with the bearing. If you find a cup that is loose in its hub, the hub must be replaced. This is because the cup is made of very hard steel and the hub is made of cast iron. If the cup turns in the hub, the relatively soft cast iron will wear and thus it will not provide a tight fit for a new cup.

Some manufacturers recommend the use of special pullers to remove bearing cups. These pullers have hooklike fingers or *jaws* that grab the inner edges of the cup. The jaws are extended until they have a firm grip on the cup. Then the tool and cup are pulled out together. (See Figure 9.48.)

Lacking special pullers, you can remove a bearing cup by carefully driving it out with a punch. The inner edge of the cup is raised a little above the inner surface of the hub. Some hubs have notches that expose portions of the edge of the cup. A punch with a flat end can be used to drive the cup out. The edge of the punch is placed against the inner edge of the cup and struck with a hammer. The punch is then shifted to the other side of the cup and struck again. This eases the cup out of the hub. Do not try to drive the cup out too fast. You must move it slowly and keep it as straight as possible. By shifting the punch back and forth, you will not cock the cup in its bore. If the cup is cocked, it may damage the hub.

After the cup has been removed, the hub should be carefully cleaned. Special cup drivers are available to drive the new cup in place. These tools are shown in Figure 9.49. The use of cup drivers is recommended because they make the job easier, and they guard the cup against damage.

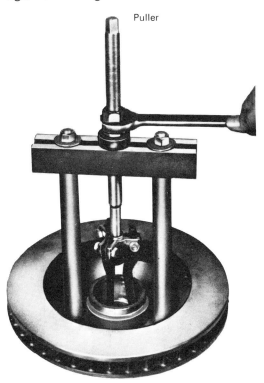

Figure 9.48 Removing an inner bearing cup with a puller (Ford Motor Company).

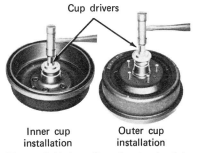

Figure 9.49 Installing front wheel bearing cups with cup drivers (Ford Motor Company).

Because all shops do not have cup drivers, you can use a brass punch to install the cups. When you install a new cup, be sure it is facing the correct way. The thickest edge of the cup always goes into the hub first. Because the outer edge of the cup is much thinner than the inner edge, it is sometimes difficult to keep the punch from slipping. If you keep the corners of your punch ground or filed square, the punch will be less likely to slip.

Another method of installing a new cup is to use the old cup as a driver. The old cup is held, thick side down, against the new cup. The new cup must be driven all the way down into its bore. You will know when it hits bottom by the different sound you will hear when you hit the punch or old cup with your hammer. If you use the old cup as a driver, you may have to drive it out after the new cup is all the way in. To do this, turn the drum or rotor around and drive the old cup out again. It will come out easily if you remembered to place the thick side down.

Job 9f

REPLACE A BEARING CUP

SATISFACTORY PERFORMANCE
A satisfactory performance on this job requires that you do the following:

1 Replace a wheel bearing cup in the drum or rotor assigned.
2 Following the steps in the "Performance Outline," complete the job within 30 minutes. At the completion of the job, the cup should be bottomed in its bore and the cup and the hub should exhibit no damage.
3 Fill in the blanks under "Information."

PERFORMANCE OUTLINE
1 Remove the assigned bearing cup.
2 Clean and inspect the hub.
3 Install the replacement bearing cup.
4 Present the hub for inspection.

INFORMATION

Hub identification _____

Bearing cup(s) replaced _____Inner _____Outer

Method used to remove bearing cup(s)

_____Puller _____Punch

Method used to install bearing cup(s)

_____Driver _____Punch _____Old cup

SUMMARY

In completing the jobs in this chapter, you have learned how bearings are used to mount the front hubs on a car. You have also learned how tapered roller bearings handle both radial and thrust loads. You have developed skills in adjusting wheel bearings, repacking wheel bearings, and replacing wheel bearing cups, and you can perform these jobs on cars with different brake systems.

SELF-TEST

Each incomplete statement or question in this test is followed by four suggested completions or answers. In each case select the *one* that best completes the sentence or answers the question.

1 Two mechanics are discussing tapered roller bearings.
Mechanic A says that tapered roller bearings can handle radial loads.
Mechanic B says that tapered roller bearings are used as front wheel bearings because of the thrust loads imposed when a car is turning a corner.
Who is right?
A. A only
B. B only
C. Both A and B
D. Neither A nor B

2 Whenever wheel bearings are repacked, you should replace the
A. nut lock
B. bearing cup
C. bearing cone
D. grease retainer

3 Two mechanics are discussing wheel bearing adjustment.
Mechanic A says that the adjusting nut should be tightened to a torque of 25 foot-pounds, backed off one-half turn, and secured with the nut lock and cotter pin.
Mechanic B says that the wheel should be turning while the adjustment nut is being tightened.
Who is right?

A. A only
B. B only
C. Both A and B
D. Neither A nor B

4 Two mechanics are discussing the parts of a front hub.
Mechanic A says that the bearing cups are threaded into the hub.
Mechanic B says that grease retainers should be driven into the hub until they are flush with the hub surface.
Who is right?
A. A only
B. B only
C. Both A and B
D. Neither A nor B

5 When removing a front hub from a car with disc brakes, the
A. rotor must be removed from the hub
B. caliper must be removed from the rotor
C. piston must be removed from the caliper
D. spindle must be removed from the control arm

6 Two mechanics are discussing wheel bearing service.
Mechanic A says that nut locks are not used with castellated nuts.
Mechanic B says that when a bearing cup is found loose in the hub, the hub should be replaced.
Who is right?
A. A only
B. B only
C. Both A and B
D. Neither A nor B

7 Two mechanics are discussing wheel bearing service.
Mechanic A says that the function of the keyed spindle washer is to keep the outer bearing cup from turning.
Mechanic B says that when inspecting a cone-and-roller assembly, the rollers should be removed from the cage.
Who is right?
A. A only

B. B only
C. Both A and B
D. Neither A nor B

8 Two mechanics are discussing the replacement of bearing cups.
Mechanic A says that bearing cups can be removed with a cup driver.
Mechanic B says that bearing cups can be installed with a blunt punch.
Who is right?
A. A only
B. B only
C. Both A and B
D. Neither A nor B

9 While inspecting a set of wheel bearings, a mechanic finds that the inner wheel bearing cage is bent. This damage was most likely caused by
A. inner race misalignment
B. impact loading of the rollers
C. improper handling or tool usage
D. improper bearing fit on the spindle

10 Two mechanics are discussing wheel bearing service.
Mechanic A says that the grease retainer should be installed so that the sharp edge of the seal faces the bearing.
Mechanic B says that the retainer should be driven in until it bottoms in the hub.
Who is right?
A. A only
B. B only
C. Both A and B
D. Neither A nor B

Chapter 10 Brake System Services

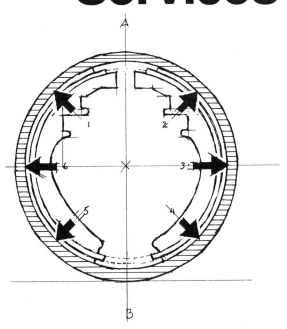

The brake system is probably the most important system in an automobile. A failure in the brake system can cause property damage, serious injury, and even death. Because of the importance of the brake system, routine maintenance is a necessity. The importance of your work can be measured only in terms of safety.

Different types of brake systems are used on different cars. This chapter will acquaint you with those systems. It will provide you with the means to gain the knowledge and to develop the diagnostic and repair skills necessary to provide the routine services required. Your specific objectives are to perform the following jobs:

1
Identify the parts of a typical drum brake assembly.
2
Adjust service brakes.
3
Inspect front brake lining—drum brakes.
4
Inspect rear brake lining—drum brakes.
5
Identify the parts in a typical disc brake assembly.
6
Inspect front brake lining—disc brakes.
7
Adjust parking brakes.

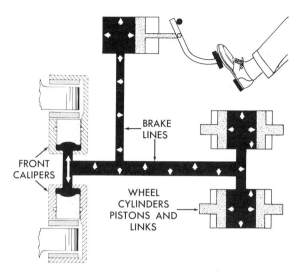
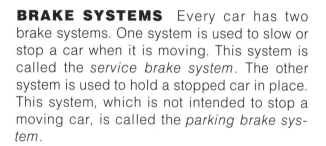

Figure 10.1 A hydraulic system transmits the driver's effort to the brakes at the wheels (Chevrolet Service Manual, Chevrolet Division, GM).

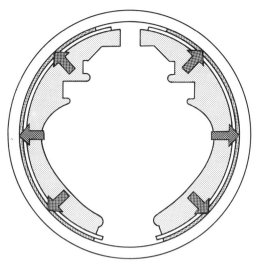

Figure 10.2 The action of a drum brake. Two shoes move outward to contact the inner surface of a drum (Management and Marketing Institute).

BRAKE SYSTEMS Every car has two brake systems. One system is used to slow or stop a car when it is moving. This system is called the *service brake system*. The other system is used to hold a stopped car in place. This system, which is not intended to stop a moving car, is called the *parking brake system*.

The Service Brake System The service brakes are applied by pushing down on the service brake pedal. This action causes brake shoes at all four wheels to be forced against *drums* or *rotors* behind the wheels. The contact of the shoes against the drums or rotors creates friction, which stops the wheels from turning.

The force the driver applies to the brake pedal is carried to each wheel by a *hydraulic system*, as shown in Figure 10.1. A hydraulic system is one that transmits pressure by means of a fluid. In a previous chapter you checked and adjusted the fluid level in a master cylinder reservoir. It is this fluid that transmits the pressure in a brake system.

Drum Brakes In a drum brake, the brake shoes are forced against the inside surface of a drum. The action of a drum brake is shown

in Figure 10.2. As you learned when you worked with wheel bearings, a drum is a ring that is attached to the inside of a wheel and rotates with it. The friction between the brake shoes and the drum causes the drum to slow down and stop turning. Because the wheel is bolted to the drum, the wheel stops rolling.

Disc Brakes In a disc brake, two brake shoes are forced against opposite sides of a rotor. The action of a disc brake is shown in Figure 10.3. As you also learned in the previous chapter, a rotor is a disc that is attached to the inside of a wheel and rotates with it. The brake shoes squeeze the rotor between them. The friction between the shoes and the rotor causes the rotor to slow down and stop turning. Because the wheel is bolted to the rotor, the wheel stops turning.

Combination Brake Systems Most cars have combination brake systems. A combination brake system uses disc brakes on the front wheels and drum brakes on the rear wheels. Each type of brake has certain braking characteristics, including some advantages, that the other does not have. Combining the two types of brakes enables the manufacturer to take advantage of both types.

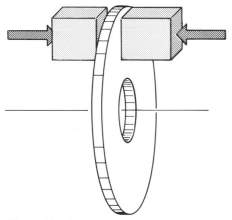

Figure 10.3 The action of a disc brake. Two shoes move together to contact the surfaces of a rotor or disc (Management and Marketing Institute).

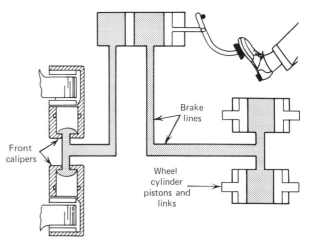

Figure 10.4 A dual hydraulic brake system. One system operates the front brakes. The other system operates the rear brakes.

Dual Hydraulic Systems All cars in current production have dual hydraulic systems. When you worked with master cylinders, you found that they had dual reservoirs. Each reservoir stores fluid for a separate system. On some cars, a separate hydraulic system is provided for the front brakes and another for the rear brakes. This arrangement is shown in Figure 10.4. On other cars, the hydraulic systems are arranged so that each system serves one front brake and the opposite rear brake. A system of that type is shown in Figure 10.5

Although one of the dual systems can stop the car if the other system fails, the stopping distance is increased. Consequently, there is an increased possibility of an accident. There are two indications that one of the systems has failed. First, the driver notices increased pedal travel and a need to apply greater effort to the pedal. Second, a warning light in the instrument panel turns on.

The Parking Brake System The parking brake system is entirely mechanical. The driver applies the parking brakes by pulling a lever or by stepping on a pedal. The parking brakes generally operate on the rear wheels only. They use cables pulled by levers to carry the driver-applied force to the wheels. A hydraulic system is not used. Parking brakes normally use the same brake shoes that the

service brakes use on the rear wheels. A typical parking brake system is shown in Figure 10.6.

DRUM BRAKES Except for slight changes to enable different self-adjuster parts to be fitted, most manufacturers use a drum brake of the type shown in Figure 10.7. The brake assembly shown is typical of those used for front wheels. Rear wheel brake assemblies are similar, but contain extra parts for the parking brake system. You should study Figure 10.7

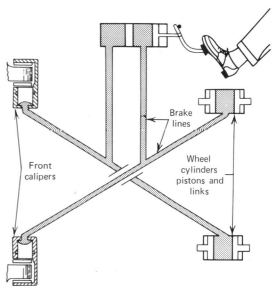

Figure 10.5 A dual hydraulic brake system. One system operates the left front brake and the right rear brake. The other system operates the right front brake and the left rear brake.

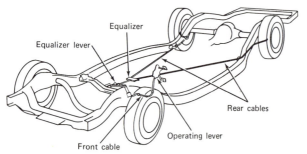

Figure 10.6 A typical parking brake system. Note that the system is entirely mechanical and uses cables and levers (Ford Motor Company).

so that you will become familiar with the parts and their location.

Drum Brake Parts All the parts are mounted on a *backing plate*, which is a round piece of pressed steel that is attached to the car. A typical backing plate is shown in Figure 10.8. At a front wheel, the backing plate is bolted to the spindle, or *steering knuckle*. At the rear of a car, the backing plates are bolted

to the rear axle housing. The backing plate holds all of the brake parts except the drum, which is bolted to the wheel.

An *anchor pin* is located at the top of the backing plate. The anchor pin takes the full load of the braking forces and must be securely attached to the backing plate. Many anchor pins are welded or riveted in place. The backing plate has six little raised platforms called *bosses*, or *ledges*. These bosses, shown in Figure 10.9, contact the edges of the brake shoes and support the shoes when they are installed.

Hold-down assemblies hold the brake shoes to the backing plate. The *retaining spring* holds the bottom of the brake shoes in contact with the *star wheel adjuster*. The star wheel adjuster is a threaded device that can be expanded to push the shoes farther apart as the lining wears.

The *wheel cylinder*, mounted near the top of the backing plate, is a hydraulic device. It contains two pistons that move outward when the driver steps on the brake pedal. This out-

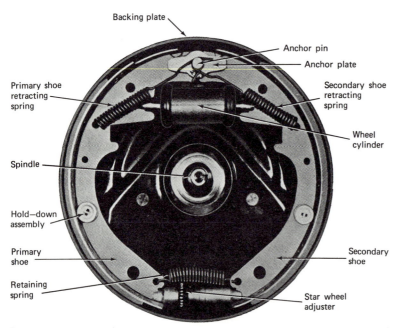

Figure 10.7 A typical drum brake assembly (Automotive Aftermarket Division, Raybestos Friction Materials Co., A Raybestos-Manhattan Company).

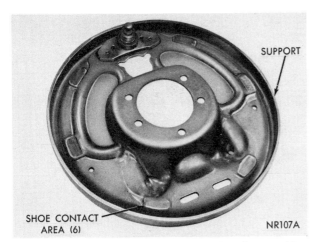

Figure 10.8 A typical backing plate. A backing plate provides the mounting for the brake parts at each wheel (courtesy Chrysler Corporation).

Figure 10.9 A backing plate has small platforms that support the brake shoes and keep them aligned (Chevrolet Service Manual, Chevrolet Motor Division, GM).

ward movement pushes the brake shoes against the brake drum. The *retracting springs* pull the shoes away from the drum and force the pistons back in the wheel cylinder when the driver releases the pedal.

Brake Shoes and Lining The most widely used brake shoe is made of two pieces of stamped steel arc welded together. These pieces are called the platform and the web, and are shown in Figure 10.10. The web is made of heavy gauge metal and is shaped and drilled so that the various springs and self-adjusting mechanisms can be anchored to it. The platform is formed to the desired curve, centered on the web, and welded to it. The platform provides the surface to which the lining is attached.

The material most commonly used in brake lining is asbestos. Asbestos provides just about the right amount of friction when used with cast iron brake drums and rotors. For use in different braking systems, the friction provided by the lining is changed by the addition of other materials to the asbestos. Asbestos is used for another reason. The friction of braking produces a great amount of heat. Actually, the energy of the car in motion must be converted to heat to bring the car to a stop. Asbestos will withstand very high temperatures without

burning or failing. Although asbestos may be ideal for use in brake lining, it creates a health hazard. Breathing asbestos dust may cause asbestosis and cancer. During brake servicing, an air purifying respirator should be worn during all procedures, starting with the removal of the wheels and including reassembly.

There are two methods used to hold the lining to the shoe. One method is to use rivets. The other is to use a *bonding* agent, or cement. Linings held to their shoes by each method are shown in Figure 10.11.

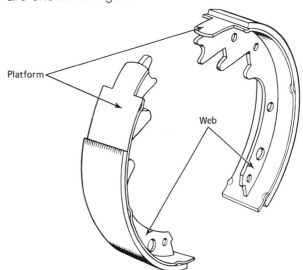

Figure 10.10 A pair of brake shoes showing the platform and the web (courtesy Chrysler Corporation).

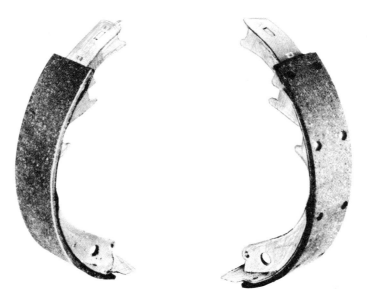

Lining bonded to shoe   Lining riveted to shoe

Figures 10.11 Lined brake shoes (Automotive Aftermarket Division, Raybestos Friction Materials Co., A Raybestos-Manhattan Company).

Job 10a

IDENTIFY THE PARTS OF A TYPICAL DRUM BRAKE ASSEMBLY

SATISFACTORY PERFORMANCE

A satisfactory performance on this job requires that you do the following:

1 Identify the numbered parts on the drawing by placing the number of each part in front of the correct part name listed below.

2 Correctly identify 9 of the 11 parts within 15 minutes.

PERFORMANCE SITUATION

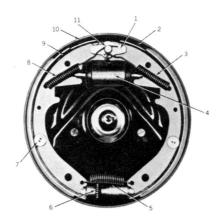

_____Backing plate	_____Primary shoe
_____Secondary shoe retracting spring	_____Primary shoe retracting spring
_____Secondary shoe	_____Anchor pin
_____Star wheel adjuster	_____Retaining spring
_____Wheel cylinder	_____Hold-down assembly
_____Cam plate	_____Anchor plate

Brake Adjustment A well-adjusted brake system allows a driver to stop a car without pushing the brake pedal too far toward the floor. This brake condition is called _pedal reserve_, but most mechanics refer to it as a "high pedal." To have a high pedal, the brake linings must be positioned very close to the drums when the brakes are released. Then, when the brake pedal is pressed down, the linings have only a short distance to travel before they contact the drums.

As you know, the brake shoes are held in position by the anchor pin and the star wheel adjuster. Because the retracting springs always pull the shoes back to contact the anchor pin, any wear on the linings increases the distance between the linings and the drums. As the linings wear, however, the star wheel adjuster can be expanded to push the shoes farther apart at the bottom of the brake assembly. This brings them closer to the drums and makes up for the lining that is worn away.

Star Wheel Adjusters Star wheel adjusters get their name from the star-like, or gear-shaped, appearance of the head of the ad-

Figure 10.12 A typical star wheel adjuster (courtesy American Motors Corporation).

justing screw. An example of a star wheel adjuster is shown in Figure 10.12. Most cars are fitted with self-adjusting brakes. The parts of a typical self-adjusting mechanism are shown in Figure 10.13. When a self-adjuster is working properly, it advances the star wheel adjuster as the lining wears away. However, the use of self-adjusters has not entirely eliminated the need for adjusting brakes by hand.

Because brakes must sometimes be adjusted by hand, all automobile manufacturers have provided a means by which you can gain ac-

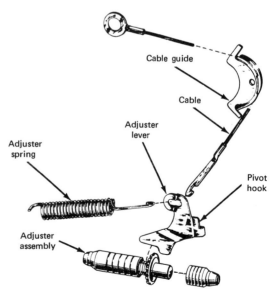

Figure 10.13 A typical self-adjusting mechanism (courtesy American Motors Corporation).

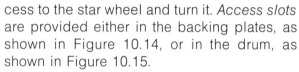

Access slot

Figure 10.14 A typical access slot in a backing plate (Chevrolet Service Manual, Chevrolet Motor Division, GM).

Figure 10.15 A typical access slot in a drum (Oldsmobile Motor Division, GM).

cess to the star wheel and turn it. *Access slots* are provided either in the backing plates, as shown in Figure 10.14, or in the drum, as shown in Figure 10.15.

Access slots are covered by metal or rubber plugs. These plugs are usually called *dust covers*. They help to prevent dirt and water from entering the brake assembly. A typical rubber dust cover is shown in Figure 10.16. Dust covers are easily removed. A thin screwdriver can be used, as shown in Figure 10.17. Dust covers should always be reinserted after a brake adjustment. If you find dust covers missing from the car on which you are working, install new dust covers. If the access slot is in the backing plate, a rubber or metal plug may be used to cover it. If the slot is in the drum, only a metal plug should be used.

Some manufacturers do not completely punch out the access slots in the drums. They provide *lanced*, or semi-punched, slots. Such slots still have a piece of metal in them. They must be opened by punching out the piece of metal with a hammer and punch. Whenever you open a lanced slot, you must remove the drum and discard the piece of metal you

punched out of the slot. If the piece of metal were left in the brake assembly, it could be caught between the lining and the drum. This would prevent the brake from working properly, and would damage the drum.

Turning the Star Wheel If the access slot is in the drum, a screwdriver can often be used to turn the star wheel. If the slot is in the backing plate, a special tool called a brake spoon probably must be used. A brake spoon is a curved metal lever. On many cars, parts of the suspension system obstruct the access slot. On these cars you must use a curved brake spoon so that you can work around the obstruction. You will need several different types of spoons in your tool kit. Some of the most commonly used types are shown in Figure 10.18.

When you try to adjust brakes on a car with self-adjusters, you will find that the star wheel can be moved in only one direction. The lever in the self-adjusting mechanism acts as a ratchet, and it allows you to tighten the adjustment but not to loosen it. Any attempt to loosen the adjustment will cause the lever to lock the star wheel. To loosen the adjustment,

Figure 10.16 A rubber dust cover used to plug an access slot in a backing plate.

Figure 10.17 Removing a rubber dust cover from a backing plate (Ford Motor Company).

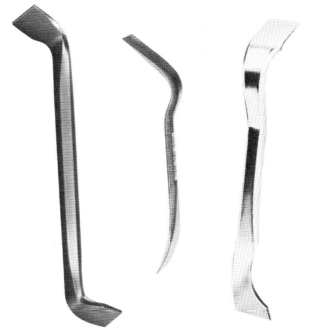

Figure 10.18 Various types of brake spoons (courtesy of KD Tools).

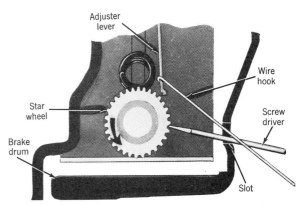

Figure 10.19 Loosening a brake adjustment through an access slot in the drum. Note how the hook is used to hold the lever away from the star wheel (Chevrolet Service Manual, Chevrolet Motor Division, GM).

you must hold the lever away from the star wheel.

If the access slot is in the drum, a small hook can be inserted through the slot and used to pull the lever away from the star wheel. This operation is shown in Figure 10.19. A suitable hook can be made from a piece of coat hanger wire or welding rod.

If the access slot is in the backing plate, the lever must be pushed away from the star wheel, as shown in Figure 10.20. A screwdriver can be used, but a piece of wire will leave more room for your brake spoon. This is shown in Figure 10.21.

Adjusting brakes to obtain a high pedal is not the only reason for releasing the lever from the star wheel. Often you will try to remove a drum only to find that it will not come off, even though it appears to be loose. When this happens, it is usually because the drum has been badly worn or *scored* and the shoes have been adjusted outward so far that the edge of the drum will not slide over the lining. When this

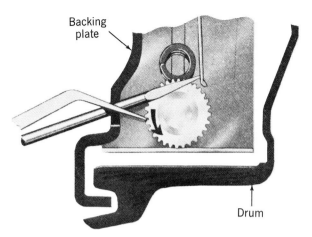

Figure 10.20 Loosening a brake adjustment through an access slot in the backing plate (Chevrolet Service Manual, Chevrolet Motor Division, GM).

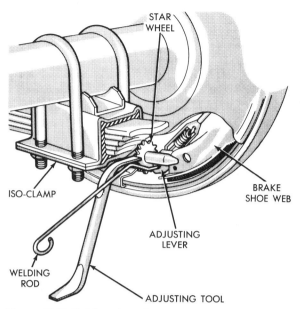

Figure 10.21 Holding the adjuster lever away from the star wheel with a tool made from a piece of welding rod (courtesy Chrysler Corporation).

condition is found, you must *back-off*, or loosen, the adjuster. This procedure will increase the clearance between the lining and the drum. Never use force to pull a drum over the lining.

ADJUSTING BRAKES The following steps outline a typical procedure for adjusting the brakes on a car equipped with self-adjusters. You should consult an appropriate manual for the procedure specified for the car on which you are working:

1 Raise the car and support it with car stands.

2 Remove the dust cover from the backing plate or drum at one wheel.

3 Insert a stiff piece of wire or a thin screwdriver into the access slot and hold the adjuster lever away from the star wheel. Using a brake spoon, tighten the adjustment until you feel a heavy drag when you try to turn the wheel.

4 Continue to hold the adjuster lever away from the star wheel. Loosen the adjustment about 20 or 30 notches (teeth) until the wheel spins freely.

5 Install the dust cover.

6 Repeat steps 2 through 5 at the remaining wheels.

7 Lower the car to the floor.

8 Make the final adjustment by driving the car, making numerous forward and reverse stops. Apply the brakes firmly until you obtain a high pedal.

Manual Adjusters   Some cars do not have self-adjusting brakes. Those cars may include police cars, taxicabs, and cars with heavy-duty suspension systems. Brakes on these cars are adjusted in the same way as those with self-adjusters. However, manual adjusters do not have a lever to prevent the star wheel from turning backward. Therefore, you do not need a wire to release the adjuster.

As with self-adjusting brakes, you should tighten the star wheel adjusting screw until you feel a heavy drag when you try to turn the wheel. Then you should back off on the adjustment until the wheel turns freely. On cars with manual adjusters, you may have to back off from 8 to 12 notches. You should check the manufacturer's manual for the recommended procedure.

Job 10b

ADJUST SERVICE BRAKES

SATISFACTORY PERFORMANCE

A satisfactory performance on this job requires that you do the following:

1 Adjust the service brakes on the car assigned.
2 Following the steps in the "Performance Outline" and the manufacturer's procedure and specifications, complete the job within 200% of the manufacturer's suggested time.
3 Fill in the blanks under "Information."

PERFORMANCE OUTLINE

1 Raise and support the car.
2 Adjust the brakes.
3 Lower the car to the floor.
4 Check the pedal reserve.

INFORMATION

Vehicle identification _____

Were the brakes fitted with self-adjusters? Yes_____ No_____

Reference used_____ Page(s)_____

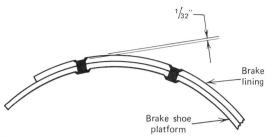

Figure 10.22 Riveted brake lining worn to less than 1/32 of an inch (about 1 mm) as shown should be replaced.

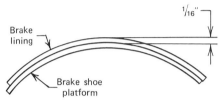

Figure 10.24 Bonded brake lining worn to less than 1/16 of an inch (about 2 mm) measured as shown should be replaced.

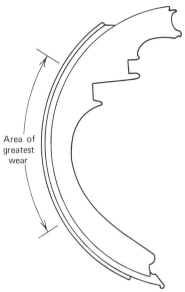

Figure 10.23 The greatest amount of lining wear usually occurs in this area.

Brake Lining Inspection Each time the brakes are applied on a moving car, a slight amount of brake lining is worn away. Depending on the type of use to which the car is subjected and the skills of the driver, brake lining life will average from 20,000 to 40,000 miles (32,000 to 64,000 km). The inspection of brake lining is an important part of routine maintenance. Worn lining can decrease the effectiveness of braking and may cause an accident. Worn lining is not only dangerous, but it can cause excessive drum wear, requiring the replacement of these expensive parts.

When a car has been driven over 20,000 miles (32,000 km), the brake lining should be inspected. Because the front wheels of a car do most of the braking, the front brakes are subject to the most wear. Because of road crown, the right front brake lining usually wears faster than the lining at the left front. But because this is not always the case, you should always remove both front drums for a brake inspection. Many mechanics combine a brake inspection with a wheel bearing repack. By combining these jobs you can save a great amount of time.

Riveted Lining Riveted lining should be replaced if it is worn to less than 1/32 of an inch (about 1 mm) over the heads of the rivets. This measurement is shown in Figure 10.22. If the lining is allowed to wear down to the rivets, the rivets can damage the drum. Because brake lining does not always wear evenly, you should check all the rivet holes. Normally, the center section of the lining on the secondary shoe will show the greatest wear. This area is shown in Figure 10.23.

Bonded Lining Because bonded lining has no rivets, it usually has a longer service life. Bonded lining should be replaced when it is worn to less than 1/16 of an inch (about 2 mm) in thickness. This measurement is shown in Figure 10.24. As with riveted lining, bonded lining does not always wear out evenly. Usually, the center section of the lining on the secondary shoe will show the greatest wear. (Refer to Figure 10.23.)

Worn linings are not the only ones that should be replaced. You should recommend replacement of any lining that is contaminated by grease or brake fluid. In addition, the cause of the contamination must be determined and repaired. If the brake lining at one wheel requires replacement, the lining at the opposite wheel should also be replaced, even if it appears to be in good condition. Replacing lin-ing at only one wheel will almost always result in a pull to one side when the brakes are applied.

INSPECTING FRONT LINING The following steps outline a procedure for inspecting the lining of drum brakes used at front wheels. You should consult an appropriate manual for the specific procedures that may be necessary for the car on which you are working:

1 Remove the front wheel covers and loosen the lug nuts holding the front wheels to the hubs.

2 Raise the front of the car and support it with car stands.

3 Remove one front wheel.

4 Remove the hub cap, cotter pin, nut lock, nut, washer, and outer wheel bearing.

Note: If the bearings are not to be cleaned, inspected, and re-packed, wrap the outer bearing and its retaining parts in a clean paper towel so that they will not become contaminated with dirt.

5 Remove the drum from the spindle.

Note: Be sure that you wear a respirator mask during this step and those subsequent steps that expose you to asbestos dust.

6 Inspect the inner surface of the drum for grooves or scoring. A scored drum should be machined or replaced.

7 Inspect the backing plate for brake fluid leakage. A leaking wheel cylinder must be rebuilt or replaced.

8 Inspect the brake hose behind the backing plate. There should be no evidence of leakage, and the hose should have no cracks, abrasions, or bulges. A leaking or damaged hose should be replaced.

9 Inspect the linings for grease or brake fluid contamination. Contaminated linings should be replaced and the cause of the contamination should be located and repaired.

Note: If the linings at one wheel require replacement, the linings at the opposite wheel must also be replaced to obtain equal braking.

10 Inspect the linings for wear. (Refer to Figures 10.22, 10.23, and 10.24.) Linings that exhibit excessive wear should be replaced.

11 Install the drum on the spindle.

12 Install the outer bearing, washer, and nut.

13 Adjust the bearings and secure the adjustment with the nut lock and a new cotter pin.

14 Install the hub cap.

15 Install the wheel and run the lug nuts up snug.

16 Repeat steps 3 through 15 at the remaining wheel.

17 Lower the car to the floor.

18 Tighten the lug nuts on both front wheels to the torque specification of the manufacturer.

19 Install the wheel covers.

Job 10c

INSPECT FRONT BRAKE LINING—DRUM BRAKES

SATISFACTORY PERFORMANCE

A satisfactory performance on this job requires that you do the following:

1 Inspect the brake lining in the front brakes of the car assigned.

2 Following the steps in the "Performance Outline" and the procedure and specifications of the manufacturer, complete the job within 60 minutes.

3 Fill in the blanks under "Information."

PERFORMANCE OUTLINE

1 Raise and support the car.

2 Remove the front wheels.

3 Remove the front drums.

4 Inspect the drums and lining.

5 Install all the parts removed.

6 Adjust the wheel bearings.

7 Lower the car to the floor.

8 Tighten the lug nuts to the manufacturer's torque specification.

INFORMATION

Vehicle identification _____

Reference used_____ Page(s)_____

Type of lining   Riveted_____ Bonded_____

Was the lining contaminated? Left_____ Right_____

Minimum lining thickness found

    Riveted lining _____ over rivet heads

    Bonded lining _____ over shoe platform

Should the lining be replaced? Yes_____ No_____

Drum condition _____Scored _____Not scored

Should the drums be machined or replaced?

 Yes_____ No_____

Wheel lug nut torque specification _____

INSPECTING REAR LINING Rear drum brake assemblies are similar to front brake assemblies except that they have a few more parts. Rear brake drums, however, are mounted differently from front drums, and they require different removal procedures. There are several types of rear brake drums, but the type you will encounter most often is called a *floating drum*. A floating drum has no hub. It is mounted on a *flange* at the end of a rear axle shaft as shown in Figure 10.25.

The drum is held in place by the wheel. Because the drum has no hub, it has no bearings. The bearings for the rear wheels are on the axle shaft. They do not require repacking and adjustment as do front wheel bearings.

Floating drums usually come off easily. Because they are held on by the rear wheels, you must first remove the wheels. With the parking brake released, you should be able to pull the drums off by hand.

When a rear axle assembly is built at the factory, two or three flat, pressed steel nuts called *Tinnerman nuts*, are usually installed on the rear wheel studs. These pressed steel nuts are needed only to keep the drums in place during storage and shipping. Once the

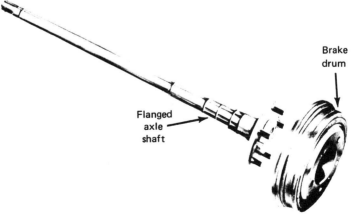

Figure 10.25 View of a floating drum and a flanged axle shaft (courtesy American Motors Corporation).

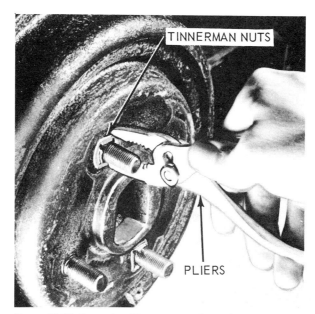

Figure 10.26 Removing Tinnerman nuts so that a rear drum can be removed (Ford Motor Company).

wheels have been installed, the pressed steel nuts serve no purpose. If you find these nuts in place after you remove a rear wheel, you must remove them before the drum will come off. (See Figure 10.26.)

You will sometimes find floating drums that will not come off the axle flange. As you learned when working with the front drums, you should never force a drum off. There are three reasons why a floating drum may not come off:

1 The parking brake may still be applied. If the drum will not come off, check the parking brake to be sure that it is released. If the brake is released, the drum should turn freely.

2 The brake shoes may have been expanded or adjusted into a badly worn or scored drum. If the drum will not come off and the parking brake is not set, back off on the brake adjustment until the drum slides off.

3 The drum may be "frozen" on the axle shaft. The center hole in the drum fits snugly on a round protrusion on the axle flange. Sometimes rust forms between the drum and the flange, causing the drum to resist normal efforts to remove it. The easiest way of removing a frozen drum is to apply heat to the drum around the center hole. An acetylene torch works best. The heat expands the drum so that it releases its grip on the axle flange. Figure 10.27 shows where heat should be applied to release a frozen drum.

Be sure to clean all traces of rust from the center hole and from the axle flange before you put the drum back on. A light coating of brake lubricant or similar light grease at the center hole will keep this trouble from recurring.

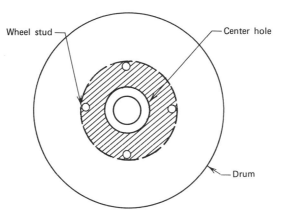

Figure 10.27 Where to apply heat to a brake drum that is "frozen" to an axle flange. The shaded area represents the proper place to apply heat.

The following steps outline a procedure for inspecting the lining of drum brakes used at rear wheels. You should consult an appropriate manual for the specific procedure that may be necessary for the car on which you are working:

1 Remove the rear wheel covers and loosen the lug nuts on both rear wheels.

2 Raise the rear of the car and support it with car stands.

3 Check to see that the parking brake is released.

4 Remove the rear wheels.

5 Remove the pressed steel Tinnerman nuts if they are still present. (Refer to Figure 10.26.)

6 Rotate the drums to determine if the parking brake is fully released.

7 Remove the drums. (Be sure to wear a respirator.)

Note: If the drums are loose on the flange but will not slide over the lining, back off on the brake adjustment. (Refer to Figures 10.19 and 10.20.) If the drum is frozen to the axle flange, heat the drum around the center hole until it expands enough to be pulled free. (Refer to Figure 10.27.)

8 Inspect the inner surfaces of the drums for scoring. A scored drum should be machined or replaced.

9 Inspect the linings for grease or brake fluid contamination. Contaminated linings should be replaced and the cause of the contamination should be located and repaired.

10 Inspect the linings for wear. (Refer to Figures 10.22, 10.23, and 10.24.) Linings that exhibit excessive wear should be replaced.

11 Clean and lubricate the center hole in the drums.

12 Install the drums on the axle flanges.

13 Install the rear wheels and run the lug nuts up snug.

14 Lower the car to the floor.

15 Tighten the lug nuts on both wheels to the torque specifications of the manufacturer.

16 Install the wheel covers.

Job 10d

INSPECT REAR BRAKE LINING—DRUM BRAKES

SATISFACTORY PERFORMANCE

A satisfactory performance on this job requires that you do the following:

1 Inspect the brake lining at the rear wheels of the car assigned.
2 Following the steps in the "Performance Outline" and the procedure and specifications of the manufacturer, complete the job within 60 minutes.
3 Fill in the blanks under "Information."

PERFORMANCE OUTLINE

1 Raise and support the rear of the car.
2 Remove the rear wheels.
3 Remove the rear drums.
4 Inspect the drums and lining.
5 Install all the parts removed.
6 Lower the car to the floor.
7 Tighten the lug nuts to the torque specifications of the manufacturer.

INFORMATION

Vehicle identification _____

Reference used_____ Page(s)_____

How were the rear drums removed?

By hand_____ By use of a puller_____ By use of heat_____

Type of lining _____Riveted _____Bonded

Was the lining contaminated? _____Left _____Right

Minimum lining thickness found

    Riveted lining _____ over rivet heads

    Bonded lining _____ over shoe platform

Should the lining be replaced? Yes_____ No_____

Drum condition   Scored_____ Not scored_____

Should the drums be machined or replaced?

Yes_____ No_____

Wheel lug torque specification _____

DISC BRAKES Disc brakes differ from drum brakes in that a disc, or rotor, is used instead of a drum. The most commonly used type of disc brake is shown in Figure 10.28. The brake shoes, sometimes called *pads*, are held in a hydraulically operated *caliper*, or clamp. The caliper bridges the rotor like a vise. Applying the brakes causes the caliper to squeeze the shoes together. The shoes grasp the rotor and slow or stop its motion. You should study Figure 10.28 to become familiar with the parts and their locations.

Disc Brake Parts The rotor is usually made in one piece with the hub. Some small, light cars use solid rotors similar to the one shown in Figure 10.29. Rotors used on heavy or fast cars are usually ventilated. As shown in Figure 10.30, a ventilated rotor is made with cooling fins between the friction surfaces. This design allows the rotor to act as its own cooling fan. As the rotor revolves, the fins pull air in from the inner edge and discharge it at the outer edge. One advantage of disc brakes is that a rotor can pass off the heat developed in braking much faster than a drum.

There are calipers with one, two, or four pistons. However, the type with one piston is most common. The operation of a single piston caliper is shown in Figure 10.31. When the brake pedal is depressed, hydraulic pressure acts equally against the bottom of the piston and the bottom of the cylinder. The pressure applied to the piston pushes the piston outward and forces the inboard shoe against the inner surface of the rotor. The pressure applied to the bottom of the cylinder causes the caliper to slide inward. This movement forces the outboard shoe against the outer surface of the rotor. Thus, equal force is applied to both sides of the rotor.

The piston and caliper move very slightly. When the brakes are released, the caliper relaxes. But the shoes do not move away from the rotor. There are no retracting springs to pull the shoes away from the rotor or to push the piston back into its cylinder. Even so, the shoes do not drag on the rotor. If they did, they would quickly wear out.

Two factors act to establish a slight but sufficient clearance between the shoes and the rotor. One is the slight amount of rotor *runout*, or wobble. It pushes the shoes away from the rotor surfaces. The other is the action of the *piston seal* fitted into the cylinder wall. The outward movement of the piston during brake application distorts the seal. When the brakes are released, the seal returns to its original shape and thus returns the piston to its original position. This function of the piston seal is shown in Figure 10.32.

Both the construction of the caliper and the action of the piston seal automatically compensate for lining wear. As the linings wear, the piston moves farther out in its cylinder bore on brake applications. The piston slips through the seal far enough to compensate for the wear. When the brake pedal is released, the piston returns only as far as the seal was

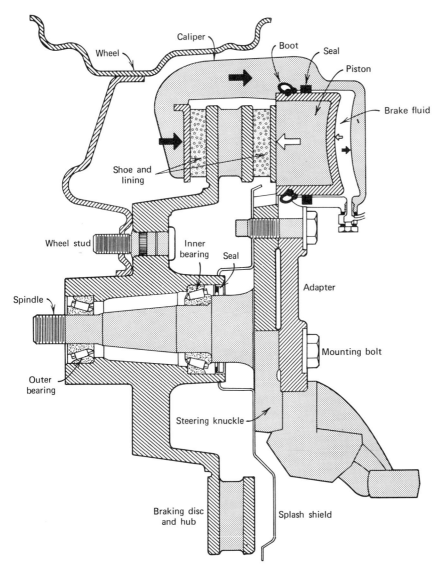

Figure 10.28 A front-sectional view of a disc brake assembly (courtesy Chrysler Corporation).

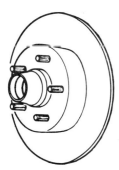

Figure 10.29 A solid rotor. Rotors of this type are found on small, light cars.

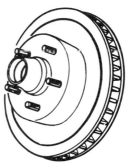

Figure 10.30 A ventilated rotor. Rotors of this type are usually found on heavy, fast cars (Chevrolet Service Manual, Chevrolet Motor Division, GM).

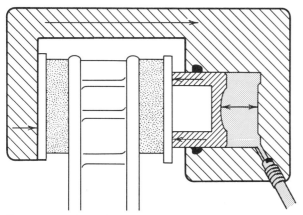

Figure 10.31 Operation of a single piston caliper. Note that because the pressure is equal, the forces pushing the shoes against the rotor are equal (Pontiac Motor Division, GM).

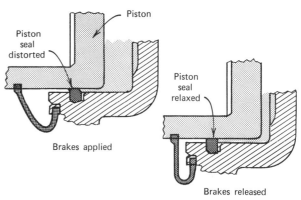

Figure 10.32 The action of the piston seal in retracting the piston. The distance the piston actually moves is exaggerated in this drawing for emphasis (Ford Motor Company).

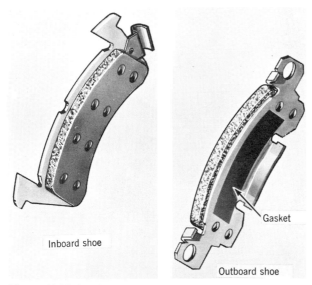

Figure 10.33 A pair of disc brake shoes (Oldsmobile Motor Division, GM).

distorted. This action makes up for lining wear, maintains the correct lining-to-rotor clearance, and eliminates the need for brake adjustment.

The brake shoes, or pads, used with disc brakes consist of flat metal plates with pieces of lining riveted or bonded to them. A typical pair of disc brake shoes are shown in Figure 10.33. Some shoes have retaining tabs to hold the shoes in position in the caliper. Others have holes or slots for positioning pins or bolts. In some instances, the shoes have an

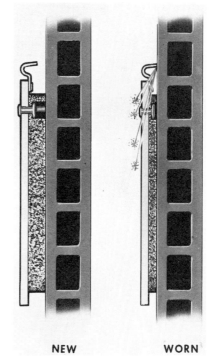

Figure 10.34 The operation of a wear sensing device. When the lining wears to a predetermined thinness, the spring or tab contacts the rotor and causes a squeal (Oldsmobile Motor Division, GM).

extra tab or spring that acts as a wear sensing device. As shown in Figure 10.34, wear sensing tabs touch the rotor when the lining wears to a predetermined thinness. The resulting noise warns the driver that the shoes require replacement.

Job 10e

IDENTIFY THE PARTS OF A TYPICAL DISC BRAKE ASSEMBLY

SATISFACTORY PERFORMANCE

A satisfactory performance on this job requires that you do the following:

1 Identify the numbered parts on the drawing by placing the number of each part in front of the correct part name listed below.
2 Correctly identify 13 of the 17 parts within 15 minutes.

PERFORMANCE SITUATION

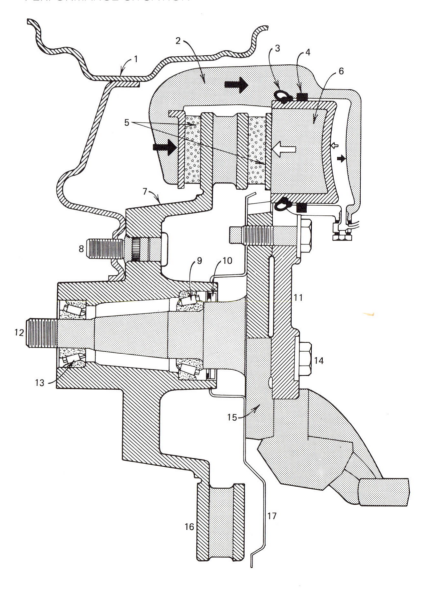

_____Caliper

_____Spindle

_____Steering knuckle

_____Rotor and hub
assembly

_____Wheel

_____Inner bearing

_____Backing plate

_____Mounting bolt

_____Brake fluid

_____Dust boot

_____Piston seal

_____Wheel stud

_____Shoes and lining

_____Adapter or mount

_____Outer bearing

_____Guide plate

_____Splash shield

_____Grease retainer

_____Piston

_____Reaction arm

Disc Brake Lining Inspection Usually, the thickness of the lining remaining on disc brake shoes can be observed when the wheel is removed. Most calipers have an *inspection port*, or hole, as shown in Figure 10.35. As shown in Figure 10.36, the lining on the inboard shoe can be seen through this port. The lining on the outboard shoe can be seen at the side of the caliper. The lining on the outboard shoe should be checked at both the leading and trailing edges. These are the points where the greatest wear occurs. Lining inspection points are shown in Figure 10.37. Because the lining is sometimes difficult to see, you should always perform the inspection with the aid of a flashlight or a drop light. Inspecting the lining exposes you to asbestos dust, so be sure to wear a respirator.

When you check the leading and trailing edges of the shoes, you will often find that the lining is worn unevenly. This is called a *tapered wear pattern*. In most cases it can be considered normal. You will often find that the lining is worn more on the trailing edge of the

Figure 10.35 The location of the inspection port in a caliper (courtesy American Motors Corporation).

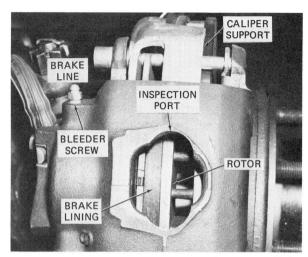

Figure 10.36 The lining on the inboard shoe can easily be seen through the inspection port (courtesy American Motors Corporation).

shoe than on the leading edge. This is caused by the higher temperatures at the trailing edge of the shoe, as shown in Figure 10.38. Sometimes you will find that the lining is worn more at the leading edge of the inner shoe and at the trailing edge of the outer shoe, as shown in Figure 10.39. This wear pattern is caused by the design and mounting of the caliper, which allows the caliper to twist slightly on brake applications. Because of the various wear patterns, you should always check the leading and trailing edges of both shoes. One edge could appear safe, but the other edge could be dangerously worn.

Not only do disc brake shoes sometimes wear unevenly, but they do not always wear at the same rate. The type and rate of wear vary considerably with different cars and under different driving conditions. Brake shoes should be replaced when the lining is worn to the minimal thickness allowed by the manufacturer. This specification depends on the type of brakes fitted and on whether bonded or riveted lining is used. Always check an appropriate manual for this specification. Allowing lining to wear beyond this point could cause rotor damage.

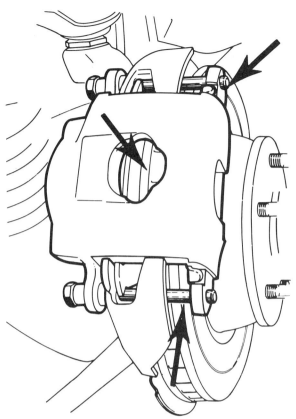

Figure 10.37 Lining inspection areas on a typical disc brake assembly (Pontiac Motor Division, GM).

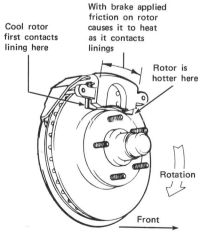

Figure 10.38 The heat pattern in an operating disc brake. This can cause excessive wear at the trailing edge of the shoes (Pontiac Motor Division, GM).

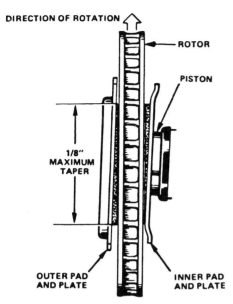

DIRECTION OF ROTATION

ROTOR

PISTON

1/8"
MAXIMUM
TAPER

OUTER PAD
AND PLATE

INNER PAD
AND PLATE

Figure 10.39 The twist of a caliper during braking can cause tapered shoe wear (courtesy of the Bendix Corporation).

INSPECTING DISC BRAKE LINING The following steps outline a procedure for inspecting the lining in disc brakes. You should consult an appropriate manual for the specific procedure and specifications that apply to the car on which you are working:

1 Remove the front wheel covers and loosen the lug nuts on both front wheels.

2 Raise the front of the car and support it with car stands.

3 Remove one front wheel.

4 With the aid of a flashlight or a drop light, inspect the lining on the inboard and outboard shoes. Be sure to inspect both the leading and trailing edges. (Refer to Figure 10.37.) (Be sure to wear a respirator.)

5 Install the wheel and run the lug nuts up snug.

6 Repeat steps 3 through 5 at the remaining wheel.

7 Lower the car to the floor.

8 Tighten the lug nuts on both wheels to the torque specifications of the manufacturer.

9 Install the wheel covers.

Job 10f

INSPECT FRONT BRAKE LINING—DISC BRAKES

SATISFACTORY PERFORMANCE

A satisfactory performance on this job requires that you do the following:

1 Inspect the brake lining in the front brakes of the car assigned.
2 Following the steps in the "Performance Outline" and the procedure and specifications of the manufacturer, complete the job within 60 minutes.
3 Fill in the blanks under "Information."

PERFORMANCE OUTLINE

1 Raise and support the car.
2 Remove the front wheels.
3 Inspect the brake lining.
4 Install the wheels.
5 Lower the car to the floor.
6 Tighten the lug nuts to the manufacturer's torque specification.

INFORMATION

Vehicle identification _____

Reference used_____ Page(s)_____

Type of lining _____Riveted _____Bonded

Minimum lining thickness specification _____

Minimum lining thickness found _____

Should the lining be replaced? _____Yes _____No

Wheel lug torque specification _____

PARKING BRAKES The parking brake system used by most manufacturers is a mechanical system that expands the rear shoes inside their drums. When the driver of a car applies the parking brake, that motion is transmitted to the rear brake shoes by cables. Levers in the system multiply the physical effort of the driver enough to force the shoes into tight contact with the drums. A typical brake cable and lever system is shown in Figure 10.40.

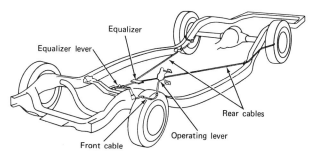

Figure 10.40 A typical parking brake cable-and-lever system. Note how the rear cables are joined at the equalizer (Ford Motor Company).

Compared with service brake systems, parking brake systems are relatively inefficient. The force with which they are applied depends on the strength of the driver. A parking brake system in good condition may fail to hold a parked car if the brakes are improperly applied. The service brakes should be applied before the parking brakes are applied. This action allows the more efficient hydraulic system to force the shoes into contact with the drums. Then, the less efficient mechanical system merely holds them in place.

PARKING BRAKE ADJUSTMENT A parking brake is considered properly adjusted when it meets the following criteria:

1 The brakes are fully applied and holding after the pedal or lever has been moved through less than half its possible travel.

2 The brakes are fully released when the pedal or lever is in the released position.

Because the parking brakes actuate the rear brake shoes, the service brakes should have the proper lining-to-drum clearance. Therefore, before attempting to adjust a parking brake, you should inspect the lining, drums, and related parts. You should check the operation of the star adjusters and you should adjust the brakes to obtain the proper lining-to-drum clearance.

In most instances, parking brake adjustment consists of shortening the length of one or more of the cables to remove unnecessary *slack* or looseness. The adjustment is usually made by means of an adjusting nut at the *equalizer*. A typical equalizer, adjusting nut, and lock nut are shown in Figure 10.41. This adjustment is easy to reach once the car has been raised.

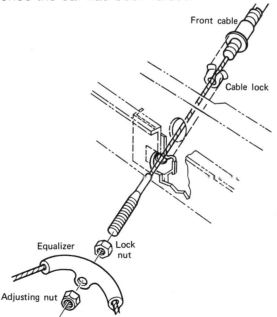

Figure 10.41 Typical provision for parking brake adjustment at the equalizer (courtesy Chrysler Corporation).

Parking brake adjustment, however, involves more than just turning the adjusting nut until you obtain the desired braking action. The operation of self-adjusting mechanisms can be affected by an improperly adjusted parking brake cable. Most manufacturers have established specific procedures for adjusting the parking brakes on their various models. For this reason, you should always follow the procedure given in the appropriate shop manual.

The following is a typical procedure for adjusting parking brakes in drum brake systems:

1 Raise the car and support it with car stands placed under the suspension.

2 Set the transmission selector lever in the NEUTRAL position.

3 Set the parking brake lever in the released position.

4 Loosen the lock nut at the adjustment. (Refer to Figure 10.41.)

5 Tighten the adjusting nut against the equalizer until the rear brakes barely start to drag. The drag can be detected by turning the rear wheels during the adjustment.

6 Loosen the adjusting nut until the brakes are fully released.

7 Tighten the lock nut to retain the adjustment.

8 Check the operation of the parking brake.

9 Lower the car to the floor.

Job 10g

ADJUST A PARKING BRAKE

SATISFACTORY PERFORMANCE

A satisfactory performance on this job requires that you do the following:

1 Adjust the parking brake on the car assigned.
2 Following the steps in the "Performance Outline" and the manufacturer's procedure and specifications, complete the job within 200 percent of the manufacturer's suggested time.
3 Fill in the blanks under "Information."

PERFORMANCE OUTLINE

1 Raise the car and support it with car stands.
2 Place the transmission selector lever and the parking brake lever in their proper positions.
3 Check the service brake operation.
4 Adjust the parking brake.
5 Check the brake operation.
6 Lower the car to the floor.

INFORMATION

Vehicle identification _____

Reference used_____ Page(s)_____

Location of adjustment_____

Was the service brake adjusted? Yes_____ No_____

How was the lining checked? _____

What was the approximate thickness of the lining? _____

SUMMARY

By completing this chapter, you have learned how to perform the routine maintenance inspections and adjustments in the service brake and parking brake systems. You now know the major components of both drum and disc brakes and their functions. You can inspect the lining used in both systems and can determine if it is excessively worn. You can adjust service brakes to obtain a high pedal, and can adjust parking brakes to hold a stopped car. You have gained knowledge, diagnostic skills, and repair skills.

SELF-TEST

Each incomplete statement or question in this test is followed by four suggested completions or answers. In each case select the *one* that best completes the sentence or answers the question.

1 Two mechanics are discussing drum brake systems.
Mechanic A says that the backing plates for the front brakes are bolted to the spindles.
Mechanic B says that backing plates for rear brakes are bolted to the rear axle housing.
Who is right?

A. A only
B. B only
C. Both A and B
D. Neither A nor B

2 Two mechanics are discussing drum brake operation.
Mechanic A says that the retracting springs pull the brake shoes away from the drum when the brakes are released.
Mechanic B says that the retracting springs push the wheel cylinder pistons back into the cylinder when the brakes are released.
Who is right?
A. A only
B. B only
C. Both A and B
D. Neither A nor B

3 To compensate for lining wear, most drum brakes are fitted with
A. anchor pins
B. hold-down springs
C. retracting springs
D. star wheel adjusters

4 On cars fitted with self-adjusting brakes, the star wheel is prevented from turning backward by the
A. anchor pin

B. cable guide
C. adjusting lever
D. hold-down spring

5 Two mechanics are discussing the operation of disc brakes.
Mechanic A says that when the brake pedal is released, the piston moves back in the caliper bore because of the action of the piston seal.
Mechanic B says that the piston is pushed back in the caliper bore by rotor runout.
Who is right?
A. A only
B. B only
C. Both A and B
D. Neither A nor B

6 The outboard shoe of a single piston disc brake is pushed against the rotor by the
A. piston
B. caliper
C. push rod
D. caliper mounting

7 Single piston disc brakes are adjusted by
A. star wheel adjusters
B. torquing the guide pins
C. self-adjusting mechanisms
D. piston movement through the seal

8 Two mechanics are discussing disc brakes.

Mechanic A says that the disc brake caliper is attached to the spindle or steering knuckle.
Mechanic B says that the rotor must be removed to inspect the brake lining.
Who is right?
A. A only
B. B only
C. Both A and B
D. Neither A nor B

9 Excess slack in the parking brake cables can be eliminated by an adjustment at the
A. link
B. equalizer
C. operating lever
D. star wheel adjuster

10 Two mechanics are discussing parking brake systems.
Mechanic A says that the service brakes should be checked and adjusted before the parking brake is adjusted.
Mechanic B says that when adjusting parking brakes, the car should be supported by car stands placed under the frame.
Who is right?
A. A only
B. B only
C. Both A and B
D. Neither A nor B

Chapter 11 Suspension and Steering System Services

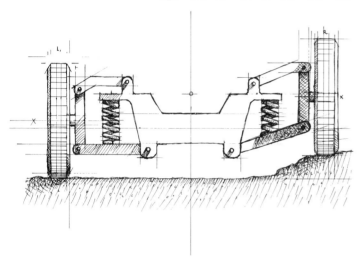

The suspension system holds the wheels of a car in their proper relationship to the car and to the road. This relationship must be maintained regardless of the road surface, the direction of travel, or the speed of the car. The steering system provides the link between the driver and the front wheels of the car. It must provide a sensitive but positive means of moving the wheels the exact distance required for steering.

Routine maintenance of the suspension and steering systems requires a knowledge of the parts in the systems and the function of those parts. In this chapter you will gain some of this knowledge and apply it in performing certain jobs. The performance of these jobs will help you to develop additional skills. Your specific objectives are to perform the following jobs:

1
Identify front suspension system parts.
2
Identify the methods used to unload ball joints.
3
Check wear indicating lower ball joints.
4
Check ball joint play.
5
Test and inspect shock absorbers.
6
Replace shock absorbers.
7
Identify steering system parts.
8
Adjust a power steering pump belt.

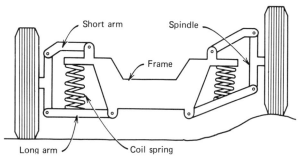

Figure 11.1 A long and short arm independent front suspension system (Ford Motor Company).

FRONT SUSPENSION SYSTEMS A

front suspension system must allow the wheels to turn in steering, even while they are moving up and down at different rates and for different distances. To obtain this motion in different planes, the parts of the system that serves one wheel must be independent of the parts of the system that serves the other wheel. Instead of one front suspension system, there must be two—an independent system for each wheel.

Long and Short Arm Suspension Systems The most commonly used type of independent front suspension system is referred to as *long and short arm suspension*. Each wheel is mounted on a spindle. The spindle is attached to the frame of the car by a long arm on the bottom and a short arm on the top. These arms, called *control arms*, are pivoted

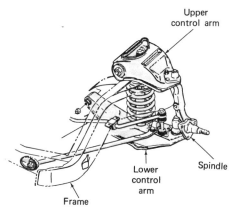

Figure 11.2 A typical left front suspension system using a coil spring mounted between the frame and the lower control arm (Ford Motor Company).

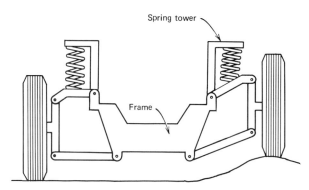

Figure 11.3 A long and short arm independent front suspension system with the spring mounted between the upper control arm and a spring tower.

at both ends. This permits the spindles to move up and down without moving the frame. Figure 11.1 shows the operation of this type of system.

The length of the control arms and the placement of their pivot points are such that the point of contact between the tires and the road does not change as the wheels move up and down. This arrangement eliminates scuffing of the tires, as the suspension system allows the wheels to rise and fall with the road surface.

Coil Springs The compact design of a coil spring makes it ideal for use in front suspension systems. Two types of coil spring mountings are commonly used. In the first type, the spring is positioned between the frame and the lower control arm, as shown in Figure 11.1. Figure 11.2 shows this type of mounting as it actually appears on a car.

The second type of mounting is shown in Figure 11.3. In this mounting, the coil spring is positioned between the upper control arm and a *spring tower* formed in the inner section of the fender. Its actual appearance is shown in Figure 11.4.

Torsion Bars. Some cars do not use coil springs in the front suspension system. They use *torsion bars* instead. A torsion bar is a spring steel bar that is twisted to give spring

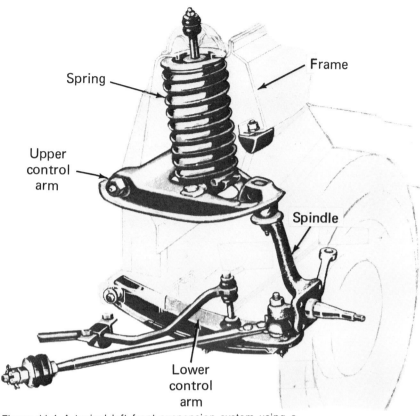

Spring

Frame

Upper
control
arm

Spindle

Lower
control
arm

Figure 11.4 A typical left front suspension system using a coil spring mounted between the upper control arm and a spring tower (Ford Motor Company).

action. It can be likened to a coil spring that has been unwound. The action of a torsion bar is shown in Figure 11.5.

Usually a torsion bar is mounted parallel to the sides of the frame. The forward end of the bar is connected to a lower control arm. The opposite end is connected to the frame. Figure 11.6 shows one type of torsion bar as it is mounted in a front suspension system. In some suspension systems, the torsion bar is mounted *transversely*, or across the frame, as shown in Figure 11.7.

Control Arms The upper control arms are usually triangular-shaped, as shown in Figure 11.8. The base of the control arm is fitted with a pivot shaft or bolts that allow the arm to swing up and down on bushings. The pivot shaft is attached to the car frame. The outer end of the arm is fitted with a *ball joint* that connects the upper arm to the spindle.

Lower control arms also may be triangular-shaped, as shown in Figure 11.9, or they may be straight, as shown in Figure 11.10. Both types are attached to the car frame by pivot shafts or bolts so that they are free to swing up and down. The outer end of the lower control arm is also fitted with a ball joint. Lacking the broad, stable base provided by a triangular shape, a straight lower control arm tends to move back and forth. This movement is prevented by a brace called a *strut*. The strut is connected to the outer end of the lower control arm and to the frame as shown in Figure 11.11.

Spindles Spindles are forged in one piece. They have a vertical brace that is attached to the ball joints of the control arms. Many car

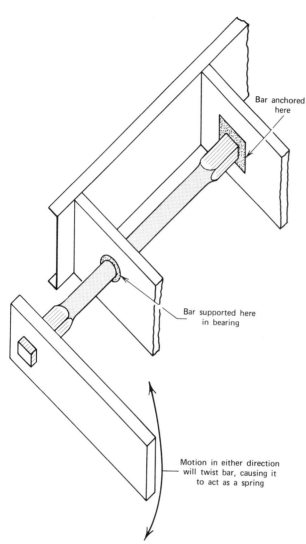

Figure 11.5 The action of a torsion bar.

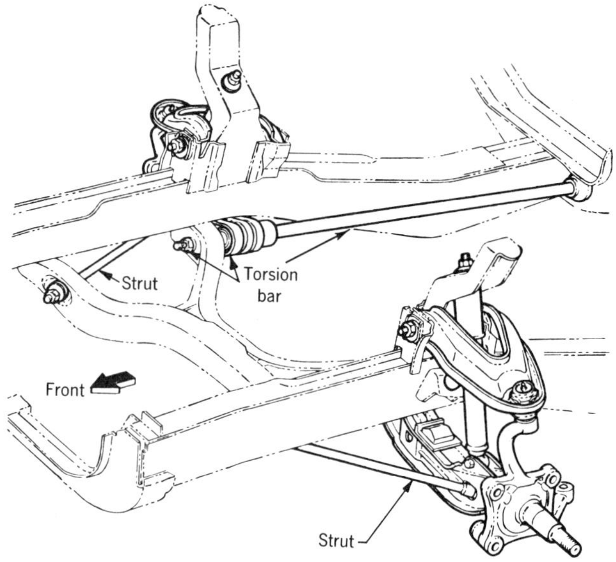

Figure 11.6 A front suspension system using torsion bars mounted parallel to the sides of the frame (courtesy Chrysler Corporation).

makers refer to spindles as *steering knuckles*. Both terms are commonly used. A typical spindle is shown in Figure 11.12.

Spindles perform many jobs. They connect the upper and lower control arms in the suspension system. Moved by the steering arms, they turn the front wheels. From your work with wheel bearings, you know that the spindles provide the axles for the front wheels. From your work with brakes you know that the spin-

dles serve as mounts for the anchor pins and the backing plates for drum brake systems. With disc brake systems, the spindles support the calipers and provide a mounting for the splash shields. As you can see, the spindles are part of the steering and brake systems as well as the suspension system.

To become more familiar with the parts of an independent front suspension system, you should carefully study Figure 11.13.

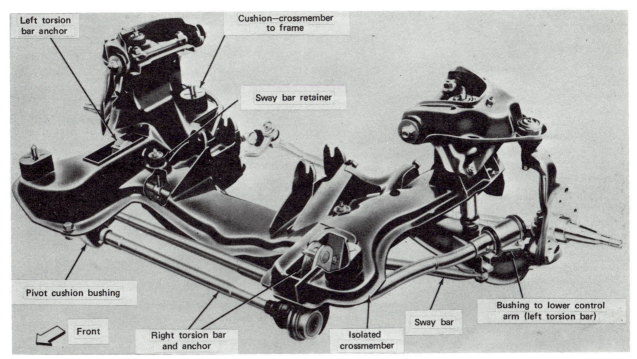

Figure 11.7 A front suspension system using torsion bars mounted across the frame (courtesy Chrysler Corporation).

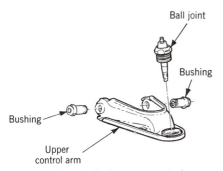

Figure 11.8 A typical upper control arm assembly (courtesy Chrysler Corporation).

Figure 11.9 A triangle-shaped lower control arm (Chevrolet Service Manual, Chevrolet Motor Division, GM).

Figure 11.10 A straight lower control arm (Ford Motor Company).

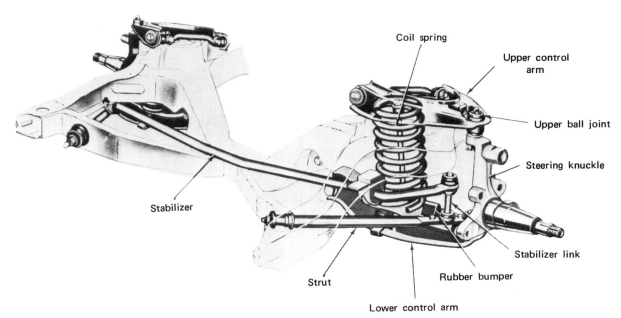

Figure 11.11 A front suspension system using a strut to control the movement of the straight lower control arm (Buick Motor Division, GM).

Figure 11.12 A typical spindle, or steering knuckle (Ford Motor Company).

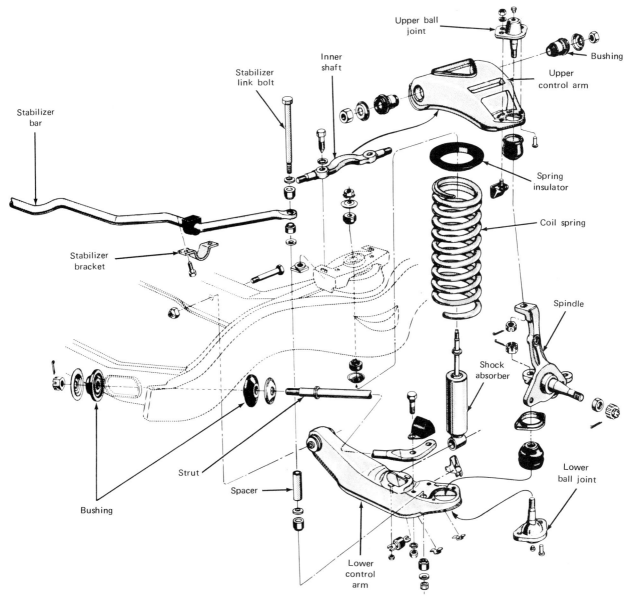

Figure 11.13 An exploded view of a left front independent suspension system using a coil spring mounted between the frame and the lower control arm (Ford Motor Company).

Job 11a

IDENTIFY FRONT SUSPENSION SYSTEM PARTS

SATISFACTORY PERFORMANCE

A satisfactory performance on this job requires that you do the following:

1 Identify the numbered parts on the drawing by placing the number of each part in front of the correct part name.

2 Correctly identify all the parts within 15 minutes.
PERFORMANCE SITUATION

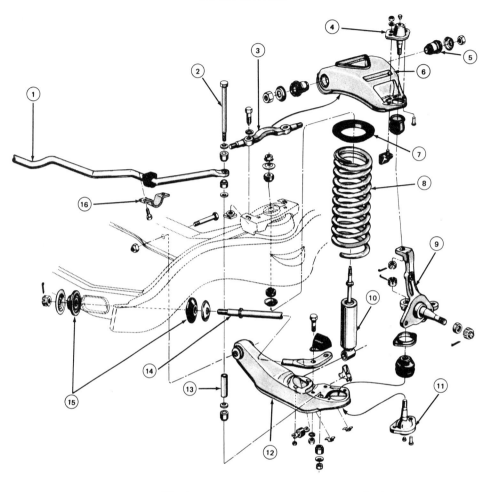

_____Strut   _____Spindle

_____Upper ball joint   _____Lower ball joint

_____Shock absorber   _____Stabilizer link spacer

_____Inner shaft   _____Stabilizer link bolt

_____Lower control arm   _____Upper control arm bushing

_____Upper control arm   _____Stabilizer bar

_____Stabilizer bracket   _____Spring insulator

_____Strut bushings   _____Coil spring

BALL JOINTS Almost all independent front suspension systems use ball joints to connect the spindles to the control arms. A ball joint, shown in Figure 11.14, is similar to the ball-and-socket joint in your shoulder. You can raise and lower your arm, move it forward and backward, twist it, or swing it. A ball joint allows movement in varying planes. Because of it, a spindle can turn, even when the suspension system is moving up and down.

There are many different types of ball joints, but they all fit into two classifications. These classifications are (1) *load-carrying ball joints* and (2) *nonload-carrying ball joints*.

Load-Carrying Ball Joints A load-carrying ball joint is one that supports the weight of the car. That weight is transmitted through a spring or torsion bar to a control arm. The control arm, in turn, transmits the weight to the spindle, or steering knuckle, through a ball joint. When the spring or torsion bar is positioned between the frame and the lower control arm, as shown in Figure 11.15, the lower ball joint is the load-carrying ball joint. When the spring is positioned between the frame and the upper control arm, as shown in Figure 11.16, the upper ball joint is the load-carrying ball joint.

Load-carrying ball joints are subject to considerable wear. Usually, they must be replaced before nonload-carrying ball joints. As shown in Figure 11.17, the weight of the car holds the ball joint tightly in its socket. Any wear on the ball or in the socket is not apparent under casual observation. Improper lubrication or the presence of water or dirt in the joint increases wear. This wear can result in a failure of the joint and in a collapse of the suspension system.

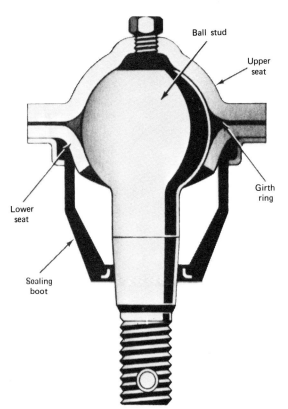

Figure 11.14 A typical ball joint (courtesy American Motors Corporation).

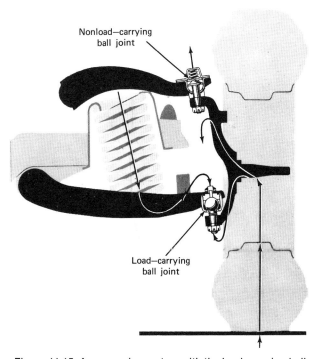

Figure 11.15 A suspension system with the load-carrying ball joint at the lower control arm. Note how the weight of the car is transmitted through the lower ball joint (courtesy Moog Automotive, Inc.).

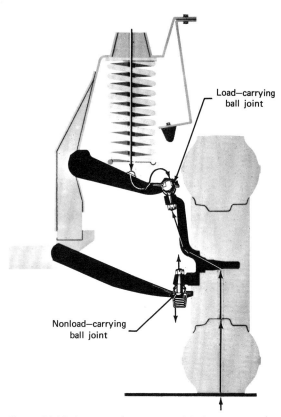

Figure 11.16 A suspension system with the load-carrying ball joint at the upper control arm. Note how the weight of the car is transmitted through the upper ball joint (courtesy Moog Automotive, Inc.).

There are two types of load-carrying ball joints. One design, shown in Figure 11.18, uses the weight of the car to pull the ball stud into its housing. This design is called a *tension-type ball joint*. The second design is called a *compression-type ball joint*. This design uses the weight of the car to push the ball stud into its housing, as shown in Figure 11.19.

Nonload-Carrying Ball Joints One of the ball joints in each suspension system does not support any of the car's weight. It acts to hold the other end of the spindle in place and to maintain the proper steering axis angles. Nonload-carrying ball joints are referred to as *follower joints, pilot joints*, and *friction joints* by different manufacturers. Most nonload-carrying ball joints are *preloaded*. This means that some method is used to hold the ball stud tight against its socket. In some cases, a spring is used to preload the ball joint, as shown in Figure 11.20. Other ball joints are preloaded by means of a rubber pressure ring, or cushion, as shown in Figure 11.21.

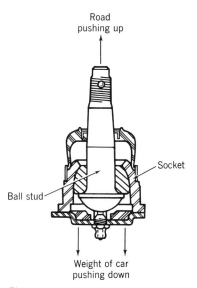

Figure 11.17 A typical load-carrying ball joint. The ball is kept in contact with its socket by the weight of the car (Chevrolet Service Manual, Chevrolet Motor Division, GM).

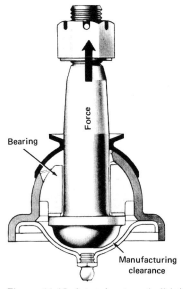

Figure 11.18 A tension-type ball joint. Note how the weight of the car applies a force that pulls the ball stud into its socket (courtesy TRW Inc., Cleveland, Ohio).

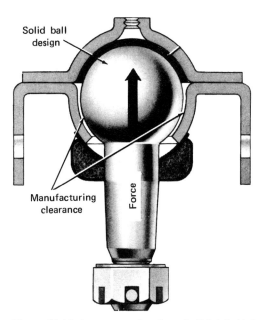

Figure 11.19 A compression type ball joint. Note how the weight of the car applies a force that pushes the ball stud into its socket (courtesy TRW Inc., Cleveland, Ohio).

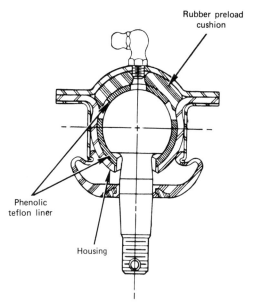

Figure 11.21 A nonload-carrying ball joint preloaded by a rubber ring (Pontiac Motor Division, GM).

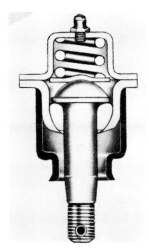

Figure 11.20 A nonload-carrying ball joint preloaded by a coil spring (Buick Motor Division, GM).

Ball joints are preloaded to provide a definite turning resistance. This turning resistance is determined by the manufacturer to ensure proper handling and steering.

Unloading Ball Joints A ball joint must move in its socket without excessive *play*, or looseness. The weight of the car holds load-carrying ball joints in compression or tension. Because of this, any looseness in the ball joint will not become apparent until the weight has been removed from the joint. Because of side-thrust forces in the suspension system, even worn nonload-carrying ball joints may appear to be in good condition until the weight of the car is removed.

Routine maintenance of the suspension and steering systems requires the frequent inspection of ball joints. Before ball joints can be effectively inspected, they must be *unloaded*. In other words, the car must be raised and

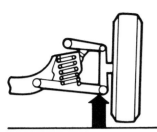

Figure 11.22 Jack position for checking ball joints of a suspension system that uses coil springs or torsion bars between the frame and the lower control arms (Ford Motor Company).

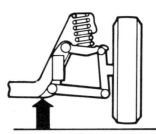

Figure 11.23 Jack position for checking ball joints of a suspension system that uses coil springs between the frame and the upper control arms (Ford Motor Company).

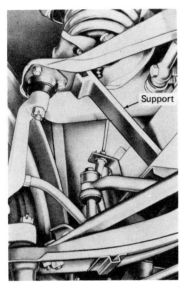

Figure 11.24 A steel support used to hold a coil spring in compression while checking ball joints (Ford Motor Company).

Figure 11.25 To completely unload the ball joints, a wood block can be used as shown on some cars (Ford Motor Company).

supported so that the weight normally borne by the ball joints is held by a jack or car stands. The placement of the support depends on the location of the load-carrying ball joint. On a suspension system that uses a coil spring or a torsion bar between the frame and the lower control arm, the jack should be positioned under the lower control arm, as shown in Figure 11.22. On a suspension system that uses coil springs between the frame and the upper control arms, the jack should be placed under the frame, as shown in Figure 11.23. Often, a brace, or support, must be placed between the upper control arm and the frame, as shown in Figure 11.24. This brace is necessary to hold the spring in compression and to remove the load from the ball joint. On some cars, a block of wood can be used to provide this support. (See Figure 11.25.) Be sure to check the manufacturer's manual for specific instructions.

Job 11b

IDENTIFY THE METHODS USED TO UNLOAD BALL JOINTS

SATISFACTORY PERFORMANCE

A satisfactory performance on this job requires that you do the following:

1 Identify the methods used to unload ball joints by matching each of the sentences below with one of the drawings showing jack placement.
2 Correctly match all the sentences with the drawings within 5 minutes.

PERFORMANCE SITUATION

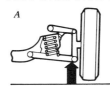 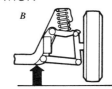

(Ford Motor Company)

_____This drawing shows the proper jack placement when the lower ball joint is the load-carrying joint.

_____This drawing shows the proper jack placement when a torsion bar is used between the frame and the lower control arm.

_____This drawing shows the proper jack placement when the upper ball joint is the load-carrying ball joint.

_____This drawing shows the proper jack placement when the upper ball joint is the follower joint.

_____This drawing shows the proper jack placement on cars that require a support between the upper control arm and the frame.

BALL JOINT INSPECTION Ball joints should be inspected as a part of routine maintenance. They should also be inspected as a part of diagnosing any problems in the suspension and steering systems. Worn ball joints allow the spindles to change position, which in turn changes the angles of wheel alignment. The latter change affects the handling of the car and causes abnormal tire wear. Excessively worn ball joints can fail and cause loss of car control. Most states which have compulsory motor vehicle inspections include ball joints on their list of parts to be checked.

Ball joint inspection should always include a check of wheel bearing adjustment. In most cases, worn or loose wheel bearings do not

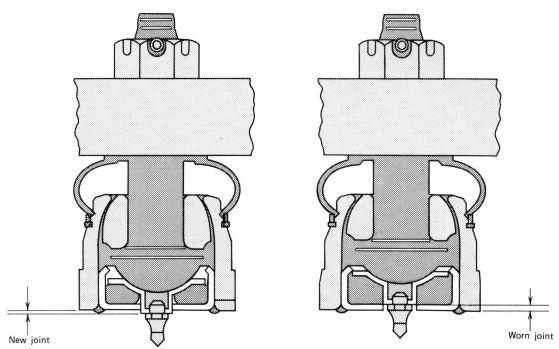

New joint

Worn joint

Figure 11.26 A visual wear indicating lower ball joint. Notice how the nipple extends beyond the ball joint cover when new, but is flush with or below the cover when the ball joint is worn (Buick Motor Division, GM).

allow an accurate ball joint check. As you learned when you lubricated ball joints, each joint is fitted with a boot, or seal. These boots not only keep the grease in the ball joint, but they keep water and dirt out. If a boot is torn or otherwise damaged so that it cannot do its job, the ball joint should be replaced.

Wear-Indicating Ball Joints   Some cars are fitted with load-carrying ball joints that incorporate a visual wear indicator, as shown in Figure 11.26. The wear indicator usually consists of a nipple about ½ of 1 inch (12.5 mm) in diameter that protrudes from the bottom of the ball joint. The nipple, drilled and threaded for a grease fitting, extends .050 in. (1.27 mm) from the surface of the ball joint when the joint is new. Wear on the interior surfaces of the ball and its socket allows the nipple to retract, or move in. The amount of retraction is equal to the amount of wear in the joint. When the nipple is level with or lower than the surface of the joint, the joint has worn .050 in. (1.27 mm) or more, and it should be replaced.

CHECKING WEAR-INDICATING LOWER BALL JOINTS   The steps that follow outline a procedure for checking lower ball joints made with wear indicators. You should check an appropriate manual for specific instructions that may be necessary for the car on which you are working:

1 Raise and support the car by the frame.

Note: **This method of supporting the car keeps the ball joints loaded as they would be if the car were on the floor.**

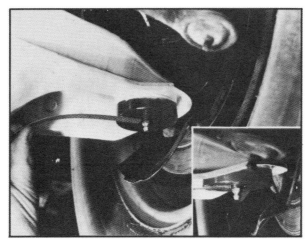

Figure 11.27 Checking the protrusion of the nipple on a wear-indicating ball joint (Pontiac Motor Division, GM).

2 Check the condition of the ball joint boots.

Note: A ruptured, or torn, boot will require that the joint be replaced.

3 Clean the base of the ball joints, making sure that the nipples and the grease fittings are free of all grease and dirt.

4 Check the position of the nipples.

Note: If the protrusion cannot be seen, you might detect any existing protrusion with your fingernail, a small screwdriver, or a steel scale, as shown in Figure 11.27. If a nipple is even with or below the surface of a ball joint, the joint should be replaced. If even one ball joint has excessive wear, both joints should be replaced.

Job 11c

CHECK WEAR INDICATING LOWER BALL JOINTS

SATISFACTORY PERFORMANCE

A satisfactory performance on this job requires that you do the following:

1 Check the lower ball joints on the car assigned.
2 Following the steps in the "Performance Outline," complete the inspection within 30 minutes.
3 Fill in the blanks under "Information."

PERFORMANCE OUTLINE

1 Raise and support the car.
2 Clean the ball joints.
3 Inspect the boots.
4 Check the protrusion of the nipples.
5 Lower the car to the floor.

INFORMATION

Vehicle identification _____

Condition of ball joints

    Left side _____Serviceable _____Unserviceable

    Right side _____Serviceable _____Unserviceable

Recommendations _____

Conventional Ball Joints Each auto manufacturer sets the specifications for allowable wear in ball joints, and also sets the procedures for checking this wear. These specifications and procedures vary, even with different models from the same manufacturer. Therefore, you must use an appropriate manual if you are to perform the inspection correctly. In most cases, conventional ball joints should be checked for *radial*, or side-to-side movement. Some manufacturers provide specifications and procedures for checking *axial*, or up-and-down movement.

When checking ball joints other than those with wear indicators, you must unload the joints. This ensures that the ball stud will be free to move in its socket and that any wear can be detected.

Radial Play Radial play, or side-to-side movement, can be detected by grasping the tire at the top and the bottom and by rocking the wheel in and out. Figures 11.28 and 11.29 show radial play at the load-carrying ball joints.

Load-carrying ball joints are constructed to allow for a certain amount of wear. If the allowable wear in a given joint is exceeded, the joint must be replaced. Any play found in a nonload-carrying ball joint indicates a loss in preload. Most car makers specify that nonload-carrying ball joints which have lost their preload should be replaced.

The amount of play in ball joints can be ac-

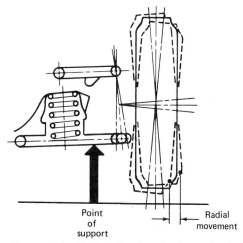

Figure 11.28 Radial play in a load-carrying ball joint (Ford Motor Company).

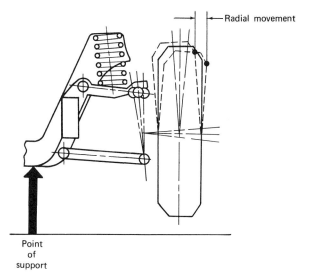

Figure 11.29 Radial play in a load-carrying upper ball joint (Ford Motor Company).

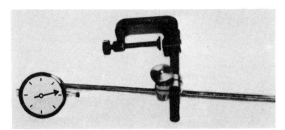

Figure 11.30 A typical dial indicator (courtesy Chrysler Corporation).

curately measured by several methods. The most accurate method requires the use of a *dial indicator*. A dial indicator, shown in Figure 11.30, is an instrument that measures movement in small increments, or additions. Most dial indicators measure increments of 1 thousandth of 1 inch (.001 in.). The movement is indicated by a pointer that moves on a dial face. Various means of anchoring the dial indicator are provided so the instrument can be positioned where desired.

Another method of measuring the amount of play in ball joints requires the use of a *ball joint checking gauge*. Such gauge, shown in Figure 11.31, indicates movement by a pointer on a scale. It is usually graduated in increments of 1 thirty-second of 1 inch ($\frac{1}{32}$ in.).

Figure 11.31 A ball joint checking gauge (courtesy AMMCO Tools, Inc.).

CHECKING RADIAL PLAY IN BALL JOINTS The steps that follow outline typical procedures for checking radial movement in ball joints. You should consult an appropriate manual for the exact procedures and specifications for the car on which you are working:

Preliminary Steps 1 Raise and support the car so that the ball joints are unloaded.

2 Check the adjustment of the front wheel bearings.

3 Adjust the wheel bearings if they are loose.

4 Check the condition of the ball joint boots.

Note: A torn or ruptured boot requires that the joint be replaced.

Nonload-Carrying Ball Joints 1 Ask an assistant to grasp the tire at the top and bottom and to slowly rock the wheel in and out to obtain the movement shown in Figures 11.28 and 11.29.

2 While the assistant is rocking the wheel, carefully observe the

nonload carrying ball joint for any sign of movement.

Note: Ignore any movement at the load-carrying ball joint.

3 Repeat steps 1 and 2 at the remaining wheel.

Note: Most manufacturers recommend replacing nonload-carrying ball joints that show any evidence of radial play.

Load-Carrying Ball Joints 1 Attach a dial indicator to the control arm containing the load-carrying ball joint.

2 Position the indicator plunger so that it contacts the inner side of the wheel rim next to the ball joint.

3 Zero the dial indicator.

Note: This can be accomplished by turning the rim of the dial face.

4 Ask an assistant to grasp the tire at the top and bottom and to slowly rock the wheel in and out to obtain the movement shown in Figures 11.28 and 11.29.

5 Note the amount of movement shown in the dial indicator.

6 Repeat steps 1 through 5 at the opposite wheel.

7 Compare the readings obtained with the specifications for allowable play. If the movement exceeds specifications, the ball joints should be replaced.

Axial Play You can detect axial play by moving the wheel up and down. This is easily done by using a lever or a pry bar placed between the center of the tire and the floor. If the wheel is alternately raised and lowered, any axial movement in the ball joints can be observed. Axial movement is shown in Figures 11.32 and 11.33.

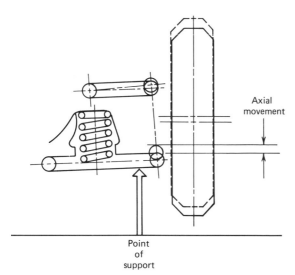

Figure 11.32 Axial play in a load-carrying lower ball joint (Ford Motor Company).

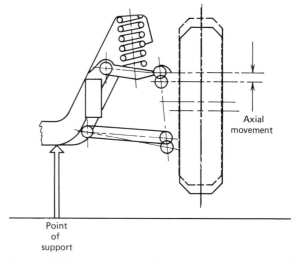

Figure 11.33 Axial play in a load-carrying upper ball joint (Ford Motor Company).

CHECKING AXIAL PLAY IN BALL JOINTS The steps that follow outline a typical procedure for checking axial play in ball joints. However, consult an appropriate manual for the specific procedure and specifications for the car on which you are working:

Preliminary Steps 1 Raise and support the car so that the ball joints are unloaded.

2 Check the adjustment of the front wheel bearings.

3 Adjust the front wheel bearings if they are loose.

4 Check the condition of the ball joint boots.

Note: A torn or ruptured boot requires that the ball joint be replaced.

Measuring Axial Movement 1 Attach a dial indicator to the control arm near the load-carrying ball joint.

2 Position the plunger of the dial indicator so that it contacts the spindle or the ball joint housing as shown in Figure 11.34.

3 Zero the dial indicator.

Note: This can be accomplished by turning the rim of the dial face.

4 Have an assistant move the wheel up and down with a lever or a pry bar to obtain the movement shown in Figures 11.32 and 11.33.

5 Note the movement indicated by the dial indicator.

6 Repeat steps 1 through 5 at the opposite wheel.

7 Compare the readings obtained with the specifications for allowable axial play.

Note: If the movement exceeds specifications, the ball joints should be replaced.

Figure 11.34 A dial indicator positioned to measure axial play in a lower ball joint (courtesy Chrysler Corporation).

Job 11d

CHECK BALL JOINT PLAY

SATISFACTORY PERFORMANCE

A satisfactory performance on this job requires that you do the following:

1 Check the radial and axial play in the ball joints of the car assigned.
2 Following the steps in the "Performance Outline," complete the inspection within 60 minutes.
3 Fill in the blanks under "Information."

PERFORMANCE OUTLINE

1 Raise and support the car so that the ball joints are unloaded.
2 Inspect the wheel bearings and adjust them if they are loose.
3 Check the radial play in the nonload-carrying ball joints.
4 Check the radial play in the load-carrying ball joints.
5 Check the axial play in the load-carrying ball joints.
6 Lower the car to the floor.

INFORMATION

Vehicle identification _____

Location of the load-carrying ball joints

_____Upper _____Lower

Ball Joint	Radial Play Found	Amount Allowable
Left upper	_____	_____
Left lower	_____	_____
Right upper	_____	_____
Right lower	_____	_____

Ball Joint	Axial Play Found	Amount Allowable
Left upper	_____	_____

Left lower _____ _____

Right upper _____ _____

Right lower _____ _____

Reference used_____ Page(s)_____

Recommendations _____

SHOCK ABSORBERS When a wheel on a moving auto hits a bump in the road, the wheel is thrust upward. As it rises, the spring in its suspension system is *compressed*, or squeezed. By compressing, the spring absorbs some of the energy that would otherwise be transmitted to the frame of the car as a jolt or shock. After the spring is compressed, it releases the stored energy by *rebounding*, or returning, to its original length and even beyond. In doing so, it forces the tire back down, actually bouncing it on the road. As the tire bounces, it rises again, and again it compresses the spring. This bouncing, shown in Figure 11.35, could continue, similar to the bouncing of a dropped ball.

The type of spring action that has been described is objectionable for several reasons. These reasons are as follows:

1 When a tire bounces, it loses contact with the road. Because of this, the driver may lose control of the car. A tire can transmit driving, steering, and braking forces to the road only when it is in firm contact with the road.

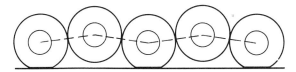

Figure 11.35 Without a shock absorber to control the rebound of its spring, a wheel and tire assembly would tend to bounce.

2 The spring may *flex*, or bend, beyond the elastic limit of its material and then break.

3 The frame of the car moves in relation to the spring motion. Therefore, the driver and the passengers experience a wavy ride.

For the reasons that have been listed, all automobile suspension systems have *shock absorbers*, commonly called "shocks." Shock absorbers control spring action and therefore limit wheel bouncing.

A shock absorber is a hydraulic device consisting of a piston in an oil-filled cylinder. The cylinder is attached to the suspension system, and the piston is attached to the car frame, or underbody. As the suspension system moves up and down, the piston is pushed and pulled up and down in the cylinder. In order to move, the piston must displace the oil in the cylinder. Oil displacement is made possible by means of valves. By varying the size of the valves and the tension of the valve springs, a manufacturer can control the speed at which the piston moves. The piston speed, in turn, controls the speed at which the suspension system moves.

Although there are many types of shock absorbers, the most commonly used are of the telescoping type, called *direct-action* shock absorbers. This type of shock absorber is pictured in Figure 11.36. It is called a direct-action shock absorber because it is installed directly between the suspension system and the car frame, or underbody. Most shocks of this type are also referred to as *double-action*

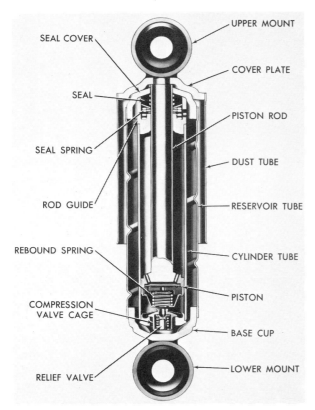

Figure 11.36 A typical direct-action shock absorber (Chevrolet Service Manual, Chevrolet Motor Division, GM).

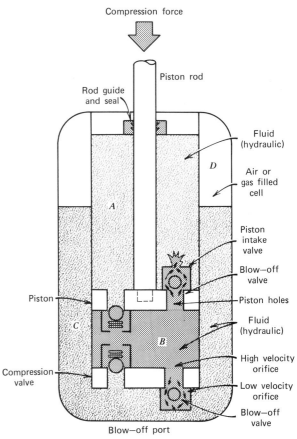

Figure 11.37 The operation of a shock absorber during the compression stroke (Chevrolet Service Manual, Chevrolet Motor Division, GM).

shocks. They are given the name because they control the action between the car frame and the suspension system both when the spring is being compressed and when it rebounds. The operation of a double-action shock is shown in Figures 11.37 and 11.38.

Most shock absorbers used as standard equipment on cars cannot be adjusted, refilled, or repaired. If a shock is leaking or if testing reveals that it is weak, the shock must be replaced.

Testing Shock Absorbers Shock absorbers can be tested by evaluating their effectiveness during a road test, but most mechanics perform (1) a bounce test, (2) a visual inspection, and (3) a manual inspection.

Bounce Test The bounce test is quick, and simple to perform. Lift up and push down on

one end of a bumper, bouncing one corner of the car. Continue until the maximum of movement is reached. Then let go of the bumper and watch the up-and-down motion. If the motion stops rather quickly, the shock absorber at that corner of the car can be considered to be in good condition. If the bouncing continues, the shock is defective.

After bouncing one corner of a car, bounce the opposite corner, using the other end of the same bumper. Compare the bounce at that corner with the bounce at the other corner. The bouncing motion should be the same at both sides. No comparison should be made between the bouncing at a front corner and the bouncing at a rear corner. The action of front shocks may be different from the action of rear shocks.

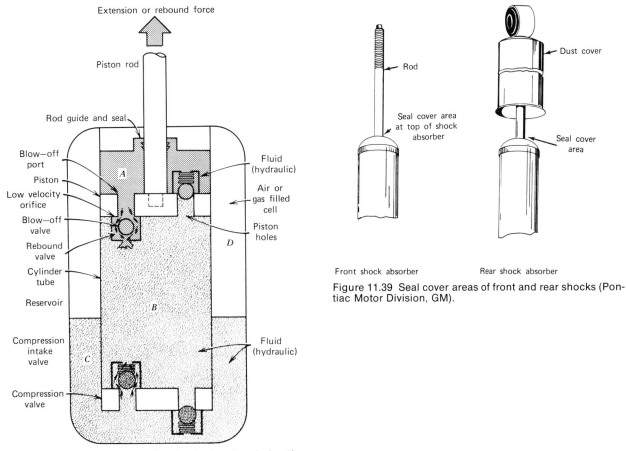

Extension or rebound force

Piston rod

Rod guide and seal

Blow—off port

Piston

Low velocity orifice

Blow—off valve

Rebound valve

Cylinder tube

Reservoir

Compression intake valve

Compression valve

Fluid (hydraulic)

Air or gas filled cell

Piston holes

Fluid (hydraulic)

Figure 11.38 The operation of a shock absorber during the rebound stroke (Chevrolet Service Manual, Chevrolet Motor Division, GM).

Rod

Seal cover area at top of shock absorber

Dust cover

Seal cover area

Front shock absorber   Rear shock absorber

Figure 11.39 Seal cover areas of front and rear shocks (Pontiac Motor Division, GM).

VISUAL INSPECTION A visual inspection may disclose a damaged shock, a leaking shock, or a loose shock mounting. The following steps will enable you to perform a thorough visual inspection:

1 Raise the car and support it by the suspension system so that the shocks are not fully extended.

2 Check for worn or missing rubber bushings and for loose mounting bolts and nuts at the top and bottom of the shock.

3 If the shock is exposed, grasp it and twist it to further check its mountings.

4 Check the shocks for fluid stains or wetness, which may indicate leakage.

5 Raise the car and change the position of the car stands so that the car is supported by the frame. When the car is supported in this manner, the shocks are fully extended.

6 Check the seal cover area, shown in Figure 11.39, for leakage.

Note: Slight traces of fluid around the seal cover area are normal. It does not require that the shock be replaced. The seal at the shock rod is designed to permit a slight seepage of fluid to lubricate the rod. Shocks are filled with sufficient fluid to compensate for this amount of leakage.

7 Lower the car to the floor.

MANUAL INSPECTION A manual inspection is sometimes the only way to detect a weak shock or a shock that is noisy. The following steps outline the procedure for a manual inspection:

1 Raise the car and support it by the suspension system so that the shocks are not fully extended.

2 Disconnect the lower end of the shock.

3 Manually extend and compress the shock, feeling for any change in the resistance to its motion. The shock should offer a definite resistance to motion in both directions, and should have no "tight" or "loose" spots.

Note: If you find that you cannot get a good grip on the shock, you can attach a temporary handle to it as shown in Figure 11.40.

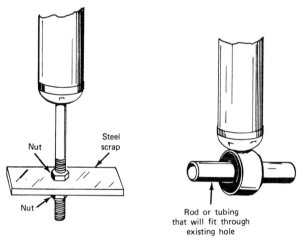

Figure 11.40 Temporary handles for manually operating shock absorbers (Pontiac Motor Division, GM).

Job 11e

TEST AND INSPECT SHOCK ABSORBERS

SATISFACTORY PERFORMANCE

A satisfactory performance on this job requires that you do the following:

1 Test and inspect the shock absorbers on the car assigned.

2 Following the steps in the "Performance Outline," complete the job within 30 minutes.

3 Fill in the blanks under "Information."

PERFORMANCE OUTLINE

1 Bounce-test all four shocks.

2 Inspect the shock mountings.

3 Inspect the shocks for leakage.

INFORMATION

Vehicle identification _____

Test and Inspection Results

Location	Bounce Test	Mounting	Leakage
Left front	_____	_____	_____
Right front	_____	_____	_____
Left rear	_____	_____	_____
Right rear	_____	_____	_____

REMOVING AND INSTALLING SHOCK ABSORBERS The following steps outline procedures for removing and installing shock absorbers. You should check an appropriate manual for any specific procedures that may be necessary for the car on which you are working:

Removing Rear Shock Absorbers

1 Raise the rear of the car with a jack and support the car with car stands placed under the axle housing.

2 Apply penetrating oil to the mounting bolts and nuts.

3 Remove the nut and washer from the lower end of one of the shocks. (See Figure 11.41.)

4 Remove the attaching bolts from the upper end of the shock. (Refer to Figure 11.41.)

5 Remove the shock.

6 Repeat steps 3 through 5 to remove the remaining shock.

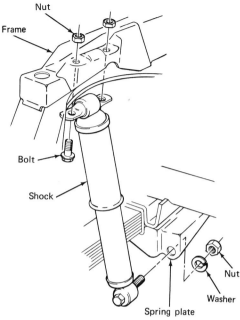

Figure 11.41 A typical rear shock absorber mounting (Buick Motor Division, GM).

Installing Rear Shock Absorbers

1 Hold the upper end of the replacement shock in position, and install the attaching bolts and nuts.

2 Tighten the attaching bolts to the manufacturer's torque specification.

3 Connect the lower end of the shock to the spring plate.

4 Install the attaching washer and nut.

5 Tighten the nut to the manufacturer's torque specification.

6 Repeat steps 1 through 5 to install the remaining shock.

7 Raise the rear of the car with a jack, remove the car stands, and lower the car to the floor.

Removing Front Shock Absorbers

1 Apply penetrating oil to the threads at the upper end of both shocks.

2 Remove the nut from the upper end of each shock. (See Figure 11.42.)

3 Raise the front of the car with a jack, and support the car with car stands placed under the suspension system.

Note: Position the car stands so that they will not interfere with the removal of the shocks.

4 Apply penetrating oil to the threads of the screws that hold the lower end of the shocks to the control arms.

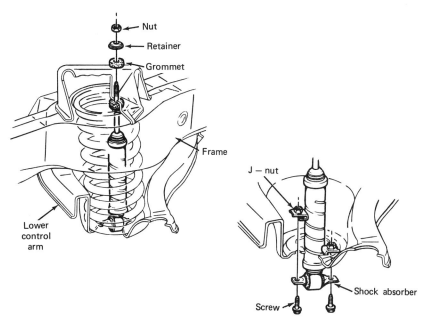

Figure 11.42 A typical method of mounting a front shock absorber. Note the use of "J" nuts at the lower mounting (Buick Motor Division, GM).

5 Remove the attaching screws. (Refer to Figure 11.42.)

6 Remove the shocks by lowering them through the opening in the control arms.

Installing Front Shock Absorbers

1 Extend a replacement shock by pulling the piston rod out to its limit.

2 Install a retaining washer, concave (cupped) side up, on the piston rod, as shown in Figure 11.43.

3 Install a new rubber grommet on the piston rod. (Refer to Figure 11.43 for the correct placement.)

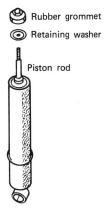

Figure 11.43 The correct positioning of the retaining washer and grommet on a shock absorber piston rod.

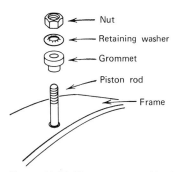

Figure 11.44 The correct positioning of the grommet, retaining washer, and nut on a shock absorber piston rod.

4 Insert the shock up through the opening in the control arm, making sure that the piston rod enters its mounting hole in the frame.

5 Install the attaching screws to hold the lower end of the shock to the control arm.

6 Tighten the attaching screws to the manufacturer's torque specification.

7 Install a new rubber grommet on the end of the piston rod as shown in Figure 11.44.

8 Install a retaining washer, concave side down, on the piston rod. (Refer to Figure 11.44.)

9 Install the nut and tighten it to the manufacturer's torque specification.

10 Install the *Pal* nut, or lock nut, if provided.

11 Repeat steps 1 through 10 to install the remaining shock.

12 Raise the front of the car with a jack, remove the car stands, and lower the car to the floor.

Job 11f

REPLACE SHOCK ABSORBERS

SATISFACTORY PERFORMANCE

A satisfactory performance on this job requires that you do the following:

1 Replace the designated shock absorbers on the car assigned.

2 Following the steps in the "Performance Outline" and the manufacturer's procedure and specifications, complete the job within 200 percent of the manufacturer's suggested time.

3 Fill in the blanks under "Information."

PERFORMANCE OUTLINE
1 Raise the car and support it so that the shocks are not extended.
2 Remove the designated shock absorbers.
3 Install the replacement shock absorbers.
4 Tighten all the mounting bolts and nuts to the manufacturer's torque specifications.
5 Lower the car to the floor.

INFORMATION

Vehicle identification _____

Reference used_____ Page(s)_____

Shock absorber(s) replaced _____Left front

_____Right front

_____Left rear

_____Right rear

Torque specifications Upper_____ Lower_____

STEERING SYSTEMS The steering gear increases the steering effort of the driver. The steering linkage transmits this effort to the front wheels. During your work with chassis lubrication, you lubricated some of the parts of the steering system. Further work on steering systems requires that you know the names of these parts and their functions.

Steering Linkage The steering linkage transmits the movement of the steering gear to the front wheels. Although there are many different steering linkage designs, the *parallelogram type*, shown in Figure 11.45, is the most widely used. This type is so named because if all the common pivot points on one side of the car are connected by lines to their corresponding points on the other side of the car, the lines will be parallel. This parallelism is shown in Figure 11.46.

The parallelogram design offers many advantages. It provides duplicate motion on both sides of a car. In addition, the placement of the pivot points can easily be aligned with the pivot points of the suspension system. This allows the steering system to transmit the same motion to both front wheels regardless of their vertical position. Therefore, the steering motion at each front wheel is the same

Figure 11.45 A parallelogram steering system (Ford Motor Company).

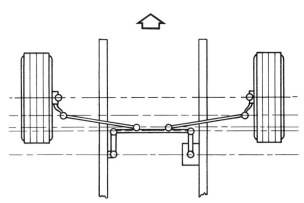

Figure 11.46 The alignment of the pivot points in a parallelogram steering system. Note that the lines connecting all common points are parallel (Chevrolet Service Manual, Chevrolet Motor Division, GM).

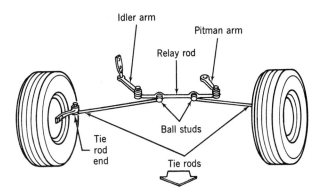

Figure 11.47 The location of the parts in a parallelogram steering system (Chevrolet Service Manual, Chevrolet Motor Division, GM).

even when the suspension system on one side is up and the system on the other side is down.

All the parts in the steering linkage are subject to wear and damage, and should be inspected at regular intervals. The names of these parts and their location in the system are shown in Figure 11.47. Their relationship to one another is shown in Figure 11.48.

Pitman Arm The Pitman arm is the first lever in the steering system. It changes the rotating motion at the steering gear to *linear*, or side-to-side motion. The Pitman arm moves in an arc and pushes or pulls the *relay rod*, which is sometimes called a *center link*.

Relay Rod The relay rod is a rigid steel bar attached at one end of the Pitman arm by a *ball stud*. A ball stud is similar to a small ball joint in that it allows movement in many directions. The opposite end of the relay rod is supported by the *idler arm*. The relay rod moves back and forth across the bottom of the car as the steering wheel is turned. Two holes are drilled through the relay rod so that the tie rods can be attached, as shown in Figure 11.48.

Idler Arm The idler arm merely supports the end of the relay rod, but it is important because it keeps the relay rod aligned. As shown in Figure 11.48, the idler arm is constructed so that it duplicates the Pitman arm. It is mounted on the frame so that it moves in the same plane and thus parallels its motion.

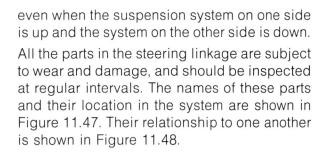

Figure 11.48 An assembled view of typical parallelogram steering linkage components (Chevrolet Service Manual, Chevrolet Motor Division, GM).

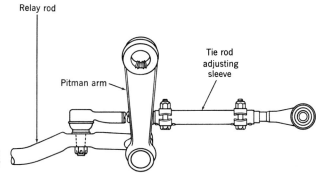

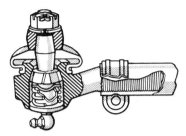

Figure 11.49 A cut-away view of a tie rod end (Ford Motor Company).

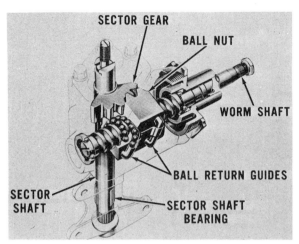

Figure 11.50 A recirculating ball steering gear (Ford Motor Company).

Tie Rods The tie rods are steel bars that connect the relay rod to the *steering arms*. Movement at the relay rod is allowed by ball studs, usually formed in one end of the tie rods. The opposite end of the tie rods is threaded for *adjusting sleeves*. These adjusting sleeves provide a means of changing the length of the assembled tie rods. The adjustment is necessary to provide the correct *toe-in*, a function of wheel alignment.

Tie Rod Ends As shown in Figure 11.49, tie rod ends are ball and socket joints (ball studs) provided with threaded stems. The threaded stem fits into the tie rod adjusting sleeves, and the tapered stud fits into a matching hole in the steering arm.

The Steering Gear The steering gear serves two functions. First, it converts the rotating motion of the steering wheel to lateral, or side-to-side motion. Second, it multiplies the steering effort of the driver. The gear system which performs these tasks also minimizes the road shock that is passed back to the steering wheel. Two types of steering gear designs are in common use: (1) the recirculating ball type and (2) the rack and pinion type.

Recirculating Ball Steering Gear Most cars use a steering gear of this design, shown in Figure 11.50. The principle of operation is very simple. It can be likened to a nut that has been threaded on a bolt. When the bolt is turned,

the nut moves up or down the threads of the bolt. The rotary motion of the bolt is converted to the lateral motion of the nut. Some steering gears of earlier design operated in just this manner. But the friction between the moving parts required excessive steering effort and caused rapid wear.

In the recirculating ball steering gear the bolt, called a *worm shaft*, and the nut, called a *ball nut*, never contact each other. They are separated by steel ball bearings, which roll and keep friction between the shaft and the nut very low. As shown in Figure 11.51, the grooves on the worm shaft and in the ball nut are in the form of threads. The steel balls fit into these threads. When the driver turns the steering wheel, the worm shaft turns. The ball

Figure 11.51 A ball nut and worm shaft disassembled. Note the threads in the nut and on the shaft (Ford Motor Company).

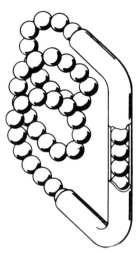

Figure 11.52 A typical ball circuit. Note that the balls are recirculated through a guide (Ford Motor Company).

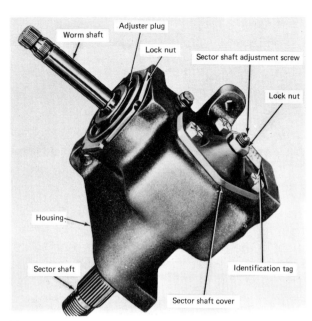

Figure 11.53 A manual steering gear (Ford Motor Company).

nut moves up or down, and the balls roll in their grooves. Two loops of balls are usually used, as shown in Figure 11.52. To keep the balls from rolling out of the ends of the ball nut, *guides* are attached to the outside of the nut. When the balls reach the end of their *circuit*, or loop, they are directed back into the grooves at the other end of the nut. In this way, the balls are constantly recirculated.

As shown in Figure 11.50, the ball nut has teeth cut on one side. These teeth mesh with the teeth on the *sector shaft*. The sector shaft is sometimes called the *cross shaft*. As the ball nut moves up or down on the worm shaft, the sector gear turns the sector shaft. Because the Pitman arm is attached to the end of the sector shaft, the steering linkage moves when the sector shaft is turned.

All the parts of the steering gear are contained in a cast housing, as shown in Figure 11.53. The housing is provided with mounting lugs, or "ears," so that it can be bolted to the frame. Two adjusting devices are provided and on some units, a filler hole is provided so that the gear lubricant can be checked and replenished.

Rack and Pinion Steering Gear Rack and pinion steering gears of the type shown in Figure 11.54 offer some advantages over recirculating ball steering gears. They provide fast, sensitive steering, and they do not require extensive linkage systems. Rack and pinion steering gears also have certain disadvantages. Their basic design limits the amount of steering effort reduction that can be provided. They also transmit more road shock back to the steering wheel than do recirculating ball types. For these reasons, rack and pinion steering gears are usually found only on small, light cars.

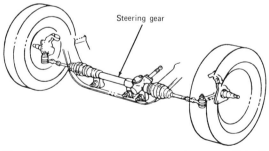

Figure 11.54 A rack and pinion steering gear. Note that the tie rods are connected directly to the steering gear (Ford Motor Company).

Job 11g

IDENTIFY STEERING SYSTEM PARTS

SATISFACTORY PERFORMANCE
A satisfactory performance on this job requires that you do the following:

1 Identify the numbered parts on the drawing by placing the number of each part in front of the correct part name.
2 Correctly identify all the parts within 15 minutes.

PERFORMANCE SITUATION

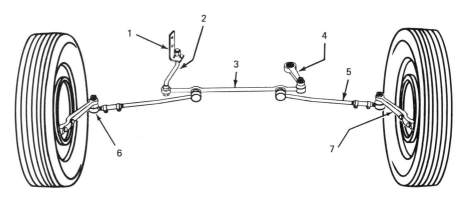

_____Tie rod end   _____Steering arm

_____Idler arm bracket   _____Relay rod

_____Pitman arm   _____Idler arm

_____Strut   _____Tie rod

POWER STEERING SYSTEMS Cars that have power steering are fitted with a booster unit in the steering system. When the effort required to turn the steering wheel exceeds a certain limit, a hydraulic device boosts the effort of the driver. This booster unit provides most of the force required for steering. The hydraulic pressure is provided by a pump driven by the engine. When the steering wheel is turned, a control valve directs the hydraulic pressure to one side of a piston. The piston then applies to the steering system a force that aids in turning the front wheels.

Three types of power steering systems are in common use. The most commonly used system is an *integral system*. In an integral system the control valve and the power piston are internal parts of the steering gear. This type of power steering system is shown in Figure 11.55.

The second type of power steering system in common use is a *nonintegral system*. It is usually referred to as a *linkage-type system*.

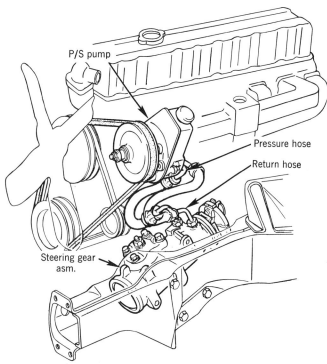

Figure 11.55 A typical integral power steering system. The control valve and the power piston are contained in the steering gear (Chevrolet Service Manual, Chevrolet Motor Division, GM).

This type of system uses externally mounted components that are attached to the steering linkage. The control valve and the power piston are connected by hoses or tubing. A typical linkage-type system is shown in Figure 11.56.

The third type of power steering system is an *integral power rack and pinion system*. Although the control valve and the power piston are contained in the same housing, they are connected externally by tubing. A system of this type is shown in Figure 11.57.

In all power steering systems, hydraulic pressure is provided by a pump mounted near the front of the engine. You are familiar with this location from your work in checking and adjusting the power steering fluid level. A typical pump, shown in Figure 11.58, is driven by a V-belt from the crankshaft pulley. The pump is connected to the control valve by means of two hoses. One hose delivers the hydraulic fluid to the control valve. The second hose returns the fluid to the reservoir.

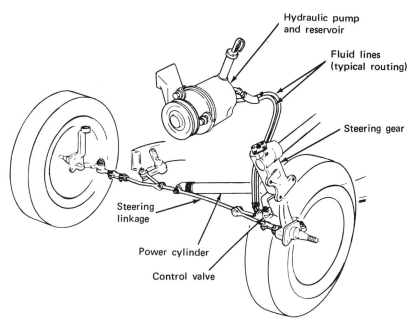

Figure 11.56 A typical linkage-type power steering system. Note that the control valve and the power cylinder are mounted separately on the steering linkage (Ford Motor Company).

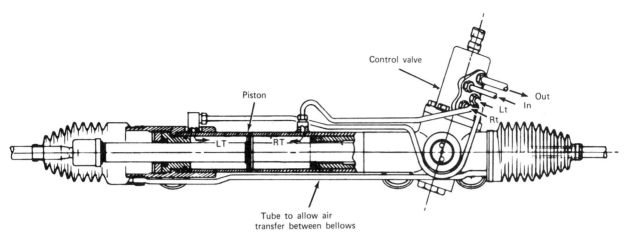

Control valve

Piston

Out
In
Lt
Rt

Tube to allow air
transfer between bellows

Figure 11.57 A typical integral power rack and pinion steering gear. Note the external connections (Ford Motor Company).

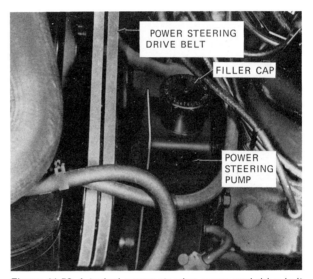

POWER STEERING
DRIVE BELT

FILLER CAP

POWER
STEERING
PUMP

Figure 11.58 A typical power steering pump and drive belt (Cadillac Motor Car Division, GM).

ADJUSTING A POWER STEERING PUMP BELT Because the power steering pump is driven by a belt, a failure of the belt results in a failure of the entire power steering system. Before any attempt is made to adjust a belt, the belt should be inspected.

As with a fan belt, a power steering belt should exhibit no cracks or glazing, and should not be oil-soaked. In most cases an oilsoaked belt indicates that the seal on the pump shaft is leaking. The exact location of the leak must be found and the required repair performed. A belt with any of these defects should be replaced.

A loose belt cannot drive the pump properly. Therefore, a belt that is not cracked, glazed, or oil-soaked should be adjusted to increase

Figure 11.59 Positioning a belt tension gauge on a power steering pump belt (courtesy American Motors Corporation).

its tension. Most manufacturers specify the tension to which the power steering belt on their cars should be adjusted. The belt tension gauge used to adjust a fan belt should be used for this job.

The steps that follow outline a typical procedure for adjusting a power steering pump drive belt. You should consult an appropriate manual for the particular procedure and specifications necessary for the car on which you are working:

1 Position a belt tension gauge on the power steering belt. (See Figure 11.59.)

2 Loosen the adjustment nuts or bolts slightly so that the pump can be moved in or out on its bracket. (See Figure 11.60.)

3 Carefully move the pump until the correct tension is indicated on the gauge.

Note: Do not apply any force to the reservoir or filler neck. On some cars you must pry the pump out as shown in Figure 11.61. The pry bar or special tool must be placed so that it does not contact the reservoir. Any force applied to the reservoir could damage its thin metal or plastic housing and cause leakage. On some cars, a ½-in. square hole is provided in the pump bracket so that a ratchet handle can be inserted and used as a lever. An adjustment feature of this type is shown in Figure 11.62.

4 Tighten the adjustment nuts or bolts to the manufacturer's torque specification while maintaining the correct tension.

5 Remove the belt tension gauge.

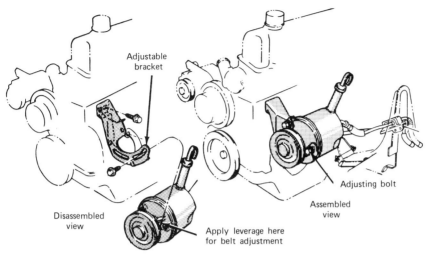

Figure 11.60 Typical provisions for power steering belt adjustment. Note the slotted holes in the adjustment bracket (Ford Motor Company).

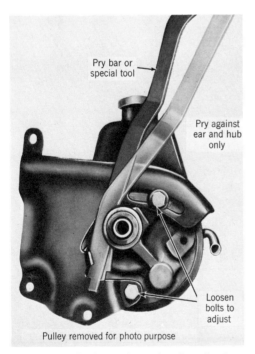

Figure 11.61 Typical prying points for adjusting power steering pump belts (Oldsmobile Division, GM).

Figure 11.62 A power steering pump mounting bracket that allows the use of a ratchet handle to provide leverage for adjustment (courtesy American Motors Corporation).

Job 11h

ADJUST A POWER STEERING PUMP BELT

SATISFACTORY PERFORMANCE

A satisfactory performance on this job requires that you do the following:

1 Adjust the power steering belt tension on the car assigned.
2 Following the steps in the "Performance Outline" and the manufacturer's procedure and specifications, complete the job within 200 percent of the manufacturer's suggested time.
3 Fill in the blanks under "Information."

PERFORMANCE OUTLINE

1 Measure the belt tension.
2 Compare the tension with the specification.
3 Loosen the adjusting bolts or nuts.
4 Adjust the belt tension to the specification.
5 Tighten the adjusting bolts or nuts to the torque specification.
6 Remove the gauge.

INFORMATION

Vehicle identification _____

Reference used_____ Page(s)_____

Belt tension at the start of the job _____

Belt tension specification _____

Belt tension at the completion of the job _____

SUMMARY

By completing the jobs in this chapter, you gained knowledge of the suspension and steering systems. You can identify many of the parts in these systems, and understand the function of these parts. You performed diagnostic and repair jobs and developed additional skills. You have proved that you can inspect ball joints and shock absorbers. You can replace shock absorbers, and you can adjust power steering pump drive belts.

SELF-TEST

Each incomplete statement or question in this test is followed by four suggested completions or answers. In each case select the *one* that best completes the sentence or answers the question.

1 Two mechanics are discussing long and short arm suspension systems.
Mechanic A says that some systems use coil springs between the frame and the lower control arms.
Mechanic B says that some systems use torsion bars between the frame and the upper control arms.
Who is right?
A. A only
B. B only
C. Both A and B
D. Neither A nor B

2 The upper control arm is connected to the spindle by
A. a relay rod
B. a Pitman arm
C. a ball joint
D. an idler arm

3 Two mechanics are discussing ball joints.
Mechanic A says that some ball joints are preloaded to provide a definite turning resistance.
Mechanic B says that load-carrying ball joints should be checked for radial and axial play.

Who is right?
A. A only
B. B only
C. Both A and B
D. Neither A nor B

4 Two mechanics are discussing wear-indicating ball joints.
Mechanic A says that they should be replaced when the nipple protrudes approximately .050 in. (1.27 mm) from the base of the ball joint.
Mechanic B says that they should be checked when the ball joint is unloaded.
Who is right?
A. A only
B. B only
C. Both A and B
D. Neither A nor B

5 Two mechanics are discussing the installation of front shock absorbers.
Mechanic A says that the first retaining washer should be placed on the upper threaded end of the shock with the concave, or cupped, side facing up.
Mechanic B says that many manufacturers use "J" nuts to attach the shock absorbers to the lower control arms.
Who is right?
A. A only
B. B only
C. Both A and B
D. Neither A nor B

6 Two mechanics are discussing the installation of front shock absorbers.
Mechanic A says that most front shock absorbers are connected between the upper and lower control arms.
Mechanic B says that when replacing front shock absorbers, a car should be supported by the frame.
Who is right?
A. A only
B. B only
C. Both A and B
D. Neither A nor B

7 The Pitman arm transmits the motion of the sector shaft to the
A. tie rod
B. relay rod
C. idler arm
D. steering arm

8 Two mechanics are discussing a parallelogram steering linkage system.
Mechanic A says that the relay rod connects the Pitman arm to the idler arm.
Mechanic B says that the idler arm duplicates the motion of the Pitman arm.
Who is right?
A. A only
B. B only
C. Both A and B
D. Neither A nor B

9 Two mechanics are discussing steering gears.
Mechanic A says that on cars with rack and pinion steering, the tie rods are connected directly to the steering gear.

Mechanic B says that on cars with a recirculating ball steering gear, the sector shaft and the ball nut are separated by steel ball bearings.
Who is right?
A. A only
B. B only
C. Both A and B
D. Neither A nor B

10 Two mechanics are discussing the adjustment of a power steering pump drive belt.
Mechanic A says that the belt should be adjusted while using a belt tension gauge.
Mechanic B says that the pump should be moved in its mounting by prying on the reservoir or the filler neck.
Who is right?
A. A only
B. B only
C. Both A and B
D. Neither A nor B

Chapter 12 Ignition System Service-Secondary Circuit

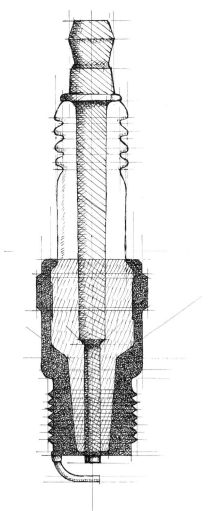

The ignition system supplies the spark that ignites the fuel-air mixture in the engine's cylinders. If the spark is too weak, or if it occurs at the wrong time, the engine will run poorly or it may not run at all. Thus, engine performance is largely dependent on the proper functioning of the ignition system. In addition to causing poor performance, a faulty ignition system can increase fuel consumption and cause unburned fuel to pollute the atmosphere.

All ignition systems require routine maintenance. The services required may vary from simple checks and adjustments to the replacement of parts. This chapter covers the most commonly performed secondary circuit services. You will learn about ignition system parts and their functions. You will test and replace these parts. And you will adjust these parts to specifications.

Your specific objectives are to perform the following jobs:

1
Identify the parts in a basic ignition system
2
Identify the function of ignition system parts
3
Identify spark plug operating conditions
4
Replace spark plugs
5
Recondition used spark plugs
6
Inspect and test spark plug wires
7
Replace a distributor cap

THE IGNITION SYSTEM There are many different ignition systems in use. However, all of these systems operate on the same principle. Battery voltage is boosted to high voltage that may at times exceed 30,000 volts. This high voltage is transmitted, at the proper time, to a spark plug in each of the engine's cylinders. Most ignition systems contain two circuits. A *primary circuit* handles battery voltage. A *secondary circuit* handles the high voltage needed to fire the spark plugs.

The Primary Circuit The primary circuit is actually the control circuit of the ignition system. Two types of primary circuits are used in automotive ignition systems. Most older cars have a primary circuit that uses a set of mechanically operated breaker points. Cars in current production do not use breaker points. Electronic components eliminate the need for these mechanically operated parts. Maintenance of ignition systems requires that you be familiar with the function of the parts in both types of circuits.

A primary circuit using breaker points consists of the *battery,* the *ignition switch,* the *ignition coil*, a set of *points*, and a *condenser*. These parts are connected by wires, as shown in Figure 12.1.

A primary circuit using electronic components consists of the *battery,* the *ignition switch,* the *ignition coil*, the *electronic control unit.* (or *module*), and a *magnetic triggering device*. These parts are connected by wires, as shown in Figure 12.2.

Primary Circuit Components

Battery The battery supplies the energy to operate the system during starting and during those times when the charging system is not producing sufficient current.

Ignition Switch The ignition switch enables the driver to turn the system, and thus the engine, on and off. On most cars, the starter switch is built into the ignition switch.

Ignition Coil The ignition coil boosts the battery voltage to the high voltage needed to fire the spark plugs. Because the coil handles both low and high voltages, it is actually a part of both the primary and secondary circuits.

A typical coil, shown in Figure 12.3, consists of two separate windings of insulated wire. These windings are wrapped around a laminated iron core. One winding is part of the primary circuit. The other winding is part of the secondary circuit. The primary winding

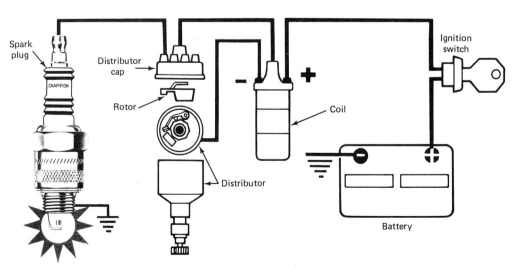

Figure 12.1 A basic breaker point ignition system (courtesy of Champion Spark Plug Company).

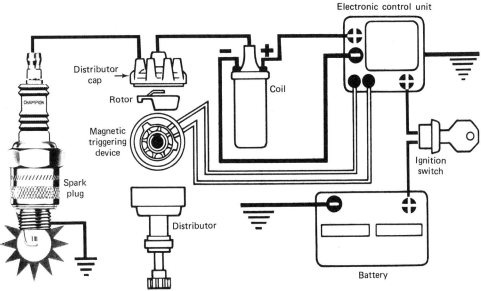

Figure 12.2 A basic electronic ignition system (courtesy of Champion Spark Plug Company).

consists of about 100 turns of heavy gauge wire. The secondary winding consists of several thousand turns of very fine wire. When current from the battery flows through the primary winding, a strong magnetic field is produced. That magnetic field is illustrated in Figure 12.4. When the flow of current through the primary winding is interrupted, the magnetic field collapses. When the magnetic field collapses, a surge of voltage is *induced*, or generated, in the secondary winding. Because of the difference in the number of turns of wire in the two windings, this induced voltage is very high.

Points   The points are a pair of switch contacts located in the distributor. Through the action of a rotating cam, these contacts are brought together and then separated, as shown in Figure 12.5. This action takes place when the engine is running and when it is being cranked by the starter motor. The alternate closing and opening of the points turns the primary circuit on and off, building and collapsing the magnetic field in the coil.

Condenser   The condenser, shown in Figure 12.6, is usually located in the distributor. The

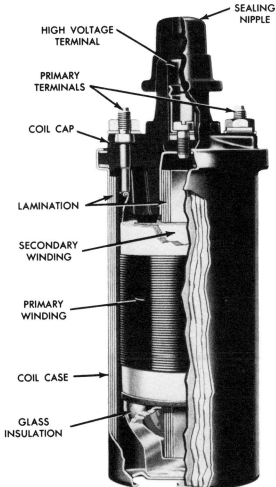

Figure 12.3 A typical ignition coil (Chevrolet Service Manual, Chevrolet Motor Division, GM).

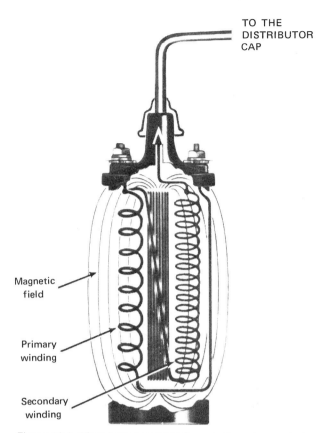

Figure 12.4 When battery current flows in the primary winding of a coil, a magnetic field is created. When the current is cut off, the magnetic field collapses, inducing high voltage in the secondary winding (Chevrolet Service Manual, Chevrolet Motor Division, GM).

condenser acts as an electrical "shock absorber" in the primary circuit. As shown in Figure 12.7, it provides an alternate path for the flow of current when the points start to open. In performing this function, the condenser reduces *arcing*, or sparking, at the points, extending their life. In addition, the action of the condenser helps to induce a higher voltage in the secondary coil winding.

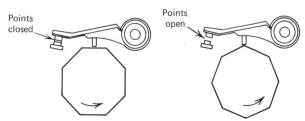

Figure 12.5 The points in a distributor are closed and opened by the action of a rotating cam.

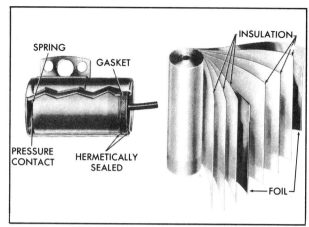

Figure 12.6 A typical condenser. A condenser is connected across the points to minimize arcing when the points open (Chevrolet Service Manual, Chevrolet Motor Division, GM).

Electronic Control Unit In a breakerless system, the electronic control unit, or module, takes the place of the points. The electronic control unit uses a *transistor* to turn the primary circuit on and off. A transistor can be compared with an electrical valve. Because a transistor has no moving parts, it does not require adjustment or replacement because of wear. Typical electronic control units are shown in Figures 12.8 and 12.9.

Magnetic Triggering Device The magnetic triggering device usually consists of a *pickup assembly*, or *sensor*, and an *armature*, or *trigger wheel*. These parts are shown in Figures 12.10 and 12.11. The sensor is mounted in the distributor, and detects changes in a magnetic field caused by the trigger wheel. The trigger wheel is rotated by the distributor shaft as is the cam in a breaker point system. The operation of one type of magnetic triggering device is shown in Figures 12.12, 12.13, and 12.14.

Secondary Circuit The secondary circuit in both breaker point systems and electronic systems is the same. The function of the secondary circuit is to distribute the high voltage surges produced by the coil to each cylinder, where it can ignite the fuel-air mixture. The

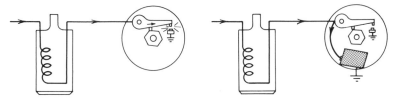

Figure 12.7 The action of the condenser. When the points open, the condenser acts to provide an alternate path for the current flowing in the primary circuit. This minimizes arcing at the points.

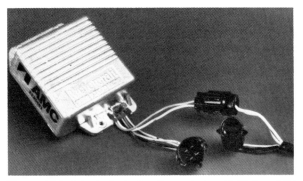

Figure 12.8 A typical electronic control unit. Units of this design are mounted on an inner fender panel or on the firewall and connected to the distributor with a wiring harness (courtesy American Motors Corporation).

Figure 12.10 A typical sensor mounted on a distributor breaker plate (courtesy American Motors Corporation).

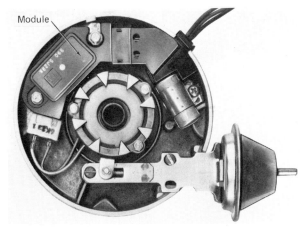

Figure 12.9 A variant control unit. Units of this type are usually called modules and are mounted inside the distributor (Pontiac Motor Division, GM).

Figure 12.11 A typical armature or trigger wheel. The trigger wheel is mounted on the distributor shaft (courtesy American Motors Corporation).

secondary circuit consists of the *ignition coil*, the *distributor cap*, the *rotor*, the *spark plugs*, and the *high tension wires* connecting those parts.

Secondary Circuit Components

Ignition Coil   As you learned previously, the coil is shared by both the primary and the sec-

ondary circuits. The high voltage induced in the coil secondary winding flows out through the tower at the top of the coil. (Refer to Figures 12.1 and 12.3.) The high voltage surges are carried from the coil to the center tower of the distributor cap by a high tension wire.

Distributor Cap   The distributor cap, shown in Figure 12.15, is made of plastic or another in-

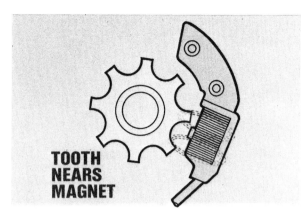

Figure 12.12 The first stage in the operation of a magnetic triggering device. As a trigger wheel tooth approaches the magnet in the sensor, the magnetic field shifts toward the tooth (courtesy American Motors Corporation).

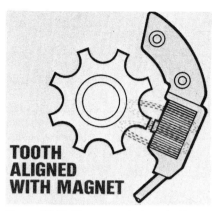

Figure 12.13 The second stage in the operation of a magnetic triggering device. When the tooth is aligned with the magnet in the sensor, the magnetic field has shifted to its maximum (courtesy American Motors Corporation).

Figure 12.14 The third stage in the operation of a magnetic triggering device. As the tooth passes the magnet in the sensor, the magnetic field moves back to its normal position (courtesy American Motors Corporation).

Figure 12.15 Secondary circuit components of a six-cylinder engine (courtesy American Motors Corporation).

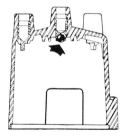

Figure 12.16 A cutaway view of a distributor cap showing the terminals (Chevrolet Service Manual, Chevrolet Motor Division, GM).

Figure 12.17 Typical distributor rotors (reprinted with permission from AC-Delco Division, General Motors Corporation).

sulating material. In addition to the center tower, a distributor cap has other towers or terminals spaced around its circumference. One tower or terminal is provided for each of the engine's cylinders. Inside the cap, at the base of each of these towers, is a metal post, shown in Figure 12.16. These posts, one at a

time, receive a surge of high voltage from the center tower by means of a rotating contact called a *rotor*.

Rotor The rotor, usually made of plastic, is mounted on the distributor shaft and turns with it. Some typical rotors are shown in Figure

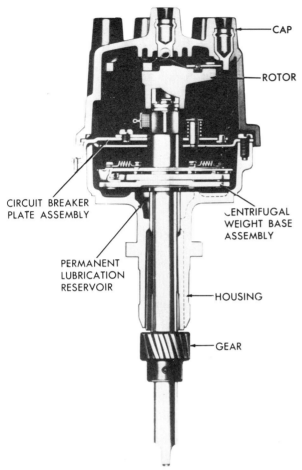

CAP

ROTOR

CIRCUIT BREAKER
PLATE ASSEMBLY

CENTRIFUGAL
WEIGHT BASE
ASSEMBLY

PERMANENT
LUBRICATION
RESERVOIR

HOUSING

GEAR

Figure 12.18 A sectioned view of a distributor used on a six-cylinder engine. Note the position of the rotor and the distributor cap terminals (Chevrolet Service Manual, Chevrolet Motor Division, GM).

GAP

Figure 12.19 A typical spark plug. A spark occurs when high voltage jumps the gap between the two electrodes (Chevrolet Service Manual, Chevrolet Motor Division, GM).

12.17. A metal strip or spring on the rotor contacts a *button* or *brush* at the base of the center tower of the distributor cap. As the distributor shaft rotates, the tip of the rotor passes from one outer terminal to the next. This allows a high voltage surge to flow to each terminal in turn. Thus, in one turn of the distributor shaft, high voltage is distributed to all the outer terminals. The relationship of the rotor and the distributor cap is shown in Figure 12.18.

Spark Plugs Although there are many types of spark plugs, they all serve the same purpose. A spark plug provides the *gap*, or air space, across which the high voltage produced by the coil can jump. A spark occurs when the high voltage jumps the gap. The gap is formed by two electrodes as shown in Figure 12.19. Spark plugs are threaded so that they can be screwed into the cylinder head(s) of an engine. This places the gap inside the combustion chamber, as shown in Figure 12.20.

High Tension Wires Because the secondary circuit may handle in excess of 30,000 volts, special high tension wires must be used. These wires, commonly called *spark plug wires*, must have extra insulation to prevent any leakage of this high voltage. Factory installed spark plug wires have a nonmetallic conductor. Some replacement spark plug wires have a metal conductor. The construction of these two types of spark plug wires is shown in Figure 12.21. To provide good connections at the distributor cap and at the spark plugs, special terminals are used at the ends of the wires. These terminals are shown in Figure 12.22.

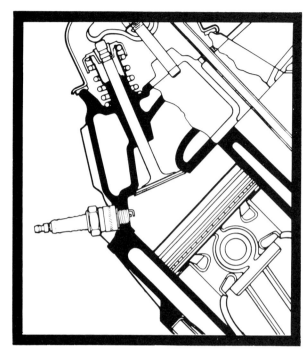

Figure 12.20 The position of the spark plug inside a typical combustion chamber (courtesy of Champion Spark Plug Company).

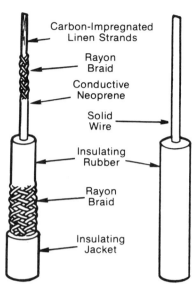

Figure 12.21 Construction of the two types of high tension wire used in the secondary circuit. Note that the conductor has a very small cross section compared with the cross section of the insulation (reprinted with permission from AC-Delco Division, General Motors Corporation).

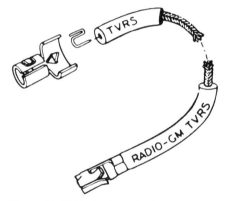

Figure 12.22 Typical terminals used with high tension wire. Note that a wire insert is used to obtain a good electrical connection between the wire core and the terminal (reprinted with permission from AC-Delco Division, General Motors Corporation).

Job 12a

IDENTIFY THE PARTS IN A BASIC IGNITION SYSTEM

SATISFACTORY PERFORMANCE

A satisfactory performance on this job requires that you do the following:

1 Identify the numbered parts on the drawing by placing the number of each part in front of the correct part name listed below.

2 Correctly identify all of the parts within 10 minutes.

PERFORMANCE SITUATION

_____Coil tower   _____Ignition coil

_____Spark plug   _____High tension wire

_____Relay   _____Distributor cap

_____Primary circuit wire   _____Battery

_____Distributor   _____Ignition switch

Job 12b

IDENTIFY THE FUNCTION OF THE IGNITION SYSTEM PARTS

SATISFACTORY PERFORMANCE
A satisfactory performance on this job requires that you do the following:

1 Identify the function of the ignition system parts listed below by placing the part number in the space provided beside the correct part function.
2 Complete the job by correctly identifying the function of all the parts within 15 minutes.

PERFORMANCE SITUATION

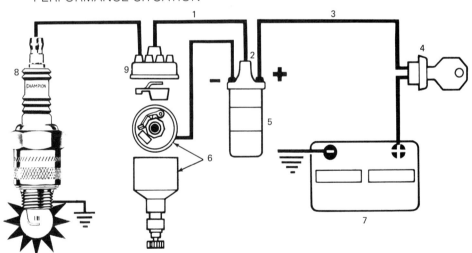

1 Ignition coil
2 Electronic control unit
3 Breaker points
4 High tension wires
5 Condenser

6 Spark plug
7 Primary wires
8 Armature and sensor
9 Ignition switch
10 Battery

_____Provides current for the ignition system while the engine is cranking

_____Conducts high voltage from the distributor cap to the spark plugs

_____Generates high voltage through induction

_____Minimizes arcing at the points

_____Conducts battery voltage through the system

_____Allows the driver to turn the system on and off

_____Makes and breaks the primary circuit in a breakerless ignition system

_____Generates high voltage in the primary circuit

_____Makes and breaks the primary circuit in an ignition system using breaker points

_____Provides a gap for the high voltage to jump

_____Triggers the electronic control unit.

SPARK PLUGS Of all the parts in an ignition system, the spark plugs usually require the most service and the most frequent replacement. This is understandable when you consider the conditions under which they operate.

When the average car has traveled 10,000 miles (16,000 km), each spark plug in the engine has fired about 15 to 20 million times. Each time a plug fires, the spark is pushed across the gap by a voltage surge that can exceed 30,000 volts. During the combustion of the fuel-air mixture, the plug is exposed to temperatures of over 5000°F (2760°C) and subjected to pressures that can exceed 700 psi (4226 kPa).

Spark plug service and replacement are considered by many to be a part of routine maintenance. The skills required are easily developed, but the application of these skills must be based on an understanding of spark plug construction and operation.

Spark Plug Construction As shown in Figure 12.23, a spark plug consists of a _center electrode_ enclosed in a ceramic _insulator_ held by a steel _shell_. The center electrode provides one side of the gap the spark must jump. The remaining side of the gap is formed by a _side electrode_, or ground electrode, which is welded to the shell.

The lower part of the shell is threaded to fit a threaded hole in the cylinder head. The upper part of the shell is six-sided, or _hexagonal_. The "hex" allows you to use a socket to remove and install the plug. Special spark plug sockets, shown in Figure 12.24, are made for this task. They have a rubber sleeve inside to hold the plug and to offer protection against insulator breakage. Some spark plug sockets are made with a hex-shaped head so that they can be be turned with a box wrench when the location of the plug makes the use of a ratchet handle difficult. Most cars require the use of a ⅝-inch or a $^{13}/_{16}$-inch spark plug socket. The

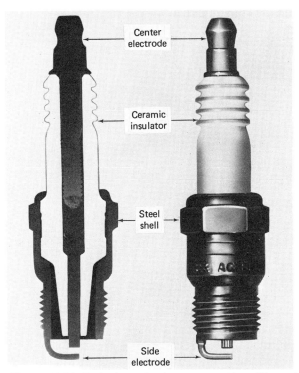

Figure 12.23 Typical spark plug construction (Chevrolet Service Manual, Chevrolet Motor Division, GM).

Spark plug socket
for 5/8" hex
spark plugs

Spark plug socket
for 13/16" hex
spark plugs

Figure 12.24 Special spark plug sockets (courtesy of Champion Spark Plug Company).

addition of these two sockets to your tool kit will enable you to service the spark plugs in most cars.

Spark Plug Design Differences Although most spark plugs may appear similar, they have many design differences. Some of these differences are not apparent. Although a certain spark plug may appear to fit a particular engine, its use may cause poor engine performance and even serious engine damage.

Thread Size   Thread size, or thread diameter, is the most obvious design difference. Most car manufacturers have adopted two sizes as standard. As shown in Figure 12.25, these sizes are 14 mm and 18 mm. Spark plugs of other sizes are available, but they are rarely used in automobiles.

Seat Types   When a spark plug is installed in an engine, it must provide a perfect seal against the pressures of compression and combustion. This seal must also allow heat to

flow from the plug to the cylinder head. A tight, heat conducting seal is provided between the spark plug seat and a matching seat machined in the cylinder head. In some engines, gaskets made of soft metal are used between the seats. In other engines, no gaskets are used.

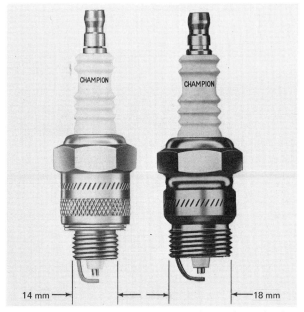

Figure 12.25 The two most commonly used spark plug thread sizes are 14 mm and 18 mm (courtesy of Champion Spark Plug Company).

14 mm
flat seat

14 mm
tapered seat

18 mm
tapered seat

Figure 12.26 Examples of flat and tapered seat plug designs. Note that the plug with the flat seat is fitted with a gasket (courtesy of Champion Spark Plug Company).

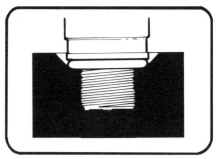

Figure 12.28 A spark plug with a short reach installed in a cylinder head designed for a spark plug with a longer reach (reprinted with permission from AC-Delco Division, General Motors Corporation).

Two commonly used seat designs are shown in Figure 12.26. On plugs that use gaskets, the seat is flat. The gasket is compressed between the seat on the plug and a matching flat seat in the cylinder head. On plugs that do not use gaskets, the seat is tapered. A tapered seat spark plug is designed to wedge into a similar taper formed in the cylinder head. Because the seats in all cylinder heads are not the same, the selection of plugs with the

wrong seat will allow leakage around the spark plug threads and will restrict heat flow.

Reach Reach, or thread length, is the distance between the seat and the end of the thread. Figure 12.27 shows some of the thread lengths in common use. If the reach of a spark plug is too short for a particular engine, the electrodes will not be properly positioned in the combustion chamber. This condition is shown in Figure 12.28. Moreover, the exposed threads in the cylinder head will become filled with carbon and other deposits of combustion. These deposits will make it difficult for you to install the correct plug at a later date.

If the reach of a spark plug is too long, as

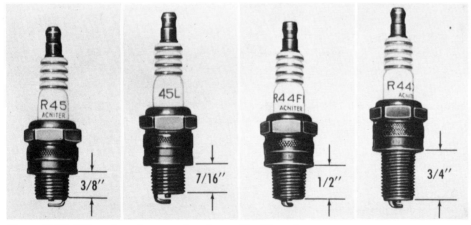

Figure 12.27 Different engines require plugs with different thread length or reach (reprinted with permission from AC-Delco Division, General Motors Corporation).

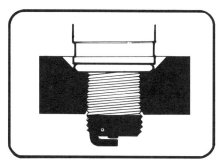

Figure 12.29 A spark plug with a long reach installed in a cylinder head designed for a spark plug with a shorter reach (reprinted with permission from AC-Delco Division, General Motors Corporation).

Figure 12.30 A fouled spark plug (Ford Motor Company).

Figure 12.31 Pre-ignition damage caused by the installation of a plug whose heat range was too high (Ford Motor Company).

shown in Figure 12.29, the plug will extend too far into the combustion chamber. This can cause problems in several ways: (1) The threads of the plug will become filled with combustion deposits. This will make it difficult to remove the plug. (2) The exposed threads may glow when heated, causing the fuel-air mixture to ignite before the spark jumps the gap. This early firing is called *pre-ignition*, and can cause damage to the spark plug and to the piston. (3) The end of the plug may contact the valves or the piston when the engine is running. This contact can cause serious engine damage.

Heat Range Spark plug heat range is the range of temperature within which a spark plug normally operates. Heat range is determined by the plug's ability to dissipate heat. To provide good performance, the spark plugs in a particular engine must operate within a certain temperature range. If a spark plug's operating temperature is too low, the plug will become *fouled*. As shown in Figure 12.30, fouling is a buildup of oil, carbon, and other combustion deposits on the insulator tip and in the shell. These deposits conduct electricity and allow secondary voltage to leak to ground. Because the spark does not jump the gap, the plug misfires and combustion does not occur.

If the operating temperature of a spark plug is too high, the electrodes wear rapidly. Under extreme conditions, pre-ignition, spark plug

failure, and engine damage will result. Figure 12.31 shows a spark plug whose heat range was too high for the engine in which it was installed.

The heat range of a spark plug is usually determined by the length of its lower insulator. As shown in Figure 12.32, the short insulator tip in the "cold" plug provides a short path for heat to flow from the insulator tip to the cylinder head, where it is dissipated in the coolant. Because the plug can pass off its heat

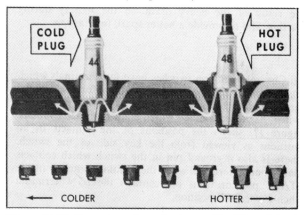

Figure 12.32 Examples of spark plugs with different heat ranges. The ability of the plug to dissipate heat is determined by the length of its insulator tip (Chevrolet Service Manual, Chevrolet Motor Division, GM).

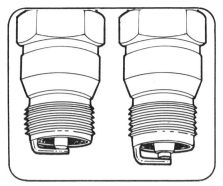

Figure 12.33 Conventional and extended tip design spark plugs (reprinted with permission from AC-Delco Division, General Motors Corporation).

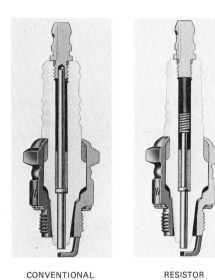

CONVENTIONAL
DESIGN

RESISTOR
DESIGN

Figure 12.34 A comparison of a conventional spark plug and a resistor spark plug. The resistor forms a part of the center electrode (courtesy of Champion Spark Plug Company).

MODEL	Resistor	Regular	Gap
CADILLAC			
V-8 Engines			
1977-78 425 cu.in. 4-bbl. or F.I. . . .	**RN-14Y6**	---	.060
1976-78 350 cu.in. 4-bbl. or F.I. . . .	**RJ-18Y6**	---	.060
1975-76 500 cu.in. 4-bbl. or F.I. . . .	**RN-14Y6**	---	.060
1975 350 cu.in. 4-bbl. or F.I. . . .	**RJ-18Y8**	---	.080
1969-74 472, 500 cu.in.	**RN-12Y**	---	.035
1968 472 cu.in.	RN-12Y	**N-12Y**	.035
1957-67 390, 429 cu.in.	RJ-12Y	**J-12Y**	.035
1951-56 All	RJ-18Y	**J-18Y**	.035

Figure 12.35 A typical listing of the spark plugs specified for a particular make of car (courtesy of Champion Spark Plug Company).

rather quickly, its operating temperature remains low. The "hot" plug has a long insulator which requires heat to travel a greater distance before it is dissipated. Thus, its operating temperature remains high.

Extended Tips On some spark plugs, the electrodes and the tip of the insulator are extended so that they project farther beyond the end of the shell. A spark plug of this design is shown in Figure 12.33. In some engines, this design extends the heat range of the plug. When the engine is running at low speed, the extended tip retains more heat and acts as a hotter plug. This prevents fouling, which is common when an engine is operated at low speeds. At higher speeds, when a colder plug is desirable, the extended tip is cooled by the flow of the incoming fuel-air mixture. Because of engine design differences, extended tip plugs cannot be used in all engines.

Resistor Types Some spark plugs have a built-in resistor. The resistor forms a part of the center electrode, as shown in Figure 12.34. The resistor serves two purposes: (1) It reduces radio and television interference caused by the ignition system, and (2) it reduces electrode wear and thus extends spark plug life.

Spark Plug Selection The correct spark plugs for a particular engine are determined by the engine manufacturer. Spark plugs are identified by code numbers and letters. The identifying code is a specification and can be found in owner's manuals, shop manuals, and the catalogs of spark plug manufacturers. Examples of some of these listings are shown in Figures 12.35 and 12.36.

Spark Plug Catalogs The catalogs distributed by the manufacturers of spark plugs are as important as the tools you use to replace spark plugs. Even though there may be copies available for use in the shop where you are work-

MAKE, YEAR AND MODEL	PLUG TYPE		PLUG GAP
	ACNITER	STD	

CHEVROLET

MAKE, YEAR AND MODEL				ACNITER	STD	GAP
1976.....Chevette ....L4 1400, 1600 ....1-Bbl.				R43TS	–	.035
Vega ....L4 140 ....1 or 2-Bbl.				R43TS	–	.035
Monza ....L4 140 ....1 or 2-Bbl.				R43TS	–	.035
V8 262 ....2-Bbl.				R45TS	–	.045
Cosworth Vega ....L4 122 ....Twin Cam				R43LTS	–	.035
Nova ....L6 250 ....1-Bbl.				R46TS	–	.035
V8 305, 350 ....2 or 4-Bbl.				R45TS	–	.045
Camaro ....L6 250 ....1-Bbl.				R46TS	–	.035
V8 305, 350 ....2 or 4-Bbl.				R45TS	–	.045
Malibu (Chevelle) ....L6 250 ....1-Bbl.				R46TS	–	.035
V8 305, 350, 400 ...2 or 4-Bbl.				R45TS	–	.045
Monte Carlo ....V8 305 ....2-Bbl.				R45TS	–	.045
V8 350, 400 ....2 or 4-Bbl.				R45TS	–	.045
Impala, Caprice ....V8 350, 400, 454 ...2 or 4-Bbl.				R45TS	–	.045
Corvette ....V8 350 ....4-Bbl.				R45TS .	–	.045

Figure 12.36 This listing of spark plugs covers the cars built by one maker for a specific year (reprinted with permission from AC-Delco Division, General Motors Corporation).

ing, you should obtain copies for your personal reference library. Different spark plug manufacturers use different code systems, and explain their systems in their catalogs. An example of one of these code systems is shown in Figure 12.37.

At times, the replacement plugs you have available may be of a different brand than those specified by the engine manufacturer. In these instances, you must be able to convert from one code system to another. The catalogs contain conversion charts so that you can easily locate the correct identification code for the replacement plugs.

"Reading" Spark Plugs Occasionally you will find that an engine requires spark plugs that are different than those specified by the manufacturer. Usually the problem is one of incorrect heat range. The condition of the electrodes and of the insulators of the plugs you remove from an engine provides a fairly accurate means of determining (1) the condi-

PREFIX

B	Series Gap
C	Commercial
CS	Chain Saw
G	Gas Engine
H	High altitude or weatherproof (shield connector, ¾-20 thread)
M	Marine
LM	Lawn mower type
R	Resistor (ACniter)
S	Shielded (⅝-24 thread)
S	Sport vehicle type
V	Surface Gap
W	Waterproof (shield connector, ⅝-24 thread)

SUFFIX

E	Engineer Corps. Shielded (Not an Aircraft type)
F	½-inch reach with pilot design (14mm.) (Foreign)
FF	½-inch reach fully threaded (14mm.)
G	Pin gap
I	Iridium Electrode
K	Hi-Perf. Marine
L	Long reach ($^7/_{16}$-inch for 14mm., ¾-inch for 18mm.)
LTS	Long reach, taper seat, extended tip
M	Special center electrode
XL	Extra long reach (¾" for 14mm.)
N	Extra long reach (14mm.) (¾-inch reach with ⅜-inch thread length)
R	Resistor
P	Platinum Electrodes
S	Extended tip
S	(⅞-inch) Moderate long reach ($^{23}/_{32}$-inch)
T	Tapered engine seat
TS	Taper seat with extended tip
W	Recessed termination
X	Special gap
Y	3-prong cloverleaf electrode

Thread Size—First Digits in the AC Type Number

TYPE NUMBER STARTS WITH	THREAD SIZE
2	½-inch
4	14mm
5	½-inch
6	¾-inch
7	⅞-inch
8	18mm
10	10mm
12	12mm

Heat Range—Last Digit in the AC Type Number

The last digit of the AC type number is the heat range of the spark plug. Read these numbers like a thermometer . . . the higher the last number, the "hotter" the spark plug will operate, the lower the last number, the "cooler" the spark plug will operate. For example, an 8 indicates a hot spark plug, 6 medium hot, 4 medium cold, and 2 cold, etc.

Figure 12.37 The code system used to identify AC spark plugs (reprinted with permission from AC-Delco Division, General Motors Corporation).

Figure 12.38 A spark plug with normal deposits. The insulator tip is light tan or gray in color (Ford Motor Company).

Figure 12.39 An oil-fouled spark plug. Wet, oily carbon deposits cover the firing tip (Ford Motor Company).

Figure 12.40 A carbon-fouled spark plug. The firing tip is coated with dry, fluffy carbon deposits (Ford Motor Company).

Figure 12.41 A spark plug that has been overheated. The insulator is white or light gray with random colored specks (Ford Motor Company).

tion of the engine and (2) the type of service to which the engine is subjected. With a little practice you can learn to "read" a spark plug and select the correct replacement.

Normal Appearance The spark plug shown in Figure 12.38 was removed from an engine which is in good condition and is in average service. The insulator tip has a light tan or gray color and the electrodes are not excessively burned. There are no heavy deposits present. Obviously, the heat range of this plug is correct for the engine from which it was removed. The replacement plug should be of the same heat range.

Oil Fouled Worn piston rings, cylinder walls, bearings, and valve guides may allow excessive amounts of oil to enter the combustion chambers of an engine. This oil is not completely burned during combustion, and oily carbon deposits build up on the spark plug tip. In a short time, the plug becomes oil fouled and misfires. A typical oil-fouled plug is shown in Figure 12.39. An oil-fouled plug usually indicates a need for major engine re-

pairs. When it is not practical for these repairs to be made, the use of a hotter plug may help to burn off the oil-fouling deposits before the plug misfires.

Carbon Fouled As shown in Figure 12.40, a carbon-fouled plug has dry, fluffy carbon deposits on the insulator, shell, and electrodes. This condition may be caused by excessive idling or low speed operation. If this is the case, a hotter spark plug may be appropriate. Because the dry, fluffy carbon is caused by unburned fuel, you should also check for a plugged air filter and other faults which may cause the fuel-air mixture to be too rich.

Overheating A plug that is operating at too high a temperature will exhibit a white insulator tip containing random colored specks. The electrodes may appear burned. A plug that has been overheated is shown in Figure 12.41. An overheated plug usually indicates excessive combustion chamber temperatures and may indicate that the plug is too hot. A plug that shows overheating should be replaced with a colder plug, but the engine and

CARBON FOULED

IDENTIFIED BY BLACK, DRY FLUFFY CARBON DEPOSITS ON INSULATOR TIPS, EXPOSED SHELL SURFACES AND ELECTRODES. CAUSED BY TOO COLD A PLUG, WEAK IGNITION, DIRTY AIR CLEANER, DEFECTIVE FUEL PUMP, TOO RICH A FUEL MIXTURE, IMPROPERLY OPERATING HEAT RISER OR EXCESS IDLING. CAN BE CLEANED.

GAP BRIDGED

IDENTIFIED BY DEPOSIT BUILD-UP CLOSING GAP BETWEEN ELECTRODES. CAUSED BY OIL, OR CARBON FOULING. IF DEPOSITS ARE NOT EXCESSIVE, THE PLUG CAN BE CLEANED.

OIL FOULED

IDENTIFIED BY WET BLACK DEPOSITS ON THE INSULATOR SHELL BORE ELECTRODES. CAUSED BY EXCESSIVE OIL ENTERING COMBUSTION CHAMBER THROUGH WORN RINGS AND PISTONS, EXCESSIVE CLEARANCE BETWEEN VALVE GUIDES AND STEMS, OR WORN OR LOOSE BEARINGS. CAN BE CLEANED. IF ENGINE IS NOT REPAIRED, USE A HOTTER PLUG.

LEAD FOULED

IDENTIFIED BY DARK GRAY, BLACK, YELLOW OR TAN DEPOSITS OR A FUSED GLAZE COATING ON THE INSULATOR TIP. CAUSED BY HIGHLY LEADED GASOLINE. CAN BE CLEANED.

NORMAL

IDENTIFIED BY LIGHT TAN OR GRAY DEPOSITS ON THE FIRING TIP. CAN BE CLEANED.

WORN

IDENTIFIED BY SEVERELY ERODED OR WORN ELECTRODES. CAUSED BY NORMAL WEAR. SHOULD BE REPLACED.

FUSED SPOT DEPOSIT

IDENTIFIED BY MELTED OR SPOTTY DEPOSITS RESEMBLING BUBBLES OR BLISTERS. CAUSED BY SUDDEN ACCELERATION. CAN BE CLEANED.

OVERHEATING

IDENTIFIED BY A WHITE OR LIGHT GRAY INSULATOR WITH SMALL BLACK OR GRAY BROWN SPOTS AND WITH BLUISH-BURNT APPEARANCE OF ELECTRODES, CAUSED BY ENGINE OVERHEATING, WRONG TYPE OF FUEL, LOOSE SPARK PLUGS, TOO HOT A PLUG, LOW FUEL PUMP PRESSURE OR INCORRECT IGNITION TIMING. REPLACE THE PLUG.

PRE-IGNITION

IDENTIFIED BY MELTED ELECTRODES AND POSSIBLY BLISTERED INSULATOR. METALLIC DEPOSITS ON INSULATOR INDICATE ENGINE DAMAGE. CAUSED BY WRONG TYPE OF FUEL, INCORRECT IGNITION TIMING OR ADVANCE, TOO HOT A PLUG, BURNT VALVES OR ENGINE OVERHEATING. REPLACE THE PLUG.

Figure 12.42 Diagnostic chart for "reading" used spark plugs (Ford Motor Company).

its accessories should be checked for other causes of high combustion temperatures.

Figure 12.42 provides additional illustrations of spark plugs which have been removed from various engines. Each illustration depicts a different engine operating condition. By studying these illustrations you can become skilled at reading spark plugs.

Job 12c

IDENTIFY SPARK PLUG OPERATING CONDITIONS

SATISFACTORY PERFORMANCE

A satisfactory performance on this job requires that you do the following:

1 Identify the operating conditions of the spark plugs shown below by placing the number of each plug in front of the description of its condition.
2 Correctly identify four of the five conditions indicated within 5 minutes.

PERFORMANCE SITUATION

1   2   3   4   5

Plug #1 Wet, black deposits on the insulator, shell interior, and electrodes
Plug #2 Black, dry, fluffy deposits on the insulator, shell interior, and electrodes
Plug #3 Melted electrodes, blistered insulator
Plug #4 White or light gray insulator with small black or gray-brown spots
Plug #5 Light tan or gray deposits on the insulator tip

_____Overheating   _____Pre-ignition

_____Ceramic fusing   _____Normal appearance

_____Carbon fouled   _____Oil fouled

SPARK PLUG SERVICES Routine maintenance of the ignition system includes three spark plug services. These services are (1) the adjustment of spark plug gap, (2) the installation of new spark plugs, and (3) the reconditioning of used spark plugs.

Adjusting Spark Plug Gaps The distance between the spark plug electrodes must be adjusted to a specification. Although the gap on all new spark plugs is pre-set by the plug manufacturer, the gap may not be correct for the engine on which you are working. Also,

Figure 12.43 Checking the gap on a spark plug (courtesy American Motors Corporation).

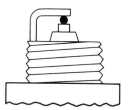

Figure 12.44 A correctly adjusted gap. The gauge wire slides between the electrodes and touches both of them.

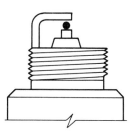

Figure 12.45 A gap that is too wide. The gauge wire does not contact both electrodes.

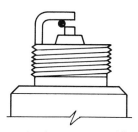

Figure 12.46 A gap that is too narrow. The gauge wire does not fit between the electrodes.

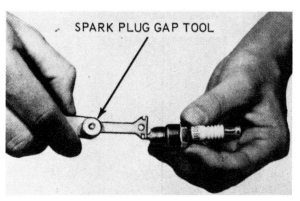

Figure 12.47 Adjusting spark plug gap by bending the side electrode (Ford Motor Company).

the plugs may have been dropped during handling and shipping and the gap may have changed. Different gap measurements are required for different engines. The correct measurement may range from .025 in. (.635 mm) to .080 in. (2.03 mm). It is important that you refer to a shop manual or a spark plug catalog for the gap measurement specified for the engine on which you are working. To insure the quality of your work, you should always check the

gap of a new spark plug and adjust it if adjustment is required.

Spark plug gap is easily measured by using a wire *feeler gauge* or a *spark plug gap gauge* of the type shown in Figure 12.43. A wire of the correct gap measurement is passed between the electrodes. If the wire passes through with a slight drag, as shown in Figure 12.44, the gap is correct. If, as shown in Figure 12.45, the wire passes through loosely, with-

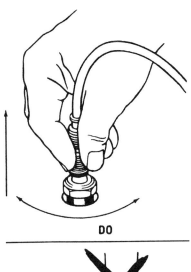

DO

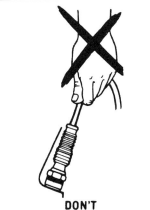

DON'T

Figure 12.48 A spark plug wire should be removed from a spark plug by twisting and pulling the boot. Never attempt to remove a wire by pulling on the wire (reprinted with permission from AC-Delco Division, General Motors Corporation).

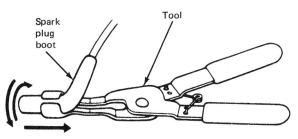

TWIST & PULL

Figure 12.49 Spark plug boots can be removed from spark plugs without damage to the wire by the use of special pliers (Ford Motor Company).

out touching both electrodes, the gap is too large. If the wire will not pass between the electrodes, as shown in Figure 12.46, the gap is too small.

The gap of a spark plug is adjusted by bending the side electrode. This is easily done with the bending tool attached to the spark plug gap gauge. The use of this tool is shown in Figure 12.47. After you have adjusted the gaps of several sets of plugs, you will have developed a skill that will enable you to make this adjustment quickly and accurately.

REPLACING SPARK PLUGS Spark plugs are probably the most frequently replaced parts in a car. As a mechanic, you will replace plugs in all types of engines. The accessibility of the spark plugs will vary from car to car, but the procedure you follow will be the same. The steps listed below outline that procedure, but you should refer to an appropriate manual for the specifications required for the car on which you are working:

Removal 1 Grasp the rubber boot at the end of the spark plug wire and twist it as shown in Figure 12.48. This will loosen the boot on the plug. Continue twisting the boot and pull it off the spark plug.

Note: Special pliers such as those shown in Figure 12.49 can be used for this operation. If you attempt to remove the boot from the plug by pulling on the wire, you may pull the wire from the boot or cause the wire to break within the insulation.

2 Label the wire with a piece of masking tape numbered to the

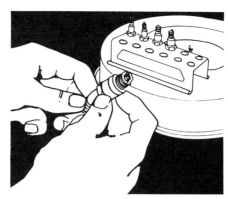

Figure 12.50 When removing spark plugs, you should place them in a tray or rack so that you can identify any cylinders that may have trouble (reprinted with permission from AC-Delco Division, General Motors Corporation).

cylinder number, or position the wire so that you can reinstall it on the correct plug.

3 Remove and label or position the remaining wires in the same manner.

4 Using a spark plug socket, loosen all the spark plugs about one full turn.

5 Using a compressed air blowgun, blow away all dirt from around the base of the plugs. This will minimize the possibility of dirt entering the engine when the plugs are removed.

Note: Be sure to wear your safety goggles during this step.

6 Using a spark plug socket, remove all the plugs and arrange them in the position they were in when in the engine. The use of a rack similar to the one shown in Figure 12.50 is suggested.

Note: By arranging the plugs in order, you can determine which cylinder(s) may be causing problems if one or more of the plugs have an abnormal reading.

7 Read the spark plugs to determine if they are of the correct heat range and if engine defects are indicated.

Installation The replacement spark plugs should be of the type specified by the engine manufacturer. If, by reading the old plugs, you have determined that hotter or colder plugs are required, consult an appropriate spark plug catalog to find the identification code of the correct plug. It is suggested that you change heat range by only one step or number. Too great a change may cause poor performance or possible engine damage.

1 Check to be sure that the gap of all the replacement plugs meets the engine manufacturer's specification. Adjust the gaps as necessary. (Refer to Figure 12.47.)

2 Thread all the spark plugs into place using finger pressure only.

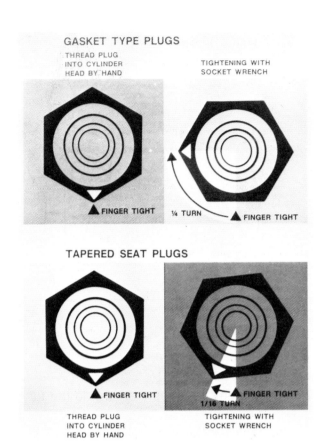

GASKET TYPE PLUGS

THREAD PLUG INTO CYLINDER HEAD BY HAND

TIGHTENING WITH SOCKET WRENCH

▲ FINGER TIGHT

¼ TURN ▲ FINGER TIGHT

TAPERED SEAT PLUGS

▲ FINGER TIGHT

1/16 TURN ▲ FINGER TIGHT

THREAD PLUG INTO CYLINDER HEAD BY HAND

TIGHTENING WITH SOCKET WRENCH

Figure 12.51 Suggested methods of tightening spark plugs when a torque wrench cannot be used (courtesy of Champion Spark Plug Company).

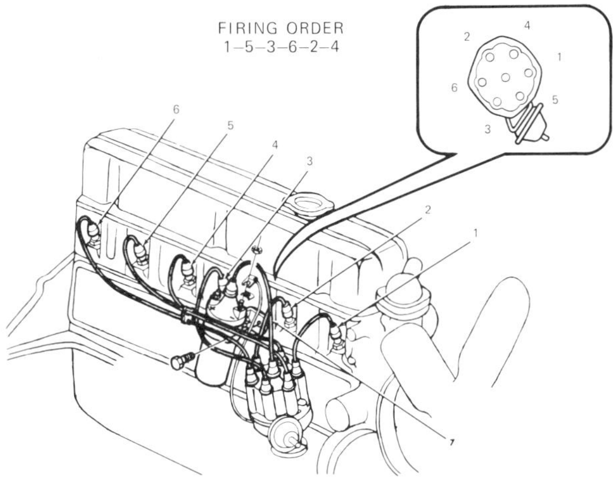

FIRING ORDER 1–5–3–6–2–4

Figure 12.52 The firing order and spark plug wire locations on a typical in-line six-cylinder engine (Chevrolet Service Manual, Chevrolet Motor Division, GM).

Note: Do not use a wrench for this step. Spark plugs should be started in their holes by using your fingers. If access to the spark plug holes is difficult, you can use a spark plug socket and an extension, turning these tools with your fingers. The use of a wrench or a ratchet handle to install spark plugs may result in your stripping the threads on the plugs and in the spark plug holes.

3 After all the plugs have been threaded into their holes, tighten the plugs to the torque specification of the engine manufacturer.

Note: Where the use of a torque wrench proves difficult, you can apply the proper torque by an alternate method shown in Figure 12.51.

4 Install the spark plug wires on the plugs, making sure that they are installed in their original locations.

Note: Spark plug wires must be installed to conform to the *firing order* of the engine. The firing order specifies the sequence in which the spark plugs fire. This specification can be found in an appropriate manual. Typical firing orders and wire locations are shown in Figures 12.52 and 12.53.

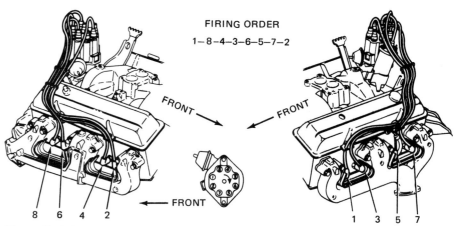

Figure 12.53 The firing order and spark plug wire locations on a typical eight-cylinder engine (Chevrolet Service Manual, Chevrolet Motor Division, GM).

Job 12d

REPLACE SPARK PLUGS

SATISFACTORY PERFORMANCE

A satisfactory performance on this job requires that you do the following:

1 Replace the spark plugs in the engine assigned.
2 Following the steps in the "Performance Outline" and the procedure and specifications of the manufacturer, complete the job within 200 percent of the manufacturer's suggested time.
3 Fill in the blanks under "Information."

PERFORMANCE OUTLINE

1 Disconnect the wires from the spark plugs.
2 Loosen the plugs and blow away the dirt from around the base of the plugs.
3 Remove the spark plugs.
4 Read the spark plugs.
5 Select the correct replacement plugs.
6 Check the gap on the replacement plugs and adjust the gap if necessary.
7 Install the spark plugs.
8 Tighten the plugs to the manufacturer's torque specification.
9 Install the wires.

INFORMATION

Vehicle identification _____

Engine identification _____

Reference used_____ Page(s)_____

Spark plug brand and identification code specified

_____

Spark plug gap specification _____

Spark plug torque specification _____

Brand and identification code of spark plugs removed

_____

Spark plugs removed were

_____Normal _____Too hot _____Too cold

Brand and identification code of spark plugs installed

_____

RECONDITIONING USED SPARK PLUGS In some instances, used spark plugs can be reconditioned and reinstalled for further use. Spark plugs used in engines with breaker point ignition systems have an average life of 10,000 miles (16,000 km). When used in engines with certain electronic systems, the efficient life of a spark plug may exceed 20,000 miles (32,000 km). Within these mileage limits you may find plugs that are dirty or fouled. It is usually possible to recondition these plugs and return them to service.

Regardless of the mileage, the condition of the electrodes usually determines whether a plug can be successfully reconditioned. As shown in Figure 12.54, the edges of the electrodes should be sharp and square. Electrode edges that are slightly rounded can be corrected by filing, but a plug which shows excessive electrode wear

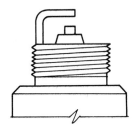

Figure 12.54 The electrodes of a spark plug should be square and have sharp corners.

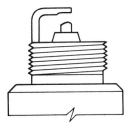

Figure 12.55 Normal electrode wear. In most instances electrodes with this degree of wear can be restored by filing.

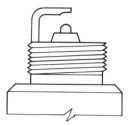

Figure 12.56 Excessive electrode wear. Electrodes worn to this degree cannot be restored by filing.

Figure 12.57 A typical spark plug cleaner (courtesy of Champion Spark Plug Company).

should be discarded. These conditions are shown in Figures 12.55 and 12.56.

Fouling and other combustion deposits on the insulator tip, inside the shell, and on the electrodes can be removed by the use of a spark plug cleaner. A spark plug cleaner, shown in Figure 12.57, is a machine that directs a blast of abrasive sand or grit into the open end of a spark plug. The abrasive blast chips away the deposits on the plug surfaces.

Spark plugs that do not exhibit excessive electrode wear can be reconditioned by performing the following operations:

1 Clean the exterior surfaces of the plug.
2 Clean the interior surfaces of the plug.
3 File the electrodes.
4 Adjust the gap.
5 Clean the threads.

The procedures for performing these operations are outlined in the following steps:

1 Clean the exterior surfaces of the plug with a rag or wiper dipped in solvent. All deposits should be removed from the insulator.

2 Examine the insulator for cracks. Discard any plug that has a cracked insulator.

3 Determine the thread size of the plug and select the correct adapter for the spark plug cleaner. (See Figure 12.58.)

Figure 12.58 Rubber adapters allow plugs with different thread sizes to be cleaned (courtesy of Champion Spark Plug Company).

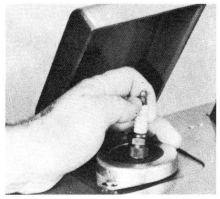

Figure 12.59 Installing a spark plug in the adapter (courtesy of Champion Spark Plug Company).

4 Install the adapter in the spark plug cleaner.

5 Position the plug in the adapter as shown in Figure 12.59.

Note: Be sure to wear your safety goggles during the following operations. Most spark plug cleaners operate as sand blasters, and if the plug or the adapter should slip, the abrasive sand could be blown into your eyes.

6 Holding the plug in place in the adapter, move the cleaner control valve to the "Cleaning Blast" or "Abrasive Blast" position.

Note: Some spark plug cleaners of the type shown in Figure 12.60 have the control valve built into a safety cover.

Figure 12.60 A spark plug cleaner that has the control valve built into the safety cover (reprinted with permission from AC-Delco Division, General Motors Corporation).

Figure 12.61 Cleaning a spark plug. Tipping and rotating the plug allows the abrasive blast to reach all parts of the insulator and shell (courtesy of Champion Spark Plug Company).

Figure 12.62 Cleaning the threads of a spark plug on a wire wheel (reprinted with permission from AC-Delco Division, General Motors Corporation).

7 Rotate the plug in the adapter and rock it from side to side while holding the valve in the "Cleaning Blast" position. (See Figure 12.61.)

8 After about three or four seconds of cleaning, move the control valve to the "Air Blast" position.

Note: **This step is necessary to blow out any abrasive sand that may be lodged between the insulator and the shell.**

9 Continue to rotate and rock the plug while holding the valve in the "Air Blast" position for about 5 seconds.

10 Release the control valve.

11 Remove the plug from the adapter.

12 Examine the nose of the plug. If all deposits have not been removed, repeat steps 5 through 12 until the nose of the plug is clean.

13 Inspect the insulator tip. Discard the plug if the tip of the insulator is cracked or chipped.

14 Clean the threads of the plug with a stiff brush or with a wire wheel as shown in Figure 12.62.

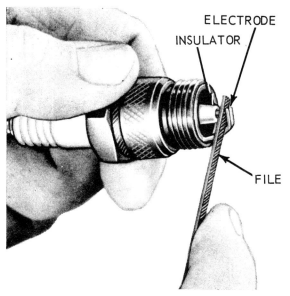

Figure 12.63 Cleaning and squaring spark plug electrodes with a file (Ford Motor Company).

15 Using a small file, clean the firing surfaces of the electrodes as shown in Figure 12.63. It may be necessary to open the gap slightly to provide clearance for the file.

Note: This operation is necessary to flatten and square the electrode surfaces.

16 Adjust the gap to the manufacturer's specification.

Job 12e

RECONDITION USED SPARK PLUGS

SATISFACTORY PERFORMANCE

A satisfactory performance on this job requires that you do the following:

1 Recondition the spark plugs assigned.
2 Following the steps in the "Performance Outline" and the specifications of the manufacturer, complete the job within 60 minutes.
3 Fill in the blanks under "Information."

PERFORMANCE OUTLINE

1 Remove the plugs from the engine.
2 Inspect the plugs.
3 Clean the plugs.
4 File the electrodes.
5 Adjust the gaps to the manufacturer's specification.
6 Install the plugs.

INFORMATION

Vehicle identification _____

Engine identification _____

Reference used _____ Page(s) _____

Spark plug brand and identification code _____

Spark plug gap specification _____

Spark plug torque specification _____

SPARK PLUG WIRES, DISTRIBUTOR CAPS, AND ROTORS

The spark plug wires, the distributor cap, and the rotor are responsible for delivering high voltage to the spark plug. Excessive resistance in these parts may prevent a spark from jumping the plug gap. Defects in the insulation of these parts may allow the voltage to leak to ground before it reaches the plug. Routine maintenance of the ignition system requires that you inspect and test these parts and replace those found defective.

Spark Plug Wires Most spark plug wires used as original equipment have a non-metallic conductor. As shown in Figure 12.64, the core of these wires is usually made of carbon-impregnated linen strands. The carbon conducts electricity, but has a relatively high resistance. These *resistance wires* (1) *suppress*, or reduce, radio and television interference caused by the ignition system and (2) reduce spark plug electrode wear. The core of a spark plug wire is easily broken, and can be pulled loose from its terminals. Because of this, spark plug wires should be handled carefully and should be removed from spark plugs only by pulling on the boots. (Refer to Figures 12.48 and 12.49.)

Spark plug wires must handle over 30,000 volts while being subjected to almost continuous vibration. The wires are also exposed to

extremes in temperature and are often wet with fuel, oil, and water. Because of these severe service conditions, spark plug wires deteriorate and will occasionally require replacement. A spark plug wire may fail in several ways:

1 The insulation may fail. Heat may cause the wire insulation and the boots and nipples to dry and crack. Oil and fuel may cause the insulation to become porous. Any failure of the insulation can allow voltage to leak to ground and cause the spark plug to misfire.

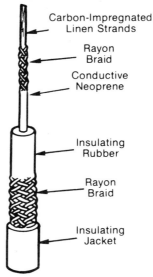

Figure 12.64 Construction of a typical resistance wire. Wires of this type are usually marked TVRS to indicate Television Radio Suppression (reprinted with permission from AC-Delco Division, General Motors Corporation).

2 The resistance of the wire may increase. Vibration and stress may cause the carbon particles in the core to separate slightly. This separation increases the resistance of the conductor and thus increases the voltage required to fire the plug. When the required voltage exceeds the voltage available from the coil, the plug will misfire.

3 The continuity of the wire may be lost. The conductive core may have an internal break or may have been pulled loose from one of its terminals. Current must then jump the gap in the wire as well as the gap of the plug. The break in the wire will burn increasingly larger until the available voltage can no longer jump both gaps. The plug will then misfire.

The condition of the insulation can be checked visually. The resistance and continuity can be checked with an *Ohmmeter*. An Ohmmeter, shown in Figure 12.65, is an instrument that measures resistance. The scale of an Ohmmeter is calibrated in Ohms (Ω) from Zero (0) to Infinity (∞). An Ohmmeter is self-powered. It contains a small battery to

Figure 12.65 A typical automotive ohmmeter (courtesy of Snap-on Tools Corporation).

push current through the part being tested. If the part has no resistance to the flow of that current, the meter will indicate Zero (0). If the part does not allow the flow of any current, the meter will indicate Infinity (∞). If the part has resistance which allows a partial flow of current, that resistance will be indicated in Ohms (Ω).

INSPECTING AND TESTING SPARK PLUG WIRES The following steps outline a procedure for inspecting and testing the spark plug wires used on most cars. The specifications for wire resistance should be obtained from an appropriate manual. When two or more wires on an engine fail to pass the inspection or the tests, it is advisable to replace the entire set. The remaining wires have been subjected to equal service, and they will most likely fail within a short time:

1 Carefully remove one spark plug wire from the spark plug.

2 Remove the remaining end of the wire from its distributor cap tower.

Note: **The manufacturers of some cars with electronic ignition systems do not recommend removing the wires from the cap for testing. On these cars, the distributor cap can be removed to gain access to the inner tower terminals. Be sure to check an appropriate manual for the alternate procedure.**

3 If the wire is dirty or oil soaked, clean the insulation with a rag or wiper dipped in cleaning solvent and dry the wire.

4 Examine the wire insulation, the boot, and the nipple for cracks, abrasions, porosity, and other damage. Check the metal terminals at the ends of the wire. They should be clean and bright and show no corrosion.

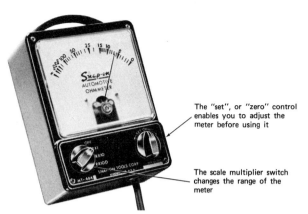

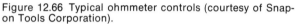

The "set", or "zero" control enables you to adjust the meter before using it

The scale multiplier switch changes the range of the meter

Figure 12.66 Typical ohmmeter controls (courtesy of Snap-on Tools Corporation).

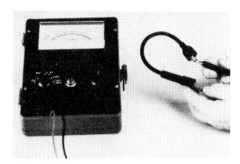

Figure 12.67 Using an Ohmmeter to check the resistance of a spark plug wire (courtesy American Motors Corporation).

5 Turn the selector switch on the Ohmmeter to the "X 1000" scale. (See Figure 12.66.)

6 Clip the ends of the Ohmmeter test leads together and turn the "Zero Adjustment" knob so that the meter indicates Zero (0). (Refer to Figure 12.66.)

7 Connect the Ohmmeter test leads to the terminals on the ends of the spark plug wire as shown in Figure 12.67.

Note: It may be necessary to insert an adapter or a short piece of stiff wire into the spark plug boot to contact the terminal at that end.

8 Read and record the resistance indicated by the meter.

Note: Be sure to multiply the meter reading by 1000 because the meter is set on the "X 1000" scale.

A reading of Zero (0) indicates that the wire is not a resistance wire, but contains a metallic conductor.

A reading of Infinity (∞) indicates that the wire lacks continuity—that there is a break in the wire.

9 Compare the resistance of the wire with the manufacturer's specifications. Figure 12.68 shows the wire resistance specifications established by one automobile manufacturer.

WIRE LENGTH	RESISTANCE (Ω)
6 to 15 in. (15 to 38 cm)	3000 to 10000
15 to 25 in. (38 to 63 cm)	4000 to 15000
25 to 35 in. (63 to 88 cm)	6000 to 20000
Over 35 in. (Over 88 cm)	8000 to 25000

Figure 12.68 Typical spark plug wire resistance specifications.

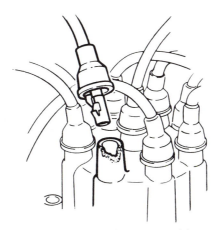

Figure 12.69 A distributor cap with an eroded or cracked tower should be replaced (reprinted with permission from AC-Delco Division, General Motors Corporation).

Note: These specifications will vary, but as a general rule, the resistance should not exceed 8000 Ohms per 12 in. (30 cm).

10 Inspect the distributor cap tower. The tower should not be cracked or eroded, as shown in Figure 12.69. The metal insert in the tower should be clean and have no corrosion.

Note: The use of a mirror and a droplight or flashlight will enable you to inspect the inside of a distributor cap tower when it is otherwise impossible to do so.

11 Slide the nipple up on the wire.

12 Insert the wire into the cap tower, pushing it firmly down into place until you feel the terminal bottom in the tower.

13 Slide the nipple down over the tower, squeezing it to expel any air that may be trapped inside.

Note: Some manufacturers recommend coating the inside of the nipple with silicone grease. Be sure to check the manual for this recommendation.

14 Install the remaining end of the wire on the spark plug, pushing the boot firmly over the insulator.

Note: Some manufacturers recommend that the inside of the boot be coated with silicone grease.

15 Position the wire so that it will not contact the exhaust manifold and secure it in any guides or wire holders that may be present.

16 Repeat the previous steps on the remaining wires.

Note: It is advisable to remove, test, and install each wire one at a time. By following this procedure you will maintain the correct firing order and wire positions.

Job 12f

INSPECT AND TEST SPARK PLUG WIRES

SATISFACTORY PERFORMANCE

A satisfactory performance on this job requires that you do the following:

1 Inspect and test the spark plug wires on the car assigned.
2 Following the steps in the "Performance Outline" and the procedure and specifications of the car manufacturer, complete the job within 60 minutes.
3 Fill in the blanks under "Information."

PERFORMANCE OUTLINE
1 Disconnect one wire.
2 Clean and inspect the wire.
3 Test the wire for continuity and resistance.
4 Connect the wire.
5 Repeat the above steps on the remaining wires.

INFORMATION

Vehicle identification _____

Wire resistance specifications_____

Reference used_____ Page(s)_____

Test results

Wire#	Insulation	Length	Continuity	Resistance
1	____OK ____NG	_____	____Yes ____No	_____
2	____OK ____NG	_____	____Yes ____No	_____
3	____OK ____NG	_____	____Yes ____No	_____
4	____OK ____NG	_____	____Yes ____No	_____
5	____OK ____NG	_____	____Yes ____No	_____
6	____OK ____NG	_____	____Yes ____No	_____
7	____OK ____NG	_____	____Yes ____No	_____
8	____OK ____NG	_____	____Yes ____No	_____

Is the resistance of all the wires within specifications?

_____Yes _____No

Which wires, if any should be replaced?

Distributor Caps and Rotors Distributor caps and rotors should be inspected for cracks, erosion, corrosion, and damage. Cracks and erosion on these parts provide a path for voltage to leak to ground. Corrosion increases the resistance of current flow. These defects can usually be located by a visual inspection.

Inspecting Distributor Caps A distributor cap may be cracked and eroded internally without any external sign of these defects. Because of this, the distributor cap must be removed from the distributor for a thorough inspection.

The following three methods are commonly used to hold a distributor cap in place on a distributor:

Spring Clips The most commonly used method of retaining a distributor cap is by spring clips, as shown in Figure 12.70. Hinged at the distributor, these clips hook into projections on the side of the cap. They are easily removed by prying them loose with a screwdriver. When you wish to install the cap, the spring clips can be snapped back into position.

Spring Loaded Hooks As shown in Figure 12.71, some caps are fitted with spring loaded hooks. These hooks engage in notches on the bottom of the distributor. Caps retained in this manner are removed by turning the slotted

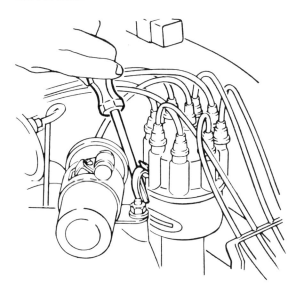

Figure 12.70 A distributor cap retained by spring clips. The clips can be released by prying with a screwdriver as shown (reprinted with permission from AC-Delco Division, General Motors Corporation).

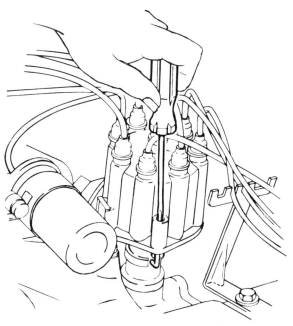

Figure 12.71 Some distributor caps are retained by spring-loaded hooks. They are released by using a screwdriver (reprinted with permission from AC-Delco Division, General Motors Corporation).

head of the hooks 180° with a screwdriver. When installing these caps, the hooks are pushed down with a screwdriver and turned so that they fit into their notches under the distributor.

Screws   Some distributor caps are held to the distributor by screws. In most instances, these screws are built into the cap so that they cannot be dropped and lost. A cap of this type is shown in Figure 12.72.

All distributor caps are made with a tab or key that aligns with a notch in the distributor. When installing a distributor cap, you should check the position of the cap before you attempt to secure it. A properly positioned cap cannot be rotated on the distributor.

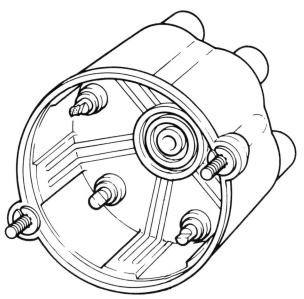

Figure 12.72 A distributor cap that is retained by screws (courtesy American Motors Corporation).

DISTRIBUTOR CAP INSPECTION   The following steps outline a procedure for inspecting a distributor cap that has been removed from a distributor. A cap which exhibits cracks, erosion, carbon paths, corrosion, or damage should be replaced:

1 Clean the outside surface of the cap, carefully examining it for cracks and erosion.

Note: Cracks and erosion are usually indicated by the presence of a carbon path, as shown in Figure 12.73. A carbon path is formed when high voltage leaks along a crack or flaw in the cap and erodes the cap surface.

2 Clean the inside of the cap with a wiper or with a compressed air blowgun, as shown in Figure 12.74. Check for cracks, carbon paths, and erosion of the terminals.

Figure 12.73 The outside of a distributor cap should be cleaned and checked for cracks and carbon paths (Chevrolet Service Manual, Chevrolet Motor Division, GM).

Figure 12.74 The inside of a distributor cap should be cleaned and checked for cracks, carbon paths, and burned or eroded terminals (Chevrolet Service Manual, Chevrolet Motor Division, GM).

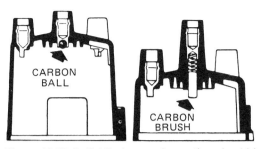

Figure 12.75 A distributor cap inspection should include a check of the carbon ball or brush under the center tower (reprinted with permission from AC-Delco Division, General Motors Corporation).

Note: Be sure to wear your safety goggles when cleaning parts with compressed air.

3 Check the carbon ball or brush under the center tower.

Note: Where a carbon brush is used, it is backed by a small spring that holds the brush in contact with the rotor. In caps of this type, the brush should be checked for freedom of movement. (See Figure 12.75.)

Inspecting Rotors While the distributor cap is off, the rotor should be removed and inspected. Many different types of rotors are used. Those shown in Figure 12.76 are merely pushed on over the distributor shaft. They are positioned by a projection or key that fits into a matching flat or keyway on the shaft. Rotors of this type are removed by pulling them off the shaft, as shown in Figure 12.77.

Rotors of the type shown in Figure 12.78 are held by two screws. Correct positioning is obtained by two protrusions molded into the bottom of the rotor. One protrusion is round; the other square. These protrusions fit into matching holes in a plate on the distributor shaft.

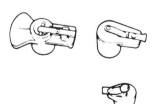

Figure 12.76 Examples of distributor rotors that slide over the distributor shaft. They are positioned by a flat or a keyway on the shaft (reprinted with permission from AC-Delco Division, General Motors Corporation).

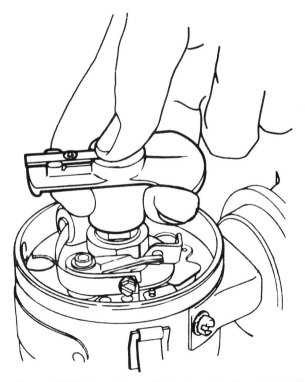

Figure 12.77 Removing a distributor rotor (reprinted with permission from AC-Delco Division, General Motors Corporation).

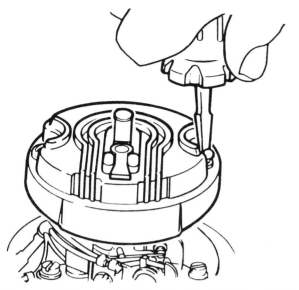

Figure 12.78 A rotor that is held to the distributor shaft by screws (reprinted with permission from AC-Delco Division, General Motors Corporation).

After the screws are removed, the rotor can be lifted from the distributor.

When installing a rotor, you should be sure that it is correctly positioned and securely in place. Failure to do so may result in damage to the rotor and to the cap.

The rotor should be cleaned and inspected for cracks, corrosion, and insufficient spring tension, as shown in Figure 12.79.

Replacing Distributor Caps Replacing a distributor cap is an easy job. But if each spark plug wire is not installed in the correct tower, the engine will not run on all cylinders. To avoid mixing the wires, each wire should be removed from the old cap and immediately installed in the replacement cap. The old cap and the replacement cap should be aligned and held side by side, as shown in Figure 12.80. Then the wires should be transferred one at a time. If space permits, the new cap can be installed on the distributor before the wires are transferred.

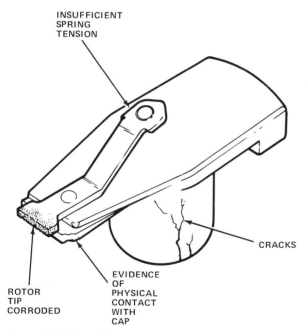

Figure 12.79 Possible rotor defects (courtesy American Motors Corporation).

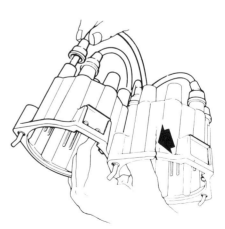

Figure 12.80 Replacing a distributor cap. The new cap should be aligned with the old cap and the wires transfered one at a time (Chevrolet Service Manual, Chevrolet Motor Division, GM).

Job 12g

REPLACE A DISTRIBUTOR CAP

SATISFACTORY PERFORMANCE

A satisfactory performance on this job requires that you do the following:

1 Replace the distributor cap on the car assigned.
2 Following the steps in the "Performance Outline" and the procedure and specifications of the manufacturer, complete the job within 200 percent of the manufacturer's suggested time.
3 Fill in the blanks under "Information."

PERFORMANCE OUTLINE

1 Remove and inspect the distributor cap.
2 Remove and inspect the rotor.
3 Install the rotor.
4 Install the replacement distributor cap.
5 Check the firing order and wire positions.

INFORMATION

Vehicle identification _____

Engine identification _____

Reference used_____ Page(s)_____

Results of distributor cap inspection

_____Defective _____Suitable for reuse

Defect found _____

Engine firing order _____

Cap was secured by _____Spring clips _____Screws

_____Spring loaded hooks

SUMMARY

By completing this chapter you learned about ignition systems. You understand the operation of the primary and secondary circuits. You learned to identify the parts in these circuits and are knowledgeable as to their construction and function. You have gained diagnostic skills. You can now read spark plugs to determine engine operating conditions. You can inspect and test secondary circuit parts. You have gained repair skills. You can now replace spark plugs, recondition used plugs, and replace spark plug wires, distributor caps, and rotors.

SELF-TEST

Each incomplete statement or question in this test is followed by four suggested completions or answers. In each case select the *one* that best completes the sentence or answers the question.

1 Two mechanics are discussing the operation of an ignition system.
Mechanic A says that high voltage is induced in the coil secondary winding when the distributor points open.
Mechanic B says that the condenser reduces arcing at the distributor points.
Who is right?
A. A only
B. B only
C. Both A and B
D. Neither A nor B

2 Which of the following components is *not* a part of the primary circuit?
A. Rotor
B. Points
C. Condenser
D. Ignition switch

3 Two mechanics are discussing ignition systems.
Mechanic A says that the ignition coil is part of the primary circuit.
Mechanic B says that the ignition coil is part of the secondary circuit.
Who is right?

A. A only
B. B only
C. Both A and B
D. Neither A nor B

4 Two mechanics are discussing ignition systems.
Mechanic A says that the points in a distributor are opened by the rotor.
Mechanic B says that the rotor is turned by the distributor shaft.
Who is right?
A. A only
B. B only
C. Both A and B
D. Neither A nor B

5 The most commonly used spark plug thread sizes are
A. 10 mm and 14 mm
B. 14 mm and 18 mm
C. 18 mm and 22 mm
D. 22 mm and 26 mm

6 Spark plugs removed from an engine have dry, fluffy carbon deposits on the insulator tip, inside the shell, and on the electrodes. This condition could be caused by
A. worn piston rings
B. a plugged air cleaner
C. excessive wire resistance
D. excessive combustion chamber temperatures

7 Two mechanics are discussing resistance-type spark plug wires.
Mechanic A says that resistance wires are used to suppress radio and television interference caused by the ignition system.
Mechanic B says that resistance wires are used to reduce spark plug electrode wear.
Who is right?
A. A only
B. B only
C. Both A and B
D. Neither A nor B

8 When tested with an Ohmmeter, a spark plug wire is found to have a resistance of 0 Ohms (Ω). The wire
A. lacks continuity
B. has a metallic core

C. has excessive resistance

D. has a carbon-impregnated linen core

9 When tested with an Ohmmeter, a spark plug wire is found to have a resistance of Infinity (∞). The wire

A. lacks continuity

B. has a metallic core

C. has insufficient resistance

D. has a carbon-impregnated linen core

10 Two mechanics are discussing distributor caps.

Mechanic A says that some distributor caps are attached to the distributor by spring loaded hooks.

Mechanic B says that a carbon path on the surface of the distributor cap indicates that high voltage has been leaking.

Who is right?

A. A only

B. B only

C. Both A and B

D. Neither A nor B

Chapter 13 Ignition System Service– Primary Circuit

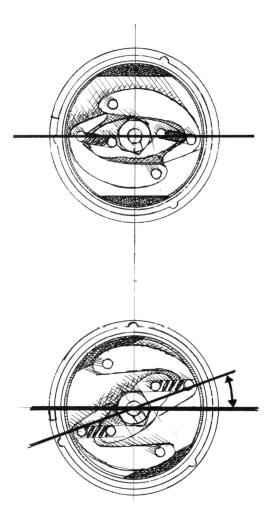

In the previous chapter you learned about and worked with the various parts that make up the secondary circuit of an ignition system. This system distributes high voltage and uses it to ignite the fuel-air mixture in the engine's cylinders. The high voltage is produced by the primary circuit. It is produced, one surge at a time, exactly when it is needed by the engine. In this chapter, you will learn about the components of the primary circuit. You will then check their function and adjust them to meet the specifications of the engine manufacturer.

The primary circuits of electronic ignition systems require very little maintenance. But the primary circuits of systems using breaker points require frequent checks and adjustments. In this chapter you will perform these checks and these adjustments. Your specific objectives are to perform the following jobs:

1
Identify the definition of terms relating to the primary circuit
2
Perform a primary circuit inspection
3
Measure dwell
4
Adjust dwell—external adjustment
5
Adjust dwell—internal adjustment
6
Identify the definition of terms relating to spark timing
7
Check and adjust timing

page 13-1

PRIMARY CIRCUIT FUNCTIONS The primary circuit is actually the "control" circuit of the ignition system. As such, it performs the following functions:

1 It provides current to the primary winding in the coil so that a strong magnetic field is created.
2 It interrupts the flow of that current so that the magnetic field collapses.
3 It times the occurrence of the first two functions so that a high surge is produced in the secondary circuit at the exact instant it is required.

To appreciate the performance of the primary circuit, you must consider the speed at which it operates. At highway cruising speed in a car with an eight-cylinder engine, the primary circuit must perform its functions about 200 times per second.

Primary Circuit Components and Their Function The primary circuits of the various electronic ignition systems are designed to require practically no maintenance. Each of these systems was designed to meet the needs of the manufacturer. Thus, the components and circuitry differ greatly. When service is required in the primary circuits of these systems, a detailed procedure established by the manufacturer must be followed. These procedures are listed in appropriate factory manuals.

Systems using breaker points require the frequent inspection and adjustment of certain components. All of these systems use similar components and circuitry. Therefore, common procedures are followed in the maintenance of these systems. A knowledge of the components used in the primary circuit of breaker point systems is necessary if you are to follow these procedures correctly.

The Points The points, or breaker points, form the contacts of a mechanical switch. A typical set of points is shown in Figure 13.1. As mentioned in the previous chapter, when the points are *closed*, or together, current flows in the primary circuit. When the points

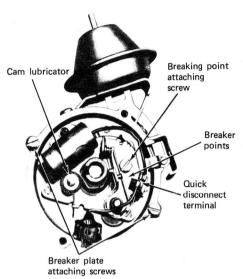

Figure 13.1 A typical set of ignition system breaker points installed in a distributor (Chevrolet Service Manual, Chevrolet Motor Division, GM).

are *open*, or separated, the current flow is stopped. This action is shown in Figure 13.2. It is not enough that the points merely open and close. Three things must be considered if the points are to function properly; (1) point resistance, (2) dwell, and (3) point gap.

Point Resistance Resistance in an electrical circuit will limit the amount of current that flows in that circuit. When you worked with

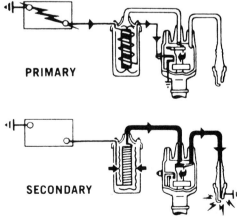

Figure 13.2 The operation of the points in an ignition system. Current flows in the primary circuit when the points are closed. The current flow stops when the points are opened (reprinted with permission from AC-Delco Division, General Motors Corporation).

batteries and with spark plug wires, you learned about resistance. If the surfaces of the points are dirty, burned, or misaligned, they may provide a resistance to current flow. This resistance could limit the current available to the coil primary winding. If insufficient current flows in the primary winding, a weak magnetic field will be produced. The collapse of a weak magnetic field may not induce sufficient voltage in the secondary winding. Point resistance is easily measured. In most instances, points with excessive resistance should be replaced.

Dwell Dwell refers to the amount of time the points remain closed. The points must remain closed for a certain amount of time to allow the primary winding to build a strong magnetic field. When the strongest possible magnetic field is produced in a coil, the coil is said to be *saturated*. The collapse of a saturated magnetic field induces the highest voltage in the secondary winding.

If the points do not remain closed for a sufficient amount of time, the secondary voltage will be low. If the points remain closed for too long a period of time, saturation of the coil will not be increased. But excessive arcing and burning of the points will usually occur. This problem occurs because of the relationship between dwell and point gap.

Dwell, sometimes called *cam angle*, is measured in degrees of distributor cam rotation, as shown in Figure 13.3. An ignition system will operate properly only when the dwell is maintained within specifications. Dwell is easily measured and adjusted.

Point Gap Point gap is the distance between the points when they are held open by the highest point of a cam lobe. This position is shown in Figure 13.4. Point gap is measured with a feeler gauge in much the same manner you measured the gap of spark plugs. Figure 13.5 illustrates the measurement of point gap. Point gap is adjustable. In most instances, the

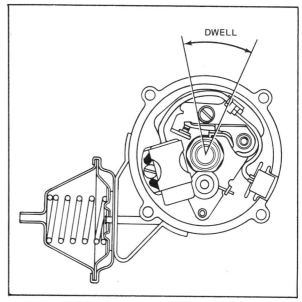

Figure 13.3 Dwell is the amount of time the points remain closed measured in degrees of cam rotation (Chevrolet Service Manual, Chevrolet Motor Division, GM).

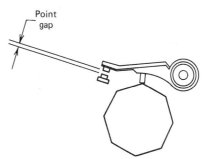

Figure 13.4 Point gap is the distance between the point surfaces when the points are held open by the highest point of the cam lobe.

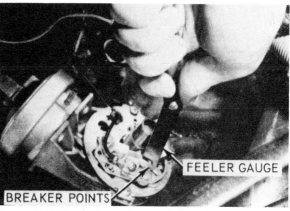

Figure 13.5 Measuring point gap with a flat feeler gauge (Ford Motor Company).

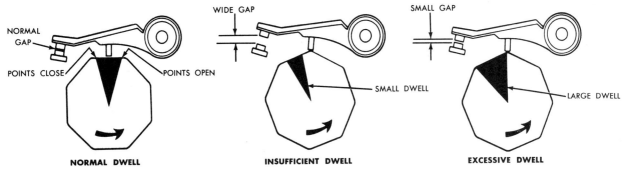

▼ = **DWELL ANGLE** (POINTS ARE CLOSED DURING THIS PERIOD OF CAM ROTATION)

Figure 13.6 Dwell and point gap are related. A wide gap results in insufficient dwell. A small gap results in excessive dwell (Ford Motor Company).

stationary point can be moved closer to, or farther away from, the movable point. As shown in Figure 13.6, point gap and dwell are related. Closing the gap of a set of points increases the dwell. Opening the gap decreases the dwell.

In most instances, a set of points adjusted to the correct dwell specification will have the correct gap. This does not mean that the point gap can be ignored. Both the dwell and the gap should be checked. If the gap is too small, current may jump the gap after the points start to open. This current flow interferes with the collapse of the magnetic field in the coil, resulting in low secondary voltage. Current jumping the gap also causes arcing and burning of the points.

The Condenser The flow of current in the primary circuit is sufficient to jump the small gap formed by the points as they start to open. Connected across the points, as shown in Figure 13.7, the condenser provides an alternate path for the flow of this current.

A typical condenser, shown in Figure 13.8, is made of two strips of conductive foil separated by strips of insulation. The strips of foil form a large conductive area that will temporarily store electricity. The foil and the insulation are rolled and sealed in a small cylinder. The cylinder body contacts one foil strip and is grounded to the distributor. The other foil strip is connected to a wire lead which is

attached to the terminal for the movable point. Some condensers are not made as a separate part. They are combined with the points in one assembly. An assembly of this type is shown in Figure 13.9.

As mentioned in the previous chapter, the condenser in an ignition system performs two functions:

1 It reduces arcing at the points and thereby extends their life. It does this by providing an alternate path for the flow of primary current at the instant of point opening.
2 It aids in the collapse of the magnetic field in the coil. This increases the voltage induced in the secondary winding.

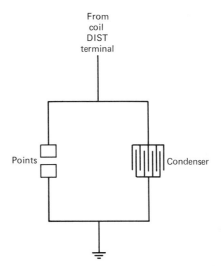

Figure 13.7 A condenser is connected in parallel with the points.

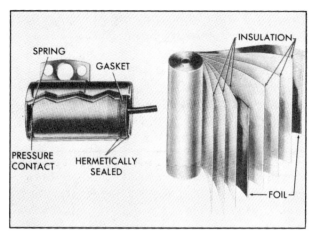

Figure 13.8 A typical condenser and its construction (Chevrolet Service Manual, Chevrolet Motor Division, GM).

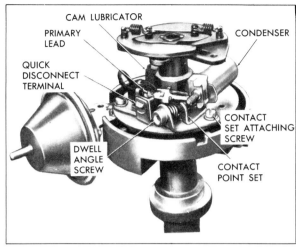

Figure 13.9 A distributor containing a set of points and a condenser combined in one assembly (Chevrolet Service Manual, Chevrolet Motor Division, GM).

Job 13a

IDENTIFY THE DEFINITION OF TERMS RELATING TO THE PRIMARY CIRCUIT

SATISFACTORY PERFORMANCE
A satisfactory performance on this job requires that you do the following:

1 Identify the definition of terms relating to the primary circuit by placing the number of each listed term in front of its correct definition.
2 Correctly identify all the terms within 10 minutes.

PERFORMANCE SITUATION

1 Points   5 Point gap
2 Condenser   6 Dwell
3 Saturation   7 Arcing
4 Induction   8 Resistance

_____Sparks that occur when an electrical connection is broken

_____The amount of time that points remain open

_____The point where a magnetic field is at full strength

_____Contacts that control the flow of current in the primary circuit

_____The creation of current by means of magnetism

_____The amount of time that points remain closed

_____The distance between points when they are at their widest opening

_____A device that minimizes arcing at the points

_____The opposition to the flow of current

_____The creation of magnetism by means of electricity

PRIMARY CIRCUIT INSPECTION Primary circuit inspection includes those checks and tests that enable you to determine if the circuit is operating within the manufacturer's specifications. Based on the results of this inspection, you can make the necessary adjustments and replace the required parts.

VISUAL INSPECTION A visual inspection may reveal obvious problems and should be performed before any electrical tests are made. The following steps outline a procedure that can be followed on any breaker point system:

1 Check for dirty, corroded, and loose connections at the battery terminals. Clean the terminal and clamps, and tighten the clamps, if necessary.

2 Check for dirty and loose connections at the battery ground cable, the starter solenoid, and the coil. Clean and tighten those connections as required.

3 Check all the connecting wires for broken or frayed insulation. Replace any damaged wires.

4 Remove the distributor cap and rotor.

5 Using a small screwdriver or a hook made from stiff wire, separate the points. Check the condition of the point surfaces.

Note: The surfaces of used points normally appear gray or "frosted." They may also exhibit slight *pitting*, or metal transfer. Points that are burned or exhibit excessive pitting should be replaced. (See Figures 13.10 and 13.11.)

6 Check the connections of the primary wire and the condenser lead at the points. Tighten the connection if it is loose.

7 Check the mounting of the condenser. Tighten the mounting screw if it is loose.

Point Resistance A test of point resistance will give you an accurate indication of the electrical condition of the point contact surfaces. Point resistance is checked while the points are closed. While the distributor cap and the rotor are off, you should check the position of the points. If the points are not closed, you can "tap" or "bump" the engine over with the starter.

A *remote starter switch*, similar to the one shown in Figure 13.12, will enable you to crank the engine while you watch the points:

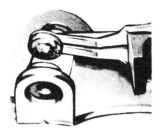

Figure 13.10 Burned points. Burned points can be caused by oil or dirt on the point surfaces (Ford Motor Company).

Figure 13.11 Points with excessive pitting. Pitting, or metal transfer, can be caused by a condenser of the wrong capacity (Ford Motor Company).

A remote starter switch allows you to operate the starter motor from under the hood. The switch is connected to the starter solenoid or starter relay. Because different cars use different starting circuits, these connections will vary.

The solenoid shown in Figure 13.13 is similar to those used on most cars built by Ford Motor Company and by American Motors Corporation. It is located between the battery and the starter motor, and is usually mounted on an inner fender panel near the battery. It can easily be found by following the cable from the battery. The remote starter switch should be connected to the BAT terminal and to the S terminal as shown.

Figure 13.14 shows the front view of the so-lenoid used in most cars built by General Motors Corporation. This solenoid is attached to the starter motor. The remote starter switch should be connected to the battery terminal and to the solenoid (S) terminal. On four-cylinder and six-cylinder engines, the solenoid is quite accessible. On eight-cylinder engines, the solenoid is usually hidden by an exhaust manifold. When working on a car with an eight-cylinder engine, you may have to go under the car to make these connections.

Most cars built by Chrysler Corporation use a starter relay with terminals arranged as shown in Figure 13.15. This relay is usually mounted on the left inner fender panel or on the left side of the firewall. Connections for a remote starter switch should be made to the battery and solenoid terminals as shown.

Figure 13.12 A remote starter switch (courtesy of Snap-on Tools Corporation).

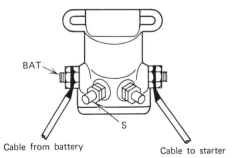

Cable from battery   Cable to starter

Figure 13.13 A starter solenoid of the type used by Ford Motor Company and by American Motors Corporation. Remote starter switch connections should be made at the BAT and S terminals as shown.

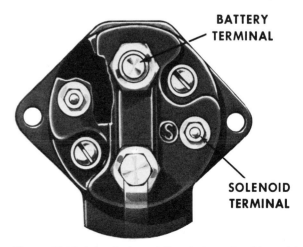

BATTERY TERMINAL

SOLENOID TERMINAL

Figure 13.14 A front view of the starter solenoid used by most cars built by General Motors Corporation. When using a remote starter switch, the switch should be connected to the battery terminal and to the solenoid (S) terminal as shown (Chevrolet Service Manual, Chevrolet Motor Division, GM).

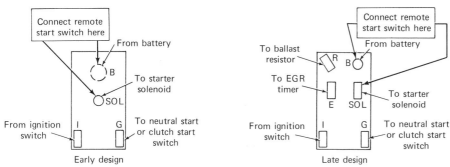

Figure 13.15 Relays of two different designs can be found on cars built by Chrysler Corporation. Remote starter switch connections should be made at the battery and solenoid terminals (courtesy Chrysler Corporation).

As an anti-theft feature, some cars are wired so that the use of a remote starter switch could damage certain parts of the ignition system. To eliminate the possibility of damage, the ignition switch should be turned to the ON position before using a remote starter switch. To prevent the engine from starting, the coil secondary wire, shown in Figure 13.16, should be removed from the center tower of the distributor cap. A jumper wire should be used to connect the coil wire to ground.

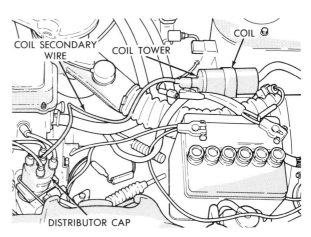

Figure 13.16 An ignition system can be temporarily disabled by removing the coil secondary wire from the distributor cap. The wire should be grounded by means of a jumper wire (courtesy Chrysler Corporation).

TESTING POINT RESISTANCE WITH A DWELL METER As its name implies, a Dwell Meter is an instrument that measures dwell. Most shops use an instrument that combines a Tachometer with a Dwell Meter. That instrument is called a *Tach-Dwell Meter*. A typical Tach-Dwell Meter is shown in Figure 13.17. You may have used a Tach-Dwell Meter when you adjusted carburetors. Most Tach-Dwell Meters have a function switch, as shown in Figure 13.18. This switch allows you to match the meter to the test you wish to perform. The following steps outline a procedure for testing point resistance with a Tach-Dwell Meter:

1 Place the function switch on the Tach-Dwell Meter in the POINT RESISTANCE position. (Refer to Figure 13.18.)

2 Apply the parking brake.

3 If the car has an automatic transmission, place the transmission selector lever in the PARK position. If the car has a standard transmission, place the shift lever in the NEUTRAL position.

4 Connect the Tach-Dwell Meter to the DIST (−) terminal on the coil and to a good ground, as shown in Figure 13.19.

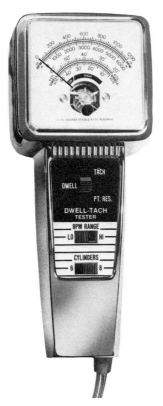

Figure 13.17 A typical Tach-Dwell meter (Kal-Equip Company).

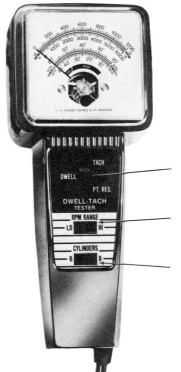

The function switch enables you to select the test you wish to perform

The tachometer scale switch enables you to select a low (under 1000 rpm) or high (over 1000 rpm) scale

The cylinder selector switch enables you to match the meter to the number of cylinders in the engine

Figure 13.18 Typical Tach-Dwell controls (Kal Equip Company).

5 Check the position of the points. If the points are not closed, "tap" or "bump" the engine over with the starter motor until the distributor cam is not holding the points open.

Note: A remote starter switch can be helpful in performing this step. Where space permits, you can use a wrench on the crankshaft pulley retaining bolt to turn the engine, as shown in Figure 13.20. In some instances, you can turn the engine over by carefully pulling on a fan blade.

6 Turn the ignition switch to the ON position.

7 Read the point resistance on the meter scale.

Note: Most meter scales have a small box or band that indicates acceptable point resistance. If the meter pointer falls outside that box or band, the point resistance is excessive. (See Figure 13.21.)

8 Turn the ignition switch to the OFF position.

9 Disconnect and remove the Tach-Dwell Meter.

10 Install the distributor cap.

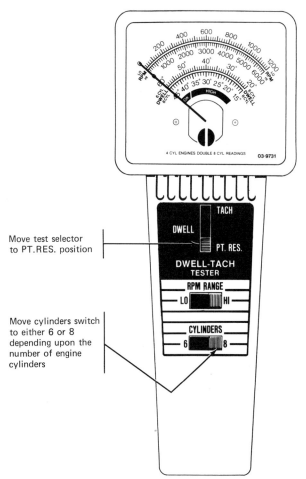

Move test selector to PT.RES. position

Move cylinders switch to either 6 or 8 depending upon the number of engine cylinders

Figure 13.19 Tach-Dwell switch positions for measuring point resistance (Kal-Equip Company).

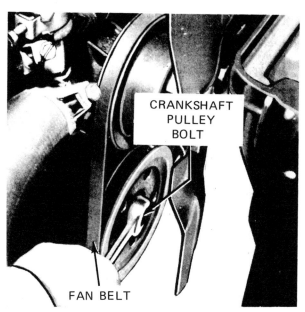

Figure 13.20 On some engines, you can turn the crankshaft by turning the pulley retaining bolt with a wrench (Ford Motor Company).

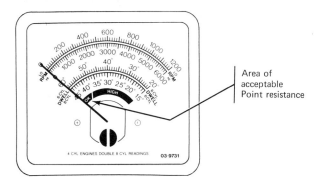

Area of acceptable Point resistance

Figure 13.21 On most Tach-Dwell Meters, acceptable point resistance is indicated when the pointer remains inside a small box or band (Kal-Equip Company).

Job 13b

PERFORM A PRIMARY CIRCUIT INSPECTION

SATISFACTORY PERFORMANCE

A satisfactory performance on this job requires that you do the following:

1 Perform a primary circuit inspection on the car assigned.
2 Following the steps in the "Performance Outline" and the procedure and specifications of the manufacturer, complete the job within 20 minutes.
3 Fill in the blanks under "Information."

PERFORMANCE OUTLINE

1 Check the battery terminals and cables. Clean and tighten the connections where necessary.
2 Check the primary wiring and connections. Clean and tighten connections where necessary.
3 Check the condition of the point surfaces.
4 Check the condenser connection and mounting. Clean and tighten the connection and mounting where necessary.
5 Test the point resistance.

INFORMATION

Vehicle identification _____

Reference used_____ Page(s)_____

Condition of parts and services performed

Battery cables and connections _____OK

_____Cleaned and tightened

Primary wiring and connections _____OK

_____Cleaned and tightened

Point surfaces _____OK (normal wear)

_____Burned

_____Excessively pitted

Condenser connections _____Wire lead tight

_____Mounting screw tight

Point resistance _____Acceptable

_____Excessive

DWELL AND POINT GAP As you know, dwell and point gap are related. Dwell is measured electrically with a Dwell Meter. Point gap is measured manually with a feeler gauge. The use of a Dwell Meter eliminates the mechanical and human error that can affect the measurement of point gap. A Dwell Meter provides another advantage. It can be used while an engine is running or while an engine is being cranked by the starter motor. The use of a feeler gauge to measure point gap requires that you remove the distributor cap. It also requires that you "tap" or "bump" the engine over with the starter motor until the points are held open by the highest point of one of the cam lobes. Most mechanics use a Dwell Meter to save time and to obtain a more accurate measurement.

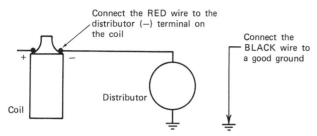

Connect the RED wire to the distributor (−) terminal on the coil

Connect the BLACK wire to a good ground

+ −

Coil

Distributor

Figure 13.22 Meter connections for measuring dwell.

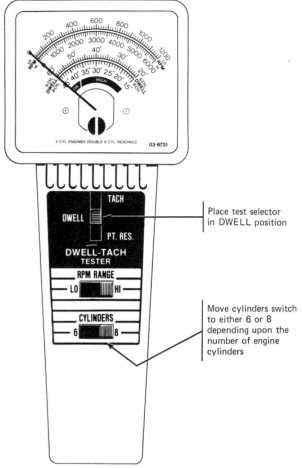

Place test selector in DWELL position

Move cylinders switch to either 6 or 8 depending upon the number of engine cylinders

Figure 13.23 Tach-Dwell Meter function switches positioned so the meter will measure dwell (Kal-Equip Company).

MEASURING DWELL Dwell should be checked as a part of routine maintenance of the ignition system. The meter connections for measuring dwell are shown in Figure 13.22. These connections are the same as those you made when you measured point resistance. To save time, the measurement of dwell should follow that test. Dwell measurement then requires only that you change the position of the function switch, as shown in Figure 13.23.

As you may remember from your work in adjusting carburetors, most Tach-Dwell Meters require that you adjust the meter to the number of cylinders in the engine. Typical switches for this purpose are shown in Figure 13.24. Some Tach-Dwell Meters allow you to select only six or eight cylinders. When using these meters, the dwell on four-cylinder engines is measured as follows:

1 Place the switch in the eight-cylinder position.

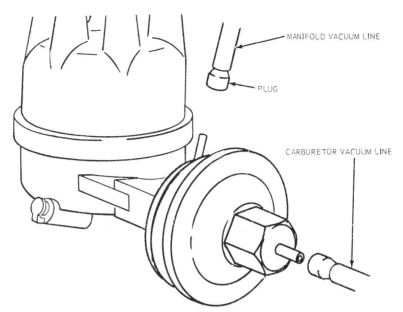

Figure 13.24 When checking dwell or timing, the hose(s) at the distributor diaphragm should be disconnected and plugged (Ford Motor Company).

2 Double the dwell indicated on the meter. As an example, an indicated dwell of 25° would be doubled to obtain the actual dwell of 50°.

The dwell specification for any engine is determined by the engine manufacturer. For four-cylinder engines, dwell specifications range from 40° to 60°. Specifications for dwell on six-cylinder engines range from 31° to 47°. Eight cylinder engines usually require from 24° to 32°. Because of the wide range of dwell specifications, the correct dwell for the engine on which you are working should be obtained from the engine decal or from an appropriate manual.

The following steps outline a procedure for measuring dwell:

1 Determine the dwell specification for the engine on which you are working.

2 Place the function switch on the meter in the DWELL position. (Refer to Figure 13.24.)

3 Position the cylinder selector switch to match the number of cylinders in the engine.

Note: Remember that on some meters you must place the switch in the eight-cylinder position and double the indicated dwell when working on four-cylinder engines.

4 Connect the meter to the DIST (−) terminal on the coil and to a good ground. (Refer to Figure 13.22.)

5 Disconnect and plug the vacuum hose(s) that are connected to the distributor diaphragm. (See Figure 13.25.)

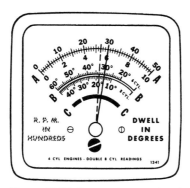

Figure 13.25 On most cars, the dwell should not change more than 3° as the engine is accelerated from idle speed to 2000 rpm (Kal Equip Company).

Note: This step must be performed because some advance mechanisms change the dwell and thus may cause a false dwell measurement.

6 Apply the parking brake.

7 If the car has an automatic transmission, place the transmission selector lever in the PARK position. If the car has a standard transmission, place the shift lever in the NEUTRAL position.

8 Start the engine and allow it to operate at idle speed.

9 Read the dwell indicated on the meter and compare it with the specification.

10 Slowly accelerate the engine to approximately 2000 rpm while observing the meter. The dwell should not change more than 3°.

Note: A change of more than 3° may indicate wear in the distributor shaft bushings or in the breaker plate. Such wear may require the overhaul or replacement of the distributor.

11 Turn the ignition switch to the OFF position.

12 Connect the vacuum hose(s) to the distributor diaphragm.

13 Disconnect and remove the Tach-Dwell Meter.

Job 13c

MEASURE DWELL

SATISFACTORY PERFORMANCE
A satisfactory performance on this job requires that you do the following:

1 Measure the dwell on the car assigned.
2 Following the steps in the "Performance Outline" and the procedure and specifications of the manufacturer, complete the job within 15 minutes.

3 Fill in the blanks under "Information."

PERFORMANCE OUTLINE

1 Adjust the meter and connect it to the engine.

2 Read the indicated dwell at idle and while accelerating.

3 Compare the indicated dwell with the specifications.

INFORMATION

Vehicle identification _____

Reference used_____ Page(s)_____

Dwell specification _____

Indicated dwell at idle _____

Dwell change while accelerating _____

Indicated dwell is _____Within specifications

_____Too high

_____Too low

Based on the indicated dwell reading, the point gap is

_____Within specifications

_____Too wide

_____Too narrow

Based on the indicated dwell reading while accelerating, the distributor

_____appears to be in good condition

_____requires further inspection

Adjusting Dwell Dwell is not adjustable on electronic ignition systems. The correct dwell is maintained by the electronic control unit. On breaker point systems, dwell is adjusted by changing the point gap. Closing the gap increases the amount of time that the points remain closed, increasing the dwell. Opening the point gap decreases the amount of time the points remain closed, decreasing the dwell. (Refer to Figure 13.6.)

EXTERNAL ADJUSTMENT Some distributors are designed so that you can adjust points externally, without having to remove the distributor cap. This design allows you to adjust the dwell while the engine is running. Distributors of this design use a set of points similar to those shown in Figure 13.26. These points have an adjusting screw that can be turned with a ⅛-inch *Allen wrench*, or hex-type wrench. A set of these wrenches is shown in Figure 13.27. Access to the points is provided by a window in the distributor cap. When the window is opened, an Allen wrench can be inserted in the adjusting screw, as shown in Figure 13.28. Turning the screw clockwise closes the point gap, increasing the dwell. Turning the screw counterclockwise opens the point gap, decreasing the dwell.

The following steps outline a procedure for adjusting dwell where an external adjustment is provided:

1 Determine the dwell specification for the engine.

2 Adjust a Tach-Dwell Meter and connect it to the DIST (−) terminal on the coil and to a good ground. (Refer to Figure 13.22.)

3 Disconnect and plug the vacuum hose(s) that are connected to the distributor diaphragm. (Refer to Figure 13.25.)

4 Raise the window on the distributor cap and insert a ⅛-inch Allen wrench into the head of the adjusting screw. (Refer to Figure 13.28.)

Note: A special point adjusting tool similar to the one shown in Figure 13.29 can be used when it is difficult to gain access to the window.

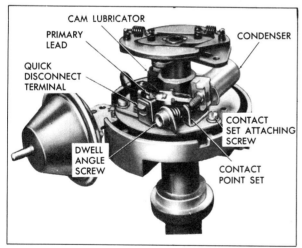

Figure 13.26 A distributor that uses points that are adjusted externally. The distributor cap and rotor have been removed (Chevrolet Service Manual, Chevrolet Motor Division, GM).

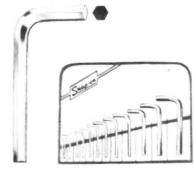

Figure 13.27 A set of Allen wrenches, or hex-type wrenches (courtesy of Snap-on Tools Corporation).

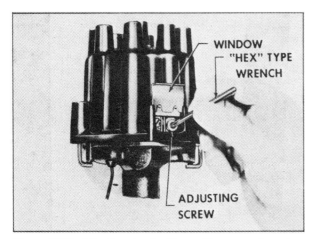
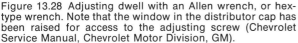

Figure 13.28 Adjusting dwell with an Allen wrench, or hex-type wrench. Note that the window in the distributor cap has been raised for access to the adjusting screw (Chevrolet Service Manual, Chevrolet Motor Division, GM).

Figure 13.29 A distributor adjusting tool. A ⅛-inch Allen wrench is mounted at the end of the flexible shaft, allowing the tool to be used where access to the distributor cap window is limited (courtesy of Snap-on Tools Corporation).

5 Apply the parking brake.

6 If the car has an automatic transmission, place the transmission selector lever in the PARK position. If the car has a standard transmission, place the shift lever in the NEUTRAL position.

7 Start the engine and allow it to run at idle speed.

8 Read the dwell indicated on the meter and compare it with the specification.

9 Adjust the dwell to the specification by turning the adjusting screw.

Note: Turning the screw clockwise increases the dwell. Turning the screw counterclockwise decreases the dwell.

Caution: On some engines, the distributor is mounted close to the fan and to the fan belts. If your hand comes in contact with these parts while they are moving you could be seriously injured. On these engines it is best to turn the engine OFF and make an approximate adjustment while the engine is not running. The engine can then be restarted to check the adjustment. This procedure should be repeated until the adjustment is correct.

10 Turn the ignition switch to the OFF position.

11 Remove the Allen wrench and close the window.

12 Disconnect and remove the Tach-Dwell Meter.

13 Connect the vacuum hose(s) to the distributor diaphragm.

Job 13d

ADJUST DWELL—EXTERNAL ADJUSTMENT

SATISFACTORY PERFORMANCE

A satisfactory performance on this job requires that you do the following:

1 Adjust the dwell on the car assigned.
2 Following the steps in the "Performance Outline" and the procedure and specifications of the manufacturer, complete the job within 15 minutes.
3 Fill in the blanks under "Information."

PERFORMANCE OUTLINE

1 Determine the dwell specification.
2 Measure the dwell and determine the correction needed.
3 Adjust the dwell to the manufacturer's specification.

INFORMATION

Vehicle identification _____

Reference used_____ Page(s)_____

Dwell specification_____

Actual dwell indicated _____

Direction adjusting screw was turned

_____Clockwise _____Counterclockwise

Dwell at completion of adjustment _____

INTERNAL ADJUSTMENT On most distributors, the dwell can be adjusted only after removing the distributor cap. A distributor of this type is shown in Figure 13.30. Dwell is adjusted by moving the stationary point closer to, or farther away from, the movable point. In order to move the stationary point, the attaching screw(s) must be loosened. A screwdriver can then be used, as shown in Figure 13.31, to pry the stationary point in the required direction. Because the distributor cap must be removed, the engine cannot be running while the adjustment is being made.

One method of adjusting dwell in a distributor of this type requires that you adjust the point gap with a feeler gauge. You must then install the cap and measure the dwell with the engine running. If the dwell is not as specified, the point gap must be readjusted and the

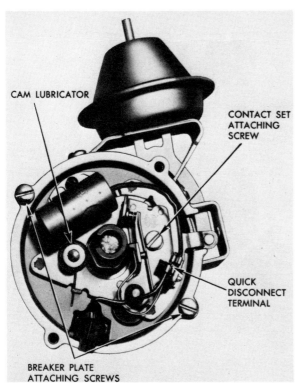

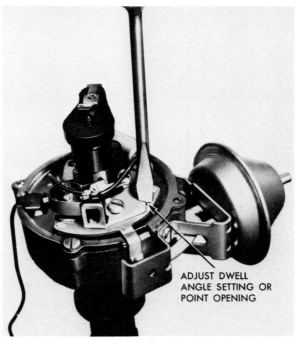

Figure 13.31 Using a screwdriver to move the stationary point (Chevrolet Service Manual, Chevrolet Motor Division, GM).

Figure 13.30 A top view of a distributor which has internally adjusted points (Chevrolet Service Manual, Chevrolet Motor Division, GM).

dwell rechecked. This procedure must be repeated until the dwell is correct. This method works fairly well when the points are new. The gap between new point surfaces can be accurately measured with a feeler gauge, as shown in Figure 13.32. When the points are used, the slight roughness or pitting on their surfaces does not allow you to make an accurate measurement. That condition is shown in Figure 13.33.

Even though the engine cannot be started, a Tach-Dwell Meter can be used to obtain an accurate dwell adjustment. Dwell will be indicated on the meter while the engine is being cranked by the starter motor. The use of a Tach-Dwell Meter in this manner will enable you to accurately adjust dwell even when the points are rough or pitted. The steps that follow outline a procedure for adjusting dwell while the distributor cap is off:

1 Determine the dwell specification for the engine.

2 Adjust a Tach-Dwell Meter and connect it to the DIST (−) terminal on the coil and to a good ground. (Refer to Figure 13.24.)

3 Remove the coil wire from the center tower in the distributor cap.

4 Ground the coil wire using a jumper wire.

5 Remove the distributor cap and the rotor.

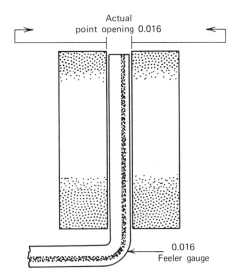

Figure 13.32 A feeler gauge will provide accurate measurement of point gap only when the points have smooth, parallel surfaces.

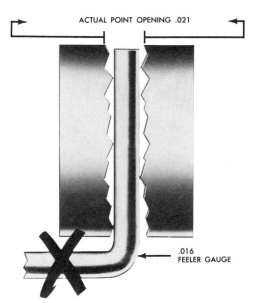

Figure 13.33 The gap between points with rough or pitted surfaces cannot be accurately measured with a feeler gauge (Chevrolet Service Manual, Chevrolet Motor Division, GM).

6 Apply the parking brake.

7 If the car has an automatic transmission, place the transmission selector lever in the PARK position. If the car has a standard transmission, place the shift lever in the NEUTRAL position.

8 Turn the ignition switch to the ON position.

9 Using a remote starter switch, crank the engine with the starter motor and observe the dwell indicated on the meter.

Note: Dwell indicated while an engine is being cranked by the starter motor will usually be about 2° higher than the actual dwell. For example, an actual dwell of 32° will be indicated on the meter as 34°.

10 Compare the dwell with the specification.

11 Determine the direction you must move the stationary point.

Note: Moving the stationary point toward the movable point increases the dwell. Moving the stationary point away from the movable point decreases the dwell.

12 Slightly loosen the point attaching screw(s). (Refer to Figure 13.30.)

Note: Loosen the screw(s) only enough to permit movement of the stationary point by a screwdriver. This helps keep the adjustment from slipping before you tighten the screw(s) to lock your adjustment.

13 Place a screwdriver in the notch at the base of the stationary point. (Refer to Figure 13.31.)

14 While cranking the engine with the starter motor, move the stationary point in the desired direction until the correct dwell reading is obtained.

15 Tighten the point attaching screw(s).

16 Crank the engine and observe the meter. If the dwell is not correct, repeat steps 10 through 16. If the dwell is correct, continue with step 17.

17 Install the rotor and the distributor cap.

18 Remove the jumper wire from the coil wire and install the coil wire in the center tower of the distributor cap.

19 Start the engine and check the dwell adjustment. If the dwell is incorrect, repeat steps 3 through 19. If the dwell is correct, continue with step 20.

20 Turn the ignition switch to OFF position.

21 Disconnect and remove the Tach-Dwell Meter.

22 Disconnect and remove the remote starter switch.

Job 13e

ADJUST DWELL—INTERNAL ADJUSTMENT

SATISFACTORY PERFORMANCE

A satisfactory performance on this job requires that you do the following:

1 Adjust the dwell on the car assigned.
2 Following the steps in the "Performance Outline" and the procedure and specifications of the manufacturer, complete the job within 30 minutes.
3 Fill in the blanks under "Information."

PERFORMANCE OUTLINE

1 Determine the dwell specification.
2 Measure the dwell and determine the correction needed.
3 Adjust the dwell to the manufacturer's specification.

INFORMATION

Vehicle identification _____

Reference used_____ Page(s)_____

Dwell specification_____

Actual dwell indicated _____

Direction stationary point was moved

_____Toward movable point

_____Away from movable point

Dwell at completion of adjustment _____

TIMING The fuel-air mixture in each combustion chamber is ignited by a spark delivered by the ignition system. As you know, that spark must occur at the end of each compression stroke. If the spark is timed to occur when each piston reaches top dead center (TDC), the engine will run. But it will not run well. Actually, the spark must occur at different times before each piston reaches TDC. The exact time the spark must occur depends on (1) the speed at which the engine is running, and (2) the load under which the engine is operating.

Engine speed and engine load are subject to constant change while driving. Because of this, a means of automatically adjusting the timing to match these changes must be provided in every ignition system. Two methods of providing automatic adjustment are usually used: centrifugal spark advance and vacuum spark advance.

Centrifugal Spark Advance The centrifugal spark advance mechanism changes the spark timing to match engine speed. When an engine is running at idle speed, a spark timed to occur at, or slightly before, TDC is satisfactory. When the speed of an engine is increased, the timing must be moved ahead, or *advanced*, so that the spark occurs earlier. This is because there is less time available for the fuel-air mixture to burn. You learned earlier that the mixture does not explode, but burns rapidly. The average burning time of the fuel-air mixture is .003 of a second. That means

that the maximum force is exerted on a piston .003 of a second after the mixture is ignited.

An engine runs most efficiently when the maximum force is exerted on a piston while the crankshaft is located approximately 10° after TDC. During the .003 of a second burning time, the crankshaft of an engine idling at 550 rpm rotates about 10°. If the spark is timed to occur when the piston is at TDC (0°), the crankshaft will be 10° past TDC when the maximum force is applied to the piston. Given that situation (illustrated in Figure 13.34), you may assume that a spark timed to occur at TDC will be correct for an engine operating at 550 rpm. But will that timing be correct when the speed of the engine is increased?

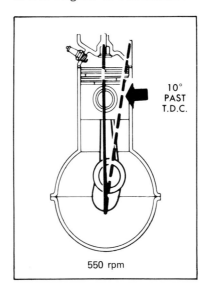

550 rpm

Figure 13.34 To obtain the maximum force on a piston when the crankshaft is 10° past TDC, the mixture in an engine operating at 550 rpm must be ignited at about TDC (Chevrolet Service Manual, Chevrolet Motor Division, GM).

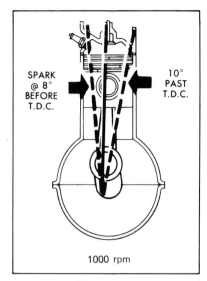

Figure 13.35 To obtain the maximum force on a piston when the crankshaft is 10° past TDC, the mixture in an engine operating at 1000 rpm must be ignited at about 8° before TDC (Chevrolet Service Manual, Chevrolet Motor Division, GM).

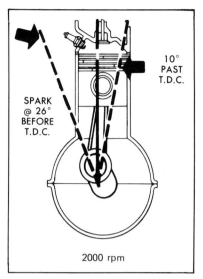

Figure 13.36 To obtain the maximum force on a piston when the crankshaft is 10° past TDC, the mixture in an engine operating at 2000 rpm must be ignited at about 26° before TDC (Chevrolet Service Manual, Chevrolet Motor Division, GM).

When an engine is operated at 1000 rpm, its crankshaft turns 18° in .003 of a second. If the spark occurs at TDC, the crankshaft will be 8° past the point where the piston should receive the maximum force. To achieve the greatest efficiency, the spark should be timed to ignite the mixture 8° before TDC. This need for spark advance is shown in Figure 13.35.

If the engine speed is increased to 2000 rpm, the crankshaft now turns 36° while the fuel is burning. This requires that the spark occur 26° before TDC if the mixture is to be completely burned by the time the crankshaft reaches 10° after TDC. This is shown in Figure 13.36.

Because automobile engines operate at constantly varying speeds, the spark timing must change with the speed. This is accomplished by the use of *centrifugal force*. Centrifugal force is a force that tends to cause a body to move away from its center of rotation. You may have seen the effect of centrifugal force when you placed a small article on a spinning record. Centrifugal force caused the article to move to the edge of the record and slide off.

Most distributors use two weights, two springs, and a cam to harness centrifugal

force. These parts are shown in Figure 13.37. In some distributors, these parts are housed under the breaker plate, as shown in Figure 13.38. In other distributors they are mounted on the top of the distributor shaft, as shown in Figure 13.39. The weights are held close to the shaft by the springs. As engine speed increases, the weights tend to move outward, against the tension of the springs. The move-

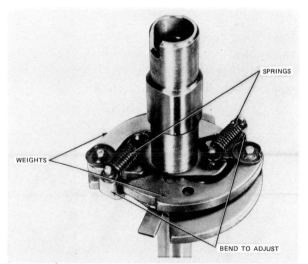

Figure 13.37 A typical centrifugal spark mechanism. Note that the springs hold the weights in toward the shaft while the unit is at rest (Ford Motor Company).

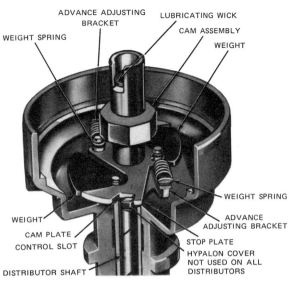

Figure 13.38 A centrifugal spark advance mechanism installed in the base of a distributor (Ford Motor Company).

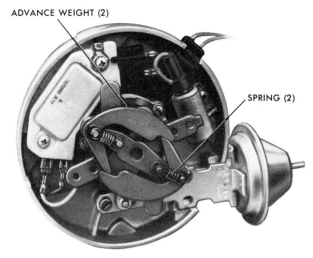

Figure 13.39 A centrifugal spark advance mechanism installed on the top of a distributor shaft (Chevrolet Service Manual, Chevrolet Motor Division, GM).

ment of the weights turns the cam. In breaker point distributors, this cam turns the cam that opens the points so that the points open earlier. In the distributors of electronic systems, this cam turns the trigger wheel so that it passes the sensor earlier. The action of the weights is shown in Figure 13.40. As the engine speed decreases, the springs return the weights toward their original position. As the weights move inward, they move the cam toward its original position.

The actual centrifugal spark advance required varies with different engines. Each engine manufacturer selects the weights, springs, and cam best suited for a particular engine

design. These parts are then adjusted so that the spark advance provides the best performance at all engine speeds. Figure 13.41 shows a centrifugal spark advance curve established by one manufacturer for a particular engine.

Vacuum Spark Advance Automobile engines operate under constantly changing loads. An engine running at 2000 rpm in a car going uphill is subjected to a far greater load than if it were running at 2000 rpm in a car coasting downhill. Some driving conditions, such as acceleration and hill climbing, place heavy loads on an engine. But during most driving, an engine is subjected to light or moderate loads. An engine that is running un-

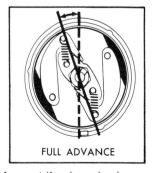

Figure 13.40 The operation of a centrifugal spark advance mechanism. Note that as the weights move outward, they "advance" the position of the cam on the distributor shaft (Chevrolet Service Manual, Chevrolet Motor Division, GM).

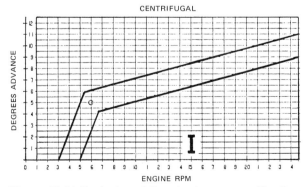

Figure 13.41 Typical centrifugal advance specifications (Cadillac Motor Car Division, GM).

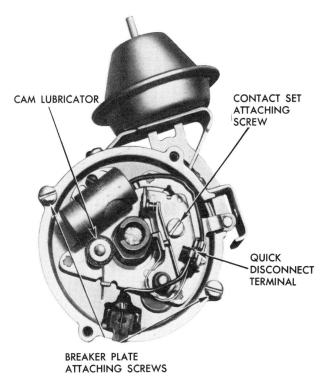

Figure 13.42 A typical vacuum advance mechanism. When vacuum pulls the diaphragm, the link rotates the breaker plate, causing the points to open earlier (Chevrolet Service Manual, Chevrolet Motor Division, GM).

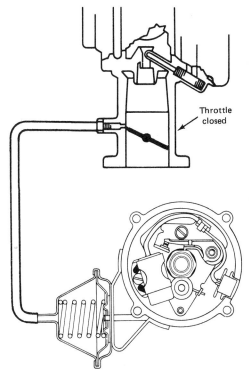

Figure 13.43 The vacuum spark advance is operated by vacuum from the carburetor. Note that when the throttle is closed, no vacuum is available and no additional advance is provided (Chevrolet Service Manual, Chevrolet Motor Division, GM).

der light or moderate load conditions can be given additional spark advance. This additional spark advance usually results in increased fuel economy.

The centrifugal spark advance mechanism is sensitive only to speed, and cannot detect engine load conditions. Therefore, a different method of providing additional spark advance must be used. Most manufacturers use a vacuum advance mechanism of the type shown in Figure 13.42. This mechanism consists of a spring-loaded diaphragm that is connected by a link to the breaker plate. When vacuum is applied to the diaphragm, the breaker plate is pulled in the direction opposite that of cam rotation. This advances the spark timing by causing the points to open earlier (or by causing the trigger wheel to pass the sensor earlier). The diaphragm is connected to an opening, or *port*, in the carburetor. As shown in Figure 13.43, this port is located so that it is

above the throttle plate when the throttle is in the idle or closed position. When the throttle is in this position, there is no vacuum available to pull the diaphragm. Thus, there is no additional spark advance at that speed.

When the engine is operated under a light load with the throttle partially open, manifold vacuum is relatively high. As shown in Figure 13.44, vacuum is present at the port under those conditions. When the throttle is wide open, as it is when the engine is heavily loaded, manifold vacuum is very low. No vacuum is available to provide additional spark advance. This condition is shown in Figure 13.45.

At any engine speed above idle, both the centrifugal and the vacuum system may function. The centrifugal system will advance the spark in relation to engine speed. The vacuum system will further advance the spark in relation to throttle opening and engine load.

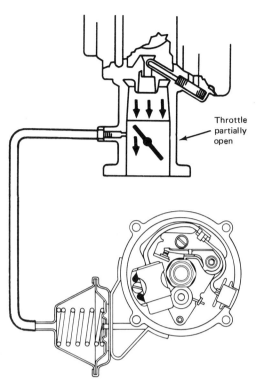

Figure 13.44 When the throttle is partially opened and the engine is operating under a light load, vacuum is present at the vacuum advance port (Chevrolet Service Manual, Chevrolet Motor Division, GM).

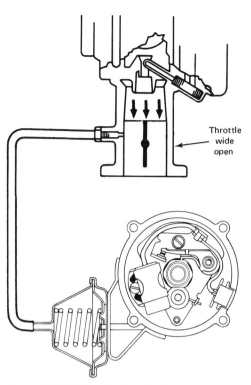

Figure 13.45 When the throttle is wide open, manifold vacuum is so low that none is present at the vacuum advance port (Chevrolet Service Manual, Chevrolet Motor Division, GM).

Job 13f

IDENTIFY THE DEFINITION OF TERMS RELATING TO SPARK TIMING

SATISFACTORY PERFORMANCE

A satisfactory performance on this job requires that you do the following:

1 Identify the definition of terms relating to spark timing by placing the number of each listed term in front of its correct definition.

2 Correctly identify all the terms within 10 minutes.

PERFORMANCE SITUATION

1 TDC
2 Distributor diaphragm
3 Centrifugal advance
4 .003 of a second

5 Vacuum advance
6 0°
7 Centrifugal weights and cam
8 Spark advance

_____ Timing the spark to occur before the piston reaches TDC

_____Moves the breaker plate to advance the spark timing

_____Total discharge condenser

_____A method of advancing spark timing in relation to engine speed

_____The approximate time required for the fuel-air mixture to burn

_____Top dead center

_____The approximate time required for the piston to move from TDC to BDC

_____The position of the crankshaft when the piston is at TDC

_____Moves the breaker point cam or the trigger wheel to advance the spark timing

_____A method of providing additional spark advance during periods of light engine load

CHECKING SPARK TIMING All engines are provided with a means by which spark timing can be checked. Most engines have timing marks on the crankshaft pulley and on the front of the engine. Figure 13.46 shows how those marks may appear. On some engines, the pulley is marked in degrees of crankshaft rotation. These degree markings usually extend both before TDC (BTDC) and after TDC (ATDC). The desired degree marking can be aligned with a pointer attached to the front of the engine. Timing marks of this type are shown in Figure 13.47. Other engines have a single mark or notch on the pulley as shown in

Figure 13.46 Typical timing marks used on a six-cylinder engine (Pontiac Motor Division, GM).

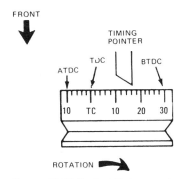

Figure 13.47 Typical timing marks as found on a crankshaft pulley. These marks can be aligned with a pointer attached to the engine. Note that in this drawing the crankshaft is at 16° before top dead center (BTDC) (Ford Motor Company).

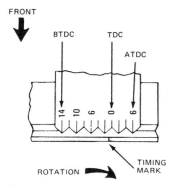

Figure 13.48 Typical timing marks as found on the front of an engine. The mark or pointer on the crankshaft pulley can be aligned with these marks. Note that in this drawing the crankshaft is at 1° before top dead center (BTDC) (Ford Motor Company).

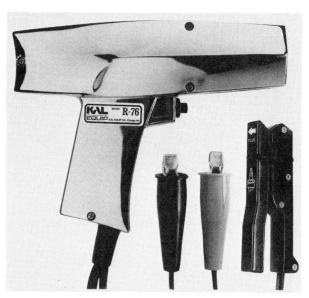

Figure 13.49 A typical power timing light. The two small wires are attached to the car battery. The remaining wire is connected to the spark plug wire for the #1 cylinder. The induction pickup shown merely clamps over the wire (Kal-Equip Company).

Figure 13.48. This mark can be aligned with the desired marking on a degree scale attached to the engine.

Timing marks are used to check the *initial spark timing*. Initial spark timing is the starting point for all spark timing. It indicates when the spark occurs while an engine is idling and before the centrifugal and vacuum advance mechanisms begin to function. The specifications for initial spark timing vary with different engines and with different engine applications. The specifications for a particular car should be obtained from the tune-up decal or from an appropriate manual.

Initial spark timing can be checked and adjusted while the engine is not running. This method is known as *static timing*. Static timing may be necessary after a distributor has been replaced, but it is rarely used during routine service.

Most mechanics check spark timing *dynamically*, or while the engine is running. Because the marks cannot be aligned while the crankshaft is turning, a *timing light*, or *strobe light*, is used to "stop" the pulley. A typical timing light is shown in Figure 13.49. A timing light provides brilliant flashes of light. When this light is directed at moving parts, the parts appear to be at rest.

A timing light is connected to the car battery and to the spark plug wire that leads to #1 cylinder. When the high voltage surge flows to the #1 plug, it triggers the light. Thus, the light flashes at exactly the same time that the plug fires. When the light flashes, the timing

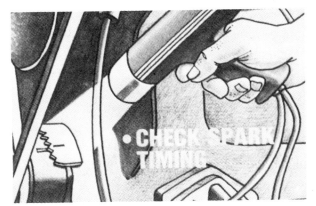

Figure 13.50 A timing light "stops" the motion of the crank-shaft pulley so the timing marks can be aligned (courtesy American Motors Corporation).

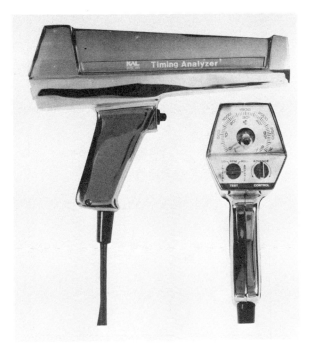

Figure 13.51 A timing light combined with a spark advance meter. This instrument will check initial spark timing and measure both centrifugal and vacuum spark advance (Kal-Equip Company).

marks can easily be seen. The alignment of the marks indicates when the plug fires in relation to the position of the crankshaft. If the spark occurs when the piston is at TDC, the timing marks will be illuminated at the instant the pointer is aligned with the TDC mark. Figure 13.50 shows a timing light in use.

A timing light can also be used to check the operation of the centrifugal and vacuum advance mechanisms. As the engine is accelerated, the change in spark timing causes the timing marks to move. This movement can be observed and, with some timing lights, measured. Figure 13.51 shows a timing light combined with an advance meter.

The following steps outline a procedure for checking spark timing with a timing light. Timing specifications and the location and type of timing marks vary with different engines. This information should be obtained from an appropriate manual:

Note: Any change in dwell will cause the timing to change. Before the timing can be accurately checked, the dwell must be checked and, if necessary, adjusted to specifications.

1 Locate the initial timing specification and the information giving the type of timing marks used and their location. (Refer to Figures 13.47 and 13.48.)

2 Using a drop light or a flashlight, locate the timing marks on the engine and on the pulley.

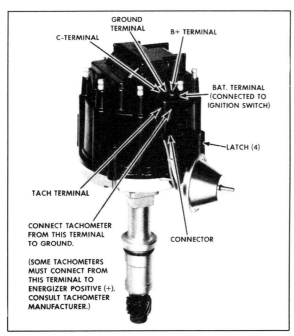

Figure 13.52 In an electronic ignition system using a distributor of this type, the coil is housed inside the distributor cap. This type system is disabled by unplugging the connector (Pontiac Motor Division, GM).

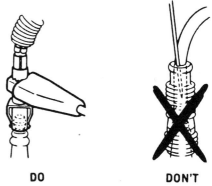

Figure 13.53 When you connect test equipment to a spark plug wire, use an adaptor between the wire and the plug or between the wire and the distributor cap tower. Never pierce a wire or insert a probe between the wire and a boot or nipple (reprinted with permission from AC-Delco Division, General Motors Corporation).

Note: On some engines, it is easier to locate the pulley markings from under the car. A remote starter switch will be of help in "tapping" the engine over while looking for the pulley markings. If you use a remote starter switch, don't forget to disconnect the coil wire from the distributor cap and to ground it with a jumper wire. This will prevent the engine from starting. If the engine is equipped with an electronic ignition system which uses a distributor similar to the one shown in Figure 13.52, you can disable the ignition system by unplugging the connector.

3 Thoroughly clean the markings on the engine and the pulley.

Note: It is suggested that you accent the pointer and the degree mark specified. A sharp piece of chalk or a piece of stiff wire dipped in light-colored paint can be used. The accented marks are easier to see when the engine is running.

4 Connect the timing light battery leads to the battery terminals.

5 Connect the remaining timing light lead to the wire that runs to the spark plug in #1 cylinder.

Note: If the timing light is equipped with an induction pickup, merely clamp the pickup over the wire. (Refer to Figure 13.49.) If the timing light does not have an induction pickup, you must disconnect the spark plug wire from the plug or from the distributor cap. An adaptor can then be used, as shown in Figure 13.53.

Never pierce a spark plug wire or attempt to insert a probe between the boot and the wire. To do so will damage the wire.

6 Position the timing light so that it cannot fall when the engine is started.

7 Install the coil wire or connect the connector if you disabled the ignition system while you were looking for the timing marks.

8 Disconnect and plug the vacuum hose(s) that are connected to the distributor diaphragm. (Refer to Figure 13.24.)

Note: Failure to disconnect the hose(s) may result in a false timing indication.

9 Connect a Tach-Dwell Meter to the DIST (−) terminal on the coil and to a good ground. (Refer to Figure 13.21.)

10 Set the meter function switch to TACH and the cylinder selector switch to the number of cylinders in the engine. (Refer to Figure 13.22.)

11 Apply the parking brake.

12 If the car has an automatic transmission, place the transmission selector lever in the PARK position. If the car has a standard transmission, place the shift lever in the NEUTRAL position.

13 Start the engine and allow it to idle.

14 Check the idle speed and, if necessary, adjust it to specifications.

Note: If the idle speed is too high, the centrifugal advance mechanism may advance the spark timing, causing a false reading when you check the initial timing.

15 Aim the timing light at the timing marks and observe their position. The pointer and the specified degree mark should be aligned.

Note: If the marks are not aligned, the initial spark timing must be adjusted. The procedure for this adjustment follows the completion of the procedure for checking timing.

16 Check the operation of the centrifugal spark advance mechanism. Slowly accelerate the engine while watching the timing marks. The marks should move in the BTDC direction and may even move beyond the range of the markings. When the engine speed is returned to idle, the marks should return to their original position.

17 Check the operation of the vacuum advance mechanism. Operate the engine at about 2000 rpm and observe the location of the timing marks. Unplug and connect the hose(s) that provide vacuum for the diaphragm. The marks should move farther ahead in the BTDC direction. Allow the engine to return to idle. The marks should return to their original position.

18 Turn the ignition switch to the OFF position.

19 If the initial spark timing is correct, disconnect and remove the

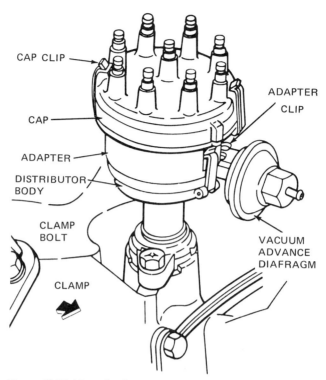

Figure 13.54 Most distributors are held in place by a clamp. After loosening the clamp, the distributor can be rotated to adjust the initial timing (Ford Motor Company).

timing light and the Tach-Dwell Meter. If the initial spark timing requires adjustment, continue with the procedure that follows.

Adjusting Spark Timing Initial spark timing is adjusted by rotating the distributor. The distributor is held in position by a clamp, as shown in Figure 13.54. After loosening the clamp, the distributor can be rotated in either direction. The following steps outline a procedure for adjusting initial spark timing. These steps are a continuation of the previously listed steps for checking initial spark timing:

20 Disconnect and plug the vacuum hose(s) that are connected to the distributor diaphragm. (Refer to Figure 13.24.)

Note: Failure to disconnect the hose(s) may result in an incorrect adjustment.

21 Loosen the bolt or nut that secures the distributor clamp.

Note: On some engines, access to that bolt or nut is extremely limited. A special distributor wrench similar to those shown in Figure 13.55 may be required.

22 Start the engine and allow it to idle.

23 Check the idle speed and, if necessary, adjust it to specifications.

24 While watching the timing marks, carefully rotate the distributor until the specified degree mark and the pointer are aligned.

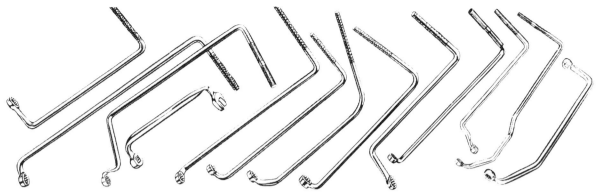

Figure 13.55 Special distributor wrenches are needed for some engines (courtesy of Snap-on Tools Corporation).

Note: To advance timing, the distributor should be rotated in the direction opposite that of shaft rotation. Rotating the distributor in the same direction as shaft rotation will retard the timing.

25 Tighten the bolt or nut that holds the distributor clamp.

26 Recheck the alignment of the timing marks.

27 Recheck the idle speed and, if necessary, adjust it to specifications.

28 Turn the ignition switch to the OFF position.

29 Connect the vacuum hose(s) to the distributor diaphragm.

30 Disconnect and remove the timing light and the Tach-Dwell Meter.

Job 13g

CHECK AND ADJUST TIMING

SATISFACTORY PERFORMANCE

A satisfactory performance on this job requires that you do the following:

1 Check and, if necessary, adjust the timing on the car assigned.
2 Following the steps in the "Performance Outline" and the procedure and specifications of the manufacturer, complete the job within 30 minutes.
3 Fill in the blanks under "Information."

PERFORMANCE OUTLINE

1 Check and, if necessary, adjust the dwell and the engine idle speed.
2 Check the initial spark timing and compare it with the specifications.
3 Check the operation of the centrifugal and vacuum advance mechanisms.
4 Adjust the initial spark timing if necessary.

INFORMATION

Vehicle identification _____

Reference used_____ Page(s)_____

Specifications Dwell_____

    Initial timing _____

    Idle speed _____

Measurements taken Dwell _____

    Initial timing_____

    Idle speed _____

Adjustments made Dwell _____

    Initial timing _____

    Idle speed_____

Operation of advance mechanisms

    Centrifugal_____

    Vacuum _____

SUMMARY

In completing this chapter, you have gained additional knowledge of ignition systems and their operation. You have learned about various primary circuit components and their functions. And you are aware of the different methods used to advance spark timing.

You have also gained additional diagnostic and repair skills. These skills include the measurement of dwell, the adjustment of dwell, and the adjustment of timing.

SELF-TEST

Each incomplete statement or question in this test is followed by four suggested completions or answers. In each case select the *one* that best completes the sentence or answers the question.

1 Two mechanics are discussing dwell.
  Mechanic A says that excessive dwell will cause the magnetic field in the coil to become oversaturated.
  Mechanic B says that insufficient dwell will cause the points to arc and burn.
  Who is right?

A. A only
B. B only
C. Both A and B
D. Neither A nor B

2 Cam angle refers to the number of degrees that the
   A. distributor shaft rotates while the points remain open
   B. crankshaft rotates while a piston moves from TDC to BDC
   C. distributor shaft rotates while the points remain closed
   D. crankshaft rotates while the fuel-air mixture is burning

3 Two mechanics are discussing the function of the condenser in a breaker point ignition system.
   Mechanic A says that the condenser reduces arcing at the points.
   Mechanic B says that the condenser aids in the collapse of the magnetic field in the coil.
   Who is right?
   A. A only
   B. B only
   C. Both A and B
   D. Neither A nor B

4 When measuring dwell on a breaker point ignition system, the meter should be connected to the
   A. BAT (+) terminal on the coil and to a good ground
   B. BAT (+) terminal on the coil and to the S terminal on the solenoid
   C. DIST (−) terminal on the coil and to a good ground
   D. DIST (−) terminal on the coil and to the S terminal on the solenoid

5 Two mechanics are discussing the adjustment of dwell.
   Mechanic A says that closing the gap of the points will increase the dwell.

Mechanic B says that on distributors which have a window in the cap for dwell adjustment, the dwell is increased by turning the adjusting screw clockwise.
Who is right?
   A. A only
   B. B only
   C. Both A and B
   D. Neither A nor B

6 Two mechanics are discussing spark advance.
   Mechanic A says that when an engine is operated under a heavy load, it requires more spark advance.
   Mechanic B says that when an engine is operated at high speed, it requires more spark advance.
   Who is right?
   A. A only
   B. B only
   C. Both A and B
   D. Neither A nor B

7 An engine is operating under a heavy load at 2000 rpm with the throttle wide open. Under these conditions, additional spark advance is provided
   A. only by the vacuum advance mechanism
   B. only by the centrifugal advance mechanism
   C. both the vacuum and the centrifugal advance mechanism
   D. neither the vacuum nor the centrifugal advance mechanisms

8 Two mechanics are discussing the procedure for checking initial spark timing.
   Mechanic A says that the dwell must be checked and, if necessary, adjusted before checking the timing.
   Mechanic B says that the idle speed must be checked and, if necessary, adjusted before checking the timing.

Who is right?
A. A only
B. B only
C. Both A and B
D. Neither A nor B

9 Initial spark timing is adjusted by rotating the
A. cap on the distributor
B. distributor in the engine
C. cam on the distributor shaft
D. breaker plate in the distributor

10 Two mechanics are discussing methods of checking advance mechanisms by using a timing light.

Mechanic A says that when an engine is accelerated, the timing marks should move in the ATDC direction.

Mechanic B says that the vacuum hose(s) at the distributor diaphragm should be disconnected while checking the centrifugal advance.

Who is right?
A. A only
B. B only
C. Both A and B
D. Neither A nor B

Chapter 14 Starting System Service

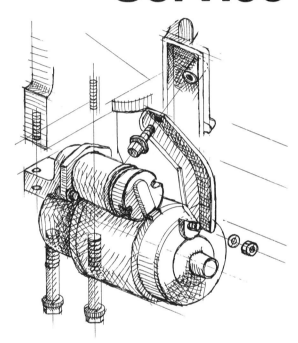

The starting system converts electrical energy to mechanical energy and uses that energy to crank the engine. The engine must be cranked to start the four-stroke cycle. Once the fuel-air mixture in the cylinders burns and exerts sufficient pressure on the pistons, the starting system is no longer needed.

If the starting system cannot crank the engine fast enough, or for a sufficient length of time, the engine will not start. Proper maintenance of the starting system will minimize system failure. And correct diagnostic procedure will enable you to locate the cause of any problems that may occur.

In this chapter you will learn how the starting system operates. You will learn about the circuits used and their components. Based on this knowledge, you will perform diagnostic tests and replace defective parts. Your specific objectives are to perform the following jobs:

1
Identify the parts in a starting system
2
Identify the function of the parts in a starting system
3
Test starter current draw
4
Test the voltage drop in a starting system
5
Replace a starter relay
6
Replace a starter motor

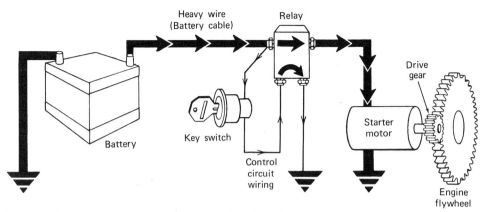

Figure 14.1 A diagram of a typical starting system. Note that the system contains two circuits. The motor circuit has its parts connected by heavy wire or cables. The control circuit uses small size wiring (Chevrolet Service Manual, Chevrolet Motor Division, GM).

THE STARTING SYSTEM The starting system consists of two circuits. One circuit operates the starter motor. Through a gear system, the motor cranks the engine. The other circuit is a control circuit. It enables the driver to turn the motor circuit on and off by means of a small switch. This switch is usually incorporated in the ignition switch. Figure 14.1 shows the two circuits in a typical starting system.

Two circuits are needed because the starter motor requires a large amount of current to crank the engine. A simple switch could be used as a control in the starting system. But the switch would have to be quite large to handle the large amounts of current without being damaged. In addition, long, heavy cables would have to be used to conduct the current to and from the switch. Figure 14.2 shows the location of both circuits in a typical automobile.

Motor Circuit The motor circuit consists of the battery, the relay, and the starter motor. These parts are connected by heavy cables which can handle large amounts of current. (Refer to Figure 14.1.)

Battery The battery is the power source in the circuit. It supplies the electrical energy needed by the starter motor. As you know from your work with batteries, a battery converts chemical energy to electrical energy. In the starting system, the starter motor converts electrical energy to mechanical energy.

A fully charged battery can deliver large amounts of energy in the form of electrical current. But this current can be delivered for only a short amount of time. If the battery is partially discharged, it may not deliver sufficient current to crank the engine fast enough to start.

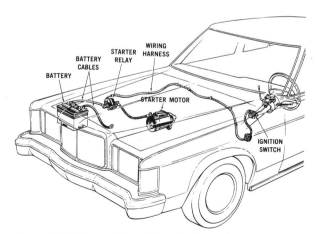

Figure 14.2 The location of the starting system components in a typical automobile. Note that the parts in the motor circuit are close together in the engine compartment. The parts of the control circuit are widely separated and are connected by wires in a wiring harness (Ford Motor Company).

Or it may not be able to deliver the current for a long enough period of time. Because the battery provides the energy that cranks the engine, its state of charge is very important.

Relay The relay is a magnetically operated, heavy-duty switch. Many types of relays are used, but they all serve the same function. They allow a small amount of current in the control circuit to control a large amount of current in the motor circuit. When the driver turns the ignition switch to the START position, a small amount of current energizes the magnet in the relay. The magnet closes a switch with large contacts and current flows to the starter motor.

Starter Motor The starter motor is a heavy-duty electric motor. Figure 14.3 shows one type of starter motor. The starter motor turns a small gear. This gear, often called the *drive*

pinion, turns the engine flywheel. (Refer to Figure 14.1.) The drive pinion is part of a drive system that shifts the pinion in and out of mesh with the flywheel gear. When the motor circuit is energized, the drive pinion is moved into mesh with the flywheel. When the starter switch is released, the drive pinion is moved back out of mesh.

Cables All the parts of the motor circuit must be connected by conductors capable of handling large amounts of current. Small wires offer too much resistance to the flow of current required. If small wires were used, the starter motor would not be able to crank the engine. And the wires would overheat and possibly melt.

Control Circuit The control circuit consists of the battery, the relay, and the starter switch. On cars with automatic transmissions and on

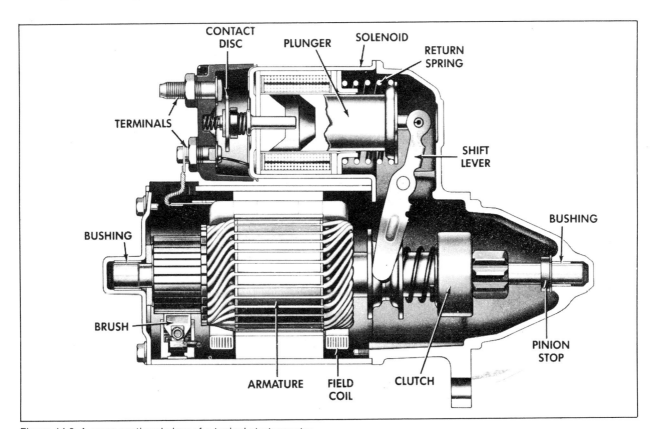

Figure 14.3 A cross-sectional view of a typical starter motor (Pontiac Motor Division, GM).

some other cars, a *neutral safety switch* is used. This switch is placed in series in the circuit. It prevents the circuit from operating unless the transmission selector lever is in the NEUTRAL or PARK position. Because the control circuit requires very little current, the parts are connected by small size wires. (Refer to Figure 14.1.)

Battery The battery is shared by both circuits. It is the common power source.

Relay The relay is also shared by both circuits. The control circuit supplies current to the relay. (Refer to Figure 14.1.)

Starter Switch The starter switch closes and opens the control circuit. In most cars it is a light-duty switch built into the ignition switch. When the driver turns the key to the START position, the starter switch contacts are brought together. A spring returns the switch to the IGNITION position when the key is released.

Job 14a

IDENTIFY THE PARTS IN A STARTING SYSTEM

SATISFACTORY PERFORMANCE

A satisfactory performance on this job requires that you do the following:

1 Identify the numbered parts in the drawing below by placing the number of each part in front of the correct part name.
2 Complete the job by correctly identifying all the parts within 10 minutes.

PERFORMANCE SITUATION

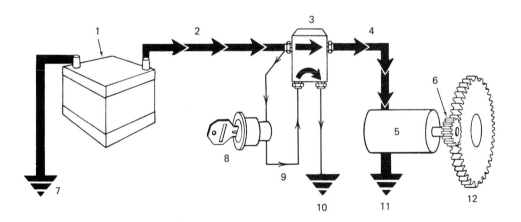

_____Control circuit wiring	_____Drive pinion
_____Starter cable	_____Battery
_____Flywheel	_____Starter motor ground

_____Circuit resistor _____Relay

_____Control circuit ground _____Starter switch

_____Battery cable _____Battery ground

_____Neutral safety switch _____Starter motor

Job 14b

IDENTIFY THE FUNCTION OF THE PARTS IN A STARTING SYSTEM

SATISFACTORY PERFORMANCE
A satisfactory performance on this job requires that you do the following:

1 Identify the function of the listed starting system parts by placing the number of each part in front of the phrase that best describes its function.
2 Complete the job by correctly identifying all the parts within 10 minutes.

PERFORMANCE SITUATION

1 Battery 7 Starter motor ground
2 Control circuit ground 8 Starter cable
3 Control circuit wiring 9 Flywheel
4 Battery cable 10 Battery ground
5 Starter switch 11 Relay
6 Drive pinion 12 Starter motor

_____Provides a path for the return of current to the battery

_____Conducts current to the relay

_____Provides a path for the return of control circuit current

_____Turns the flywheel

_____Provides a bypass for excess starter current

_____Conducts current to the starter motor

_____Provides the control in the control circuit

_____Conducts current in the control circuit

_____Provides a path for the return of motor circuit current

_____Turns the crankshaft

_____Provides the energy for the system

_____Provides the control in the motor circuit

_____Converts electrical energy to mechanical energy

STARTING SYSTEM COMPONENTS All starting systems in late model cars have two circuits and operate in the same manner. But the systems used by various manufacturers are different and use different components. To properly service these systems, you must be aware of these differences.

Relays If you used a remote starter switch when you worked on ignition systems, you are familiar with starter relays. Relays are magnetic switches. They use magnetism to close switch contacts. These contacts can handle large amounts of current. Two types of relays are commonly used. One type, shown in Figure 14.4, uses an electromagnet to move an armature, which causes two switch contacts to come together. A relay of this type is used on most cars built by Chrysler Corporation. On

these cars, the relay is mounted on an inner fender panel or on the firewall.

The other type of relay is commonly called a _solenoid_. A solenoid is an electromagnet with a movable core. Figure 14.5 shows a relay of this type. A large metal disc is attached to the core. When magnetism pulls the core, the disc contacts two large terminals. A solenoid is used as a relay on most cars built by Ford Motor Company and by American Motors Corporation. It is usually mounted on the inner fender panel near the battery. (Refer to Figure 14.2.)

A solenoid can exert a very strong pull. On many cars, a large solenoid is mounted on the starter motor. This solenoid is used to shift the starter drive pinion into mesh with the gear teeth on the flywheel. In some applications, the solenoid on the starter motor performs an

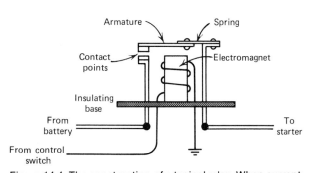

Figure 14.4 The construction of a typical relay. When current flows from the control switch, the electromagnet pulls the armature down, closing the contact points. Current then flows from the battery to the starter.

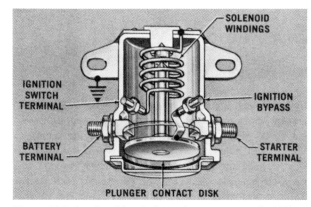

Figure 14.5 A solenoid switch used as a starter relay. When current passes through the solenoid windings, the plunger and the disc are pulled upward. The disc then contacts the two large terminals (Ford Motor Company).

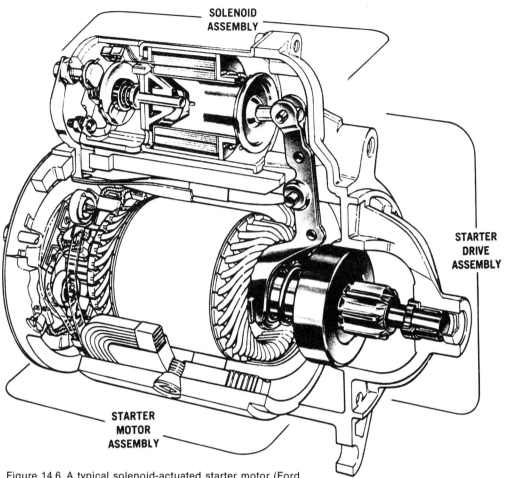

SOLENOID
ASSEMBLY

STARTER
DRIVE
ASSEMBLY

STARTER
MOTOR
ASSEMBLY

Figure 14.6 A typical solenoid-actuated starter motor (Ford Motor Company).

additional task. It also acts as a relay, thus eliminating the need for a separate part. Most cars built by General Motors Corporation use the solenoid to perform both functions.

Starter Motors Many different starter motor designs are used. But most of them can be classified in three distinct types:

Starters Actuated by a Solenoid Figure 14.6 shows a typical solenoid starter. An externally mounted solenoid operates a shift fork to slide the drive pinion out, as shown in Figure 14.7. Starters of this type are used on cars built by General Motors Corporation and on some cars built by Ford Motor Company.

Gear Reduction Starters Actuated by a Solenoid As shown in Figure 14.8, starters of this type use an internally mounted solenoid and incorporate a gear reduction system. Gear reduction starter motors are used on cars built by Chrysler Corporation.

Starters Actuated by a Movable Field Pole Shoe Starters of this type, shown in Figure 14.9, do not use a separate solenoid. One of the field windings in the starter motor acts as a solenoid winding. A movable pole shoe takes the place of a solenoid plunger. Starter motors of this type are used on cars built by Ford Motor Company and by American Motors Corporation.

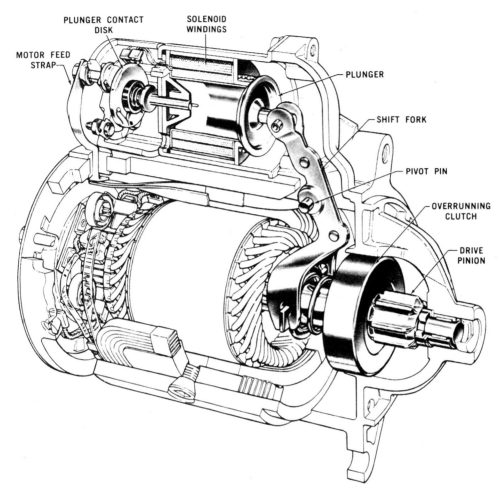

PLUNGER CONTACT DISK

SOLENOID WINDINGS

MOTOR FEED STRAP

PLUNGER

SHIFT FORK

PIVOT PIN

OVERRUNNING CLUTCH

DRIVE PINION

Figure 14.7 A solenoid-actuated started motor with the solenoid energized. Note that the shift fork has moved the drive pinion outward (Ford Motor Company).

Starter Drive Clutches If the starter motor is to crank the engine, the drive pinion must be held in mesh with the flywheel. The solenoid serves this function as long as the ignition switch is held in the START position. This means that when the engine starts, the flywheel turns the drive pinion until the driver releases the switch.

Because of the gear ratio between the drive pinion and the flywheel, the drive pinion is turned at a very high rate of speed. If the starter armature is rotated at this speed, it will be destroyed by centrifugal force. Therefore, the armature must be disconnected from the drive pinion when the engine starts. This function is performed by an *overrunning clutch*.

An overrunning clutch, shown in Figure 14.10, is a device that allows torque to be transmitted in only one direction. The clutch locks to allow the starter armature to turn the drive pinion. But it releases when the pinion tries to turn the armature.

STARTING SYSTEM SERVICE The starting system requires very little maintenance. The maintenance consists of (1) keeping the battery in a high state of charge and (2) keeping all the electrical connections in the system clean and tight. You learned how to perform these services when you worked with batteries.

In addition to maintaining the battery and the

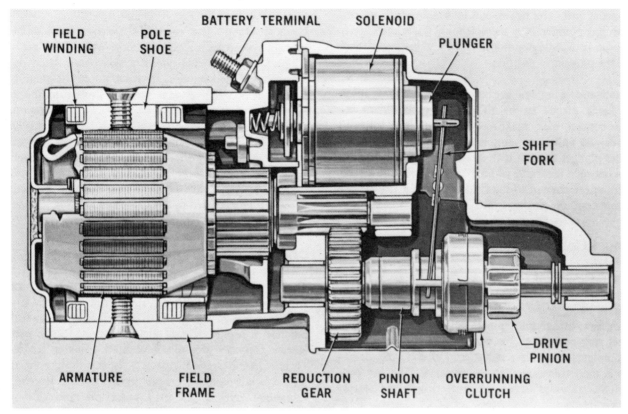

Figure 14.8 A gear reduction starter motor. Note that the solenoid is enclosed (Ford Motor Company).

connections, other services may be required when problems arise in the system. These services include the replacement of parts. But before you attempt to replace any part, you should determine if the part is defective.

Diagnosis of starting system problems is easy if you understand how the system operates and if you follow a logical test procedure.

TESTING STARTER CURRENT DRAW A starter current draw test provides a quick check of the entire starting system. This test is performed with a Battery-Starter Tester of the type shown in Figure 14.11. You used a tester of this type when you load tested batteries. The following steps outline a procedure for performing a starter current draw test. You should consult the manual furnished with the tester you have available for any special procedure which may be necessary with that instrument. The specifications for starter current draw should be obtained from an appropriate service manual:

1 Test the specific gravity of the battery. If the specific gravity is less than 1.200, the battery should be charged before a starter current draw test is attempted.

2 Check the battery terminals and cable clamps. Clean and tighten the clamps, if necessary.

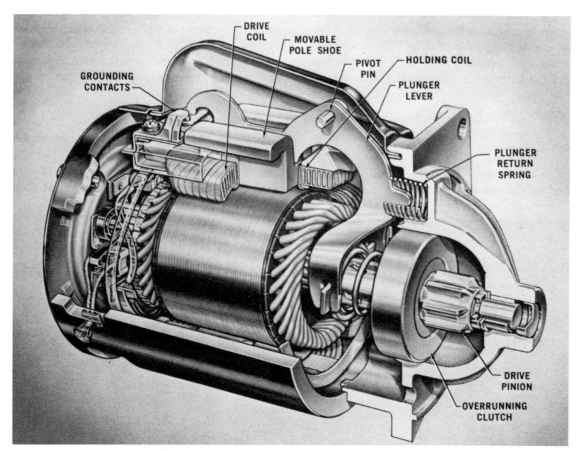

Figure 14.9 A starter actuated by a movable pole shoe. The function of the solenoid is performed by a field coil winding and the movable pole shoe (Ford Motor Company).

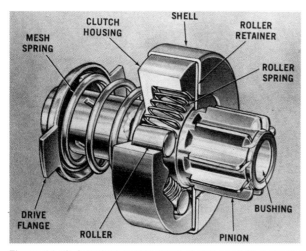

Figure 14.10 A typical overrunning clutch used in a starter drive system (Ford Motor Company).

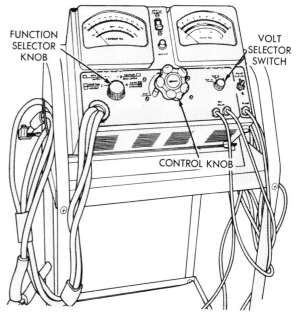

Figure 14.11 A typical tester used to test batteries and starting systems (courtesy Chrysler Corporation).

Note: The battery connections must be clean and tight to obtain accurate test results.

3 Turn the carbon pile control knob on the tester to the OFF position.

4 If the tester is fitted with a function control switch, turn the switch to the STARTER TEST position.

5 If the tester is fitted with a volt selector switch, turn the switch so that a voltage exceeding battery voltage is selected.

6 Connect the heavy ammeter leads to the battery terminals. The positive (+) lead must be connected to the positive (+) terminal, the negative (−) lead to the negative (−) terminal.

7 Connect the voltmeter leads to the battery terminals. The positive (+) lead must be connected to the positive (+) terminal, the negative (−) lead to the negative (−) terminal.

Note: **The voltmeter leads should contact the battery terminals, as shown in Figure 14.12. If the voltmeter leads are connected to the clamps on the ammeter leads, an inaccurate voltmeter reading may be obtained.**

8 Disable the ignition system by removing the center wire from the distributor cap and grounding it.

Note: **An alternate disabling procedure may be used.**

9 Apply the parking brake.

10 If the car has an automatic transmission, place the transmission selector lever in the PARK position. If the car has a standard transmission, place the shift lever in the NEUTRAL position.

11 Crank the engine for about 3 seconds while observing the voltmeter. Record the voltage indicated.

Note: **A remote starter switch may be used for this step.**

Figure 14.12 Connections for performing a starter current draw test. Note that the voltmeter leads are not attached to the ammeter leads, but are in contact with the battery posts (courtesy American Motors Corporation).

12 Turn the carbon pile control knob clockwise until the voltmeter indicates the recorded voltage. Read the current indicated by the ammeter and immediately turn the control knob counterclockwise to the OFF position.

13 Record the current indicated by the ammeter.

14 Compare the meter reading with the manufacturer's specification for starter current draw.

15 Disconnect and remove the tester.

16 Restore the ignition system to operating condition.

Interpretation of Test Results The specifications for starter current draw vary with different engines produced by different manufacturers. Starter motors on six-cylinder engines usually draw from 150 to 180 amperes. Starter motors on eight-cylinder engines usually draw from 160 to 210 amperes. These specifications are averages for cars with 12-volt systems.

Three test results are possible. The indicated starter current draw may be within specifications, above specifications, or below specifications.

Within Specifications If the ammeter reading falls within the manufacturer's specified range, the starting circuit is in good condition and should require no repairs.

Above Specifications If the indicated current draw exceeds the manufacturer's specifications, several problems may be indicated. In most instances, the starter motor is faulty and will require repair or replacement. High current draw may also be caused by the use of oil that is too heavy, high engine temperature, or internal engine damage.

Below Specifications If the starter current draw falls below the specifications of the manufacturer, it is usually an indication of high resistance in the motor circuit. All the connections, including the ground connections, should be checked, cleaned, and tightened.

Job 14c

TEST STARTER CURRENT DRAW

SATISFACTORY PERFORMANCE
A satisfactory performance on this job requires that you do the following:

1 Perform a starter current draw test on the car assigned.
2 Following the steps in the "Performance Outline" and the specifications of the manufacturer, complete the job within 15 minutes.
3 Fill in the blanks under "Information."

PERFORMANCE OUTLINE
1 Test the specific gravity of the battery.
2 Connect the tester.

3 Disable the ignition system.

4 Read the voltage while the starter motor is cranking the engine.

5 Read the amperage while using the carbon pile to duplicate the voltage reading.

6 Compare the reading with the manufacturer's specifications.

INFORMATION

Vehicle identification _____

Engine identification _____

Reference used_____ Page(s)_____

Specification for starter current draw_____Amperes

Starter current draw indicated by test_____Amperes

Recommendations _____

TESTING VOLTAGE DROP All conductors have resistance, but their resistance is usually very low. When conductors are connected, those connections offer more resistance. If the connections are clean and tight, the additional resistance will also be slight. But if the connections are dirty, loose, or corroded, the resistance may increase to where current flow is restricted.

The starter motor requires large amounts of current. If there is high resistance in the motor circuit, the starter motor will be unable to receive the current it requires. Any resistance in a circuit will cause a drop in voltage. Therefore, a voltage drop test can be used to detect resistance.

The steps that follow outline the procedure for a series of four voltage drop tests in a starting system. These tests will enable you to find the exact location of any high resistance. Because the voltmeter readings taken will be in tenths of 1 volt, a voltmeter with a low scale is required for accuracy:

Preparation 1 Test the specific gravity of the battery. If the specific gravity is less than 1.200, the battery should be charged.

2 Disable the ignition system by removing the center wire from the distributor cap and grounding it.

Note: An alternate disabling procedure may be used.

3 Apply the parking brake.

4 If the car has an automatic transmission, place the transmission selector lever in the PARK position. If the car has a standard transmission, place the shift lever in the NEUTRAL position.

5 Connect a remote starter switch to the relay.

6 Adjust the voltmeter to the low scale.

Test 1 This test measures the voltage drop in the "hot" side of the motor circuit.

1 Connect the positive (+) voltmeter lead to the positive (+) battery post, as shown in Figure 14.13.

Note: **The voltmeter lead must contact the battery post, not the cable clamp.**

2 Connect the negative (−) voltmeter lead to the terminal bolt on the starter motor. (Refer to Figure 14.13.)

Note: **The voltmeter lead should contact the starter terminal bolt and not the terminal on the end of the cable.**

3 Crank the engine and observe the voltmeter reading. Record the voltage indicated.

4 Disconnect the negative (−) voltmeter lead.

Test 2 This test measures the voltage drop between the battery and the starter side of the relay.

1 Connect the negative (−) voltmeter lead to the terminal bolt on the starter side of the relay, as shown in Figure 14.14.

2 Crank the engine and observe the voltmeter reading. Record the voltage indicated.

3 Disconnect the negative (−) voltmeter lead.

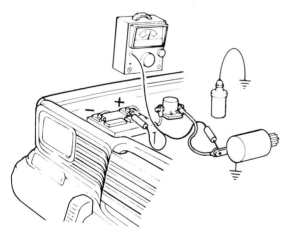

Figure 14.13 Meter connections for performing a voltage drop test of the "hot" side of the starting system motor circuit (courtesy American Motors Corporation).

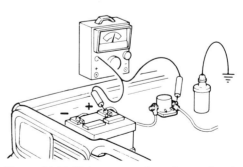

Figure 14.14 Meter connections for performing a voltage drop test of the "hot" side of the motor circuit between the battery and the starter side of the relay (courtesy American Motors Corporation).

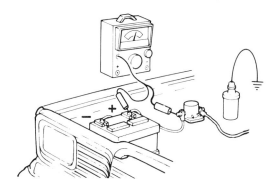

Figure 14.15 Meter connections for performing a voltage drop test of the "hot" side of the motor circuit between the battery and the battery side of the relay (courtesy American Motors Corporation).

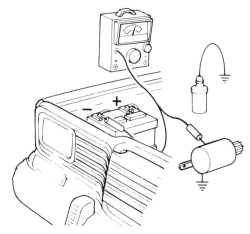

Figure 14.16 Meter connections for performing a voltage drop test of the ground side of the motor circuit (courtesy American Motors Corporation).

Test 3 This test measures the voltage drop between the battery and the battery side of the relay.

1 Connect the negative (−) voltmeter lead to the terminal bolt on the battery side of the relay, as shown in Figure 14.15.

2 Crank the engine and observe the voltmeter reading. Record the voltage indicated.

3 Disconnect both voltmeter leads.

Test 4 This test measures the voltage drop in the ground side of the motor circuit.

1 Connect the positive (+) voltmeter lead to the starter motor housing as shown in Figure 14.16.

2 Connect the negative (−) voltmeter lead to the negative (−) battery post. (Refer to Figure 14.16.)

Note: The voltmeter lead must contact the battery post, not the cable clamp.

3 Crank the engine and observe the voltmeter reading. Record the voltage indicated.

4 Disconnect both voltmeter leads.

5 Restore the ignition system to operating condition.

Interpretation of Test Results

Test 1   The indicated voltage should not exceed .5 volts.

A reading of .5 volts or less indicates that the resistance in the "hot" side of the motor circuit is acceptable. The readings of Test 2 and Test 3 can be disregarded. Move to Test 4.

A reading of more than .5 volts indicates excessive resistance in the "hot" side of the motor circuit. Move to Test 2.

Test 2 The indicated voltage should not exceed .3 volts.

A reading of .3 volts or less indicates that excessive resistance is present between the relay and the starter motor. The starter cable connections should be cleaned and tightened. The cable should be replaced if necessary.

A reading of more than .3 volts indicates excessive resistance between the battery and the starter terminal on the relay. Move to Test 3.

Test 3 The indicated voltage should not exceed .2 volts. A reading of .2 volts or less indicates that excessive resistance is present in the relay or in the relay connections. The connections should be cleaned and tightened. The relay should be replaced if necessary.

A reading of more than .2 volts indicates excessive resistance is present between the battery and the relay. The battery cable connections should be cleaned and tightened. The battery cable should be replaced if necessary. Move to Test 4.

Test 4 The indicated voltage should not exceed .3 volts.

A reading of .3 volts or less indicates that the resistance in the ground side of the motor circuit is acceptable.

A reading of more than .3 volts indicates excessive resistance in the ground connections. The battery ground cable should be cleaned and tightened. The ground cable should be replaced if necessary. The starter mounting bolts should be checked and tightened.

Verification of Repair The appropriate voltage drop test should be repeated after any repair has been made.

Job 14d

TEST THE VOLTAGE DROP IN A STARTING SYSTEM

SATISFACTORY PERFORMANCE

A satisfactory performance on this job requires that you do the following:

1 Test the voltage drop in the motor circuit of the starting system on the car assigned.
2 Following the steps in the "Performance Outline" and the specifications of the manufacturer, complete the job within 20 minutes.
3 Fill in the blanks under "Information."

PERFORMANCE OUTLINE

1 Prepare the vehicle and the meter for the test.
2 Measure the voltage drop in the entire "hot" side of the motor circuit.
3 Measure the voltage drop between the battery and the starter side of the relay.
4 Measure the voltage drop between the battery and the battery side of the relay.
5 Measure the voltage drop in the ground side of the motor circuit.
6 Restore the vehicle to operating condition.

7 Compare your readings with the specifications of the manufacturer.

INFORMATION

Vehicle identification _____

Reference used_____ Page(s)_____

Meter identification_____

Voltmeter scale used _____

	Test Performed	Test Result	Specification
	Voltage drop in entire "hot" side of circuit	_____volts	_____volts
	Voltage drop between battery and starter side of relay	_____volts	_____volts
	Voltage drop between battery and battery side of relay	_____volts	_____volts
	Voltage drop in ground side of circuit	_____volts	_____volts

INTERPRETATION OF TEST RESULTS

_____Resistance of entire motor circuit is within specifications

Excessive resistance may be present in the

_____Positive battery post and the cable clamp connection

_____Battery cable

_____Battery cable connection at the relay

_____Relay

_____Starter cable connection at the relay

_____Starter cable

_____Starter cable connection at the starter motor

_____Negative battery post and the cable clamp connection

_____Ground cable

_____Ground cable connection at the engine

_____Starter motor mounting

REPLACING A RELAY The steps that follow outline typical procedures for replacing starter relays. An appropriate service manual should be consulted for specific procedures that may be necessary on particular cars:

Solenoid Relays of the Type Used on Vehicles Built by Ford Motor Company and by American Motors Corporation
1 Disconnect the ground cable from the battery.
2 Disconnect the wires and cables from the relay.
Note: Arrange the wires so that they will be installed in the same position.
3 Remove the relay.
4 Install the replacement relay.
5 Install the cables and wires.
6 Connect the battery ground cable.

Relays of the Type Used on Vehicles Built by Chrysler Corporation
1 Disconnect the ground cable from the battery.
2 Disconnect the wires from the relay.
Note: The late model relays plug into a quick disconnect socket on a wiring harness.
3 Remove the relay.
4 Install the replacement relay.
5 Install the wires.
6 Connect the battery ground cable.

Job 14e

REPLACE A STARTER RELAY

SATISFACTORY PERFORMANCE
A satisfactory performance on this job requires that you do the following:

1 Replace the starter relay on the car assigned.
2 Following the steps in the "Performance Outline," complete the job within 20 minutes.
3 Fill in the blanks under "Information."

PERFORMANCE OUTLINE
1 Disconnect the battery ground cable.
2 Remove the relay.
3 Install the replacement relay.
4 Connect the battery ground cable.
5 Test the operation of the relay.

INFORMATION

Vehicle identification _____

Reference used_____ Page(s)_____

REPLACING A STARTER MOTOR Removing a starter motor from an engine and installing a replacement is a relatively simple job. But when the engine is located in a crowded engine compartment, the job becomes more difficult. The starter motor on some cars can be removed by working under the hood. On others, you must raise the car, support it, and work underneath.

Two methods of mounting a starter on an engine are commonly used. One method uses two or three short bolts to hold the starter to the front of the flywheel housing, as shown in Figure 14.17. The other method uses two long bolts to hold the starter to the bottom of the flywheel housing. As shown in Figure 14.18, a reinforcement bracket is often used with this latter method.

On some cars, the steering linkage blocks the removal of the starter motor. Turning the wheels to the extreme left or to the extreme right may provide sufficient clearance. In some instances, the steering linkage must be disconnected and moved.

There are many variables in engine and chassis design, even

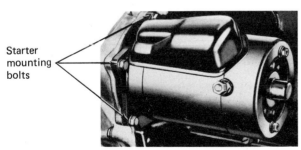

Starter mounting bolts

Figure 14.17 In this installation, the starter motor is held to the front of the flywheel housing by three bolts (Ford Motor Company).

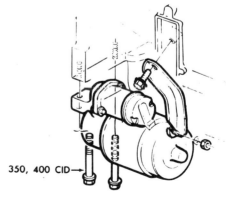

350, 400 CID

Figure 14.18 In this installation, the starter motor is held to the bottom of the flywheel housing by two bolts. A bracket reinforces the mounting (Chevrolet Service Manual, Chevrolet Motor Division, GM).

among cars built by the same manufacturer. Many of these variables require different starter motor replacement procedures. The steps that follow outline a general procedure. You should consult an appropriate service manual for the specific procedure required for the car on which you are working:

Removal 1 Disconnect the battery ground cable.

2 If the starter must be removed from under the car, raise the car and support it with car stands.

Note: On some cars, placing the car stands under the frame will provide more clearance at the steering linkage and allow easier starter removal.

3 Remove any reinforcing brackets, braces, or heat shields present.

4 Disconnect the wires and cables connected to the starter.

Note: Be sure to observe the location of each wire so that you can install them in the correct location on the replacement starter.

5 Remove the bolts holding the starter to the flywheel housing.

Note: On some engines, shims are used between the starter motor and the flywheel housing, as shown in Figure 14.19. Be sure to save any shims present so that you can install them with the replacement starter.

6 Remove the starter motor.

Note: Starter removal may be blocked by other engine and chassis components. Consult an appropriate service manual for the manufacturer's recommended removal procedure.

Installation 1 Clean the starter mounting surface on the flywheel housing.

2 Position the replacement starter against the flywheel housing and start the mounting bolts.

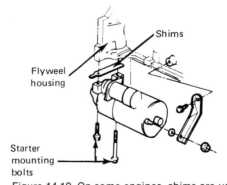

Figure 14.19 On some engines, shims are used between the starter motor and the flywheel housing to provide a means for adjusting gear mesh (Pontiac Motor Division, GM).

Note: Install any shims that were removed with the original starter motor.

3 Turn all the bolts into place gradually, holding the starter in position.

4 Tighten the bolts to the manufacturer's torque specification.

5 Install the wires and cables.

6 Install any brackets, braces, and heat shields removed. Tighten the attaching bolts to the torque specifications of the manufacturer.

7 Install any engine and chassis components removed to allow starter removal.

8 Connect the battery ground cable.

9 Check the operation of the starter motor.

10 Raise the car, remove the car stands, and lower the car to the floor.

Job 14f

REPLACE A STARTER MOTOR

SATISFACTORY PERFORMANCE

A satisfactory performance on this job requires that you do the following:

1 Replace the starter motor on the car assigned.
2 Following the steps in the "Performance Outline" and the procedure and specifications of the manufacturer, complete the job within 200 percent of the manufacturer's suggested time.
3 Fill in the blanks under "Information."

PERFORMANCE OUTLINE

1 Disconnect the battery ground cable.
2 Raise and support the car if necessary.
3 Remove all parts necessary to gain access to starter.
4 Remove starter.
5 Install starter.
6 Install all parts removed to gain access.
7 Connect battery ground cable.
8 Check starter operation.
9 Lower car to floor.

INFORMATION

Vehicle identification _____

Reference used_____ Page(s)_____

SUMMARY

By performing the jobs in this chapter, you learned how to perform many of the services necessary to maintain starting systems. You now have knowledge of how the systems function. You are aware of the many different components used and can identify those components. You have also developed skills. You can perform starter current draw tests and voltage drop tests. And you can interpret the results of these tests to diagnose problems in the starting system. In addition, you have gained repair skills in the replacement of defective components.

SELF-TEST

Each incomplete statement or question in this test is followed by four suggested completions or answers. In each case select the *one* that best completes the sentence or answers the question.

1 Which of the following parts is NOT a part of the control circuit?
   A. Relay
   B. Battery
   C. Starter motor
   D. Starter switch

2 Two mechanics are discussing starting systems.
   Mechanic A says that on most cars, a relay is used to complete the motor circuit so current can flow to the starter motor.
   Mechanic B says that on some cars, a neutral safety switch is used in the motor circuit.
   Who is right?
   A. A only
   B. B only
   C. Both A and B
   D. Neither A nor B

3 Starter motors with a gear reduction drive are used on cars built by
   A. Ford Motor Company
   B. Chrysler Corporation
   C. General Motors Corporation
   D. American Motors Corporation

4 When an engine starts, the drive pinion is disconnected from the starter armature by the
   A. field pole shoe
   B. torque converter
   C. overrunning clutch
   D. solenoid return spring

5 A starter current draw test should not be performed unless the battery specific gravity is at least
   A. 1.000
   B. 1.100
   C. 1.200
   D. 1.300

6 When performing a starter current draw test, the voltmeter leads should be connected to the
   A. relay terminals
   B. battery terminals
   C. ammeter lead terminals
   D. starter motor terminals

7 A test of a starting system reveals that the starter current draw is below specifications. The most probable cause of that finding is
   A. low resistance in the motor circuit
   B. high resistance in the motor circuit
   C. low resistance in the control circuit
   D. high resistance in the control circuit

8 A test of a starting system reveals that the voltage drop between the battery positive (+) post and the starter motor terminal is excessive. The most probable cause of that finding is
   A. low resistance in the motor circuit
   B. high resistance in the motor circuit

C. low resistance in the control circuit

D. high resistance in the control circuit

9 A test of a starting system reveals that the voltage drop between the battery negative (−) terminal and the starter motor housing is .2 volts.

Mechanic A says that the system has excessive resistance in the ground side of the motor circuit.

Mechanic B says that the system has excessive resistance in the ground side of the control circuit.

Who is right?

A. A only

B. B only

C. Both A and B

D. Neither A nor B

10 Two mechanics are discussing starter motor replacement.

Mechanic A says that on some engines, shims are placed between the solenoid and the starter motor to adjust the movement of the drive pinion.

Mechanic B says that on some engines, shims are placed between the starter motor and the flywheel housing to adjust the mesh of the drive pinion.

Who is right?

A. A only

B. B only

C. Both A and B

D. Neither A nor B

Chapter 15
Charging System Service

Automotive charging systems use alternators to convert mechanical energy to electrical energy. This electrical energy is needed to operate the other electrical systems and to maintain the state of charge of the battery.

If the charging system fails, the battery will soon fail. Without an electrical power source, the car will not run. Charging system failure can be minimized by proper maintenance. Any required repairs should be based on a diagnosis of the cause of the particular problem. And the diagnosis must be based on knowledge.

In this chapter you will learn how charging systems operate. You will learn about the components used and how they function. And you will diagnose the cause of problems, isolate these causes, and perform the needed repairs. Your specific objectives are to perform the following jobs:

1
Identify the parts in a charging system
2
Identify the function of the parts in a charging system
3
Perform a three-stage charging circuit test
4
Determine the cause of undercharging
5
Determine the cause of overcharging
6
Replace an alternator

THE CHARGING SYSTEM The charging system is responsible for maintaining the state of charge of the battery. If the charging system should fail, the battery can provide energy for only a limited time. Repairs to the charging system should be based on diagnosis. And the diagnosis is based on a knowledge of the system, its components, and their function.

Charging System Components Most automotive charging systems include four major components. Those components are: (1) the alternator, (2) the regulator, (3) the battery, and (4) the indicating device. Figure 15.1 shows the location of those components in a typical charging system.

The Alternator An alternator, shown in Figure 15.2, is a generator that produces alternating current. For this reason, it is sometimes referred to as an *AC generator*. The alternator is driven by a belt from the engine crankshaft, as shown in Figure 15.3. Through magnetism, the alternator converts mechanical energy to electrical energy. Some of this electrical energy is used by the various other electrical systems. And some of this energy is converted to chemical energy and stored in the battery.

The Regulator The regulator acts as an automatic control in the charging system. Without a regulator, an alternator will always operate at its highest possible output. It will do

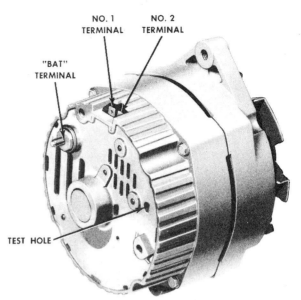

Figure 15.2 A Delcotron alternator. Alternators of this type have integral regulators and are used on vehicles built by General Motors Corporation (Pontiac Motor Division, GM).

this even when the energy it produces is not needed. Uncontrolled, alternator output voltage will exceed the limits of the other electrical systems in a car. Bulbs and other components will burn out. The battery will be damaged by overcharging. And, within a very short time, the alternator will burn itself out. Figure 15.4 shows a typical regulator.

The Battery Although the battery converts and stores energy, it also acts as a "cushion" or "shock absorber" in the system. The battery does this by balancing out slight differences in the energy supplied by the alternator and the energy demanded by the other systems.

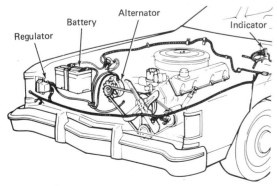

Figure 15.1 The location of the components in a typical charging system (Ford Motor Company).

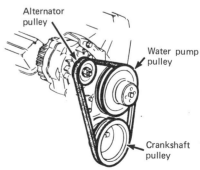

Figure 15.3 The alternator is driven by a belt from the crankshaft (Pontiac Motor Division, GM).

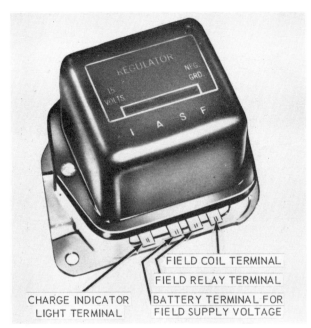

Figure 15.4 A typical alternator regulator (Ford Motor Company).

The Indicating Device The indicating device provides the driver with some indication of system failure. On most cars, the indicating device consists of a warning light on the instrument panel. If this light remains on while the engine is running, it indicates that the alternator is not charging the battery.

Some cars have an ammeter as an indicating device. These meters are usually not as accurate as those you use for testing. But they do inform the driver of the approximate amount of current that is flowing in the electrical system. Ammeters used on instrument panels show current flow in two directions. Current flowing into the battery moves the meter needle to the CHARGE side of the dial. When the needle moves to the DISCHARGE side, it means that current is flowing out of the battery.

On other cars, a voltmeter is provided as the indicating device. The voltmeter indicates system voltage, usually on a scale divided into voltage ranges.

Charging System Circuits Many different circuits are used to connect the components in the charging system. These circuits vary even among cars built by the same manufacturer. Figures 15.5 and 15.6 show two typical circuits. Different circuits require different

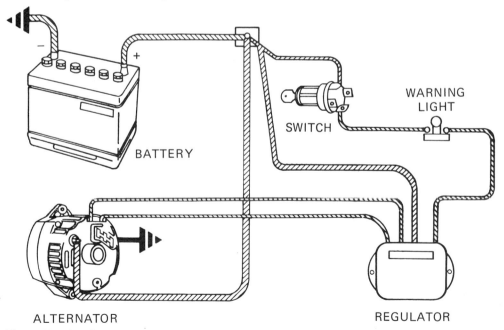

Figure 15.5 A typical charging system circuit (Pontiac Motor Division, GM).

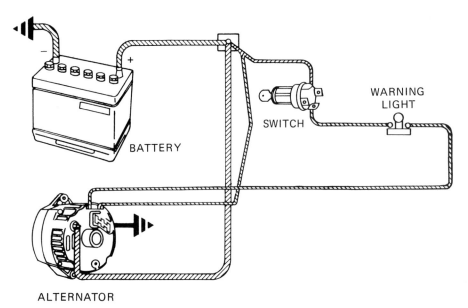

Figure 15.6 A charging system circuit used when the regulator is housed within the alternator (Pontiac Motor Division, GM).

testing procedures. These procedures are covered later in this chapter.

CHARGING SYSTEM COMPONENT OPERATION
Many different types of alternators and regulators are used in automotive charging systems. Because of the different service procedures required, a knowledge of how those components operate is important.

Alternators When a magnetic field is moved across a conductor, a current is induced in this conductor. You learned this principle when you studied ignition coils. In an alternator, an electromagnet, called a *rotor*, turns inside a set of wire coils, or windings, called a *stator*. These parts are shown in Figure 15.7. As the rotor turns, its magnetic lines of force move across all the windings in the stator. This action induces current in the windings.

As the rotor turns, the poles of its magnetic field at the stator continuously alternate from north to south. Because of this, the current induced in the stator windings is *alternating current*. The polarity of alternating current continuously changes back and forth from positive (+) to negative (−). The battery and the electrical systems in the car require *direct current*. Direct current does not change polarity.

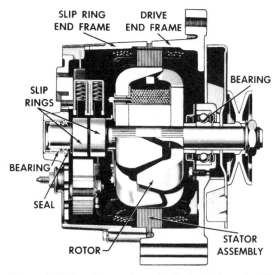

Figure 15.7 A cutaway view of a typical alternator (Pontiac Motor Division, GM).

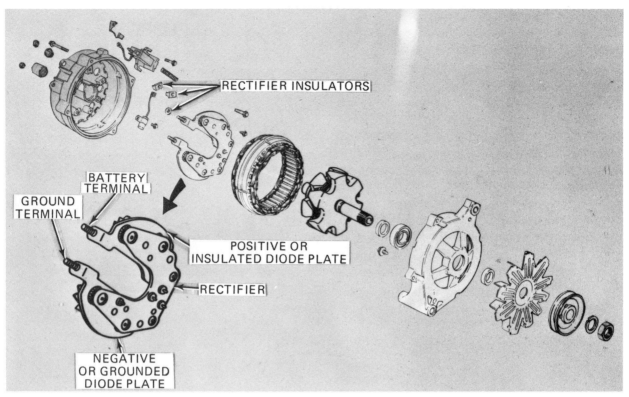

Figure 15.8 A typical rectifier assembly and its location in an alternator (Ford Motor Company).

To be useful in automotive electrical systems, alternating current must be *rectified*, or converted to direct current. A *rectifier* is used for this task. Figure 15.8 shows a rectifier and its location in an alternator. A rectifier consists of a group of *diodes*. A diode is an electrical check valve that conducts current in only one direction. Both positive (+) and negative (−) diodes are used in pairs to "split" the alternating current. Most rectifiers contain six or eight diodes. Half the diodes conduct positive (+) current and half conduct negative (−) current. Thus, the alternating current is converted to direct current before it leaves the alternator.

The voltage produced by an alternator depends largely on the strength of the rotor's magnetic field. This magnetic field is created by a coil of wire inside the rotor. Figure 15.9 shows this *field coil*. Battery voltage is conducted to the field coil by a pair of brushes that contact slip rings on the rotor shaft. (Refer to Figure 15.7.) By controlling the amount of current that flows through the field coil, the output voltage of the alternator is controlled. Current flow through the field coil is controlled automatically by a regulator.

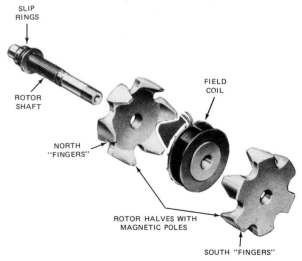

Figure 15.9 Exploded view of a rotor (Ford Motor Company).

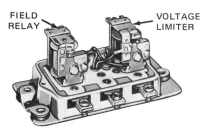

Figure 15.10 A typical electromechanical regulator (Ford Motor Company).

Regulators As mentioned above, regulators control alternator output by controlling the amount of current that flows in the field winding. But regulators have other functions. In some systems they turn off the field current when the engine stops running. And they are also used to operate the warning light on the instrument panel.

There are many types of alternator regulators, but they can be classified in three distinct types as follows:

Electromechanical Regulators Figure 15.10 shows a typical electromechanical regulator. These regulators use magnetically operated switches. One switch functions as a voltage limiter. By directing current through various resistors, it limits the voltage that flows to the field winding. The remaining switch opens the circuit to the field winding when the alternator is not operating. This switch is usually called the field relay. Figure 15.11 shows the wiring

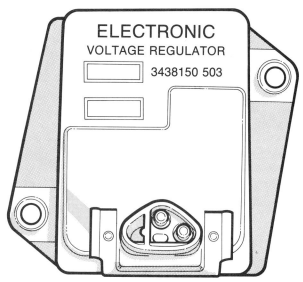

Figure 15.12 A typical transistorized regulator. The unit is sealed and has no moving parts (courtesy Chrysler Corporation).

diagram of a typical electromechanical regulator.

Transistorized Regulators Transistorized regulators, often called electronic regulators, do not have any moving parts. They use transistorized circuits to replace the mechanical switches. Many types of transistorized regulators are used. Some are mounted separately from the alternator. A regulator of this type is shown in Figure 15.12. Others are mounted

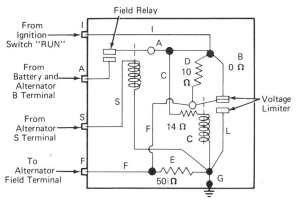

Figure 15.11 An internal wiring diagram of a typical electromechanical regulator (Ford Motor Company).

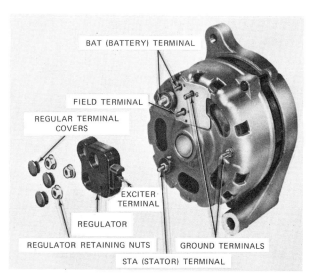

Figure 15.13 A transistorized regulator that is mounted on the rear of an alternator (Ford Motor Company).

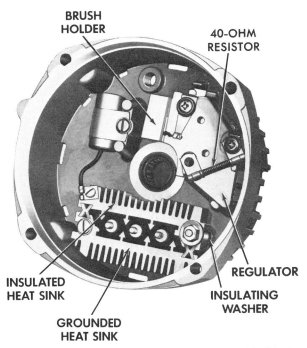

Figure 15.14 A transistorized regulator mounted inside the rear housing of an alternator (Chevrolet Service Manual, Chevrolet Motor Division, GM).

externally on the rear of the alternator, as shown in Figure 15.13. Still others are mounted inside the alternator as an integral part of the assembly. A regulator of this type is shown in Figure 15.14.

Composite Regulators As shown in Figure 15.15, some regulators contain both transis-

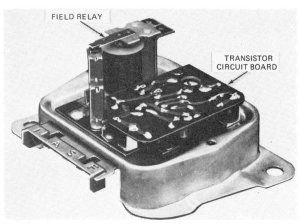

Figure 15.15 A composite regulator. A mechanical field relay is used together with a transistorized voltage limiter circuit board (Ford Motor Company).

torized and electromechanical parts. Regulators of this type are mounted separately from the alternator.

Warning Lights Most cars have a warning light on the instrument panel to warn the driver of any system failure. Figure 15.16 shows the three phases of warning light operation.

SWITCH	ENGINE	LAMP
Off	Stopped	Off
On	Stopped	On
On	Running	Off

Figure 15.16 The charging system warning light operates in three phases.

Job 15a

IDENTIFY THE PARTS IN A CHARGING SYSTEM

SATISFACTORY PERFORMANCE

A satisfactory performance on this job requires that you do the following:

1 Identify the numbered parts in the drawing below by placing the number of each part in front of the correct part name.
2 Complete the job by correctly identifying all the parts within 5 minutes.

PERFORMANCE SITUATION

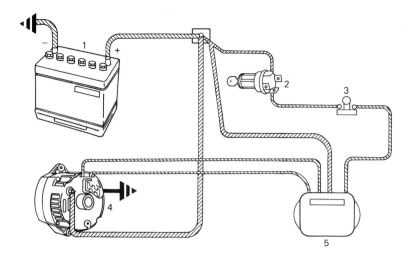

_____Ignition switch   _____Solenoid

_____Battery   _____Alternator

_____Regulator   _____Warning light

Job 15b

IDENTIFY THE FUNCTION OF THE PARTS IN A CHARGING SYSTEM

SATISFACTORY PERFORMANCE

A satisfactory performance on this job requires that you do the following:

1 Identify the function of the listed charging system parts by placing the number of each part in front of the phrase that best describes its function.
2 Complete the job by correctly identifying all the parts within 10 minutes.

PERFORMANCE SITUATION

1 Alternator   6 Battery
2 Stator   7 Electromechanical regulator
3 Rotor   8 Transistorized regulator
4 Diode   9 Field winding
5 Rectifier   10 Brushes and slip rings

_____Converts and stores energy

_____Uses magnetically operated switches to control voltage

_____Conducts current to the field winding

_____Converts alternating current to direct current

_____Conducts current to the stator

_____Converts mechanical energy to electrical energy

_____Acts as an electrical check valve

_____Creates a magnetic field in the rotor

_____Uses transistorized circuits to control voltage

_____Moves a magnetic field across the stator windings

_____Receives current through induction

CHARGING SYSTEM SERVICE Routine maintenance of the charging system consists of (1) keeping the alternator belt in adjustment and (2) keeping all the electrical connections in the system clean and tight. You developed skills in those jobs when you worked with cooling systems and batteries.

Other services may be required when problems arise in the system. These services include the replacement of parts. But before you attempt to replace any part, you should determine if the part is defective.

You now have a knowledge of the parts in the charging system and how they function. Based on this knowledge, you can diagnose most charging system problems by following a logical test procedure.

PRELIMINARY CHECKS
Test the Battery If the battery is discharged, an accurate test of the charging system cannot be made. Check the specific gravity of the battery electrolyte and charge the battery if necessary. If the battery is defective, the alternator will be unable to keep it charged. Load test the battery and replace it if it is defective.

Check the Battery Posts and Cable Clamps Loose, dirty, and corroded connections will prevent the alternator from maintaining the state of charge of a battery. Clean and tighten the connections as necessary.

Test the Voltage Drop in the Cables and Their Connections Even though battery cable connections may appear to be clean and tight, they may have excessive resistance. The steps that follow outline a procedure similar to the one used when you tested for voltage drop in the starting system:

1 Disable the ignition system by removing the center wire from the distributor cap and grounding it.

Note: An alternate disabling procedure may be used.

2 Apply the parking brake.

3 If the car has an automatic transmission, place the transmission selector lever in the PARK position. If the car has a standard transmission, place the shift lever in the NEUTRAL position.

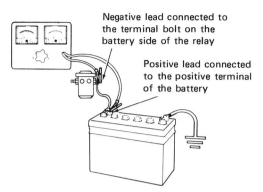

Negative lead connected to
the terminal bolt on the
battery side of the relay

Positive lead connected
to the positive terminal
of the battery

Figure 15.17 Connections for checking voltage drop in the
battery cable and its connections (Ford Motor Company).

4 Connect a remote starter switch to the starter relay.

5 Adjust a voltmeter to the low scale.

6 Connect the positive (+) voltmeter lead to the positive (+) battery post, as shown in Figure 15.17.

Note: The voltmeter lead must contact the battery post, not the cable clamp.

7 Connect the negative (−) voltmeter lead to the terminal bolt on the battery side of the starter relay. (Refer to Figure 15.17.)

Note: The voltmeter lead must cotact the terminal bolt, not the battery cable terminal.

8 Crank the engine and observe the voltmeter reading.

Note: The voltage reading should not exceed .2 volts. A reading of more than .2 volts indicates excessive resistance in the cable or its connections. Clean and tighten the connections. Replace the cable if necessary.

9 Disconnect the voltmeter.

10 Connect the positive (+) voltmeter lead to a good ground on the engine, as shown in Figure 15.18.

11 Connect the negative (−) voltmeter lead to the negative (−) battery post. (Refer to Figure 15.18.)

Note: The voltmeter lead must contact the battery post, not the cable clamp.

12 Crank the engine and observe the voltmeter reading.

Note: The voltage reading should not exceed .2 volts. A reading of more than .2 volts indicates excessive resistance in the battery ground cable or its connections. Clean and tighten the connections. Replace the cable if necessary.

13 Remove the voltmeter.

14 Restore the ignition system to operating condition.

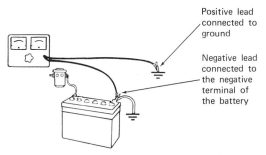

Figure 15.18 Connections for checking voltage drop in the battery ground cable and its connections (Ford Motor Company).

Positive lead connected to ground

Negative lead connected to the negative terminal of the battery

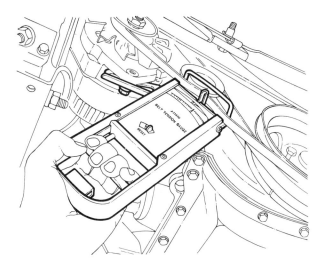

Figure 15.19 Using a gauge to check the tension of an alternator belt (courtesy American Motors Corporation).

Check the Alternator Drive Belt A loose belt will slip and the alternator will not be driven at the proper speed. Use a belt tension gauge to check the belt tension, as shown in Figure 15.19. Adjust the belt if the tension is not within specifications. Replace the belt if it is glazed or damaged.

Check the Wiring An open circuit or a short circuit in the wiring is a common cause of charging system problems. Check for loose connections and damaged wires. Clean and tighten loose connections, and repair or replace damaged wires. Some cars have *fusible links* in the charging circuit. As shown in Figure 15.20, these links are short lengths of special wire that burn out when excessive current flows in the circuit. The gauge and length of the wire used as a fusible link varies with different cars and with different systems. When you find

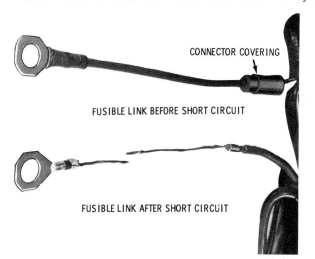

CONNECTOR COVERING

FUSIBLE LINK BEFORE SHORT CIRCUIT

FUSIBLE LINK AFTER SHORT CIRCUIT

Figure 15.20 On some cars, fusible links are used in the charging circuit to protect the parts from damage by excessive current (Oldsmobile Division, GM).

a burned fusible link, you must consult an appropriate manual for those specifications and for the correct replacement procedure.

In performing the preliminary checks, you may have found and corrected some problems. You should now perform a three-stage charging test. This test will tell you if the charging system is operating correctly. By performing this test, you can verify your repairs and check for other problems which may be present.

PERFORMING A THREE-STAGE CHARGING TEST The following steps outline a procedure for performing a three-stage charging test:

Stage 1 This part of the test provides you with a base voltage reading to which you can compare the readings you obtain in stages 2 and 3.

1 Adjust the voltmeter to a scale exceeding battery voltage.

2 Connect the voltmeter to the battery terminals as shown in Figure 15.21.

3 Read the voltmeter and record the reading as the base voltage. (See Figure 15.22.)

Note: **The engine should not be running and all accessories should be turned off.**

Stage 2 This part of the test provides you with a no-load voltage reading with the engine running.

1 Apply the parking brake.

2 If the car has an automatic transmission, place the transmission selector lever in the PARK position. If the car has a standard transmission, place the shift lever in the NEUTRAL position.

3 Start the engine and run it at approximately 2000 rpm.

Note: **Be sure that all accessories are turned off.**

4 Read the voltmeter and record the reading as the no-load voltage.

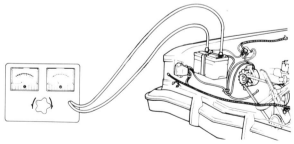

Figure 15.21 All the readings taken during a Three-Stage Charging test are taken with a voltmeter connected to the battery (Ford Motor Company).

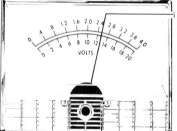

BASE VOLTAGE
With engine and all electrical loads turned off.

Figure 15.22 The Base Voltage reading is a measurement of battery voltage. It is taken with the engine and all electrical loads off (Ford Motor Company).

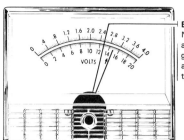

BASE VOLTAGE
Not more than 2.0 volts above base voltage with engine running @2000 RPM and all electrical loads turned off.

Figure 15.23 The No-Load Voltage reading is a measurement of the charging circuit voltage taken while the engine is running approximately 2000 rpm with all electrical loads off (Ford Motor Company).

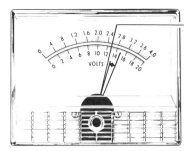

BASE VOLTAGE
At least 0.5 volt above base voltage with engine running @2000 RPM and headlights and blower turned on.

Figure 15.24 The Load Voltage reading is a measurement of the charging circuit voltage taken while the engine is running approximately 2000 rpm with a heavy load on the circuit (Ford Motor Company).

Note: You may have to let the engine run for a short time if the voltmeter reading keeps rising. Read the voltmeter when the needle stops rising.

5 Compare the no-load voltage with the base voltage. (See Figure 15.23.)

Note: The no-load voltage should exceed the base voltage, but by no more than 2.0 volts. A no-load voltage of more than 2.0 volts over the base voltage may indicate an overcharging condition. The reading obtained in Stage 3 will verify this.

Stage 3 This part of the test provides you with a load voltage reading while the engine is running and with a heavy load on the charging system.

1 Turn the headlights on in the high beam position.

2 Turn the heater blower switch to the HIGH position.

3 Run the engine at approximately 2000 rpm.

4 Read the voltmeter and record the reading as the load voltage.

5 Turn off the engine, the headlights, and the heater blower.

6 Disconnect the voltmeter.

7 Compare the load voltage with the base voltage. (See Figure 15.24.)

Note: The load voltage should exceed the base voltage by at least .5 volts, but not more than 2.0 volts. If the load voltage is within this range, the charging system is operating correctly. If the difference is less than .5 volts, the system is undercharging. If the difference is more than 2.0 volts, the system is overcharging. Additional tests are required in both instances.

Job 15c

PERFORM A THREE-STAGE CHARGING CIRCUIT TEST
SATISFACTORY PERFORMANCE
A satisfactory performance on this job requires that you do the following:

1 Perform a three-stage test on the charging circuit of the car assigned.
2 Following the steps in the "Performance Outline," complete the job within 45 minutes exclusive of any charging time required.
3 Fill in the blanks under "Information."

PERFORMANCE OUTLINE
1 Perform the preliminary circuit checks.
2 Perform any repairs required.
3 Measure the base voltage.
4 Measure the no-load voltage.
5 Measure the load voltage.
6 Compare the readings.

INFORMATION

Vehicle identification _____

Reference used_____ Page(s)_____

Specific gravity of electrolyte Cell #1 _____

Cell #2 _____

Cell #3 _____

Cell #4 _____

Cell #5 _____

Cell #6 _____

Battery required charging _____Yes _____No

Was battery charged? _____Yes _____No

Load Test

Battery ampere hour capacity _____

Discharge rate (Test load) _____

Amount of time load was maintained _____

Voltage indicated while under load_____

Approximate battery temperature_____

Recommendations _____Battery is serviceable

_____Battery should be replaced

Battery terminals and connections

_____Were found clean and tight

_____Were cleaned and tightened

Voltage drop test results

Battery positive cable_____

Battery ground cable _____

Were cable services required? _____Yes _____No

Alternator drive belt

Belt tension specification _____

Belt tension measurement _____

Was belt adjusted?   _____Yes _____No

Belt condition _____Good _____Glazed _____ Damaged

Three-stage charging test

Base voltage _____

No-load voltage_____

Load voltage _____

Interpretation of test results _____

TESTING FOR THE CAUSE OF UNDERCHARGING The test procedures that follow are typical of those recommended by the various manufacturers. There are many different types of charging systems in use. And these systems use a variety of components. For these reasons you should consult an appropriate manual for the specific test procedures recommended for the system on which you are working. In all instances, these test procedures should not be attempted until the preliminary checks and the three-stage charging test have been performed:

Systems Using Alternators with Integral Regulators (Delcotron) Alternators of the type shown in Figure 15.25 have a *test hole* in the slip ring end frame. This hole allows you to by-pass the integral regulator. The following procedure should be used:

1 Locate the test hole in the rear of the alternator.

Note: On some cars, access to the test hole is blocked. On these cars, the alternator must be removed for bench testing.

2 Insert a small screwdriver into the test hole, as shown in Figure 15.26. Check to see that it will touch both the side of the hole and the *test tab* inside the alternator.

Note: The test tab is about ¾ inch (19 mm) inside the hole. Do not insert the screwdriver into the hole for a distance of more than 1 inch (25 mm). To do so may damage internal parts. If you cannot touch the test tab, the alternator must be removed for bench testing.

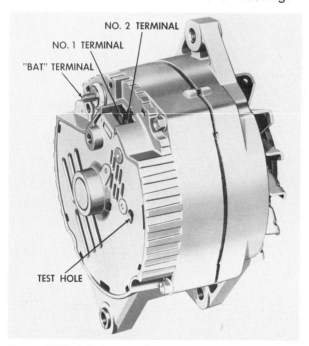

Figure 15.25 A Delcotron alternator with an integral regulator. A test hole is provided so that the regulator can be bypassed for testing (Pontiac Motor Division, GM).

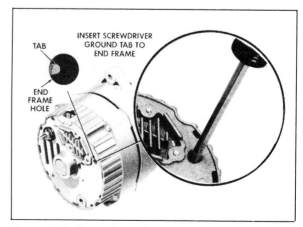

Figure 15.26 Bypassing an integral regulator (Pontiac Motor Division, GM).

3 Adjust a voltmeter to a scale exceeding battery voltage.

4 Connect the voltmeter to the battery terminals. (Refer to Figure 15.21.)

5 Apply the parking brake.

6 If the car has an automatic transmission, place the transmission selector lever in the PARK position. If the car has a standard transmission, place the shift lever in the NEUTRAL position.

7 Start the engine and allow it to idle.

8 Insert the small screwdriver into the test hole so that it contacts both the side of the hole and the test tab. (Refer to Figure 15.26.)

9 Gradually accelerate the engine and observe the voltmeter while holding the screwdriver in place. The reading should rise at least 2.0 volts above the battery voltage.

10 Remove the screwdriver and turn off the engine.

Interpretation of Test Results If the voltage rises considerably, the regulator in the alternator is defective. If the voltage does not rise, and the wiring is known to be in good condition, the alternator is defective. In both instances the alternator must be repaired or replaced.

Systems Using Alternators with Separate Regulators (Ford and Motorcraft) Alternators of the type shown in Figures 15.27 and 15.28 are controlled by regulators mounted separately. The following procedure explains how those regulators can be by-passed with jumper wires:

1 Determine the location of the battery (BAT) terminal and the field

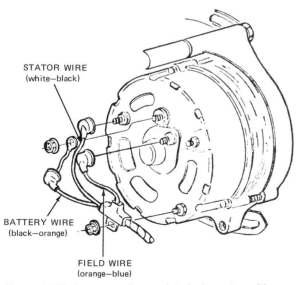

Figure 15.27 An externally regulated alternator with rear-mounted terminals. Alternators of this type are used on some vehicles built by Ford Motor Company and by American Motors Corporation (Ford Motor Company).

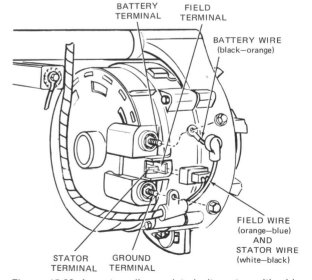

Figure 15.28 An externally regulated alternator with side-mounted terminals. Alternators of this type are used on some vehicles built by Ford Motor Company (Ford Motor Company).

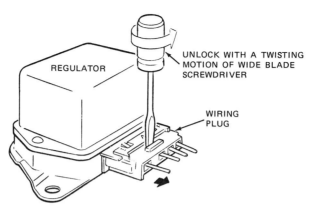

Figure 15.29 On some cars, the wiring plug is disconnected from the regulator by using a screwdriver as shown (Ford Motor Company).

(FLD) terminal on the alternator. (Refer to Figures 15.27 and 15.28.)

2 Disconnect the regulator from the circuit.

Note: Most wiring harnesses have a plug that connects to the regulator. This plug can be unlocked by using a screwdriver, as shown in Figure 15.29.

3 Adjust a voltmeter to a scale exceeding battery voltage.

4 Connect the voltmeter to the battery terminals. (Refer to Figure 15.21.)

5 Apply the parking brake.

6 If the car has an automatic transmission, place the transmission selector lever in the PARK position. If the car has a standard transmission, place the shift lever in the NEUTRAL position.

7 Start the engine and allow it to idle.

8 Connect a jumper wire to the battery (BAT) and the field (FLD) terminals, as shown in Figure 15.30.

9 Gradually accelerate the engine and observe the voltmeter reading. The reading should rise at least 2.0 volts above the battery voltage.

10 Remove the jumper wire and turn off the engine.

Interpretation of Test Results If the voltage does not rise, the alternator is defective and must be repaired or replaced. If the voltage rises considerably, the alternator is functioning properly. The cause of undercharging lies either in the regulator or in the wires connecting the regulator to the alternator. To isolate the problem, continue with step 11.

11 Connect a jumper wire between the "A" and "F" contacts in the plug that you disconnected from the regulator. (See Figure 15.31.)

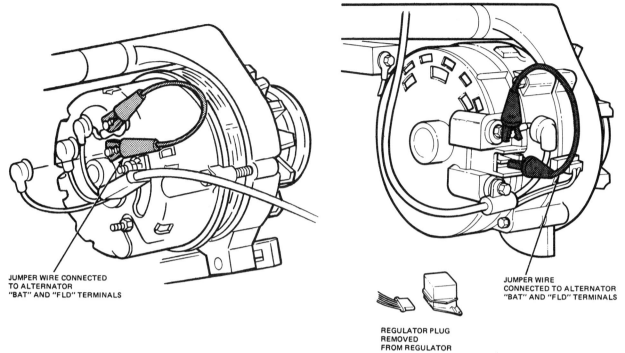

JUMPER WIRE CONNECTED
TO ALTERNATOR
"BAT" AND "FLD" TERMINALS

REGULATOR PLUG
REMOVED
FROM REGULATOR

JUMPER WIRE
CONNECTED TO ALTERNATOR
"BAT" AND "FLD" TERMINALS

Figure 15.30 Jumper wire connections for checking alternator output (Ford Motor Company).

12 Restart the engine.

13 Gradually accelerate the engine and observe the voltmeter reading.

14 Turn off the engine and remove the jumper wire.

Interpretation of If the voltage rises considerably, the regulator is defective and
Test Results should be replaced. If the voltage does not rise, the problem is
caused by a break in the "A" wire or in the "F" wire. To isolate the
problem, continue with step 15.

15 Connect a jumper wire to the "F" contact in the plug and to the
positive (+) battery terminal, as shown in Figure 15.32.

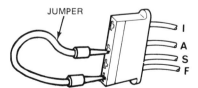

JUMPER

I
A
S
F

Figure 15.31 Jumper wire connections for bypassing the
regulator at the wiring harness plug (Ford Motor Company).

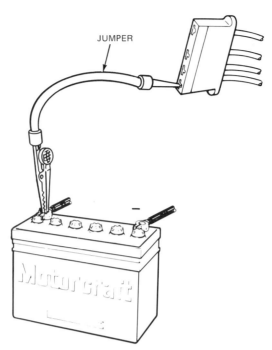

JUMPER

Figure 15.32 Jumper wire connections for testing the wires between the regulator and the alternator (Ford Motor Company).

16 Restart the engine.

17 Gradually accelerate the engine and observe the voltmeter reading.

18 Turn off the engine and remove the jumper wire.

Interpretation of Test Results If the voltage does not rise, the problem is caused by a break in the "F" wire. If the voltage rises, the problem is caused by a break in the "A" wire. Perform the needed repair. Verify the repair by performing a three-stage charging circuit test.

Systems Using Alternators with Separate Regulators (Chrysler) Alternators of the type shown in Figure 15.33 are controlled by regulators mounted separately. These regulators control the alternator field through its ground circuit. The following procedure explains how these regulators can be by-passed with a jumper wire:

1 Determine the location of the field (FLD) terminal on the rear of the alternator. (Refer to Figure 15.33.)

2 Disconnect (unplug) the wire from the field (FLD) terminal.

3 Adjust a voltmeter to a scale exceeding battery voltage.

4 Connect the voltmeter to the battery terminals. (Refer to Figure 15.21.)

5 Apply the parking brake.

6 If the car has an automatic transmission, place the transmission

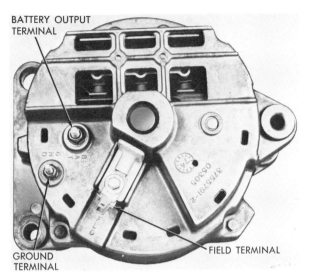

BATTERY OUTPUT
TERMINAL

GROUND
TERMINAL

FIELD TERMINAL

Figure 15.33 The rear view of an externally regulated alternator used on some vehicles built by Chrysler Corporation (courtesy Chrysler Corporation).

selector lever in the PARK position. If the car has a standard transmission, place the shift lever in the NEUTRAL position.

7 Start the engine and allow it to idle.

8 Connect a jumper to the field (FLD) terminal on the alternator and to a good ground.

9 Gradually accelerate the engine and observe the voltmeter. The reading should rise at least 2.0 volts above the battery voltage.

10 Remove the jumper wire and turn off the engine.

Interpretation of Test Results If the voltage does not rise, the alternator is defective and must be repaired or replaced. If the voltage rises considerably, the alternator is functioning properly. The cause of undercharging lies either in the regulator ground, in the regulator, or in the wire that connects the field terminal to the regulator. To isolate the problem, continue with step 11.

11 Connect the field wire to the field (FLD) terminal.

12 Connect a jumper wire between the base of the regulator and a good ground.

13 Start the engine.

14 Gradually accelerate the engine and observe the voltmeter. The reading should rise at least 2.0 volts above the battery voltage.

15 Turn off the engine and remove the jumper wire.

Interpretation of Test Results If the voltage rises considerably, the regulator has a poor ground. Remove the regulator and clean the regulator base to obtain a good connection with the body. The use of lock washers on the attaching

Figure 15.34 A typical electronic regulator. Note the locking tab which must be released to remove the plug (courtesy Chrysler Corporation).

bolts is recommended. Verify the repair by performing the three-stage charging test. If the voltage does not rise, the cause of the undercharging lies in the regulator or in the wire connecting the regulator to the field (FLD) terminal. To isolate the cause of the problem, continue with step 16.

16 Disconnect the field wire from the regulator.

Note: On vehicles with an electromechanical regulator, remove the green wire from the terminal. On vehicles with an electronic regulator, disconnect the wiring plug by releasing the locking tab. (See Figure 15.34.)

17 Turn the ignition switch to the ON position, but do not start the engine.

18 Remove the positive (+) voltmeter lead from the battery and touch it to the disconnected wire.

19 Observe the voltmeter reading. Battery voltage should be indicated.

20 Turn the ignition switch to the OFF position.

Interpretation of Test Results If battery voltage is indicated, the regulator is defective and should be replaced. If no voltage is indicated, the wire connecting the regulator to the field (FLD) terminal is broken and should be repaired. Verify the replacement or the repair by performing a three-stage charging test.

Job 15d

DETERMINE THE CAUSE OF UNDERCHARGING

SATISFACTORY PERFORMANCE

A satisfactory performance on this job requires that you do the following:

1 Determine the cause of undercharging indicated by a three-stage charging circuit test.
2 Following the steps in the "Performance Outline" and the procedure and specifications of the manufacturer, complete the tests required within 30 minutes.
3 Fill in the blanks under "Information."

PERFORMANCE OUTLINE

1 By-pass the regulator.
2 Check the system with the regulator by-passed

INFORMATION

Vehicle identification _____

Reference used_____ Page(s)_____

Test results   Alternator _____OK _____NG

Regulator _____OK _____NG

Wiring _____OK _____NG

Recommendations _____

TESTING FOR THE CAUSE OF OVERCHARGING The following test procedures are typical of those recommended by the various manufacturers. You should consult an appropriate manual for the specific procedures recommended for the system on which you are working. In all instances, these procedures should be attempted only after the preliminary checks and the three-stage charging circuit test have been performed.

Systems Using Alternators with Integral Regulators (Delcotron) Overcharging in systems using alternators of this type (refer to Figure 15.25) is usually caused by an internal failure in the alternator. The alternator should be repaired or replaced.

Systems Using Alternators with Separate Regulators (Ford and Motorcraft) The following steps outline a procedure for determining the cause of overcharging in systems using alternators of this type: (Refer to Figures 15.27 and 15.28.)

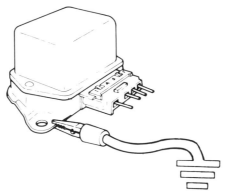

Figure 15.35 A poor regulator ground can be detected by grounding the regulator with a jumper wire (Ford Motor Company).

1 Adjust a voltmeter to a scale exceeding battery voltage.

2 Connect the voltmeter to the battery terminals. (Refer to Figure 15.21.)

3 Read the voltmeter and record the reading as the base voltage.

4 Connect a jumper wire to the base of the regulator and to a good ground. (See Figure 15.35.)

5 Apply the parking brake.

6 If the car has an automatic transmission, place the transmission selector lever in the PARK position. If the car has a standard transmission, place the shift lever in the NEUTRAL position.

7 Start the engine and run it at approximately 2000 rpm.

8 Read the voltmeter. The indicated voltage should not exceed 2.0 volts above the base voltage.

9 Turn off the engine and remove the jumper wire.

Interpretation of Test Results If the voltage does not exceed 2.0 volts over the base voltage, the regulator has a bad ground. Remove the regulator and clean the regulator base to obtain a good connection with the body. The use of lock washers on the attaching bolts is recommended. Verify your repair by repeating steps 7 and 8. If the voltage rises above the base voltage, continue with step 10.

10 Disconnect the wiring plug from the regulator. (Refer to Figure 15.29.)

11 Start the engine and run it at approximately 2000 rpm.

12 Read the voltmeter. The voltage should not rise above the base voltage.

13 Turn off the engine.

Interpretation of Test Results If the voltage rises above the base voltage, there is a short circuit in the wiring between the regulator and the alternator. Most likely, the "A" and "F" wires are in contact with each other. Check the wiring and perform the needed repairs. Verify your repair by repeating steps 11 through 13. If the voltage does not rise, the regulator is defective and should be replaced. Verify your repairs by performing a three-stage charging circuit test.

Systems Using Alternators with Separate Regulators (Chrysler)

The following steps outline a procedure for determining the cause of overcharging in systems using alternators of this type: (Refer to Figure 15.33.)

1 Adjust a voltmeter to a scale exceeding battery voltage.

2 Connect the voltmeter to the battery terminals. (Refer to Figure 15.21.)

3 Read the voltmeter and record the reading as the base voltage.

4 Disconnect the wire from the field (FLD) terminal on the alternator. (Refer to Figure 15.33.)

5 Apply the parking brake.

6 If the car has an automatic transmission, place the transmission selector lever in the PARK position. If the car has a standard transmission, place the shift lever in the NEUTRAL position.

7 Start the engine and allow it to idle.

8 Gradually accelerate the engine and observe the voltmeter. The reading should remain at the base voltage.

9 Turn off the engine.

Interpretation of Test Results

If the voltage rises above the base voltage, the alternator is defective and should be repaired or replaced. Verify your repair by performing a three-stage charging circuit test. If the voltage does not rise above the base voltage, continue with step 10.

10 Disconnect the field wire from the regulator.

Note: **On vehicles with an electromechanical regulator, remove the green wire from the terminal. On vehicles with an electronic regulator, disconnect the wiring plug by releasing the locking tab. (Refer to Figure 15.34.)**

11 Disconnect the negative (−) voltmeter lead from the battery and connect it to the field wire.

12 Read the voltmeter. The voltmeter should indicate no voltage.

13 Disconnect the voltmeter lead.

Interpretation of Test Results

If voltage is indicated by the voltmeter, the field wire between the regulator and the alternator is grounded. Repair the wire. Verify your repair by repeating steps 11 through 13. If the voltmeter indicates no voltage, the regulator is defective and should be replaced. Connect the field wire to the field (FLD) terminal on the alternator and verify any repairs by performing a three-stage charging circuit test.

Job 15e

DETERMINE THE CAUSE OF OVERCHARGING

SATISFACTORY PERFORMANCE

A satisfactory performance on this job requires that you do the following:

1 Determine the causes of overcharging indicated by a three-stage charging circuit test.
2 Following the steps in the "Performance Outline" and the procedure and specifications of the manufacturer, complete the tests required within 30 minutes.
3 Fill in the blanks under "Information."

PERFORMANCE OUTLINE

1 By-pass the regulator as required.
2 Check the system to isolate the defect.

INFORMATION

Vehicle identification _____

Reference used_____ Page(s)_____

Test result Alternator _____OK _____NG

Regulator _____OK _____NG

Wiring _____OK _____NG

Grounds _____OK _____NG

Required repairs_____

_____

REPLACING AN ALTERNATOR On some cars, the alternator is mounted so that it is accessible from under the hood. On other cars, it must be removed from under the car. Figures 15.36 and 15.37 show typical alternator installations and the attaching hardware. Cars equipped with power steering and air conditioning may have the alternator mounted in a different location.

The following steps outline a procedure for replacing an alternator. There are many variations in alternator mountings. Because of this, you should consult an appropriate service manual for the procedure required for the car on which you are working:

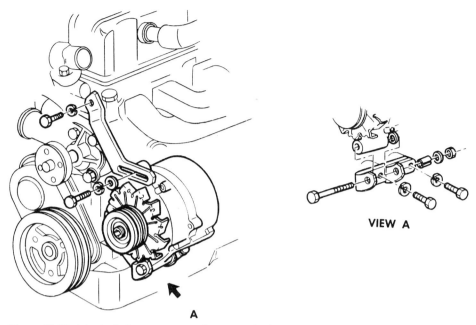

Figure 15.36 A typical alternator mounting on an in-line engine (Chevrolet Service Manual, Chevrolet Motor Division, GM).

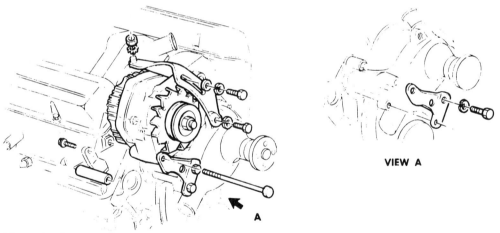

Figure 15.37 A typical alternator mounting on a V-type engine (Chevrolet Service Manual, Chevrolet Motor Division, GM).

Removal 1 Disconnect the battery ground cable.

2 If the alternator must be removed from under the car, raise the car and support it with car stands.

3 Loosen the alternator adjustment bolts and remove the belt from the alternator pulley.

4 Disconnect the wires from the alternator.

5 Remove any brackets, braces, or shields as necessary.

6 Remove the alternator.

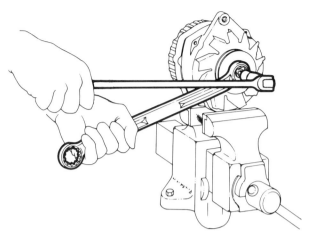

Figure 15.38 Removing an alternator pulley nut. Note that the nut is turned with a box wrench while the rotor is held by an Allen wrench socket (courtesy American Motors Corporation).

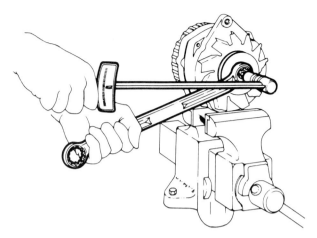

Figure 15.39 Tightening an alternator pulley nut. A torque wrench can be used on the Allen wrench socket (courtesy American Motors Corporation).

Preparation for Installation Many replacement alternators are supplied without a pulley. The pulley must be removed from the old alternator and installed on the replacement alternator.

On most alternators, the pulley is held on the rotor shaft by a nut. (Refer to Figure 15.7.) The rotor shaft usually has a hex-shaped hole in its end. This hole enables you to hold the shaft with an Allen (or hex) wrench. As shown in Figure 15.38, the nut can then be removed with a box wrench. When the pulley is installed on the replacement alternator, it should be tightened to the manufacturer's torque specification. Figure 15.39 shows how a torque wrench can be used on an Allen socket.

Some alternators do not use a nut to retain the pulley. The hole in the pulley is slightly smaller than the diameter of the rotor shaft. The pulley is forced on the shaft to obtain a very tight *interference fit*. A puller is required to remove the pulley. A small groove is machined near the end of some pulleys. Figure 15.40 shows how a puller fits on a pulley of that type. As shown in Figure 15.41, other pulleys require a special puller that fits inside the pulley. Pulleys of this type are removed as shown in Figure 15.42.

The installation of interference fit pulleys requires the use of a press, as shown in Figure 15.43. The alternator must be disassembled so that the rear of the rotor shaft is supported.

Installation 1 Hold the alternator in position and install the mounting bolts by hand.

Note: Do not attempt to tighten any of the bolts until all the bolts have been installed.

2 Alternately tighten the bolts until they are all snug.

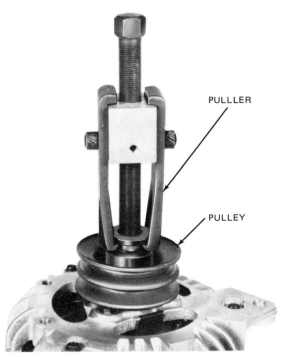

Figure 15.40 A puller installed on an interference fit alternator pulley (courtesy Chrysler Corporation).

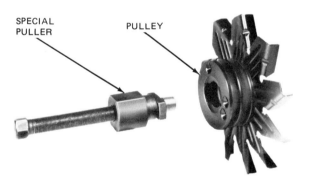

Figure 15.41 Some pulleys require a special puller that fits inside the pulley (courtesy Chrysler Corporation).

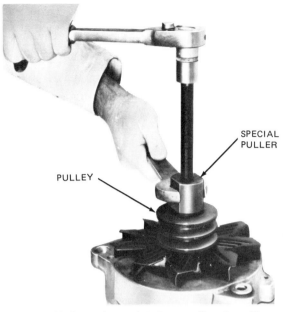

Figure 15.42 Removing an interference fit pulley with a special puller (courtesy Chrysler Corporation).

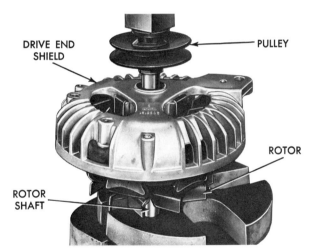

Figure 15.43 Using a press to install an interference fit pulley. Note that the alternator has been disassembled so the rotor shaft can be supported on the press table (courtesy Chrysler Corporation).

3 Install the belt on the pulley.

4 Adjust the belt tension.

5 Tighten all the bolts to the torque specifications of the manufacturer.

6 Connect the battery ground cable.

7 Check the operation of the alternator.

8 If the car is off the floor, lower the car to the floor.

Job 15f

REPLACE AN ALTERNATOR

SATISFACTORY PERFORMANCE

A satisfactory performance on this job requires that you do the following:

1 Replace the alternator on the car assigned.
2 Following the steps in the "Performance Outline" and the procedure and specifications of the manufacturer, complete the job within 200 percent of the manufacturer's suggested time.
3 Fill in the blanks under "Information."

PERFORMANCE OUTLINE

1 Disconnect the battery ground cable.
2 Raise and support the car if necessary.
3 Remove the alternator.
4 Remove the alternator pulley and install it on the replacement alternator if necessary.
5 Install the alternator.
6 Connect the battery ground cable.
7 Check the operation of the alternator.
8 Lower the car to the floor.

INFORMATION

Vehicle identification _____

Reference used_____ Page(s)_____

Was the pulley exchanged? _____Yes _____No

Does the replacement alternator operate correctly?

_____Yes _____No

SUMMARY

By completing this chapter, you have gained knowledge and developed diagnostic and repair skills in maintaining charging systems. You have an understanding of how the various systems operate. You are aware of the many different types of components used in those systems. And you can identify these components and their functions. You are knowledgeable as to the various tests used to diagnose the cause of problems in charging systems. And you can perform these tests, isolate problems, and perform necessary repairs.

SELF-TEST

Each incomplete statement or question in this test is followed by four suggested completions or answers. In each case select the *one* that best completes the sentence or answers the question.

1 In an alternator, current is induced in the
   A. diode
   B. rotor
   C. stator
   D. rectifier

2 Current is conducted to the field winding by means of
   A. lines of force
   B. the stator windings
   C. diodes and rectifiers
   D. brushes and slip rings

3 The strength of the magnetic field in an alternator is determined by the amount of current that flows through the
   A. solenoid
   B. rectifier
   C. field winding
   D. stator windings

4 Two mechanics are discussing alternator regulators.
   Mechanic A says that regulators control the current that flows through the field winding.
   Mechanic B says that regulators convert alternating current to direct current.
   Who is right?
   A. A only
   B. B only
   C. Both A and B
   D. Neither A nor B

5 Two mechanics are discussing alternator regulators.
   Mechanic A says that electromechanical regulators use magnetically operated switches to control voltage.
   Mechanic B says that electronic regulators use transistorized circuits to control voltage.

Who is right?
   A. A only
   B. B only
   C. Both A and B
   D. Neither A nor B

6 In an alternator, alternating current is converted to direct current by the
   A. stator
   B. brushes
   C. rectifier
   D. regulator

7 Two mechanics are discussing preliminary charging system checks.
   Mechanic A says that the resistance of the field coil should be checked.
   Mechanic B says that the voltage drop in the stator windings should be checked.
   Who is right?
   A. A only
   B. B only
   C. Both A and B
   D. Neither A nor B

8 When performing a three-stage charging circuit test, a voltmeter should be connected to the
   A. field (FLD) terminal and ground
   B. stator (STA) and field (FLD) terminals
   C. field (FLD) and battery (BAT) terminals
   D. positive (+) and negative (−) battery terminals

9 Which of the following measurements are NOT taken as a part of a three-stage charging circuit test?
   A. Base voltage
   B. Load voltage
   C. Field voltage
   D. No-load voltage

10 Some rotor shafts have a hex-shaped hole to aid in
   A. removing the pulley
   B. adjusting the diodes
   C. aligning the brushes
   D. installing the stator

Appendix
Reference
Material

Throughout this text you are constantly advised to consult various manuals. As a mechanic, you should have these manuals available so that you can refer to them for the information you may need on a particular job. You should start now to build your reference library so that you will be well equipped when you start to work.

MANUFACTURER'S SERVICE MANUALS Most car manufacturers publish complete service manuals for each model year of the cars they build. Information on the availability and price of these manuals can be obtained by contacting the manufacturers at the following addresses:

American Motors	American Motors Corporation 14250 Plymouth Road Detroit, Michigan 48232
Buick	Buick Motor Division General Motors Corporation Flint, Michigan 48550
Cadillac	Cadillac Motor Car Division General Motors Corporation 2860 Clark Avenue Detroit, Michigan 48232
Chevrolet	Chevrolet Motor Division General Motors Corporation General Motors Building Detroit, Michigan 48202
Chrysler	Chrysler Corporation P.O. Box 1919 Detroit, Michigan 48231

page A-1

Dodge	Dodge Division Chrysler Motors Corporation P.O. Box 857 Detroit, Michigan 48231
Ford	Ford Motor Company The American Road Dearborn, Michigan 48121
Jeep	Jeep Corporation American Motors Corporation Toledo, Ohio 43600
Lincoln and Mercury	Lincoln-Mercury Division Ford Motor Company 3000 Schaefer Road Dearborn, Michigan 48216
Oldsmobile	Oldsmobile Division General Motors Corporation 920 Townsend Street Lansing, Michigan 48921
Plymouth	Plymouth Division Chrysler Motors Corporation P.O. Box 857 Detroit, Michigan 48231
Pontiac	Pontiac Motor Division General Motors Corporation 1 Pontiac Plaza Pontiac, Michigan 48053

COMPREHENSIVE SHOP MANUALS The most commonly used specifications and the procedures for the most frequently performed service operations for recent model cars are compiled in these manuals. Published yearly, they provide the best single source of reference material you will need in your daily work. The two most widely used manuals are as follows:

Motor Auto Repair Manual	Motor 1790 Broadway New York, New York 10019
Chilton's Automotive Service Manual	Chilton Book Company Chilton Way Radnor, Pennsylvania 19089

MANUALS AND CATALOGS PUBLISHED BY MANUFACTURERS OF AUTOMOTIVE PARTS, TOOLS, AND EQUIPMENT The makers of the parts, tools, and equipment you use in servicing automobiles offer a variety of reference materials. Many of these materials are available free of charge upon request from the following companies:

AC-Delco Division General Motors Corporation 400 Renaissance Center Detroit, Michigan 48243	Electrical test equipment, batteries, fuel pumps, tools, spark plugs, spark plug cleaners, alternators, starting motors
Albertson and Company, Incorporated Sioux City, Iowa 51102	Engine tools and equipment
Alemite Division Stewart-Warner Corporation 1826 W. Diversey Parkway Chicago, Illinois 60614	Lubrication equipment
Allen Electric and Equipment Company 2101 N. Pitcher Street Kalamazoo, Michigan 49007	Electrical test equipment
Ammco Tools, Incorporated 2100 Commonwealth Avenue North Chicago, Illinois 60064	Hand tools, brake service equipment, alignment equipment
Arvin Industries, Incorporated Automotive Aftermarket Division Columbus, Indiana 47201	Exhaust system parts
Auto Specialties Manufacturing Company St. Joseph, Michigan 49085	Jacks, stands, lifts, cranes, presses, hydraulic equipment
Auto-Test Incorporated 411 West 8th Street Neillsville, Wisconsin 54456	Automotive test equipment
Balcrank Products Wheelabrator-Frye Incorporated 400 South Byrkit Avenue Mishawaka, Indiana 46544	Lubrication equipment and accessories

John Bean Division FMC Corporation Lansing, Michigan 48900	Alignment and brake service equipment
Bear Manufacturing Corporation 2830 Fifth Street Rock Island, Illinois 61201	Alignment equipment, balancing equipment
Bendix Automotive Aftermarket 1217 So. Walnut Street South Bend, Indiana 46620	Tune-up parts, brake parts, chemicals
Black and Decker Manufacturing Company Towson, Maryland, 21204	Air and electric power tools and accessories
Blackhawk Manufacturing Company Applied Power Industries, Incorporated Box 8720 Milwaukee, Wisconsin 53227	Hand and power tools, jacks and car stands
Brookstone Company 127 Vose Farm Road Peterborough, New Hampshire 03458	Hand tools
Carter Carburetor Division ACF Industries, Incorporated Educational Aids Department P.O. Box 16092 Clayton, Missouri 63105	Carburetors, fuel pumps, fuel system parts
Champion Spark Plug Company P.O. Box 910 Toledo, Ohio 43601	Spark plugs, spark plug cleaners, tools
Chicago Rawhide Manufacturing Company 900 North State Street Elgin, Illinois 60120	Grease and oil seals
The Cooper Tire Company Division of Cooper Tire and Rubber Company Findlay, Ohio 45840	Tires

CRC Chemicals Division of C. J. Webb, Incorporated Limekiln Pike P.O. Box 100 Dresher, Pennsylvania 19025	Lubricants, penetrants, cleaners
Dana Parts Corporation P.O. Box 500 Hagerstown, Indiana 47346	Automotive parts
Dresser Industries Hand Tool Division 3201 North Wolf Road Franklin Park, Illinois 60131	Hand tools
Echlin Manufacturing Company Branford, Connecticut 06405	Electrical system parts
E. Edelmann and Company Chicago, Illinois 60647	Hydrometers, tubing, fittings, tools
EIS Corporation Middlefield, Connecticut 06455	Brake system parts, brake fluid
ESB Brands Incorporated P.O. Box 6949 Cleveland, Ohio 44101	Batteries
Everco Industries, Incorporated 4916 West Belmont Avenue Chicago, Illinois 60641	Power steering hoses
Fel-Pro Incorporated Skokie, Illinois 60076	Gaskets, sealers, adhesives
Fox Valley Instrument Company Sheboygan, Michigan 49721	Automotive test equipment
Gabriel Division Maremont Corporation 1283 Murfreesboro Road Nashville, Tennessee 37217	Shock absorbers
The Gates Rubber Company 999 South Broadway Denver, Colorado 80217	Belts, power steering hoses
Gibson Products Corporation Division of Rolero,	Brake system parts

Incorporated
P.O. Box 7187
Cleveland, Ohio 44128

The Goodyear Tire and Rubber Company Akron, Ohio 44309	Tires
Grey-Rock Division Raybestos Manhattan, Incorporated P.O. Box 9140 Bridgeport, Connecticut 06603	Brake lining
Harrison Radiator Division General Motors Corporation Lockport, New York 14094	Radiators, heaters, air conditioners
Hein-Werner Corporation Waukesha, Wisconsin 53186	Jacks, presses, cranes, car stands
Hennessy Industries Incorporated The Coats Company Incorporated 1601 J. P. Hennessy Drive La Vergne, Tennessee 37086	Tire changing machines
Hunter Engineering Company 1350 Hunter Drive Bridgton, Missouri 63044	Alignment equipment, balancing equipment
Ideal Corporation 1000 Pennsylvania Avenue Brooklyn, New York 11207	Thermostats, hose clamps, flashers
Ingersol Rand/Proto Tool Company 2309 Santa Fe Avenue Los Angeles, California 90058	Hand and power tools
Kal-Equip Company 411 Washington Street Otsego, Michigan 49078	Automotive test equipment
K-D Manufacturing Company Hempland Road Lancaster, Pennsylvania 17604	Hand tools

Kelsey Products Division Kelsey-Hayes Company 38481 Huron River Drive Romulus, Michigan 48174	Brake parts
Kem Manufacturing Company Incorporated Fair Lawn, New Jersey 07410	Filters, fuel pumps, starter drives, ignition parts, electrical parts
Lockheed Products Wagner Electric Corporation 6400 Plymouth Avenue St. Louis, Missouri 63100	Brake parts
Marquette Corporation 307 East Hennepin Avenue Minneapolis, Minnesota 55414	Electrical test equipment, battery chargers
Milwaukee Hydraulic Products Corporation Milwaukee, Wisconsin 53214	Jacks, lifts, presses
Moog Industries Box 7224 St. Louis, Missouri 63177	Steering and suspension parts and tools
Owatonna Tool Company P.O. Box 268 Owatonna, Minnesota 55060	Hand tools and pullers
P & C Hand Tool Company P.O. Box 22066 Portland, Oregon 93222	Hand tools
Pennzoil Oil City, Pennsylvania 16301	Lubricants and solvents
Proto Tool Division Ingersol Rand Corporation 3900 Wesley Terrace Schiller Park, Illinois 60176	Hand tools and pullers
Quaker State Oil Refining Corporation Oil City, Pennsylvania 16301	Lubricants
Raybestos Division Raybestos Manhattan, Incorporated Bridgeport, Connecticut 06603	Brake lining

Robertshaw Controls Company P.O. Box 400 2318 Kingston Pike Knoxville, Tennessee 37901	Radiator, fuel tank, and oil filter caps
Rockwell International Power Tool Division 6263 Poplar Avenue Memphis, Tennessee 37901	Air and electric power tools
The Russell Manufacturing Company Middletown, Connecticut 06457	Brake lining
Snap-On Tools Corporation 8028 28th Avenue Kenosha, Wisconsin 53140	Hand and power tools, and automotive service equipment
Standard Motor Products, Incorporated 37-18 Northern Boulevard Long Island City, New York 11101	Automotive tune-up parts
Standard-Thomson Corporation 152 Grove Street Waltham, Massachusetts 02154	Thermostats
Stant Manufacturing Company Incorporated Connersville, Indiana 47331	Radiator pressure caps, pressure testers, thermostats
Stewart-Warner Corporation Alemite and Instrument Division 1826 Diversey Parkway Chicago, Illinois 60614	Alignment equipment, balancing equipment, and lubrication equipment
Sun Electric Corporation Harlem and Avondale Chicago, Illinois 60631	Automotive test equipment
TRW Inc. Replacement Division 8001 East Pleasant Valley Road Cleveland, Ohio 44131	Automotive replacement parts
Union Carbide Consumer Products Company	Anti-freeze, chemicals

Division of Union Carbide
Corporation
270 Park Avenue
New York, New York 10017

Valvoline Oil Company   Lubricants
Division of Ashland Oil
Company
Ashland, Kentucky 41101

Walker Manufacturing   Jacks, cars stands, cranes, and
Company   presses
1201 Michigan Boulevard
Racine, Wisconsin 53402

Weaver Division   Jacks and car stands
Dura Corporation
2171 South 9th Street
Springfield, Illinois 62705

Metric System—SI The International System of Units (Système International
d'Unités) officially abbreviated "SI" in all languages—the modern metric system

QUANTITY	EXAMPLES OF APPLICATIONS	METRIC UNIT	SYMBOL
Length	Dimensions Tire rolling circumference Turning circle/radius Braking distance	meter	m
	Greater than 999 meter	kilometer	km
	Dimensions	millimeter	mm
	Depth of surface finish	micrometer	μm
Area	Glass & Fabrics Brake & Clutch linings Radiator area etc.	square centimeter	cm²
	Small areas	square millimeter	mm²
Volume	Car Luggage Capacity	cubic meter	m³
	Vehicle fluid capacity	liter	l
	Engine Capacity	cubic centimeter	cm³
Volume Flow	Gas & Liquid	liter per second	l/s
Time Interval	Measurement of elapsed time	second	s
		minute	min
		hour	h
		day	d
Velocity	General use	meter per second	m/s
	Road speed	kilometer per hour	km/h
Acceleration & Deceleration	General use	meter per second squared	m/s²
Frequency	Electronics	hertz	Hz
		kilohertz	kHz
		megahertz	mHz

Rotational Speed	General use	revolution per minute	rpm
		revolution per second	rps
Mass	Vehicle mass	megagram	t
	Legal load rating		
	General use	kilogram	kg
	Small masses	gram	g
		milligram	mg
Density	General use	kilogram per cubic meter	kg/m³
		gram per cubic centimeter	g/cm³
		kilogram per liter	kg/l
Force	Pedal effort	newton	N
	Clutch spring force		
	Handbrake lever effort		
	etc.		
Moment of Force (Torque)	Torque	newton meter	N-m
Power, Heat Flow Rate	General use	watt	W
	Bulbs	kilowatt	kW
	Alternator output		
	Engine performance		
	Starter performance		
Celsius Temperature	General use	degree Celsius	°C
Thermodynamic Temperature	General use	kelvin	k
Electric Current	General use	ampere	A
		milliampere	mA
		microampere	μA
Potential Difference (Electromotive Force)	General use	kilovolt	kV
		volt	V
		millivolt	mV
		microvolt	μV
Electric Resistance	General use	megohm	MΩ
		kilohm	kΩ
		ohm	Ω
Electric Capacitance	General use	farad	F
		microfarad	μF
		picofarad	pF
Fuel Consumption	Vehicle performance	liter per 100 kilometer	l/100 km
Oil Consumption	Vehicle performance	liter per 1000 kilometer	1/1000 km
Stiffness	Linear stiffness	kilonewton meter	kN/m
Tire Revolutions	Tire Data	revolution per kilometer	rev/km
Pressure	Tire	kilopascal	kPa
	Coolant		
	Lubricating oil		
	Fuel pump delivery		
	Engine compression		
	Manifold		
	Brake line (hydraulic)		
	Car heating & ventilation		
	Barometric pressure		
Luminous Intensity	Bulbs	candela	cd
Accumulator Storage Rating	Battery	ampere hour	A-h

QUANTITY	**U.S.A./Metric Comparison**		
	USA	METRIC—SYMBOL	
Length	Inch-Foot-Mile	Meter	m
Weight (mass)	Ounce-Pound	Kilogram	Kg
Area	Square inch/Foot	Square Meter	m²
Volume-Dry	Cubic inch/Foot	Cubic Meter	m³
-Liquid	Ounce-Pint-Quart-Gallon	Liter	l
Velocity	Feet Per Second	Meter per Second	m/s
Road Speed	Miles Per Hour	Kilometer per Hour	km/h
Force	Pound-Force	Newton	N
Torque	Foot-Pounds	Newton meter	N-m
Power	Horsepower	Kilowatt	kW
Pressure	Pounds Per Square Inch	Kilopascal	kPa
Temperature	Degrees Fahrenheit	Degrees Kelvin	K
		and Celsius	°C

Decimal Equivalents

MILLIMETER	DECIMAL	FRACTION	DRILL SIZE
.1	.0039		
.15	.0059		
.2	.0079		
.25	.0098		
.3	.0118		
	.0135		80
.35	.0138		
	.0145		79
.39	.0156	1/64	
.4	.0157		
	.0160		78
.45	.0177		
	.0180		77
.5	.0197		
	.0200		76
	.0210		75
.55	.0217		
	.0225		74
.6	.0236		
	.0240		73
	.0250		72
.65	.0256		
	.0260		71
.7	.0276		
	.0280		70
	.0292		69
.75	.0295		
	.0310		68
.79	.0312	1/32	
.8	.0315		
	.0320		67
	.0330		66
1.75	.0689		
	.0700		50
1.8	.0709		
1.85	.0728		
	.0730		49
1.9	.0748		
	.0760		48
1.95	.0767		
1.98	.0781	5/64	
	.0785		47
2.0	.0787		
2.05	.0807		
	.0810		46
	.0820		45
2.1	.0827		
2.15	.0846		
	.0860		44
2.2	.0866		
2.25	.0885		
	.0890		43
2.3	.0905		
2.35	.0925		
	.0935		42
2.38	.0937	3/32	
2.4	.0945		
	.0960		41
2.45	.0964		
	.0980		40
2.5	.0984		
	.0995		39
	.1015		38
2.6	.1024		
	.1570		22
4.0	.1575		
	.1590		21
	.1610		20
4.1	.1614		
4.2	.1654		
	.1660		19
4.25	.1673		
4.3	.1693		
	.1695		18
4.37	.1719	11/64	
	.1730		17
4.4	.1732		
	.1770		16
4.5	.1771		
	.1800		15
4.6	.1811		
	.1820		14
4.7	.1850		13
4.75	.1870		
4.76	.1875	3/16	
4.8	.1890		12
	.1910		11
4.9	.1935		10
	.1960		9
5.0	.1968		
	.1990		8
5.1	.2008		
	.2010		7
5.16	.2031	13/64	
	.2040		6
6.8	.2677		
6.9	.2716		
	.2720		I
7.0	.2756		
	.2770		J
7.1	.2795		
7.14	.2811		
	.2812	9/32	K
7.2	.2835		
7.25	.2854		
7.3	.2874		
	.2900		L
7.4	.2913		
	.2950		M
7.5	.2953		
7.54	.2968	19/64	
7.6	.2992		
	.3020		N
7.7	.3031		
7.75	.3051		
7.8	.3071		
7.9	.3110		
7.94	.3125	5/16	
8.0	.3150		
	.3160		O
8.1	.3189		
8.2	.3228		
	.3230		P
8.25	.3248		
8.3	.3268		
8.33	.3281	21/64	
8.4	.3307		
10.72	.4210	27/64	
11.0	.4330		
11.11	.4375	7/16	
11.5	.4528		
11.51	.4531	29/64	
11.91	.4687	15/32	
12.0	.4724		
12.30	.4843	31/64	
12.5	.4921		
12.7	.5000	1/2	
13.0	.5118		
13.10	.5156	33/64	
13.49	.5312	17/62	
13.5	.5315		
13.89	.5469	35/64	
14.0	.5512		
14.29	.5625	9/16	
14.5	.5709		
14.68	.5781	37/64	
15.0	.5906		
15.08	.5937	19/32	
15.48	.6094	39/64	
15.5	.6102		
15.88	.6250	5/8	
16.0	.6299		
16.27	.6406	41/64	
16.5	.6496		
16.67	.6562	21/32	
17.0	.6693		
17.06	.6719	43/64	
17.46	.6875	11/16	
17.5	.6890		

Decimal Equivalents

MILLI-METER	DECI-MAL	FRAC-TION	DRILL SIZE	MILLI-METER	DEC-IMAL	FRAC-TION	DRILL SIZE	MILLI-METER	DEC-IMAL	FRAC-TION	DRILL SIZE	MILLI-METER	DEC-IMAL	FRAC-TION	DRILL SIZE	MILLI-METER	DEC-IMAL	FRAC-TION
.85	.0335				.1040		37	5.2	.2047				.3320		Q	17.86	.7031	45/64
	.0350		65	2.7	.1063				.2055		5	8.5	.3346			18.0	.7087	
.9	.0354				.1065		36	5.25	.2067			8.6	.3386			18.26	.7187	23/32
	.0360		64	2.75	.1082			5.3	.2086				.3390		R	18.5	.7283	
	.0370		63	2.78	.1094	7/64			.2090		4	8.7	.3425			18.65	.7344	47/64
.95	.0374				.1100		35	5.4	.2126			8.73	.3437	11/32		19.0	.7480	
	.0380		62	2.8	.1102				.2130		3	8.75	.3445			19.05	.7500	3/4
	.0390		61		.1110		34	5.5	.2165			8.8	.3465			19.45	.7656	49/64
1.0	.0394				.1130		33	5.56	.2187	7/32			.3480		S	19.5	.7677	
	.0400		60	2.9	.1141			5.6	.2205			8.9	.3504			19.84	.7812	25/32
	.0410		59		.1160		32		.2210		2	9.0	.3543			20.0	.7874	
1.05	.0413			3.0	.1181			5.7	.2244				.3580		T	20.24	.7969	51/64
	.0420		58		.1200		31	5.75	.2263			9.1	.3583			20.5	.8071	
	.0430		57	3.1	.1220				.2280		1	9.13	.3594	23/64		20.64	.8125	13/16
1.1	.0433			3.18	.1250	1/8		5.8	.2283			9.2	.3622			21.0	.8268	
1.15	.0452			3.2	.1260			5.9	.2323			9.25	.3641			21.03	.8281	53/64
	.0465		56	3.25	.1279				.2340		A	9.3	.3661			21.43	.8437	27/32
1.19	.0469	3/64			.1285		30	5.95	.2344	15/64			.3680		U	21.5	.8465	
1.2	.0472			3.3	.1299			6.0	.2362			9.4	.3701			21.83	.8594	55/64
1.25	.0492			3.4	.1338				.2380		B	9.5	.3740			22.0	.8661	
1.3	.0512				.1360		29	6.1	.2401			9.53	.3750	3/8		22.23	.8750	7/8
	.0520		55	3.5	.1378				.2420		C		.3770		V	22.5	.8858	
1.35	.0531				.1405		28	6.2	.2441			9.6	.3780			22.62	.8906	57/64
	.0550		54	3.57	.1406	9/64		6.25	.2460		D	9.7	.3819			23.0	.9055	
1.4	.0551			3.6	.1417			6.3	.2480		E	9.75	.3838			23.02	.9062	29/32
1.45	.0570				.1440		27	6.35	.2500	1/4		9.8	.3858			23.42	.9219	59/64
1.5	.0591			3.7	.1457			6.4	.2520				.3860		W	23.5	.9252	
	.0595		53		.1470		26	6.5	.2559			9.9	.3898			23.81	.9375	15/16
1.55	.0610			3.75	.1476				.2570		F	9.92	.3906	25/64		24.0	.9449	
1.59	.0625	1/16			.1495		25	6.6	.2598			10.0	.3937			24.21	.9531	61/64
1.6	.0629			3.8	.1496				.2610		G		.3970		X	24.5	.9446	
	.0635		52		.1520		24	6.7	.2638				.4040		Y	24.61	.9687	31/32
1.65	.0649			3.9	.1535			6.75	.2657	17/64		10.32	.4062	13/32		25.0	.9843	
1.7	.0669				.1540		23	6.75	.2657				.4130		Z	25.03	.9844	63/64
	.0670		51	3.97	.1562	5/32			.2660		H	10.5	.4134			25.4	1.0000	1

HOW TO USE CONVERSION CHARTS

Left Column is units of 10, (0,10,20,30 etc.); Top Row is in units of one (0, 1, 2, 3, etc.).

Example: Feet to Inches Conversion Chart

feet	0	1	2	3	4	5	6	7	8	9	feet
	inches	inches	inches	inches	inches	inches	inches	inches	inches	inches	
		12	24	36	48	60	72	84	96	108	
10	120	132	144	156	168	180	192	204	216	228	10
20	240	252	264	276	288	300	312	324	336	348	20
30	360	372	384	396	408	420	432	444	456	468	30
40	480	492	504	516	528	540	552	564	576	588	40
50	600	612	624	636	648	660	672	684	696	708	50

12 feet equals 144 inches. Read across from
10 and down from 2.
6 feet equals 72 inches. Read down from 6.

Feet to Meters

ft	0	1	2	3	4	5	6	7	8	9	ft
	m	m	m	m	m	m	m	m	m	m	
		0.305	0.610	0.914	1.219	1.524	1.829	2.134	2.438	2.743	
10	3.048	3.353	3.658	3.962	4.267	4.572	4.877	5.182	5.486	5.791	10
20	6.096	6.401	6.706	7.010	7.315	7.620	7.925	8.230	8.534	8.839	20
30	9.144	9.449	9.754	10.058	10.363	10.668	10.973	11.278	11.582	11.887	30
40	12.192	12.497	12.802	13.106	13.411	13.716	14.021	14.326	14.630	14.935	40
50	15.240	15.545	15.850	16.154	16.459	16.764	17.069	17.374	17.678	17.933	50
60	18.288	18.593	18.898	19.202	19.507	19.812	20.117	20.422	20.726	21.031	60
70	21.336	21.641	21.946	22.250	22.555	22.860	23.165	23.470	23.774	24.079	70
80	24.384	24.689	24.994	25.298	25.603	25.908	26.213	26.518	26.822	27.127	80
90	27.432	27.737	28.042	28.346	28.651	28.956	29.261	29.566	29.870	30.175	90
100	30.480	30.785	31.090	31.394	31.699	32.004	32.309	32.614	32.918	33.223	100

Meters to Feet

m	0	1	2	3	4	5	6	7	8	9	m
	ft	ft	ft	ft	ft	ft	ft	ft	ft	ft	
		3.2808	6.5617	9.8425	13.1234	16.4042	19.6850	22.9659	26.2467	29.5276	
10	32.8084	36.0892	39.3701	42.6509	45.9318	49.2126	52.4934	55.7743	59.0551	62.3360	10
20	65.6168	68.8976	72.1785	75.4593	78.7402	82.0210	85.3018	88.5827	91.8635	95.1444	20
30	98.4252	101.7060	104.9869	108.2677	111.5486	114.8294	118.1102	121.3911	124.6719	127.9528	30
40	131.2336	134.5144	137.7953	141.0761	144.3570	147.6378	150.9186	154.1995	157.4803	160.7612	40
50	164.0420	167.3228	170.6037	173.8845	177.1654	180.4462	183.7270	187.0079	190.2887	193.5696	50
60	196.8504	200.1312	203.4121	206.6929	209.9738	213.2546	216.5354	219.8163	223.0971	226.3780	60
70	229.6588	232.9396	236.2205	239.5013	242.7822	246.0630	249.3438	252.6247	255.9055	259.1864	70
80	262.4672	265.7480	269.0289	272.3097	275.5906	278.8714	282.1522	285.4331	288.7139	291.9948	80
90	295.2756	298.5564	301.8373	305.1181	308.3990	311.6798	314.9606	318.2415	321.5223	324.8032	90
100	328.0840	331.3648	334.6457	337.9265	341.2074	344.4882	347.7690	351.0499	354.3307	357.6116	100

Miles to Kilometers

mile	0	1	2	3	4	5	6	7	8	9	mile
	km	km	km	km	km	km	km	km	km	km	
		1.609	3.219	4.828	6.437	8.047	9.656	11.265	12.875	14.484	
10	16.093	17.703	19.312	20.921	22.531	24.140	25.750	27.359	28.968	30.578	10
20	32.187	33.796	35.406	37.015	38.624	40.234	41.843	43.452	45.062	46.671	20
30	48.280	49.890	51.499	53.108	54.718	56.327	57.936	59.546	61.155	62.764	30
40	64.374	65.983	67.593	69.202	70.811	72.421	74.030	75.639	77.249	78.858	40
50	80.467	82.077	83.686	85.295	86.905	88.514	90.123	91.733	93.342	94.951	50
60	96.561	98.170	99.779	101.39	103.00	104.61	106.22	107.83	109.44	111.04	60
70	112.65	114.26	115.87	117.48	119.09	120.70	122.31	123.92	125.53	127.14	70
80	128.75	130.36	131.97	133.58	135.19	136.79	138.40	140.01	141.62	143.23	80
90	144.84	146.45	148.06	149.67	151.28	152.89	154.50	156.11	157.72	159.33	90
100	160.93	162.54	164.15	165.76	167.37	168.98	170.59	172.20	173.81	175.42	100

Kilometers to Miles

km	0	1	2	3	4	5	6	7	8	9	km
	mil	mil	mil	mil	mil	mil	mil	mil	mil	mil	
		0.621	1.243	1.864	2.486	3.107	3.728	4.350	4.971	5.592	
10	6.214	6.835	7.457	8.078	8.699	9.321	9.942	10.562	11.185	11.805	10
20	12.427	13.049	13.670	14.292	14.913	15.534	16.156	16.776	17.399	18.019	20
30	18.641	19.263	19.884	20.506	21.127	21.748	22.370	22.990	23.613	24.233	30
40	24.855	25.477	26.098	26.720	27.341	27.962	28.584	29.204	29.827	30.447	40
50	31.069	31.690	32.311	32.933	33.554	34.175	34.797	35.417	36.040	36.660	50
60	37.282	37.904	38.525	39.147	39.768	40.389	41.011	41.631	42.254	42.874	60
70	43.497	44.118	44.739	45.361	45.982	46.603	47.225	47.845	48.468	49.088	70
80	49.711	50.332	50.953	51.575	52.196	52.817	53.439	54.059	54.682	55.302	80
90	55.924	56.545	57.166	57.788	58.409	59.030	59.652	60.272	60.895	61.515	90
100	62.138	62.759	63.380	64.002	64.623	65.244	65.866	66.486	67.109	67.729	100

Gallons (U.S.) to Liters

U.S. gal	0	1	2	3	4	5	6	7	8	9	U.S. gal
	L	L	L	L	L	L	L	L	L	L	
		3.7854	7.5709	11.3563	15.1417	18.9271	22.7126	26.4980	30.2834	34.0638	
10	37.8543	41.6397	45.4251	49.2105	52.9960	56.7814	60.5668	64.3523	68.1377	71.9231	10
20	75.7085	79.4940	83.2794	87.0648	90.8502	94.6357	98.4211	102.2065	105.9920	109.7774	20
30	113.5528	117.3482	121.1337	124.9191	128.7045	132.4899	136.2754	140.0608	143.8462	147.6316	30
40	151.4171	155.2025	158.9879	162.7734	166.5588	170.3442	174.1296	177.9151	181.7005	185.4859	40
50	189.2713	193.0568	196.8422	200.6276	204.4131	208.1985	211.9839	215.7693	219.5548	223.3402	50
60	227.1256	230.9110	234.6965	238.4819	242.2673	246.0527	249.8382	253.6236	257.4090	261.1945	60
70	264.9799	268.7653	272.5507	276.3362	280.1216	283.9070	287.6924	291.4779	295.2633	299.0487	70
80	302.8342	306.6196	310.4050	314.1904	317.9759	321.7613	325.5467	329.3321	333.1176	336.9030	80
90	340.6884	344.4738	348.2593	352.0447	355.8301	359.6156	363.4010	367.1864	370.9718	374.7573	90
100	378.5427	382.3281	386.1135	389.8990	393.6844	397.4698	401.2553	405.0407	408.8261	412.6115	100

Liters to Gallons (U.S.)

L	0	1	2	3	4	5	6	7	8	9	L
	gal	gal	gal	gal	gal	gal	gal	gal	gal	gal	
—		0.2642	0.5283	0.7925	1.0567	1.3209	1.5850	1.8492	2.1134	2.3775	—
10	2.6417	2.9059	3.1701	3.4342	3.6984	3.9626	4.2267	4.4909	4.7551	5.0192	10
20	5.2834	5.5476	5.8118	6.0759	6.3401	6.6043	6.8684	7.1326	7.3968	7.6610	20
30	7.9251	8.1893	8.4535	8.7176	8.9818	9.2460	9.5102	9.7743	10.0385	10.3027	30
40	10.5668	10.8310	11.0952	11.3594	11.6235	11.8877	12.1519	12.4160	12.6802	12.9444	40
50	13.2086	13.4727	13.7369	14.0011	14.2652	14.5294	14.7936	15.0577	15.3219	15.5861	50
60	15.8503	16.1144	16.3786	16.6428	16.9069	17.1711	17.4353	17.6995	17.9636	18.2278	60
70	18.4920	18.7561	19.0203	19.2845	19.5487	19.8128	20.0770	20.3412	20.6053	20.8695	70
80	21.1337	21.3979	21.6620	21.9262	22.1904	22.4545	22.7187	22.9829	23.2470	23.5112	80
90	23.7754	24.0396	24.3037	24.5679	24.8321	25.0962	25.3604	25.6246	25.8888	26.1529	90
100	26.4171	26.6813	26.9454	27.2096	27.4738	27.7380	28.0021	28.2663	28.5305	28.7946	100

Gallons (Imp.) to Liters

IMP gal	0	1	2	3	4	5	6	7	8	9	IMP gal
	L	L	L	L	L	L	L	L	L	L	
—		4.5460	9.0919	13.6379	18.1838	22.7298	27.2758	31.8217	36.3677	40.9136	—
10	45.4596	50.0056	54.5515	59.0975	63.6434	68.1894	72.2354	77.2813	81.8275	86.3732	10
20	90.9192	95.4652	100.0111	104.5571	109.1030	113.6490	118.1950	122.7409	127.2869	131.8328	20
30	136.3788	140.9248	145.4707	150.0167	154.5626	159.1086	163.6546	168.0005	172.7465	177.2924	30
40	181.8384	186.3844	190.9303	195.4763	200.0222	204.5682	209.1142	213.6601	218.2061	222.7520	40
50	227.2980	231.8440	236.3899	240.9359	245.4818	250.0278	254.5738	259.1197	263.6657	268.2116	50
60	272.7576	277.3036	281.8495	286.3955	290.9414	295.4874	300.0334	304.5793	309.1253	313.6712	60
70	318.2172	322.7632	327.3091	331.8551	336.4010	340.9470	345.4930	350.0389	354.5849	359.1308	70
80	363.6768	368.2223	372.7687	377.3147	381.8606	386.4066	390.9526	395.4985	400.0445	404.5904	80
90	409.1364	413.6824	418.2283	422.7743	427.3202	431.8662	436.4122	440.9581	445.9041	450.0500	90
100	454.5960	459.1420	463.6879	468.2339	472.7798	477.3258	481.8718	486.4177	490.9637	495.5096	100

Liters to Gallons (Imp.)

L	0	1	2	3	4	5	6	7	8	9	L
	gal	gal	gal	gal	gal	gal	gal	gal	gal	gal	
—		0.2200	0.4400	0.6599	0.8799	1.0999	1.3199	1.5398	1.7598	1.9798	—
10	2.1998	2.4197	2.6397	2.8597	3.0797	3.2996	3.5196	3.7396	3.9596	4.1795	10
20	4.3995	4.6195	4.8395	5.0594	5.2794	5.4994	5.7194	5.9394	6.1593	6.3793	20
30	6.5593	6.8193	7.0392	7.2592	7.4792	7.6992	7.9191	8.1391	8.3591	8.5791	30
40	8.7990	9.0190	9.2390	9.4590	9.6789	9.8989	10.9189	10.3389	10.5588	10.7788	40
50	10.9988	11.2188	11.4388	11.6587	11.8787	12.0987	12.3187	12.5386	12.7586	12.9786	50
60	13.1986	13.4185	13.6385	13.8585	14.0785	14.2984	14.5184	14.7384	14.9584	15.1783	60
70	15.3983	15.6183	15.8383	16.0582	16.2782	16.4982	16.7182	16.9382	17.1581	17.3781	70
80	17.5981	17.8181	18.0380	18.2580	18.4780	18.6980	18.9179	19.1379	19.3579	19.5779	80
90	19.7978	20.0178	20.2378	20.4578	20.6777	20.8977	21.1177	21.3377	21.5576	21.7776	90
100	21.9976	22.2176	22.4376	22.6575	22.8775	23.0975	23.3175	23.5374	23.7574	23.9774	100

Pounds to Kilograms

lb	0	1	2	3	4	5	6	7	8	9	lb
	kg	kg	kg	kg	kg	kg	kg	kg	kg	kg	
—		0.454	0.907	1.361	1.814	2.268	2.722	3.175	3.629	4.082	—
10	4.536	4.990	5.443	5.897	6.350	6.804	7.257	7.711	8.165	8.618	10
20	9.072	9.525	9.979	10.433	10.886	11.340	11.793	12.247	12.701	13.154	20
30	13.608	14.061	14.515	14.969	15.422	15.876	16.329	16.783	17.237	17.690	30
40	18.144	18.597	19.051	19.504	19.958	20.412	20.865	21.319	21.772	22.226	40
50	22.680	23.133	23.587	24.040	24.494	24.948	25.401	25.855	26.308	26.762	50
60	27.216	27.669	28.123	28.576	29.030	29.484	29.937	30.391	30.844	31.298	60
70	31.751	32.205	32.659	33.112	33.566	34.019	34.473	34.927	35.380	35.834	70
80	36.287	36.741	37.195	37.648	38.102	38.555	39.009	39.463	39.916	40.370	80
90	40.823	41.277	41.730	42.184	42.638	43.092	43.545	43.998	44.453	44.906	90
100	45.359	45.813	46.266	46.720	47.174	47.627	48.081	48.534	48.988	49.442	100

Kilograms to Pounds

kg	0	1	2	3	4	5	6	7	8	9	kg
	lb	lb	lb	lb	lb	lb	lb	lb	lb	lb	
—		2.205	4.409	6.614	8.818	11.023	13.228	15.432	17.637	19.842	—
10	22.046	24.251	26.455	28.660	30.865	33.069	35.274	37.479	39.683	41.888	10
20	44.092	46.297	48.502	50.706	52.911	55.116	57.320	59.525	61.729	63.934	20
30	66.139	68.343	70.548	72.752	74.957	77.162	79.366	81.571	83.776	85.980	30
40	88.185	90.389	92.594	94.799	97.003	99.208	101.41	103.62	105.82	108.03	40
50	110.23	112.44	114.64	116.84	119.05	121.25	123.46	125.66	127.87	130.07	50
60	132.28	134.48	136.69	138.89	141.10	143.30	145.51	147.71	149.91	152.12	60
70	154.32	156.53	158.73	160.94	163.14	165.35	167.55	169.76	171.96	174.17	70
80	176.37	178.57	180.78	182.98	185.19	187.39	189.60	191.80	194.01	196.21	80
90	198.42	200.62	202.83	205.03	207.23	209.44	211.64	213.85	216.05	218.26	90
100	220.46	222.67	224.87	227.08	229.28	231.49	233.69	235.89	238.10	240.30	100

Pounds per Square Inches to Kilopascals

lb/in²	0	1	2	3	4	5	6	7	8	9	lb/in²
	kPa	kPa	kPa	kPa	kPa	kPa	kPa	kPa	kPa	kPa	
—	0.000	6.8948	13.7895	20.6843	27.5790	34.4738	41.3685	48.2663	55.1581	62.0528	—
10	68.9476	75.8423	82.7371	89.6318	96.5266	103.4214	110.3161	117.2109	124.1056	131.0004	10
20	137.8951	144.7899	151.6847	158.5794	165.4742	172.3689	179.2637	186.1584	193.0532	199.9480	20
30	206.8427	213.7375	220.6322	227.5270	234.4217	241.3165	248.2113	255.1060	262.0008	268.8955	30
40	275.7903	282.6850	289.5798	296.4746	303.3693	310.2641	317.1588	324.0536	330.9483	337.8431	40
50	344.7379	351.6326	358.5274	365.4221	372.3169	379.2116	386.1064	393.0012	399.8959	406.7907	50
60	412.6854	420.5802	427.4749	434.3697	441.2645	448.1592	455.0540	461.9487	468.8435	475.7382	60
70	482.6330	489.5278	496.4225	503.3173	510.2120	517.1068	524.0015	530.8963	537.7911	544.6858	70
80	551.5806	558.4753	565.3701	572.2648	579.1596	586.0544	592.9491	599.8439	606.7386	613.6334	80
90	620.5281	627.4229	634.3177	641.2124	648.1072	655.0019	661.8967	668.7914	675.6862	682.5810	90
100	689.4757	696.3705	703.2653	710.1601	717.0549	723.9497	730.8445	737.7393	744.6341	751.5289	100

Kilopascals to Pounds per Square Inches

kPa	0	1	2	3	4	5	6	7	8	9	kPa
	lb/in²	lb/in²	lb/in²	lb/in²	lb/in²	lb/in²	lb/in²	lb/in²	lb/in²	lb/in²	
—		.1450	.2901	.4351	.5801	.7252	.8702	1.0153	1.1603	1.3053	—
10	1.4504	1.5954	1.7404	1.8855	2.0305	2.1556	2.3206	2.4656	2.6107	2.7557	10
20	2.9007	3.0458	3.1908	3.3359	3.4809	3.6259	3.7710	3.9160	4.0610	4.2061	20
30	4.3511	4.4961	4.6412	4.7862	4.9313	5.0763	5.2213	5.3664	5.5114	5.6564	30
40	5.8015	5.9465	6.0916	6.2366	6.3816	6.5267	6.6717	6.8167	6.9618	7.1068	40
50	7.2518	7.3969	7.5419	7.6870	7.8320	7.9770	8.1221	8.2671	8.4121	8.5572	50
60	8.7022	8.8473	8.9923	9.1373	9.1824	9.4274	9.5724	9.7175	9.8625	10.0076	60
70	10.1526	10.2976	10.4427	10.5877	10.7327	10.8778	11.0228	11.1678	11.3129	11.4579	70
80	11.6030	11.7480	11.8930	12.0381	12.1831	12.3281	12.4732	12.6182	12.7633	12.9083	80
90	13.0533	13.1984	13.3434	13.4884	13.6335	13.7785	13.9236	14.0686	14.2136	14.3587	90
100	14.5037	14.6487	14.7938	14.9388	15.0838	15.2289	15.3739	15.5190	15.6640	15.8090	100

Pound Feet to Newton-Meters

ft-lb	0	1	2	3	4	5	6	7	8	9	ft-lb
	N-m	N-m	N-m	N-m	N-m	N-m	N-m	N-m	N-m	N-m	
—		1.3558	2.7116	4.0675	5.4233	6.7791	8.1349	9.4907	10.8465	12.2024	—
10	13.5582	14.9140	16.2698	17.6256	18.9815	20.3373	21.6931	23.0489	24.4047	25.7605	10
20	27.1164	28.4722	29.8280	31.1838	32.5396	33.8954	35.2513	36.6071	37.9629	39.3187	20
30	40.6745	42.0304	43.3862	44.7420	46.0978	47.4536	48.8094	50.1653	51.5211	52.8769	30
40	54.2327	55.5885	56.9444	58.3002	59.6560	61.0118	62.3676	63.7234	65.0793	66.4351	40
50	67.7909	69.1467	70.5025	71.8584	73.2142	74.5700	75.9258	77.2816	78.6374	79.9933	50
60	81.3491	82.7049	84.0607	85.4165	86.7724	88.1282	89.4840	90.3898	92.1956	93.5514	60
70	94.9073	96.2631	97.6189	98.9747	100.3305	101.6863	103.0422	104.3980	105.7538	107.1096	70
80	108.4654	109.8213	111.1771	112.5329	113.8887	115.2445	116.6003	117.9562	119.3120	120.6678	80
90	122.0236	123.3794	124.7353	126.0911	127.4469	128.8027	130.1585	131.5143	132.8702	134.2260	90
100	135.5818	136.9376	138.2934	139.6493	141.0051	142.3609	143.7167	145.0725	146.4283	147.7842	100

Newton-Meters to Pound Feet

N-m	0	1	2	3	4	5	6	7	8	9	N-m
	ft-lb	ft-lb	ft-lb	ft-lb	ft-lb	ft-lb	ft-lb	ft-lb	ft-lb	ft-lb	
—		.7376	1.4751	2.2127	2.9502	3.6878	4.4254	5.1692	5.9005	6.6381	—
10	7.3756	8.1132	8.8507	9.5883	10.3258	11.0634	11.8010	12.5385	13.2761	14.0136	10
20	14.7512	15.4888	16.2264	16.9639	17.7015	18.4390	19.1766	19.9142	20.6517	21.3893	20
30	22.1269	22.8644	23.6020	24.3395	25.0771	25.8147	26.5522	27.2898	28.0274	28.7649	30
40	29.5025	30.2400	30.9776	31.7152	32.4527	33.1903	33.9279	34.6654	35.4030	36.1405	40
50	36.8781	37.6157	38.3532	39.0908	39.8283	40.5659	41.3035	42.0410	42.7786	43.5162	50
60	44.2537	44.9913	45.7288	46.4664	47.2040	47.9415	48.6791	49.4167	50.1542	50.8918	60
70	51.6293	52.3669	53.1045	53.8420	54.5796	55.3171	56.0547	56.7923	57.5298	58.2674	70
80	59.0050	59.7425	60.4801	61.2176	61.9552	62.6928	63.4303	64.1679	64.9055	65.6430	80
90	66.3806	67.1181	67.8557	68.5933	69.3308	70.0684	70.8060	71.5435	72.2811	73.0186	90
100	73.7562	74.4938	75.2313	75.9689	76.7064	77.4440	78.1816	78.9191	79.6567	80.3943	100

Metric—English Conversion Table

Multiply	by	to get equivalent number of:	Multiply	by	to get equivalent number of:
Length			*Acceleration*		
Inch	25.4	millimeters (mm)	Foot/sec²	0.304 8	meter/sec² (m/s²)
Foot	0.304 8	meters (m)	Inch/sec²	0.025 4	meter/sec²
Yard	0.914 4	meters			
Mile	1.609	kilometers (km)	*Torque*		
Area			Pound-inch	0.112 98	newton-meters (N-m)
			Pound-foot	1.355 8	newton-meters
Inch²	645.2	millimeters² (mm²)			
	6.45	centimeters² (cm²)	*Power*		
Foot²	0.092 9	meters² (m²)			
Yard²	0.836 1	meters²	Horsepower	0.746	kilowatts (kW)
Volume			*Pressure or Stress*		
Inch³	16 387.	mm³	Inches of water	0.249 1	kilopascals (kPa)
	16.387	cm³	Pounds/sq.in.	6.895	kilopascals
	0.016 4	liters (l)			
Quart	0.946 4	liters	*Energy or work*		
Gallon	3.785 4	liters			
Yard³	0.764 6	meters³ (m³)	BTU	1 055	joules (J)
			Foot-pound	1.355 8	joules
			Kilowatt-hour	3 600 000.	joules (J = one W's)
Mass				or 3.6 × 10⁶	
Pound	0.453 6	kilograms (kg)	*Light*		
Ton	907.18	kilograms (kg)			
Ton	0.907	tonne (t)	Foot candle	1.076 4	lumens/meter² (lm/m²)
Force			*Fuel Performance*		
Kilogram	9.807	newtons (N)	Miles/gal	0.425 1	kilometres/litre (km/l)
Ounce	0.278 0	newtons	Gal/mile	2.352 7	liters/kilometer (l/km)
Pound	4.448	newtons			
Temperature			*Velocity*		
Degree Fahrenheit	(†°F-32) ÷ 1.8	degree Celsius (C)	Miles/hour	1.609 3	kilometers/hr. (km/h)

°F −40 0 32 40 80 98.6 120 160 200 212 °F

°C −40 −20 0 20 37 40 60 80 100 °C

GLOSSARY

AC Alternating current.

Accelerator prop A telescopic rod used to hold the accelerator pedal depressed.

Accelerator pump A small pump in the carburetor that forces an additional amount of fuel into the fuel-air mixture when the accelerator pedal is pushed down.

Access slots Openings in the backing plates or drums that allow access to the star wheel adjusters.

Accumulator A chamber in a hydraulically operated brake booster unit that stores a small quantity of fluid under pressure.

Ackerman principle The geometric principle used to provide toe-out on turns. The ends of the steering arms are angled so that the inside wheel turns more than the outside wheel when a car is making a turn.

Additive Anything added to a product in an attempt to improve the product.

Advance (Spark) To change the ignition timing so that the spark occurs earlier.

Air cleaner A device that removes dirt and dust from the air.

Air horn The upper portion of a carburetor. Usually contains the choke plate.

Air spring An air-filled device, usually a rubber bag, that is pressurized to provide spring action.

Align To bring into position. To adjust to a specification.

Alignment The adjustment of components to bring them into a predetermined position. Usually considered a combination of camber, caster, and toe-in adjustments.

Allen wrench A hex-shaped tool or bit that fits into a hex-shaped hole in the head of a bolt or screw.

Alternating current An electrical current that alternately changes polarity.

Alternator A device that converts mechanical energy to electrical energy in the form of alternating current.

Ammeter An instrument that measures current flow in amperes.

Ampere A unit of measurement of electrical current flow. With a pressure of 1 volt, 1 ampere will flow in a circuit that has a resistance of 1 Ohm.

Ampere hour capacity A measurement of a battery's ability to deliver a specified amount of current for a specified time.

Anchor pin A steel pin, or stud, mounted on the backing plate. The anchor pin keeps the brake shoes from turning with the drum.

Antifreeze A chemical added to water to lower its freezing point.

Arbor press A piece of equipment used to apply pressure through leverage.

Arc grinder See **Brake shoe grinder**.

Arc grinding The machining operation by which the lining on a pair of brake shoes is ground to fit the drum in which they will be used.

Arcing The spark formed when electricity jumps a gap. Arcing usually occurs when a circuit is broken.

Asbestos A nonflammable, heat-resistant mineral used in making brake lining and clutch facings.

ATDC After top dead center.

Atmospheric pressure The pressure exerted by the weight of the atmosphere; 14.7 psi at sea level.

Available voltage The maximum voltage produced by the ignition system.

Axial play Movement that is parallel to the axis of rotation.

Axle, front A crossbeam that is designed to support the weight of the front of a car. Steerable spindles are mounted at each end.

Axle, rear A shaft that transmits the driving force from the differential to a rear wheel.

Backing plate A pressed-steel plate upon which the brake shoes, wheel cylinder, and anchor pin are mounted.

Bail The spring-wire loop used to secure the cover on most master cylinder reservoirs.

Ball bearing An antifriction bearing that uses a series of steel balls held between the inner and outer bearing races.

Ball joint A joint, or connection, where a ball moves within a socket so as to allow rotary motion while the angle of the axis of rotation changes.

Ball joint inclination See **Steering axis inclination**.

Ball joint press A tool used to remove and install ball joints that are pressed into control arms.

Barrel shape A brake drum defect caused by excessive wear at the center of the friction surface.

Battery An electrochemical device that converts electrical energy to chemical energy while charging, and converts chemical energy to electrical energy while discharging.

BDC Bottom dead center.

Bead The part of a tire that contacts the rim of a wheel.

Bearing A device that acts to reduce friction between two moving parts.

Bearing clearance The space allowed for the lubricating film between a bearing and a shaft or journal.

Bearing cone The inner race for a ball or roller bearing.

Bearing cup The outer race for a ball or roller bearing.

Bearing race The inner or outer ring that provides the smooth, hard contact surface for the balls or rollers in a bearing.

Bell housing The cover at the rear of an engine that encloses the flywheel and the clutch assembly.

Bell mouth A brake drum defect caused by excessive wear, expansion, or both at the open end of a brake drum.

Bellows A movable cover or seal, usually of a rubberlike material, that is pleated or folded like an accordion to allow for expansion and contraction.

Bellows seal An expanding diaphragm used as a seal between the master cylinder reservoir and the reservoir cover. It prevents air from contacting the fluid, yet it allows the fluid to change in volume.

BHP Brake horsepower.

Bias belted tire A bias ply tire that has reinforcing strips or belts placed over the plies at the tread section.

Bias ply tire A tire constructed of alternate plies positioned so that the cords cross the centerline of the tire at an angle of about 35°.

Bimetallic Made of two different metals.

Bleeder hose A length of rubber tubing used in bleeding brakes.

Bleeder jar A glass or transparent plastic container used to detect the escape of air while bleeding brakes.

Bleeder screw See **Bleeder valve**.

Bleeder tank See **Pressure bleeder**.

Bleeder valve A valve placed in a hydraulic system where it can be opened to allow the release of air.

Bleeder wrench A tool used to open bleeder valves.

Bleeding The procedure by which air is purged from a hydraulic system.

Block See **Cylinder block**.

Blow-by The leakage of compression and combustion pressure past the piston rings.

Blower A supercharger.

Body roll The tipping of a car body to one side, usually in a turn.

Boiling point The exact temperature at which a liquid begins to turn to a vapor.

Bonded lining Brake lining that is attached to a brake shoe by an adhesive.

Booster A power brake unit.

Booster battery An auxiliary battery used to start the engine of a car that has a discharged battery.

Booster cables See **Jumper cables**.

Boot A flexible rubber or plastic cover used over the open ends of master cylinders and wheel cylinders to keep out water and other foreign matter.

Bore The walls of a cylinder. Also used to refer to the diameter of a cylinder.

Bore diameter The diameter of a cylinder.

Brake drum A ring-shaped housing that rotates around fixed brake shoes and is slowed or stopped when the shoes are expanded.

Brake drum lathe A machine that is used to refinish the inner surface of a brake drum.

Brake fluid A special liquid used in hydraulic brake systems.

Brake hose Flexible tubing used to transmit pressure in the hydraulic part of a brake system.

Brake line Special rigid steel tubing used to transmit pressure in the hydraulic part of a brake system.

Brake lining A friction material, usually asbestos, that is fastened to the brake shoes.

Brake shoe The metal form to which the brake lining is attached.

Brake shoe grinder A machine used to grind the lining on a brake shoe so that it will fit a particular drum.

Brake spoon A tool used to turn star wheel adjusters and thus to adjust the brake lining-to-drum clearance.

Breaker arm The movable part of a pair of ignition breaker points.

Breaker points A pair of contact points that are opened and closed by the action of a cam.

Brush An electrical conductor that contacts a commutator or a slip ring.

BTDC Before top dead center.

Caliper (brake) The actuating device of a disc brake. A hydraulically actuated clamp that forces brake shoes into contact with a disc brake rotor.

Caliper (tool) An adjustable measuring device.

Cam angle See **Dwell**.

Cam bolt A bolt fitted with an eccentric that will cause parts to change position when the bolt is turned.

Camber The inward or outward tilt of a wheel. The angle formed by the centerline of the wheel and the true vertical.

Camber roll The inherent characteristic of independent suspension systems to change camber angles when cornering.

Camber wear Wear on one side of a tire tread caused by the angle at which the tire tread contacts the road surface.

Camshaft A shaft machined to have a series of cam lobes. The rotation of a camshaft opens the valves in an engine.

Canister A container of activated charcoal used to absorb and store fuel evaporation emissions.

Car stands Pedestal-type supports for holding up a car once the car has been raised.

Carbon pile A variable resistance unit used to perform certain electrical tests.

Carburetor A device that measures and mixes fuel and air.

Castellated nut A nut that has slots through which a cotter pin may be passed to secure the nut to its bolt or stud.

Caster The forward or backward tilt of the steering axis centerline. The angle formed by the centerline of the steering axis and the true vertical when viewed from the side.

Catalytic converter A chamber in an exhaust system that contains a catalyst. The catalyst decreases the amount of unburned hydrocarbons in the exhaust gases by increasing their rate of oxidation.

Cell One unit or compartment of a battery.

Center bolt The bolt that maintains the alignment of the leaves in a leaf spring. It also maintains the position of the axle housing on the spring.

Center link See **Relay rod**.

Center of gravity The point about which the weight of a car is evenly distributed. The point of balance.

Centrifugal advance A system that uses centrifugal force to advance spark timing as engine speed increases.

Centrifugal force The outward force from the center of a rotating object.

Chassis The frame, suspension systems, engine, and drive train of a vehicle. The assembled parts of an automobile without the body.

Check valve A valve that opens to allow passage in one direction but closes to prohibit flow in a reverse direction.

Choke A valve used to reduce the amount of air that enters a carburetor.

CID Cubic inch displacement.

Circuit A connection of conductors that provides a complete path for current to flow from a power source, through a load, and return to the power source.

Clutch A friction device used to connect and disconnect the engine and the transmission.

Clutch cover assembly The assembly of the pressure plate, springs, and release levers that acts to engage and disengage a clutch.

Clutch disc The driven member in an automotive clutch.

Clutch fork The lever that holds and moves the clutch release bearing.

Clutch housing See **Bell housing**.

Clutch pedal play The distance a clutch pedal can be depressed before the release bearing contacts the levers of the cover assembly.

Clutch pressure plate The spring loaded part of a clutch assembly that holds the clutch disc against the flywheel.

Clutch release bearing The bearing that contacts the levers or fingers of a clutch cover assembly.

Coefficient of friction A relative measurement of the friction developed between two objects in contact with each other.

Coil (ignition) A transformer that multiplies battery voltage to a voltage sufficient to push current across the gap of a spark plug.

Coil spring A length of spring-steel wire wound in the shape of a spiral.

Coil spring compressor A tool for compressing a coil spring to allow its removal and installation.

Color code Color markings used to identify wires in a circuit.

Combination brake system A dual brake system that uses disc brakes at the front wheels and drum brakes at the rear wheels.

Combination valve A valve used in combination brake systems that combines two or more valves in a common housing. A combination valve may contain a pressure differential valve, a proportioning valve, and a metering valve.

Combustion Rapid burning.

Combustion chamber The area provided for combustion to occur above the top of a piston.

Commutator A series of metal bars or segments that are connected to the windings of an armature.

Compression The application of pressure to a gas.

Compression (springs) The loading, or storing of energy, in a spring.

Compression gauge An instrument used to measure the compression in the cylinders of an engine.

Compression ratio The ratio between the volume of a combustion chamber and a cylinder when the piston is at BDC, and the volume of the combustion chamber when the piston is at TDC.

Compression test A comparison qof the compression measured in all the cylinders of an engine.

Concentric Having the same center.

Condensation The conversion of a vapor to a liquid.

Condenser An electrical device that can absorb and store surges of current.

Conductor Any material that allows the flow of electrical current.

Connecting rod The link between a piston and the crankshaft.

Contact area The portion of a tire that contacts the road at any given time.

Control arms, front The horizontal arms that connect the front wheels to the car and which support the weight of the front of the car.

Control arms, rear The horizontal arms that connect the rear axle housing to the frame when coil springs are used in the rear suspension system. The arms maintain axle alignment and handle the driving and torque loads.

Coolant The mixture of water and antifreeze used in a cooling system.

Core (radiator) The tubular section of a radiator where the coolant transfers its heat to the air.

Cotter pin A round locking pin formed by a folded semicircular steel wire. The pin is locked by spreading the paired ends of the wire.

Crankcase The lower housing of an engine. The crankcase houses the crankshaft and often holds the oil supply.

Crankshaft The offset or cranklike shaft by which an engine delivers power. By means of connecting rods, the crankshaft converts the reciprocating motion of the pistons to rotating motion.

Crossmember A structural part of a frame that connects the side rails.

Crowfoot wrench A short open end wrench that can be attached to a handle or an extension.

Curb weight The weight of a vehicle with a full supply of fuel, oil, and coolant but with no driver, passengers, or luggage.

Current The flow of electrons through a conductor.

Cylinder A hole in which a piston moves.

Cylinder block The engine casting that contains the cylinders.

Cylinder head The upper casting of an engine. The combustion chambers are usually formed in the cylinder head.

Cylinder hone A rotating tool that uses abrasive stones to remove minor imperfections and to polish the bores of cylinders.

DC Direct current.

Deflection See **Distortion**.

Deflection, tire The difference between the free diameter and the rolling diameter of a tire.

Degree A unit used to measure angles. It is 1/360th of a circle. Usually abbreviated by the symbol ° placed behind a number.

Detonation The violent combustion of the fuel-air mixture in a cylinder.

Diagnosis The scientific process of determining the causes of problems.

Dial indicator A precision instrument that indicates linear measurement on a dial face.

Diaphragm A flexible membrane that separates two chambers and yet allows the volume of each chamber to change.

Die (thread) A tool for cutting threads on a shaft.

Differential A gear device that allows the driving wheels on a common axle to rotate at different speeds.

Direct current An electrical current that maintains a constant polarity.

Directional stability The ability of a car to travel in a straight line with a minimum of driver control.

Disc See **Rotor**.

Disc brake A brake system that utilizes a disc, or rotor, attached to the wheel. The car is slowed or stopped when brake shoes, or pads, grasp the rotor with a clamping action.

Displacement See **Piston displacement**.

Distortion A twisting or bending condition.

Distributor (ignition) A rotating switching device that opens and closes the primary circuit and distributes secondary circuit voltage to the spark plugs.

DOHC Double overhead camshafts.

DOT Department of Transportation.

Double flare The expanded end of tubing that is folded back to provide a double thickness.

Drag link See **Relay rod**.

Drift See **Pull**.

Drive shaft The shaft connecting the transmission to the driving axle.

Drive train The system of parts that transmits power from the engine to the driving wheels.

Drop center rim A common wheel design in which the center of the rim is lower than the edges, or flanges.

Dropped center The lowered area in the center section of a wheel rim.

Drum brake A brake system that uses curved shoes that are expanded to contact the inside of a rotating drum or ring.

Dual brake system A brake system that utilizes two separate hydraulic systems.

Dual master cylinder A master cylinder that has two reservoirs and two pistons, usually in tandem. Dual master cylinders are used with dual brake systems.

Duo-servo A brake design that provides servo action regardless of the direction of drum rotation.

Dust covers Small plugs made of rubber or metal, used to cover the access holes in backing plates and drums.

Dwell The amount of time, measured in degrees of distributor cam rotation, that the ignition points remain closed.

Dwell meter An instrument that measures dwell.

Dynamic balance Balance in motion. The balance of a wheel while it is rotating. The total weight distributed evenly over both the axis of rotation and the centerline of the wheel.

Eccentric Off-center.

Eccentric bolt See **Cam bolt**.

Electrode A conductor used to form one side of an air gap.

Electrolyte A mixture of sulfuric acid and water used in a lead/ acid battery.

Electromagnet A nonpermanent magnet consisting of a coil of wire wrapped around a soft iron core. Magnetism is present only while current flows through the coil.

Electronic ignition system A system that uses solid state electronic components in the primary circuit to eliminate the need for breaker points.

End play See **Axial play**.

Energy The ability to do work.

Energy absorbing steering column A steering column that is designed to collapse, or telescope, at a controlled rate in the event of a frontal collision.

Engine A device that converts heat energy to mechanical energy.

Engine displacement The total displacement of all the cylinders in an engine.

Equalizer A device used in parking brake systems to equalize the pull of both rear brake cables.

Ethylene glycol A chemical compound used as the major ingredient in permanent antifreeze.

Evaporation The conversion of a liquid to a vapor.

Exhaust manifold The system of passages that connects each cylinder of an engine to the exhaust pipe.

Exhaust pipe The pipe connecting the exhaust manifold to the muffler.

Feather-edge wear pattern See **Saw-tooth wear pattern**.

Feeler gauge A thin strip of metal of known thickness used to measure the clearance between two parts.

Field The area of magnetic force that surrounds a magnet.

Filament The wire conductor in a bulb. The filament glows to produce light.

Filter A straining device that removes foreign matter from a liquid or from a gas.

Firewall That body panel that separates the engine compartment from the passenger compartment.

Firing order The sequence in which the cylinders of an engine fire.

Fixed anchor A nonadjustable anchor pin. It may be riveted or welded to the backing plate, or it may pass through the backing plate and attach to a part of the suspension system.

Flare The expanded, funnel-shaped end of a piece of tubing.

Flare nut wrench See **Tubing wrench**.

Flaring tool A tool used to give the ends of tubing a flared shape.

Floating caliper A single-piston caliper positioned by pins, bolts, or ways.

Flushing A method of cleaning a system by pumping a liquid through the system to wash away foreign matter.

Flywheel The heavy wheel attached to a crankshaft. The flywheel smooths out the rotation between power strokes through its momentum.

Foot pound A unit of measurement for torque. In tightening a bolt or a nut, 1 foot pound is the torque obtained by a pulling force of 1 pound applied to a wrench handle 12 inches long.

Force A pulling or pushing effort measured in pounds.

Four stroke cycle A term used to describe the operation of a particular type of internal combustion engine. The strokes indicate the action that occurs with each movement of the piston: (1) intake, (2) compression, (3) power, and (4) exhaust.

Frame The foundation of an automobile. The steel structure to which the body is attached.

Free diameter The outer diameter of a tire that is not under load.

Friction The resistance to motion between two objects in contact with each other.

Fuel pump The device that pulls fuel from the fuel tank and forces it to the carburetor.

Fuse An electrical safety depice. A fuse will allow a limited amount of current to flow through it. If the current flow exceeds that limit, the fuse melts, or "bltws," breaking the circuit.

Gasket A liner or packing that is sandwiched between two parts to obtain a leakproof joint.

Generator A device that converts mechanical energy to electrical energy.

Ground A common return route in electrical circuits. The metal parts of a car are usually used as a ground to provide a return path to the negative (−) battery terminal.

Hard spots Scattered bumps on the friction surface of a brake drum that become apparent after machining. Hard spots are caused by excessive heat and pressure, which change the molecular structure of the cast iron.

Heat dissipation The transfer of heat, usually to the surrounding air.

Heat range The operating temperature range of a spark plug.

Heat riser The part of the intake manifold that is heated by exhaust gases to aid vaporization while the engine is cold.

Heel The end of a brake shoe nearest the anchor pin.

High pedal The condition in which the brakes are applied when the brake pedal is depressed only a slight amount.

High tension wires See **Secondary wires**.

Hone To remove metal with a fine abrasive stone.

Horses See **Car stands**.

Hotchkiss drive A rear axle suspension system in which the driving force and axle torque are handled by leaf springs.

Hub The central part of a wheel. The housing for the bearings upon which the wheel rotates around a spindle.

Hubbed drum A brake drum that is mounted on a hub.

Hydraulic Using fluids to transmit force and motion.

Hydraulics The science of the use of fluids to transmit force and motion.

Hydraulic brakes Brakes that are actuated by hydraulic pressure.

Hydrocarbons A chemical compound made up of hydrogen and carbon.

Hydrometer An instrument used to measure the specific gravity of a liquid.

Hydroscopic The tendency to absorb water.

ID Inside diameter.

Idle speed The slowest engine operating speed.

Idler arm An arm or lever that can rotate about its support and that is used to support one end of a relay rod. It usually duplicates the motion of the Pitman arm.

Ignition system The system that boosts battery voltage and distributes it to each spark plug at the proper time.

Impact puller A tool designed to loosen or separate parts by impact. One part is struck to cause sudden movement.

Impact wrench A power tool that turns nuts or bolts by means of a series of blows.

Included angle The sum of the angles of camber and steering axis inclination.

Independent suspension Suspension systems by which a wheel on one side of a car can move vertically without affecting the wheel on the other side of the car.

Induction The transfer of electricity by means of magnetism.

Inertia The tendency of a body at rest to remain at rest, and the tendency of a body in motion to remain in motion.

In-line engine An engine whose cylinders are arranged in a single row.

Insulation A material that does not conduct electricity.

Intake manifold The system of passages that connects the carburetor to each of the cylinders in an engine.

Integral Made in one piece. A combination of two or more parts made as one unit.

Interleaf friction The friction between the leaves of a leaf spring.

Intermediate link See **Relay rod**.

Jack A device for raising a car.

Jam nut (jamb nut) See **Lock nut**.

Journal That part of a shaft which contacts a bearing.

Jumper cables Cables used to start a car that has a discharged battery.

Kinetic balance Balance of the radial forces on a spinning tire. Determined by an electronic balancer.

Kinetic energy The energy of a mass in motion.

Kingpin A pin or shaft upon which the steering spindle assembly rotates.

Kingpin inclination See **Steering axis inclination**.

Knock-off puller A type of impact puller consisting of an internally threaded cap that is installed on a threaded shaft. The cap is struck with a hammer until the impact loosens the fit between the shaft and its adjacent part.

KPI Kingpin inclination.

Lash Movement, or play, between parts. The clearance between moving parts, such as meshing gear teeth.

Lateral Side.

Lateral runout Wobble, or side-to-side movement, of a rotating wheel or of a rotating wheel and tire assembly.

Lead A slight pull to one side.

Leaf spring A spring made of individual strips, or leaves, of flat spring steel.

Limited slip differential A differential that utilizes a clutch device to deliver power to either rear wheel when the opposite wheel is spinning.

Linkage A system of rods and levers used to transmit motion or force.

Load range An alphabetic system used to identify the service limitations of a tire.

Load test A measurement of battery voltage taken while the battery is delivering a specified amount of current.

Lock nut A second nut threaded on a bolt or stud. The lock nut is tightened against the nut which secures the bolt or stud and locks that nut in place.

Lock washer A washer designed to prevent a nut or a bolt from loosening.

Long and short arm suspension An independent suspension system that utilizes short upper control arms and long lower control arms.

Low pedal The condition in which the brake pedal must travel very far or very close to the floor before the brakes are applied.

Low profile tire A tire designed with less height and a wider cross section than conventional tires.

Lubricant Any material, usually liquid or semiliquid, that reduces friction when placed between two moving parts.

Main leaf The longest leaf in a leaf spring. The leaf in a leaf spring that has its ends rolled into eyes.

Manual bleeding A method of purging air from a hydraulic system by manually operating the brake pedal.

Master cylinder The part of the hydraulic system that converts the force of the driver to hydraulic pressure.

Mechanical advance See **Centrifugal advance**.

Mechanical brakes A brake system that is actuated mechanically, usually by rods or cables.

Metering valve A valve used in combination brake systems which shuts off the flow of fluid to the front calipers during light pedal applications. It acts to delay the operation of the front brakes until the rear brakes have started to apply.

Micrometer A precision instrument for linear measurement.

Millimeter A metric unit of measurement equal to 0.039370 inches. Usually found abbreviated as mm, as in 1 mm.

Minute An angle measure equal to 1/60th of 1 degree. Usually found abbreviated as ' following a number, as in 30'.

Motor A device that converts electrical energy to mechanical energy.

Muffler A device used to silence the noise of engine exhaust gases.

Needle bearing An antifriction bearing that utilizes a series of very thin steel rollers.

NIASE National Institute for Automotive Service Excellence.

Octane rating A measurement of the ability of a fuel to resist detonation.

OD Outside diameter.

Ohm A unit of measurement of resistance. A pressure of 1 volt is required to push a current of 1 ampere through a resistance of 1 Ohm.

Ohmmeter An instrument that measures resistance in Ohms.

Oil filter A straining device that removes foreign matter from oil.

Oil pan See **Crankcase**.

Open circuit A circuit in which a break prevents the flow of current.

Oscillate To move back and forth.

Out-of-round (brakes) A drum defect in which the friction surface is not round, but has worn or warped into an oval or elliptical shape.

Out-of-round (journal) A defect on a shaft where the journal has worn to an oval or elliptical shape.

Out-of-round (wheel and tire) A defect in which the wheel or tire is not round.

Overinflation The condition of a tire that is inflated to more than the recommended pressure.

Overrunning clutch A clutch that will transmit motion when turned in one direction, but will slip when turned in the opposite direction.

Oversteer The tendency of a car to turn more sharply than the driver intends while negotiating a turn.

Pad A common term for a brake shoe used in disc brakes.

Parallel circuit An electrical circuit that provides a separate path for current flow to and return from each of two or more loads.

Parallelism The parallel alignment of the two surfaces of a disc brake rotor.

Parallelogram steering linkage A commonly used steering linkage system that utilizes a relay rod or center link to connect the Pitman arm to an idler arm which duplicates the Pitman arm's length and motion. Separate tie rods connect the steering arms to the relay rod. The assembled linkage resembles a parallelogram in shape, and the centerlines of the pivot points are parallel.

Parking brake A mechanical brake system used to keep a parked car from moving.

Pascal's Law A basic law of hydraulics: "When pressure is exerted on a confined fluid, the pressure is transmitted equally and in all directions."

Patch area See **Contact area**.

PCV Positive crankcase ventilation.

Pedal reserve See **High pedal**.

Penetrating oil A very thin oil that is used to penetrate rust and corrosion and to free rusted parts.

Petcock A drain valve.

Pinging The metallic knocking caused by detonation.

Piston A movable plug that fits in a cylinder.

Piston cup A rubber cup-shaped part that seals a brake cylinder and eliminates leakage between the piston and the cylinder walls.

Piston displacement The volume displaced by a piston when it moves from BDC to TDC.

Piston pin The pin that connects the piston to the connecting rod.

Piston rings Expanding metal rings that fit in grooves cut around a piston. The rings provide a tight seal against the cylinder walls.

Piston skirt The part of a piston below the piston rings.

Pitman arm The arm connected to the steering gear sector shaft that transforms the rotating motion of the shaft into lateral motion at the relay rod.

Pits The holes or roughness left on a surface as a result of rust or corrosion.

Plates The metal grids in a battery. Positive plates are composed of lead peroxide. Negative plates are composed of sponge lead.

Play Movement between parts.

Plies The layers of cord that make up the carcass, or body, of a tire.

Ply rating A method of indicating relative tire strength. The ply rating usually does not indicate the actual number of plies.

Positive crankcase ventilation system An emission control system that pulls fumes from the crankcase and burns them in the engine.

Power brakes A hydraulic brake system that utilizes engine intake manifold vacuum or an external hydraulic power source to boost the braking effort of the driver.

Power steering A steering system that utilizes hydraulic pressure to boost the steering effort of the driver.

Preignition Ignition of the fuel-air mixture before the spark jumps the plug gap.

Preload A thrust load applied to bearings that support a rotating part to eliminate axial play or movement.

Pressure The amount of force applied to a definite area. It is measured in pounds per square inch.

Pressure bleeder A tank that stores brake fluid under pressure. When connected to the master cylinder, the fluid is forced through the system and facilitates bleeding.

Pressure bleeding A method of purging air from a hydraulic system by forcing fluid through the system by means of a pressure bleeder.

Pressure cap A radiator cap designed to hold in some of the pressure exerted by expanded coolant.

Pressure differential valve A spool-type valve used in dual brake systems to detect any difference in pressure between the systems. Its motion usually operates a switch that sends current to a warning lamp on the instrument panel.

Primary brake shoe In self-energizing brakes, the primary brake shoe is the one that is pulled away from the anchor by the rotation of the drum. Usually it is the forward shoe.

Primary circuit The circuit in the ignition system that creates the magnetic field in the coil.

Primary winding The winding in an ignition coil that uses battery current to create a magnetic field.

Primary wires The wires that form the conductors in the primary circuit.

Propeller shaft See **Driveshaft**.

Proportioning valve A valve used in dual brake systems that decreases the pressure at the rear brakes in proportion to pedal force.

PSI Pounds per square inch.

Pull The tendency of a car to veer to one side.

Puller A tool used to remove parts from a shaft or from a hole.

Pushrod (master cylinder) The rod that transmits the movement and force of the driver from the brake pedal lever to the master cylinder piston.

Pushrod (valve) The rod that transmits the movement of the valve lifter to the rocker arm.

Pushrod (wheel cylinder) The rod that transmits the movement and force of the wheel cylinder piston to the brake shoe.

Race See **Bearing race**.

Rack and pinion steering gear A steering gear design that utilizes a small pinion gear attached to the steering shaft to move a long toothed bar, called the rack gear. The ends of the rack gear are attached to the steering arms by means of tie rods.

Radial force variation The difference in stiffness at two or more points on a tire.

Radial load A load that is applied at 90° to an axis of rotation.

Radial play Movement at 90° to an axis of rotation.

Radial ply tire A tire constructed of alternate plies positioned so that the cords cross the tire centerline at an angle of 90°.

Radial runout Variation in the radius of a wheel or a wheel and tire assembly. Out-of-round.

Radiator A heat exchanger that allows the heat in the coolant to be passed off into the air.

Rag joint A flexible coupling that contains a rubberized fabric disc, or wafer. Usually found in steering systems.

Rate The softness or stiffness of a spring. The load required to cause a spring to deflect 1 inch.

Reach The distance between the firing end of a spark plug and its seat.

Rebound The motion of a spring when suddenly released after compression. The release of energy from a compressed spring.

Recirculating ball steering gear A commonly used steering gear design that utilizes a series of ball bearings to connect the worm gear to the ball nut. The balls, recirculated through tubes, provide rolling friction between the worm gear and the ball nut.

Rectifier A device used to change AC to DC.

Regulator (alternator) A device used to control output voltage.

Relay An electromagnetic switch.

Relay rod The part of a steering linkage that connects the Pitman arm to the idler arm.

Required voltage The voltage necessary to force current across the gap of a spark plug.

Reservoir A storage area.

Residual pressure The slight pressure that remains in a hydraulic system after the brake pedal has been released.

Residual pressure (check) valve A valve which is in the master cylinder and that acts to maintain a slight pressure in the system at all times.

Resistance The ability of a conductor to restrict the flow of current.

Retard (spark) To change the ignition timing so that the spark occurs later.

Riding height See **Suspension height**.

Rim diameter The diameter of a wheel measured at the base of the rim flange.

Rivet A fastening device used to secure brake lining to a brake shoe. A headed pin that is placed through holes in two objects. The end opposite the head is expanded to secure the pin.

Road crown The slope, or pitch, of a road from its center to the curbs or shoulders.

Road feel The feeling transmitted back to the steering wheel by the wheels of the car.

Road shock A shock or movement transmitted from the road surface to the steering wheel through the steering gear and linkage.

Rocker arm A lever that transmits the movement of a push rod to a valve.

Roller bearing An antifriction bearing that uses a series of steel rollers held between inner and outer bearing races.

Rotor (alternator) The rotating field coil that creates a moving magnetic field.

Rotor (brake) A disc that is attached to a wheel or hub to provide a friction surface for a brake system.

Rotor (distributor) The rotating switch contact that distributes the high voltage produced in the coil to each of the spark plug wires.

Rotor lathe A machine that is used to refinish the surfaces of a brake rotor.

RPM Revolutions per minute.

Runout Any variation in the movement of the surface of a rotating object.

Saddle That portion of an axle or axle housing which mounts on the spring.

SAE Society of Automotive Engineers.

Safety rim A wheel design in which the rim has two ridges inside the flanged edges. The bead of the tire is held between the flange and the ridge, and is restrained from slipping into the dropped center in the event of a blowout.

Saw-tooth wear pattern A tire wear pattern in which the tread ribs wear more on one side than on the other side. Usually caused by incorrect toe-in.

Score A scratch or groove. Commonly found on cylinder walls and on the friction surfaces of drums, rotors, and flywheels.

Scrub radius The distance between the extended centerline of the steering axis and the centerline of the tire at the point where the tire contacts the road.

Scrub rib A protective rib, or ridge, on the sidewall of a tire. It is designed to protect the sidewall when the tire comes in contact with a curb.

Sealed beam bulb A unitized bulb consisting of a lens, reflector, and a filament.

Sealed bearing A bearing that has been lubricated and sealed at the time of manufacture.

Secondary brake shoe In self-energizing brakes, the brake shoe that is pushed into contact with an anchor by the rotation of the drum. Usually the rear shoe.

Secondary circuit The ignition system circuit that transmits the high voltage from the coil to the spark plugs.

Secondary wires The conductors in the secondary circuit.

Self-adjusting brake A brake that automatically maintains the proper lining-to-drum clearance.

Self-energizing brake A brake design in which the brake shoes, through leverage and wedging action, are applied with a greater force than that furnished by the wheel cylinder.

Semi-elliptical spring A leaf spring that is formed in the shape of one-half an ellipse.

Separators Insulators in a battery that prevent the plates from contacting each other.

Series circuit An electrical circuit that provides only one path for the flow of current through two or more loads.

Serrations Grooves, or teeth, formed in parts so that they do not shift positions when they are tightened together.

Servo action A braking action in which one shoe serves to add to the application force of another. This action provides a high brake application force without requiring high pedal effort on the part of the driver.

Shackle A movable link used to attach one end of a leaf spring to the frame while allowing it to change in length.

Shim A spacer used to adjust the distance between two parts.

Shimmy A rapid oscillation, or wobble, of a wheel and tire assembly about the steering axis.

Shock absorber A device used to dampen the oscillations of a spring.

Short circuit A defect in an electrical circuit that allows current to return to the power source before passing through the load.

Side rails The structural members that comprise the sides of a frame.

Sliding caliper A single piston caliper that is positioned by machined surfaces on its anchor plate.

Slip angle The angle between the true centerline of the tire and the actual path followed by the tire while rounding a turn.

Snap ring A split ring that is held in a groove by its own tension. Internal snap rings are used in grooves cut around the bore of a hole. External snap rings are used in grooves cut around a shaft.

Soft pedal The soft, springy feeling detected when the brake pedal is depressed and when air is present in the hydraulic system.

Solenoid An electromagnet with a movable core.

Solid-axle suspension A suspension in which the wheels are mounted at each end of a solid, or undivided, axle or axle housing.

Spanner A wrench. A tool designed to turn a nut or threaded ring by means of holes or notches in the part.

Spark plug A device that provides a fixed air gap across which current jumps to provide a spark.

Specific gravity The weight of a substance compared with the weight of an equal volume of water.

Spindle That part of a front suspension system about which a front wheel rotates. A shaft or pin about which another part rotates.

Spindle bolt See **King pin**.

Spinner An electrically driven drum or roller used to spin a wheel and tire assembly on the car to check for imbalance.

Splash shield A metal deflector used to protect a disc brake rotor from road splash.

Spongy pedal See **Soft pedal**.

Spoon See **Brake spoon**.

Spring bolt The bolt used to attach the fixed end of a leaf spring to the car frame.

Spring clips Clamps or straps used on leaf springs to prevent the ends of the leaves from separating when the spring rebounds.

Spring hanger The mounting to which the fixed end of a leaf spring is attached by the spring bolt.

Spring liners Strips of soft metal or plastic used to separate the leaves in a leaf spring.

Spring pockets Formed sections of a frame designed to retain one end of a coil spring.

Spring seats See **Spring pockets**.

Spring steel A type of steel which has properties that allow it to withstand a great amount of deflection and still return to its original shape.

Spring towers See **Spring pockets**.

Spring wind-up The deflection of a leaf spring during acceleration and deceleration.

Sprung weight The total weight of all the parts of a car supported by the springs.

Stability The property of a body that causes it, when disturbed from a condition of equilibrium or steady motion, to develop forces or tendencies to restore it to its original condition.

Stabilizer A device that uses the torsional resistance of a steel bar to reduce the roll of a car and to prevent too great a difference in the spring action at the two front wheels.

Stake To secure a part by burring or distorting adjacent surfaces.

Static At rest; stationary.

Static balance Balance at rest. A distribution of weight around the axis of rotation so that a wheel has no tendency to rotate by itself, regardless of its position.

Stator (alternator) The stationary winding in which current is induced by a moving magnetic field.

Steering angle See **Toe-out on turns**.

Steering arms The arms that transmit the steering motion from the tie rods to the steering knuckles.

Steering axis inclination The tilt of the centerline of the steering axis toward the centerline of the car. The angle formed by the centerline of the steering axis and the true vertical when viewed from the front.

Steering column The support for the steering wheel. It includes the mast jacket, steering shaft, and shift tube. It also serves as a mounting for other controls.

Steering gear A device made of gears to transmit steering effort to the steering linkage.

Steering geometry A term used to describe the relationships of the various measurements and angles in the steering and suspension systems.

Steering knuckle A forging consisting of a spindle and its mounting. It is mounted between the upper and lower ball joints and pivots for steering.

Steering linkage A system of links, rods, and levers used to transmit motion from the steering gear to the steering knuckles.

Steering shaft A steel rod that connects the steering wheel to the steering gear.

Steering system The combination of the steering gear, steering wheel, and steering linkage, which enables the driver to turn the front wheels.

Steering wheel play Any movement of the steering wheel that does not produce movement of the front wheels.

Stroke The distance a piston travels as it moves from TDC to BDC.

Strut A brace used between a control arm and the frame.

Stud A headless bolt that is threaded on both ends.

Sulfated The condition of a battery when the composition of the plates has changed to lead sulfate.

Supercharger A device that forces the fuel-air mixture into the intake manifold.

Suspension height The distance from a specified point on a car to the road surface when the car is at curb weight.

Tach-Dwell meter An instrument that measures both engine speed and ignition system dwell.

Tachometer An instrument for measuring engine speed.

Tailpipe The outlet pipe from a muffler.

Tap (thread) A tool used to cut threads in a hole.

Taper A lack of parallelism. A cylinder defect in which one end of a cylinder has a larger diameter than the opposite end. A drum defect in which the diameter at the outer edge is different from the diameter at the inner edge.

Tapered roller bearing An anti-friction bearing that uses a series of tapered steel rollers held between tapered inner and outer races.

TDC Top dead center.

Thermostat A temperature operated valve that controls the flow of coolant in a cooling system.

Throttle The valve in the carburetor that controls the flow of fuel-air mixture into the intake manifold.

Thrust load A load that is applied in line with an axis of rotation.

Tie rod A rod used to connect the relay rod to a steering arm.

Tie rod end The ball-and-socket joint at the end of a tie rod.

Tie rod fork A fork-shaped wedge used to remove a ball stud from its mounting hole.

Tie rod sleeves Tubes or pipes with internal threads into which the tie rods and tie rod ends are threaded. Turning the sleeves extends or retracts the tie rod, changing its length.

Timing chain The chain that connects the crankshaft to the camshaft.

Timing gears The gears that connect the crankshaft to the camshaft.

Timing light A strobe light used to "stop" the motion of a crankshaft pulley so that the alignment of the timing marks can be observed.

Timing marks Marks, usually on the crankshaft pulley and on the front of the engine, that indicate the position of the crankshaft.

Tire bead See **Bead**.

Tire casing The body of a tire exclusive of its tread.

Tire print The pattern made by the tire at the point of road contact.

Tire problem detector (TPD) An instrument that measures the radial force variation of a mounted tire.

Tire rotation The system by which wheel and tire assemblies are moved to different locations at regular intervals. Tire rotation equalizes wear and thus extends tire life.

Tire sidewall The portion of the tire between the bead and the tread.

Tire tread The portion of a tire that contacts the road surface.

Tire wear pattern The characteristics of the wear shown by the tread of a tire.

Toe (alignment) The difference between the measurements taken between the front and the rear of the tires mounted on a common axle.

Toe (brakes) The end of a brake shoe that is not adjacent to its anchor.

Toe-in A condition in which the front of the wheels on a common axle are closer together than the rear of the wheels.

Toe-out A condition in which the front of the wheels on a common axle are farther apart than the rear of the wheels.

Toe-out on turns The difference between the turning angle of the inside wheel and the outside wheel during a turn. This angle is usually measured while the inner wheel is turned 20°.

Tolerance A permissible variation, usually stated as extremes of a specification.

Torque A force that tends to produce a twisting or turning motion.

Torque sequence The order in which a series of bolts or nuts should be tightened.

Torque wrench A wrench or handle that indicates the amount of torque applied to a bolt or nut. A tool used to tighten bolts and nuts to a specific torque.

Torsion bar A spring steel bar that is supported and anchored at one end, whereas the other end is supported but allowed to twist. The bar's resistance to any torque or twisting effort provides spring action.

Torsion bar suspension A suspension system that utilizes torsion bars in place of springs.

Tracking The relationship of the paths taken by the front wheels and the rear wheels. The alignment of the center of the tread distance of the front wheels with the center of the tread distance of the rear wheels.

Tramp See **Wheel tramp**.

Transmission A device used to adjust engine speed and torque to particular driving situations.

Transverse torsion bars Torsion bars mounted so that they extend across the frame.

Tread The distance between the centerlines of the wheels on a common axle.

Tread wear indicators Ridges molded into the grooves between the ribs of a tire tread. The indicators become visible when the tread is worn to a depth of less than $1/16$ in. (1.6 mm).

Tubing bender A tool used to bend tubing without kinking or deforming its walls.

Tubing cutter A tool used to cut tubing. In operation, the tubing is held between a pair of rollers and a sharp wheel. The tool is moved around the tubing, and the wheel cuts the tubing cleanly and without distortion.

Tubing wrench A wrench used to turn fittings on tubing. A tubing wrench distributes the turning forces evenly around the fitting, and thus minimizes the possibility of damage.

Turbosupercharger A supercharger driven by the pressure of exhaust gases.

Turning angle See **Toe-out on turns**.

Turning radius Usually given as the diameter of the smallest circle in which a car can travel.

U-bolt A steel shaft, threaded at both ends, that is bent 180° (U-shaped). Used to attach an axle housing to a leaf spring.

Underinflation The condition of a tire which is inflated to less than the recommended pressure.

Understeer The tendency of a car to turn less sharply than the driver intends while negotiating a turn.

Unit body A design that does not use a frame. The body of the car, reinforced at appropriate points, provides the mounting for the suspension systems.

Universal joint A connection that allows power to be transmitted through an angle.

Unsprung weight The weight of the parts in the suspension system that are not supported by the springs.

Vacuum A pressure less than atmospheric pressure.

Vacuum advance A system that utilizes engine vacuum to advance spark timing as engine load decreases.

Valve (engine) A movable plug or door that opens and closes a port in the combustion chamber. Most engines have two valves for each cylinder. An intake valve opens to let the fuel-air mixture in, and an exhaust valve opens to let the burned gases out.

Valve lifter The part that is moved by the lobe on a camshaft. A cam follower.

Valve spring The spring that closes a valve and holds it closed.

Ventilated rotor A disc brake rotor that is formed with cooling fins cast between its friction surfaces.

Viscosity A measurement of the ability of a liquid to flow.

Volt A unit of measurement of electrical pressure. A pressure of 1 volt is required to push 1 ampere of current through a resistance of 1 Ohm.

Voltage drop The loss in electrical pressure as it pushes current through resistance.

Voltmeter An instrument that measures electrical pressure in volts.

Vulcanizing The process used to bond rubber by means of chemical action under heat and pressure.

Waddle Side-to-side movement of a car. Usually caused by a tire that has a belt which has been installed crookedly.

Wander The tendency of a car to veer, or drift, to either side from a straight path.

Water jacket The hollow areas surrounding the cylinders and combustion chambers of an engine. Coolant flows through the water jackets to carry off excess heat.

Weave See **Wander**.

Wheel alignment See **Alignment**.

Wheel alignment rack Equipment which supports and positions a car so that accurate measurements can be made of the relationships of parts in the steering and suspension systems.

Wheel balancer A machine used to check and correct the balance of a wheel and tire assembly.

Wheel cylinder The output cylinder in a hydraulic brake system.

Wheel tramp The vertical movement of a spindle caused by static imbalance.

Wheel weights Weights made of lead alloy. They are attached to a wheel rim flange to balance a wheel and tire assembly.

Wheelbase The distance between the centers of the front and rear wheels.

Worm and sector steering A steering gear design which utilizes a worm shaft that engages a sector shaft.

Zerk fittings Grease fittings.

Answer Key
With Text References

Chapter 1
1 A page 1-3
2 B page 1-5
3 C page 1-6
4 A page 1-7
5 C page 1-8
6 A page 1-8
7 C page 1-14 & 1-18
8 A page 1-14
9 B page 1-21
10 C page 1-22

Chapter 2
1 D page 2-5
2 D page 2-4
3 C page 2-10
4 A page 2-13
5 B page 2-17
6 D page 2-18
7 A page 2-21
8 C page 2-26
9 C page 2-27
10 A page 2-28

Chapter 3
1 D page 3-2 & 3-3
2 D page 3-5
3 D page 3-3 & 3-5
4 B page 3-8 & 3-9
5 A page 3-21
6 B page 3-22
7 C page 3-20
8 B page 3-24
9 B page 3-28
10 D page 3-26

Chapter 4
1 C page 4-5
2 B page 4-6
3 B page 4-8
4 B page 4-17
5 C page 4-13 & 4-14
6 D page 4-18
7 B page 4-16
8 A page 4-20 & 4-22
9 D page 4-29
10 A page 4-33 & 4-34

Chapter 5
1 C page 5-2
2 C page 5-4
3 D page 5-6
4 D page 5-15
5 B page 5-16
6 C page 5-14
7 D page 5-20
8 A page 5-22
9 D page 5-16 & 5-25
10 C page 5-29

Chapter 6
1 A page 6-2
2 D page 6-3
3 D page 6-4
4 A page 6-7 & 6-8
5 C page 6-8
6 C page 6-12
7 A page 6-17
8 A page 6-19
9 B page 6-24
10 C page 6-29

Chapter 7
1 B page 7-2
2 A page 7-2 & 7-3
3 A page 7-6
4 D page 7-8
5 D page 7-6 & 7-7
6 B page 7-14
7 A page 7-14
8 C page 7-31
9 D page 7-34
10 A page 7-34

Chapter 8
1 D page 8-2
2 B page 8-2
3 A page 8-3
4 C page 8-5 & 8-6
5 C page 8-10
6 D page 8-13 & 8-14
7 C page 8-17 & 8-18
8 C page 8-22
9 A page 8-19
10 A page 8-26

Chapter 9
1 C page 9-5
2 D page 9-3
3 B page 9-8
4 B page 9-15 & 9-29
5 B page 9-17
6 C page 9-3 & 9-29
7 D page 9-3 & 9-2
8 B page 9-29
9 C page 9-12
10 A page 9-14 & 9-15

Chapter 10
1 C page 10-4
2 C page 10-5
3 D page 10-4
4 C page 10-8
5 C page 10-19
6 B page 10-19
7 D page 10-19
8 A page 10-20 & 10-23
9 B page 10-27
10 A page 10-27 & 10-28

Chapter 11
1 A page 11-2 & 11-3
2 C page 11-3
3 C page 11-11 & 11-16
4 D page 11-14
5 C page 11-27
6 D page 11-21 & 11-26
7 B page 11-30
8 C page 11-30
9 A page 11-31 & 11-32
10 A page 11-36

Chapter 12
1 C page 12-3 & 12-4
2 A page 12-6
3 C page 12-2
4 B page 12-3 & 12-6
5 B page 12-11
6 B page 12-17
7 C page 12-30
8 B page 12-32
9 A page 12-32
10 C page 12-35 & 12-36

Chapter 13
1 D page 13-3
2 C page 13-3
3 C page 13-4
4 C page 13-13
5 C page 13-15 & 13-17
6 B page 13-22 & 13-25
7 B page 13-25
8 C page 13-29 & 13-31
9 B page 13-31
10 B page 13-31

Chapter 14
1 C page 14-3
2 A page 14-3 & 14-4
3 B page 14-7
4 C page 14-8
5 C page 14-9
6 B page 14-11
7 B page 14-12
8 B page 14-15
9 D page 14-16
10 B page 14-20

Chapter 15
1 C page 15-4
2 D page 15-5
3 C page 15-5
4 A page 15-4 & 15-5
5 C page 15-6
6 C page 15-5
7 D page 15-9
8 D page 15-12
9 C page 15-12 & 15-13
10 A page 15-28

Index